THE NEW BOOK OF KNOWLEDGE

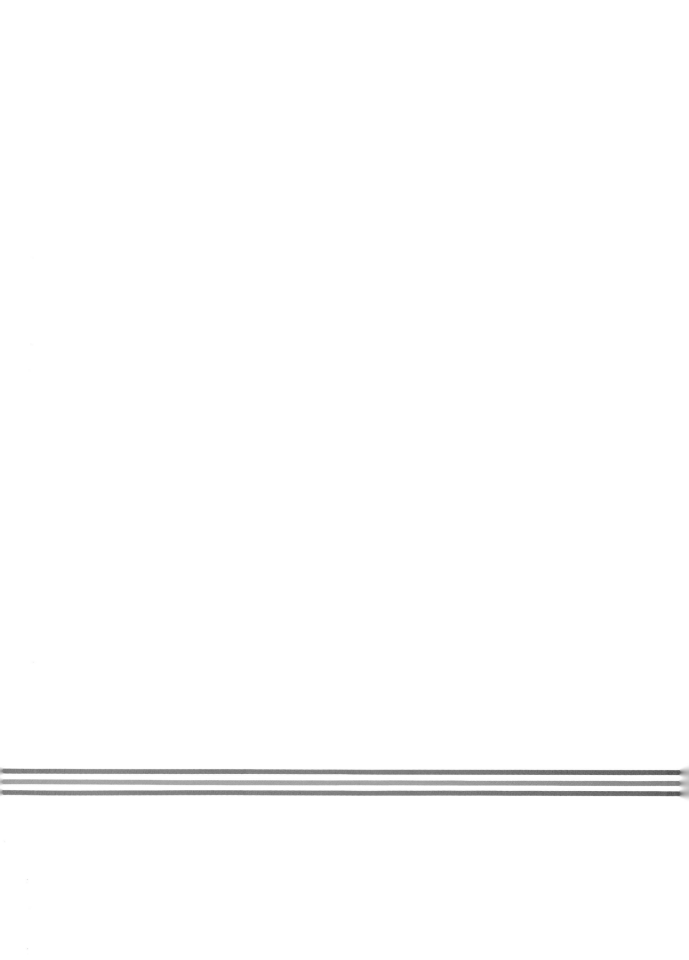

THE NEW BOOK OF KNOWLEDGE

Grolier Publishing Company, Inc.
An Imprint of Scholastic Library Publishing
Danbury, Connecticut

VOLUME 1

A

Library of Congress Cataloging-in-Publication Data

The new book of knowledge.
p. cm.
Includes index.
Summary: An illustrated encyclopedia with articles on history, literature, art and music, geography, mathematics, science, sports, and other topics. Some articles include activities, games, or experiments.
ISBN 0-7172-0535-5 (alk. paper)
1. Children's encyclopedias and dictionaries. [1. Encyclopedias and dictionaries.] I. Grolier Publishing Company, Inc.
AG5.N273 2003
031—dc21 2002029741

ISBN 0-7172-0535-5 (set)

PRINTED AND MANUFACTURED IN THE UNITED STATES OF AMERICA

The publishers wish to thank the following for permission to use copyrighted material:
Harcourt, Brace & World, Inc., and Alfred J. Bedard for "The Emperor's New Clothes" from *It's Perfectly True and Other Stories* by Hans Christian Andersen, translated by Paul Leyssac, copyright 1938 by Paul Leyssac.
Harcourt Brace Jovanovich, Inc., for excerpt on measuring star distances from *Space in Your Future* by Leo Schneider, copyright 1961 by Leo Schneider.
Little, Brown and Company for excerpt from *Little Women* by Louisa May Alcott.
David McKay Company, Inc., for excerpts from *Arabian Nights,* edited by Andrew Lang, new edition 1946, copyright 1898, 1946, Longmans Green and Company, Inc., now David McKay Company, Inc.

PREFACE

THE NEW BOOK OF KNOWLEDGE is uniquely related to the needs of modern young people, both in school and at home. The children and teenagers of today are standing on the threshold of a new world, and they must learn to cope with it successfully. Knowledge in every field is bursting its bounds. Old "truths" are becoming invalid; new "truths" are opening vistas never before imagined. Our youth need an encyclopedia that will help them understand the constantly changing realities of the world around them. For that purpose, more than one thousand advisers and contributors, together with a staff of editors, artists, and other specialists, have worked together to create and sustain THE NEW BOOK OF KNOWLEDGE—an encyclopedia designed for the young people of today.

SCOPE

THE NEW BOOK OF KNOWLEDGE is designed for the library and the classroom as well as for practical and educational use at home. It will be useful to a wide range of readers, from very young children to students ready for an adult encyclopedia. The content of the encyclopedia was selected by educators who analyzed the curriculum requirements of school systems across the nation, by librarians familiar with the research needs of children and young adults, and by cultural specialists who considered the interests and needs of the set's users beyond school and library settings. Students will find a wealth of information and clarifications of concepts that will be important and useful in their schoolwork. In addition, the articles have been enriched by many informative projects, experiments, and illustrations.

For children, and the young child in all of us, there are carefully selected illustrations, games, and activities, as well as selections from well-known and much-loved stories, myths, fables, and other classic works of literature. Parents will find much material to use with and read aloud to their children, both for enjoyment and as answers to their questions. These materials will provide important additions to every child's growing-up experiences. They will also help children learn the value of books as sources of information, imagination, and pleasure.

AUTHORITY

The articles in THE NEW BOOK OF KNOWLEDGE are written or reviewed by experts eminent in their fields who understand how to address and write about their subjects in a way that is both informative and interesting to our readership. Almost all of the articles are signed, and the contributor's or reviewer's position appears with each signature so that readers can see the person's authority. Many articles are signed not only by an author but also by a reviewer. The few unsigned articles are written by staff editors who are familiar with the needs and ability levels of young readers and are subject-matter specialists. A complete list of contributors, consultants, and reviewers appears in Volume 20.

ACCURACY

To ensure utmost accuracy, every article, map, drawing, photograph, diagram, chart, and fact box is checked by skilled researchers so that the information provided is correct and current. Where authorities disagree or information is unknown, the reader is so informed. Editorial policy is to present fact, not opinion.

READABILITY

Reading consultants to the encyclopedia have helped the staff design a set that is comprehensible, informative, and interesting. Articles whose subjects appeal to younger children are at lower levels of comprehension, whereas other articles, especially those with a technical vocabulary, are at higher levels. In addition, the editors strive to provide the background information necessary to ensure a complete understanding of every article. They realize that for information to become knowledge, it must be understood so well that its seekers can both use it correctly and communicate it to others. The editors also make every effort to present information in a style that will capture the reader's interest and imagination. To further assure pleasurable reading, the type in which the set is printed was chosen after careful research in typeface legibility.

ARRANGEMENT and AVAILABILITY of INFORMATION

THE NEW BOOK OF KNOWLEDGE is organized alphabetically in unit letter volumes. Each volume contains an Index that is cross-referenced to the entire contents of the set. Blue paper is used for the Index pages so that they can be easily identified. Articles and Index entries are arranged in alphabetical order, letter by letter to the comma, ignoring hierarchical orders. In addition, there is extensive use of *See also* references following articles.

The encyclopedia also includes standing cross-references. These are printed in the same type as article headings and refer the reader to the article or articles where the subject is covered. Other devices that assist the search for information include placing word guides at the bottom of each page close to the page number; placing a page number on every page or, where this is not possible, on one out of every double spread of pages; organizing long articles into shorter units through the use of boldface headings; and presenting information in concise forms such as fact summaries, chronologies, charts, graphs, and lists. Finally, the Wonder Questions, which have been a part of the set since the original 1911 edition of THE BOOK OF KNOWLEDGE, appeal to one's curiosity and provide concise information throughout the set about a wide range of topics.

MAPS

THE NEW BOOK OF KNOWLEDGE presents a map program planned especially to meet the needs of its readers. Maps are prepared by skilled cartographers in collaboration with geographers and subject editors. The maps are clear, accurate, informative, attractive, and easy to understand. Information of various kinds is presented on different but related maps, not crowded onto one map. Pictorial symbols, decorative insets, and rich color make the maps appealing to the eye and also provide additional information. There are almost one thousand maps of all kinds in the encyclopedia, and most are in color.

ILLUSTRATIONS

THE NEW BOOK OF KNOWLEDGE is printed on a full-color press so that color can be available throughout. There are more than thirteen thousand color illustrations in the set. All of the photographs, illustrations, and maps were selected to complement and add information to the text and were as carefully checked for accuracy as the text itself. The illustrations appear near the information they illustrate, and they are large enough to show details clearly. Most of the artwork was commissioned especially for this publication.

BIBLIOGRAPHY

A comprehensive bibliography in the Home and School Reading and Study Guides points the way to further reading on more than a thousand topics. The recommended readings are grouped by general levels—primary, intermediate, and advanced. These references emphasize that THE NEW BOOK OF KNOWLEDGE is a springboard to learning that will stimulate the curiosity of its readers and lead them to further study.

The Editors

FIRST EDITION STAFF

Martha Glauber Shapp, M.A.
Editor in Chief

Cathleen FitzGerald, B.A., H. Dip. Ed.
Managing Editor

Ben Feder
Designer and Graphic Arts Consultant

Lowell A. Martin, Ph.D.
Vice President and Editorial Director, Grolier, Inc.

EDITORIAL

SOCIAL STUDIES

Chief Editor: Dorothy W. Furman, B.S.

Senior Editors: Sue Brandt, B.A.; F. Richard Hsu, M.A.; Mary B. Irving, B.A.; Jerome Z. Neibrief, B.S.; John Ratti, M.A.; Eugenio C. Villicaña, M.A.

Associate Editors: Jay Bennett; Joyce Berry, B.A.; Claudia H. Cohl, B.A.; Mary-Stuart Garden, B.A.; Carol Z. Rothkopf, M.A.

Assistant Editors: Lorraine Abelson Abraham, B.A.; Marcus Anton Cohen, B.A.; Ellen Gendell, B.A.; Bryna Mandel, B.A.; Paul Schmel, B.A.; Amy Small, B.A.; Annette Stiefbold, M.A.

Editorial Assistants: Cecilia H. Bustos; Judith Glickman, B.A.; Mada Levine, B.A.; Barbara Mathes, B.A.

LANGUAGE AND LITERATURE

Senior Editor: James E. Jarnagin, M.A.

Associate Editors: Marcia B. Marks, B.A.; Janet Stone, B.A.

Assistant Editors: Carol Smith Bundy, B.A.; Lis Shabecoff, B.A.

TECHNOLOGY

Senior Editor: Peter R. Limburg, B.S.F.S., M.A.

Associate Editor: Sara L. Hannum, B.A.

Assistant Editors: Marion Bowman; Arthur G. Hudgins, M.A., Winifred B. Luhrmann, B.A.; Anthony M. Quintavalla, B.A.

EDITORIAL COORDINATOR

Lois C. Schwartz, B.A.

SCIENCE AND MATHEMATICS

Chief Editor: Patricia G. Lauber, B.A.

Senior Editor: Herbert Kondo, M.A.

Administrative Assistant: Anita Sedler

Associate Editors: John S. Bowman, B.A.; Barbara Land, M.S.; Rebecca Marcus, B.A.; Elizabeth Shepherd, B.A.

Assistant Editors: Chica Minnerly, B.A.; Steven Moll, B.A.; Harvey M. Weiss, M.A.

Editorial Assistants: Larry Baker, B.A.; Larry Blaser, M.A.; Stephen Kreitzman, B.A.; Ruth Plager, B.A.

MUSIC AND ART

Senior Music Editor: David L. Buckley, B.A.

Senior Art Editor: David Jacobs, B.F.A.

Associate Editor: Gwendolyn E. Reed, B.A. (Art)

Assistant Editors: Sara Friedman, B.A. (Art); Barbara Kaye, B.A. (Art); Joseph H. Markham, B.A. (Music); Robert Porter, B.F.A. (Art)

SPORTS AND LEISURE; HEALTH, HOME, AND COMMUNITY

Senior Editor: Helen Hull Jacobs

Associate Editors: Eleanor Felder, M.S.; Virginia Gurnee; Sylvia Rosenthal, B.A.

Assistant Editor: Noemie Emery, M.A.

STAFF EDITORS

Elisabeth Freidel Earley, M.A.; Susan Elliott, B.A.; Rosalyn Heith, B.A.; Fay Leviero; Sarah Lee McSweeney, B.A.

COPY EDITORS

Chief Copy Editor: Patricia Ellsworth, B.A.

Senior Copy Editors: Paule H. Jones, M.A.; Sandra L. Russell, B.A.; Damsey Wilson

Staff Members: Philip G. Anthony; Marcy Benstock, B.A.; Jeane Pavelle Garment, B.A.; Philip C. Johnson, B.A.; Naomi Kassabian, M.A.; Marian Klein, B.A.; Martin S. Mitchell, B.A.; Thomas W. Wyckoff

RESEARCHERS

Chief Researcher: Marshall Tulloch, B.A.

Senior Researcher: Thomas Cuddihy, B.A.

Staff Members: Margaret Anderson, B.A.; Lydia Cohen, B.A.; Helen McVey Colvin, B.A.; Margaret Covode, B.A.; Susan Day, B.A.; David Diao, B.A.; Edward Diaz, B.A.; Stephen Elliott, B.A.; Imre Horvath, M.A.; Rita Horvath, B.A.; Leland Lowther, M.A.; Susan Nergaard, B.F.A.; Peter Scarlet, B.A.; Ralph Slayton, B.S.; Camilla Turnbull, B.A.; Sally Valentine, B.A.

PROOFREADERS

Chief Proofreader: Martha L. Moffett, B.S.

Staff Members: Elizabeth M. Elkind, B.A.; Patricia M. Godfrey, B.A.; Susan F. Heimann, M.A.; Louise Oblan-Shor, B.A.

INDEXERS

Chief Indexer: Ruth Hines, M.L.S.

Consulting Indexer: Sarita Robinson, M.A.

Dictionary Index Editor: Sybil Rhoads, B.S.

Staff Members: Diane Gilroy, M.A.; Janet Hadley; Zohreh Kerendian, B.S.; Brenda Kurz, B.A.; Martin S. Mitchell, B.A.; Barbara Paskell, B.A.; Margaret Reed; Carole Schindeler, M.A.; Toni Strauss, B.S.; Barbra Wood, B.A.

MAPS

Map Designer: George Buctel, B.A.

Editor: Linda Keim, B.A.

Assistant Editors: Emily Wood Corbin, A.A.; Margo Dryden, A.A.; Cyril Edoho, M.A.; Arlene Zuckerman, B.A.

OFFICE MANAGER

Joanne Burns

STAFF ASSISTANTS

Kiki Barroso; Rose Ann Bonetti; Sheridan Cogan; Willie May Elcock; Louisa Folta; Anne Hegarty; Ruth Heim; Aline Moyler; Mitzi L. Sanchez; Dorothy Schatten; Minna Sedler; Stephanie Shaffer

ART AND PRODUCTION

Art and Production Director: Verne Bowman, B.F.A.

Production Manager: Charles Behre, B.A.

Assistant Art Director: Chester Prosinski, B.F.A.

Art Coordinator: Rita Maduro, B.S.

Typography Manager: Barbara Effron, B.S.

Typography Coordinators
Tema Harris, B.F.A.; Geraldine Felder Smith

Layout Designers
Susan Colton, B.A.; Ronald Cooper, A.A.S.; Sue Crooks; Nancy Ferguson, B.A.; Mary Ann Joulwan; Sidney Miller; Miriam Troner, B.A.

Staff Artist
Irmgard Lochner

PHOTO EDITORS

Chief Editor: Isabelle Rubin, M.A.

Administrative Assistant: Susan Lewis West, B.A.

Staff Members: Anne Alpert, B.A.; Carol Baker, B.A.; Beverly Bayne, B.A., B.S.; Laura Bustard; Lois Davis, M.A.; Wesley Day, B.A.; Monika Dillon, B.A.; Iris Eaton; Ada Fridman, M.D.; Richard Green, B.A.; Elizabeth Heskett, M.A.; Gloria Hoffman, B.A.; Dorothy Kalins, B.A.; Jane Latta; Diana Lee, B.A.; Alice Lundoff, M.S.; Ivy Minely, B.A.; Barbara Nagelsmith, B.S.; Marjorie Goreff Neuwirth, B.A.; Joan Scafarello, B.A.; Lisl Steiner, B.A.; Patricia Walsh, M.A.

STAFF ASSISTANTS

Linda Bokor; Nancy Hammalian, B.A.; Michael Harvest; Lynn Jacobs, B.S.; Laura Johnson, B.A.; Franklin Schmidt; Marcy Waxman, B.A.; Marjorie Williams

MANUFACTURING

Director: Ed McKenna

Staff: Raymond Labott; Walter Stork

ABBOTT, SIR JOHN JOSEPH CALDWELL.
See Canada, Government of (Profiles).

ABBREVIATIONS

Abbreviations are shortened forms of words and phrases. In the past, when all writing was done by hand, abbreviations saved time and space. Today, although most of what we read is printed, so much information is available that we need abbreviations for much the same reasons.

There are various ways of abbreviating words. A part of the whole word followed by a period may be used. It is often the first syllable or letters, as in Mon. for Monday, Jan. for January, co. for company or county. Some words are shortened to the first and last letters: pr. for pair, yr. for year, Mr. for Mister. In other cases key letters are selected: TV for *te*le*v*ision, pkg. for package. Modern abbreviations often use initials, and many omit periods (CB, mpg, UFO).

Initials for many Latin phrases are used as abbreviations. Here the period is retained. For example, the letters i.e. stand for the Latin *id est*, which means "that is." No., meaning number, goes back to *numero*, the Latin word meaning "by number."

People often make up their own abbreviations, and some of these, like VIP (*v*ery *i*mportant *p*erson), come into general usage. Your notebook may contain abbreviations that you have made up yourself.

An **acronym** is a word formed from the initial letters in a phrase or title. It is pronounced as a single word, not as a series of letters. OPEC, one such form, stands for the name *O*rganization of *P*etroleum *E*xporting *C*ountries. This acronym, like many others, omits periods.

Some common abbreviations and acronyms are listed below. Others may be found in the dictionary, in the regular alphabetical order of words or in a special appendix.

Isabelle Forst
Former Assistant Superintendent of Schools
New York City

See also Chemistry for abbreviations of chemical elements; Postal Service for abbreviations of state names; articles on letters of the alphabet for abbreviations beginning with those letters.

AAA—American Automobile Association
A.A.U.—Amateur Athletic Union
ABC—American Broadcasting Company
AC—alternating current
ACLU—American Civil Liberties Union
A.D., A.D.—*anno Domini* (Latin, "in the year of our Lord")
ad, advt.—advertisement
adj.—adjective
aka—also known as
ALA—American Library Association
alt.—altitude
A.M., a.m.—*ante meridiem* (Latin, "before noon")
AMA—American Medical Association
anon.—anonymous (giving no name)
AP—Associated Press
assn., assoc.—association
asst.—assistant
att., atty.—attorney
attn.—attention
ATV—all-terrain vehicle
Ave., Av.—Avenue
AWOL—absent without leave
b.—born
B.A., A.B.—Bachelor of Arts
BBC—British Broadcasting Corporation
B.C., B.C.—before Christ
B.C.E.—before (the) common era
bldg.—building
Blvd.—Boulevard
B.S., B.Sc.—Bachelor of Science
C—Celsius
c., ca.—*circa* (Latin,"about")
cap.—capital
Capt.—Captain
CB—citizens band (radio frequency)
CBC—Canadian Broadcasting Corporation
CBS—Columbia Broadcasting System
CD—certificate of deposit; compact disc
cf.—*confer* (Latin,"compare")
chap.—chapter
CO—Commanding Officer
co.—company; county
c/o.—care of
Col.—Colonel
col.—college; column
cop., ©—copyright
CORE—Congress of Racial Equality
corp.—corporation; corporal
C.P.A.—certified public accountant
CPR—cardiopulmonary resuscitation
CPU—central processing unit
CST—central standard time
d.—died; day
D.A.—District Attorney
D.A.R.—Daughters of the American Revolution
DC—direct current
D.D.—Doctor of Divinity
D.D.S.—Doctor of Dental Surgery
dec.—deceased
Dem.—Democrat
dept.—department
dia., diam.—diameter
DNA—deoxyribonucleic acid (chemical carrying genetic information)
Dr.—Doctor
DST—daylight saving time
e.g.—*exempli gratia* (Latin, "for example")
EKG—electrocardiogram
elev.—elevation
EPA—Environmental Protection Agency
ERA—Equal Rights Amendment
Esq.—Esquire
est.—established; estimated
EST—eastern standard time
ETA—estimated time of arrival
et al.—*et alii* (Latin, "and other")
etc.—*et cetera* (Latin, "and the rest")
F—Fahrenheit
FBI—Federal Bureau of Investigation
FCC—Federal Communications Commission
fed.—federal

ff.—following (pages)
FHA—Federal Housing Administration
Fig.—Figure
Gen.—General
GI—government issue
GNP—gross national product
G.O.P.—Grand Old Party, nickname for present Republican Party in the United States
Gov.—Governor
H.M.S.—His (or Her) Majesty's Service; His (or Her) Majesty's Ship
Hon.—Honorable
hosp.—hospital
H.P., HP, h.p.—horsepower
hr.—hour(s)
H.R.H.—His (or Her) Royal Highness
ht.—height
ibid.—*ibidem* (Latin, "in the same place")
ICBM—intercontinental ballistic missile
i.e.—*id est* (Latin, "that is")
ill., illus.—illustrated; illustration
inc.—incorporated; including
I.N.R.I.—*Iesus Nazarenus Rex Iudaeorum* (Latin, "Jesus of Nazareth, King of the Jews")
intro.—introduction
IOU—I owe you
IQ—intelligence quotient
IRA—individual retirement account
I.R.A.—Irish Republican Army
IRS—Internal Revenue Service
J.P.—justice of the peace
Jr.—Junior
KO—knockout
kwhr., kwh.—kilowatt-hour(s)
l., ll.—line, lines
lab—laboratory
Lat.—Latin
lat.—latitude
Lieut., Lt.—Lieutenant
lit.—literary
lon., long.—longitude
L.P.N.—licensed practical nurse
Ltd.—limited
m.—married, meter
M.A., A.M.—Master of Arts
Maj.—Major
max.—maximum
M.B.A.—Master of Business Administration
M.D.—Doctor of Medicine
med.—medical; medicine
mfg., manuf.—manufacturing
mgr.—manager
MIA—missing in action
min.—minimum; minute(s)
misc.—miscellaneous
mo.—month(s)
M.O.—*modus operandi* (Latin, "method of operation"); mail order
MP—military police
M.P.—member of Parliament
mpg—miles per gallon
mph—miles per hour
Mr.—Mister
Mrs.—Mistress (the original term for a married or unmarried woman)
M.S.—Master of Science
Ms.—Miss or Mrs.
MS, ms; MSS, mss—manuscript; manuscripts
MST—mountain standard time
Mt., mt.—mount; mountain
n.—noun
NAACP—National Association for the Advancement of Colored People
NASA—National Aeronautics and Space Administration
natl.—national
NATO—North Atlantic Treaty Organization
N.B.—*nota bene* (Latin, "note well")
NBC—National Broadcasting Company
NFL—National Football League
NOW—National Organization for Women
OAS—Organization of American States
op. cit.—*opere citato* (Latin, "in the work cited")
OPEC—Organization of Petroleum Exporting Countries
p., pp.—page; pages
P.A.—physician's assistant
par.—paragraph; parallel
PBS—Public Broadcasting Service
PC—personal computer
pd.—paid
Pfc.—Private, First Class
Ph.D.—Doctor of Philosophy
pkg.—package
pl.—plural
P.M.—Prime Minister
P.M., p.m.—*post meridiem* (Latin, "after noon")
P.O.—Post Office
pop.—population
POW—prisoner of war
pr.—pair
pres.—president
prof.—professor
pron.—pronoun
pro tem.—*pro tempore* (Latin, "for the time being"; "temporarily")
P.S.—postscript; Public School
pseud.—pseudonym
PST—Pacific standard time
PTA—Parent-Teacher Association
pub.—public; publisher; published
Q.E.D.—*quod erat demonstrandum* (Latin, "which was to be shown or proved")
q.v.—*quod vide* (Latin, "which see")
RAF—Royal Air Force
rd.—road
RDA—recommended dietary allowance
recd.—received
Rep.—Republican; Representative
Rev.—Reverend
rev.—revenue; revised
R.N.—Registered Nurse
RNA—ribonucleic acid (in cells, chemical used to build protein)
R.O.T.C.—Reserve Officers' Training Corps
rpm—revolutions per minute
R.R.—railroad; rural route
R.S.V.P.—*Répondez, s'il vous plaît* (French, "please reply")
RV—recreational vehicle
SEC—Securities and Exchange Commission
sec.—second
sec., secy.—secretary
Sen.—Senator
sing.—singular
soc.—society
SPCA—Society for the Prevention of Cruelty to Animals
SPCC—Society for the Prevention of Cruelty to Children
sq.—square
Sr.—Senior
SST—supersonic transport
St.—Saint; Street
Ste.—Sainte (French, feminine of Saint)
subj.—subject
supt.—superintendent
syn.—synonym
tbs., T—tablespoon(s)
temp.—temperature
tr.—translation; transpose
treas.—treasury; treasurer
tsp., t—teaspoon(s)
U., univ.—university
UFO—unidentified flying object
UHF—ultrahigh frequency
U.N.—United Nations
UPI—United Press International
USPS—United States Postal Service
U.S.S.—United States Ship
v.—verb; verse
VA—Veterans Administration
VAT—value-added tax
VCR—videocassette recorder
VFW—Veterans of Foreign Wars
VHF—very high frequency
vid.—*vide* (Latin, "see"; used to direct attention, as *vide p. 40*)
VISTA—Volunteers in Service to America
viz.—*videlicet* (Latin, "namely")
v.p.—vice president
vs.—*versus* (Latin, "against")
wk.—week
wt.—weight
yr.—year

ABERNATHY, RALPH DAVID. See ALABAMA (Famous People).

ABNAKI INDIANS. See INDIANS, AMERICAN (The Algonkians).

ABOLITION MOVEMENT

The abolition movement in United States history was a two-hundred-year campaign to free American blacks from the practice of slavery, or forced labor. The movement, which began in the late 1600's, evolved through several increasingly militant stages before the Civil War (1861–65) brought the issue to a climax. After four years of bloodshed, the victory of the Union forces made possible the ratification of the 13th Amendment (1865), which finally declared slavery illegal in the United States.

Early Activities and Accomplishments

The first recorded abolition meeting took place in 1688 in Germantown, Pennsylvania, among a group of Quakers and Mennonites, whose religious beliefs equated slavery with sin. "What thing in the world," they inquired of other colonists, "can be done worse toward us, than if men should rob or steal us away and sell us for slaves to strange countries?" For the next one hundred years, individuals continued to speak out against forced servitude, but no formal antislavery organization was founded until Benjamin Franklin helped organize the Pennsylvania Society for Promoting the Abolition of Slavery in Philadelphia in 1775. Dozens of similar protest organizations soon sprang up in other Northern states, gaining members beyond religious circles.

The three primary goals of these pioneer antislavery societies were to improve the living conditions of the black population, both slave and free; to challenge suspected false claims of slave ownership; and to petition legislative bodies to emancipate, or free, slaves within their jurisdictions. These initial movements were highly successful, and by 1804 slavery had been abolished in Rhode Island, Vermont, Pennsylvania, Massachusetts, New Hampshire,

At Boston's Tremont Temple in 1860, police and a hostile mob broke up an abolitionist meeting held in memory of the first anniversary of John Brown's execution.

Connecticut, and New Jersey. In addition, the importation of slaves from Africa ended in 1808, according to the terms of the U.S. Constitution (Article I, Section 9).

Militant Abolitionism

A more militant stage of the antislavery movement began in 1829 with the publication of *An Appeal to the Colored People of the World*. Written by David Walker, a freeborn black, the *Appeal* called for a slave revolt in the United States similar to the violent uprisings that had freed Haitian slaves from French colonial rule in the late 1700's. Legislators in Georgia and North Carolina enacted laws to censor what they termed incendiary, or explosive, publications, and African Americans in the South were arrested for distributing copies of Walker's pamphlet.

On January 1, 1831, a young and outspoken white abolitionist from Massachusetts named William Lloyd Garrison published the first issue of his antislavery newspaper, *The Liberator*. The following year he helped organize the New England Anti-Slavery Society in Boston.

In 1833 representatives from eleven states met in Philadelphia to form a national organization, the American

This moving emblem of a man in chains became the unofficial symbol of the abolition movement. It was used to illustrate a wide variety of antislavery publications.

Profiles

Frederick Douglass

John Brown

John Brown (1800–59), born in Torrington, Conn., was the most radical of the militant white abolitionists and a hero to the slaves. A biography of John Brown appears in Volume B.

Frederick Douglass (Frederick Augustus Washington Bailey) (1817–95), born a slave in Tuckahoe, Md., escaped to the North in 1838. An orator and editor of the antislavery newspaper the *North Star*, he was the most influential of the black abolitionists. A biography of Frederick Douglass appears in Volume D.

James Forten (1766–1842), a free black, born in Philadelphia, Pa., was a major financial contributor to the abolition movement. As a teenager, he served on an American ship during the Revolutionary War and was taken prisoner by the British. After the war, he returned to Philadelphia and became an apprentice to a sailmaker. By 1798 he owned the business and had become quite wealthy. Forten was opposed to the movement to colonize American blacks in Africa. He assisted blacks escaping from the South and became a major financial backer of William Lloyd Garrison's newspaper, *The Liberator*.

Henry Highland Garnet (1815–82), born a slave in Kent County, Md., escaped to New York in 1824 and later became a Presbyterian minister and professional speaker with the American Anti-Slavery Society. At an 1843 National Convention of Free Colored People, he called upon slaves to rise up and "strike for your lives and liberties!" Garnet was the first African American to address the U.S. House of Representatives (1865).

William Lloyd Garrison (1805–79), born in Newburyport, Mass., was perhaps the most outspoken white champion of the abolitionist cause. In the first edition (1831) of his newspaper, *The Liberator*, Garrison declared slavery an abomination in God's sight. He demanded immediate emancipation, vowing never to be silenced. "I am in earnest—I will not equivocate—I will not excuse—I will not retreat a single inch; and I will be heard!" He cofounded the American Anti-Slavery Society in 1833. For additional information, see the article MASSACHUSETTS (Famous People) in Volume M.

Elijah Parish Lovejoy (1802–37), born in Albion, Me., was a white Presbyterian minister and abolitionist. Opposition to his views in St. Louis, Mo., forced Lovejoy to abandon his position there as editor of a religious newspaper. In 1837 he relocated to Alton, Ill., where he began publishing the *Alton Observer* and tried to establish a chapter of the American Anti-Slavery Society. Within the year, Lovejoy was killed by a mob that came to seize his printing press. He became a martyr to the abolitionist cause.

Robert Purvis (1810–98), a freeborn South Carolinian of a well-to-do family, moved to Philadelphia and became an antislavery activist. He was one of three African Americans who helped organize the American Anti-Slavery Society (1833). Purvis also headed (1838–44) the Philadelphia Vigilance Committee, which assisted hundreds of fugitive slaves on the Underground Railroad. "Slavery," he said, "will be abolished in this land, and with it, that twin relic of barbarism—prejudice against color."

John Brown Russwurm (1799–1851), born in Port Antonio, Jamaica, was a cofounder of *Freedom's Journal*, the first newspaper owned and operated by African Americans. The first issue was published in New York on March 16, 1827. Seeking freedom for slaves, Russwurm favored the back-to-Africa movement of the day, for which he was burned in effigy by activists opposed to colonization. In 1829 he moved to Liberia, in West Africa.

William Lloyd Garrison

Harriet Beecher Stowe

Harriet Beecher Stowe (1811–96), born in Litchfield, Ct., gained international renown for her novel *Uncle Tom's Cabin*. Published in 1852 in reaction to the Fugitive Slave Law, the book increased popular support for ending slavery. A biography of Harriet Beecher Stowe appears in Volume S.

Sojourner Truth (Isabella Van Wagener) (1797?–1883), born a slave in Ulster County, N.Y., became the most famous antislavery spokeswoman. In 1843 she said that God called upon her to "travel up and down the land" and preach his word. She changed her name to Sojourner (meaning traveler) Truth and set out on a lecture tour to speak out about religion, slavery, and women's issues. Although she could neither read nor write, she was a captivating orator. Truth touched her audiences with such declarations as, "I have borne 13 children and seen them most all sold off into slavery, and when I cried out with a mother's grief, none but Jesus heard!"

David Walker (1785–1830), a free black, born in Wilmington, N.C. , settled in Boston in 1827. He became a charter member of the Massachusetts Colored General Association and contributed to *Freedom's Journal*. In 1829, Walker published a 76-page pamphlet, *An Appeal to the Colored People of the World*, urging slaves to rise up against their oppressors, convinced that violence was the only sure way to gain freedom. Walker's *Appeal* outraged slaveholders. He died mysteriously in 1830. Most abolitionists believed he had been poisoned.

William Lloyd Garrison's *The Liberator* was the most militant antislavery publication. Founded in 1831, it was published until emancipation was achieved in 1865.

Anti-Slavery Society. Three African Americans took part in the proceedings, making it the nation's first interracial public advocacy group. Most of its members believed that persistent "moral persuasion" would eventually convince slaveholders of the immorality of slavery, and that the practice would gradually disappear. Others, however, insisted on taking political action and called for the creation of an abolitionist political party.

Political Abolitionism

In 1840 the Liberty Party was organized in Albany, New York. The new party nominated a reformed ex-slaveholder, James G. Birney, for president. Despite the tens of thousands of Americans who called themselves abolitionists, only 7,000 cast their vote for Birney. Even fewer voted for him in 1844.

In 1846, as Congress was preparing to administer the transfer of territory from Mexico, David Wilmot, a U.S. representative from Pennsylvania, offered a provision that would prohibit slavery in land added to the Union.

WONDER QUESTION

What were the Gag Rules?

By 1836, the U.S. Congress had been overwhelmed by the number of petitions from citizens requesting that slavery not be extended into new U.S. territories. Because the reading of these petitions took up so much time, that year the House of Representatives passed a series of resolutions, known as the Gag Rules, to prevent further discussion of the issue. Opponents, led by House member and former president John Quincy Adams, argued that the Gag Rules violated the citizens' First Amendment right to petition the federal government for "redress of grievances." The measures were repealed in 1844.

This Wilmot Proviso became the basis of the new Free Soil Party, which attracted former Liberty Party members as well as antislavery Democrats, known as the Barnburners.

In 1848 the Free Soil Party endorsed former president Martin Van Buren under the slogan "Free Soil, Free Speech, Free Labor, and Free Men." However, when Van Buren drew only slightly more than 10 percent of the vote, support for the Free Soil Party dwindled. By 1856 most of its members had joined the Republican Party, which was organized in 1854 in opposition to the Kansas-Nebraska Act.

The Kansas-Nebraska Act (1854), which overturned the Missouri Compromise of 1820, allowed settlers to vote for or against slavery in their own territories. Nebraskans voted no, but Kansans voted yes. The growing number of "free staters" were enraged, notably John Brown, whose subsequent attacks on Kansas slaveholders gave rise to the name Bleeding Kansas.

Abolitionists already were embittered by the passage of the Fugitive Slave Act (1850) that had made it illegal for any American to assist fugitive slaves. Outrage over this law actually increased support for the Underground Railroad, a secret network of people dedicated to helping slaves escape to the North. Abolitionists were further outraged when the U.S. Supreme Court ruled in 1857, in the Dred Scott Decision, that the Constitution protected slave property throughout the United States. Each of these actions propelled the North and South toward a civil war, which began in April 1861.

On September 22, 1862, as a military measure, U.S. president Abraham Lincoln issued his Emancipation Proclamation, declaring that as of January 1, 1863, any slave residing in a Confederate state would be "forever free." Enforcement of this policy, however, depended upon which side won the war.

On April 9, 1865, the Confederates surrendered to the Union forces and the Civil War came to an end. Eight months later, on December 18, 1865, abolition was assured with the ratification of the 13th Amendment to the Constitution.

RUSSELL L. ADAMS
Chair, Department of Afro-American Studies
Howard University

See also EMANCIPATION PROCLAMATION; UNDERGROUND RAILROAD.

ABORIGINES, AUSTRALIAN

The Australian Aborigines were the earliest known inhabitants of Australia and today are regarded as the native people of that continent. The term "aborigine," which comes from the Latin words *ab origine*, means "from the beginning" and can be applied to the native peoples of any region.

It is believed that Australia's first Aborigines migrated from Southeast Asia more than 75,000 years ago. They probably crossed the Indian Ocean and the various seas in between by raft or dugout canoe.

TRADITIONAL WAY OF LIFE

Traditionally the Aborigines were divided into about 500 tribal groups, each with its own language or dialect. Each tribe claimed its own territory and moved from place to place within that area to hunt, fish, and gather food.

Each tribe was an extended family made up of several clans. Clan members lived in family groups of thirty to forty people. Each clan had an emblem called a totem—perhaps an animal or a plant. The totem was honored as a clan member and served as a reminder of the clan's common ancestry. The Aborigines believed that all things—people, animals, plants, and even rocks—were important parts of nature and of the spirit world.

The Aborigines survived by adapting to Australia's often harsh conditions. They were one of the few early peoples to use the lever, as part of a woomera (spear-thrower). They also used several types of boomerangs, flat, curved throwing sticks made of hardwood. One type, the returning boomerang, was used for sport. When thrown properly, this kind spins through the air and returns to the thrower in a perfect arc. The Aborigines also used non-returning boomerang-type weapons for hunting, fighting, and other purposes, but they were not the only early culture to use such a tool. The Aborigines also left a rich heritage of artwork in the form of rock carvings and bark and cave paintings.

In 1788, when the first European settlers came to Australia, there were perhaps more than 300,000 Aborigines living there. As the Europeans spread out, many natives were driven from their lands into remote areas. Many others died from foreign diseases.

In Australia's Aboriginal societies, adult males are the principal guardians of sacred rites and culture. Ritual dances and body painting are two forms of expression that create a spiritual connection to ancestral origins.

ABORIGINES IN MODERN AUSTRALIA

Today there are about 265,000 Aboriginal peoples in Australia. About one-third of them are considered full-blooded. The remainder are of mixed Aboriginal-European ancestry.

All together, Aborigines make up only about 1.5 percent of Australia's population. Most live in cities and towns, although a few are trying to preserve some form of the old, nomadic way of life.

The standard of living for most Aborigines lags far behind that of other Australian citizens. In the past few decades, the government has sponsored a number of programs to help the Aborigines compete for jobs and housing opportunities.

In recent years, efforts also have been made on the part of the Aborigines to regain title to their ancestral lands. They have been successful in regaining ownership of some parts of the Northern Territory and of South Australia. Since 1980, these lands have been administered by the Aboriginal Development Commission. In 1992 the Australian High Court ruled that the Aborigines owned Australia before European settlement began, and in 1994 they were given the right to claim land under "native" title.

CAROL PERKINS
Author, *The Sound of Boomerangs*

See also AUSTRALIA (The Aborigines).

ABORTION

Abortion is the ending of a pregnancy before the fetus (unborn child) has developed and grown enough to live outside the mother. If abortion happens naturally, before the 20th week of pregnancy, it is called a spontaneous abortion, or miscarriage. If it happens naturally after the 20th week, it is termed a late fetal death or a stillbirth.

If abortion is caused by artificial means, generally by medical procedure, it is called an induced abortion. Most induced abortions in the United States are performed in the first trimester of the pregnancy.

In the United States, a debate rages over the ethical and legal aspects of induced abortion. Members of the right-to-life movement believe that abortion is morally wrong and should be restricted or prohibited because it ends the life of a human being. They have influenced a number of states to vote on bills that would outlaw abortion except for pregnancies caused by criminal acts, or when the mother's life is at risk. People who refer to themselves as pro-choice may also believe that abortion is morally wrong. But they believe that the law should protect the woman's right to medical privacy and the right to choose for herself whether to have an abortion. They also argue that statistics show fewer pregnancy-related deaths wherever abortion is legal.

In 1973, in the *Roe* v. *Wade* case, the U.S. Supreme Court ruled that a woman could not be prevented from having an induced abortion during her first trimester. Prevention, the Court said, would violate the woman's right to privacy. States could, however, restrict second trimester abortions and prohibit third trimester abortions. In 1992 the Court allowed additional restrictions. Some states may now require a 24-hour waiting period or permission from the parents of a pregnant teenager or the father of the fetus. The abortion-inducing drug RU-486 was approved for use in the United States in 2000.

ANN E. WEISS
Author, *Bioethics: Dilemmas in Modern Medicine*

ABRAHAM

Abraham is called the father of the Jews and is considered the founder of the Jewish religion. He was the first to believe in one all-powerful God instead of many gods.

Abraham's story is found in the book of Genesis, the first book of the Bible. When Abraham was 75 years old, God commanded him to leave Haran in search of a new home. God promised that a great nation would arise in the new land. Abraham set out with his wife, Sarah, his nephew Lot, and some followers. They traveled into the land of Canaan. God told Abraham that this was the land he would give to Abraham's descendants. Abraham journeyed on toward the south, building altars to God wherever he went. When a famine came, he went into Egypt. He grew rich in cattle, silver, and gold.

When Abraham and his followers left Egypt, both Abraham and Lot grew very prosperous. They acquired so many sheep that their shepherds quarreled over grazing land. Abraham and Lot agreed to separate and live in different places.

The story of Abraham is told in Genesis, the first book of the Bible. Here Abraham is shown receiving a message from God, promising him a son.

Abraham settled in Hebron. Lot and his family settled in Sodom. When Sodom was attacked by the armies of four great kings, Lot was taken captive. Abraham went to his rescue with 318 men and brought Lot and all his goods back to Sodom.

The people of Sodom and neighboring Gomorrah grew very wicked. God told Abraham that he would destroy both cities because no righteous people could be found in them. But God warned Lot to escape with his wife and two daughters, forbidding them to look behind as they fled. Lot's wife looked back, and she became a pillar of salt.

When Abraham and Sarah had grown very old and were still childless, God promised them a son. God also said that Abraham would have as many descendants as there were stars in the sky and that one day they would dwell in the Promised Land. In time, a son was born to Abraham and Sarah and was named Isaac. God told Abraham that he would keep his promise with Isaac and his descendants.

While Isaac was still a boy, God tested Abraham again. He told Abraham to take Isaac to the top of a mountain and sacrifice him. Abraham loved his son, but he could not disobey God's command. At the place of sacrifice, Isaac asked, "Where is the lamb for a burnt offering?" Abraham answered that God would provide it. Then he built an altar, bound up Isaac, and laid him on top of the altar. Just as he was about to put the knife to his son, God stopped him. God said, "Lay not thine hand upon the lad, neither do thou any thing unto him: for now I know that thou fearest God, seeing thou hast not withheld thy son, thine only son, from me." Abraham looked up and saw a ram caught in a thicket. He offered the ram in sacrifice. God blessed Abraham for his obedience.

When Sarah and Abraham died, they were buried in the cave of Machpelah in Hebron. After Abraham's death, God blessed Isaac.

Christians and Muslims also honor Abraham and trace their belief in one God back to him. The Arabs claim descent from Ishmael, who was Abraham's son by Hagar, Sarah's handmaiden. Sarah had given Hagar to Abraham when she thought she herself would have no children.

Abraham's life is regarded as an example of the proving of faith through trial. Because Abraham listened to God, he is called the Friend of God. His unquestioning obedience to God's commands is taken as proof of genuine righteousness.

Reviewed by MORTIMER J. COHEN
Author, *Pathways Through the Bible*

ACCIDENTS. See FIRST AID; SAFETY.

ACCOUNTING. See BOOKKEEPING AND ACCOUNTING.

ACHAEMENIDS. See PERSIA, ANCIENT.

ACHILLES. See GREEK MYTHOLOGY.

ACID RAIN

Acid rain is a general term for rain or other precipitation that has been polluted by chemicals called acids. This environmental problem can pollute lakes, rivers, and streams; damage metals and other construction materials; and even pose a health risk to people.

Acid rain forms when certain pollutants, such as sulfur oxides and nitrogen oxides, mix with tiny droplets of water vapor in the atmosphere. Power plants are the main source of pollutants causing acid rain. Smoke from factories, exhaust fumes from automobiles and trucks, and even gases given off by chemical fertilizers also put pollutants into the air. The pollutants change the clean, fresh water to droplets of acid. These acids fall to the ground as rain, snow, or sleet. Even fog can contain acids.

Rain normally contains some naturally occurring acids, which are not considered a problem. However, sulfuric and nitric acids in rain are a problem. Acid rain soaks the ground and can make soil, lakes, and rivers abnormally acidic. In badly affected regions, plants and many types of aquatic animals are harmed. Entire lakes and some forest trees can be affected. Even buildings and statues can be damaged by acid rain.

Pollution That Causes Acid Rain. When fossil fuels—oil, coal, and gas—are burned, in industrial plants or automobile engines, for example, sulfur oxides and nitrogen oxides are released into the air.

Nitrogen oxides and other acid-forming chemicals also enter the air from the breakdown of agricultural fertilizers. Hydrochloric acid often comes directly from smokestacks.

Acid rain weakened these trees (*above*), leaving them unable to survive a deadly insect infestation. Sculptures (*right*) that existed intact for centuries are decaying at an alarming rate due to acid rain and other pollution.

Carbon monoxide and carbon dioxide are produced by motor vehicles.

Because pollutants can travel over hundreds and even thousands of miles, acid rain often affects areas that are far from power plants and heavy automobile exhaust. Pollutants in smoke enter the air high above the ground through tall smokestacks and are carried by winds for great distances. Pollutants from the midwestern United States are regularly carried to New York, New England, and southeastern Canada. Similarly, pollution from Canada is carried by winds into the United States. Norway and Sweden have received acid rain created by pollutants from England, Germany, Italy, France, and Austria.

The Effects of Acid Rain. Millions of tons of acids fall in rain on the United States and Canada each year. The concentrations of these acids are too weak to cause burns, but they do produce other less severe effects.

When acid rain falls on metal objects, the objects can be damaged. Shiny objects become dull and, if the process continues for many years, the metal objects can corrode and lose strength or crumble. Acid rain also affects the surfaces of stone statues and stone or brick buildings.

The way in which acid rain reacts with aluminum can cause serious ecological problems. Aluminum is normally present in soil. If acid rain causes soil acidification, the aluminum in the soil may dissolve in water and be absorbed by plants, where it can damage root cells. Animal cells are also very sensitive to aluminum. In lakes and streams, it can kill the eggs of many kinds of fish and the embryos of salamanders and other amphibians. Aluminum affects mature fish by causing the gills to clog with mucus, preventing breathing. It also disrupts eggshell formation in birds.

Human beings may also be at risk from the effects of acid rain. In moist air, high levels of pollutants from acidic aerosols have been found to affect lung function in experimental studies. People who suffer from asthma, emphysema, and chronic bronchitis are more sensitive to acid environments.

Stopping Acid Rain. In 1990, the United States passed the Clean Air Act Amendments. This was a law that required significant annual reductions in air pollution. One measure to fight acid rain is to remove from the air those sulfur and nitrogen compounds that become acids. Some of these compounds can be taken out of fuel before the fuel is burned. Or the pollutants can be removed from smoke before the smoke enters the air. Each individual also can play a role in reducing air pollution by conserving energy through such activities as cutting back on the use of electricity and carpooling or using public transportation.

Reviewed by Patricia M. Irving
Director, National Acid Precipitation Assessment Program

ACIDS. See Chemistry.

ACNE. See Diseases (Descriptions of Some Diseases).

ACOUSTICS. See Sound and Ultrasonics.

ADAMS, CHARLES FRANCIS (1807–1886)

Charles Francis Adams was an American historian and diplomat. The son of President John Quincy Adams and the grandson of President John Adams, he was born in Boston, Massachusetts, on August 18, 1807. He graduated from Harvard in 1825, became a lawyer, and later entered politics, serving in the Massachusetts state legislature (1840–45) as a Whig. Adams, who opposed slavery, switched over to the Free Soil Party and ran unsuccessfully as its vice-presidential candidate in 1848. Later he served in the U.S. House of Representatives as a Republican (1859–61).

Adams performed his most important work during the U.S. Civil War. In 1861 he was appointed ambassador to Great Britain by President Abraham Lincoln. The British government had declared itself neutral in the American conflict, yet many prominent Britons openly supported the Confederate states, and several Confederate navy ships were built in England. Adams persuaded the British government not to intervene diplomatically on the Confederate side and to officially ban further shipbuilding for the Confederates (although several ships continued to slip through on the black market).

In 1872 Adams represented the United States on an international committee that settled the so-called *Alabama* claims for damages caused by British-built Confederate ships during the Civil War. The committee assessed Great Britain $15.5 million for damages for building the *Alabama* and other ships, which had violated international neutrality laws.

Adams edited many letters, papers, and diaries of his famous parents and grandparents. Among the most notable is his 12-volume *Memoirs of John Quincy Adams* (1864–67). He died in Boston on November 21, 1886.

MICHAEL WINSHIP
Cornell University

ADAMS, HENRY (1838–1918)

Henry Brooks Adams—historian, novelist, and philosopher—was born on February 16, 1838, in Boston, Massachusetts. Adams came from a distinguished family. His grandfather, John Quincy Adams, and his great grandfather, John Adams, both were former presidents of the United States; his father, Charles Francis Adams, was a historian, diplomat, and politician. Not surprisingly, Henry Adams grew up assuming that he, too, would be an important person one day.

When Adams graduated from Harvard in 1858, he entered a world in which he felt he did not belong. He tried a number of careers, first as his father's private secretary (1861–68). He later became a journalist, and then for seven years he taught history at Harvard.

Finally in 1877, Adams settled down in Washington, D.C. There he suffered a great personal tragedy in 1885 when his beloved wife Marian committed suicide. Adams devoted himself to writing books. In his *Mont-Saint-Michel and Chartres: A Story of 13th Century Unity* (1913), he described the Middle Ages as a time of beauty and spiritual unity, very much unlike the chaotic times in which he felt he lived. It seemed to him that America was a harsh place where only the most brutal and energetic people could succeed, not the most intelligent and idealistic. In *The Education of Henry Adams* (1918), he explored this observation, trying to understand how the world had changed and why he could not adapt to the new society.

In 1919, a year after Henry Adams' death, *The Education of Henry Adams* was awarded a Pulitzer prize. It is still considered a classic among autobiographies.

Among Adams' other works were two novels, *Democracy, an American Novel* (1880), a political satire; and *Esther* (1884), the story of a woman's search for religious truth. His most important historical work was the multi-volume *History of the United States during the Administrations of Jefferson and Madison* (1884–1891). Adams died in Washington, D.C., on March 27, 1918.

MICHAEL WINSHIP
Cornell University

JOHN ADAMS (1735-1826)

2nd President of the United States

FACTS ABOUT JOHN ADAMS

Birthplace: Braintree (now Quincy), Massachusetts *(below)*
Religion: Unitarian
College Attended: Harvard College, Cambridge, Massachusetts
Occupation: Lawyer
Married: Abigail Smith
Children: Abigail, John Quincy, Susanna, Charles, Thomas
Political Party: Federalist
Office Held Before Becoming President: Vice President
President Who Preceded Him: George Washington
Age on Becoming President: 61
Years in the Presidency: 1797–1801
Vice President: Thomas Jefferson
President Who Succeeded Him: Thomas Jefferson
Age at Death: 90
Burial Place: First Unitarian Church, Quincy, Massachusetts

John Adams

DURING JOHN ADAMS' PRESIDENCY

The first cast-iron plow was patented by Charles Newbold (1797). *Below:* Disputes between the United States and France led to an undeclared naval war between the two nations and the creation of the Navy Department (1798). *Left:* The U.S. Marine Corps was established as a permanent service by Congress (1798). The Mississippi Territory, including what is now Mississippi and Alabama, was created (1798). The Indiana Territory, including all or parts of present-day Indiana, Wisconsin, Illinois, Michigan, and Minnesota, was created (1800). The capital was moved from Philadelphia to Washington, D.C. (1800).

ADAMS, JOHN. Of all the early presidents of the United States, John Adams has been the least understood and appreciated. His reputation, both during his lifetime and after, has suffered from this lack of understanding. Yet he was a remarkable man who contributed greatly to the creation of the United States during the American Revolution and in its formative years.

▶ EARLY YEARS

Adams was born on October 30, 1735, in Braintree (now Quincy), Massachusetts. His great-grandfather Henry Adams had emigrated from England. But both his grandfather Joseph Adams and his father, John Adams, had been born in Braintree. His mother, Susanna Boylston Adams, came from the nearby city of Boston.

Adams grew up on his father's farm, doing the usual country chores, including feeding the horses, milking the cows, and chopping wood. In 1751, at the age of 16, he entered Harvard, then a small college, and graduated four years later. He then taught school during the day and studied law at night. In 1758 he became a lawyer. Perhaps his most famous case, which showed Adams' characteristic courage, was his successful defense of the British soldiers who were arrested after the Boston Massacre in 1770.

In 1764, Adams married Abigail Smith. She was an intelligent and sprightly woman whose letters are still a source of interesting information. The marriage was happy and successful. It lasted 54 years, until Abigail Adams' death in 1818. Their eldest son, John Quincy, later became the sixth president.

▶ POLITICAL BEGINNINGS

Altogether, Adams spent about 25 years in public life. He became interested in politics quite early in his career as a lawyer. In 1765 a crisis arose when the British Government passed the Stamp Act. This was an unpopular tax on public documents, newspapers, licenses, insurance policies, and even playing cards. Adams wrote powerful articles against the tax in the Boston *Gazette*. These articles

Abigail Adams was the wife of one president, John Adams, and the mother of a second, John Quincy Adams. She was the first First Lady to occupy the White House.

helped to establish his reputation as a political thinker, as an opponent of Britain's colonial policies in America, and as a champion of individual liberties.

The Continental Congress. Adams served as a delegate from Massachusetts to the First Continental Congress in Philadelphia in 1774 and to the Second Continental Congress, which met in 1775. With brilliance and persistence, he argued for American independence from Britain. When the fighting broke out in 1775 that marked the beginning of the Revolutionary War, Adams proposed George Washington as the commander of American military forces.

Adams was a member of the committee that drafted the Declaration of Independence. Although the Declaration was written chiefly by Thomas Jefferson, Adams bore the burden of defending it on the floor of the Continental Congress. It was adopted on July 4, 1776.

Diplomatic Service. Adams' diplomatic career began in 1778 when he was sent to France to help negotiate a treaty of alliance. In 1780 he returned to Europe as minister to arrange for loans and trade agreements in France and the Netherlands. Two years later Adams, together with Benjamin Franklin and John Jay, signed the preliminary peace treaty with Britain. The treaty, known as the Treaty of Paris, was finally concluded in 1783. It ended the Revolutionary War and crowned Adams' long struggle for American independence.

In 1785, Adams was appointed the first U.S. minister to Britain. He tried to win British friendship and economic co-operation, but without success. One reason was that he was too outspoken in defense of American interests. He was happy to return home in 1788, after having spent some ten years abroad.

Vice President. In the first presidential election in the United States, in 1788, George Washington won all the electoral votes cast for president. Adams became vice president. Both men were re-elected in 1792.

In spite of his general agreement with Washington's policies, Adams was impatient with his position as vice president. Adams was eager to lead and to act. Instead, he had to confine himself to the largely ceremonial job of presiding over the U.S. Senate.

PRESIDENT

Adams' frustration was ended by his victory in the presidential election of 1796. Running as the Federalist candidate, he edged out Thomas Jefferson, leader of the Democratic-Republicans (also called the Republicans). According to the laws of the time, Jefferson thus became vice president. As a result, the new president and vice president belonged to opposing political parties.

John Adams was the first president to occupy the White House. He and Abigail moved in near the end of his term, in the fall of 1800. The President's Palace, as it was then known, was still unfinished and littered with debris.

Adams' one term as president was marked by troubles, both international and domestic. The foreign affairs crisis involved American neutrality at a time when Britain and France were at war. French attacks on American ships stirred up a warlike atmosphere in the United States, even inside Adams' own Cabinet. The situation was aggravated by the so-called XYZ Affair.

The XYZ Affair. Adams had sent a diplomatic mission to France to arrange a treaty. There the diplomats were visited by three agents of the French foreign minister Talleyrand. These agents, known as X, Y, and Z, asked for a bribe of $240,000. When news of this XYZ Affair reached America, it caused an uproar and led to an undeclared war between the United States and France. But despite immense pressure, including that of members of his own Federalist Party, President Adams knew that the United States was not strong enough to fight the French Empire. He persisted in his efforts for peace, which was finally achieved by the Convention of 1800. Adams considered it his great accomplishment. He said, "I desire no other inscription over my gravestone than: 'Here lies John Adams, who took upon himself the responsibility of the peace with France in the year 1800.' "

Adams' courageous but unpopular peace policy and his stubborn independence in other political matters cost him the support of his own party. The leading Federalists, including the powerful Alexander Hamilton, turned bitterly against him. This led to a hopeless split in their party.

The Alien and Sedition Acts. President Adams' unpopularity was aggravated by the Alien and Sedition Acts. These acts were a direct result of the excitement over the trouble with France. The country was divided into pro-French and pro-British groups. Adams' Federalist Party was strongly anti-French. The opposition Democratic-Republican Party, led by Jefferson, was just as strongly anti-British.

The Federalists were convinced that opposition against them was aroused by the French and Irish living in America. They were sure that the country swarmed with French spies. The Federalists controlled Congress. In 1798 they decided to crush the opposition through legislation that came to be known as the Alien and Sedition Acts.

The Alien Act contained three provisions. One required that the period of naturalization for foreigners be changed from 5 to 14 years. The second authorized the president to deport all aliens considered dangerous to the peace and security of the country. The third gave the president the power to imprison or banish citizens of an enemy country in time of war.

More serious was the Sedition Act, which was aimed at American opponents of the government. This act made it a crime to oppose the administration directly or indirectly. Even those who voiced criticism in print were made subject to harsh penalties.

The Sedition Act resulted in the prosecution of 25 persons and the conviction of 10 of them. All were prominent Democratic-Republicans.

These acts were violently unpopular. They were considered an attack on the basic liberties of the American people. President Adams was not personally responsible for them, but they were passed by his party and he signed them. Therefore the blame fell upon him. In the election of 1800, Adams and his party suffered disastrous defeat. The Federalist Party never recovered.

On March 4, 1801, after the inauguration of President Jefferson, Adams retired from public life. He returned to Braintree and devoted the remaining 25 years of his life to

Final plans for the White House (*below*) were drawn up by Irish architect James Hoban. Construction began in 1792, and the Adams family became its first occupants in 1800.

John Adams (*standing, in rust-colored suit*) and the four other members of the drafting committee present the Declaration of Independence to the Second Continental Congress.

intellectual pursuits, mainly reading (philosophy, religion, political thought, science) and letter writing. He resumed his friendship and correspondence with Thomas Jefferson in 1812. The two men had been separated for 12 years because of political differences. On July 4, 1826—the 50th anniversary of the Declaration of Independence—John Adams died at Quincy. That same day Jefferson died at Monticello, Virginia.

HIS POLITICAL PHILOSOPHY

Adams expressed his ideas in a number of essays and books, as well as in his letters. There are three main elements in his philosophy. One is Adams' view of human nature. Another is his conception of inequality. The third is his idea of government.

IMPORTANT DATES IN THE LIFE OF JOHN ADAMS

1735	Born at Braintree (now Quincy), Massachusetts, October 30.
1755	Graduated from Harvard College.
1758	Began practicing law.
1764	Married Abigail Smith.
1765	Attacked the Stamp Act in articles in the Boston *Gazette*.
1774–1777	Served in the Continental Congress.
1780	Minister to the Netherlands.
1782	Went to Paris (with John Jay and Benjamin Franklin) to arrange peace treaty with Great Britain ending the Revolutionary War. Treaty of Paris concluded 1783.
1785–1788	Minister to Great Britain.
1789–1797	Vice-president of the United States.
1797–1801	2nd president of the United States.
1826	Died at Quincy, Massachusetts, July 4.

Adams did not agree with democrats like Jefferson that human beings were naturally good and decent. On the contrary, he believed that people were basically selfish and only good because of necessity.

Adams also denied the democratic idea of equality. He pointed out that among all nations the people were "naturally divided into two sorts, the gentlemen and the simple men." The gentlemen, being superior in abilities, education, and other advantages, were therefore qualified to rule.

These views underlay Adams' philosophy of government. Since human beings were greedy and selfish, it was necessary for society to keep them in check. The average person, he felt, could not be entrusted with power.

Adams believed in liberty and was opposed to tyranny. Though he was sometimes accused of being a monarchist, he actually preferred a republic. But instead of a Jefferson-type democracy, Adams favored a republican government run by an aristocracy of talented men.

Such views, expressed with his typical bluntness, gained Adams unpopularity and even hostility among the American people. But he was not one to seek popular favor. He died as he had lived, an independent, tough-minded, somewhat opinionated and irritable Yankee—but always a courageous patriot and scholar.

SAUL K. PADOVER
Editor, *The World of the Founding Fathers*

JOHN QUINCY ADAMS (1767-1848)

6th President of the United States

FACTS ABOUT JOHN QUINCY ADAMS
Birthplace: Braintree (now Quincy), Massachusetts *(center)*
Religion: Unitarian
College Attended: Harvard College, Cambridge, Massachusetts
Occupation: Lawyer
Married: Louisa Catherine Johnson
Children: George, John, Charles Francis, Louisa Catherine
Political Party: Federalist, Democratic-Republican (National Republican), Whig
Nickname: "Old Man Eloquent"
Office Held Before Becoming President: Secretary of State
President Who Preceded Him: James Monroe
Age on Becoming President: 57
Years in the Presidency: 1825-1829
Vice President: John C. Calhoun
President Who Succeeded Him: Andrew Jackson
Age at Death: 80
Burial Place: Quincy, Massachusetts

DURING JOHN QUINCY ADAMS' PRESIDENCY

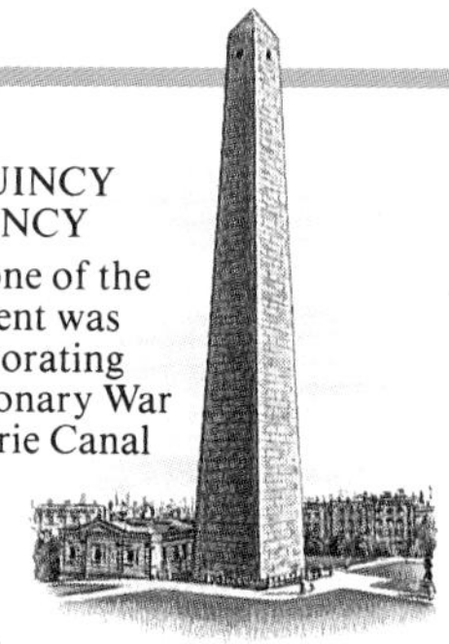

Right: The cornerstone of the Bunker Hill Monument was laid (1825), commemorating the famous Revolutionary War battle. *Below:* The Erie Canal was opened (1825), linking New York with Lake Erie and the other Great Lakes and increasing trade with and settlement of the growing Midwest. The first iron vessel, built of sheet iron, in the United States, the steamboat *Codorus,* was tested (1825) on the Susquehanna River. Construction of the Baltimore and Ohio Railroad, the first commercial passenger and freight railroad in the United States, was begun (1828).

ADAMS, JOHN QUINCY. Many Americans have sought the office of president of the United States and have deliberately shaped their lives to that end. John Quincy Adams' parents prepared him for the presidency from boyhood. But although Adams achieved his goal of becoming president, his term in the White House was overshadowed by his two other political careers—as America's greatest diplomat and as its greatest defender of human freedom in the U.S. House of Representatives.

AN UNUSUAL CHILDHOOD

John Quincy Adams was born on July 11, 1767, in Braintree (now Quincy), Massachusetts. His father was John Adams, who would later become the second president of the United States. His mother, Abigail Smith Adams, was the most accomplished American woman of her time. Young Adams grew up as a child of the American Revolution, which began when he was 7 years old.

John Quincy's education began in the village school and continued under his mother's guidance. His education was inspired by letters from his father, who had been serving in the Continental Congress in Philadelphia since 1774.

During the Revolutionary War, John Quincy accompanied his father on two diplomatic missions to Europe. In 1781, at the age of 14, he acted as French interpreter to his father on a mission to Russia. In 1783, John Quincy served as his father's secretary when the elder Adams was minister to France. Young Adams was present at the signing of the Treaty of Paris in 1783, which ended the Revolutionary War.

In Paris, John Quincy Adams began his famous diary. He was to continue it for over 60 years. On the title page of the first volume was the proverb that ruled his life: "Sweet is indolence [laziness] and cruel its consequences." Adams never had a lazy day.

Young Adams returned to Massachusetts in 1785 to complete his education at Harvard College. He graduated in 1787 and then studied law.

HIS EARLY DIPLOMATIC CAREER

He had barely developed a law practice when the French Revolution broke out. Articles Adams wrote for a Boston newspaper attracted the attention of President George Washington. In 1794 Washington appointed the 28-year-old John Quincy Adams minister to the Netherlands. Adams' official dispatches and his letters from the Dutch capital at The Hague convinced the President that this young man would one day stand at the head of the American diplomatic corps.

In 1797, while on a mission from the Netherlands to England, Adams married Louisa Catherine Johnson, daughter of the American consul in London.

From The Hague Adams (whose father was now president) was assigned to the Court of Prussia. There he negotiated a treaty of friendship and commerce. He continued his letters and dispatches about the war of the French Revolution. Because of political reasons, John Adams recalled him after Thomas Jefferson was elected president in 1800.

Adams' experiences had convinced him that the United States must never be caught in the "vortex" of European rivalries and wars. This lesson guided him through his later diplomatic career and influenced United States policy for a century afterwards.

A SHORT TERM IN THE SENATE

When he returned to Boston, Adams found the practice of law frustrating. He had a strong desire to enter politics. In 1803 the Massachusetts legislature elected him to the United States Senate. Though elected as a Federalist, Adams felt that party politics stopped at the ocean's edge. To the disgust of Massachusetts Federalists, he voted for President Jefferson's Embargo of 1807. The embargo was aimed at protecting United States neutrality in the wars between England and France. It stopped all American trade with the two countries. Adams' vote in favor of the embargo cost him his Senate seat. The legislature held a special election ahead of time to replace him with a more faithful Federalist.

DIPLOMAT AGAIN

In 1809 President James Madison appointed Adams the first American minister to Russia. Adams was in Russia when the War of 1812 broke out between the United States and Great Britain. He served on the delegation that brought about the Peace of Ghent in 1814. The following year he became minister to Great Britain, where he served until 1817.

By now Adams was in his 50th year. He was without question the most experienced man in the United States diplomatic service. Because of his European experience, Adams had become a confirmed isolationist. He felt that the future of the United States lay in expansion across the North American continent rather than in European alliances.

SECRETARY OF STATE

In 1817 President James Monroe called Adams home to become secretary of state. The most important achievements of Secretary Adams were the treaties he negotiated, which brought much of the Far West under American control. The famous Transcontinental Treaty of 1819 (ratified 1821) with Spain gave the United States access to the Pacific Ocean. This was the greatest diplomatic triumph ever achieved by one man in the history of the United States. Adams was also responsible for treaties with the newly independent countries of Latin America.

The Monroe Doctrine

John Quincy Adams had a major role in forming the Monroe Doctrine. Adams' words in that famous document made it clear that the United States would not tolerate any new European colonization in the Americas. The doctrine properly bears President Monroe's name. For it was Monroe who in 1823 first declared its principles to the world as American foreign policy.

The Election of 1824

Adams was never a dynamic politician. But his accomplishments brought him before the people in the national election of 1824. There was no real party contest. The old political parties had disappeared during the so-called Era of Good Feeling of Monroe's administration. It was a contest of leaders.

General Andrew Jackson, the hero of the battle of New Orleans during the War of 1812, received a majority of the popular vote. But no candidate received the necessary ma-

The 79-year-old Adams sat for this photograph in 1847, a year before he died.

This portrait of Louisa Catherine Adams, the President's wife, dates from the 1820's. The harp and book symbolize her love of music and literature.

jority in the electoral college. Jackson had 99 electoral votes; Adams, 84; William H. Crawford of Georgia, 41; and Henry Clay of Kentucky, 37. Under the Constitution the election had to be decided by the House of Representatives. The voting there was by states and was limited to the first three candidates. On February 9, 1825, Adams was elected president by a bare majority of states.

John Adams, then 90 years old, was delighted at his son's victory. But Abigail Adams did not live to see the presidency come to rest on her son's shoulders. She had died in 1818.

HIS TERM AS PRESIDENT

President John Quincy Adams appointed Henry Clay secretary of state. Clay had thrown the votes of his supporters in the House of Representatives to Adams rather than Jackson. At once Jackson and his followers raised the cry of "corrupt bargain." That there was a political deal seems fairly certain. But there is nothing to show that it was dishonest.

The charge of corrupt bargain was the beginning of a quarrel with Jackson that marred Adams' administration. Jackson had strong support among the voters of the newly admitted states. Adams, after all, had not received a majority of the popular vote. The Jacksonians were out to get rid of Adams and seize office themselves.

The 4 years of Adams' presidency were prosperous and generally happy years for the United States. Adams' ambition was to govern "as a man of the whole nation," not as the leader of a political party. He believed in liberty with power. He favored more power for the federal government in the disposal of public lands and in building new roads and canals to keep up with the westward movement. He supported federal control and protection of the Indian groups against invasion of their lands by the states.

This program hit at the narrow interpretation of the Constitution under the old Jeffersonian concept of states' rights. It thus aroused Adams' opponents. In the election of 1828, Andrew Jackson was elected president by an overwhelming majority.

With his term as president over, Adams' career seemed finished. He returned sadly to

Quincy, Massachusetts. However, he was still willing to serve his country in any office, large or small. In 1830 he was elected to the House of Representatives. Nothing could have been more pleasing to Adams, for the ghost of the presidency still haunted him. He hoped for the nomination again. But these hopes soon faded.

"OLD MAN ELOQUENT"

During Adams' years in the House of Representatives, the stormy issue of slavery faced the United States. At heart Adams was an abolitionist: he wished to do away completely with slavery. But he was politically prudent, and did not say so publicly. He became a leader of the antislavery forces in Congress but limited his efforts to constitutional means. He sought to abolish slavery in the District of Columbia. He opposed its expansion into the territories of the United States. And he championed the right of petition to Congress for abolition of slavery.

As secretary of state and as president, Adams had tried to obtain Texas from Mexico. But in Congress he resisted to the last the movement for annexation of Texas. By that time the entry of Texas into the Union would have meant the creation of one or more new slave states. On the other hand, he championed the annexation of Oregon, where slavery did not exist. "I want the country for our Western pioneers," he said.

Adams was a patron and supporter in Congress of scientific activities, especially in the fields of weights and measures, and astronomy. He led the movement for establishment of the Smithsonian Institution, in Washington, D.C., one of the nation's foremost centers of learning.

Adams' long career of public service ended in the U.S. House of Representatives. He was elected to Congress in 1830 and died there on February 23, 1848.

"Old Man Eloquent," as Adams was called, opposed the war with Mexico that followed the annexation of Texas in 1845. He considered it an unjust war. On February 21, 1848, while protesting the award of swords of honor to the American generals who had won the war, Adams collapsed on the floor of the House of Representatives. He died two days later in the Capitol.

During most of his early career as a diplomat, Adams was little known throughout the country. His term as president was unpopular. Always a reserved man, he seemed cold and aloof to the people. His career in the House of Representatives made him a violently controversial figure. It was not until the final years of his life that Adams won esteem and almost affection, especially in the hearts and minds of the millions who hated slavery. Representatives of both political parties journeyed to Quincy, Massachusetts, for his funeral. In death, John Quincy Adams seemed at last to belong to the whole nation.

SAMUEL FLAGG BEMIS
Yale University
Author, *John Quincy Adams and the Union*

See also MONROE DOCTRINE.

IMPORTANT DATES IN THE LIFE OF JOHN QUINCY ADAMS

1767	Born at Braintree (later Quincy), Massachusetts, July 11.
1787	Graduated from Harvard College.
1794	Appointed minister to the Netherlands.
1797	Married Louisa Catherine Johnson.
1797–1801	Minister to Prussia.
1803–1808	Served in the United States Senate.
1809–1814	Minister to Russia.
1814	Headed American delegation that negotiated the Peace of Ghent, ending the War of 1812.
1815–1817	Minister to Great Britain.
1817–1825	Secretary of state.
1825–1829	6th president of the United States.
1831–1848	Served in the U.S. House of Representatives.
1848	Died at Washington, D.C., February 23.

ADOLESCENCE

The time between childhood and adulthood is known as adolescence. It is a period of physical growth. But it is also a time that the mind and behavior mature. The length of time for this period of development varies. Adolescence can start at 9 and end at 18. It can start at 14 and end at 25.

Young people may grow quickly in some ways and slowly in others. This is why children who may be only 9, 10, or 11 years old may be adolescents in some ways already, while teenagers of 13 or 14 may just be reaching adolescence.

Making friends and being a friend take on special importance during adolescence. Friendships are often formed with those who have similar interests and ideas.

For example, 11-year-old Sue is already 5 feet 4 inches (163 centimeters) tall. Her body is fully developed. But sometimes she acts very babyish. She has not yet learned to concentrate, so her schoolwork is far below that of others in her class.

On the other hand, Ricky, at 14, looks much younger than he is. But he is the brightest boy in his class. He is editor of his school newspaper, and his teachers and friends know that he is reliable and capable.

Sue is an adolescent because of her physical growth, and Ricky is one because he is mature in his thinking and behavior. When they "catch up with themselves," they will be well on the way to adulthood.

During adolescence, young people begin to find out about themselves and what they want to do, and what kind of people they want to be. It can be a time of self-expression, curiosity, and exploration, a time of discovery and adventure. Slowly but surely, boys and girls accept more and more responsibility for their own behavior.

THE BODY BEGINS TO CHANGE

Only a short time ago, the adolescent boy or girl had the body of a child. Now many physical changes begin to take place. Girls begin to develop breasts and have more of a waistline. They also begin to grow pubic hair and hair under their arms. Boys may notice that their voices are becoming deeper and that they are growing hair on their faces and other parts of their bodies. This period of dramatic physical development is called puberty.

Before, during, or after some of these changes, girls will begin to menstruate and boys will begin to mature sexually. These are normal glandular changes. They show that the organs of reproduction are being prepared for the part they will someday play.

Both boys and girls may feel that their arms and legs are growing too fast for the rest of their bodies. They may feel clumsy and awkward. Glandular changes sometimes cause acne, a skin disturbance. The skin may become oily, and pimples may appear. It is natural for young people to feel strange and uncomfortable about these physical changes. But part of growing during adolescence is getting acquainted with the new self that is appearing and gradually accepting the changes that are taking place.

FEELINGS ARE CHANGING, TOO

These body changes affect feelings as well as appearance. The glands and hormones that are bringing about external physical changes are also working toward a new internal balance. This is hard work for the body. There are times when adolescents feel very tired and seem to need a lot of sleep. At times they may feel happy and lively, at other times gloomy and depressed. Ups and downs are natural during adolescence, but eventually boys and girls begin to have more control over their feelings.

Adolescents still feel unsure of themselves, so they are annoyed at anything that makes them feel exceptional or different, whether it is wearing glasses or braces or having many freckles. As young people mature and gain self-confidence, they begin to accept themselves as they are.

ADOLESCENTS CAN HELP THEMSELVES

There are many ways boys and girls can help themselves handle the changes of adolescence. If they are tired, they can get extra sleep and relaxation. If they feel full of energy, they can participate in sports or go dancing. They can eat sensibly and take proper care of their bodies.

They can also help themselves by seeking information and advice about any questions and worries. They are often concerned about their role as adults, and about their future careers and adult relationships. Many adolescents are also troubled by their new feelings about sex. It is quite normal for people at this age to begin to feel strong physical desires.

Both boys and girls need reassurance and information. They can get information from reading. Or they can talk to their parents. But sometimes it is hard to talk freely and openly with parents because the relationship is so close. Then an understanding adult who is not part of the family may be able to help. It may be easier to confide in a favorite teacher or camp counselor. The person whose advice an adolescent seeks should be someone whom she or he trusts and who has enough background and experience to be of help.

If boys and girls feel guilty and unhappy about some of their thoughts and keep all their fears and confusions to themselves, they will make this an unnecessarily difficult time.

GROWING UP WITH OTHERS

This is a time that will influence a boy's or girl's choice of adult companions, of a vocation, and even of a marriage partner.

Friends

Making friends and learning how to be a friend take on special importance during adolescence. It is the time that the center of their social world changes from their home environment to their peer group environment. At first the most important thing is popularity. Boys and girls want to be well liked. They want to do what their friends want to do, and be what their friends want to be. This is all part of feeling unsure.

Later on, young people become more selective about their friends. They begin to choose those who have the same ideas and interests or those who are interesting because they have different backgrounds. As boys and girls develop their own standards, popularity becomes less important to them than the genuine affection of individuals they admire.

Young people often need to make friends among those of their own sex before they feel ready for relationships with the opposite sex. It is natural to feel more at ease with those who are having the same experiences and feelings. Later, girl-boy friendships may begin and become more intense and personal. At this time a young person may face some important issues and decisions.

Dating is one of these issues. Many girls and boys hope that they will be attractive and appealing to members of the opposite sex, but feel confused and uncertain about just how this can be accomplished. Also, they may wonder whether they should date only one person because it makes them feel safe and popular or because everyone else in the crowd is dating only one person. Or should they go out with many different kinds of people in order to learn more about themselves, to find out what relationships give them the most satisfaction?

The intimacy that develops between a girl and a boy who go out only with each other can create a problem. How far should an adolescent girl and boy permit this intimacy to lead them? Girls and boys are often very curious about sex and their sexual drive can be very strong. It is a powerful and sometimes disturbing feeling. They have certain worries and fears about it, too.

As boys and girls mature they try to understand their feelings about sex. They try to find answers to their questions so that they can set standards for their own behavior. The more responsible and mature they become, the more they think about long-range goals. They are willing to give up immediate satisfactions for something that is more important to them in the future. The more they care about their own feelings and needs, the more sensitive they are to other people. They understand the need for making choices seriously, rather than on a sudden impulse, to avoid hurting themselves and others.

Family

All adolescents have mixed feelings about their families. There are times when boys and girls feel that they could manage very well if only their parents would leave them alone. At other times young people feel uncertain and confused. They wish their parents would take over and tell them what to do.

Many conflicts with parents come up over social relationships. Teenagers are often so eager to belong to a group that they do not always use good judgment in making friends. Then their parents have to step in and help them by keeping some control over their activities. This is especially true when matters of health and safety are concerned. But when boys and girls show signs of greater maturity and sounder judgment, parents usually have more confidence in them and allow them to make more decisions and choices.

Family chores and responsibilities are other common causes of conflict. Teenagers sometimes forget that as members of the family group they have certain obligations. At times they feel they are being nagged about everything. Their rooms are untidy, their clothes are not neat, they sleep too late, they talk on the phone too much, they go to bed too late, they are careless with money, they do not allow enough time for homework. At times teenagers feel overwhelmed with criticism. But at other times they may sense that all their parents' comments are really signs of loving and caring.

Sometimes younger brothers and sisters seem to be a nuisance. Teenagers resent baby-sitting. It interferes with their privacy and cuts into their free time. Older sisters and brothers may tease teenagers, and this makes them feel young and foolish. But all this is only one side of the picture. Adolescents still need their families and the love a family gives, and their families still need them.

Some rebellion against adult authority is healthy—within limits. An adolescent wants to become a strong and independent person, and that is right. But this is not accomplished by fighting against adults. Being cooperative is much more effective.

But adolescents cannot grow up alone. They need the help and understanding of the adults who are closest to them. Parents can help their teenagers as they mature. One of the best ways is simply by acting as parents. This means being strong and firm when necessary. Children may call their parents old-fashioned. They may say, "You don't understand me." But wise parents overlook such expressions. They know that many times teenagers ask for permission to do something they are not ready for. They ask because the whole crowd is asking, and they do not want to be different. But secretly the teenagers want their parents to say "No," to set limits for them. They need to feel that their parents have authority and will use this authority wisely. Teenagers also need to know that their parents will not take a firm stand one day and then give in the next day. They want their parents to be consistent.

Being firm, of course, does not mean being too strict, and being consistent does not mean being stubborn. Understanding parents also give their teenagers love and encouragement and let them feel that they are free to grow.

▶ LOOKING AHEAD

A young child finds it hard to imagine being grown up. Adulthood seems so far away and strange. To a child what happens each day matters most. The child is not really interested in what will happen next month, next year, or in the next ten years.

During adolescence all that changes. The subjects boys and girls study in school and the marks they get have a great deal to do with their plans for a vocation. Their friendships with other boys and girls and their dating have a clear relationship to adult love and the choice of a marriage partner.

One of the most exciting things about adolescence is that it suddenly brings the future so much closer. That is what makes adolescence such a special time.

EDA J. LESHAN
Author, *You and Your Feelings*

See also FAMILY.

ADOPTION

Adoption is a way for children who cannot be cared for by their birth parents to become members of another family. Certain laws and procedures create the same legal relation between adoptive parents and a child as the biological one that exists between birth parents and a child. Adoption ends the child's ties to his former parents. After adoption the child has a new and permanent home.

WHY CHILDREN NEED ADOPTION

In most countries children are brought up in families that are made up of a father, a mother, and the children born to them. Some birth parents, however, cannot give the love and care that every child needs. They are often very young and unmarried. They did not think ahead of time about the responsibilities of being parents. These parents may decide, after much sorrow, to give up their child for adoption. They want the child to have a chance to grow up in a family that can provide love and the potential to fulfill the child's needs for security and permanence.

Other children may lose their parents by death, accident, illness, war, or some other disaster. Sometimes parents with serious personal problems neglect or abandon a child. Children may be left for a long time in temporary foster homes or institutions. Then it may become clear that their parents will never be able to take them home. In all these cases someone other than the parents has to decide that adoption will be best for the child.

Families have to be found for children who no longer have parents to care for them. There are many childless people who wish to adopt. They have a desire to love and raise a child and to have a child who loves them. Also, some parents who already have children want to share their love and family life with another child who needs parents.

WHO IS ADOPTED

The children who are adopted in the United States are mostly white babies. They go into their new homes shortly after birth. It has usually been difficult to find families for older, handicapped, or nonwhite children. Recently, however, a greater number of these children—especially African American, Native American, and Asian children—are being adopted.

The total number of children adopted each year in the United States is almost 130,000. About half are adopted by a stepparent, by grandparents, or by other relatives. The others are adopted by unrelated people.

HOW ADOPTION TAKES PLACE

Children needing families and people seeking children may be brought together in several ways. The majority of the adoptions by nonrelatives now take place through recognized social agencies.

Physicians, lawyers, clergymen, and other well-meaning individuals have frequently arranged adoptions. Sometimes a dishonest person tries to make money by finding a child for someone willing to pay a high price. Such transactions are illegal.

Arrangements by individuals have in some cases been harmful to a child, to birth parents, or to adoptive parents. An individual cannot usually give the time, help, or protections needed in adoption. Many difficulties are prevented when social agencies are responsible for planning an adoption and selecting adoptive parents.

Social agencies are established and supported by concerned people in a community or by state governments. Some agencies have been given the duty by law to protect children and to provide adoption and other social services. Such agencies are known as child-welfare agencies, children's aid societies, or family and children's services.

ADOPTION SERVICES

The purpose of an adoption service is to help children, birth parents, and adoptive parents. Social workers, who have special training and experience, provide the service. They know how to study children and find out what may be best for each child. They work with physicians, psychologists, and lawyers. They use the advice of other experts in selecting suitable parents for a particular child. Then they help adoptive parents take the necessary steps to complete a legal adoption. Agencies usually charge a fee for this service, based on ability to pay.

Parents and older children especially may need continuing help as they become a family. Most problems that occur are the usual ones that all parents and children have. Some of the problems have to do with adoption. For example, adoptive parents are encouraged to help a child understand, as soon as the child is able, what it means to be adopted. It is not easy to explain about adoption. Many adoptive parents would like to keep it a secret. Sooner or later, however, adopted children discover that they have not been born to their parents. Many become upset about it. They wonder why their birth parents gave them up. They may imagine that they would have been happier with those other parents, and they are curious about their heredity.

It takes time for children to feel comfortable about being adopted. They have to learn that true parents are the people who help a child grow up and feel loved. They have to know why their birth parents made an adoption plan for them. Usually it is because they care about the child and want him or her to have a better family life than they could ever provide.

LEGAL PROCESS

An adoption must take place according to law. In each state and in most countries, laws have been passed that say how the relationship of parent and child can be ended and a new one created. The laws require certain procedures to be followed. These are designed to protect the various people, and especially the child, involved in an adoption.

The parent-child relation is very important in our society. The law requires that a judge must decide whether it should be broken. A judge must also grant an adoption decree to make the adoption legal and final.

After the adoption has been arranged, either by agreement between the biological and adoptive parents or through an agency, the adoptive parents must go to court and ask that lasting family ties between the child and them be established. They must first wait until the child has lived with them for a set period of time. Then the judge has to make sure that the adoption is likely to benefit the child.

The judge considers all the facts obtained in a study of the case and talks with a child if he or she is old enough to understand. In most states, after the decree is granted all court records are sealed. No one can see these without a court order. Then a new birth certificate for the child is issued with the names of the adoptive parents. Lawyers are used in an adoption to see that all legal procedures are properly carried out.

TRENDS IN ADOPTION

Formerly, the purpose of adoption was to enhance the family unit by providing a childless family with an heir to inherit property or to continue a family name. It was not until 1851, in Massachusetts, that the first adoption law to protect children was passed. Since then people have become more concerned about the child's welfare in adoption.

Gradually ideas about adoption have changed. Adoption is now considered a way to find families for children. Communities and social agencies are trying to give more children the benefits of adoption. One reason is the belief that every child has a right to a caring and supportive family.

Social agencies are using new methods to find families to care for an older child, a sibling group, or a child with handicaps. Legislation has been passed to help families who choose to adopt children with special needs. The adoptive parents of such children are given allowances to help meet the costs of including the child in their family.

People who are members of minority groups are being encouraged to adopt children. Also, in some states, the law allows single persons to adopt children.

Various organizations are engaged in research to find out how to make adoption as satisfactory as possible for children and their biological and adoptive families.

Recently, there has been a trend toward the re-establishment of a relationship, later in life, between adoptees and their birth parents. A few states have passed "open records" legislation that allows the examination of certain adoption records. This makes it easier for adult adoptees and their birth parents to secure the information needed to conduct a search for each other. Some states have adoption registries that take information from, and provide information to, any person engaged in such a search.

ZITHA R. TURITZ
Former Director, Standards Development
Child Welfare League of America, Inc.
Reviewed by BEVERLY STUBBEE
Child Welfare Specialist

Magazine advertisements, such as this one for crayons, must be eye-catching in order to attract the attention of the parents and children who will buy the product.

ADVERTISING

Advertising is part of our daily lives. To realize this fact, simply count the television and radio commercials you see and hear in one day, or leaf through the pages of a magazine or newspaper. Most people receive hundreds of advertising messages every day.

WHAT IS ADVERTISING?

Advertising is the difficult business of bringing information to great numbers of people. The purpose of an advertisement is to make people respond—to make them react to an idea, such as helping to prevent forest fires, or to affect their attitudes toward a certain product or service.

At the beginning of the 1900's, advertising was described as salesmanship in print. If this definition were expanded to include television and radio, it would still stand today. The most effective way to sell something is through person-to-person contact. But the cost of person-to-person selling is high. Because it takes a great deal of time, it increases the cost of the product or service. Advertising distributes the selling message to many people at one time.

THE MEDIA

To bring their messages to the public, advertisers must use carriers, such as television, radio, magazines and newspapers, and direct mail. The carrier of a message is called a **medium** of communication, or simply a medium. The five media (plural of medium) just mentioned are the ones most commonly used. Other media include billboards, posters, printed bulletins, and, especially in Europe, films. Unusual methods that have been used to attract attention include skywriting and messages painted on the sails of boats or trailed from high-flying kites.

When advertisers select a medium or a group of media to carry a message, they must think of the kind of product they are selling and the kind of people who are most likely to buy it. They must figure out how to reach the largest possible number of these people at the lowest possible cost. The cost of reaching a thousand people—the cost per thousand—is different in each medium. In print media such as newspapers and magazines, advertisers buy **space** (pages or parts of pages) in which to display their messages. In the broadcast media—radio and television—they buy **time** in which to present them.

Meanwhile, media planners at the agency decide on the most efficient way to reach the target group. They also determine the size, color, and dates for printed advertisements; the time periods for broadcast commercials; and the costs in each case. These media recommendations must also be approved by the client. The materials for the completed advertisement are then shipped to the media with authorization for their use on specific dates or for specific periods of time at agreed-upon rates or prices.

The agency checks to make sure that each advertisement or commercial actually appears. If everything is satisfactory, the agency then bills the client. The total cost includes the agency commission; when the agency pays the media, the agency's commission for its service is deducted. Some agencies work for flat fees rather than commissions, and the client pays the agency a sum of money in addition to the cost of producing the advertising.

What Makes Customers Buy?

Advertisers and their agencies have spent great amounts of time, money, and effort trying to determine what makes potential customers want a product. There is no single answer. To find the special quality of a product that will cause people to buy, advertisers often turn to research.

Several kinds of research are employed in advertising. **Marketing research** explores sales patterns, sales problems, and sales possibilities for a product. **Product research** is designed to discover how the public feels about a product. **Copy research** discovers how well an advertisement gets its message across. **Motivational research** unearths the reasons people behave as they do.

A consumer may buy a certain brand of face soap because it is used by a glamorous movie star or sports figure. When selecting a new refrigerator, that same consumer may be attracted to a sleek or colorful style. Or perhaps that consumer is most concerned with how much food the refrigerator will hold and how efficiently a particular model uses energy.

Some advertisements appeal to logic through straightforward presentation of facts about a product. Others appeal more to the emotions. Most advertisements combine logical and emotional approaches. Advertisements offer consumers an opportunity to make their purchasing decisions from among a wide range of choices. One of the important roles of advertising is to provide the consumer with a free and abundant choice.

▶ADVERTISING AS A CAREER

Advertising is a big business—and a fascinating business. It combines writing, art, show business, and science.

The average advertising agency has a need for people with many different kinds of experience and talent. But opportunities are limited. Some estimates suggest that there are probably not more than a few thousand places for newcomers in advertising each year.

Most advertising jobs require the ability to use language with skill. Other important qualities are curiosity and the ability to use imagination in analyzing situations. Retail selling experience is excellent preparation for a career in advertising. The American Association of Advertising Agencies, in New York City, offers information about careers in advertising.

▶HISTORY

Advertising is very old. It can be traced back as far as the public criers of ancient Greece—who, for a fee, shouted out messages about their clients' wares. It first became important in the late 1400's, when the merchants of the rapidly growing cities and towns needed a way to tell people where their goods could be bought.

The first printed advertisement in the English language appeared in 1478. This early ad was the work of William Caxton, England's first printer, who used it to advertise religious books from his own workshop. Caxton posted small printed notices along London's main streets. Besides advertising his product, he identified his shop with a red-striped shield so that customers could find it easily.

This same sort of simple, informational advertising is still used. Examples are the roadside signs that tell travelers that they can buy eggs or take flying lessons just down the road.

The Industrial Revolution, in the 1700's and 1800's, brought a new kind of advertising. Large factories took the place of small workshops, and goods were produced in large quantities. Manufacturers used the newly built railroads to distribute their products over wide areas. They had to find many thousands of customers in order to stay in business. They

REVERE
Paul Revere & Son,
At their BELL and CANNON FOUNDERY, at the North Part of BOSTON,
CAST BELLS, of all ſizes; every kind of Braſs ORDNANCE, and every kind of Compoſition Work, for SHIPS, &c. at the ſhorteſt notice; Manufacture COPPER into SHEETS, BOLTS, SPIKES, NAILS, RIVETS, DOVETAILS, &c. from Malleable Copper.
They always keep, by them, every kind of Copper faſtening for Ships. They have now on hand, a number of Church and Ship Bells, of different ſizes; a large quantity of Sheathing Copper, from 16 up to 30 ounce; Bolts, Spikes, Nails, &c of all ſizes, which they warrant equal to Engliſh manufacture.
Caſh and the higheſt price given for old Copper and Braſs. march 10

This early advertisement is a simple listing of the products and services available from Paul Revere's foundry. Compare it to today's advertisements.

could not simply tell people where shoes or cloth or tea could be bought—they had to learn how to make people want to buy a specific product. Thus modern advertising was born. Advertising created new markets and helped to raise standards of living as people came to feel that they had a right to new and better products.

Advertising agencies began to develop in the United States just after the Civil War. At first these agencies merely sold space in the various media, mainly newspapers and magazines. But they soon added the service of writing and producing advertisements. From these beginnings, advertising has developed into a highly specialized profession.

PROS AND CONS OF ADVERTISING

Advertising has received a great deal of criticism from various sources. Its critics say that it appeals to unworthy motives like vanity, snobbery, and the fear of being "left out." And they say that high-pressure advertising makes people buy some things that they do not really need and cannot afford. Another common criticism is that some advertising is deceitful.

Most people who work in advertising feel that it can certainly help shape attitudes toward products. But they know from experience that it is not possible to sell a poor product more than once. People may try a product because they are attracted by the advertising, but if they do not like it they simply will not buy it again. Consumers make the choices, and because of advertising they may have many more products from which to choose and are more informed about their choices.

Advertising agencies and the media work against deceptive practices by setting standards within the industry. In the United States there is also some government regulation. Consumers are protected by such agencies as the Federal Trade Commission, the Federal Communications Commission, and the U.S. Postal Service. State and local agencies, as well as private organizations, work to prevent false or misleading advertising.

Advertising is used for public service messages as well as for commercial ones. Smokey the Bear, who for many years warned the public against the dangers of forest fires, was a creation of the advertising industry. Advertising agencies produce the campaigns for organizations such as the Red Cross, helping them to gather money. And advertising is an efficient way of telling large numbers of people about new ideas, useful inventions, and scientific discoveries. Defenders of advertising say that it stimulates the economy by helping to keep production and employment high.

Advertising is an important part of life in a complex society. Often a word or phrase from an advertisement will enter the language, at least for a time. Songs written for use in advertising may become popular apart from their original use. A character seen or heard in advertising may become a favorite with the public. These are some of the ways advertising becomes part of popular culture.

Advertising has been described as the news of the marketplace. Partly because of the influence of advertising, people have learned to want ever better products and services, to take better care of their health, and to improve their way of living. Advertising is an important economic and social force.

Don Johnston
Chairman and Chief Executive Officer
J. Walter Thompson Company

See also Mail Order; Sales and Marketing.

AFGHANISTAN

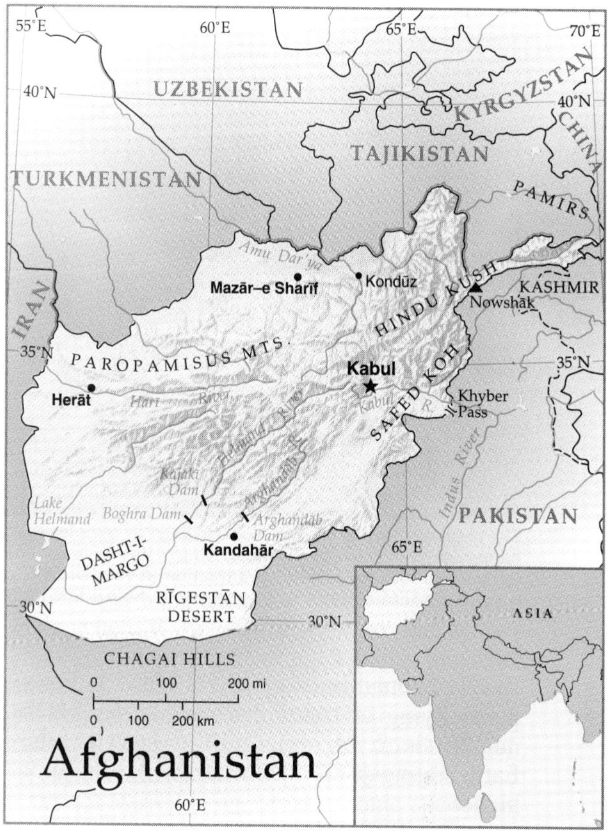

Afghanistan is a rugged, landlocked nation in west central Asia. Historically, the area has been a crossroads, connecting China, Central Asia, South Asia, and the Middle East.

Many centuries of regional migration, trade, and continuous invasions by outsiders produced a proud and independent society of many races, tribal groups, and languages. But years of political upheaval and war brought little but enduring hardship, starvation, and poverty for the majority of Afghan civilians. In the late 1900's, occupation by the Soviet Union (1979–89) and civil wars among various Afghan tribal groups weakened the central government. Neighboring countries, particularly Pakistan and Iran, became more influential in Afghanistan's internal affairs.

In 1996, the Taliban, a radical Islamic group supported by Pakistan, gained control over most of Afghanistan. But in 2001, the United States and its allies went to war against the Taliban for harboring members of the terrorist group responsible for the September 11 attacks on the World Trade Center and the Pentagon. Afghanistan has since been ruled by a temporary interim government supported by the United Nations.

▸ PEOPLE

Afghanistan has more than a dozen different tribal groups. The Pashtuns, the largest group, make up nearly 40 percent of the population. Most live across southern Afghanistan. The Tajiks, the second largest group, are

Below: **The Blue Mosque in Mazār-e Sharīf is revered by Muslims as the burial site of Hazrat Ali, son-in-law of Mohammed.** ***Right:*** **Pashtuns form the largest group among Afghanistan's many tribes.**

an Indo-Iranian people (related to the Tajiks found in Tajikistan). They live mainly in the northeast. The Hazaras, believed to be descendants of the Mongols, inhabit the central mountain region. Uzbeks, Turkomans, and others live on the northern plains.

Language. The Pashtuns speak Pashto, an Indo-Iranian-based language. The Tajiks speak Dari, which is an Afghan form of Persian, also known as Farsi. Other Persian/Farsi dialects are spoken by the Hazaras. The Uzbeks and Turkomans speak languages related to Turkish.

Religion. Although Afghanistan is not an Arab country, most Afghans belong to the Sunni branch of Islam. About 15 percent are members of the Shi'a sect. Afghanistan also has small communities of Hindus, Sikhs, and Jews.

Education. Under the rule of the Taliban, education was supervised by religious leaders. Boys learned to read and write the language of the Koran (Qur'an), but they did not learn mathematics, history, or science. Girls were not allowed to attend formal school past the age of 8. Some parents risked jail and other forms of punishment in order to educate their daughters in secret. When the Taliban government fell, boys and girls of all ages eagerly returned to school.

Way of Life. Although some Afghans still live a traditional nomadic life, most are now settled farmers, plowing their small fields with wooden plows drawn by oxen or cutting their wheat crops by hand with sickles.

In the countryside, a typical Afghan house is built of mud or mud brick and has three or four rooms, furnished with rugs and pillows. Round flat bread and rice are staple foods, together with mutton (sheep), goat meat, chicken, yogurt, and fruit. Traditional clothing for men consists of a turban wound around either a skullcap or a karakul cap (made out of lambskin), and a long shirt worn outside the trousers. Village women wear long dresses over trousers and large scarves over their hair.

LAND

Afghanistan is bordered by Iran to the west; Turkmenistan, Uzbekistan, Tajikistan, and China to the north; and Pakistan to the south and east.

Land Regions. The three major land regions of Afghanistan are the dry and dusty Northern Plains; the Central Highlands, which cover approximately two-thirds of the land; and the desert Southwestern Lowlands. The country's most fertile areas are in the east and southwest.

Farmers with oxen plow their fields in the Bāmiān valley in northeastern Afghanistan. The Hindu Kush mountains rise in the background.

The towering, snowcapped Hindu Kush range rises in the northeast, reaching heights greater than 20,000 feet (6,100 meters). It contains Mount Nowshāk, the country's highest peak, rising 24,551 feet (7,483 meters) above sea level. The twisting Khyber Pass, which cuts through the Safed Koh range in the east, links Afghanistan with Pakistan in the southeast.

Rivers. Because much of Afghanistan is arid (dry), farmers depend on the rivers to provide irrigation for growing crops. Afghani-

FACTS and figures

REPUBLIC OF AFGHANISTAN is the official name of the country.
LOCATION: South central Asia.
AREA: 251,773 sq mi (652,090 km^2).
POPULATION: 27,000,000 (estimate).
CAPITAL AND LARGEST CITY: Kabul.
MAJOR LANGUAGES: Pashto, Dari.
MAJOR RELIGIOUS GROUP: Muslim.
GOVERNMENT: Republic. **Head of state and government**—president. A Transitional Authority, established by a *loya jirga* (grand council), will rule Afghanistan until a new constitution is approved.
CHIEF PRODUCTS: Agricultural—wheat, rice, and other grains; cotton; fruits; nuts; karakul pelts; wool; mutton. **Manufactured**—textiles, processed foods. **Mineral**—natural gas, petroleum, coal, iron ore, copper, chromium.
MONETARY UNIT: Afghani (1 afghani = 100 puls).

stan has several rivers. But only the Amu Dar'ya (known in ancient times as the Oxus) can be used by ships. Other major rivers include the Helmand, Harī, Arghandāb, and Kabul rivers.

Climate. Afghanistan's climate is generally marked by extremes—very cold, snowy winters and hot, dry summers. Average temperatures are higher in the lowlands. Precipitation is slight, ranging from 2 to 9 inches (50 to 230 millimeters) per year.

Natural Resources. Most of Afghanistan's known resources have not been developed. Minerals include natural gas, coal, iron ore, copper, chromium, petroleum, and small amounts of gold and silver. Precious gems, including lapis lazuli, emeralds, and rubies, are also found.

At one time Afghanistan had great areas of forest. But these have long since been cut down to provide lumber and fuel, causing erosion of the soil.

ECONOMY

Afghanistan was once one of the few developing nations that was self-sufficient, with its own food supply. But after the wars began in the 1970's, trade was interrupted. Nearly one-third of the population eventually fled the country, causing severe labor shortages. Farmlands were bombarded and laced with landmines. Agriculture was further damaged by several years of drought.

MAJOR CITIES

Kabul, Afghanistan's capital and largest city, has a population of more than 1 million. For the past 200 years, Kabul has been the commercial, cultural, political, and educational center of the country. But in recent years the city was almost completely destroyed. One of the priorities of the Afghan interim government was to restore Kabul to its previous stature so that it might function as the seat of a centralized government.

Kandahār, situated in a fertile valley in the southeast, has long been a trading center for Pakistan and Iran. With a population of about 190,000, it is Afghanistan's second largest city. Kandahār once served as the capital before it was moved to Kabul in 1776. It served as headquarters for the Taliban regime.

CULTURAL HERITAGE

Because Afghanistan is situated at the crossroads of many different lands, it shares many cultural traditions with its neighbors. From religion and languages to clothing and food, many similarities can be found with Iranians, Pakistanis, and other peoples of Central Asia.

The national dance is called the *attan*. Intense and warlike, the *attan* reminds Afghans of their long and hard fight for freedom and independence.

HISTORY AND GOVERNMENT

Afghanistan has known many conquerors and many rulers. With each invasion came new peoples and new influences. Great cities were built, and a prosperous agricultural economy based on irrigation was developed. But these achievements were destroyed by invading Mongols in the 1200's and 1300's.

Independence. In 1747 the Pashtun tribes made Afghanistan an independent kingdom. But the Afghans, situated between the expanding superpowers of the region, Russia and Great Britain, struggled hard to keep their independence. They fought two wars against the British before Great Britain took control of Afghanistan's foreign affairs in the late 1800's. In 1919, after World War I (1914–

18), Afghanistan successfully asserted its full independence again.

After World War II (1939–45), Afghanistan and Pakistan disagreed over their border. Pakistan sometimes refused to allow imported goods to reach Afghanistan. This forced Afghanistan to approach the Soviet Union, which sent imports through its country.

A Communist Government. Afghanistan remained a kingdom until 1973, when a military coup toppled the monarchy. The leader of the coup, General Mohammed Daoud Khan, was named president and prime minister. Daoud was killed during another coup in 1978, and the government was taken over by a leftist group, which signed a treaty of peace and friendship with the Soviet Union. But most Afghans opposed the new government, and a revolt, led in part by tribal, civilian, and religious leaders, erupted. By the middle of 1979, opposition forces controlled the countryside. In December 1979, thousands of Soviet troops were airlifted into Afghanistan in an attempt to stop the spreading Afghan resistance to the Soviet-supported government.

The Struggle for Control. Between 1979 and 1989, more than 100,000 Soviet troops were engaged in Afghanistan, battling Afghan resistance forces called *mujahideen*, who were fighting for independence. The economy was devastated, and more than 5 million Afghans fled the country, most settling in refugee camps in neighboring Pakistan and Iran.

After the Soviets withdrew in 1989, a struggle for control began between the *mujahideen* and the Communists, led by President Najibullah. In 1992, Kabul was occupied by *mujahideen* forces, and Afghanistan was declared an Islamic state. A struggle for power then broke out among *mujahideen* factions, and in 1996 a new force, the Taliban (supported by Pakistan), captured Kabul. Najibullah was executed, and strict laws in the name of Islam were imposed throughout much of the country. These laws offended most mainstream Muslim people. Most international governments, including Muslim states, refused to recognize the Taliban's government, citing its harsh treatment of women, its destruction of non-Muslim art treasures, and its harboring of international terrorists.

On September 11, 2001, terrorists attacked the United States, killing thousands of people. The attackers were linked to Osama bin Laden, a Muslim militant living in Afghanistan under the Taliban's protection. After the crisis, U.S. president George W. Bush declared war on terrorists and warned the Taliban that if they did not turn over bin Laden to the proper international authorities, they would risk the same fate as the terrorists themselves.

When the Taliban failed to respond by October 7, U.S. and British forces initiated air strikes against them and bin Laden. The regime finally collapsed on December 7, although bin Laden and Taliban leader Mullah Omar had not yet been captured.

Various anti-Taliban Afghan leaders, including the exiled king, agreed to share

After the Taliban regime collapsed in 2001 during the War on Terrorism, Muslim women were free to lift the veils of their burkas for the first time in five years.

power until a *loya jirga* (grand council) could be assembled to elect a transitional leader who would rule until a new constitution could be written. In June 2002, Pashtun tribal leader Hamid Karzai was elected president of the Transitional Authority. His first priorities were to settle internal differences, distribute humanitarian aid, accommodate returning refugees, and rebuild Afghanistan's devastated economy. Meanwhile, warfare continued within Afghanistan's borders.

Reviewed by Alam Payind
Jennifer Nichols
Middle East Studies Center
The Ohio State University

See also Terrorism, War on.

Scattered across the barren desert areas of northern Africa are fertile oases, watered by underground streams. This oasis is in Morocco.

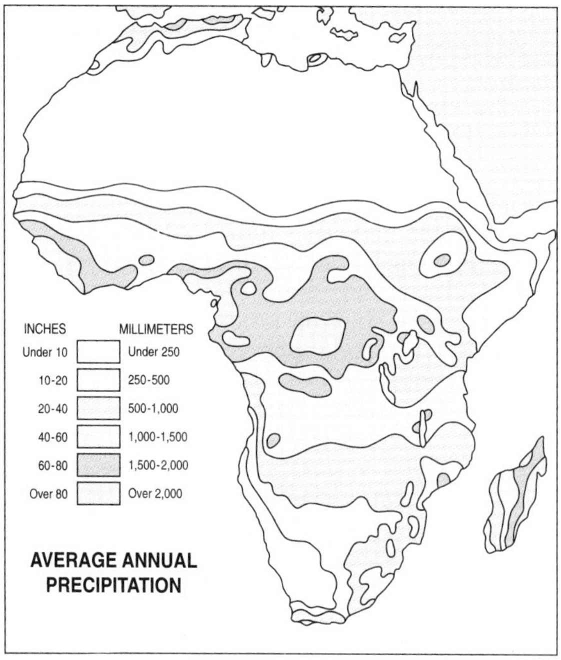

INDEX TO AFRICA PHYSICAL MAP

Aden, Gulf of F3
Agulhas, Cape D8
Ahaggar Mountains C2
Albert, Lake E4
Ankaratra Highlands F6
Arabian Desert E2
Atlas Mountains B1
Bab el Mandeb F3
Bauchi Plateau C4
Benue River C4
Blue Nile River E3
Bié Plateau C6
Bodélé Depression D3
Canary Islands A1
Chad, Lake C3
Chari River D3
Congo Basin D4
Congo River D4
Drakensberg E7
Edward, Lake E4
Elgon, Mt. E4
Emi Koussi D2
Erg Iguidi B2
Ethiopian Highlands E4
Fouta Djallon A3
Gibralter, Strait of B1
Great Karroo D8
Great Rift Valley E4
Good Hope, Cape of D8
Gough Island B8
Guardafui, Cape F3
Guinea, Gulf of B4
Kalahari Desert D7
Kariba, Lake E6
Kasai River D5
Kenya, Mt. E5
Kilimanjaro, Mt. E5
Kivu, Lake E5
Libyan Desert D2
Limpopo River E7
Mediterranean Sea D1
Molopo River D7
Mozambique Channel F6
Mweru, Lake E5
Namib Desert C7
Nasser, Lake E2
Niger River B3
Nile River E3
Nubian Desert E2
Nyasa, Lake E6
Okavango Basin D7
Okavango River D6
Orange River D7
Prince Edward Islands E8
Qattara Depression D2
Ras Dashan E3
Red Sea E2
Ruwenzori E4
Senegal River A3
Serengeti Plain E5
Shebeli River F4
Sidra, Gulf of D1
Sinai Peninsula E2
Suez Canal E1
Tahat C2
Tana, Lake E3
Tanganyika, Lake E5
Tibesti Massif D2
Turkana, Lake E4
Uele River D4
Vaal River D7
Victoria Falls D6
Victoria, Lake E5
Volta River B4
White Nile River E4
Zambezi River E6

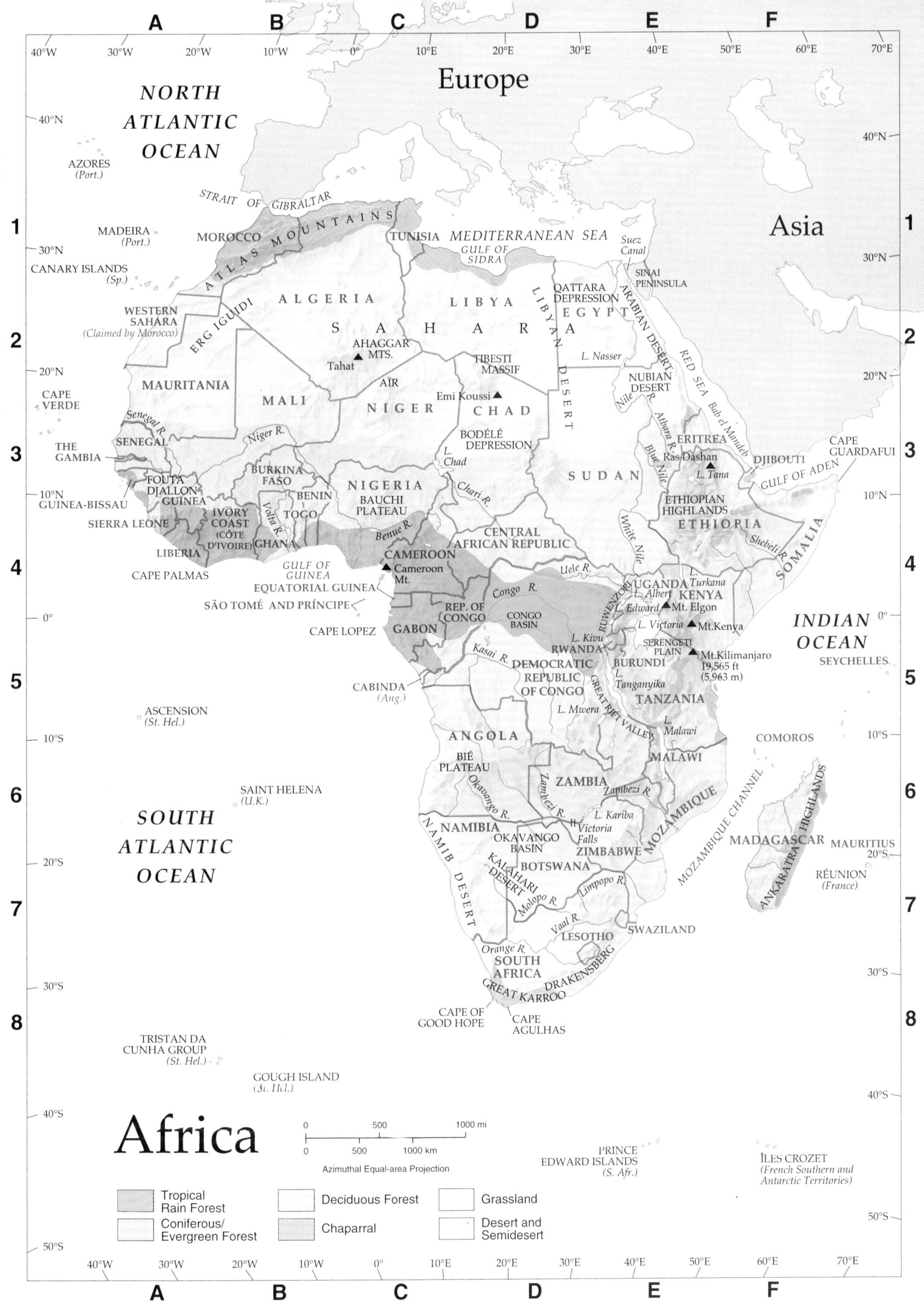

A
B
C
D
E
F
1
2
3
4
5
6
7
8
40°W
30°W
20°W
10°W
0°
10°E
20°E
30°E
40°E
50°E
60°E
70°E
40°N
30°N
20°N
10°N
0°
10°S
20°S
30°S
40°S
50°S
Europe
Asia
NORTH ATLANTIC OCEAN
SOUTH ATLANTIC OCEAN
INDIAN OCEAN
AZORES (Port.)
MADEIRA (Port.)
CANARY ISLANDS (Sp.)
STRAIT OF GIBRALTAR
MOROCCO
ATLAS MOUNTAINS
TUNISIA
MEDITERRANEAN SEA
GULF OF SIDRA
Suez Canal
SINAI PENINSULA
WESTERN SAHARA (Claimed by Morocco)
ERG IGUIDI
ALGERIA
LIBYA
QATTARA DEPRESSION
EGYPT
ARABIAN DESERT
LIBYAN DESERT
S A H A R A
AHAGGAR MTS.
Tahat
TIBESTI MASSIF
L. Nasser
RED SEA
NUBIAN DESERT
Nile R.
MAURITANIA
AÏR
MALI
NIGER
Emi Koussi
CHAD
CAPE VERDE
Senegal R.
SENEGAL
THE GAMBIA
Niger R.
BODÉLÉ DEPRESSION
L. Chad
Atbara R.
Blue Nile
ERITREA
Bab el Mandeb
Ras Dashan
L. Tana
DJIBOUTI
CAPE GUARDAFUI
GULF OF ADEN
SUDAN
BURKINA FASO
FOUTA DJALLON
GUINEA
GUINEA-BISSAU
NIGERIA
BENIN
TOGO
BAUCHI PLATEAU
Chari R.
ETHIOPIAN HIGHLANDS
ETHIOPIA
SIERRA LEONE
IVORY COAST (CÔTE D'IVOIRE)
Volta R.
GHANA
LIBERIA
Benue R.
CENTRAL AFRICAN REPUBLIC
White Nile
Shebeli R.
SOMALIA
CAMEROON
Cameroon Mt.
GULF OF GUINEA
CAPE PALMAS
EQUATORIAL GUINEA
SÃO TOMÉ AND PRÍNCIPE
Uele R.
L. Turkana
UGANDA
KENYA
RUWENZORI
L. Albert
L. Edward
Mt. Elgon
Congo R.
REP. OF CONGO
CONGO BASIN
GABON
CAPE LOPEZ
L. Victoria
Mt.Kenya
L. Kivu
RWANDA
SERENGETI PLAIN
Mt.Kilimanjaro 19,565 ft (5,963 m)
SEYCHELLES
Kasai R.
DEMOCRATIC REPUBLIC OF CONGO
BURUNDI
L. Tanganyika
TANZANIA
CABINDA (Ang.)
ASCENSION (St. Hel.)
L. Mwera
GREAT RIFT VALLEY
L. Malawi
ANGOLA
COMOROS
BIÉ PLATEAU
MALAWI
Zambezi R.
ZAMBIA
Okavango R.
SAINT HELENA (U.K.)
L. Kariba
MOZAMBIQUE
MOZAMBIQUE CHANNEL
NAMIBIA
Victoria Falls
OKAVANGO BASIN
ZIMBABWE
MADAGASCAR
ANKARATRA HIGHLANDS
MAURITIUS
NAMIB DESERT
KALAHARI DESERT
BOTSWANA
Limpopo R.
RÉUNION (France)
Molopo R.
Vaal R.
SWAZILAND
LESOTHO
Orange R.
SOUTH AFRICA
DRAKENSBERG
GREAT KARROO
CAPE OF GOOD HOPE
CAPE AGULHAS
TRISTAN DA CUNHA GROUP (St. Hel.)
GOUGH ISLAND (St. Hel.)
Africa
0 500 1000 mi
0 500 1000 km
Azimuthal Equal-area Projection
PRINCE EDWARD ISLANDS (S. Afr.)
ÎLES CROZET (French Southern and Antarctic Territories)
Tropical Rain Forest
Coniferous/ Evergreen Forest
Deciduous Forest
Chaparral
Grassland
Desert and Semidesert

Cape Town (*left*), the legislative capital of South Africa, lies on the southernmost tip of the continent. Nairobi (*above*) is Kenya's capital and largest city and one of the chief cities of eastern Africa.

CITIES

In spite of a largely rural population, Africa also has a considerable culture based on urban life. Cairo, the capital of Egypt, is the continent's largest city and continues to attract increasing numbers of people from the countryside. Alexandria, Egypt's chief port, is an ancient center of learning and commerce, named for Alexander the Great. Other important cities of the north are Casablanca, Morocco's principal city and port; and Algiers and Tunis, the capitals, respectively, of Algeria and Tunisia.

Southern Africa's major cities include Cape Town, located at the southernmost tip of the continent, and Johannesburg, both in South Africa. Lagos, Nigeria's largest city and chief port, and Abidjan, capital of Ivory Coast, are western Africa's largest urban centers. Dakar, Senegal's capital, is a leading port situated on Africa's most westerly point of land.

Eastern Africa has several major cities. Dar es Salaam, Tanzania's capital and largest city, is one of the region's leading ports. Nairobi is Kenya's chief city and capital, and Addis Ababa is the largest city, commercial center, and capital of Ethiopia. Central Africa's largest city, Kinshasa, is the capital of the Democratic Republic of Congo.

THE ECONOMY

Although rich in terms of its natural resources, most of Africa is in the developing stage, economically. The continent has emerged in only relatively recent times from the colonial period, when it served mainly as a source of raw materials for Europe's industry and as a market for its manufactured goods. Aside from South Africa, the most highly industrialized of the African countries, the continent in general has only begun to develop a modern industrial economy. Agriculture and the mining of its mineral wealth are still the main sources of Africa's income.

Agriculture

Most Africans earn their livelihood from the soil. The great majority practice subsistence farming, growing basic food crops for their own use, generally on small plots of land. Commercial crops, intended for export, are often grown on large plantations. Ordinarily, a variety of crops can be grown in some regions of the continent. In others, the thinness of the soil, the arid climate, and frequent drought make farming difficult.

Northern and Western Regions. Wheat, barley, and grapes flourish on the Mediterranean coast. Date palms, fig trees, and wheat, cotton, and vegetables can be grown in the scattered oases, or watered areas, of the desert regions. In the rainy, tropical areas of western Africa, the main food crops are yams, cassava (a starchy root), and rice. Commercial crops grown here include cacao (from which chocolate is made), coffee, rubber, and palm oil. Ivory Coast is the world's leading producer of cacao, while Nigeria is a major producer of coffee and natural rubber. In the drier savanna, important crops include such grains as millet, sorghum, and corn, peanuts, and cotton.

Eastern and Southern Regions. Corn and wheat, along with millet, cassava, and vegetables, are the major food crops of eastern Africa. Commercial crops include sisal (a fiber from which cord and twine are made), cotton, coffee, tea, and pyrethrum (used in making insecticides). Winter wheat, wine grapes, and other fruits are grown in South Africa's southern Cape province, which has a Mediterranean-type climate. Sugarcane is an important crop in the coastal region of Mozambique and along the eastern coast of South Africa.

Livestock Raising. Livestock raising is an important element of African agriculture, particularly in the savanna and steppe regions. Goats are grazed in the arid Sahel, while farther north, in the Sahara itself, semi-nomadic peoples regularly migrate, seeking pasture for their herds of camels and sheep. Eastern Africa has a distinctive cattle culture, especially among the Masai of Kenya and Tanzania, where ownership of cattle is a sign of wealth and prestige. Smaller domestic livestock, such as pigs and chickens, are kept as part of the traditional subsistance farming. Large-scale commercial cattle- and sheep-raising is carried out in South Africa.

Livestock raising (*left*) is an important part of African agriculture, particularly in regions of limited rainfall. In more fertile areas, such as the Nile Valley (*below*), a variety of crops can be grown.

was succeeded by the empire of Mali, one of whose chief cities was the fabled Timbuktu. Mali held sway until it was replaced, in turn, as the most powerful western state by Songhai, which at its height during the early 1500's stretched from the Atlantic coast to northern Nigeria. Two modern African nations, Ghana and Mali, have taken their names from these old kingdoms.

European Exploration

European exploration along the coast of Africa began with the Portuguese, who were looking for a convenient water route to India. Bartholomeu Dias rounded the Cape of Good Hope at the southern tip of Africa in 1488. Another Portuguese explorer, Vasco da Gama, visited the eastern coast and reached India in 1498. Soon afterward, the Portuguese established coastal settlements and began trading in gold, spices, ivory, and slaves.

Other European powers began to compete with the Portuguese, establishing forts and trading posts along the coast. But the dense rain forests, disease, and hostility by Africans long kept Europeans from penetrating to the inland areas.

European exploration of the interior of Africa first began in the second half of the 1700's, with the discoveries of two Scots—James Bruce, who explored the region of the Blue Nile; and Mungo Park, who traveled down the Niger River. The Scottish missionary and doctor David Livingstone made extensive discoveries in central Africa and the lake region of southeastern Africa in the mid-1800's. He was joined by Henry Morton Stanley, who later explored the vast Congo region. Sir Richard Burton and John Speke both sought the source of the Nile.

Scc EXPLORATION AND DISCOVERY (Exploring Africa) in Volume E. An article on Stanley and Livingstone appears in Volume S. An article on Sir Richard Burton appears in Volume B.

The Slave Trade

The slave trade was a by-product of the opening of Africa. Arabs had long been established in the trade in slaves in eastern Africa. By the 1600's and 1700's, the Portuguese, British, Dutch, and French had joined them. Millions of black Africans were to become its victims before the trade was banned by most European countries in the 1800's. For more information on the slave trade, see the article SLAVERY (The African Slave Trade and other sections) in Volume S.

Top: The British explorer Richard Burton (1821–90) spent years searching for the source of the Nile. His discoveries included Lake Tanganyika. *Right:* The slave trade was one of the tragic episodes of African history, lasting from the 1600's until it was abolished by most European countries in the 1800's.

IMPORTANT DATES

About 3200 B.C. Egypt united under King Menes.

About 2000 B.C. Rise of kingdom of Kush (Nubia).

814 B.C. Phoenicians settle the colony of Carthage in northern Africa.

About 600 B.C. Greeks replace Phoenicians in trade and exploration of Africa.

264–146 B.C. Punic Wars involve Rome and Carthage in a struggle for control of the Mediterranean. Victorious Roman armies destroy Carthage.

168 B.C. Romans conquer Egypt.

A.D. 300's–1000's Kingdom of Ghana flourishes in western Africa.

300's Kingdom of Aksum (in northern Ethiopia) converted to Christianity.

429–439 Vandals conquer northern Africa, which had been part of the Roman Empire.

About 500 Decline of Vandals; northern Africa becomes part of the Byzantine Empire.

640–710 Period of the Arab conquest of northern Africa; introduction of Islam and the Arabic language.

1000's Mali empire conquers Ghana.

1415 Prince Henry the Navigator sends Portuguese expeditions down the western coast of Africa.

1487–88 Bartholomeu Dias of Portugal discovers Cape of Good Hope.

1497–98 Portugal's Vasco da Gama sails around the Cape of Good Hope to India.

1500's Songhai kingdom overthrows Mali.

1517 Ottoman Turks conquer Egypt.

1520–26 Francisco Alvarez of Portugal explores Ethiopia.

1535 Spain conquers Tunis.

1595 First Dutch settlement established on the Guinea coast.

1626 French settle in Senegal.

1652 Cape Town founded by the Dutch.

1660 Rise of the Bambara kingdoms on the upper Niger.

1697 France completes conquest of Senegal.

1768–73 James Bruce explores the Blue Nile.

1787 Home for freed African slaves set up in Sierra Leone.

1792 Denmark becomes the first country to abolish the slave trade.

1795, 1805 Mungo Park explores the Niger River.

1807, 1811 Britain abolishes slave trade.

1814 Cape Colony becomes a British possession.

1815 France, Spain, and Portugal abolish slave trade.

1821 Freed American slaves arrive in Liberia.

1830–47 France conquers Algeria.

1834 Britain frees all slaves in its colonies.

1836–40 Great Trek of Boers (descendants of Dutch settlers) to interior of what is now South Africa.

1841 David Livingstone begins exploration of Africa.

1847 Liberia becomes the first independent black republic.

1849 The French establish a home for freed slaves at Libreville in Gabon.

1850's Richard Burton and John Hanning Speke explore source of the Nile.

1866 Diamonds are found in South Africa.

1869 Suez Canal opens.

1871 Henry M. Stanley's search for Livingstone ends successfully in Tanganyika.

1871 Cecil Rhodes starts building his fortune and empire in southern Africa.

1884 Germany annexes South-West Africa, gains control of Togoland and the Cameroons.

1885 King Leopold II of Belgium establishes the Congo Free State as his personal property. Germany acquires Tanganyika.

1886 Gold discovered in South Africa—gold rush begins.

1898 Fashoda Crisis on the upper Nile brings Britain and France to the brink of war.

1899–1902 Boer War: Britain's defeat of Boers gives it control of South Africa.

1908 Congo Free State is turned over to the Belgian government and renamed the Belgian Congo.

1910 The British colonies in South Africa are united to form the Union of South Africa.

1922 Egypt gains independence from Britain.

1935 Italy invades Ethiopia.

1941–43 North African campaign of World War II fought.

1948 South Africa formally adopts policy of apartheid, or racial separation.

1951 Libya gains independence.

1954–62 Period of Algerian war of independence.

1956 Tunisia, Morocco, Sudan gain independence. Egypt nationalizes the Suez Canal, touching off a Middle East war.

1957 Ghana gains independence.

1958 Guinea gains independence.

1960 Belgian Congo, Cameroon, Central African Republic, Chad, Congo, Dahomey (now Benin), Gabon, Ivory Coast, Malagasy Republic (now Madagascar), Mali, Mauritania, Niger, Nigeria, Senegal, Somalia, Togo, and Upper Volta (now Burkina Faso) gain independence.

1961 Sierra Leone and Tanganyika gain independence. South Africa becomes a republic.

1962 Algeria, Burundi, Rwanda, and Uganda gain independence.

1963 African leaders form the Organization of African Unity (OAU). Zanzibar and Kenya gain independence.

1964 Zanzibar and Tanganyika united as Tanzania. Malawi and Zambia gain independence.

1965 The Gambia gains independence. Rhodesia unilaterally declares independence.

1966 Botswana and Lesotho gain independence.

1967–70 Civil war rages in Nigeria.

1968 Equatorial Guinea, Mauritius, and Swaziland gain independence.

1971 Egypt's Aswan Dam formally opened.

1974 Guinea-Bissau gains independence.

1975 Comoros, Mozambique, Sāo Tomé and Príncipe, Angola, and Cape Verde gain independence.

1976 Seychelles gains independence.

1977 Djibouti gains independence.

1980 Zimbabwe (former Rhodesia) gains independence under black majority rule.

1990 Namibia gains independence.

1993 Eritrea wins independence from Ethiopia.

1994 Inauguration of Nelson Mandela as first black president of South Africa.

1998 Civil war resumes in the Democratic Republic of Congo (formerly Zaïre).

2001 OAU is dissolved to make way for a new African Union.

The Colonial Era

The "scramble for Africa," as the rivalry for African possessions was called, began in the mid-1800's. During the next 50 years, the continent came almost completely under European domination. France and Britain were the main colonial powers, but Portugal, Germany, Spain, Italy, and Belgium also carved out large African empires that were often many times larger than the European countries themselves. By the beginning of the 1900's, the only African states that were still independent were Ethiopia and Liberia. Ethiopia had successfully resisted colonization, while Liberia had been founded, in the early 1800's, as a refuge for freed American slaves.

The March Toward Independence

The end of World War II in 1945 saw the rise of African nationalism as a mass movement. The great march toward independence began in the late 1950's and proceeded swiftly. In 1960 alone, 17 nations won independence. By 1970 most of the continent had freed itself from colonial rule. Independence was generally gained peacefully, although in a few cases it was preceded by years of guerrilla war.

The transfer of authority was usually orderly. In several instances, however, independence was followed by civil war, either immediately or some years later. In some countries, separatists sought to break away

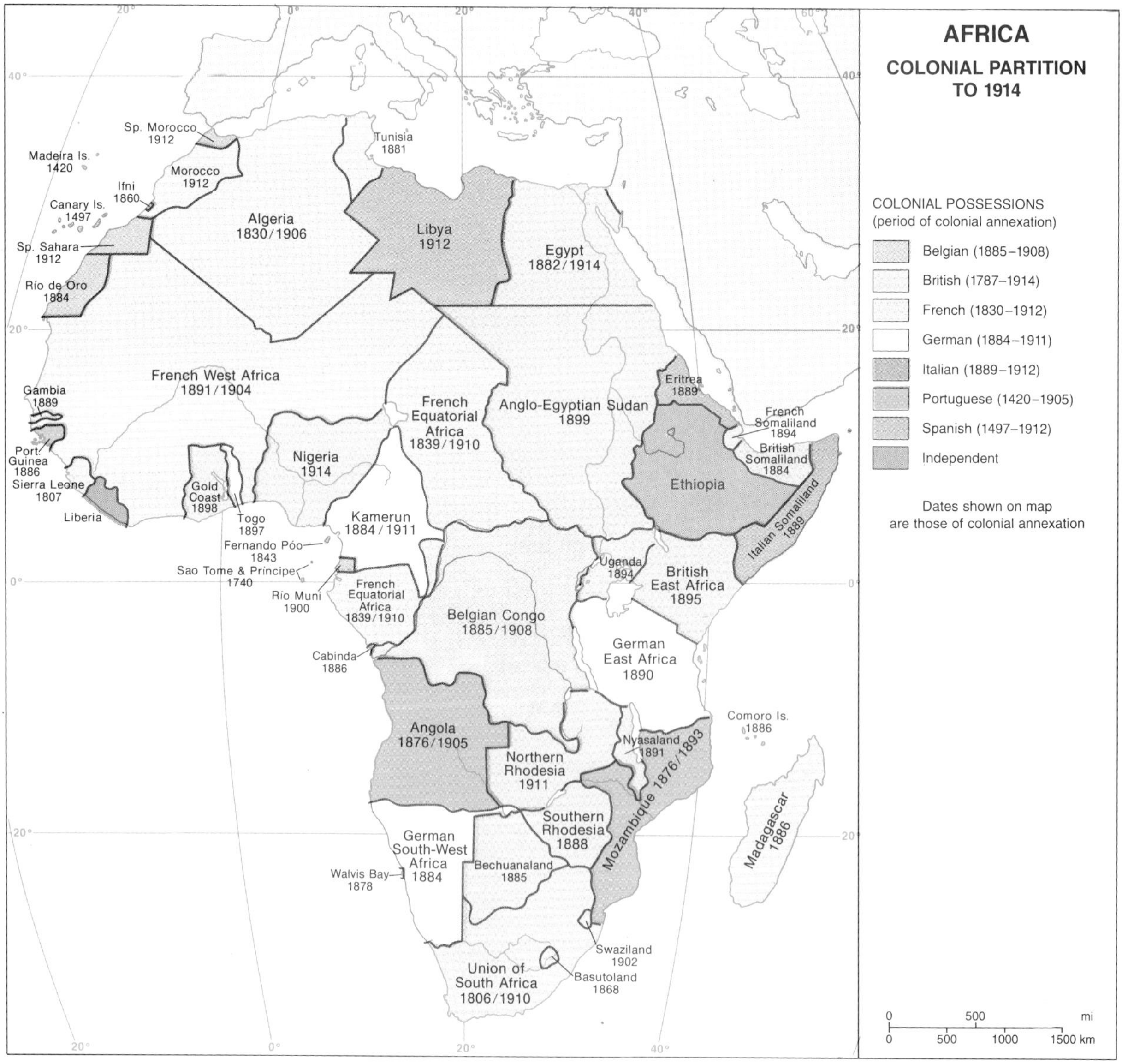

The inauguration of Nelson Mandela as South Africa's first black president in 1994 was an event of globally historic importance.

and form their own nations. This occurred in the Belgian Congo in 1960 and in Nigeria in 1967. When Angola and Mozambique won independence from Portugal in the 1970's, civil war erupted as opposing political factions fought for power.

Nevertheless, progress toward complete independence continued. Zimbabwe finally gained independence under black-majority rule in 1980. The last of the great African colonies, Namibia (a former German territory administered by South Africa) gained its independence in 1990. Africa's newest nation, Eritrea, won independence from Ethiopia in 1993, after years of fighting. In South Africa the inauguration, in 1994, of Nelson Mandela as its first black president marked a historic turning point in a country where a white minority had long been dominant.

The Future

Much remains to be done, however. Average incomes for most Africans are very low. There are still not enough schools or teachers and relatively few hospitals and doctors compared to Africa's vast size and numbers of people. Traditional ways of life have been disrupted by the migration of people from the countryside to the cities. Tribal and ethnic loyalties that sometimes cross the old European-drawn boundaries have also led to violent conflict in several regions.

Most African nations are dependent on one or two primary exports, chiefly agricultural or mineral products, for much of their income. Their economies are thus subject to changes in world prices for these products. Falling prices, together with increases in the cost of vital imports, have forced many countries to reduce needed social and economic programs. Drought has caused widespread crop failure. Famine and civil strife in such countries as Sierra Leone, Somalia, the Democratic Republic of Congo, Sudan, Liberia, Angola, Rwanda, and Burundi have caused the death of many people and created a refugee problem. AIDS has also had a devastating impact on the continent.

Africans now make up more than one-quarter of the member nations of the United Nations and have an increasingly important voice in world affairs. In 2002, the Organization of African Unity (OAU) was replaced by the African Union. It was hoped that this new organization, modeled on the European Union, would increase Africa's importance as a regional economic bloc. That same year, in a program called the New Partnership for Africa's Development, the world's leading industrial nations pledged billions of dollars to aid any African country that successfully reformed its economy and government.

Donald J. Ballas
Indiana University of Pennsylvania

Reviewed by Hugh C. Brooks
St. John's University (New York)

L. Gray Cowan
Columbia University

See also articles on individual African countries.

AFRICA, ART AND ARCHITECTURE OF

African art has developed from ancient traditions. Generations before the United States and the nations of Europe became great powers, Africa had known the rise and fall of many great kingdoms. The organization, discipline, laws, and religions of these ancient kingdoms show that Africa has been civilized for thousands of years.

The continent of Africa is often divided into two parts. To the north of the Sahara desert are the peoples known as Arabs, living in such countries as Morocco, Algeria, and Egypt. The articles EGYPTIAN ART AND ARCHITECTURE and ISLAMIC ART AND ARCHITECTURE contain information on the arts of these peoples. This article discusses the arts of the peoples living south of the Sahara.

Prehistoric rock paintings by the San people of southern Africa are the earliest existing examples of African art south of the Sahara desert.

The land varies greatly across sub-Saharan Africa. Victoria Falls, in Zimbabwe, and snowcapped mountains such as Kilimanjaro are in sharp contrast to dry plains and tropical rain forests. The differences in physical environment produced many different cultures, each with a distinct artistic tradition.

▶ THE FUNCTIONS OF AFRICAN ART

Much of the world's art was made for religious reasons, and African art is no exception. Ancestor worship, spirits, magic, and other aspects of the religion of African peoples are reflected in their art. Art was also created for marriage ceremonies, for funerals, for honoring leaders, and for celebrations.

Nearly all African art has a function. Statues are carved to honor ancestors, kings, and gods. Masks are used in rituals surrounding boys' and girls' coming-of-age ceremonies, at funerals, and for entertainment. Jewelry, clothing, hairstyles, and body painting are sometimes used to signify wealth, power, and social status.

Carved figures are used to guard containers filled with sacred relics of ancestors. Combs, spoons, bowls, stools, and other useful items are elaborately carved and decorated. Objects are made with taste and skill, regardless of their function.

African art is not anonymous, but very few African artists are known by name. Most worked alone or in a workshop composed of a master and one or more apprentices. Because their work often consisted of replacing existing objects that had deteriorated, artists were obliged to conform to the ancient artistic laws. Yet despite these restrictions, African artists managed to express individual imagination and to employ new materials and techniques. If these innovations proved to make the art more effective, they became part of an ever-growing tradition.

▶ BEGINNINGS

In prehistoric times, the nomadic San people of southern Africa left many paintings and engravings in caves and on rock faces. These works portray human figures and animals (especially antelopes) as well as mythological symbols. They show men and women hunting, fishing, gathering food, dancing, and performing ritual activities.

Other early works of art are those of the Nok culture, which flourished in northern Nigeria from about 500 B.C. to A.D. 200. The human and animal figures made of terra cotta (fired clay) that have been found in the region are the earliest known sculptures of

Artists of the ancient kingdom of Ifé used cast-metal techniques to create life-like sculpture that, in its naturalism, differs greatly from most other African art.

sub-Saharan Africa. The heads of the figures are several times larger than the heads of real human beings. This is a stylistic convention that, with slight variations, can be observed in the art of most African peoples. Although we do not know why this convention was used in the Nok culture 2,000 years ago, in most African sculpture the head is emphasized because it is the most vital part of the body.

SCULPTURE

Sculpture is Africa's greatest art. Wood is used far more than any other material. This means that much African art did not last, because wood is more easily destroyed than stone or metal. Because of this, there are some gaps in our knowledge of African art history.

An Early Tradition: Ifé and Benin

In the midwestern part of what is now Nigeria, two ancient kingdoms existed, Ifé and Benin. Artists in Ifé were casting metal sculpture by the A.D. 1000's. Archaeological evidence suggests that artists in Benin were casting metal as early as the 1300's; their earliest metal sculptures date from the 1400's.

This cast-metal plaque is characteristic of the art of the kingdom of Benin. There, too, artists followed a tradition of naturalism, often depicting events at the royal court.

The cast-metal sculpture of Ifé and Benin was naturalistic; that is, the work of art resembled the actual object it was meant to represent. For subject matter the artists used animals, birds, people, and events at the royal court. Benin artists depicted Portuguese soldiers, merchants, and other foreigners who visited the kingdom. Artists also worked in ivory, especially at Benin, where elephant tusks were carved to honor deceased kings.

Ifé and Benin sculpture represents a very different tradition from that of most other African art. In its naturalism, it is closer than any other type of art in Africa to classical Western art.

Regional Styles

Most African sculpture originated in western and central Africa, a vast area containing three main cultural regions: the Western Sudan, the Guinea Coast, and Central Africa. Figure carving is rare in eastern and southern Africa, except among a few peoples in Kenya, Tanzania, and Madagascar.

Many different styles of sculpture exist in western and central Africa, and even within each cultural region. Some stylistic characteristics, however, are common to all the regions. In addition to the "head-heavy" proportions described above, these characteristics are simplified forms, balanced and symmetrical design, and unemotional facial expression. Although the form of a face or figure may be minimal, details are both precise and abundant. For example, figures may have intricately designed hairstyles and body adornments such as necklaces and bracelets.

Western Sudan. This region extends from Senegal through Chad, ranging from semi-desert to grassland to wooded savanna. Sculpted figures tend to be angular and elongated, and the facial features are only suggested. Many of these figures are used in religious rituals; they usually have dull or encrusted surfaces

from ceremonial offerings of millet gruel or other liquid substances that have been poured over them.

Guinea Coast. This region extends along the Atlantic Ocean from Guinea-Bissau through central Nigeria and Cameroon. It includes coastal rain forests and inland wooded grasslands. Sculpted figures from this cultural region tend to be shorter and more rounded than those from the Western Sudan region. Figures often have smooth, luminous surfaces. Much art from the central part of the region, including that of the Akan people—the Baule of Ivory Coast and the Asante of Ghana—and the Yoruba people of southwestern Nigeria, was made to honor leaders. Here gold and ivory as well as wood were used to make objects of value.

The royal arts of the small kingdoms in the grasslands area of central Cameroon are bold and expressive. Colorful beadwork is used to embellish carved wood thrones and figures. The face, hands, and feet of some sculpted figures are covered with molded sheet brass.

Central Africa is an enormous area that extends down the Atlantic coast from Equatorial Guinea to northern Angola and eastward through the Democratic Republic of Congo.

In the Ogowe River basin region of Gabon, sculpted guardian figures are placed atop containers holding the sacred relics of deceased ancestors. Among the Kota people, guardian figures are flat metal-sheathed heads with minimal facial features set on lozenge-shaped bases. In contrast, those of the Fang people are single heads or complete figures that are more naturalistic in appearance.

The Kongo people predominate in the Lower Congo River basin. Their art displays a greater degree of naturalism than most African sculpture. Gesture and emotion are subtly indicated. Many figures depict a mother with a child on her lap. Because the Kongo were once part of a powerful kingdom, much of their art consists of items made for royalty.

Most African sculpture has simplified forms and a balanced design. *Top:* A terra cotta figure of a horse and rider from Mali has an elongated shape typical of sculpture from the Western Sudan region. *Far left:* A wood sculpture of a mother and child was made by the Yoruba people of Nigeria. *Left:* Much African art serves a practical purpose: In this Luba wood sculpture from the Democratic Republic of Congo, "twin" female figures form the support for a headrest.

The Kuba and the Hemba are only two peoples among hundreds in the Democratic Republic of Congo who have important sculptural traditions. Kuba figure sculpture portrays ancestral kings seated cross-legged. Standing Hemba figures are rounded naturalistic forms that serve to commemorate ancestors.

Eastern and Southern Africa. This cultural region extends south along the southern Atlantic coast and around South Africa to Ethiopia. Here, in Botswana and Namibia, are found the ancient rock paintings attributed to the San people of the Kalahari Desert. Figure carving is rare in this region. Instead, the arts of personal adornment, including body painting, and of decorating useful objects, such as headrests, spoons, and stools, are very highly developed. In Ethiopia, the art of the highlands reflects the influence of Christianity, which was introduced there in the A.D. 300's. Non-Christian Ethiopians created figurative carvings for use in their own religious worship.

MASKS

Masks are supports for spirits, which according to traditional beliefs are found in nature and in humans and animals. Some spirits are gods. Masks perform a variety of functions: They may be used in rites marking the transition from childhood to adulthood, to enforce the laws of society, to cause rain to fall during periods of drought, and to celebrate gods and ancestors.

Masks are usually worn as disguises, along with a full costume of leaves or cloth, but they are sometimes used for display. They are used in masquerades, which may be performed publicly or secretly. Generally music and dance are part of the event. Although masks may represent male or female spirits, they are almost always worn by men. During the performance, a masked dancer is no longer himself, but the spirit the mask represents.

Face masks are only one type of mask. There are also helmet, or "bucket," masks,

Masks serve a variety of important functions in African society, and distinctive styles of mask making have arisen in different regions. *Left:* A two-faced mask of painted wood was made by the Fang people of Gabon. *Above:* A painted-wood and fiber mask made by the Kuba people of the Democratic Republic of Congo is decorated with paint, beads, and shells. *Right:* A wooden mask made by the Songe people of the Democratic Republic of Congo is covered with a pattern of finely cut lines.

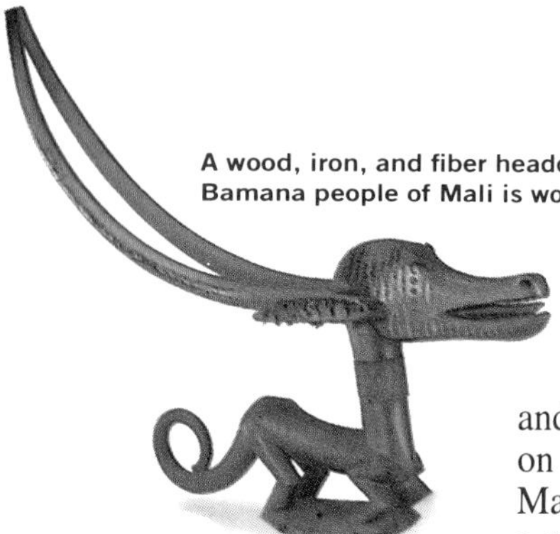

A wood, iron, and fiber headdress made by the Bamana people of Mali is worn on top of the head.

covering all or half of the head, and crest masks, worn on top of the head. Masks are made from a variety of materials. They may be carved of wood and painted with pigments made from plants or minerals. They may be decorated with animal skins, feathers, or beads. Artists also make masks out of paint fibers, tree bark, metal, or other materials.

▶ DECORATIVE ARTS

Goldwork

For centuries, African goldsmiths have used different techniques to create gold objects. They can cast solid forms, hammer gold into shapes, or press thin pieces of gold (gold leaf) onto ready-made objects.

Goldwork prevailed in areas of Africa where gold was mined and used for trade. Gold mines were located in the modern nations of Senegal, Mali, Ivory Coast, and Ghana. Ghana was so famous for its gold that it was once called the Gold Coast. A rare and expensive material, gold was used as currency and worn by kings and important religious and political officials. It was also used to make jewelry and other body ornaments, as well as to decorate weapons.

The Akan people of Ivory Coast and Ghana used metal counterweights to weigh gold dust, which was the local currency from the 1400's to the mid-1800's. Called goldweights, the counterweights were actually miniature sculptures made of cast bronze or brass. They depict animals, plants, human beings, objects, and scenes from everyday life.

Jewelry

Men, women, and children wear jewelry to decorate their bodies or as a badge of distinction. Jewelry includes a variety of objects: hair ornaments, necklaces, earrings, bracelets, rings, and anklets. Artists make jewelry from many different materials. These include gold, silver, brass, iron, and copper, carved ivory, and beads made of glass, amber, stone, or shells.

Textiles

Textiles are woven on looms by both men and women. Locally grown cotton, raffia palm, and a woody fiber called bast are the most commonly used fibers, but silk and wool are also woven.

Among the Kuba of the Democratic Republic of Congo, men and women work together to make cloth. First, men weave raffia into square or rectangular pieces. Next, the women embroider designs on the cloth with raffia thread. They can also create a cut-pile effect that resembles velvet. Although Africans commonly wear Western-style clothing, traditional apparel made from locally woven cloth is the proud national dress. Thus weaving remains a vital occupation in many parts of Africa.

Above: In gold-mining areas of western Africa, small weights such as this were used to weigh gold dust. *Right:* A carved ivory bracelet from the court of Benin.

The skill of African artisans can be seen in the beauty of everyday objects. *Far left:* A woven cotton rug from Sierra Leone has a geometric design. Textiles are woven by both men and women. *Left:* A terra cotta vessel from central Africa. Most African pottery is made by women.

Textile artists create patterns on textiles using various techniques, including weaving, dyeing, stamping, painting, embroidery, and appliqué. Patterns may be plain or extremely intricate, consisting of geometric forms or figures such as animals and birds. Materials such as metallic or glossy threads may be incorporated to enhance the design. Natural or imported dyes are used to color the cloth.

Pottery

Pottery is usually crafted by women, who have made vessels in different sizes and shapes for cooking, storing, and serving food and drink since time beyond memory. The smooth, symmetrical vessels are hand-formed; the mechanical potter's wheel has been introduced only recently.

Potters create designs on the surface of the vessel by burnishing it with a smooth pebble, by cutting lines in with a blade, or by making impressions with combs and other objects. The surface may also be decorated with slip, a thin wash of clay, in a different color than the clay of the vessel. The vessels are fired in the open and may be dipped in a vegetable solution to seal them. Because they are fired at low temperatures, African vessels made by traditional methods do not shatter when used over an open fire.

Some vessels are used for religious rituals or for display as works of art. Such vessels are decorated with modeled figures and are usually made by especially skilled potters.

Basketry

Like pottery and weaving, basketry is a very old craft that is practiced by both men and women. Baskets are essential household objects, used for storage, for preparing or serving food, and for carrying objects.

The techniques and materials used to make baskets are determined by how the basket will be used. There are three basic techniques: coiling, twining, and plaiting (braiding). Vegetable fibers, such as grasses and raffia, are the main materials used. Leather, wood, or other materials may be added for both decoration and strengthening.

PAINTING

Although easel painting was introduced only at the beginning of the 1900's, Africans have always painted. The most ancient evidence is in the prehistoric San rock paintings in southern Africa. In Christian Ethiopia, artists illustrated Bible stories in books, on scrolls, and later on canvas.

African artists have always used paint to decorate surfaces. People painted their bodies when they participated in religious or social rituals and ceremonies, or simply to make themselves more attractive. They have traditionally painted the internal and external walls of their houses and places of worship. Sculpted figures and masks were also painted.

Until European paints were introduced, artists obtained their colors from natural sources, including clay, plant leaves and roots, stones, and minerals.

▶ARCHITECTURE

A wide range of architectural forms can be found in Africa. The simplest houses are the beehive-shaped houses of the Pygmies of central Africa. The frames of such houses are constructed with flexible branches that are covered with large, fresh leaves. This type of temporary housing suits the Pygmies' nomadic way of life. Agricultural people, in contrast, require sturdy, permanent houses.

Houses may be built with thick mud walls or with sturdy bamboo frames. Roofs may be thatched or covered with corrugated metal. The spacious Islamic mosques in Mali are perhaps the most dramatic example of mud architecture. The royal palaces of the Cameroon grassfields, some of which reach heights of more than 25 feet, are outstanding examples of bamboo-frame structures.

The most noteworthy stone architecture is the complex of buildings constructed during the 1100's to the 1400's at the ancient city of Great Zimbabwe in southern Africa. It is remarkable because of its great size and because the stone walls were assembled without mortar.

Important buildings are ornamented with carved and painted doors, door frames, and posts to support the veranda roofs. Kings and other sponsors of elaborate architecture often brought specially skilled sculptors from great distances to work for them.

A wide variety of architecture can be found in Africa. The Ndebele people of southern Africa have traditionally painted the clay walls of their houses with striking geometric designs. Inside walls may also be decorated with painted designs.

▶CONTEMPORARY TRENDS

The traditional art of Africa has had a great impact on modern art. In the early 1900's, European artists came into increased contact with the art of Africa. Artists such as Pablo Picasso and Henri Matisse incorporated elements of African art into their works.

Contemporary Africans create art in a variety of styles. In some societies, traditional religion and social practices have prevailed (usually with modern modifications), and there is a need for sculptors to create masks for initiations and sculptures for shrines, much as their predecessors did. However, they may use modern innovations such as imported paints. Sign painters, graphic artists, photographers, and textile and fashion designers also are part of the contemporary visual art scene.

Some artists are like their counterparts in Europe and America. They are self-taught or trained at universities and art schools. They display their art at exhibitions in art galleries and museums at home and abroad, and have local and foreign patrons. The content of their art may be African or not; it may be realistic or non-representational—the choice is theirs. The African art that caused a revolution in Western art early in the 1900's continues to inspire artists all over the world, including those born in Africa.

ROSLYN WALKER
Curator, National Museum of African Art

Storytellers play a key role in traditional African society. The stories they perform dramatize important truths, teach moral lessons, and transmit the history of the community. For many years, these stories were not written down but were passed on from one generation to the next by word of mouth. This oral tradition is a vital part of African literature.

AFRICA, LITERATURE OF

This article concerns both the oral traditions and the written literature of the peoples of Africa. While literature is generally considered to be a written body of work, it can also be defined more broadly. This fact is of special significance when discussing the nonwritten oral tradition by which Africans transmit history, culture, and duty from one generation to the next.

THE ORAL TRADITION (ORATURE)

In many parts of Africa, the spoken word is considered to be much more powerful than the written word. For centuries, a great deal of the traditional literature of Africa was not written down. It was performed, and passed on by word of mouth. That is why an African philosopher once said, "Whenever an old man dies, it is as though a library had been burned to the ground."

(It should be noted, however, that not all of Africa's literature was of the oral tradition alone. Throughout the many dynasties and civilizations along the Nile River, written literature flourished for centuries and continues to be written in Ethiopia today.)

In recent years, a major debate has taken place among scholars of African literature as to whether the term "literature" should be used to define the oral tradition. The term **orature** emerged from the debate, giving the spoken tradition its own name. African orature serves an important social, religious, and educational purpose. The truths by which the people have always lived are dramatized, providing valuable lessons for social behavior.

The performer or storyteller relies on common experience and shared tradition. As he tells the story to his audience, he also acts out the narrative by means of gestures, facial expressions, body movement, mime, voice modulation, song, and dance. The members of the audience understand according to their ages and social circumstances. A story may mean one thing to the teller, another to the adults, and still another to the children. Everyone learns something from the performance. The good storyteller makes certain that learning takes place by punctuating his performance with proverbs that underscore the social value of the story.

In Africa the spoken word is an art and a celebration of life, to be shared by all who live in the community. Like life, this art constantly changes. When a story is repeated, it will be different because it will have been adapted to the changes in society. The ancestral wisdom, however, is not lost in the changed version. It, too, will have been adapted to the circumstances of the changed times. The actively participating audience, joining in singing and clapping, will be different, too. Each listener will be older and wiser than the last time. In this way, the past and the present remain harmoniously linked in a balanced expression of culture and duty.

Although most people in African society are capable of storytelling, not everyone becomes an expert performer in public. Those who do must be specially trained in the art of eloquence and must learn to sing and play one or more musical instruments because of the importance of music to the oral tradition.

FORMS OF THE ORAL TRADITION

Although there are many different forms of orature in Africa, they all share certain themes. Universal traits of human behavior—honesty and dishonesty, charity and greed, bravery and cowardice, wisdom and foolishness—are exposed and examined. The main forms of orature are proverbs, riddles, folktales, poetry, and epics.

Proverbs and Riddles. Proverbs are extremely popular and are used in almost every kind of situation. They are short and witty and are treasured by Africans for the traditional wisdom and universal truths contained in them.

Riddles are commonly used to set the mood for performances and are especially popular with children, who are encouraged to use them to sharpen their wits. Like proverbs, riddles are usually short. Their language is poetic and indirect, relying on metaphor (a way of suggesting a likeness between two objects or ideas) as well as on subtleties of sound, rhythm, and tone. Some examples of African proverbs and riddles are given below.

Proverbs

Sierra Leone: If you climb up a tree, you must climb down the same tree.

Ghana: Only when you have crossed the river can you say the crocodile has a lump on his snout.

Ashanti: The ruin of a nation begins in the homes of its people.

Ethiopia: A fool and water go the way they are diverted.

Riddles

What talks a lot when going, but is silent when coming back? Answer: water gourds. Empty gourds rattle together—"talk"—on the way to be filled. Full gourds do not rattle.

What darts about all day and rests behind a gate of straw at night? Answer: the eye. The straw refers to the eyelashes.

Folktales. Short oral narratives commonly referred to as folktales are told in nearly all societies in Africa. They are used to teach moral lessons, expose trickery, promote heroic behavior, and tell about how or why things came to be. Or they may present a dilemma, challenging the listener to make a choice between two or more equally deserving arguments. Folktales can be purely fictional, or they can be based on real events of the past.

The main characters in fictional folktales are usually **tricksters**—small and normally weak characters endowed with cleverness, cunning, and resourcefulness, which they use to outwit their adversaries. Because they are always motivated by greed and selfishness, tricksters sometimes become the victims of their own excesses.

Trickster characters are usually animals but are sometimes human or part human. Gods may also be used as trickster characters. For example, among the Yoruba people of Nigeria, the god Elegba is the trickster. In Sudan, the clever hare is the subject of these stories. Anansi the spider is the greedy trickster from Ghana, Liberia, and Sierra Leone. In Nigeria and Cameroon, the tortoise is the mischievous hero. The Ethiopian tricksters are Totta the monkey and Koora the crow.

Some of the trickster characters were brought to the Americas by Africans. Anansi stories are still popular in Jamaica, Belize, and Suriname, and the clever hare has become Brer Rabbit in the United States.

Poetry. Poetry is one of the oldest, most highly developed, and most widespread of African oral traditions. It has many forms and is used for a variety of purposes—for religious and sacred practices as well as for such secular (nonreligious) events as birth and marriage celebrations. There is also lyric poetry, political poetry, satirical poetry, and drum poetry.

The practice of poetry requires formal training in the language, history, culture, and music of the society. Performers of poetry are usually identified with a specific social group. In Mali, these performers are called *djeli*; in eastern Democratic Republic of Congo, they are called *karisi*. The Zulu of South Africa call them *imbongi*. The bards, or heroic singers, of Cameroon and Gabon bear the same name as the instrument they play and the type of tale they recite: *mvet*. In Ethiopia, storytellers are called *amina*.

Epics. The epic, a major part of Africa's oral tradition, is found mainly in western and central Africa and, to a lesser extent, in eastern and southern Africa. An epic is a long poem that tells about the fantastic deeds of a legendary hero. Often it weaves the ideals and traditions of a people into the story. It is usually narrated to a musical accompaniment.

Sundiata is the national epic of the Malinke people of Mali. It honors the founder of the Mali empire. *Lianja* tells the fabulous story of the epic hero of the Mongo people of the Democratic Republic of Congo. Liyongo, the spear lord, gives his name to an epic sung in the languages of eastern and central Africa. These are only three of the many epics of Africa.

The famous storyteller (*djeli*, or griot) of Mali, *Djeli* Mamoudou Kouyate, describes his position and role in society just before recounting the great *Sundiata* epic:

I am a griot. It is I, *Djeli* Mamoudou Kouyate, son of Bintu Kouyate and *Djeli* Kedian Kouyate, master in the art of eloquence. Since time immemorial the Kouyates have been in the service of the Keita princes of Mali; we are vessels of speech, we are the repositories which harbour secrets many centuries old. The art of eloquence has no secrets for us; without us the names of kings would vanish into oblivion, we are the memory of mankind. I teach kings the history of their ancestors so that the lives of the ancients might serve them as an example, for the world is old, but the future springs from the past. My word is pure and free of all untruth; it is the word of my father; it is the word of my father's father. . . .

AFRICAN LITERATURE IN EUROPEAN LANGUAGES

During the colonial period, beginning in the 1700's, Europeans introduced their own written languages as tools of power, education, and government. Different peoples with different languages and cultures were grouped together in the various colonial territories. When these territories became independent, choosing one official African language proved difficult. Thus most of the new African states retained the language of their former colonizers as their official language.

The written translation of orature into these foreign languages was natural and inevitable. And as it gains recognition and popularity, orature is being written and translated into more of the major languages of the world. This rapid shift from the oral to the written tradition carries with it the danger that young Africans may choose not to become performers of orature. The risk of losing the tradition, under these circumstances, is quite real.

Learning to write the European languages also produced a new literature: short stories, poems, and novels that were never meant to be recited and plays that were meant to be performed on a stage rather than in a traditional African setting.

Some of these literary forms have been explored by African writers in their own languages. But those who write in English, French, or Portuguese can expect to have more readers. For this reason most recent African literature has been written in these languages. Ethiopia is an exception; written literature in the Ge'ez script has been practiced there for centuries, together with an oral tradition. An example is the epic story of Solomon and Mequeda, Queen of Sheba, which has also been translated into European languages.

African writing in French developed primarily in the regions of western and central Africa once occupied by the French. African literature in English comes from countries in eastern, western, and southern Africa where, for a time, English-speaking people ruled. Portuguese is used in Mozambique and Angola, former colonies of Portugal.

The Negritude Movement. Beginning in the 1930's, some African writers writing in French launched a literary movement known as negritude. Aimé Césaire, a West Indian from the island of Martinique, was the first to use the word. Césaire had been influenced by the African American literary movement of the 1920's known as the Harlem Renaissance. In his greatest poem, *Return to My Native Land* (1939), he defined negritude as a celebration of blackness.

Césaire's friend Léopold Sédar Senghor became the president of Senegal and one of the major writers of his generation. Senghor defined negritude as the cultural heritage, values, and spirit of black African civilization.

The negritude movement also expressed anger. It attacked the white world for racism, for concern with wealth and material things, and for pretending one thing but being another. This anger may be seen in the novels of Ferdinand Oyono from Cameroon, especially in *Houseboy*, the story of an African servant in a white household.

Other writers of the negritude movement include poet Tchicaya U Tam'si of the Congo and novelist Camara Laye of Guinea.

Other Views. Wole Soyinka, a Nobel Prize-winning Nigerian playwright, expressed a different view. Soyinka wrote *A Dance of the Forests* for the celebration of Nigerian independence in 1960. This play is a fantasy in which traditional gods and spirits call up a group of ancestors to accuse them of participating in the European slave trade. "Do not romanticize old Africa," the play is saying.

This no-nonsense attitude is shared by Ezekiel Mphahlele, a South African writer, and by most Africans writing in English. To them, Senghor's idea of traditional African life is unrealistic.

The Nigerian novelist Chinua Achebe has recorded the strife within the traditional African community. He says it is useless to deny social change; the problem is how to meet it. His novels *Things Fall Apart* (1958) and *Arrow of God* (1964) ask whether modern Nigerian leaders can develop the strength of character of certain old chiefs and priests who resisted European ways.

The terrible experience under colonialism and the struggle for independence provided substantial material for African novelists and poets of the new literature. In South Africa, in particular, the new literature played an extremely important role in expressing the Africans' feelings in their struggle against apartheid. But censorship and persecution forced many black writers, such as the poet Dennis Brutus, to flee the country.

White South African writers, too, voiced their objections to apartheid. Alan Paton wrote about racial conflict in *Cry, the Beloved Country* (1948) and other novels. Athol Fugard dramatized the plight of black South Africans in many plays, notably *The Blood Knot* (1961), *A Lesson from Aloes* (1978), and *The Road to Mecca* (1984). The novels and short stories of Nadine Gordimer, winner of the 1991 Nobel Prize for literature, explore these same social and political themes.

Women in African Literature. Traditionally, the position of women in orature was secondary to that of men. The early stages of the new African literature also tended to be male-dominated. Recently, however, many women novelists and poets, as well as feminist scholars and literary critics, have emerged. Notable women writers include Ama Ata Aidoo of Ghana, Buchi Emecheta of Nigeria, Martha Mvungi of Tanzania, Grace Ogot of Kenya, Bessie Head of South Africa, and Kebedech Tekleab of Ethiopia.

FILM

Filmmaking came to Africa after independence in the 1960's. Film, more than written literature, was ideally suited to accommodate the performance aspects of orature. As filmmaking in Africa gained momentum, so did the search for stories suitable for film. Both filmmakers and writers soon turned to the rich oral tradition for their material. As a result, many of the leading African films are patterned after the traditional epics and other forms of orature.

For these reasons, and because they are seen by a great number of people, African films play an important role in keeping the oral tradition alive in modern times.

The number of African filmmakers is growing steadily, along with that of novelists, poets, and playwrights. The work of all these artists constitutes a major contribution to the richness of world literature. African orature and modern literature tell about a world many people of the West have never visited, or even imagined correctly. It is a world that is well worth getting to know.

Abiyi R. Ford
School of Communications
Howard University

The traditional music of Africa is celebrated for its richness and diversity. ***Clockwise from upper left:*** Percussion instruments such as drums and xylophones are the most common African instruments. However, traditional instruments also include wind instruments such as this wooden horn as well as a variety of stringed instruments.

AFRICA, MUSIC OF

Africans perform and listen to all types of music—popular, classical, and traditional. Traditional music has its roots in the soil of Africa and is extremely diverse: There are more than 700 different languages and ethnic groups in Africa, and each is associated with a particular kind of music.

At one time, scholars assumed that all African music was the same and that it rarely changed. We now know that traditional African music has been changing for centuries. Many changes occurred even before Europeans and other outsiders visited Africa. When people come in contact with each other, through trade, war, or other circumstances, musical ideas are often exchanged. For example, the Asante people of Ghana in western Africa adopted the *donno*, a type of talking drum, from people who lived north of them.

The physical environment, occupation, and social structure of the people also affect their music making. For example, the Khoisan people of southern Africa used to be nomadic—that is, they were constantly moving from place to place to hunt and gather foods. Clans of twenty to fifty people lived together as equals, with no political leaders. The Khoisan used few musical instruments; singing was their main form of music making. While the women and girls sang and clapped their hands, the men danced and played drums.

The music of the Baganda people of Uganda, on the other hand, developed in a very different way. In earlier times, their kingdom was one of the largest in eastern Africa. The king's court included several musicians, who played a variety of instruments—drums, trumpets, flutes, harps, lyres, drum-chimes, and xylophones—for the king's private enjoyment and for official activities. Other musicians performed at community events and ceremonies.

MUSIC IN AFRICAN LIFE

Africans perform music when they come together for leisure and recreation. They also use music at religious ceremonies, festivals, and work. Music plays an important role at birth, initiation, wedding, and funeral ceremonies. Songs performed at some events help people remember their history and customs.

In many parts of Africa, adults take their children to special camps for initiation ceremonies. There the elders teach the girls and boys what they need to know about adulthood. The girls learn lullabies as part of child-care training. The boys learn historical songs to teach them the customs of their society. Through music, children may also learn about numbers and language, as well as singing and dancing techniques.

Some musicians in Africa are specialists who receive formal training from a family member or a professional musician. But music is a vital part of everyday life for all Africans. Everyone participates in a performance by dancing, singing, handclapping, or playing a musical instrument. Mothers train their children when they are infants by rocking them to music and singing songs. Among the Fon people in western Africa, children who lose their first tooth have to sing a special song to commemorate the event. Children also learn music by playing games and telling stories.

In many African communities, musicians are admired and respected for the service they perform for the community. But some people believe musicians are lazy because they spend all their time making music. Also, through their music, musicians sometimes warn and criticize people about unacceptable behavior, and this can make them unpopular. However, most people believe that musicians play an important role in society.

The Talking Drum

Some of the most interesting African drums are known as talking drums because they imitate the tones of African languages. One type of talking drum is the hourglass pressure drum, such as the *dùndún* played by the Yoruba people of Nigeria. It consists of two drum heads connected by cords on an hourglass-shaped frame. The drum is held at the performer's side under the arm. When the cords are pressed by the arm, the drum heads are stretched and the pitch of the drum is raised. Changing the pressure on the cords changes the pitch of the sound produced when the drum head is struck.

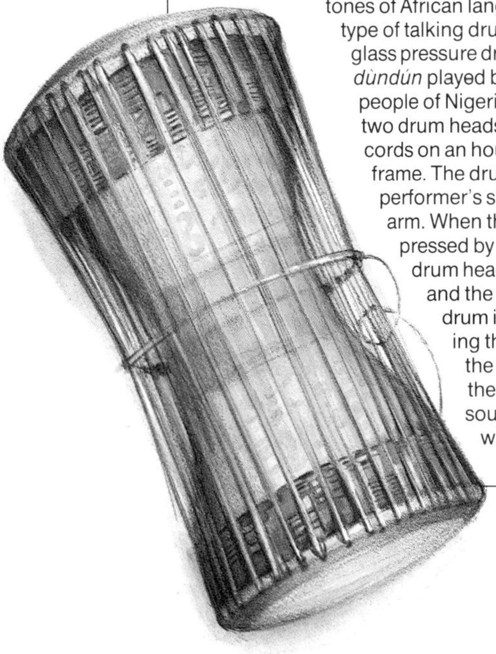

INSTRUMENTS

Africans perform music on a wide variety of percussion, stringed, and wind instruments.

Percussion Instruments are the most common instruments in Africa. Societies that do not use drums may perform on rattles, bells, sticks, clappers, and stamping tubes.

Percussion instruments are mainly used for rhythm, but some also play melodies. For example, the xylophone has wooden keys of various sizes, which produce different tones when struck with a stick. The Chopi people of eastern Africa include as many as 13 xylophones in ensembles that also include drums, rattles, and whistles. While some of the xylophone musicians play the main melody, others play a supporting repetitive part.

Drums come in a variety of sizes and shapes. Some are small and held in the hand; others are large and are placed on the ground when played. To produce a sound, musicians strike the drum head with sticks, hands, or both. Sometimes the musician scrapes or rubs the drum head with a stick to produce a sound. The Akan-speaking people of Ghana play a drum called *etwie* in honor of their king. The drum is made of wood and covered with the skin of a leopard. When the drum head is rubbed with a stick, the sound that is produced imitates the sound of the leopard. By reproducing the sound of a feared and powerful animal, *etwie* music symbolizes and praises the might and majesty of the king.

Stringed Instruments include musical bows, harps, zithers, lyres, and lutes. The musical bow is the most common stringed instrument in Africa. It has only one string, which is plucked or struck. Harps and zithers are common in eastern and central Africa; eastern Africa is also the primary location for lyres. The lute is found in societies influenced by Arab culture. Lutes can be bowed like a fiddle or plucked like a banjo. The *kora*, a 21-string harp lute, is prominent among the Mandinka people. The *kora* looks like a lute but is played like a harp.

Wind Instruments include flutes, reed pipes, horns, and trumpets. The flute is the most widespread. Flutes can be made of wood, bamboo, clay, or other materials and can have as many as seven finger holes. They are played vertically or horizonally. The reed pipe, like the lute, is located in areas influenced by Arab culture. Horns and trumpets are made of animal horns and tusks, wood, gourd, or bamboo and can be either end-blown or side-blown.

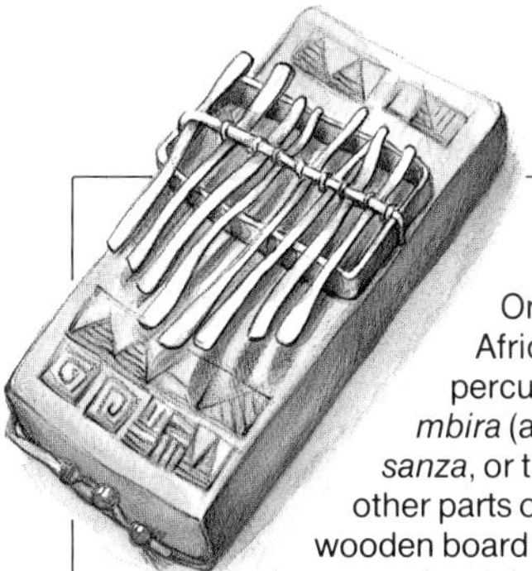

The Mbira

One of the most distinctive African instruments is a small percussion instrument called the *mbira* (also known as the *kalimba*, *sanza*, or thumb piano). Rarely found in other parts of the world, it consists of a wooden board or box over which several tongues of metal or bamboo are fastened. When the tongues are plucked (usually with the thumbs), soft sounds are produced. The sound can be modified by wrapping wire around the tongues to produce a buzzing effect, or by attaching a hollow gourd to make the sound resonate (vibrate and grow louder). Many African musicians play the *mbira* as a solo instrument or to accompany singing. Several *mbira* can also be played together in an ensemble, with singing and rattle accompaniment.

▸ CHARACTERISTICS

Singing is the most characteristic way of performing African music. Although people sing solos, singing in a group is more common. Often, one person leads a song and a group of singers responds by repeating the same theme or a variation. This arrangement is sometimes called call and response.

Language or speech serves as the basis for most African melodies and rhythms. Many African languages are **tone languages**, meaning that the pitch on which a word or a syllable is spoken determines its meaning. The high and low sounds of the rhythms played on African talking drums correspond closely to speech. In earlier times, such "talking" instruments informed African people about current events.

In an African performance, music, dance, song, and drama are all important. Although musicians include a variety of musical sounds in their ensembles, percussion is essential. The Ewe people of Ghana include singing, handclapping, rattles, bells, and four or five drums in their ensembles. The bell players perform a repetitive rhythm that serves as the base for all other parts. Some of the drummers and other musicians perform a different repetitive pattern. The leader of the group, playing the largest drum or drums, does not play a repetitive rhythm but **improvises**—spontaneously creates different but related music. When everyone performs the various rhythms and melodies together, this is called **polyphony**. African music is interesting not because of the individual parts that each person plays. Rather, Africans enjoy hearing how the parts interrelate and communicate with each other.

▸ INFLUENCES

Much of today's popular music contains African elements. This is because African Americans have greatly influenced music throughout the world. When Europeans took Africans as slaves to the Americas, Africans remembered much about the music they performed in Africa. Those in the West Indies and various parts of Central and South America continued to worship African gods and play African instruments.

In the United States, most slaves could not openly practice their African traditions. Slaveowners outlawed drums and other loud instruments when they discovered that slaves could use them to communicate. Instead of playing drums, slaves patted different parts of the body or used handclapping or foot-stomping to make music. When they sang songs, they performed them differently from European Americans. They used a different vocal quality and added bends and slurs to the melody. Also, they created their own songs and styles of music. Spirituals, blues, jazz, gospel, and other forms of popular music come from the integration of African and European elements.

Music from the United States, Europe, and Asia has influenced musicians in modern Africa. Highlife, juju, and soukous are a few of the new forms of popular music that one can hear in dance halls and nightclubs in Africa. Musicians now create new hymns for the church. Also, Africans have begun to compose their own style of classical music. Along with traditional music, each of these types of music plays an important role among the people who live in various cities, towns, and villages throughout Africa.

JACQUELINE COGDELL DJEDJE
University of California, Los Angeles

From left to right: Kathy E. Morris Wilkerson, New Orleans' first female firefighter. NBA All-Star Kevin Johnson takes time out to play with a group of young friends. Dr. James W. Mitchell, Director of Analytical Chemistry at AT&T Bell Laboratories. Farmworkers pick peppers near Atchafalaya, Louisiana.

AFRICAN AMERICANS

African Americans are citizens of the United States who trace at least part of their ancestry to the continent of Africa. Although some are recent immigrants, most are descended from Africans who were brought in slavery to the American colonies and states between the years 1619 and 1808. Today, African Americans number about 34.6 million, or 12.3 percent of the total United States population. The largest communities reside in the states in the Deep South, followed by those in the Northeast, Midwest, and West.

Over the centuries, African Americans have been known by a succession of names. Many of these name changes reflected the African Americans' desire to establish a distinctive identity and to express pride in their racial heritage. Until the early 1800's, the preferred name was African. Later the terms black, colored, and Negro (the Spanish word for "black") came into use. After the 1960's, the terms Negro and colored were largely abandoned in favor of black and Afro-American. Since the late 1980's, the term African American has been preferred.

The African heritage in North America, which dates as far back as any other except Native American, has greatly influenced the American culture through the centuries. African roots are evident in the distinctive African American styles of clothing and adornment, in cooking, and in modern dance. They also are found in African American literature and in orature, or oral history, passed down through the generations, that tell the stories of the African American experience.

Perhaps the strongest influence, however, is found in music, an art form that has always been central to the daily lives of most Africans. African roots can be found in nearly every American music form, from the early spirituals and the gospel singing of religious celebration to rhythm and blues, soul, rock and roll, rap, and the most uniquely American music form of all—jazz.

Today, in music as well as all other forms of mass popular culture, African Americans are more influential than ever. The better part of black creative expression has been directed toward widening the nation's perceptions and understanding of African Americans and their values.

OVERVIEW

For three hundred years, European colonists brought Africans to the New World as slaves

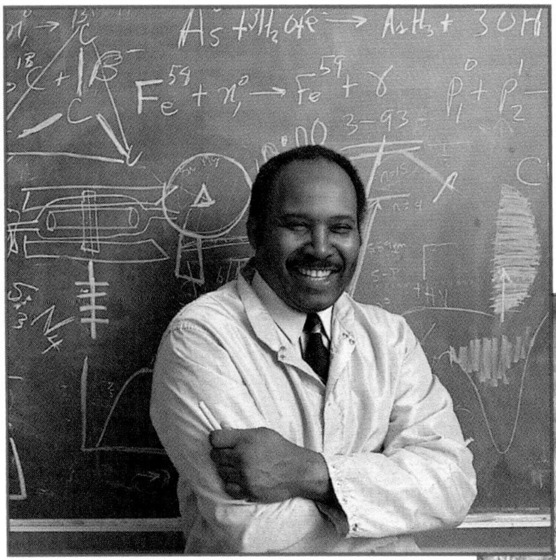

to clear vast tracts of land for the cultivation of sugar, rice, cotton, and tobacco. The black community in what is now the United States began in 1619 at Jamestown, Virginia, where 20 Africans were traded for water and supplies by Dutch seamen on their way from New York to Suriname, South America. Historians are divided on the issue of whether or not these particular immigrants were slaves or indentured servants (people who were contracted to work for a specific period of time in exchange for voyage costs, food, and lodging). One thing is certain: At least 1 million Africans became unwilling travelers to North America before the United States outlawed the importation of slaves in 1808.

Much of African American history is based on the blacks' struggle to achieve the equality and unalienable rights promised by the founders of a democratic government. In 1776, Thomas Jefferson wrote in the Declaration of Independence, "We hold these truths to be self-evident, that all men are created equal, that they are endowed by their Creator with certain unalienable Rights, that among these are Life, Liberty, and the pursuit of Happiness." Frederick Douglass, an ex-slave and the most prominent black abolitionist of the mid-1800's, challenged this notion of democracy when he declared to the white community, "The rich inheritance of justice, liberty, prosperity, and independence, bequeathed by your fathers, is shared by you, not by me."

A strong antislavery movement helped set the stage for the United States Civil War (1861–65) between the free states in the North and the slave states in the South. Emancipation, or freedom, for the slaves was assured in 1865 by the 13th Amendment to the U.S. Constitution after the North defeated the South. But it was not until the ratification of the 14th Amendment (1868) that African Americans were declared citizens in the land of their birth. The 15th Amendment (1870) assured African American men their right to vote.

Slavery had encouraged a false assumption that blacks were inferior to whites. Despite emancipation, discrimination against blacks continued to deprive African Americans of their legal rights well into the 1900's. Fundamental democratic privileges, such as the right to vote, were routinely denied them, and they were set apart from mainstream society by laws designed to keep the races socially separate and politically unequal. Their frustrations finally erupted in a civil rights movement in the 1950's and 1960's, when African Americans began demanding their proper and equal place in society.

The modern-day historian John Hope Franklin has noted, "With an optimism born in hope when only despair was in view," African Americans struggled for equal status "in the land that [African American author] James Weldon Johnson reminded them was theirs by right of birth and by right of toil."

AFRICAN AMERICAN FIRSTS

1624 William Tucker, born in Jamestown, Virginia, is believed to have been the first African American born in what is now the United States.

1770 Crispus Attucks, an American patriot, was killed by British troops in the Boston Massacre. He was the first-known African American to die in the American revolutionary movement.

1821 Thomas L. Jennings, a New York tailor, was the first black to receive a U.S. patent, for inventing a dry-cleaning process.

1827 *Freedom's Journal*, the first African American newspaper, was published by coeditors John B. Russwurm and Charles B. Ray, in New York City.

1842 Lenox Remond of Boston was hired by the American Anti-Slavery Society as the first of many black professional anti-slavery lecturers.

1853 *Clotel: A Tale of the Southern States*, written by William Wells Brown, was the first-known novel written by an African American.

1865 John S. Rock became the first African American allowed to practice law in the U.S. Supreme Court.

1868 John Willis Menard, the first African American elected to the U.S. Congress, was not permitted to take his seat in the U.S. House of Representatives.

1870 Hiram Rhoades Revels became the first African American to serve in the U.S. Senate; Joseph Hayne Rainey was the first to win election and be seated in the U.S. House of Representatives.

1872 Pinckney Benton Stewart Pinchback, the lieutenant governor of Louisiana, became the first African American elevated to the position of governor.

1893 Dr. Daniel Hale Williams performed the world's first successful heart operation.

1903 Maggie Walker founded the St. Luke Penny Thrift Savings Bank in Richmond, Va., becoming the first African American woman to head a bank.

1940 Benjamin O. Davis, Sr., became the first black brigadier general in the U.S. Army; Hattie McDaniel became the first African American to win an Academy Award for her supporting role in *Gone With the Wind*.

1947 Jackie Robinson of the Brooklyn Dodgers was the first African American to join a major league baseball team.

1950 Gwendolyn Brooks became the first African American to win a Pulitzer Prize, for her volume of poetry *Annie Allen*; Ralph Bunche became the first African American to win the Nobel Peace Prize.

1955 Marian Anderson became the first African American soloist to perform with the Metropolitan Opera in New York City.

1957 Althea Gibson became the first African American tennis player to win a singles championship at Wimbledon, in England.

1963 Sidney Poitier became the first African American to win the Academy Award for best actor.

1966 Constance Baker Motley became the first African American woman to serve as a federal judge; Robert C. Weaver became the first African American appointed to a cabinet position, as secretary of the Department of Housing and Urban Development; Edward W. Brooke, a Republican from Massachusetts, became the first African American elected to the U.S. Senate since the Reconstruction period.

1967 Thurgood Marshall became the first African American appointed to the U.S. Supreme Court; Carl Stokes, a Democrat, was elected mayor of Cleveland, the first African American to govern a major city.

1968 Shirley Chisholm, a Democrat from New York, became the first African American woman elected to the U.S. House of Representatives.

1975 Daniel "Chappie" James became the first African American four-star general (in the U.S. Air Force); Virginia Hamilton became the first African American to win a Newbery Medal, for her novel *M.C. Higgins, the Great* (1974).

1977 Patricia R. Harris became the first African American woman appointed to a president's cabinet, as secretary of Housing and Urban Development.

1983 Guion S. Bluford, Jr., became the first African American astronaut to make a space flight.

1989 The Reverend Barbara L. Harris, an African American Episcopalian priest, became the first female bishop consecrated by the worldwide Anglican community.

1990 L. Douglas Wilder, a Democrat, became the first African American elected governor of a state (Virginia).

1992 Mae C. Jemison, M.D., became the first African American woman to make a space flight; Carole Moseley Braun, a Democrat from Illinois, became the first African American woman elected to the U.S. Senate.

1993 Toni Morrison became the first African American to win the Nobel Prize for literature.

2001 General Colin L. Powell was the first African American named secretary of state, the nation's highest cabinet office.

2002 Halle Berry was the first African American to win the Academy Award for best actress.

Many African American families are active members of their churches. The church has long been a source of comfort, strength, and leadership in black communities.

THE ROLE OF THE CHURCH

When Africans were first brought to America, they were forced to abandon their native religions and were taught Christianity. Many embraced the new faith, finding spiritual comfort and hope. In the late 1700's, black churches started to form, and many became centers of African American community life. Their music—spirituals and rousing gospel songs—has since become part of the American musical tradition.

Many black churches led the fight against discrimination, and throughout their history, African Americans have often chosen their leaders from the ranks of the church.

In the 1960's the Nation of Islam challenged the black churches, claiming that Islam is the true religion of African peoples. But most worshipers have remained with the Christian churches, which continue to play an important role in many African American communities.

THE AFRICAN PAST

From the ancient civilization of Egypt of 3000 B.C. to the fall of Timbuktu in the A.D. 1600's, the African continent was the site of a succession of great inland societies, whose names still carry hints of mystery and grandeur—Meroe, Napata, Axum, and Kush. In western Africa along the Niger River, three massive societies rose and fell: ancient Ghana (A.D. 800–1200); Melle (or Mali) (1000–1400); and Songhai (1200–1600). Through trade, commerce, and warfare, these societies grew from small village kingdoms into complex empires, ruled by great kings and covering thousands of square miles. No coastal African society ever matched these inland empires in terms of size, governmental organization, and military power.

Long before Europeans appeared on Africa's Atlantic coast, traditional African societies had traded people for goods. African communities recognized ownership claims to people not belonging to their family or clan. In traditional African exchange systems, claims to the rights of individual slaves were bought and sold along with tangible goods, such as gold and ivory.

The hardships endured by slaves in Africa were softened somewhat by the cultural traditions they shared with their African slaveholders, such as religion and respect for ancestors. By contrast, the European treatment of enslaved Africans from the late 1400's on was influenced by myths of black inferiority and the promise of wealth that could be gained by using slave labor. Few Europeans had any interest in or knowledge of Africa's true history or greatness.

In the 1500's, gold and slaves were traded out of Timbuktu, the legendary city of Africa's Songhai Empire.

PLANTATION BONDAGE ERA (1619–1865)

Over a period of about 350 years, from the early 1500's to the mid-1800's, approximately 12 million Africans were forcibly transported across the Atlantic Ocean to the Americas. Of this number, about 8 percent, or approximately 1 million, were brought to North America (after 1619), with the rest going to the islands of the Caribbean and the shores of Central and South America. Collected by European slave traders working out of western Africa, millions of Africans were taken in exchange for guns, iron, beads, silks, brocades, and other cloths, knives, basins, mirrors, and the like. They were then sold as slaves to colonial plantation owners in the Americas.

The Slave Trade

The business of trading goods for people, and then selling those people as slaves for a financial profit, was initiated and funded by European royalty and merchants. They fi-

This article traces the history of African Americans, from their African roots to the present day. For more information, refer to the following articles in the appropriate volumes in *The New Book of Knowledge*: ABOLITION MOVEMENT; AFRICA; AFRICA, ART AND ARCHITECTURE OF; AFRICA, LITERATURE OF; AFRICA, MUSIC OF; AMERICAN LITERATURE; CIVIL RIGHTS; CIVIL RIGHTS MOVEMENT; CIVIL WAR, UNITED STATES; COMPROMISE OF 1850; DRED SCOTT DECISION; EMANCIPATION PROCLAMATION; HYMNS (Spiritual and Other Folk Hymns); JAZZ; KANSAS-NEBRASKA ACT; LINCOLN, ABRAHAM (The Lincoln-Douglas Debates); MISSOURI COMPROMISE; RACISM; RECONSTRUCTION PERIOD; SEGREGATION; SLAVERY; SPINGARN MEDAL; UNDERGROUND RAILROAD; UNITED STATES, HISTORY OF THE; the history sections of individual state articles; and biographies and profiles of notable individuals.

1526–39 The first Africans arrived in the Americas in the company of Spanish and Portuguese explorers.

1539 Estevanico (Little Stephen), a Moroccan slave who had escaped his Spanish captors, led the first expedition of explorers into the Southwest as far as present-day New Mexico and Arizona.

1565 Africans helped establish North America's oldest European settlement, St. Augustine, Florida.

1619 North America's first slaves were brought to Jamestown, Virginia.

1688 The first formal protest against slavery was made in Germantown, Pennsylvania.

1775–81 At least 5,000 blacks fought in the Revolutionary War, notably at the battles of Bunker Hill, Lexington, Brandywine, White Plains, Concord, and Saratoga. Two of them, Prince Whipple and Oliver Cromwell, crossed the Delaware River with George Washington on Christmas Day, 1776.

From 1619 to 1808, about 1 million black Africans were sold into slavery and shipped across the Atlantic Ocean to what is now the United States.

nanced the trading companies that outfitted ships and their crews and maintained agents on both sides of the Atlantic Ocean.

Over the years, thousands of European ships crisscrossed the Atlantic on this triangular, or three-legged, business route between Europe, Africa, and the Americas. On the journey's second leg, known as the Middle Passage, each ship carried between 200 and 300 Africans to America. During a journey lasting four to six months, the slaves traveled most of the way lying down because there was no room for standing or sitting. They were branded with hot irons, separated by gender, and fed a diet of beans, yams, and corn mush. Some were under 10 years of age. The tightly packed conditions promoted contagious diseases that killed an estimated 20 percent of the blacks as well as many of the white crew members. From the diaries of Africa-based trading company agents, scholars calculate that an additional 2 to 4 percent of the slaves died before they ever reached the ships. These losses increased the value of the slaves who survived the rigorous crossing.

On arrival in the colonies, slaves were evaluated for their strength and potential work capabilities and put up for sale on the auction block. Most slaves in North America were bought by well-to-do plantation owners living in the Southern colonies, with open areas suitable for commercial agriculture. About 10,000 planters made up the Southern ruling class, each owning 50 or more slaves. Virginia planters George Washington and Thomas Jefferson each held at least 250 slaves, even as they debated the morality of slavery.

Slave Life

Slaves engaged in three basic categories of work—domestic, mechanical, and agricultural. Domestic slaves worked around the slaveholders' homes, cooking, cleaning, and raising the white children. Other slaves were skilled artisans, trained as carpenters, millwrights, masons, tailors, and shoemakers. Most slaves, however, were engaged in some form of farming. Those who were skilled in crop production were more valuable than unskilled farm laborers, or "field hands." As such, they were treated differently, often having better food, clothing, and shelter.

The typical day for a slave began in a lineup for task or group assignments. Except for a short break for a midday meal, work continued until nightfall. Generally the slaves were not required to work on Saturday afternoons or on Sundays, except during certain stages of rice and sugarcane cultivation, when they were required to work 16 to 18 hours a day, seven days a week. If the taskmaster felt it necessary, slaves could be worked to the very limit of their strength.

Weekly food rations were a peck (eight dry quarts) of corn, three or four pounds of bacon

In 1816 the Reverend Richard Allen of Philadelphia was consecrated the first bishop of the African Methodist Episcopal (A.M.E.) Church, the first independent black religious denomination.

1777 Vermont became the first state to abolish slavery.

1787 The Free African Society was founded by Richard Allen and Absalom Jones in Philadelphia.

1817 James Forten presided over the first interstate convention of African Americans. More than 3,000 attended to protest a proposal by the American Colonization Society to deport free blacks to Africa.

1822 Denmark Vesey organized 6,000 slaves in South Carolina in a failed effort to overthrow slavery.

1826 The Massachusetts Colored General Association, established in Boston, became the nation's first African American political group.

1830 A national meeting of African American leaders in Philadelphia was the first time black leaders met to review the problems and status of black Americans.

or salt pork, and perhaps some yams and molasses. This was supplemented with vegetables and salad greens raised by the slaves themselves on patches of ground allowed them near their one-room cabins. Leisure time was enjoyed after the fall harvest season and during major holidays.

Although many slaves were not intentionally mistreated, most slaves lived in constant fear. At the word of any person in authority, a slave could be punished, physically abused, or even sold away from his or her family. Although some considerate buyers made an effort to keep family members together, often children were sold apart from their mothers, and husbands and wives were taken to separate plantations. This disregard for the slaves' emotional needs weakened the foundations of many black families. In spite of such inhumane treatment, there were relatively few slave uprisings in North America, perhaps because there were at least four times as many whites as blacks, and blacks generally did not have access to weapons.

Forced to be submissive and obedient by day, slaves created a different style of life for themselves at night. Between sundown and sunup, they tried to maintain normal family traditions and relationships. Many found comfort in religion, and community gatherings often were centered on religious celebration. They sang hymns and other religious songs called spirituals to lift their burdens and to express their suffering. Songs such as "Nobody Knows the Trouble I've Seen" and "Swing Low, Sweet Chariot" were among the first created in America.

Free Blacks

Not all of the blacks in antebellum (pre–Civil War) America were slaves. "Free blacks" lived and worked in major cities throughout the nation. The rights of free blacks, however, were strictly limited, especially in the South, where so-called Black Codes dictated their behavior. Free blacks were not allowed to express any kind of social or political viewpoint, nor were they allowed to socialize with whites or to carry weapons. Therefore, not surprisingly, black leadership became centered in the North, where blacks enjoyed a greater measure of freedom.

Although Northerners made up only 15 percent of the nation's free-black population, they set the standard for the black community's social and religious values. Free blacks financed neighborhood elementary schools in New York and many other Northern cities. Even in the slaveholding South, where "compulsory ignorance" laws prohibited black education, many blacks taught their children how to read and write during the time permitted for religious instruction. They treasured literacy, even though they were forced to hide it.

The Abolitionist Movement

In the 30 years prior to the outbreak of the Civil War in 1861, free blacks in the North played a major role in the struggle to abolish slavery in the United States. They founded organizations, such as the American Society of Free People of Color, to protest racial prejudice in the North as well as slavery in the South. Free-black churches raised money to support antislavery lecturers and news-

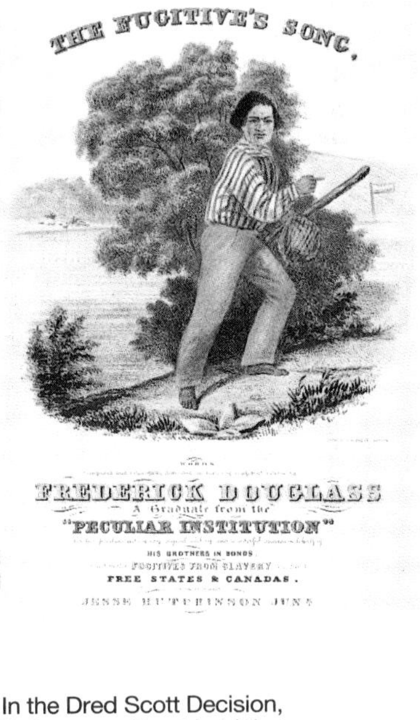

Frederick Douglass was the most famous black abolitionist of his day. In 1845 an antislavery song was published describing his escape from slavery.

1831 Nat Turner led an unsuccessful slave revolt in Southampton County, Virginia. He and many others were hanged for the deaths of more than 50 whites. The uprising led to the nation's first public debate over the morality of slavery.

1840–61 Harriet Tubman, working through the Underground Railroad, rescued more than 300 slaves from the South. She later became a spy and a nurse for the Union Army.

1850 Enactment of the Fugitive Slave Law caused many African Americans and others to flee to Canada to join the abolitionist movement against slavery in the United States.

1857 In the Dred Scott Decision, the U.S. Supreme Court held that slaves, and also free blacks, were not citizens of the United States and therefore had no rights protected by the Constitution.

This tinted photo of black Union soldiers (Company E, 4th U.S. Infantry) was taken at Fort Lincoln, District of Columbia, in 1865.

papers, such as the *North Star*, published by Frederick Douglass. The free-black communities of the North supported these publications to the limit of their resources and were the main sponsors of *The Liberator*, edited by the militant white abolitionist William Lloyd Garrison. Blacks also were instrumental in the efforts of the Underground Railroad, a secret society of people who helped thousands of slaves escape from bondage in the South.

As the abolitionist movement rapidly gained followers in the 1840's and 1850's, bitter arguments over states' rights and the existence of slavery pushed the nation ever closer to war. When the Civil War began in 1861, abolitionists prayed for a Northern victory of pro-Union forces that would bring emancipation, or freedom, to the slaves.

The Civil War and Emancipation

During the course of the Civil War (1861–65), nearly 200,000 African Americans, both slave and free, volunteered to fight for the Union against the slaveholding Confederate states in the South. Black servicemen took part in nearly every major military engagement, although until 1864 they were paid less than white soldiers. They also built fortifications, handled provisions, and served as lookouts. Some also served as spies.

The promise of emancipation was fulfilled when the Union forces won the war in 1865. By the end of that year, the 13th Amendment was ratified, abolishing slavery in the United States. In 1868 the 14th Amendment extended full legal citizenship to African Americans, and in 1870 the 15th Amendment guaranteed voting rights to black men. A profound national social revolution was set in motion.

RURAL EMANCIPATION ERA (1865–1915)

Between 1865 and 1915, many Americans left their farms and moved to a town or city, where new jobs were opening up. About 90 percent of the African Americans remained within the eleven ex-Confederate Southern states where they had been raised and where their families had lived for generations.

The Evolution of Black Education

The "social reconstruction" of former slaves began with basic education, the success of which was by far the most dramatic evidence of their new legal freedom. Tens of thousands of ex-slaves, so long forbidden to learn to read and write, now displayed a passion for knowledge so powerful that, in the words of one observer, "it was as if an entire race was trying to go to school."

The nation's first real "teacher corps" consisted of several thousand Northern-born white women who went South to instruct black students, braving the taunts and threats of white

In 1863, immigrants in New York City rioted when the U.S. government tried to draft them into the Union Army. Unwilling to fight to free the slaves, they expressed their outrage by lynching blacks in the city streets.

1861–65 Of the 200,000 blacks who served in the Union forces during the Civil War, 72% were from the slave and border states and 28% were from the Northern free states. Nearly 30,000 lost their lives; 21 received the Medal of Honor.

1863 President Abraham Lincoln's Emancipation Proclamation declared the freedom of any slave residing in a state in rebellion against the Union.

▼ The announcement of a military draft prompted Irish American attacks on blacks in New York City, leaving 74 people dead.

1865 The urgent need for food and first aid and other services prompted the federal government to establish the Bureau of Freedmen, Refugees, and Abandoned Lands (later called the Freedmen's Bureau) to assist the 4 million African Americans making the transition from slavery to freedom.

Southerners who feared that blacks would be "overeducated for their places." Within a decade, these teachers were replaced in the classrooms by many of their older black pupils. The faculties of the earliest black colleges and universities remained more white than black for a much longer period, due to the shortage of college-trained blacks.

In 1890 the Morrill Land Grant Act established 17 institutions of higher learning. These tax-supported A & I (Agricultural and Industrial) and A & M (Agricultural and Mechanical) colleges reflected the doctrine of industrial education of the sort promoted by the educator Booker T. Washington at his Tuskegee Institute in Alabama. Washington's theories directly conflicted with those of another prominent black scholar of the era, W. E. B. Du Bois, who believed that blacks should study the liberal arts. This historic debate was but one example of the emerging conflict within the black community over the proper focus of black education.

The post-emancipation educational experience produced a small but highly educated group of African Americans who supported at least a dozen black-issue-oriented newspapers. In 1910, Du Bois, at his own expense, launched *Crisis*, black America's first race-relations journal, which is still published today. These publications, financed by their readers, boldly explored race relations.

Political Advances

Prior to 1868, John M. Langston had been the only black to hold elective office anywhere in the United States. He had been a city councilman in Brownhelm, Ohio, in 1856. Then between 1868 and 1898, 22 African Americans were elected to the U.S. Congress, including two to the U.S. Senate. At the state and local levels, nearly a thousand gained public office. Many had gained political experience working in the antislavery campaigns.

In 1905, W. E. B. Du Bois, a scholar and early civil rights leader, founded the Niagara Movement, a forerunner of the NAACP, to fight discrimination.

Discrimination and Violence

After the war, during the period known as Reconstruction, blacks in the South were protected by federal troops who occupied the former Confederate states. But when those troops were withdrawn in 1877, blacks found themselves at the mercy of the Ku Klux Klan and similar white-supremacist groups. Violence against blacks became so commonplace that approximately 100,000 fled from the Carolinas, Tennessee, Alabama, and Mississippi to the safer havens of Kansas, Missouri, and Illinois. By 1892, lynchings, or unlawful executions, of African Americans by terrorist groups in the South averaged one every two days.

Two U.S. Supreme Court decisions further undermined the new freedom of African Americans. In 1883, the Court declared that the 1875 Civil Rights Act, which forbade discrimination against blacks in public facilities, was unconstitutional and that local authorities could discriminate for a variety of reasons, including that of race. Most of the former

1865 The 13th Amendment to the Constitution abolished slavery in the United States. African American and white abolitionists celebrated the victory with church programs, speeches, and parades.

1865–70 Howard University, Bowie State University, Morehouse College, Talladega College, Morgan State University, and Fisk University were among the institutions of higher learning founded to educate African Americans.

1868 The 14th Amendment to the Constitution granted citizenship to "All persons born or naturalized in the United States," overturning the Dred Scott Decision (see 1857).

1870 The 15th Amendment to the Constitution affirmed that no citizen may be denied the right to vote due to their race or color.

1875 The U.S. Congress passed the Civil Rights Act of 1875, prohibiting discrimination of blacks in public facilities.

Beginning in the late 1800's, many poor black Southern sharecroppers (*left*) moved to the cities, hoping to find economic prosperity. The oppressive conditions they found in urban centers, however, prompted early civil rights marches, such as one in Harlem in 1912 (*below*).

Confederate states quickly passed "Jim Crow" laws (named for a minstrel show character) that segregated (separated) the races in all public facilities, including schools. The trend climaxed in 1896 with the infamous Supreme Court case *Plessy* v. *Ferguson*, which declared that segregation was constitutional as long as white and black facilities were equal. Seven Southern state legislatures used additional tactics to keep blacks from voting. They began charging blacks money to vote (a poll tax), which few could afford to pay. They also instituted "grandfather clause" voting rules, meaning that voters had to demonstrate their understanding of the federal and state constitutions unless they could prove that one of their grandfathers had voted before January 1, 1867. Since African Americans were not declared citizens until July 23, 1868, few could claim kinship to such an unusual relative. These discouragement tactics successfully eliminated most blacks from the voting process.

Migration to the Cities

After the Civil War, many blacks supported themselves by working as sharecroppers, cultivating sections of other people's land in exchange for a share of the crop as payment. But after a series of economic depressions, in 1872, 1884, and 1893, many found it difficult to feed their families. After each depression cycle, thousands of blacks, as well as whites, abandoned farming and moved to the nearest industrial town or city to look for jobs in manufacturing industries. Many of the blacks who remained in the farming communities joined protest organizations, such as the Colored Farmers' Alliance, which by the 1890's had gained a membership of more than 1 million in nine states. White resistance to this union climaxed in North Carolina, the state with the highest concentration of alliance members. In 1898, after the Southern Democrats who were hostile to black issues won control of the state legislature, a riot broke out in Wilmington, North Carolina. More than 40 people were killed over a period of several days.

1883 Jan Ernest Matzeliger revolutionized the shoe industry with his invention of the shoe lasting machine, which was capable of attaching soles of shoes to their upper parts.

1896 In the ruling *Plessy* v. *Ferguson*, the U.S. Supreme Court upheld the right of a state to establish separate but equal facilities for blacks and whites, encouraging racial segregation and discrimination.

1903 W. E. B. Du Bois became a national figure with the publication of *The Souls of Black Folk*.

1905 Du Bois and other early civil rights activists launched the Niagara Movement, calling for an immediate halt to segregation and racism.

1909 The National Association for the Advancement of Colored People (NAACP) was founded by a group of whites and blacks to favorably influence public opinion and to defend the legal rights of African Americans.

Soldiers of the all-black 369th Infantry distinguished themselves at the Battle of the Argonne Forest in World War I. The entire regiment was awarded the Croix de Guerre, France's highest medal for bravery.

URBANIZATION (1915–1945)

Following the terror of the Wilmington Riot, many Southern blacks headed north to settle in Boston, Newark, Philadelphia, Pittsburgh, Cleveland, Cincinnati, Detroit, Chicago, St. Louis, and Harlem, a section of New York City. Over the next two decades, hundreds of thousands of blacks moved into these urban centers. But on arrival, most discovered overcrowded facilities, inadequate housing, and dead-end jobs. As a result, concerned individuals of both races formed the National Association for the Advancement of Colored People (NAACP) in 1909 and the National Urban League (NUL) in 1911. The NAACP was devoted to the pursuit of civic justice and the NUL to economic fairness.

World War I

When the United States entered World War I in 1917, W. E. B. Du Bois, among others, urged blacks to support the war effort "shoulder to shoulder with our white fellow citizens." Of the 2.2 million African Americans who registered for the draft following the passage of the Selective Service Act in May 1917, a total of 367,000 were actually drafted and 42,000 went overseas to fight in France. More than 600 African Americans received commissions as officers of the U.S. Army to take command of segregated black military units.

During the war, tens of thousands of black men and women found employment as coal miners and in industrial centers where war supplies, such as ammunition, ships, and motor vehicles, were manufactured. These job opportunities brought economic prosperity to many black communities for the first time. Racism, however, continued to undermine the African American community, and competition between blacks and poor whites for limited job opportunities led to a violent cycle of race riots.

Meanwhile, the Ku Klux Klan was rapidly expanding northward and its membership grew to 4 million. Northern lampposts, as well as Southern oak trees, now served as lynching gallows. In 1919 at least 70 blacks were lynched, including 10 African American war veterans wearing full uniform.

The 1920's

This wave of racial hatred divided the African American community itself. The majority of middle-class blacks believed racism could end with full integration of the races, but many working-class blacks, who felt completely removed from white society, supported a new Back-to-Africa movement led by Marcus Garvey. For nearly a million individuals, Garvey was a prophet of black pride, independence, and separatism.

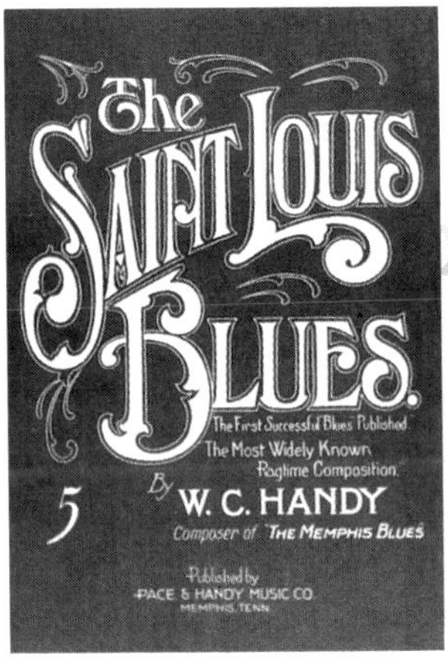

1911 The National Urban League (NUL) was founded to help African Americans find employment.

1914 W. C. Handy, known as the "father of the blues," popularized the blues style of music with the release of his classic "St. Louis Blues."

1918 Approximately 370,000 African Americans distinguished themselves in combat during World War I.

▼ Nearly 100 people lost their lives in hundreds of race riots that erupted in major U.S. cities, partly as a result of competition for jobs among returning soldiers.

About this time, the black middle class began producing a stunning collection of now-classic literary and artistic works. Because so many were created in Harlem, this period of the 1920's became known as the Harlem Renaissance. The works of Langston Hughes, Claude McKay, Countee Cullen, Jessie Fauset, and James Weldon Johnson were widely circulated. Also popular were "race movies," produced for black audiences by Oscar Micheaux.

Marcus Garvey attracted millions of followers with his Back-to-Africa movement in the 1920's.

The Depression Years

Creative expression diminished during the Great Depression of the 1930's, as jobs became increasingly scarce and racial tensions once again exploded. A riot in Harlem in 1935 was directly connected to housing shortages and to a local unemployment rate that exceeded 50 percent. Blacks also were highly frustrated because they felt generally unprotected by the law. In cases involving blacks and whites, the law courts almost always ruled in favor of the whites.

On the positive side, however, the administration of President Franklin D. Roosevelt included blacks in its economic relief efforts. In 1936 the esteemed black educator Mary McLeod Bethune, an associate of the president's wife, Eleanor Roosevelt, formed what was known as the Black Cabinet to deal with governmental problems and policies affecting African Americans. The formation of the Committee for Industrial Organization (CIO) in 1935 extended union membership to blacks who found employment in the automobile, railroad, textile, and tobacco industries and in the building trades. Before this time, they had generally been limited to service jobs, such as janitors and cooks.

World War II

America's entry into World War II in 1941 renewed an old debate concerning the role African Americans should play in defense of the nation. Black service personnel were excluded by law from the United States Marines and by custom from the Air Force. Blacks in the Navy could only aspire to be cooks and kitchen helpers. Despite these barriers, more than 1 million patriotic African Americans joined the armed forces. Pressure from the NAACP and other African American leadership groups persuaded the Marine Corps to drop its policy of discrimination and the Air Force to set up pilot training operations for blacks in Tuskegee, Alabama. By mid-1942 approximately 200 African American officers had received commissions for duty, and by 1945 nearly 500,000 African Americans were serving overseas. It did not escape their notice, however, that while they were fighting for democracy overseas, many were still living in segregation in the United States.

World War II significantly affected the lives of African Americans. Employers in the military industries were ordered by the federal

Mary McLeod Bethune

1925 The first major African American labor union, the Brotherhood of Sleeping Car Porters, was organized by A. Philip Randolph. His work paved the way for the acceptance of blacks in the labor movement of the 1930's and 1940's.

1936 Mary McLeod Bethune helped organize the National Council of Black Federal Officials, known as the Black Cabinet, during the administration of President Franklin Roosevelt.

1939 Concert singer Marian Anderson performed before 75,000 people at the Lincoln Memorial, after the Daughters of the American Revolution (DAR) refused to allow her to appear at Constitution Hall.

BREAKING THE COLOR BARRIER

By the 1940's, blacks had made inroads into mainstream popular culture. Among those who rose to the top were (*clockwise from left*) singer Sarah Vaughan, known as "the Divine One"; Richard Wright, author of the acclaimed novel *Native Son*; jazz great Count Basie and his orchestra; Jackie Robinson, the first black major league player of the 1900's; and the esteemed artist W. H. Johnson.

1940 Richard Wright published *Native Son*, describing the hostile social and economic conditions that can lead blacks into crime.

1941 President Franklin Roosevelt issued Executive Order 8802, prohibiting discrimination in government and in defense industries.

1942 The Congress of Racial Equality (CORE), led by James Farmer, was founded in Chicago to seek nonviolent, direct action to combat discrimination.

1946 The U.S. Supreme Court ruled in *Morgan* v. *Virginia* that segregation in interstate bus travel was unconstitutional.

1948 President Harry S. Truman issued Executive Order 9981, abolishing segregation in the armed forces.

1953 Ralph Ellison won a National Book Award for *Invisible Man* (1952), a story of a black man's efforts to overcome society's stereotypes and assert his individuality.

Separationism, Militancy, and Black Power

During the civil rights era, a religious group called the Nation of Islam, or Black Muslims, began to grow in strength. The group, founded by Wali D. Farad (Fard) in the 1930's, required its followers to separate themselves from whites. In the 1960's, the two most visible Black Muslim leaders were Elijah Muhammad and Malcolm X. In 1964, however, Malcolm X moved away from the separatist doctrine and founded his own movement, the Organization of Afro-American Unity (OAAU). He was assassinated at a meeting in Harlem the following year.

Also prominent during this time was a group known as the Black Panther Party for Unity and Self-Defense, organized in California by Huey P. Newton and Bobby G. Seale. The Panthers brought attention to such problems as unfair rent evictions and police brutality. Soon they were teaching black history classes and informing people of their rights. "Black Power" became a popular slogan. It was meant to encourage blacks to gain economic and political power and, more importantly, to gain self-pride and dignity. Eventually, however, the Black Panthers grew increasingly militant. They started rejecting nonviolent protest methods and urged blacks to prepare for an armed struggle against the whites. Many people began to fear them.

The civil rights movement headed North and began addressing matters of economic inequality. In response to some police encounters, rioting broke out in black neighborhoods in Harlem, Newark, and the Watts section of Los Angeles. As black ghettos went up in flames, televised newscasts showed African

Top: **The dynamic Black Muslim leader Malcolm X was in the process of re-examining his theories of black separatism when he was killed by an assassin in 1965.**

Left: **In March 1965, blacks and whites marched together from Selma to Montgomery, Alabama, to protest racial discrimination in voting procedures.**

1963 On August 20, more than 200,000 blacks and whites participated in a March on Washington, D.C., to protest the lack of federal civil rights legislation. Dr. Martin Luther King, Jr., delivered an electrifying speech, "I Have a Dream."

1964 Malcolm X left the Black Muslim organization Nation of Islam and formed the Organization of Afro-American Unity (OAAU), stressing black nationalism and social action. He was assassinated the following year.

▼ The U.S. Congress passed the Civil Rights Act of 1964, prohibiting racial discrimination in public places and in employment and education.

▼ Dr. Martin Luther King, Jr., won the Nobel Peace Prize.

1965 White resistance to a black voter registration drive led to a Freedom March, from Selma to Montgomery, Alabama, to protest discrimination at the polls.

▼ Congress passed the Voting Rights Act.

Americans chanting threatening slogans like "Burn, Baby, Burn." Then on April 4, 1968, the African American community was dealt a crushing blow when Dr. King, the principal advocate of nonviolence and social justice, was assassinated by a white man in Memphis, Tennessee. The civil rights movement had lost its most respected leader.

The Reverend Jesse Jackson founded the Rainbow Coalition in 1984 to carry on the fight for civil justice and to promote racial tolerance and understanding.

Beyond Civil Rights

During the election campaigns of 1968, it became apparent that a conservative, anti-civil rights backlash had begun to take hold of the nation. George Wallace, the defiant, pro-segregationist governor of Alabama, became a popular third-party candidate for president of the United States.

Race relations worsened in the 1970's as national support for issues concerning African Americans diminished. Racial violence returned in the 1980's and 1990's in such communities as Forsyth, Georgia; Howard Beach and Crown Heights, New York; and Los Angeles, California.

Meanwhile, black separatists also attracted new followers. By 1978, Minister Louis Farrakhan, the most influential Black Muslim leader since Malcolm X, began addressing audiences of 8,000 to 10,000 African Americans, who were seeking solutions to social problems that included poverty, drug abuse, crime, and gang violence. By 1990, Farrakhan had become a controversial figure. Many applauded his preaching the virtues of decent and law-abiding behavior. However, many others, especially within the rising and prosperous black middle class, rejected Farrakhan's notion of black superiority and racist tendencies.

A more positive force within the African American community was the Reverend Jesse Jackson. In 1984, Jackson founded the Rainbow Coalition, a political organization dedicated to social, economic, judicial, and environmental reforms to enrich the lives of African Americans and other minorities. The popular support for Jackson's candidacy for president of the United States in 1984 and 1988 brought African American issues back into the national spotlight.

While two-thirds of the African American community thrived, at least one-third was living in poverty in areas with disproportionately high rates of crime, unemployment, and welfare dependency. Routine concerns of inner-city residents were quality of housing, personal safety, and inadequacy of services.

Despite persistent problems, by the end of the 20th century, the African Americans had also achieved many goals. The community was characterized by its diversity of income levels, occupations, religious affiliations, levels of education, and lifestyles. Increasingly they were represented in the various professions and at all levels of government.

In recent years, many inner-city school systems with large enrollments of African Americans have suffered from a lack of resources and adequate funding. Efforts have been made to raise the esteem and performance levels of

The New York Times

NEW YORK, FRIDAY, APRIL 5, 1968

RTIN LUTHER KING IS SLAIN IN MEMP

WHITE IS SUSPECTED; JOHNSON URGES

Hanoi Charges U.S. Raid Far North of 20th Parallel

DISMAY IN NATION

Negroes Urge Others to Carry on Spirit

PRESIDENT'S PLEA

On TV, He Deplores 'Brutal' Murder of Negro Leader

1968 The U.S. Senate passed a civil rights bill prohibiting racial discrimination in the sale or rental of most housing.

▼ Dr. Martin Luther King, Jr., was assassinated by a white man, touching off a new wave of violence in more than one hundred cities nationwide.

1971 African American members of the House of Representatives founded the Congressional Black Caucus to focus on legislative issues affecting blacks and other under-represented groups.

1986 For the first time, the birthday of Dr. Martin Luther King, Jr., was celebrated as a national holiday (on the third Monday of every January).

1995 The Million Man March on Washington called on black men to declare responsibility for their families and communities.

A scientist studies cells in hopes of uncovering clues about the causes of aging and the factors that determine an organism's life span. Research such as this may one day help us to slow down or completely control the aging process.

we understand the immune system, we may be a lot closer to controlling the aging process.

RESEARCH ON LIFE SPANS

Another type of research on aging involves the collection of facts about ages and growth rates in animals. It is very hard to study the force of mortality in animals by keeping them for life and recording when they die, since many live half as long as we do ourselves.

What we need to find out is the force of mortality at different ages in populations of animals in captivity and in the wild. For the most part we must rely on research records, though the records are far from complete. In a few cases, however, we can tell the ages of animals by some structure on the animal's body that grows regularly. The shells, bones, or teeth of certain animals lay down a fixed number of marks or rings every year. We can tell the ages of these animals just as we can tell the age of a tree by counting its rings.

Life Spans of Organs and Cells

In addition to studying how long an entire animal or person lives, researchers are exploring the life spans of organs and cells.

Would our heart age if it were not joined to the rest of us? We know that when a healthy young heart is transplanted into an old person, it does not prevent the older person from aging. But would an older person's heart last longer in the body of a young person?

Scientists have tried to find answers to such questions by putting tissue from an old animal (a mouse, for example) in the body of a young animal. Unfortunately, the experiments have produced unclear results, so scientists have simplified their experiments and turned to studying individual cells.

When human cells are grown outside the body in a laboratory, they usually divide a limited number of times before the cell culture dies out. One reason appears to be that the tips of cell structures called chromosomes break off each time a cell divides. Eventually, these bits (called telomeres) wear down, leading to cell death. However, by injecting a substance called telomerase into cells, scientists have been able to protect the telomeres and thus create "immortal" cells that divide without limit. Telomerase also appears to enable many types of cancer cells to divide continuously, so its potential as an anti-aging medicine remains unclear.

Clearly there are still many puzzles to be solved before we have a complete picture of what controls the life span of cells, organs, or entire animals. The results of some experiments have raised more questions than they have answered.

Other experiments seem to provide valuable new information, but it cannot be safely used until we have a clearer understanding of the aging process.

▶ THE DREAM OF A LONGER LIFE

Research on aging has raised many interesting questions about how the body works and how it changes over time. But one of the most important questions is whether the ultimate goal of gerontology—to make people live longer—is really a good idea.

People have never liked to think that they would get old or that their lives would end around a fixed age. So there have always been stories about miraculously long lives and about people who regained their youth. A Greek myth tells us of Eos (Aurora), goddess of the dawn, who prayed that her husband, Tithonus, be made immortal. The prayer was granted, but unfortunately she had forgotten to ask that he stay eternally young. So he grew older and older and more and more decrepit until he prayed to be allowed to die.

Poets in the Middle Ages wrote of a Fountain of Youth in which one could bathe and become young. The fountain was a fiction. But during that time, early chemists called alchemists tried to discover the elixir of life, which would make old people young.

The alchemists failed. But many scientists, backed by governments and universities, are now carrying out serious research on aging.

Certainly if we only made people live longer, like Tithonus—instead of preventing them from aging as well—it would not be a good thing. On the other hand, there are some people of 80 who are ill or crippled because of age, while others are healthy and active. If it were possible that we could all be healthy and useful at 80—even if we lived no longer in the end—it would be a great improvement both for individuals and for society. Now we spend nearly a third of our lives learning our jobs. If we lived longer, we could do more work in a lifetime and carry out more of our plans.

However, if we lived longer lives and if birth rates remained the same, the world's increasing population would grow even faster. Such an increase would have major impacts on our society and environment.

Already, the North American population has experienced what is known as the "baby boom"—an 18-year period of rapid population growth following the end of World War II, from 1946 to 1964. During this period, many more children were born (76 million in the United States alone) than in the same period before or after.

The legendary Fountain of Youth, sought by Ponce de León, was a magic spring that would restore youth to the aged. It is one of the many myths about eternal youth.

The children of this generation, often called baby boomers, brought about much prosperity as they grew up and entered the workforce. However, as the baby boomers age and enter their retirement years, they are predicted to place a mounting burden on the rest of society, which will have to care for them in their old age.

The possibility of lengthening life raises some difficult questions. At the moment we do not know for certain whether we can ever hope to change the rate of aging. Yet everyone should think about the problems because scientists are making a serious attempt to find the means of slowing aging. It seems reasonable to think they will succeed eventually—but when and by how much nobody can yet say.

ALEX COMFORT
Author, *A Good Age*

See also OLD AGE.

AGNEW, SPIRO T. See VICE PRESIDENCY OF THE UNITED STATES.

Specialized farming of beef cattle is a huge enterprise in western regions of the United States and Canada. The structures at the rear of the feedlot are for grain storage.

such as tobacco, soybeans, or vegetables. Cash crops, as the name indicates, are raised to be sold rather than for use on the farm.

General farms usually require constant labor and often cannot use new technologies. As a result, general farms are becoming few in number. In most countries with modern agriculture systems, specialized farming is predominant.

Specialized farms concentrate on one or two products. In North America, some specialized farms are clustered by region. Wheat farms stretch across the Prairie Provinces of Canada and the High Plains of the United States, from Montana and North Dakota through Colorado, Kansas, and Oklahoma.

Sometimes two products fit well together. The dry climate most suitable for wheat lands is also suitable for the grasslands that support beef cattle. The cattle can also graze on young wheat plants. So wheat and beef production often go together.

In the U.S. Midwestern region extending from Nebraska to Ohio, which has heavier rainfall than the High Plains, corn is the favored crop. Corn is a high-yielding crop, producing as much as 200 bushels per acre (500 bushels per hectare). Another important Midwestern crop is soybeans, which sell for high prices. Soybean and corn production go together because the same farm machinery can be used for both crops and because both thrive during the long humid summer days.

Cotton and soybeans often go together on specialized farms in the humid South—in Mississippi, Arkansas, and Tennessee. Cotton and wheat go together in the dry southern plains of Oklahoma, West Texas, and New Mexico. (Cotton can grow well in dry climates if there is enough irrigation.)

The irrigated valleys of California and other Western states provide fresh fruits and vegetables—even for millions of people living across the continent on the East Coast. In the East, Florida produces vegetables and provides orange juice for the whole nation. There are also other centers for fruit and vegetable production—Michigan, for example.

While some specialized farms, such as fruit and vegetable farms, are located far away from consumers, others, such as dairy farms, tend to be located on the edges of cities. Los Angeles County in California, for example, with one of the world's largest cities, is also one of the United States' major agricultural centers. Dairies located near Los Angeles, like other specialized farms, may do just one thing —in this case they just feed and milk the cows. Many other steps are done elsewhere. For example, the dairy cows were probably born and raised on other farms, to be purchased by the dairy farm just before they were ready to be milked.

Farmers are just one of many groups involved in agriculture. Others include feed and fertilizer suppliers, truckers and shippers, food processors and packagers, distributors, and grocers. There are some kinds of specialized agriculture, in fact, that have no farmers at all. For example, in the United States today, chickens and eggs are produced largely in factories. Not long ago almost every farm had some chickens, which provided eggs and meat for the farm family. Now, however, most chickens are raised in large buildings, which may be owned by grocery store chains or by large companies. Specialized farming has greatly changed the process of food production in highly developed countries. The term **agribusiness** is now used to describe the entire industry involved in the production, distribution, and sale of agricultural products.

LAND MANAGEMENT

Plants grow in the earth's thin skin of topsoil. Because such a small portion of the earth's surface can be used to produce crops, it is very important that farmers take care of the soil so that it does not become exhausted and is not eroded away by rain and wind. All over the world, much good farmland has been lost to erosion. For example, people seeking timber and food may cut down trees and other vegetation that hold the soil, and they may plow steep hillsides that soon become eroded and barren. (For more information, see the article EROSION in Volume E.)

In the United States alone, roughly 30 percent of all cropland is considered to be at high risk of being eroded. Several billion tons of soil on U.S. cropland are lost to wind and water erosion each year. However, there are a number of soil conservation methods that farmers can practice to control erosion. These ways include changing crops from year to year (rotating crops) so that high-profit crops are followed by soil-building crops. Or, different crops can be planted side by side in narrow bands (strip cropping). Water erosion can be slowed by cultivating across, rather than up and down, the sides of hills and by digging ridges (terraces) along the sides of hills, which keep water from rushing downhill and washing away the soil.

A new practice is "minimum till," in which plant residues (remains) are not plowed under after the harvest but instead are left on the surface to protect soil from wind and rain. Minimum till is easier than other methods, so this is a popular form of soil conservation.

There are other losses of farmland, but these losses are small by comparison to erosion. For example, some farmland is being used for roads, factories, and houses. Some

A modern "chicken factory" can accommodate flocks of more than 100,000 chickens at a time. The birds remain indoors and are fed and watered by machines.

AIDS

In the mid-1970's, a new disease began to emerge—a disease that came to be called AIDS, or *a*cquired *i*mmune *d*eficiency *s*yndrome. Although not widely known at first, AIDS eventually became recognized as a major health threat. By the end of 1999, the disease had killed more than 18 million people. Over 30 million more were thought to be infected. Some parts of the world—sub-Saharan Africa, India, Thailand, the United States, and Brazil—have been more severely affected by AIDS than others. But the threat of AIDS is worldwide.

What Is AIDS? AIDS is a disease caused by a virus, the human immunodeficiency virus type 1 (HIV-1). Mainly, the virus attacks cells of the body's immune system (such as certain white blood cells) that help fight infection. When the virus attacks these cells, the immune system becomes weak, or deficient. (The name "acquired immune deficiency syndrome" describes the condition that results.) Once the immune system has been weakened by the virus, diseases of all kinds can easily take hold, including some that are rare and do not normally affect healthy people. Eventually, one of these diseases can kill the person with AIDS.

AIDS is a progressive disease. At first, a person infected with the virus shows no major signs. However, the person can spread the infection to others. Immune system cells begin waging a battle against the ever-multiplying virus. Over time, usually ten years or more, the immune system becomes weakened. Various symptoms may appear that can last a long time and may or may not be serious. Finally, the disease progresses to true AIDS. This end stage is characterized by certain life-threatening infections, such as pneumonia, and often by nervous disorders, cancers, and severe weight loss.

How AIDS Spreads. HIV is present in body fluids, and it can be spread only through an exchange of certain of those fluids. This means that it is difficult for most people to get AIDS. In fact, researchers think that HIV is spread mainly in the following ways: The virus can be transmitted from an infected person to another person during sexual intercourse. A woman who is infected with HIV can pass it to her unborn child through her blood or to her baby through breast milk. It can be transmitted by exposure to infected blood or blood products—as when drug abusers share hypodermic needles. Before 1985, when American blood banks began to screen for the virus, a number of people became infected when they received transfusions of infected blood.

The virus is rarely, if ever, transmitted by means other than those described above. As scientists have learned more about AIDS, they have been able to lay many unreasonable fears to rest. There is no need to avoid someone who has AIDS—you do not catch the disease by touching or being in a room with that person. The virus is not spread by sneezing or through food, drinking glasses, toilet seats, or swimming pools. And there is no evidence that it can be spread by insects such as mosquitoes.

You will not catch AIDS by donating blood because the needles used in this procedure are new. And screening tests for infected blood have dramatically reduced the chances of contracting the virus through a transfusion. The risk of becoming infected in a health-care setting is extremely small.

Searching for a Cure. Great progress has been made in understanding AIDS. Scientists have developed blood tests to find out if people have been infected with HIV. These tests look for HIV antibodies, substances that the body produces in an effort to fight the virus. But researchers have not yet discovered a cure for AIDS. Some drugs can slow the progress of the disease, and scientists are testing experimental vaccines that they hope will protect people from AIDS.

In 1999 researchers announced that the original source of the virus was a type of chimpanzee native to west Africa. The virus was introduced into the human population when people who hunt the animals were exposed to infected blood. Scientists hoped to learn more about preventing AIDS by determining how infected chimpanzees resist disease.

For now, however, the best defense against AIDS lies in teaching people to avoid those behaviors that spread the disease.

Reviewed by MERVYN F. SILVERMAN, M.D.
President
American Foundation for AIDS Research

See also IMMUNE SYSTEM.

AIR. See AERODYNAMICS; ATMOSPHERE.

AIR CONDITIONING

Until the mid-1900's, summers were very uncomfortable for people living in the tropics and midlatitudes in much of the world. For example, the weather in Washington, D.C., was so hot and humid during the summer months that sessions of Congress were adjourned. Today air conditioning has made it possible to be comfortable even on the hottest, stickiest days of the year. You will almost certainly find air conditioning in the movie theaters you attend, in most of the stores and office buildings where your family shops and works, in the restaurants where you eat, perhaps even in your family's home and car.

Everyone knows that air conditioning makes you feel cool. But an air conditioning system is often used for more than just cooling. It keeps the temperature and humidity, or moisture content, of the air in an enclosed space at just the right level for the comfort of the people inside. It also circulates the air with fans and removes dust from the air with filters.

Many industries depend on air conditioning to keep the air in their plants clean, cool, and at the right moisture level. For example, textile fibers such as wool and cotton will stretch or shrink as the moisture content of the air changes. This causes variations in the quality of the cloth. Electronic products, such as computer chips, may require not only controlled temperature and humidity, but also special filters to remove dust from the air. And, because people work better when they are comfortable, air conditioning helps increase worker productivity.

HISTORY OF AIR CONDITIONING

The earliest methods devised to cool buildings were based on evaporation of water. The ancient Egyptians and other desert dwellers hung woven mats soaked with water across the entrances to their houses. As the hot, dry air blew through the mats, the water evaporated, cooling the air. Modern devices based on the **evaporative cooling** method are still used in much of the American Southwest.

In more humid climates, another approach was needed. Evaporative cooling devices do not remove humidity from the air, and they do not work as well in humid conditions. For the best comfort, both temperature and relative humidity in a building must be lowered.

The first system of **mechanical air conditioning**, which keeps the humidity low and

How an Air Conditioner Works

This diagram shows how heat and humidity are removed from indoor air by an air conditioner, which then cools the air and blows it back indoors. A simple room air conditioner is shown, but all mechanical air conditioners work the same way.

1. Indoor air is cooled as it passes over an evaporator, a set of coils containing liquid refrigerant. The moisture in the air forms droplets on the coils and trickles outside through a drain hole.

2. Heat from the air causes some of the refrigerant to evaporate, and it passes into the compressor as a vapor.

3. The compressor increases the pressure of the refrigerant vapor, making it hotter. It loses that heat to the outside air, becoming a warm high-pressure liquid in the condenser.

4. The warm liquid refrigerant sprays through the expansion valve back into the evaporator. As it expands, the refrigerant turns into a mixture of cold vapor and cold liquid, and the cycle is ready to begin again.

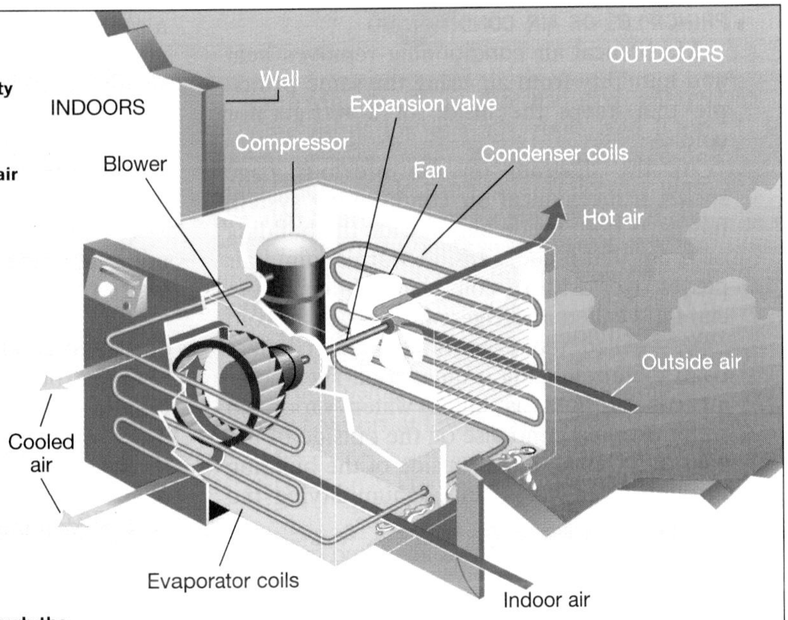

Jet Engines

Jet engines have fewer moving parts than reciprocating engines, but they burn a great deal more fuel. A jet engine burns its fuel in an enclosed space called a combustion chamber. The burning of fuel produces hot gases that rush out of the rear opening of the engine at high speed. This powerful jet exhaust pushes the engine (and the plane to which it is attached) forward.

Before leaving the engine, the gases race past a fanlike device called a **turbine,** making it turn. The turbine is mounted on a drive shaft. As the drive shaft turns, it turns another set of fans, called the **compressor,** at the front end of the engine. The spinning compressor packs enormous amounts of air into the combustion chamber, providing the oxygen needed for continuous burning of the fuel. This basic type of jet engine is called the **turbojet.** It powers some of the fastest high-altitude aircraft, such as military fighters and bombers.

The **turboprop** engine is very similar to the turbojet, but it uses the power of the jet exhaust to turn a propeller. Turboprops are used on planes that must use fuel more efficiently, but planes using them do not fly as fast.

Turbofans are jet engines with a second turbine that drives a fan near the front of the engine. This fan, which acts something like a propeller, forces air out through special openings at very high speed. The air passes around the outside of the engine and provides extra thrust without burning extra fuel. The rest of the air enters the engine. Turbofan engines are widely used in modern airliners because they burn less fuel and are usually quieter than turbojet engines used in earlier airliners.

More about how jet engines work can be found in the article JET PROPULSION in Volume J–K.

Rocket Engines

Rocket engines are used very rarely in aircraft today. Rockets require much more fuel than jet engines, so they would require much larger fuel tanks. Also, refueling a rocket is more complicated than putting jet fuel or aviation gas on an airplane. Unlike jet engines, rockets are closed at the forward end. As a solid or liquid fuel burns in the combustion chamber, hot gases rush rearward through a nozzle. Because every physical action results in an opposite reaction, the engine, and the aircraft attached to it, is pushed forward. Rocket engines have been used primarily on experimental types of aircraft such as the Bell X-1, which, in 1947, was the first plane to break the sound barrier. (Rocket engines are described in the article ROCKETS in Volume R.)

New Designs

Today, a great deal of research and development is being devoted to engines and propulsion. Because reciprocating engines are less expensive to operate than jet engines, and because jet engines often make a great deal of noise, many researchers are experimenting with high-performance propeller-driven engines. In the late 1980's, the National Aeronautics and Space Administration (NASA) and several private companies were experimenting

Most jet-powered passenger airplanes have turbofan engines similar to this one with its cowling removed for repairs (*left*). A new turboprop design (*right*) has two propellers, which move in opposite directions. It produces as much power as a turbofan at lower cost.

The *Solar Challenger* flew across the English Channel in 1981, powered only by sunlight. The black areas on the top of its wings are solar cells, which convert sunlight to electricity.

with curved propeller blades, which will be used on airliners of the future. The Beech Starship, which was developed by a private company, uses a rear-mounted **pusher prop,** which is almost as fast as a jet engine and more efficient than a propeller that pulls an airplane through the air.

There have been new developments in power for very light aircraft. Dr. Paul MacCready, an American inventor, built the *Gossamer Condor* in 1977 and the *Gossamer Albatross* in 1979. These were human-powered airplanes in which the pilot pedaled a bicycle-like mechanism that turns the propeller. A later MacCready design known as the *Solar Challenger* flew across the English Channel in 1981 entirely under solar power.

INSTRUMENTS

Aviation pioneers flew using very simple methods, such as looking for landmarks and other visual references. They also sensed the forces on the airplane through their bodies, so they said they "flew by the seat of their pants." But instruments have become more and more important in aviation. Generally, the larger the airplane, the greater the number of instruments. Even a relatively simple training airplane like a Cessna 152 contains enough instruments to confuse the nonflyer. But a highly complex airplane such as the Concorde, a supersonic airliner, contains many more instruments. As a result, the crew of the Concorde and some other large airliners includes a special crew member, the flight engineer, whose job is to monitor these instruments and make the necessary adjustments to the engines and other systems. The pilot and co-pilot fly the airplane and also give their attention to flight instruments and navigation instruments.

Engine Instruments

Each airplane, no matter how large or how small, has a number of instruments for each engine. A **tachometer** tells how many revolutions per minute the engine makes. The temperature and the pressure of the air entering the engine, the fuel pressure, the oil pressure, and the engine temperature are usually measured as well. Jet planes use gauges that measure the temperature of the exhaust gases as they exit the tail pipe. Although all aircraft also have fuel gauges, most pilots measure the amount of fuel at the beginning of the flight and mathematically compute their fuel consumption throughout the trip. They use the fuel gauge only as a backup to their own computations.

Flight Instruments

If a pilot is flying low and slow, he or she does not need many flight instruments. However, all pilots need to know four basic types of information. They must know the **heading** (the direction in which the airplane is flying), its altitude, its airspeed, and its **attitude** (pitch and bank in relation to the horizon).

This engraving of a plantation in Clarke County in the 1800's shows slaves called field hands engaged in the backbreaking task of picking cotton by hand.

tacked Fort Mims, about 50 miles (80 kilometers) north of Mobile, killing approximately 250 settlers. The Tennessee militia, led by General Andrew Jackson, marched from one Indian village to another, burning and killing. The final conflict came on March 27, 1814, when Jackson defeated the Creek at the Battle of Horseshoe Bend. The Indians signed a treaty that gave most of their territory to the U.S. government. Almost immediately, thousands more settlers poured into Alabama.

Statehood and the Trail of Tears

Settlers organized the Alabama Territory in 1817. Two years later it became a state. Between 1819 and 1846, the state capital was moved three times due to transportation difficulties and Alabama's changing centers of population. State government finally settled in Montgomery in 1846.

In the early years of statehood, settlers pushed for the removal of all Indians from Alabama. In 1830, Andrew Jackson, who was by then the president of the United States, signed the Removal Act, using his power to force the migration of most of Alabama's Indians to Oklahoma. The route the Indians took, on which many thousands died throughout the 1830's, became known as the Trail of Tears.

Cotton, Slavery, and the Civil War

Between 1820 and 1860, due to a booming cotton market, Alabama became one of the wealthiest states in the Union. However, the state's large cotton plantations would not have been as profitable without the use of slave labor. Alabamians, therefore, fiercely resisted a growing movement in the North to abolish slavery, and they objected to the federal government interfering in the affairs of the South-

INDEX TO ALABAMA MAP

Abbeville •	(Henry)	D4
Alabaster	(Shelby)	C2
Albertville	(Marshall)	C1
Alexander City	(Tallapoosa)	D3
Andalusia •	(Covington)	C4
Anniston •	(Calhoun)	D2
Arab	(Marshall)	C1
Ashland •	(Clay)	D2
Ashville •	(St. Clair)	C2
Athens •	(Limestone)	C1
Atmore	(Escambia)	B4
Attalla	(Etowah)	C1
Auburn	(Lee)	D3
Bay Minette •	(Baldwin)	B5
Bessemer	(Jefferson)	C2
Birmingham •	(Jefferson)	C2
Boaz	(Marshall)	C1
Brewton •	(Escambia)	B4
Butler •	(Choctaw)	A3
Camden •	(Wilcox)	B4
Carrollton •	(Pickens)	A2
Centre •	(Cherokee)	D1
Centrerville •	(Bibb)	B3
Chatom •	(Washington)	A4
Chickasaw	(Mobile)	A5
Clanton •	(Chilton)	C3
Clayton •	(Barbour)	D4
Columbiana •	(Shelby)	C2
Conecuh Nat'l Forest		C4
Cullman •	(Cullman)	C1
Dadeville •	(Tallapoosa)	D3
Daleville	(Dale)	D4
Daphne	(Baldwin)	B5
Decatur •	(Morgan)	C1
Demopolis	(Marengo)	B3
Dothan •	(Houston)	D4
Double Springs •	(Winston)	B1
Elba •	(Coffee)	C4
Enterprise	(Coffee)	D4
Eufaula	(Barbour)	D4
Eutaw •	(Greene)	B3
Evergreen •	(Conecuh)	C4
Fairfield	(Jefferson)	C4
Fairhope	(Baldwin)	B5
Fayette •	(Fayette)	B2
Florence •	(Lauderdale)	B1
Fort Payne •	(De Kalb)	D1
Fultondale	(Jefferson)	C2
Gadsden •	(Etowah)	C1
Gardendale	(Jefferson)	C2
Geneva •	(Geneva)	D4
Greensboro •	(Hale)	B3
Greenville •	(Butler)	C4
Grove Hill •	(Clarke)	B4
Guntersville •	(Marshall)	C1
Hamilton •	(Marion)	B1
Hartselle	(Morgan)	C1
Hayneville •	(Lowndes)	C3
Heflin •	(Cleburne)	D2
Homewood	(Jefferson)	C2
Hoover	(Jefferson)	C2
Hueytown	(Jefferson)	C2
Huntsville •	(Madison)	C1
Irondale	(Jefferson)	C2
Jackson	(Clarke)	B4
Jacksonville	(Calhoun)	D2
Jasper •	(Walker)	B2
Lafayette •	(Chambers)	D3
Lanett	(Chambers)	D3
Leeds	(Jefferson)	C2
Linden •	(Marengo)	B3
Livingston •	(Sumter)	A3
Luverne •	(Crenshaw)	C4
Madison	(Madison)	C1
Marion •	(Perry)	B3
Midfield	(Jefferson)	C2
Millbrook	(Elmore)	C3
Mobile •	(Mobile)	A5
Monroeville •	(Monroe)	B4
Montgomery★	(Montgomery)	C3
Moulton •	(Lawrence)	B1
Mountain Brook	(Jefferson)	C2
Muscle Shoals	(Colbert)	B1
Northport	(Tuscaloosa)	B2
Oneonta •	(Blount)	C2
Opelika •	(Lee)	D3
Oxford	(Calhoun)	D2
Ozark •	(Dale)	D4
Pelham	(Shelby)	C2
Pell City •	(St. Clair)	C2
Phenix City •	(Russell)	D3
Piedmont	(Calhoun)	D2
Pleasant Grove	(Jefferson)	C2
Prattville •	(Autauga)	C3
Prichard	(Mobile)	A5
Rainbow City	(Etowah)	C2
Roanoke	(Randolph)	D2
Rockford •	(Coosa)	C3
Russellville •	(Franklin)	B1
Saraland	(Mobile)	A5
Satsuma	(Mobile)	A5
Scottsboro •	(Jackson)	C1
Selma •	(Dallas)	B3
Sheffield	(Colbert)	B1
Southside	(Etowah)	C2
Sylacauga	(Talladega)	C2
Talladega •	(Talladega)	C2
Talladega Nat'l Forest		B3,D2
Tallassee	(Elmore)	D3
Tarrant	(Jefferson)	C2
Troy •	(Pike)	D4
Trussville	(Jefferson)	C2
Tuscaloosa •	(Tusculoosa)	B2
Tuscumbia •	(Colbert)	B1
Tuskegee •	(Macon)	D3
Tuskegee Nat'l Forest		D3
Union Springs •	(Bullock)	D3
Valley	(Lee)	D3
Vernon •	(Lamar)	A2
Vestavia Hills	(Jefferson)	C2
Wedowee •	(Randolf)	D2
Wetumpka •	(Elmore)	C3
Wheeler Nat'l Wildlife Refuge		C1
Wm. B. Bankhead Nat'l Forest		B1

• County Seat

Counties in parentheses

★ State Capital

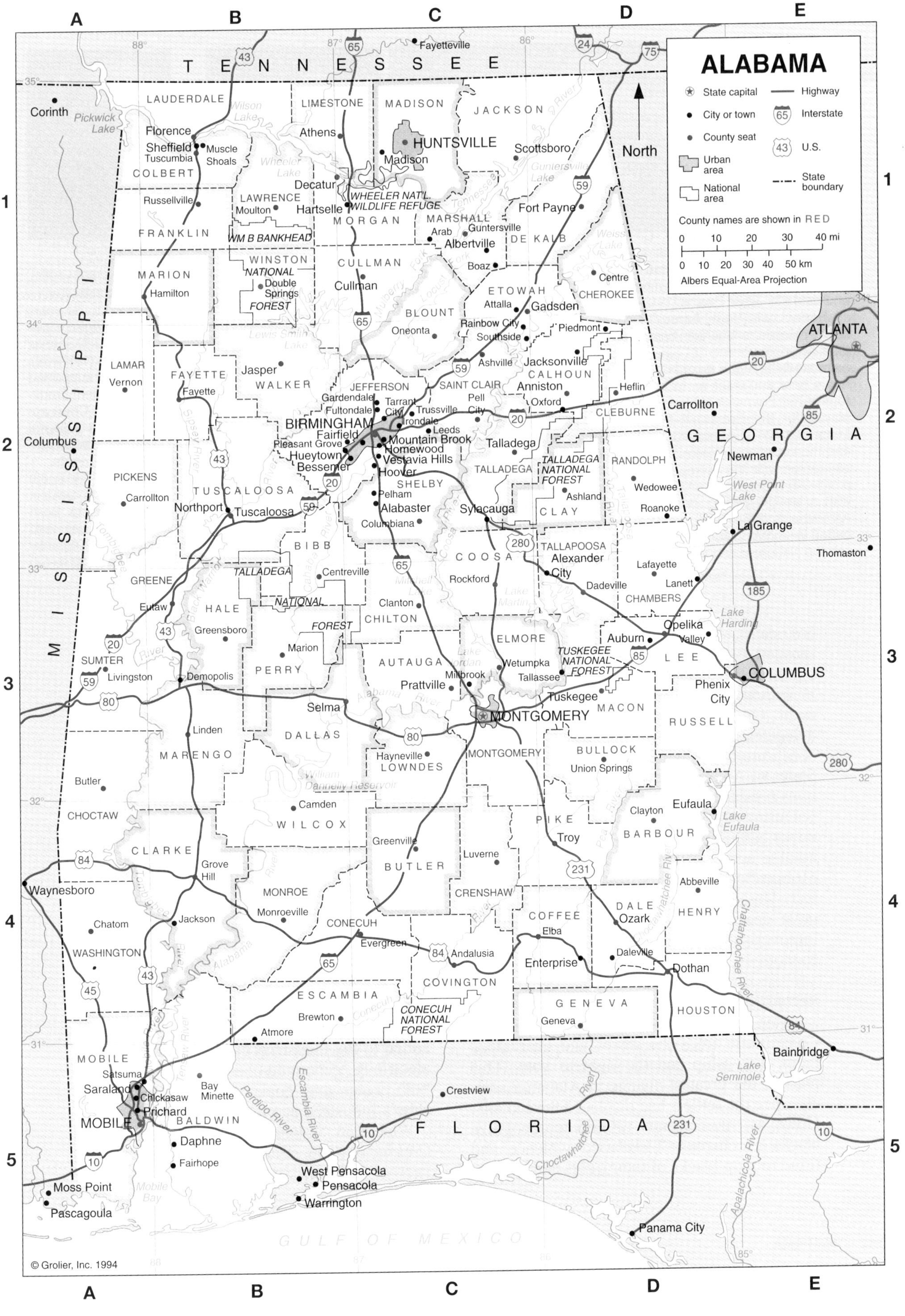
ALABAMA
State capital
City or town
County seat
Urban area
National area
Highway
Interstate
U.S.
State boundary
County names are shown in RED
0 10 20 30 40 mi
0 10 20 30 40 50 km
Albers Equal-Area Projection
North
A
B
C
D
E
1
2
3
4
5
TENNESSEE
GEORGIA
FLORIDA
MISSISSIPPI
GULF OF MEXICO
Fayetteville
Corinth
Pickwick Lake
LAUDERDALE
Wilson Lake
LIMESTONE
MADISON
JACKSON
Florence
Sheffield
Muscle Shoals
Tuscumbia
Athens
HUNTSVILLE
Madison
Scottsboro
Wheeler Lake
COLBERT
Decatur
Guntersville Lake
WHEELER NAT'L. WILDLIFE REFUGE
Russellville
LAWRENCE
Moulton
Hartselle
MORGAN
MARSHALL
Arab
Guntersville
Fort Payne
DE KALB
Albertville
FRANKLIN
WM B BANKHEAD
WINSTON
NATIONAL
Double Springs
FOREST
CULLMAN
Cullman
Boaz
Weiss Lake
Centre
CHEROKEE
MARION
Hamilton
ETOWAH
Attalla
Gadsden
BLOUNT
Oneonta
Rainbow City
Southside
Piedmont
Lewis Smith Lake
LAMAR
Vernon
FAYETTE
Fayette
Jasper
WALKER
Ashville
Jacksonville
CALHOUN
SAINT CLAIR
Anniston
Oxford
Heflin
JEFFERSON
Gardendale
Fultondale
Tarrant City
Trussville
Pell City
Irondale
CLEBURNE
Carrollton
BIRMINGHAM
Fairfield
Leeds
Pleasant Grove
Mountain Brook
Homewood
Vestavia Hills
Hueytown
Bessemer
Hoover
Talladega
TALLADEGA
TALLADEGA NATIONAL FOREST
RANDOLPH
Columbus
Newman
PICKENS
Carrollton
SHELBY
Pelham
Alabaster
Ashland
Wedowee
West Point Lake
TUSCALOOSA
Northport
Tuscaloosa
Sylacauga
CLAY
Roanoke
Columbiana
La Grange
BIBB
COOSA
TALLAPOOSA
Alexander City
Thomaston
ATLANTA
GREENE
TALLADEGA
Centreville
NATIONAL
FOREST
Rockford
Lake Martin
Dadeville
Lafayette
Lanett
CHAMBERS
Eutaw
HALE
Greensboro
Clanton
CHILTON
Mitchell Lake
Lake Harding
Opelika
Auburn
Valley
SUMTER
Livingston
Marion
PERRY
AUTAUGA
ELMORE
Wetumpka
TUSKEGEE NATIONAL FOREST
Tallassee
LEE
COLUMBUS
Demopolis
Millbrook
Prattville
Selma
MONTGOMERY
Tuskegee
MACON
Phenix City
RUSSELL
Linden
DALLAS
MARENGO
Hayneville
LOWNDES
MONTGOMERY
BULLOCK
Union Springs
Butler
William Dannelly Reservoir
Camden
CHOCTAW
WILCOX
PIKE
Clayton
Eufaula
Lake Eufaula
BARBOUR
Troy
Greenville
Luverne
CLARKE
Grove Hill
BUTLER
Waynesboro
MONROE
CRENSHAW
Abbeville
Monroeville
DALE
Ozark
HENRY
Chatom
Jackson
CONECUH
COFFEE
Elba
WASHINGTON
Evergreen
Andalusia
Enterprise
Daleville
Dothan
COVINGTON
ESCAMBIA
Brewton
CONECUH NATIONAL FOREST
GENEVA
Geneva
HOUSTON
Atmore
Bainbridge
MOBILE
Satsuma
Saraland
Bay Minette
Lake Seminole
Chickasaw
Prichard
Crestview
MOBILE
BALDWIN
Perdido River
Escambia River
Daphne
Fairhope
Moss Point
Pascagoula
Mobile Bay
West Pensacola
Pensacola
Warrington
Choctawhatchee
Apalachicola River
Chattahoochee River
Panama City
Tombigbee River
Black Warrior River
Alabama River
Sipsey River
Coosa River
Tallapoosa River
Pea River
Tennessee River
Mulberry Fork
Locust Fork
Cahaba River
Tensaw River
© Grolier, Inc. 1994

mile (10,686-kilometer) coastline is longer than that of any of the other continental states. The total shoreline, including offshore islands, bays, and inlets, is about 34,000 miles (54,720 kilometers) long.

Alaska encompasses more than 1,000 islands, mostly in the Alexander Archipelago and the Aleutian island chain. The Alexander Archipelago and the thin strip of mainland that borders British Columbia are known as the Panhandle.

Land Regions

Alaska's vast landscape contains four major land regions.

The Pacific Mountain System, in the south, contains the Coast Mountains in the southeast; the St. Elias, Wrangell, Chugach, and Kenai ranges around the Gulf of Alaska; the Aleutian Range, which sweeps southwestward through the Alaska Peninsula and the Aleutian Islands; and the Alaska Range farther inland. The Alaska Range is known for its high peaks and its many glaciers and rivers. Its crowning point is Mount McKinley. Rising 20,320 feet (6,194 meters), it is the highest peak in North America.

The Central Uplands and Lowlands, covering most of central Alaska, is made up of rolling hills, valleys, and low mountain ranges. Forests grow in its eastern and central valleys. Some areas are covered by permafrost, or permanently frozen subsoil. Others are covered with a dense growth of low vegetation.

The Rocky Mountain System reaches its northernmost extension at the Brooks Range. The highest mountains within this range are located in the northeastern part of the state and rise just above 9,000 feet (2,743 meters).

The Arctic Coastal Plain, also known as the Arctic Slope, lies entirely within the Arctic Circle. From the foot of the Brooks Range, this flat and treeless plain slopes northward to the Beaufort Sea and the Arctic Ocean. The soil is largely permafrost.

Rivers and Lakes

The Yukon is the great river of Alaska. It winds across central Alaska more than 1,200 miles (1,900 kilometers) and empties through a huge, swampy delta into Norton Sound. The largest of the Yukon's tributaries in Alaska are the Porcupine, the Koyukuk, and the Tanana rivers. Other major rivers are the Kuskokwim, Susitna, Copper, and Colville rivers.

Alaska has many natural lakes. Iliamna Lake, on the Alaska Peninsula, is the largest, covering about 1,000 square miles (2,600 square kilometers). Becharof Lake, south of Iliamna, is the second largest.

Mount McKinley is the highest mountain in all of North America. The Athabascan Indians call it *Denali*, meaning the Great One. Located in Denali National Park in the south central part of the state, it is the crowning point of the Alaska Range.

Climate

Alaska's climate varies widely from one region to another. The Panhandle and the coastal plain along the Gulf of Alaska have moderate temperatures and heavy precipitation. High mountains protect these areas from cold northerly winds, and ocean currents warm the shores. Winds off the Pacific Ocean lose their moisture as they collide with the mountains, drenching the area with rain. The average annual precipitation in this region is about 94 inches (2,388 millimeters), although some areas receive twice that amount. The average annual temperature is 41°F (5°C). The Copper River, Cook Inlet, and Bristol Bay areas have colder winters and less rainfall.

Summer and winter temperatures in the interior are more extreme. Average annual precipitation there is about 15 inches (380 millimeters). The growing season in the Tanana Valley near Fairbanks averages only about 100 days, but long hours of summer sunlight help to make up for the short season. The waters of the Arctic Ocean keep Arctic

Lichens cover the ground in the tundra regions of Alaska. This type of vegetation is an important food source for reindeer and caribou.

Places of Interest

In the vast expanse of Alaska, there are many places of scenic and historic interest, including remote arctic lands, sites of early Russian settlement, prospectors' trails, the seacoast, spectacular glaciers, and wilderness homes of Alaska's fascinating, varied, and abundant wildlife.

Denali National Park and Preserve, located midway between Anchorage and Fairbanks, contains Mount McKinley, the highest mountain in North America. Originally established in 1917 as Mount McKinley National Park, this popular park preserve contains deep lakes, glaciers, and approximately 300 peaks of the Alaska Range, as well as a wide variety of wildlife.

Gates of the Arctic National Park and Preserve lies completely north of the Arctic Circle. Located in the central Brooks Range, the area is a vast wilderness of mountains, valleys, glacial lakes, and rivers. It was designated a national park in 1980.

Glacier Bay National Park and Preserve, 100 miles (160 kilometers) west of Juneau, can be seen by boat or by air. The park contains more than forty great ice masses between two parallel mountain ranges—the St. Elias to the east and the Fairweather to the west. Whales and seals can be found in Glacier Bay.

Katmai National Park and Preserve, on the eastern shore of the Alaska Peninsula, is the site of the violent volcanic eruption in 1912 that turned green lands into the Valley of Ten Thousand Smokes. Also remarkable for its wildlife, it is the nation's largest grizzly bear sanctuary.

Totem Bight State Historical Park, near Ketchikan

Kenai Fiords National Park, south and west of Seward on the Kenai Peninsula, includes the Harding Icefield, one of the major ice caps in the United States.

Klondike Gold Rush National Historical Park, at Skagway, preserves historic buildings from the gold rush days, as well as the Chilkoot and White Pass trails, once trekked by prospectors.

Malaspina Glacier is located in the St. Elias Range on Yakutat Bay. The largest glacier in North America, it covers an area about the size of Rhode Island.

Saint Michael's Russian Orthodox Cathedral, a landmark building in Sitka, houses a beautiful collection of icons, or religious paintings.

Sitka National Historical Park, at Sitka, preserves the site where the Tlingit Indians made their last stand against the Russian settlers in 1804. The park also includes a wildlife sanctuary, beautiful spruce and hemlock trees, and a collection of Tlingit totem poles.

Totem Bight State Historical Park, north of Ketchikan, contains a unique collection of Haida and Tlingit totem poles from the 1800's.

Wrangell-St. Elias National Park and Preserve, east of Anchorage, is the largest unit of the National Park System. The Chugach, Wrangell, and St. Elias mountain ranges of the Pacific Mountain System converge here, forming North America's largest collection of peaks higher than 16,000 feet (4,877 meters).

State Parks. For information on state parks and other public lands, such as wildlife refuges, contact the Alaska Public Lands Information Center, 605 W. 4th Avenue, Anchorage, Alaska 99501.

Brown bear catching salmon, Katmai National Park and Preserve

Mendenhall Glacier, near Juneau

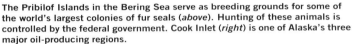

The Pribilof Islands in the Bering Sea serve as breeding grounds for some of the world's largest colonies of fur seals (*above*). Hunting of these animals is controlled by the federal government. Cook Inlet (*right*) is one of Alaska's three major oil-producing regions.

Alaska from being as bitterly cold as the interior. Precipitation in this region averages only about 7 inches (178 millimeters) a year.

Weather in the Aleutian Islands is influenced by the warm Pacific Ocean to the south and the cold Bering Sea to the north. The air is wet and foggy. Average annual temperatures are about the same as those along the Gulf of Alaska, but there is only half as much precipitation. Fierce, gusting winds called williwaws often lash the islands.

Plant and Animal Life

Forests cover about one-third of Alaska. The coastal forests—in the Panhandle and along the Gulf of Alaska —are dense, towering stands of western hemlock, Sitka spruce, and red and yellow cedar. The interior forests contain mostly white spruce, birch, aspen, poplar, and willow. Muskeg bogs, common to much of Alaska, contain spongy masses of plant life—cranberry vines, crowberries, grasses, mosses, and lichens. The dead plants decay slowly because of the low temperatures.

Alaska is home to an astounding variety of wildlife. Black-tailed deer, mountain goats, moose, black bears, and Kodiak brown bears are among the largest animals found in the southeast. Farther north, moose become more plentiful than deer, and grizzly bears and Dall sheep appear. Caribou, a type of reindeer, increase in numbers toward the north, where they travel in herds of thousands. Polar bears live in the far north. Animals that are not native to Alaska but were brought there include reindeer, elk, musk oxen, and bison.

Nearly 400 species of birds make their home in Alaska, including geese, grouse, and ptarmigan and such predatory birds as bald eagles, falcons, hawks, and owls. Wolves and foxes are found throughout most of the state. Animals that are valued for their fur include marten, mink, and beaver. Major game fish include rainbow trout and grayling. The most important commercial fish are salmon, cod, herring, halibut, crab, shrimp, clams, and scallops. Enormous numbers of marine mammals, such as walruses, whales, and seals, thrive in Alaska's bounteous waters.

Natural Resources

Traditionally, Alaska's most prized natural resources were fur, fish, and gold. Today they are petroleum and natural gas. Rich deposits have been found in Prudhoe Bay, the Kenai Peninsula, and Cook Inlet. Gold and silver are known to exist in almost every region of the state. Also, surveys have shown that Alaska holds approximately half of the nation's coal reserves.

Russians (*above*) were the first people to immigrate to Alaska, starting in the late 1700's. The Inuit (*right*) make up the largest segment of Alaska's native population. They include the Inupiat of the northern regions and three Yupik groups—Siberian, Pacific Gulf, and Central Alaskan.

PEOPLE

Although Alaska is one of the least populous states in the nation, its population has grown tremendously in recent decades. Three out of every four Alaskans live in five major urban areas. The Anchorage borough is the most densely populated, followed by the Fairbanks, Kenai Peninsula, Matanuska-Susitna, and Juneau boroughs.

Two out of every three Alaskans were born outside of the state and are descended from a variety of nationalities. Many came from other U.S. states to work in Alaska's oil fields or for the government. There are pockets of African, Hispanic, and Asian Americans in urban areas. Approximately 16 percent of the state's population is Native American. The three major groups are the Inuit, the Aleut, and various Indian communities that include the Haida, Tsimshian, and Tlingit and eleven Athabascan groups. For more information, see the articles INUIT and INDIANS, AMERICAN (North American Indians Since 1500: In the Far North and Northwest) in Volume I.

Education

The first schools in Alaska were established by the Russians after the settlement of Kodiak Island in 1784. After the United States purchased Alaska in 1867, educational work among the native peoples was carried on by missionaries. Gradually, as settlers went to Alaska during the 1880's and 1890's, the federal government established public schools. Today each borough or rural district regulates its own public-school system, according to the policies of the State Board of Education. Home schooling and correspondence-course study is common in remote areas.

The state-supported University of Alaska was founded in 1917 in Fairbanks as the Alaska Agricultural College and School of Mines. Today main campuses also are located

PEOPLE

Population: 626,932 (2000 census).

Density: 10 persons per 10 sq mi (4 per 10 km²).

Distribution: 68% urban; 32% rural.

Largest Cities (2000 census):

Anchorage 260,283	Sitka 8,835
Juneau 30,711	Ketchikan 7,922
Fairbanks 30,224	Kodiak 6,334

Persons per sq mi	Persons per km²
over 250	over 100
50-250	20-100
5-50	2-20
0-5	0-2

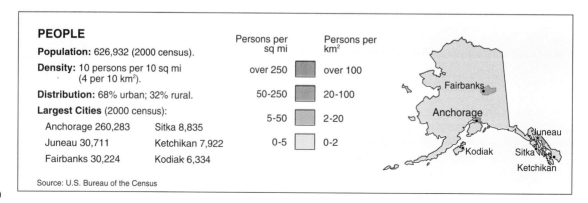

Source: U.S. Bureau of the Census

in Anchorage and Juneau, with branch campuses in several communities. The state university system offers strong programs in arctic and petroleum engineering, marine sciences, geophysics, and international business and trade. There are three private colleges in the state: Alaska Pacific University, in Anchorage; Alaska Bible College, in Glennallen; and Sheldon Jackson College, the oldest college in the state, in Sitka.

Libraries, Museums, and the Arts

Anchorage's public library system circulates more than a million books a year. Statewide, there are about ninety public libraries and branches. The Alaska State Library in Juneau houses the state's largest collection of state-related books and documents.

The Alaska State Museum in Juneau is the state's leading natural history museum. Displays cover ancient and modern native culture, pioneer and mining history, and Alaskan wildlife. The Anchorage Museum of History and Art highlights centuries of Alaskan art and history. The University of Alaska Museum in Fairbanks features Alaskan history and natural sciences. The Sheldon Jackson Museum in Sitka houses an array of native artifacts. Other museums include the Living Museum of the Arctic, in Kotzebue; and the Trail of '98 Museum, in Skagway.

ECONOMY

Petroleum is Alaska's single most important product. Royalties and taxes on oil alone provide nearly 85 percent of the state's revenues. Fish is Alaska's most valuable export.

Services

Service industries account for more than half of Alaska's annual gross state product (GSP)—the total value of goods and services produced in a year. Government is the largest segment, employing approximately 30 percent of the workforce, including national park workers. Other services, in descending order of importance, are transportation, communication, and utilities; finance, insurance, and real estate services; business, social, and personal services, which include tourism; and wholesale and retail trade.

Manufacturing

Alaska has relatively few manufacturing industries. Its most important manufactured goods are processed seafood products, such as canned salmon and smoked, salted, or frozen fish and shellfish. Wood is processed to produce round logs, lumber, wood pulp, wood chips, and paper.

Agriculture

Due to its harsh climate and rugged terrain, Alaska ranks last among the fifty states in the value of its farm production. Most of Alaska's farming is done in the Matanuska-Susitna Valley north of Anchorage and in the Tanana Valley near Fairbanks. Major farm products are milk, hay, potatoes, lettuce, greenhouse plants, and cattle.

Alaska leads the nation in the value of its seafood catch (*left*). Seaplanes (*below*) bring essential goods to people who live in Alaska's remote regions.

Alaska's fisheries, on the other hand, are extremely productive. They account for half the catch of the entire United States. Groundfish are the most valuable. These include pollack, cod, flatfish, rockfish, and sablefish. Salmon, once Alaska's leading commercial fish, now rivals shellfish for second place. Crab—tanner, king, and Dungeness—are the major shellfish catches. Alaska also supplies much of the world's halibut.

Mining and Construction

Mining contributes more to Alaska's GSP than any other single enterprise. One-fourth of all the petroleum produced in the United States comes from Alaska, making it the leading oil-producing state. More than 1.8 million barrels of crude oil are extracted from Alaska's oil fields every day. About 90 percent of all the state's oil comes from Prudhoe Bay and Kuparuk on the North Slope. They are the two largest known oil fields in North America. The state also produces about 860 million cubic feet (24.4 million cubic meters) of natural gas a day.

After petroleum, zinc is Alaska's most valuable mineral product. The Red Dog Mine near Kotzebue is the largest zinc mine in the Northern Hemisphere. Valdez Creek Placer Gold Mine is the largest gold producer in the United States, and Greens Creek Mine, near Juneau, is North America's largest silver producer.

All three phases of mining—exploration, development, and production—require construction work, including the building of housing for workers. As new mineral reserves are continually being found, construction continues to be an important support industry in the state.

The Trans-Alaska Pipeline carries oil from Prudhoe Bay on the North Slope to the port of Valdez on Prince William Sound, a distance of 800 miles (1,287 kilometers).

Transportation

Most people do not realize that Alaska is as close to major European cities as it is to major Asian cities. Air and sea traffic take the polar route across the Arctic region between Europe and Alaska every day. Anchorage and Fairbanks have international airports that provide passenger and cargo service. Modern airports also are located in Juneau, Ketchikan, Kodiak, Sitka, Wrangell, Petersburg, and Nome. Bush planes, flown by bush pilots, handle most of the travel into the rugged interior.

Alaska has one road connection to Canada and the Lower 48, the Alaska Highway. The Alaska Railroad is the principal rail line. Both extend north as far as Fairbanks. Perhaps Alaska's best-known transportation system is the Trans-Alaska Pipeline. This 800-mile (1,287-kilometer) channel transports oil from Alaska's North Slope fields to the port of Valdez for shipping. The port of Valdez is the fourth busiest port in the country. Most of its traffic is domestic, and most of its cargo is oil.

PRODUCTS AND INDUSTRIES

Manufacturing: Processed foods, wood and paper products, electrical and nonelectrical machinery, sand and gravel materials, computer equipment, handcrafted goods.

Agriculture: Seafood, milk, hay, livestock feed, potatoes.

Minerals: Petroleum, natural gas, zinc.

Services: Wholesale and retail trade; finance, insurance, and real estate; business, social, and personal services; transportation, communication, and utilities; government.

Percentage of Gross State Product* by Industry

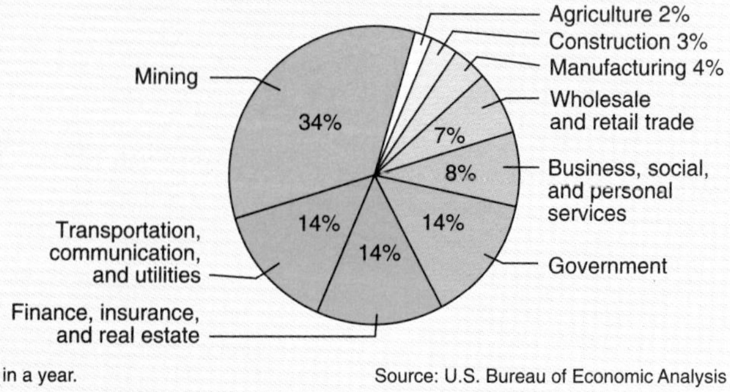

*Gross state product is the total value of goods and services produced in a year.

Source: U.S. Bureau of Economic Analysis

Communication

Among Alaska's major newspapers are the *Anchorage Daily News*, the *Anchorage Times*, and the Fairbanks *Daily News Miner*. The *Tundra Times*, Alaska's oldest statewide newspaper, reports news of interest to Alaska's Native American population. More than sixty radio stations broadcast in the state, and more than a dozen television stations have satellite transmission.

CITIES

Most of Alaska's large population centers, except for Fairbanks, are in the state's southern coastal region. Small towns and villages dot the interior and the western coast.

Juneau, located in the Panhandle, is Alaska's capital and second largest city. Founded by gold miners in 1880, it was named for Joe Juneau, one of the first prospectors to discover gold in the area.

Juneau, often called the longest city in the world, occupies a long and narrow stretch of land that slopes from the foot of Mount Juneau down to a bustling waterfront on Gastineau Channel. Douglas Island, in the channel, also is part of the city. The mountains cut the city off from the mainland, so visitors must come in by boat or airplane. Attractions include the Alaska State Museum, St. Nicholas Russian Orthodox Church, and a fascinating historic district.

Anchorage, Alaska's most populous city, is home to more than 40 percent of the state's residents. The metropolitan area, known as the Anchorage Bowl, lies between Cook Inlet to the east and the Chugach Mountains to the west. The city was founded in 1915 when the Alaska Railroad was under construction. Today it is the state's commercial and financial center. Revenues from the booming oil industry have financed the construction of the Performing Arts Center, Sullivan Sports Arena, and dozens of office towers and luxury hotels. Earthquake Park, commemorating the 1964 earthquake, offers a scenic view of the city and its surroundings.

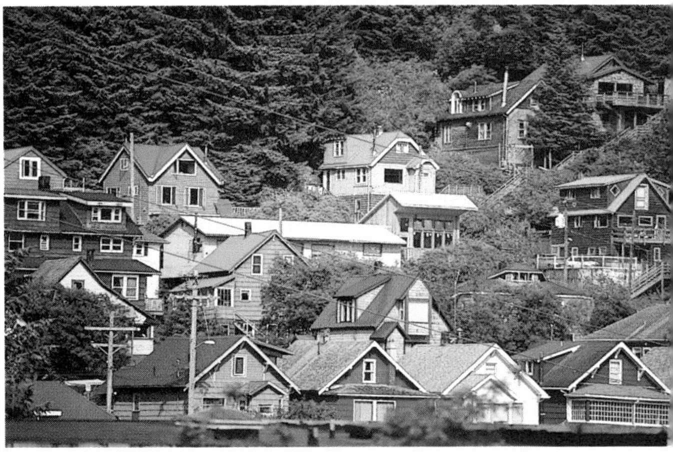

More than 40 percent of Alaska's population lives in the sprawling city of Anchorage (*top*). Juneau (*above*), the state capital, has charming hillside neighborhoods with clusters of brightly painted houses.

Fairbanks, Alaska's third largest city, is the only major population center in the interior. Fairbanks is the northern endpoint of the Alaska Railroad and the state's major highways. Thus it is a transportation hub for travel to the northern and western regions of the state. Fairbanks' international airport also provides travel to and from Asia, Europe, Arctic Alaska, and the Lower 48 states.

The city was founded in 1902 when gold was discovered there. Today it is a main trading center for the Yukon Valley. Its attractions include the main campus of the University of Alaska and a pioneer theme park called Alaskaland. It also serves as the gateway to Denali National Park and Preserve.

Four pillars of Alaskan marble and a statue of a Kodiak brown bear distinguish the entrance to the state capitol building in Juneau.

INDEX TO ALASKA MAP

Akutan C5
Alakanuk C3
Alaska Maritime Nat'l. Wildlife Refuge A5, B5, C5
Alaska Peninsula Nat'l. Wildlife Refuge D4, D5
Anchorage D4
Anderson D3
Angoon F4
Aniak C4
Aniakchak Nat'l. Monument and Preserve D4
Annette I. Indian Res. F4
Arctic Nat'l. Wildlife Refuge D2, E2
Barrow D2
Bering Land Bridge Nat'l. Preserve C3
Bethel C4
Cape Krusenstern Nat'l. Monument C2
Chevak C3
Chugach Nat'l. Forest D4, E4
Cordova E4
Craig F4
Delta Junction E3
Denali Nat'l. Park and Preserve D3
Dillingham D4
Dutch Harbor C5
Emmonak C3
Fairbanks D3
Fort Yukon E2
Galena D3
Gambell C3
Gates of the Arctic Nat'l. Park and Preserve D2
Glacier Bay Nat'l. Park and Preserve E4, F4
Haines F4
Homer D4
Hoonah F4
Hooper Bay C3
Houston D3
Izembek Nat'l. Wildlife Refuge C5
Juneau ★ F4
Kake F4
Kanuti Nat'l. Wildlife Refuge D2, D3
Katmai Nat'l Park and Preserve D4
Kenai D4
Kenai Nat'l. Wildlife Refuge D4
Kenai Fjords Nat'l. Park D4
Ketchikan F4
King Salmon D4
Klawock F4
Kobuk Valley Nat'l Park C2, D2
Kodiak D4
Kodiak Nat'l. Wildlife Refuge D4
Kotzebue C2
Kwethluk C4
Lake Clark Nat'l. Park and Preserve D4
McGrath D3
Metlakatla F4
Misty Fiords Nat'l Monument F4
Mountain Village C3
Ninilchik D4
Noatak Valley Nat'l. Park C2, D2
Nome C3
Noorvik C2
North Pole D3
Palmer D3
Petersburg F4
Point Hope C2
Quinhagak C4
St. Paul B4
Salamatof D4
Sand Point C5
Savoonga C3
Selawik C2
Selawik Nat'l. Wildlife Refuge D3
Seward D4
Sitka F4
Skagway F4
Soldotna D4
Thorne Bay F4
Togiak C4
Togiak Nat'l. Wildlife Refuge C4
Tok E3
Tongass Nat'l. Forest F4
Unalakleet C3
Unalaska C5
Valdez E4
Wasilla D3
White Mountains Nat'l Recreation Area D3
Willow D3
Wrangell F4
Wrangell-St. Elias Nat'l. Park and Preserve E3, E4
Yakutat E4
Yukon-Charley Rivers Nat'l. Preserve E3
Yukon Delta Nat'l. Wildlife Refuge C4
Yukon Flats Nat'l. Wildlife Refuge D2

★ State capital

▶ GOVERNMENT

Alaska remained a territory for 75 years before it became a state. This was the longest territorial period in the nation's history. Anxious for statehood, Alaskans adopted a constitution in 1956, three years before they joined the Union.

Like the United States government, Alaska's state government consists of three branches: executive, legislative, and judicial. The governor is the state's chief executive. Other executive branch officers include the lieutenant governor and the attorney general.

The state's legislative branch consists of a senate and a house of representatives. The legislature convenes in January of odd-numbered years. The normal 120-day lawmaking session can be extended ten days upon a two-thirds vote of the legislators.

The Alaska Supreme Court heads the judicial branch of government. There are also courts of appeals, superior courts, district courts, and local magistrates.

While most other states are divided into counties, Alaska is divided into 13 boroughs organized around population centers. Those

GOVERNMENT

State Government
Governor: 4-year term
State senators: 20; 4-year terms
State representatives: 40; 2-year terms
Number of organized boroughs: 13

Federal Government
U.S. Senators: 2
U.S. Representatives: 1
Number of electoral votes: 3

For the name of the current governor, see STATE GOVERNMENTS in Volume S. For the names of current U.S. senators and representatives, see UNITED STATES, CONGRESS OF THE in Volume U-V.

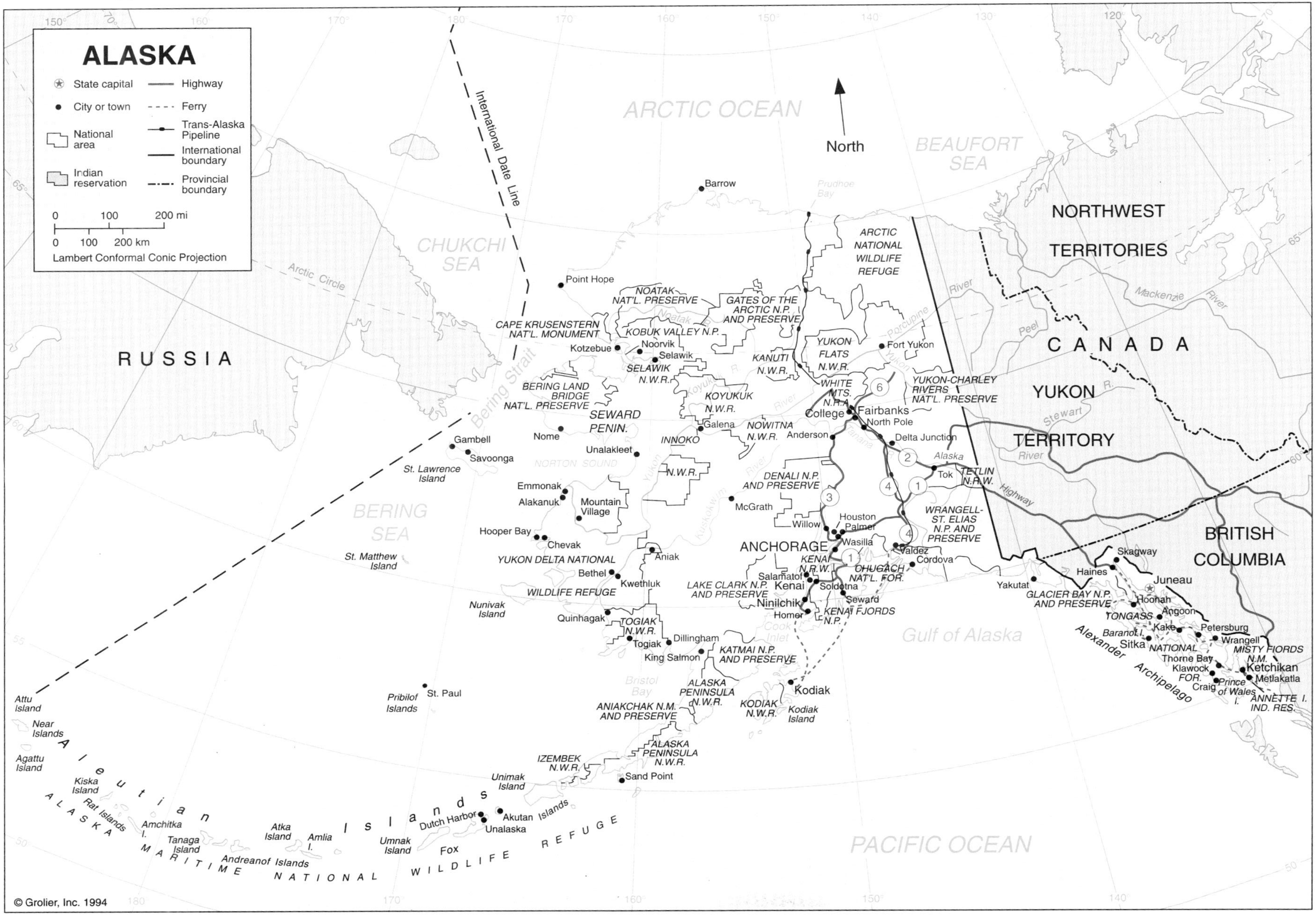
ALASKA
State capital
City or town
National area
Indian reservation
Highway
Ferry
Trans-Alaska Pipeline
International boundary
Provincial boundary
0 100 200 mi
0 100 200 km
Lambert Conformal Conic Projection
ARCTIC OCEAN
North
BEAUFORT SEA
CHUKCHI SEA
BERING SEA
Gulf of Alaska
PACIFIC OCEAN
International Date Line
Arctic Circle
Bering Strait
NORTON SOUND
RUSSIA
CANADA
NORTHWEST TERRITORIES
YUKON TERRITORY
BRITISH COLUMBIA
Barrow
Prudhoe Bay
Point Hope
Kotzebue
Noorvik
Selawik
Nome
Gambell
Savoonga
St. Lawrence Island
Unalakleet
Galena
Fort Yukon
Fairbanks
College
North Pole
Delta Junction
Anderson
Tok
McGrath
Emmonak
Alakanuk
Mountain Village
Hooper Bay
Chevak
Aniak
Bethel
Kwethluk
Quinhagak
Togiak
Dillingham
King Salmon
Houston
Palmer
Willow
Wasilla
ANCHORAGE
Valdez
Cordova
Salamatof
Kenai
Soldotna
Seward
Ninilchik
Homer
Kodiak
Kodiak Island
Yakutat
Haines
Skagway
Juneau
Hoonah
Angoon
Kake
Petersburg
Wrangell
Sitka
Baranof I.
Thorne Bay
Klawock
Craig
Prince of Wales I.
Ketchikan
Metlakatla
ANNETTE I. IND. RES.
Alexander Archipelago
St. Matthew Island
Nunivak Island
Pribilof Islands
St. Paul
Sand Point
Unimak Island
Akutan
Dutch Harbor
Unalaska
Fox Islands
Umnak Island
Amlia I.
Atka Island
Andreanof Islands
Tanaga Island
Amchitka I.
Rat Islands
Kiska Island
Agattu Island
Near Islands
Attu Island
Aleutian Islands
ALASKA MARITIME NATIONAL WILDLIFE REFUGE
NOATAK NAT'L. PRESERVE
GATES OF THE ARCTIC N.P. AND PRESERVE
ARCTIC NATIONAL WILDLIFE REFUGE
CAPE KRUSENSTERN NAT'L. MONUMENT
KOBUK VALLEY N.P.
SELAWIK N.W.R.
BERING LAND BRIDGE NAT'L. PRESERVE
SEWARD PENIN.
KOYUKUK N.W.R.
KANUTI N.W.R.
YUKON FLATS N.W.R.
WHITE MTS. N.R.A.
YUKON-CHARLEY RIVERS NAT'L. PRESERVE
INNOKO N.W.R.
NOWITNA N.W.R.
DENALI N.P. AND PRESERVE
TETLIN N.W.R.
WRANGELL-ST. ELIAS N.P. AND PRESERVE
YUKON DELTA NATIONAL WILDLIFE REFUGE
KENAI N.W.R.
CHUGACH NAT'L. FOR.
LAKE CLARK N.P. AND PRESERVE
KENAI FJORDS N.P.
TOGIAK N.W.R.
KATMAI N.P. AND PRESERVE
ALASKA PENINSULA N.W.R.
KODIAK N.W.R.
ANIAKCHAK N.M. AND PRESERVE
IZEMBEK N.W.R.
GLACIER BAY N.P. AND PRESERVE
TONGASS NATIONAL FOR.
MISTY FIORDS N.M.
Yukon
Koyukuk R.
Noatak R.
Kuskokwim River
Tanana
Porcupine
Peel River
Mackenzie River
Stewart River
Yukon R.
Alaska Highway
Cook Inlet
Bristol Bay
© Grolier, Inc. 1994

Famous People

Aleksandr Baranov

Vitus Bering

Joseph Juneau

Aleksandr Andreevich Baranov (1746–1819) became the first manager of the Russian-American Company, established in 1799, and served as the first governor (1799–1818) of Russian America. A successful fur trader, he extended Russian settlements in Alaska and sold furs to the United States, Canada, and China. Baranov's settlement at New Archangel (now Sitka) replaced Kodiak as the fur-trading capital. Baranof Island is named for him.

Vitus Bering (1680–1741), a Danish explorer employed by the Russian Navy, was the first European to set foot in Alaska. He also discovered the strait and the sea that now bear his name. A biography of Bering is included in Volume B.

Susan Howlet Butcher (1954–), a world-class sled dog racer, was born in Boston, Massachusetts, and lives in Manley Hot Springs. In 1979 she became the first person to drive a sled dog team to the top of Mount McKinley. In the annual 1,000-mile (1,600-kilometer) Anchorage-to-Nome Iditarod Trail Sled Dog Race, she took first place in 1986, 1987, 1988, and 1990, setting new course records in 1986, 1987, and 1990.

Sheldon Jackson (1834–1909), born in Minaville, New York, was a leading Presbyterian missionary. He went to Alaska in 1884 to minister to the Inuit and became known as the Bishop of All Beyond. He helped save the Inuit from starvation by urging the U.S. government to import reindeer from Siberia for domestication. In 1885 he was appointed Alaska's first superintendent of public instruction. Jackson founded many free schools and traveled widely, collecting native artifacts on his way. He was a sponsor of Sitka Industrial School, which was later renamed Sheldon Jackson College.

Joseph Juneau (1836?–99), a French Canadian gold miner born near the city of Quebec, was prospecting with Richard Harris and three Tlingit Indians in 1880 when he discovered gold near present-day Juneau, touching off the Alaska gold rush. The town that sprang up on the site was named Juneau after him. It has been the capital of Alaska since 1900.

---

parts of the state that do not belong to a particular borough are governed by the state legislature. Only one Alaskan community is organized under federal law. This is the former Tsimshian Indian reservation of Metlakatla on Annette Island. Otherwise, Alaska's Indian affairs are conducted according to the Alaska Native Claims Settlement Act.

HISTORY

It is believed that Alaska's first settlers came to the area possibly as long as 40,000 years ago. These nomadic hunters and gatherers migrated from what is now Siberia, pursuing wild game across the Bering land bridge that once existed between Asia and North America. Three distinct groups of people developed among these early settlers: the Inuit, the Aleut, and various Athabascan and other Indian groups.

Russian Exploration and Settlement

The first Europeans arrived in 1741, when Vitus Bering, a Dane serving in the Russian Navy, landed on Alaska's southern coast. Bering's crew had found not only a new land, but also a new article of trade—the luxurious fur of the sea otter. Soon, Russian hunters and traders were rushing to colonize Alaska. The newcomers took many native Aleuts as slaves, while some settled down and married native women. In 1784, Russian traders established their first permanent settlement at Three Saints Bay on Kodiak Island. This new colony became known as Russian America.

By 1799 the Russian-American Company had been chartered, with Aleksandr Baranov as its manager. Baranov expanded trade eastward into the Alexander Archipelago and built a fort near the present-day city of Sitka on Baranof Island. The native Tlingit Indians, who could not tolerate this invasion of their centuries-old homeland, attacked the fort in 1802 and won back their ground. But Baranov returned in 1804 with fully armed Russian troops and forced the Tlingit to retreat for good. Baranov rebuilt the settlement, New Archangel, which became the capital of Russian America. Later renamed Sitka, it remained the capital of Alaska until 1900.

Near right: **When U.S. Secretary of State William H. Seward bought Alaska from Russia in 1867, many people thought the purchase was extravagant and called it Seward's Folly. This cartoon shows Seward (left) and President Andrew Johnson (right) preparing to "cool down" angry congressmen with a chunk of Alaskan ice.** ***Far right:*** **In 1897, one year after gold was discovered in the Klondike region of Canada's Yukon Territory, prospectors built the town of Skagway near Chilcoot Pass, which was then the shortest route—over the mountains—to the Yukon.**

William Louis Paul, Sr. (1885–1977), a politician and lawyer born in Port Simpson, British Columbia, was the first native ever to serve (1925–29) in the Alaska territorial legislature. He fought the Literacy Act in 1925 to protect the natives' voting rights. His advocacy of Tlingit and Haida rights in 1968 paved the way for the Alaska Native Claims Settlement Act of 1971.

William Henry Seward (1801–72), a statesman and outspoken opponent of slavery, was born in Florida, New York. Having served as a New York state senator (1831–34) , as governor of New York (1839–42), and as a U.S. senator (1849–61), he was appointed U.S. secretary of state by President Abraham Lincoln in 1861. During the Civil War (1861–65), he succeeded in preventing European nations from recognizing the Confederate States of America as a legitimate nation. In 1865, Seward was injured in the same assassination plot that killed Lincoln. After his recovery he continued in his post until 1869, under President Andrew Johnson. It was during this time that Seward, a territorial expansionist, purchased Alaska for the United States (1867).

Susan Butcher

Grigori Shelekhov (1747–95), a Russian fur trader, founded the first Russian colony in Alaska at Three Saints Bay on Kodiak Island in 1784. After his death, his business, the Shelekhov-Golikov Company, formed the basis of the Russian-American Company.

The Alaska Purchase

By the mid-1800's, Russia's interest in Alaska had declined. The colony was expensive to maintain, and the fur trade had ceased to be profitable. In 1867, U.S. Secretary of State William H. Seward arranged to purchase Alaska from Russia for $7.2 million. Many Americans believed it was a foolish idea. Newspaper articles and cartoons ridiculed Alaska, calling it Seward's Folly, Seward's Icebox, Icebergia, and Walrussia. But Seward believed Alaska was a land of great potential.

The Gold Rush

Seward's Folly soon turned to fortune. In 1880, near present-day Juneau, Tlingit guides led prospectors to rich deposits of gold. Year after year, new gold strikes brought additional waves of gold rushers. In 1896, fabulous deposits were found in the Klondike region of Canada's Yukon Territory, and tens of thousands of fortune hunters swarmed through Alaska's Panhandle to get there. After gold was discovered in Nome in 1899, a tent city sprang up overnight. Within a couple of years,

PREPARING FOR THE HEATED TERM.

King Andy and his man Billy lay in a great stock of Russian ice in order to cool down the Congressional majority.

almost 18,000 prospectors had arrived. To help keep order among the gold hunters, Alaska adopted a system of courts and laws in 1900. In 1912, Congress officially declared Alaska a U.S. territory.

The Long Road to Statehood

Alaskans first appealed to Congress for statehood in 1916, but the bill failed to pass. In 1941, when America declared war on Japan and entered World War II, Alaska's strategic importance became clear. More than 150,000 American troops and civilian workers were rushed to Alaska. In only eight months, a 1,523-mile (2,451-kilometer) road was built through Canada to Fairbanks as a military supply route. Now called the Alaska Highway, it is still the only road connecting Alaska with the Lower 48 states.

In 1942, Japan bombed the American naval base at Dutch Harbor in the Aleutian Islands and invaded the islands of Attu and Kiska. Fierce American resistance, with heavy casualties on both sides, managed to free the islands again. This was the only North American territory to be invaded during the entire course of the war.

After the war ended in 1945, the United States entered into the Cold War era with the Soviet Union, reinforcing Alaska's strategic importance. In 1958, Congress approved the Alaska Statehood Act, and on January 3, 1959, President Dwight D. Eisenhower proclaimed Alaska the 49th state.

Hardship and Prosperity

On March 27, 1964, a devastating earthquake, registering about 9.2 on the Richter scale, ravaged Anchorage and much of the Gulf coast and killed 131 people. This was the strongest earthquake ever recorded in North America. In 1967, flood waters rushed through Fairbanks, killing five people.

In 1968 the state's economy boomed when massive oil and natural gas reserves were discovered at Prudhoe Bay. Due to profits from oil, the gross state product doubled between 1973 and 1975. Construction of the Trans-Alaska Pipeline began in 1974 to transport the oil to the port of Valdez, and Alaska's population and labor force soared. After the pipeline was completed in 1977, revenues began flowing into the state treasury, allowing Alaskans to abolish the state income tax.

Alaska Native Claims Settlement Act

In 1971, President Richard Nixon signed the Alaska Native Claims Settlement Act, awarding Alaska's Native Americans approximately 44 million acres (18 million hectares) of land and more than $962 million in compensation for past infringements on their land and resources. Eventually 13 regional corporations were organized to manage the money and the economic development of the natives' lands, such as mineral exploration and development. However, some communities resisted economic interests, choosing instead to preserve their territory.

Environmental Concerns

The dark side of the oil boom was its effect on the environment. For example, deep-water blasting destroyed fishing grounds. Exploration on the North Slope endangered the populations of caribou, polar bears, whales, and other animals vital to the Inupiat Inuit's survival. And leaks in the Trans-Alaska Pipeline threatened wildlife.

In 1978, 56 million acres (23 million hectares) of Alaskan land were set aside as national parks, monuments, and wildlife refuges. While this protected Alaska's natural areas, it also closed off a vast amount of territory to mineral exploration. The state of Alaska sued to retain access to these lands, but lost. Two years later the Alaska National Interest Lands Conservation Act passed into law.

In 1989 came the worst environmental disaster in Alaska's history. The oil tanker *Exxon Valdez* ran aground in Prince William Sound, spilling millions of gallons of crude oil. Hundreds of miles of shoreline—as well as thousands of birds, fish, and other animals—were coated with thick, black oil. Federal, state, and local governments, oil companies, and environmentalists all joined forces to clean up the environment and sort out the damages. The disaster only heightened the debate between land developers and environmentalists.

In 2001, President George W. Bush reignited the environmental debate when he announced his intentions to reopen the Arctic National Wildlife Refuge to oil and gas drilling in response to the rising costs of imports.

Ann Heinrichs
Author, *Alaska*

ALBANIA

Albanians call themselves Shqiptarë, which means "sons of the eagle." It is an appropriate name because many Albanians live in the high mountains just as eagles do. A fiercely independent people, the Albanians long suffered under foreign domination. For nearly 500 years Albania was a part of the Turkish Ottoman Empire, before winning its independence in 1912. In the early 1990's, Albanians freed themselves from a Communist system of government that had long ruled the country.

THE PEOPLE

Most of the people are Albanians. Greeks are the country's largest ethnic minority. The Albanians were formerly divided into two major groups—the Gegs, in the north, and the Tosks, in the south. The Shkumbi River was the dividing line between the two. The differences in speech and customs between the two groups were largely eliminated during the period of Communist rule. The population is concentrated mainly in and around the major cities of Tiranë (also spelled Tirana), Durrës, Vlorë, Elbasan, and Shkodër. Tiranë is the capital and largest city.

Many people of Albanian ancestry live outside their homeland. Most live in what was Yugoslavia. But there are also large Albanian communities in Greece, Italy, Western Europe, and the United States.

Way of life. In spite of many centuries of foreign occupation, the traditional Albanian way of life was preserved in the high mountain region. In the more isolated areas, the clan

Albania is a small, rugged country. Many of its people, like these schoolgirls, traditionally have lived in the high mountains that make up most of the land.

Métis, and missionaries. The best-known mission was St. Albert Mission, founded by Father Lacombe in 1861. It was the province's first successful agricultural settlement.

In 1873 the Canadian Government organized the North West Mounted Police. Mounted Police posts were established in Alberta at Fort Macleod, Fort Saskatchewan, and Fort Calgary. The "Mounties" brought law and order to the region. One of their first acts was to stamp out an illegal whiskey trade.

The Canadian Pacific Railway reached Calgary in 1883. This was the turning point in the growth of settlement. The first settlers to take advantage of the rail line were ranchers who settled on the rich grazing land in the south.

Toward the end of the 1800's, Canada encouraged immigration by offering land to homesteaders. This, together with more railway construction in western Canada, attracted many settlers. They came from eastern Canada, the United States, and Britain and other European countries. The population of Alberta rose rapidly from about 73,000 in 1901 to more than 375,000 in 1911.

In 1905, Alberta became a separate province. Following World War I, the Depression and drought of the 1930's slowed economic growth. However, population doubled in the years between World War I and World War II. The discovery of oil at Leduc in 1947, followed by even larger oil discoveries elsewhere, touched off the greatest period of economic growth in Alberta's history. But by the early 1980's, economic growth had slowed, due in part to a decline in oil prices. Because of this economic recession, migration increased, leading to a decline in population. A partial recovery of oil and gas prices stimulated some economic activity, as did the 1988 Winter Olympics in Calgary and a free trade agreement with the United States that began in 1989.

D. Wayne Moodie
University of Manitoba
Reviewed by A. H. Laycock
University of Alberta

ALBRIGHT, MADELEINE. See Washington, D.C. (Famous People).
ALBUQUERQUE. See New Mexico (Cities).
ALCHEMY. See Chemistry, History of.

ALCOHOL

Alcoholic beverages have been known for many centuries, but it was not until the late Middle Ages that the substance alcohol was discovered. Someone—possibly an alchemist in southern Italy—collected a colorless, flammable liquid from heated wine. This liquid, first called *aqua ardens*, or "burning water," was named alcohol in the 1500's.

Today thousands of different alcohols are known. Some are clear, colorless fluids that evaporate readily and mix freely with water. Others are thick, oily liquids that hardly dissolve in water. Some are even solid at room temperature.

Alcohols are made up of atoms of carbon, hydrogen, and oxygen. The carbon atoms form a kind of framework around which the hydrogen and oxygen atoms are arranged. Each particular type of alcohol is typically determined by the number and arrangement of these three elements.

Most alcohols are very poisonous. Ethyl alcohol, or ethanol, is found in alcoholic beverages. It is poisonous when taken in large quantities. Methyl alcohol, also called wood alcohol, is so poisonous that a small amount may cause blindness or death. Denatured alcohol, an important industrial solvent, is ethanol to which poisonous chemicals or unpleasant-tasting substances have been added to make it unfit to drink.

Alcohols are used in enormous quantities in the manufacture of plastics, medicines, synthetic fibers, paints, and other common products. Because other substances mix easily with them, alcohols are used to extract, or remove, flavoring oils, perfumes, and drugs from plant and animal products.

In the home, ethanol is an ingredient in antiseptics, flavorings, perfumes, liquors, and many medicines. Because of its low freezing point (about −179°F, or −117°C), red-tinted ethanol is usually used in outdoor thermometers. Isopropyl alcohol, or rubbing alcohol, is commonly used in both homes and hospitals.

Reviewed by Louis I. Kuslan
Southern Connecticut State University

ALCOHOLISM

Alcoholism is a chronic illness of addiction to the sedative drug alcohol. Alcohol is one of the oldest and most widely used drugs, and many adults drink alcoholic beverages without becoming addicted. Addiction can be defined as the compulsive use of a substance, which the individual cannot control. Compulsive drinkers drink in spite of knowing that drinking is affecting their lives in a harmful way. Alcoholics sometimes stop drinking, but unless treated they almost always start drinking again.

Alcoholism is often diagnosed as either alcohol **abuse** or **dependence**. Alcohol abuse is a mild form of the illness. Alcohol dependence is a more severe form and is often, but not always, marked by tolerance to the effects of alcohol as well as by a withdrawal syndrome when the use of alcohol is stopped. About 13 percent of people in the United States will suffer from the illness of alcohol abuse or dependence during their lifetime.

Although alcoholism is known to be a hereditary illness, its causes are not clearly understood. There does not seem to be a particular type of personality likely to become an alcoholic. It has been noted that some alcoholics can at first drink large amounts of alcohol without feeling the effects of the alcohol and without having a hangover. This can make them think that they can drink alcohol without negative consequences. Also, the illness may show itself only after several years of drinking.

There has been a substantial increase in the use of alcohol among young people. More people under age 21 are killed by alcohol than by illicit drugs. Although it is illegal in all of the U.S. states for anyone under 21 to purchase or possess alcohol, the drinking of alcohol, especially **binge drinking**, has become an increasing problem among high-school and college students. Binge drinking is defined as consuming five or more drinks in a row for men and four or more in a row for women.

Effects of Alcohol. Alcoholics often show personality changes once they drink compulsively. They may become angry and argumentative, quiet, or depressed. Often a small amount of alcohol causes persons with alcoholism to feel even more anxious, sad, tense, and confused. They then seek relief by drinking more.

Many medical problems affect alcoholics. Serious damage to the liver, heart, stomach, and other organs, especially the brain, can result from the overuse of alcohol. Many alcoholics do not eat properly, and some of their ills are caused by poor nutrition as well as by the direct effects of alcohol on the body.

The problem of driving a car after consuming a defined amount of alcohol is known as drunk driving, described legally as Driving While Impaired (DWI) or Driving Under the Influence (DUI). Drunk driving has received increased attention in recent years. States have enacted tougher legislation to combat the offense. Mothers Against Drunk Driving (MADD), a nationwide organization, was founded in 1980 to help keep U.S. roads safe and to support victims of drunk driving.

Treatment for Alcoholism. Alcoholism can be treated through counseling, by attendance at mutual support groups, and, much less frequently, with medications such as antidepressant drugs.

Mutual help groups, such as Alcoholics Anonymous, give patients guidance, support, and hope. Attendance at mutual help groups also counteracts the tendency of alcoholics to want to be alone as their disease progresses to the more severe stage of dependence. Doctors, psychologists, and counselors familiar with alcoholism can help motivate the patient to enter into a plan for recovery. Private rehabilitation centers have been established to help alcoholics recover. Many large businesses have set up programs to help their employees who are alcoholics.

Several programs have been formed to help the families of alcoholics better understand the disease and its problems. Al-Anon is for the family and friends of alcoholics. Alateen, a division of Al-Anon, is for young people, primarily teenagers, who live in an alcoholic family situation. Adult Children of Alcoholics (ACA) helps adults who have problems because they grew up with an alcoholic parent. Research into methods of treatment and prevention will further help those affected by this major health problem.

PETER A. MANSKY, M. D.
Department of Psychiatry
Albany Medical College of Union University

See also DRUG ABUSE.

The ruins of Hippo Regius, near present-day Annaba, are a reminder of past civilizations that ruled in Algeria. Originally settled by the Phoenicians, it later flourished under the Romans and was a center of early Christianity.

Romans in the 5th century A.D. During the 6th century, the region fell to the Byzantine, or Eastern Roman, Empire. The Arabs began their conquest of the area during the 7th century. From 1518 to 1830, Algeria was part of the Turkish Ottoman Empire.

French Rule. In 1830 the French invaded Algeria and occupied it after many years of armed resistance by the Algerians. During World War II (1939–45), Algeria was controlled briefly by Germany, but it later became headquarters for the Free French Forces under General Charles de Gaulle.

Struggle for Independence. The Algerians' struggle for independence began in earnest in 1954, when the Algerian National Liberation Front (FLN) launched a guerrilla campaign against the French. After more than seven years of bloody civil war, an agreement was reached in 1962 between the FLN and the French government under President Charles de Gaulle, providing for Algerian independence. A brief revolt led by French military officers opposed to independence was put down, and on July 3, 1962, Algeria officially became an independent country.

Algeria Since Independence. Ahmed Ben Bella, a leader in the struggle for independence, became president in 1963. He was overthrown in 1965 in a military coup led by Colonel Houari Boumedienne. Boumedienne served as head of a military government and as president of Algeria until his death in 1978. He was succeeded by Chadli Bendjedid, who became president in 1979 and was re-elected in 1984 and 1988.

Until 1989 the FLN was the only legal political party in Algeria. Under constitutional amendments approved in 1989, other political parties were permitted to organize. In local elections held in 1990, the first open elections since independence, the Islamic Front for National Salvation (FIS)—which seeks to transform Algeria into an Islamic state—won control of 32 of the country's 48 provinces.

In the first round of legislative elections, held in December 1991, FIS candidates won by a wide margin over the FLN. But in 1992 the military suspended further elections and the military-backed High Council of State (HCS) was formed to run the country. The subsequent banning of the FIS and arrest of its leaders were met with violence. From 1992 to 2001, fighting between pro-government security forces and Muslim extremists claimed more than 100,000 lives.

Multiparty legislative elections were held under a new constitution in 1997 and 2002, but the FIS was still banned. Abdelaziz Bouteflika, whom the military supported, won the 1999 presidential election by default when his opponents withdrew. Voters then approved a peace plan that included pardons for FIS fighters who gave up their weapons, but some violence still continued.

Robert S. Chauvin
Stetson University

Reviewed by Alf Andrew Heggoy
Coauthor, *Historical Dictionary of Algeria*

ALGIERS. See Algeria (Major Cities).

ALGONKIAN INDIANS. See Indians, American.

ALI, MUHAMMAD. See Boxing (Profiles).

ALIEN AND SEDITION ACTS. See Adams, John (President); United States, History of the (Founding the Republic).

ALIENS

People who are not citizens of the country in which they live are called aliens. Aliens are required to obtain government permission in order to stay in a foreign country for any lengthy period of time. In the United States the Immigration and Naturalization Service handles alien affairs. This office admits aliens in three categories.

Temporary visitors must obtain visas from the Department of State to enter the country. Visas allow them to travel, attend school, or conduct business for a limited time.

There are several million **permanent resident aliens** living in the United States. They enjoy most of the rights and privileges of American citizens, such as the right to hold a job or to own property. They also share many of the same duties, such as paying taxes. However, they cannot vote or hold most public offices. Resident aliens over the age of 18 must carry an identification card, more commonly known as a "green card."

The third category is made up of **refugees**, who have been forced to leave their homelands because of war or persecution. Most refugees are admitted into the United States under a special procedure called parole. They may eventually achieve resident-alien status.

Any alien in the United States who does not follow U.S. government laws and regulations can be deported (required to leave the country), according to the Alien Act of 1798.

An **illegal alien** is a person who enters a country without the permission of that country's government or who stays beyond the term of his or her visa (permit). Illegal aliens can cause complex problems because they place a burden on public services, such as medical facilities, without paying the taxes that support these services. The Immigration Reform and Control Act of 1986 established penalties for people who employ illegal aliens, but it also gave legal status to any illegal alien who had been living in the United States since January 1, 1982.

ROBERT RIENOW
Author, *The Great Unwanteds: Illegal Aliens and the American Challenge*

See also CITIZENSHIP; IMMIGRATION; NATURALIZATION; PASSPORTS AND VISAS.

ALLEN, ETHAN (1738–1789)

Ethan Allen was a hero of the American Revolutionary War and a leader in the fight for Vermont's statehood. He was born in Litchfield County, Connecticut, probably on January 10, 1738. As a young man he fought in the French and Indian War (1754–63).

In 1769, Allen settled in Vermont, which was then known as the "New Hampshire grants." A heated dispute arose between the colonial governors of New York and New Hampshire because each claimed that land for his own colony. Allen felt that the original settlers from New Hampshire had the strongest claim. Unfortunately for them, Britain decided otherwise and granted the land to New York.

This action prompted Allen and his friend Seth Warner to organize a militia called the Green Mountain Boys. In 1770 the group took up arms against the intruding New Yorkers to prevent them from taking over their land. The governor of New York declared Allen an outlaw and offered a reward for his arrest.

In April 1775, the Revolutionary War began. On May 10, Allen, with his Green Mountain Boys and some Connecticut militia, succeeded in capturing the British fort at Ticonderoga, New York, on Lake Champlain. Four months later, Allen and his men failed in an attempt to capture Montreal, and Allen was taken prisoner.

On his release in 1778, Allen returned to continue the fight for Vermont's independence. However, the Continental Congress refused to recognize Vermont's claim to statehood. Allen considered having Vermont annexed to Canada, but the plan fell through.

Ethan Allen died on February 12, 1789, in Burlington, Vermont. Two years later, Vermont became the 14th state of the Union.

Reviewed by RICHARD B. MORRIS
Editor, *Encyclopedia of American History*

ALLEN, RICHARD. See PENNSYLVANIA (Famous People).

ALLEN, WOODY. See MOTION PICTURES (Profiles: Directors).

ALLENTOWN. See PENNSYLVANIA (Cities).

ALLERGY. See DISEASES.

ALLIGATORS. See CROCODILES AND ALLIGATORS.

The snowcapped Alps extend across much of south central Europe. The highest Alpine peak, Mont Blanc (to left of center), lies on the border between France and Italy.

ALPS

The Alps are a great mountain system of south central Europe, famed for the spectacular beauty of their snowcapped peaks.

Extent and Divisions. From the coast of the Mediterranean Sea, the Alps stretch for a distance of about 660 miles (1,060 kilometers). They form the boundary between France and Italy and extend across Switzerland, northern Italy, southern Germany, Austria, and the Balkan peninsula. They are usually divided into three main sections: Western, Central, and Eastern Alps. Some of the principal Alpine mountain ranges are the Maritime, Ligurian, Rhaetian, Pennine, and Bernese Alps in the Western and Central Alps; and the Noric and Carnic Alps, the Hohe Tauern and Dolomites, and the Julian and Dinaric Alps in the Eastern Alps.

Peaks, Glaciers, Rivers. Mont Blanc, on the border between France and Italy, is the highest peak in the Alps, rising 15,771 feet (4,807 meters). The Matterhorn, on the Swiss-Italian border, although lower in elevation, is noted for its steep, knifelike ridges, which have long challenged mountain climbers. There are more than 1,200 Alpine glaciers, or slow-moving bodies of ice. The largest, the Aletsch Glacier, covers an area of about 66 square miles (171 square kilometers). Several important rivers, including the Rhine, the Rhône, and tributaries of the Po, rise in the Alps.

Plant and Animal Life. A variety of plant and wild animal life thrives at elevations below the highest summits. Grapes are cultivated in the southern valleys. Oak, beech, and other trees grow on the lower slopes, while evergreens are found at higher elevations. Above the tree line are meadows, often used for grazing livestock. The edelweiss is the most famous of Alpine flowers. The chamois (a kind of antelope), ibex (a wild goat), and golden eagle all live above the tree line.

Passes and Tunnels. There are about 50 Alpine passes, or natural gaps in the mountains. Some of these were used in older historical times by invading armies crossing into Italy. The best-known passes include the Brenner, between Austria and Italy; the Great St. Bernard and the Simplon, between Switzerland and Italy; the Montgenèvre, the Little St. Bernard, and the Mont Cenis, between France and Italy; the St. Gotthard in Switzerland; and the Arlberg in Austria.

Numerous railroad and highway tunnels have made travel across the Alps much easier. The Simplon Tunnel, extending for 12½ miles (20 kilometers) between Switzerland and Italy, is one of the world's longest railroad tunnels. The St. Gotthard Road Tunnel in Switzerland, completed in 1980, is the world's longest highway tunnel, with a length of 10 miles (16.3 kilometers).

Reviewed by DANIEL JACOBSON
Michigan State University

ALUMINUM

In the 1800's, people already knew that aluminum was the most abundant metal in the earth's crust. They had even been able to extract the blush-white metal from its ores. But the cost of refining it was still so high that Emperor Napoleon III of France still had his finest dinner spoons made of it in the 1860's. Metallurgists were in the position of having discovered a great treasure house of extremely useful metal without having found the key that would unlock it. When a way was found to refine the metal cheaply in 1886, aluminum became an important part of nearly every industry in the world.

Aluminum makes up between 7 and 8 percent of the earth's crust. Although it is so abundant, its existence was not suspected for a long time. This is because it is never found in nature as a pure metal but is combined with other chemical elements in compounds that are very hard to break down.

Aluminum compounds are found in many minerals, and all clay contains aluminum. Many of the most beautiful precious stones are basically nothing but colored aluminum compounds. Rubies and sapphires, for example, are aluminum oxide with traces of other elements. Emeralds contain aluminum along with beryllium, chromium and silicon.

The most important ore of aluminum is bauxite, a type of clay. It generally contains from 40 to 60 percent aluminum oxide.

The existence of aluminum was predicted in 1808 by the English scientist Sir Humphry Davy. However, he was unable to solve the problem of extracting the metal from its ore. In 1825 the Danish scientist H. C. Oersted produced the first aluminum metal the world had ever seen—but in an amount too small even to conduct experiments. The German scientist Friedrich Wöhler succeeded in extracting aluminum in powder form in 1845 and made the first discoveries about aluminum's properties.

Aluminum's career as a luxury item ended in 1886 with the simultaneous discoveries of Charles M. Hall in the United States and Paul Héroult in France. The two men had independently hit upon the same solution to the problem of converting aluminum ore into the metal aluminum cheaply enough for everyday use.

The Hall-Héroult process is basically the same one used in today's two-step process of aluminum refining. Bauxite ore is refined to produce aluminum oxide, a white powder, which is also called alumina. Alumina in turn must be further processed to produce aluminum. It was this second step that held back aluminum production for so many years.

Hall and Héroult found that alumina could be dissolved in molten cryolite, an icy-looking mineral found in Greenland, and then broken down by passing an electric current through the molten mixture. The current separates the alumina into aluminum and oxygen. The aluminum settles at the bottom of the cell and is drawn off periodically. More alumina is added to keep the process going. About 2 pounds (0.9 kilogram) of alumina are needed to make 1 pound (0.45 kilogram) of aluminum metal.

Aluminum's many characteristics combine to make it suitable for many products. An important characteristic is its light weight. Aluminum weighs two thirds less than such common metals as iron, copper, nickel, or zinc. Its lightness makes aluminum useful in the manufacture of building materials, bus and truck bodies, and automotive and airplane parts. About 90 percent of the total weight of a typical four-engine aircraft is aluminum.

Aluminum also conducts electricity well. For this reason it has replaced copper for high-voltage electric transmission lines. Since it is lighter than copper, electric lines of aluminum need fewer supporting towers.

Because it is a good conductor of heat, aluminum makes good cooking utensils. If just one edge of an aluminum pan is heated,

FACTS ABOUT ALUMINUM

CHEMICAL SYMBOL: Al

ATOMIC WEIGHT: 26.98

SPECIFIC GRAVITY: 2.7 (a little more than 2½ times as heavy as water).

COLOR: silvery white with a bluish tinge.

PROPERTIES: soft and easily shaped; resists corrosion; nonmagnetic; good conductor of heat and electricity; forms compounds that are hard to break down.

OCCURRENCE: third most abundant element in the earth's crust (after oxygen and silicon); most abundant metal in the earth's crust.

CHIEF ORE: bauxite.

CHIEF SOURCES: Australia, Guinea, Jamaica, Brazil, Russia.

In England and certain other countries, aluminum is called aluminium.

▶ EARLY NATIONAL LITERATURE

Benjamin Franklin

By the late 1700's, America's several colonies had existed as dependencies of England for almost two hundred years. America was growing rapidly in population and economic importance, but its literary culture lagged behind. The first American whose work and writing received international recognition was Benjamin Franklin. A scientist, diplomat, businessman, and writer, he rose to success from humble beginnings and seemed to embody the American dream of opportunity.

Franklin's writing, from the humorous "Dogood Papers" (1722) he published as a teenager, through the hugely popular *Poor Richard's Almanac* (1733–38), is always marked by shrewd common sense and independent thought. His *Autobiography,* written between 1771 and 1788, is one of the landmarks of American literature. Franklin's self-portrait, written in a strong, straightforward style, captures the accents of real speech. That style is his chief legacy to the nation's literary tradition.

Political Writing

As America moved toward independence, literature reflected the changing political situation. Some of the most important writing of this period was produced in support of revo-

American Literature 1700–1900

This time line follows the progress of American literature from colonial days to the dawn of the modern era. The writing produced during those 200 years reflects the sweeping changes that took place as the United States transformed from a rural society of villages and small towns into a powerful industrialized nation. Biographies of the writers listed on the time line can be found in the appropriate volumes of this encyclopedia.

Benjamin Franklin

1733 First edition of *Poor Richard's Almanac* by Benjamin Franklin (1706–90)

1776 *Common Sense* by Thomas Paine (1737–1809)

1819–20 *The Sketch Book* by Washington Irving (1783–1859)

COMMON SENSE;
ADDRESSED TO THE
INHABITANTS
OF
AMERIC
On the following interesti
SUBJEC
I. Of the Origin and Design of Go
with concise Remarks on the E
II. Of Monarchy and Hereditary S
III. Thoughts on the present State
IV. Of the present Ability of Ame
cellaneous Reflections.
Man knows no Master save crea
Or those whom choice and commo
PHILADELPHIA;
Printed, and Sold, by R. BELL, in Third-
MDCCLXXVI.

Rip Van Winkle

lution. Thomas Paine's *Common Sense,* published on the eve of the Revolutionary War in early 1776, sold more than 100,000 copies in two months and helped to lead the nation toward its demands for independence. The letters of men and women like John and Abigail Adams, Thomas Jefferson, and James Madison eloquently recorded a dangerous and pivotal period in history.

Out of the continuous discussion and debate emerged the Declaration of Independence and the Constitution, two documents of unequaled importance in political history, which have also earned a high place in American literature. The Declaration, which was officially submitted by a committee, was in fact mostly the work of one man, Thomas Jefferson. Although he was a southern aristocrat and slaveholder, Jefferson established himself as one of the nation's most articulate domestic voices. His library of about six thousand volumes served as the foundation of the Library of Congress, and his writings and building designs strongly influenced America's taste in architecture. His *Notes on the State of Virginia* (1784) made important contributions to American natural science.

Early Black Writing

The Constitution demonstrated the limits as well as the strengths of American democracy. Women were denied the vote, and black

1826 *The Last of the Mohicans* by James Fenimore Cooper (1789–1851)

1828 *American Dictionary of the English Language* by Noah Webster (1758–1843)

1832 *Poems* by William Cullen Bryant (1794–1878)

1836 *Nature* by Ralph Waldo Emerson (1803–82)

1840 *Tales of the Grotesque and Arabesque* by Edgar Allan Poe (1809–49)

1845 *Narrative of the Life of Frederick Douglass* by Frederick Douglass (1817–95)

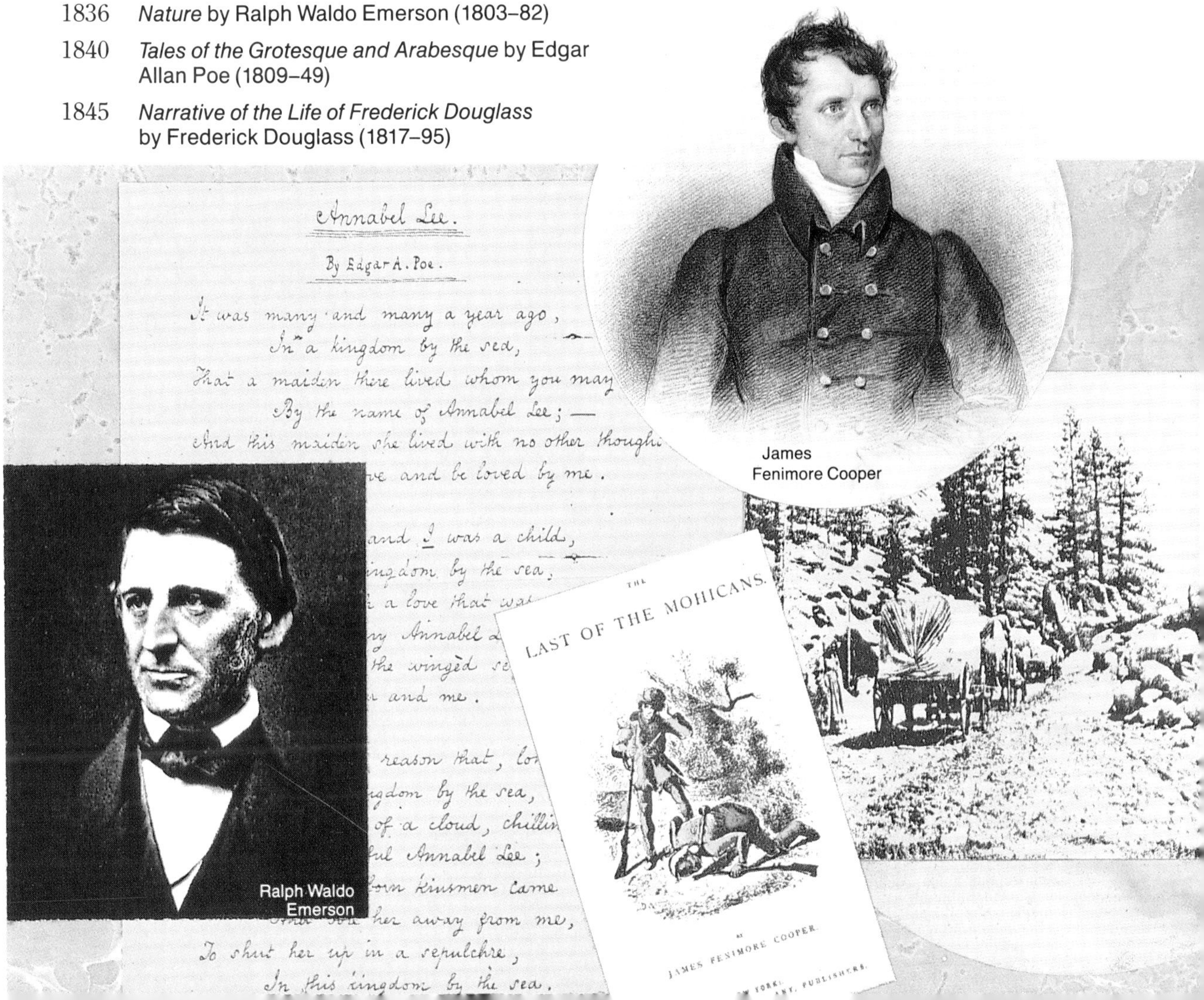

James Fenimore Cooper

Ralph Waldo Emerson

Vanderbilt, John D. Rockefeller, and J. P. Morgan became familiar figures in the daily press. Because of the country's fascination with wealth and material values, these years were sometimes called the "Gilded Age."

James and Twain

Many writers and artists found the culture of America to be unfriendly, anti-intellectual, and even uncivilized. As a result, several of them actually left the United States for longer or shorter periods to live and work in Europe. The most famous of these early expatriates was Henry James, one of the major novelists of the late 1800's and early 1900's. James used the contrast between Europe and America, which he called the "international theme," as a central subject in many of his stories and novels. He was especially interested in the psychology of his characters, and he employed a subtle prose style in order to reveal the inner life of his heroes and heroines. He also developed theories of fiction that would influence later generations of writers.

Unlike James, Mark Twain had begun as a poor boy and had worked in dozens of different jobs before finding his career as a writer. Although he believed in the promise of democracy, he was a stern critic of American society. His masterpiece, *The Adventures of Huckleberry Finn* (1884), is a brilliant comedy, but it also contains a strong attack on the slave system and the corruption of national ideals. Like all of Twain's best novels, including *The Adventures of Tom Sawyer* (1876), *Huckleberry Finn* employs a strong and believable colloquial (conversational) English. Twain said that "the soul of the people, the life of the people" was in their everyday speech, and his own greatest achievement was in his literary use of the ordinary language of America's people.

Henry James lived in England for many years. His novels often contrast the values of the young United States with the age-old traditions of Europe.

Frontier Humor

Twain's style grew out of the tall tales and frontier humor of the Old Southwest (a region stretching from Georgia to Missouri). The isolation and lawlessness of the frontier gave rise to an oral tradition of jokes and stories that eventually made its way into print. Some of the major humorists were Augustus Baldwin Longstreet, George Washington Harris, and Bret Harte. Harte's stories, such as "The Luck of Roaring Camp" (1868) and "The Outcasts of Poker Flat" (1869), were vivid portrayals of life in the mining camps of the California gold rush.

Realism

The emergence of the frontier humorists, who came from the West and South, demonstrated that American literature was becoming a more national achievement. Another important writer from the Midwest was William Dean Howells, who was born in Ohio and who eventually became one of the most influential novelists and editors of the late 1800's. In his fiction as well as his essays, Howells spoke as the champion of a new realism, which took ordinary, middle-class life as its subject. His many books include *The Rise of Silas Lapham* (1885) and *A Hazard of New Fortunes* (1890).

The years after the Civil War produced many important realist writers, including Rebecca Harding Davis, Edward Eggleston, and Hamlin Garland. Davis' "Life in the Iron Mills," which was published in the *Atlantic Monthly* magazine in 1861, was an angry work that revealed the oppression of workers. Eggleston's *Hoosier Schoolmaster* (1871) was set among the common people of Indiana, while Garland's *Main-Travelled Roads* (1891) exposed the hard and bitter lives of farmers and villagers in the Midwest.

New England Women Writers

New England continued to produce important writers in the later 1800's, including a group of remarkable women: Rose Terry Cooke, Mary E. Wilkins Freeman, and Sarah Orne Jewett. Each of these women, in different ways, explored the narrow, rural lives of men and women who had been left behind in the great changes that followed the Civil War.

Cooke's stories emphasized the loneliness and poverty of New England life. Freeman was especially interested in the sufferings of women. Her stories, collected in such volumes as *A Humble Romance* (1887) and *A New England Nun* (1891), portrayed the effects of isolation and outworn traditions on individual lives. Jewett emphasized the relationships among women that help them to cope and survive. In her masterpiece, *The Country of the Pointed Firs* (1896), men are mostly absent. The story centers on the daily lives of women, whose quiet activities—gardening, knitting, quilting, visiting, talking, praying—have replaced the more familiar adventures of male fictional heroes.

Southern Writing

Much of the literature produced by white writers in the South after the Civil War looked back affectionately at plantation life before the war. There were significant exceptions, including the work of George Washington Cable, Lafcadio Hearn, and Kate Chopin. Cable, who served in the Confederate army, later became a spokesman for black rights. His major novel, *The Grandissimes* (1880), was an attack on the racism and moral hypocrisy of the South.

Hearn was born in Greece and lived for a while in New Orleans before settling permanently in Japan. One of his early books, *Gombo Zhebes* (1885), was a collection of Creole proverbs. It was one of the earliest attempts to preserve American folk tales and treat them seriously.

Kate Chopin was born in St. Louis and also lived for a while in New Orleans. The mother of six children, she was widowed at the age of 30 and supported herself with her writing. Her most successful work, collected in *Bayou Folk* (1894) and *A Night in Acadia* (1897), was a series of sketches based on the Creole people and customs, which she had observed while she lived in New Orleans. Her tales provide vivid glimpses of the passion that lies beneath the surface of respectability. Her masterwork, *The Awakening* (1899), sympathetically explores the emotions and desires of its heroine.

Naturalism

The tremendous economic and political changes of the late 1800's were accompanied by a philosophy of competition and rugged individualism. Sometimes called "social Darwinism," this philosophy argued that human relations involved an endless struggle, in which only the "fittest" survived. Traditional concepts of justice and morality were threatened by a harsher view of human life in which individual choice mattered less than heredity and environment.

One literary outcome of this new point of view was the movement known as naturalism. Influenced by such European writers as Emile Zola and Gustave Flaubert, naturalism depicted men and women as controlled by instincts or passion, helpless in the face of economic and social circumstances.

Two of the major American naturalist writers were Stephen Crane and Frank Norris. Crane's poems and fiction continually assert the cruelty and indifference of the universe. *Maggie: A Girl of the Streets* (1893), which is set in the slums of New York's Lower East Side, tells the pitiable story of a young girl whose poverty drives her into prostitution, despair, and death. Crane's most famous novel, *The Red Badge of Courage* (1895), strips away the patriotic feeling surrounding the Civil War to reveal the horror of war's reality. The novel's young hero, Henry Fleming, experiences battle as confused, terrifying, and ultimately meaningless. Crane called the novel "a psychological portrait of fear." As such, it is a brilliant success.

Like Crane, Frank Norris believed that force ruled human lives. His major work was a projected three-volume "epic of wheat," which would take in the whole nation and its economic life. Only the first two volumes were completed before Norris' death, but the first of them, *The Octopus* (1901), is his chief work. Loosely based on California history, the novel is mainly a study in the power of destiny. In Norris' view, nature is a vast machine, and human beings are insignificant atoms in a large, mysterious design. It was a view widely shared as the 1800's ended.

The Beats, on preceding page.) A group of writers who became known as "confessional poets" published some of the most important recent verse. The confessional writers used their own lives, including their most intimate problems, as the subject matter of their poetry. The group included Robert Lowell, John Berryman, and Sylvia Plath.

Lowell's *Life Studies* (1959), which combined shocking personal revelations with superb craftsmanship, influenced a generation of writers. Berryman's *Dream Songs* (1964–68) was a kind of versified diary in which alcoholism, failure, and death are frequent topics. Plath, who committed suicide at age 30, wrote poems in which anger and despair merge in thoughts of dying; her best work was published, after her death, in *Ariel* (1965).

Black Poets. Gwendolyn Brooks won the first Pulitzer prize awarded to a black writer for her second volume of poetry, *Annie Allen* (1949). Her poetry became increasingly militant after 1967, when she and other writers in the Black Arts Movement dedicated their work to the task of social change.

Robert Hayden made extensive use of black history and folklore in his poetry; his books include *Figures of Time* (1955) and *A Ballad of Remembrance* (1962). Hayden's "Runagate, Runagate" pays tribute to Harriet Tubman, who escaped from slavery and then helped hundreds of others to freedom.

Postwar Drama

In the years following the war, the leading playwrights were Arthur Miller, Tennessee Williams, and Edward Albee. Miller's *Death of a Salesman* (1949) has been perhaps the most important play of the postwar era; the tragedy of the central character, Willy Loman, went beyond personal failure to encompass the collapse of the American dream.

Tennessee Williams wrote more than two dozen full-length plays. Several of them, including *The Glass Menagerie* (1944), *A Streetcar Named Desire* (1947), and *Cat on a Hot Tin Roof* (1955), are among the classics of recent American theater. Edward Albee wrote more experimental plays than Miller or Williams, often short works influenced by the European "theater of the absurd." In a typical Albee play, a small group of characters engage in verbal and even physical abuse, sometimes for no apparent reason.

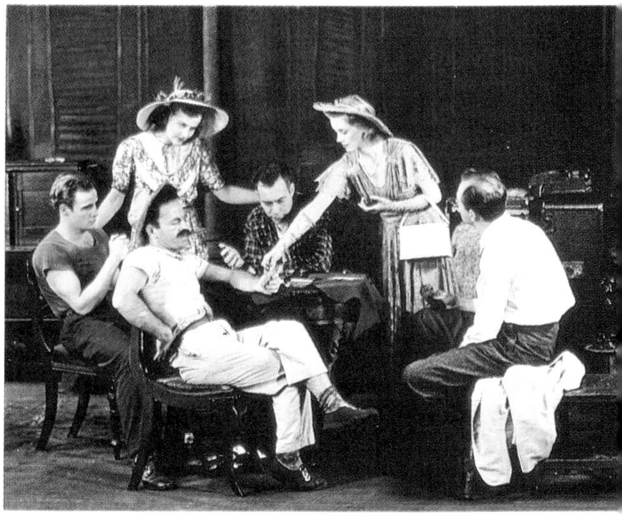

A scene from *A Streetcar Named Desire*, by Tennessee Williams. Williams wrote more than two dozen plays. Many have become classics of American theater.

More recent playwrights whose work has commanded attention include Sam Shepard and David Mamet. Many of the best contemporary dramatists have been women, including Wendy Wasserstein; Beth Henley, who won the Pulitzer prize for *Crimes of the Heart* (1981); and Marsha Norman, who won the Pulitzer for *'Night Mother* (1983).

Postwar Fiction

The early postwar mood of alienation and discontent was best captured in the 1951 novel *The Catcher in the Rye,* by J. D. Salinger, in which young Holden Caulfield dreams of protecting all the world's children from danger. Other writers of the period whose work focused on the anxieties of the middle class were John Cheever and John Updike.

Southern Fiction. Although the American economy had become increasingly national, the South remained a separate literary region after World War II. Some of the main writers of that region have included Robert Penn Warren, Eudora Welty, Flannery O'Connor, William Styron, and Walker Percy.

Warren won distinction both as a novelist and a poet. His best novels were his earliest ones, in particular the Pulitzer prize-winning *All the King's Men* (1949), a fictional account of the Louisiana politician Huey Long. Eudora Welty wrote some of the finest short stories of the century, memorably evoking the people and landscapes of the rural South. Her first collection, *A Curtain of Green and Other Stories* (1941), remains her masterpiece.

Flannery O'Connor's stories combine the grotesque and the supernatural; her work is filled with outcasts and marginal people. William Styron has chosen subjects that range from the Nazi death camps, in *Sophie's Choice* (1979), to an 1800's slave revolt, in *The Confessions of Nat Turner* (1967). Walker Percy, a physician and a Catholic, continually explored the decay of faith in the modern South. His novels include *The Moviegoer* (1961) and *The Last Gentleman* (1966).

Jewish Fiction. Among the most significant recent writers were several Jewish novelists who examined the debate over older values that followed World War II. This group included Saul Bellow, Bernard Malamud, and Philip Roth. Bellow, who won the Nobel prize in 1976, has created memorable characters and urban scenes. He writes in defense of the individual and of traditional culture; his finest novels are perhaps *Henderson the Rain King* (1959) and *Herzog* (1964).

Bernard Malamud was the son of Russian immigrants. His stories and novels often resemble folk tales and allegories. In much of his work, including his best book, *The Assistant* (1957), Malamud created characters who are defeated by circumstance but maintain their faith. Philip Roth has shown a lifelong interest in the problem of moral authority. His most famous book to date has been *Portnoy's Complaint* (1969).

Black Writers. The past few decades have been a triumphant period for black writers. In 1952, Ralph Ellison published *Invisible Man,* one of the most important novels of the postwar era. The book combines realism, folklore, and fantasy to tell the story of its narrator's life and his discovery of American racism.

James Baldwin was the son of a storefront preacher, an eloquent and bitter man. Baldwin's first and best novel, *Go Tell It on the Mountain* (1953), is based on his own childhood experiences. In addition to fiction, he produced some of the most brilliant essays of his time. Collected in such volumes as *Notes of a Native Son* (1955) and *Nobody Knows My Name* (1961), these essays make up a passionate denunciation of racial injustice.

Postwar black writing has encompassed the remarkable accomplishment of gifted women, including Toni Morrison and Alice Walker. Morrison's fiction celebrates the language and the heritage of tales that define the American black experience. Her principal novels, such as *Song of Solomon* (1977) and *Beloved* (1987), for which she received the Pulitzer prize, combine a detailed knowledge of history with myth and fantasy. Alice Walker's major novel, *The Color Purple* (1982), is written as a series of letters that reveal the oppression and liberation of a woman named Celie.

Other talented black women writers have included Margaret Walker, Paule Marshall, and Toni Cade Bambara.

Experimental Fiction. Over the past several decades, a number of writers have undertaken a wide range of technical experiments in fiction. Vladimir Nabokov, a Russian émigré, used parody, multilingual jokes, and intricate plots to focus attention on the nature of fiction itself. Donald Barthelme worked in fragments, word games, and fairy tales. His stories have been collected in such volumes as *Come Back, Dr. Caligari* (1964). John Barth has created narratives in which storytelling itself becomes the main subject.

Contemporary Diversity

The most evident hallmark of contemporary American literature is its great range and diversity. From the "minimalist" realism of Raymond Carver to the enormous and complex novels of Thomas Pynchon; from the brilliant reportage of Joan Didion to the finely crafted fables of Cynthia Ozick—recent American writing has represented the widest variety of styles and subjects.

The nation's ethnic minorities have produced distinguished work. Maxine Hong Kingston, in such books as *Woman Warrior* (1976), has dramatized the tensions between past and present in Asian-American culture. The main character of *Bless Me, Ultima* (1972), by Rudolfo Anaya, learns to base his life in the modern world on the foundation of tradition. The novels of the Native American writer Leslie Marmon Silko, including *Ceremony* (1978), combine realistic narrative with the songs and legends of the Indian past.

PETER CONN
University of Pennsylvania
Author, *Literature in America: An Illustrated History*

AMERICAN REVOLUTION. See REVOLUTIONARY WAR.

AMMUNITION. See GUNS AND AMMUNITION.

AMOEBA. See MICROBIOLOGY; PROTOZOANS.

Building Cities with Clay

There was little timber or stone on the river-bottom land where the Sumerians built their cities. But clay was plentiful. They packed moist clay into molds and dried the clay in the sun. In this way they formed flat bricks that could be stacked upon each other to build the walls of houses, shops, palaces, and the ziggurat. The main disadvantage of the sun-dried bricks was that they crumbled after a time, even in a dry climate. But the builders discovered that if they baked the moist bricks, the heat hardened the clay. The bricks then remained firm even in wet weather. A wall built of fire-baked bricks set together with asphalt would stand for a very long time. The Sumerians and Babylonians used fire-baked bricks for their more important buildings.

Writing on Clay Tablets

The Sumerians wrote on clay. They pressed the end of a stick into the soft clay, making little three-cornered marks. They combined these three-cornered marks to form signs that stood for words. Since the marks looked like wedges, this form of writing is called cuneiform, which means "wedge-shaped." The Babylonians, as well as other peoples, borrowed cuneiform writing from the Sumerians. For more than 2,000 years people in this part of the world wrote with these little wedge-shaped marks.

Clay tablets were heavy and awkward to handle, but they lasted for centuries. A paper book buried in the ground for 3,000 years would have rotted away completely. But a clay tablet, carefully dug up, remains in good condition. Scholars in modern times have found thousands of the Sumerian and Babylonian tablets. These tablets tell many things about this ancient civilization. They tell of business and trade, for there are letters from merchants to their agents. There is a "farmer's almanac," which gives instructions about each season's work in the fields. A Sumerian physician wrote down some favorite medical remedies. One of the most interesting tablets describes what children did in school 4,000 years ago. They hurried to school because their teacher would beat them with a cane if they were late. The teacher also used the cane to punish children for talking, leaving the school

King Hammurabi receives the insignia of royal office from a god. Beneath the sculpture is the Code of Hammurabi, one of the world's oldest sets of laws. The detail below shows the cuneiform writing on the stone, the earliest fully developed system of writing that is known.

without permission, and not doing lessons properly.

The Oldest Written Laws in the World

People living together in cities must have laws. The Sumerians and Babylonians wrote their laws on tablets of clay and stone. These are some of the oldest known written laws. One law provided that people would have to pay a certain amount of silver if they entered an orchard that was not their own and were caught there for stealing. The most famous collection of early laws was issued by Hammurabi, king of Babylon, around 1750 B.C. His code declared that Hammurabi was like a real father to his people. He gave them laws "to cause justice to prevail in the land, to destroy the wicked and evil, that the strong might not oppress the weak." Most of our knowledge of the code comes from a tablet found in Susa, Iran, in 1901.

All people were not equal in Babylon. Some people were aristocrats, some were commoners, and some were slaves. People were not treated in the same way by the laws. If a free man knocked out the eye of another free man, he could lose his own eye as punishment. Slaves were still less fortunate. The laws treated them like property. The Sumerians and Babylonians were not the only slave owners in ancient times. Almost all ancient civilizations allowed slavery. Frequently prisoners of war were kept as slaves rather than killed.

More Trade and Better Products

People living in a city did not have to make everything they used. Instead, they could spend their time making one kind of product that they traded for things they needed. A weaver would make cloth and trade it to the potter for dishes, to the merchant for grain, and to the metalsmith for tools. Since weavers spent their time doing only one kind of job, they learned to do it well. They made much finer cloth than part-time weavers could. The same was true of potters, smiths, barbers, and people with other skills.

In the Sumerian and Babylonian cities, artisans devoted themselves to their special jobs. The fine metalwork, jewelry, and stone carving that they produced show the skill of these specialized workers.

▸ EGYPTIAN CIVILIZATION

Civilization in Egypt is older than the oldest pyramid. About 3200 B.C. a king named Menes (also called Narmer) brought the land along the Nile River under his rule. For more than 3,000 years, Egypt remained one of the richest and most civilized lands in the world.

The Egyptians had a system of writing. Instead of using clay tablets, they wrote on sheets of papyrus. These were made from strips of the papyrus reed, which grew along the Nile. Papyrus does not last as well as clay tablets. But since the Egyptian climate is dry, many ancient writings have survived. There is a letter from a boy-king to one of his captains, asking that the captain bring back a dancing dwarf from central Africa. There are collections of wise sayings, including one that advised a young man to "think much, but keep thy mouth closed." One essay by a soldier tells how difficult it is to serve in a cold, foreign land. Such writings tell the thoughts of people who lived thousands of years ago.

The God-Kings and Their Officials

The Egyptians thought of their kings, whom they called pharaohs, as gods who had power over the Nile River. The Nile flooded each year and brought water to the fields. Since the prosperity of the people depended on the king, they had to give the king a part of what they produced.

The king supposedly ruled the entire land. But no one person could actually manage so large a kingdom alone. Egypt was in fact ruled in the king's name by an army of officials. The king's chief assistant, called a vizier, appointed the most important officials. They in turn appointed other officials, who appointed still lesser ones. Every district had its official, who was the government representative best known to the common people. The district official served as chief of police, judge, overseer of the irrigation canals, and tax collector.

Religion

The Egyptians worshiped many gods and goddesses. The most important was Re, the sun god. Egyptian kings were thought to be descended from Re, and "son of Re" was part of a king's official title. Re was associated with other gods, including Osiris, king of the underworld, and Isis, wife of Osiris.

A wall painting in the palace of Minos at Knossos depicts the acrobatic bull-fighters of ancient Crete. The painting dates from the Middle Bronze Age.

CRETAN CIVILIZATION

Four thousand years ago the people of Crete depended on the sea for both their wealth and safety. Crete is an island in the Mediterranean Sea, well situated for trade. The Cretans traded wheat, wine, linen, olive oil, and cypress timber for goods from Egypt, Syria, Italy, and lands still farther away. They also depended on the sea for defense. They built no walls around cities because they counted on their navy to keep enemies from their shores.

A statue of a young man, dating from the 500's B.C., in a temple of the god Apollo in Boeotia, Greece.

Knossos and the King's Palace

Knossos was the greatest of the Cretan cities. Thousands of people lived there. The king's palace was a rambling structure covering 5 acres (2 hectares). It contained an open court, a throne room, chapels, and apartments for the king and his attendants. There were rooms where wheat and olive oil were stored in jars nearly as tall as a human adult. Paintings showing scenes from daily life decorated the walls. Bits of the paintings that remain show us how these people looked.

The people of Knossos watched performances in outdoor theatres. They liked active sports such as boxing. They had an unusual exhibition in which acrobats turned somersaults in midair, coming down on the backs of charging bulls. "Bull leaping" would have made most rodeo contests of today look tame.

Throughout Knossos there were signs of the city's wealth. Women wore gold jewelry and elaborately ruffled skirts. The palaces and houses contained fine pottery and carved stone figures. The king and the nobles had chariots complete with spare wheels, which were necessary because of the rough cobblestone streets.

Trade was important in Crete, but most people were not traders. They worked on the land, growing wheat, olives, figs, and grapes. They tended goats and sheep and drove ox teams. The people gave the oxen such names as Dapple and Darkie, Blondie and Bawler.

Disaster Strikes: A Civilization Forgotten

The prosperity of Knossos came to an end about 1400 B.C. Disaster struck the city, but just what happened is not clear. Perhaps the sea no longer kept invaders away. People continued to live at Knossos, but the great days were past. After 1100 B.C. the old civilization disappeared and was almost entirely forgotten within a few hundred years. The world has learned of the ancient cities only since 1900, when scholars digging among the ruins found the walls of palaces and houses. Among other things, diggers found a number of clay tablets with writing on them. It was clear that there were two different kinds of writing, but both were in an unknown script. It was 1952 before anyone could read these tablets. Then scholars discovered that these ancient writers used an early form of Greek on one group of tablets. But the other writing still remains a complex mystery.

GREEK CIVILIZATION

Athens in the year 447 B.C. was not the largest city in the ancient world. But it was surely one of the liveliest and most interesting. In that year builders began working on the Parthenon, the beautiful temple built in honor of the goddess Athena. The Parthenon stands on the high rocky hill called the Acropolis. Some of the most brilliant people of the ancient world were in Athens in those days, writing books and plays and teaching. There was interesting talk in the homes, on the streets, or wherever people gathered.

Athens was a leader of the Greek cities. This does not mean that Athens ruled Greece, for in those days each city ruled itself. The city-states sometimes united against a common enemy, as when the Persians invaded Greece in 490 and 480 B.C. But they also fought among themselves. The Peloponnesian Wars (431–404 B.C.) brought two groups of

This wall carving of the Greek goddess Athena dates from the 400's B.C.

Greek vase from the 500's B.C. depicts the legendary heroes Achilles and Ajax playing dice.

Small statues of worshipers were placed in Sumerian temples. Those at right have stylized features including huge, bulging eyes. The temple statue of the ruler Gudea (*left*) is a later example. Its sculptor may have tried to carve a likeness of Gudea's features.

colored stones. Bowls, vases, bottles, and other containers (called vessels) were made of stone for religious use. The outsides of the vessels were decorated with relief carvings of animals and plants.

Around 3000 B.C. the Sumerians entered their first truly great age, called the Early Dynastic period. Sculpture during this period was created to stand in the temple of the god of the city. Sculptured worshipers stood with their hands clasped in front of their bodies—a gesture of respect before the god. Sometimes the figure held a cup that may have contained an offering to the god. Clothing was solid and stiff; there was no suggestion that a body was beneath it. Most of the artist's skill was concentrated on the head. Eyes were enormous and bulging. The long beards of men had heavy, crosswise ridges. If the figure had hair, it was long and braided, but often heads were shown shaved.

Sumerian sculpture was carved from stone, which had to be imported. There was very little stone in Mesopotamia. The most popular stone was gypsum, which is soft, satiny, and white, and looks like mother-of-pearl.

During this period sculpture gradually became more delicate and lifelike. The rocklike clothing was replaced by more natural-looking skirts, and beards were formed with hundreds of tiny curls. The mouths of these statues are slightly upturned and give life to the face.

Sumerian art reached a peak during the time of the famous ruler Gudea. The sculptures made of Gudea and his family were among the greatest achievements of Sumerian art. Sometimes the statues were seated and sometimes they were standing. Gudea's body was a heavy mass of stonelike drapery as in early Sumerian sculpture. An attempt may have been made to carve a likeness of Gudea's features on the statues.

Sumerian Architecture

Mesopotamia was a land without stone or forests. The usual materials for buildings were mud and reeds. Homes were built of reeds from the marshlands. Sometimes the reeds were tied in great bundles and set in two rows. The tops were bent together and tied. Other homes were rectangular and constructed of woven reed. Often the reed building was entirely covered with mud and painted.

Sumerian temples stood atop towering structures called ziggurats. An artist's reconstruction shows the ziggurat at Ur as it probably looked in ancient times.

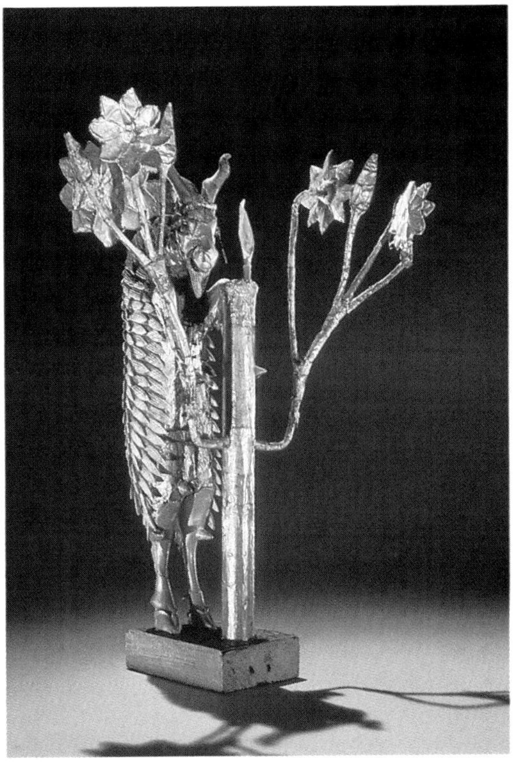

Sumerian sculptors worked with metal and colored stones. This offering stand of wood, gold, and lapis lazuli depicts a ram rearing up against a flowering tree.

The only other buildings that we know about are temples. The temple of the local god was both the spiritual and physical center of a Sumerian city. Built of bricks made of mud and dried in the sun, it stood on a raised platform or tower made of the same material. This temple tower is called a **ziggurat.** The ziggurat was an artificial mountain built in successively smaller stages, like a pyramid. At the top of the "mountain" was the temple of the city-god. Great staircases led from the ground to the summit. The brick walls of the ziggurat often were decorated with colored stones, mother-of-pearl inlays, large paintings, and rows of copper animals.

The ziggurat developed by Sumerian architects became the main form of ancient Mesopotamian architecture. As far as we know, the ziggurat at Warka was the first. The ziggurat built for the moon-god in the city of Ur during the Neo-Sumerian period has remained in better condition than earlier ones. This is because its architects had learned that bricks baked in an oven were much stronger than bricks simply dried in the sun. However, nothing survives of the shrine.

▶BABYLONIA (2000–1100 B.C.)

Three centuries of war followed the end of the Sumerian Empire. City-states within Mesopotamia fought with each other, and barbarian tribes invaded the Tigris-Euphrates region. Finally in the 18th century B.C., Hammurabi, ruler of the city of Babylon, became the ruler of Sumer and Akkad and united the warring city-states.

Sculpture during the time of Hammurabi was more naturalistic (lifelike) than ever before in Mesopotamia. Although it is not certain, the stone heads that have been found were probably meant to represent Hammurabi. The king was shown as a bearded man with very large eyelids and wearing a cap. Portraiture was unusual in Mesopotamia, but in Egypt—the great nation to the west—royal portraits were being created. It is likely that Egypt influenced Babylonian art.

In Babylonia, sculpture became increasingly naturalistic, or lifelike. This stone head was intended to represent a particular person—probably King Hammurabi.

Hammurabi recorded his famous laws on a large stone called a **stela.** The laws were written on the lower three quarters of the stone; the top quarter was carved in bold relief, with a figure of a seated god before whom Hammurabi stood. The scene was intended to give religious authority to the laws.

Like the Sumerians, the Babylonians used bronze as well as stone for their sculpture. One bronze statue from the First Dynasty was of a kneeling man. His face was covered with gold. On the base of the statue a carved inscription requested long life for the king, perhaps Hammurabi. Other surviving bronze statues include one of a spirited group of wild goats standing on their hind legs and another of a ram bearing an inscription to a god.

The Kassites, mountaineers from the east, slowly pushed their way into Babylon after the death of Hammurabi. The First Dynasty fell around 1600 B.C., and the Kassite barbarians made themselves masters of Babylonia. Although they adopted Babylonian culture, the Kassites produced very little art.

Babylonian Architecture

Only a few ruins remain of the architecture of the First and Kassite dynasties. Many Sumerian buildings were rebuilt, and the architecture of new buildings was copied from Sumerian styles. The Kassite royal palace was larger than most earlier buildings. Around 1450 B.C. a new temple was built at Warka for the worship of the mother-goddess. It was not on a ziggurat, but was small and rectangular. Reliefs in brick depicting huge gods formed a continuous band of decoration on the outside walls of the temple.

The Kassite Dynasty fell to the Assyrians in about 1100 B.C. Until the 6th century B.C., the Babylonians were attacked, overrun, crushed, and conquered many times. But they survived to rise again and to make Babylon one of the great cities of the ancient world.

▶MINOAN CIVILIZATION (2000–1200 B.C.)

More than 5,000 years ago the Mediterranean island of Crete was inhabited by people known as the Minoans. The Minoans developed a civilization around the same time that the Sumerians began theirs. Nothing was known about this civilization until the 20th

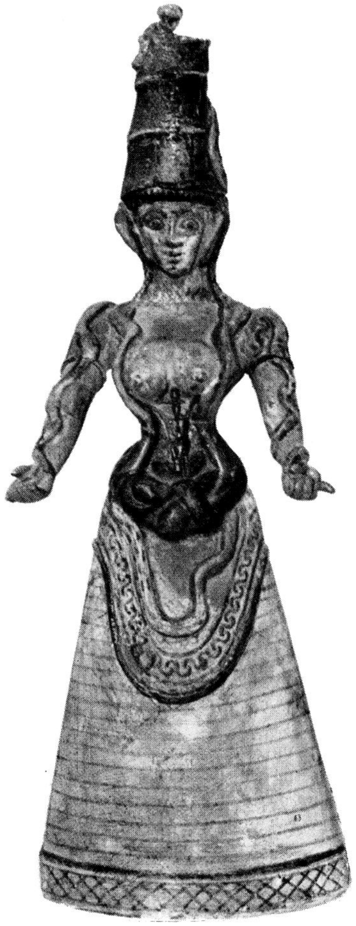

Frescoes—paintings done on wet plaster—decorated the walls of the Minoan palace at Knossos. One of the most important figures was the king-priest (*left*). Painted pottery statues known as snake-goddesses (*right*) were created by the Minoans about 1600 B.C.

century, and little is certain about its history and earliest art.

The sculpture of the Minoans—at least what has survived—is small and very different from the sculpture of Mesopotamia. Figures of animals and people were made of bronze, stone, ivory, or terra-cotta (red clay). The Minoans sometimes baked clay statuettes and painted them. In contrast to Mesopotamian sculpture, Minoan figures were shown in motion: representations of worshipers had upraised arms; animals were shown running; an acrobat was depicted jumping over a bull. Slender young men and women were portrayed with impossibly small waists and narrow hips. Figures of men had arms crossed on their chests. Women wore narrow corsets beneath their breasts, flaring skirts, and high headdresses.

Around 1600 B.C. the Minoans created statuettes known as snake-goddesses. However, these sculptures probably represented priestesses rather than goddesses. Made of painted pottery, these figures are similar to earlier Minoan work—they are dressed in the same manner—but their outstretched arms have snakes coiled around them.

Ivory figurines were originally enriched with gold details now lost. Common subjects were young athletes leaping over bulls, a child at play, or a child attended by nurses. Bronze sculpture almost always represented a Minoan at prayer.

Relief sculpture on a large scale was probably unknown to the Minoans. Most carving in relief was done on stone vessels. Subjects included farmers marching and singing, and people boxing, wrestling, bull leaping, or just standing. The Minoans also created a great many delicate, tiny seals carved on gems. Some scholars believe that all adult Minoans had their own seal designs.

Minoan Architecture

The Minoans did not build temples. Religious ceremonies were conducted outdoors or in the palaces. The palace was the center of the Minoan community. It was, of course, the residence of the royal family and the seat of government, but it was also used as a storehouse for merchandise and contained workshops where goods were manufactured.

The palace was usually built on a hillside and was made up of many low, rectangular units. Roofs were flat, and foundations were made of stone. Two or three stories was the usual height; the first story was stone and the ones above were probably of mud bricks.

A great court paved with stones was built in the center of the palace. Religious ceremonies were conducted in this court. It is thought that this central court was planned first, and as new parts were needed they were built around it. Corridor walls were decorated with large frescoes—paintings done on wet plaster. Because the building was constructed in separate parts, many staircases and corridors were needed. Walls and sometimes even floors may have been covered with alabaster. Ceilings were held up by painted wooden columns, which were circular or oval. They were unusual because they were smaller at the base than at the top. No one is certain why the columns were made in this way.

Comfort was important to the Minoans. Their palaces and country houses sprawled over large areas, and there were many passageways and windows. Sunlight poured into every part of the buildings, and there was a great feeling of spaciousness. Elaborate bathrooms—undoubtedly the first in Europe—contained terra-cotta tubs, drains, and toilets.

In the course of many centuries, the great Minoan palaces were destroyed several times. Scholars cannot be absolutely certain of the causes, but earthquakes, tidal waves, or fires were among the natural causes. There may also have been uprisings and invasions. But each time, the Minoans rebuilt their palaces. Then, around the year 1200 B.C., the Minoan civilization came to a sudden end. The Dorian tribes from the north took over Crete along with much of the Greek mainland. The Minoan buildings, along with all Minoan art, were lost for the next 30 centuries.

▶ THE HITTITES (1400–1200 B.C.)

Anatolia, a land in Asia Minor, was the home of the ancient peoples known as the Hittites. Around 1400 B.C. the Hittites extended their empire eastward as far as Mesopotamia.

Except for their statuettes in bronze, the Hittites made no sculpture-in-the-round that we know of. Hittite sculpture, in fact, was so completely a part of Hittite architecture that the two arts must be discussed together.

The Hittites built on an enormous scale. Unlike Mesopotamia, Anatolia was rich in stone and wood. The foundations of their military, civil, and religious buildings were of stone. In early Hittite buildings, stones 3 meters (10 feet) high were used in rough blocks. Later, stone that had been trimmed was used. Above the stone first level, the buildings were constructed with bricks and wood. Parts of the structure that received the most use—such as window sills and thresholds—were reinforced with stone.

Hattusas, the capital city of the Hittite Empire, was enclosed in a great wall. One of the gates was guarded by two stone lions, one on each side. The lions had been carved in very high relief from huge stones, and the remaining part of the boulders rose as high as 3 meters above the lions. Other gates were protected by sphinxes (lions with human heads) that were carved in the same way. The lions and sphinxes appeared to have grown out of the stone.

Marching figures carved in relief from stone slabs were placed along the walls of Hittite buildings on the ground level. The slabs were of either limestone or dolerite, a coarse-grained stone that had to be coated with plaster or gesso (chalk mixed with glue) to create a smooth surface. The marching figures represented a religious procession. Most of these reliefs were at Yasilikaya, which was probably a holy shrine or religious center. Gods were shown wearing flowing robes and often standing on sacred animals.

Great stone lions over 3,000 years old still stand at the ruins of Bogazkoy, a meeting place of the ancient Hittites.

Some of these reliefs were carved on the sides of cliffs at Yasilikaya, and elaborate buildings with open courts and great staircases led to the cliffs. Egyptian and Minoan designs were often included in the reliefs, a sign of trade and communication between empires. Yasilikaya may have been the coronation place of the Hittite kings.

Hittite art did not have a chance to develop fully. In the 13th century B.C., the empire was overwhelmed by invasions of barbarians from the north and by an army of mysterious peoples called the Peoples of the Sea, whose origins are unknown.

▸ ASSYRIA (900–600 B.C.)

In the centuries that followed the decline of the Hittites, the Assyrians gradually built a great empire. The Assyrians were similar to the Babylonians in language, law, and religion, but they were much more brutal. Their civilization was based on the army, and their art reflected their love of war and vio-

Marching figures were carved on the sides of cliffs at Yasilikaya, a Hittite religious center.

lence. Only a few sculptures-in-the-round have been found. One is of an early emperor, Ashurnasirpal II. In style it resembled sculpture from the Early Dynastic period of Sumer.

In the long, rectangular rooms of Assyrian buildings, there were large gypsum slabs carved in relief. The carvings often showed fierce battles or hunting scenes. Complicated and horrible scenes of torture and bloodshed and of vicious animals may have been highlighted with black, red, and yellow paint.

Assyrian reliefs give us a picture of cities, fortresses, costumes, and daily life of a people forever lost to us. From these reliefs we know the kind of furniture the Assyrians used, although only bits and pieces of real furniture have been found.

The Assyrians also carved reliefs of gigantic human-headed bulls, each with five legs. These huge creatures always appear in pairs as guardians of a palace. Placed near an entrance, they were sometimes combined with figures of men of superhuman size.

Reliefs of ivory were used by the Assyrians to decorate chests, thrones, chairs, and other furniture. Often the reliefs were gilded (coated with gold) and inlaid with colored glass and stones. Common subjects of the sculpture were plants, real and imaginary beasts, musicians, and a woman standing at a window.

Assyrian Architecture

The chief cities of Assyria were Nimrud, Khorsabad, and Nineveh, the capital. Following an ancient custom, cities were enclosed within great walls to keep enemies out. The buildings in the cities of Assyria were made of mud bricks and looked much like the buildings of Sumer. The buildings were not very high, but were spread over a large area and contained a great many rooms.

Only the ziggurat towered high over the city walls. At Khorsabad the Assyrians erected a spectacular ziggurat reaching as high as a twelve-story building of today. It was probably built in seven levels, and each one was painted a different color.

Inside and outside of every important Assyrian structure, color played an important part. Colorful glazed bricks in various patterns decorated the walls. Sometimes the outside walls were whitewashed and the inside decorated with frescoes. Ceilings were held up by wooden columns resting on stone bases. The combination of wooden columns, glazed brick, stone reliefs, and frescoes of flowers and animals created rich and impressive effects that never grew monotonous.

The stone carvings of the warlike Assyrians frequently illustrated hunting and battle scenes. This 7th century B.C. relief from Nineveh depicts King Ashurbanipal hunting.

Five-legged winged bulls with human heads (*left*) protected the gates of Assyrian palaces. A carved amber statue of the Assyrian king Ashurnasirpal II (*right*) dates from the 9th century B.C. It is one of the few surviving Assyrian sculptures-in-the-round.

In 640 B.C. the Assyrian Empire controlled more of the Middle East than it ever had before. Yet, less than 30 years later the empire no longer existed. In 612 B.C. it was invaded and crushed by a combined army of Chaldeans and Medes.

THE CHALDEANS (615–539 B.C.)

When the Chaldeans and Medes divided the Assyrian Empire in two, southern Mesopotamia and the lands west of the Euphrates River became the Chaldean, or Neo-Babylonian, Empire. The Chaldeans were the descendants of the Babylonians, who had ruled the ancient world before the rise of the Hittites and Assyrians.

Babylon was restored as the capital of a great empire. Temples from the old First and Kassite dynasties were rebuilt. The best-known Chaldean king, Nebuchadnezzar, built the Hanging Gardens of Babylon. His palace was built in levels, and each level had a terrace planted with flowers and shrubs. The pillars that supported each level were hollow and were used as wells.

Little remains of the art of the Chaldeans. Their famous ziggurat is hardly more than rubble today. It is likely that this ziggurat was the Tower of Babel mentioned in the Bible, for it was Nebuchadnezzar who conquered and destroyed Jerusalem, enslaved the Hebrews, and carried them to Babylonia. The ziggurat and palace were made of baked bricks. The exteriors were decorated with

An Egyptian wall painting shows female musicians playing the double oboe, long-necked lute, and harp.

A mosaic dating from about 2800 B.C. shows a musician of ancient Sumeria playing a lyre.

A double-reed instrument is shown in an ancient Etruscan wall painting.

on the types of scales, melodies, and rhythms the professional musician had to learn and guided him in tuning his instruments.

The Sumerians

In the ancient cities of Mesopotamia, near the Tigris and Euphrates rivers, Sumerian and later Babylonian court musicians sang and played their harps and long-necked lutes. Temple musicians participated in ceremonies honoring Shamash, the sun god; Ningirsu, the god of war; and other gods. The sacred prayers were sung by large choirs trained at the temple schools. The priests wrote their theories of religion, science, and music on clay tablets in wedge-shaped symbols. They also wrote down many prayers and hymns, often with the accompanying music written alongside the text. Unlike modern Western notation, each special sign for writing the music represented groups of notes rather than single notes. The written prayers, religious myths, and sacred music were probably kept secret and hidden from the eyes of those outside the clergy.

In addition to the harp and long-necked lute, the Sumerians favored another string instrument, the lyre. Instead of a neck the lyre has two separate arms connected by a crossbar. The flute and oboe also appeared, although wind instruments were generally not as popular as strings. Two oboes were usually bound together in a V shape and played at the same time. One of the pair probably played the melody, and the other droned a single continuous note. This melody-and-drone style of music has persisted to modern times in the Middle East and in India, where the double-wind instrument is still found.

Many of the Sumerian instruments were played at the religious ceremonies. For example, the god of wisdom, Ea, was worshiped in a sacrificial bull ritual featuring a large, goblet-shaped metal drum. Special hymns at this ceremony were accompanied by the double oboe.

The Egyptians

The civilization of ancient Egypt first appeared along the Nile River about 4000 B.C., perhaps a few hundred years later than that of Sumer. Like the Sumerian and Babylonian kings, the Egyptian pharaohs had many professional musicians. These are often shown on tomb paintings and sculptures playing, singing, and dancing in groups rather than as soloists. A typical musical group of about 2500 B.C. might have had several of the Egyptians' favorite instrument, the large curved harp, standing upright. There might also have been some flutes and a double clarinet consisting of two clarinets glued together. However, the most important part of the group was the singers, who were also conductors. These conductors accomplished more than conductors of modern times, for their special finger, hand, and arm motions were a special sign language. By holding the palm upward or making a circle of the thumb and forefinger, for example, they could indicate to the accompanists what melodies and rhythms to play. A similar sign language is still used today in Egypt and India.

Many musicians were exchanged as gifts between the kings of ancient times. Pharaoh Pepi II, who ruled Egypt for more than 90 years in the 26th and 25th centuries B.C., even received presents of skilled Pygmy dancers from the Congo. Much later, when Egypt became a conquering nation, many such gifts began to pour in. The pharaohs received hundreds of music girls and their instruments from Mesopotamia and other parts of southwest Asia after conquering this region in about 1500 B.C. Among the new instruments were the lyre, long-necked lute, double oboe, and tambourine. The girls seem to have brought with them a more exciting style of music, which the Egyptians soon adopted.

Little is known of the melodies and rhythms of the ancient Egyptians. However, their harps were tuned to one of the most popular scales of ancient times (and of modern Japan). This is one of the pentatonic, or five-note, scales, which can be illustrated on the piano by the tones A F E C B. No doubt other scales were also used by the Egyptians. Like the Sumerians, the Egyptians enjoyed a touch of harmony in their music, such as the drone. The drone is a steady, continuous note with a hypnotic effect. However, it was always merely a backdrop to the more important part of the music, the melody.

The sistrum, a rattle with jingling crossbars, was played at the festivals of the

▶THE VARIETY OF ANIMAL LIFE

Groups of animals may share some traits, yet every kind of animal has its own life-style and way of surviving. Sometimes the traits that make the living patterns different are very small; the great blue heron and the little blue heron are an example. They both are long-legged birds that wade into water to stalk small creatures, such as fish and frogs. They both live in marshes or other wetlands. However, the great blue heron is about twice the size of the little blue heron. The difference in size means that they feed in the same place, in a similar manner, but at different depths.

Each kind of animal is suited to living in a particular kind of environment, or **habitat**. An animal fits into a **niche** within its habitat—that is, it has a specific role within its community. Wetlands, such as marshes, are the habitat of herons, while their niche is that of a bird that wades to catch small water animals.

The heron's behavior and body structures enable it to survive within its particular habitat and niche. While wading, a heron will freeze its movements; motionless, it looks for a fish or a frog. When the heron sees its prey, it quickly extends its long neck and with its bill seizes the startled prey.

The climbing perch, an Asian fish, has another type of life-style. It lives in small ponds that sometimes dry up during times of drought. When this happens, the perch behaves in an unusual way for a fish: It creeps over the ground to another pond that still holds water. The climbing perch can do this because it has strong, flexible fins that act almost like legs. It also has a lunglike organ that allows it to breathe air as it travels out of water and over land.

The difference in their sizes allows the great blue heron (*top*) and the little blue heron (*bottom*) to have separate niches within the same shared habitat.

The traveling behavior, fins, and air-breathing organ of the climbing perch are like the heron's long legs and hunting behavior. They are all changes, or **adaptations**, of a living thing geared to a particular way of life. Every animal has its own special adaptations that improve its chances of survival.

Animals do not adapt on purpose; they adapt by chance. The adaptation of the giraffe's ancestors is an example. It may appear that the ancestors of the giraffe grew a long

Did you know that . . .

the bird called an oxpecker spends almost its entire life clinging to the back of a hoofed animal such as this impala? The oxpecker performs a valuable pest-removal service by removing bloodsucking ticks and blood-flies from the impala's body. In return, the impala allows the oxpecker to rest and sleep and even court and mate on its back.

There are many patterns of living within the same forest community. Some animals are most active during the day, others are most active during the night.

Animals of the Day

Clockwise from top right: woodpecker, cardinal, chipmunk, rabbit, coyote, lynx, and squirrel.

Animals of the Night

Clockwise from top right: flying squirrel, red fox, badger, woodcock, raccoon, mule deer, barn owl, and bat.

HOW ANIMALS COMMUNICATE

Animals use many signals, including some that are silent, to communicate with one another. Each species shares a language of sound and behaviors that is recognized by all its members.

Animal Calls. Each animal sound has a meaning. Calls are used for many reasons, including to warn or defend, to claim territory, to help find a mate, and to announce that food has been found. If frightened, a young alligator utters a shrill distress call. The call alerts other young alligators to the danger. The call also draws adult females to the young alligators. The nearness of the adult females provides protection for all the young, so the call serves as a warning and a defense.

A distress call can also confuse an enemy. When a frog is frightened, it lets out a loud squeak. The sudden loud sound can startle the enemy just long enough for the frog to jump away.

Animals that live in large groups such as bird flocks often use food calls that let the group know where a source of food can be found. A tern (a type of small gull) that sights a school of small fish swimming through the water utters a screamlike call.

Not all animal sounds are made with the voice. The ruffed grouse is known for its drumming sound. A male ruffed grouse trying to establish its territory or attract a mate will stand on a log and beat the air with its wings, creating a thumping sound. Although the beating is slow at first, it ends with a rapid whirring noise.

Coyotes, which live throughout the United States, Canada, and Mexico, communicate by howling. The eerie howl of the coyote is usually heard during the evening, night, or early morning.

Silent Signals. Body characteristics and behaviors provide the silent signals that many animals use to communicate. The shape of a body part, the color of fur, or a pattern of movement can send a message from one animal to another.

Some signals are used so that members of a particular species can identify one another. The horns of each species of antelope have a unique shape—some are straight spikes, others are spiraled, and still others are long and curved. Antelopes are able to recognize one another by the shape of the horns.

Scent is an important communication tool that some animals use to establish ownership. A male wolf urinates on shrubs and bushes to let other males know he is around and in charge of his territory. Scent is also used by members of the same species to identify one another and in mating.

Another silent mating signal is the flashing light that the firefly emits. Fireflies use their flashing signal to attract members of the other sex. Each species of firefly has its own pattern of flashes.

Using postures and facial expressions, animals can transmit a great number of messages that are either friendly or hostile. When a young animal whose mother is disciplining it turns over on its back exposing its soft stomach, it means the offspring knows the mother is in charge. In a meeting of two adult animals, the animal that assumes the same posture is saying "I give up."

HOW ANIMALS REPRODUCE

For a species to exist, its members must reproduce their kind. There are two main types of reproduction in the animal kingdom: asexual reproduction, in which a new offspring is produced by one parent, and sexual reproduction, in which a new offspring is produced by two parents.

Asexual Reproduction. Asexual reproduction is carried on by simple animals, such as sponges, jellyfish, flatworms, and those that make coral. When a coral animal reproduces, small projections, called buds, form on its body. The buds grow on the parent and develop their own feeding organs. Soon they split off the parent as a new, separate offspring.

During sexual reproduction, the sponge (*above*) releases sex cells into the surrounding water. The courting frigate bird (*above right*) inflates its huge red pouch to attract females. Orangutans and their young (*right*) enjoy a close relationship.

Another form of asexual reproduction is called **fragmentation**. During fragmentation, an animal, such as a flatworm, divides into two halves. After dividing, each fragment of the flatworm forms the body parts it is missing and becomes a complete new individual.

Sexual Reproduction. During sexual reproduction, two sex cells, an egg cell from a female and a sperm cell from a male, join to create a new offspring. The sperm of some animals, such as mammals, unites with the egg inside the female's body in a process called fertilization. The fertilized egg grows inside the female until the offspring is fully developed and ready for birth.

The fertilization process does not always take place inside the female during sexual reproduction. Some animals produce young without ever coming together to mate. Many fish and aquatic animals, such as frogs, release eggs and sperm into the water when individuals of both sexes are near one another. Fertilization is then a matter of luck. The chances of it occurring are increased in animals that send out signals to attract the opposite sex to them during the release of the cells. Male frogs, for example, emit mating calls that draw the females to them.

Care of the Young. Typically, animals that release sex cells but do not stay around to care for the offspring produce vast numbers of eggs. The female ocean sunfish, which can weigh 1,000 pounds (454 kilograms), can produce 28 million eggs in a single season. The unprotected eggs of the sunfish are threatened by wind, waves, and predators. But because so many eggs are produced, some have a chance of surviving and continuing the species.

Animals that have small numbers of young usually provide some sort of care for them. The female Pacific salmon builds a nest of pebbles and gravel for her 800 eggs. Birds and mammals, which may have only a few, or even a single, offspring, protect and feed their young. Some mammals, such as human beings, care for their young over many years.

A cultural anthropologist may live with a people to learn about their culture. It will take many months of fieldwork to complete a study of this Pygmy group in Zaïre.

ANTHROPOLOGY

Why are people in some parts of the world called by their mother's family name instead of by their father's? Why do people scattered over the face of the earth speak related languages? What did human beings look like when they first began to use stone tools or make pottery?

Such questions are dealt with by the science of anthropology. Scientists who work in this field are called anthropologists. The word "anthropology" comes from two Greek words —*anthropos* ("human being") and *logos* ("study"). Anthropology, then, is the study of human beings and human culture.

Anthropology is a young science, which took shape only in the mid-1800's. Until that time, few individuals had made a serious study of different peoples. European explorers had long been bringing back stories about peoples of Africa, Asia, and the Pacific islands, peoples of different sizes and colors. These people brought up their children and ran their societies in ways unknown to Europeans. Their languages had sounds that Western people had not heard before. To most Westerners then, such customs were strange, uncivilized, or even wrong. They thought that these distant peoples should learn about European ways. The goal was not to understand their ways but to change them.

By the mid-1800's, some Westerners were beginning to hold rather different ideas. Perhaps, they thought, what was best for one group of people might not be best for another. Perhaps it was not desirable to make everyone over in the European image. Perhaps other peoples and their ways should be studied for their own sakes. From such ideas grew the science of anthropology—the study of people, both past and present, near and far away.

Studying all the peoples who have lived on earth is a big job, and anthropologists approach this study in several ways. **Physical anthropologists** are concerned mainly with people as physical, biological creatures. By studying fossil remains of ancient people, physical anthropologists learn about our origins. They also try to understand the physical variations among different human groups today.

In contrast, **cultural anthropologists** study how people live throughout the world. Anthropologists who specialize in archaeology also study social life, by digging up the remains of ancient cultures. In this way, **archaeologists** are able to bring to anthropology an understanding of the human past. **Anthropological linguists** add an important view by concentrating on one aspect of human life—language. They search for the origin of human speech and of the various languages, and they study how languages change.

PHYSICAL ANTHROPOLOGY

Physical anthropologists have been working for more than a century with the bones of very ancient people. They study the shapes of heads, the sizes of brain cases, and the lengths of limbs. All these measurements give hints about how the human race has changed since its beginning. For example, anthropologists have noticed that ancient skulls held smaller brains than those of modern people. This shows that brain size increased as humans evolved.

Physical anthropologists are also interested in modern people's physical traits, such as types of skin, eyes, hair, blood, and diseases. Some of the basic information about these traits comes from the work of biologists and physicians. Physical anthropologists combine all this information and look for new patterns. Are several inherited physical traits related to one another? In what way do these traits differ around the world?

The physical anthropologist tries to find out how people's physical traits relate to their way of life. And if anthropologists can find out how people have changed in the past, they may be able to suggest how people may adapt in the future. For more information on the work of physical anthropologists, see the article PREHISTORIC PEOPLE in Volume P, and the article RACES, HUMAN in Volume R of this encyclopedia.

CULTURAL ANTHROPOLOGY

The word "culture" takes on a special meaning for the anthropologist. A **culture** is the entire way of life that a group of people learns—everything the group has, makes, thinks, believes, and passes on to children. Culture includes knowledge, belief, art, morals, law, custom, and all other habits and abilities that members of the group acquire.

Cultural anthropology has two main goals: (1) to describe the cultures of all human groups and (2) to explain the similarities and differences among them.

The first cultural anthropologists began their studies among peoples living in distant lands. Many of these groups were then considered to be "primitive" because they had not developed writing, did not use metals, or lived in villages rather than cities. Actually these cultures were highly developed in terms of art, religion, family structure, and so on. But they seemed simpler to study than larger industrial societies.

Cultural anthropologists such as Margaret Mead often went alone to some isolated island or faraway village. Often they came from universities that wanted to document and study such people. Some were sent by the government responsible for the people.

The anthropologists had to win the trust of the people they studied. The people sometimes thought the anthropologists were crazy or perhaps evil spirits because they wore funny clothes and wrote in a strange language. If the people accepted them, the anthropologists settled down to live with the people for a while, and perhaps were adopted into a family. Then the anthropologists were ready to study all the different aspects of the culture. Over the years, anthropologists have concentrated on several important aspects of people's lives.

A physical anthropologist at the National Museum in Nairobi, Kenya, compares the skull of a humanlike creature found in Africa with other ancient skulls.

glands at the tip of the gaster is injected into the victim through the sting. But not all ants have useful stings. Some have stings so small or shaped so that they cannot be inserted into prey. Some of these ants produce formic acid or other kinds of venom that are sprayed or dabbed onto prey.

Inside the Body. The nervous system of an ant consists of the brain, nerve cord, and nerves. The brain is very tiny, but compared to the ant's body size, it is one of the largest brains in the insect world. The brain serves as the control center for all the body functions and processes. From the brain, a nerve cord extends along the lower side of the ant's body to the tip of the gaster. Nerves branch out along the nerve cord, carrying messages from the brain to other parts of the body and from other body parts to the brain.

Like other animals, ants take in oxygen during the process of respiration. The oxygen enters the body through small holes called **spiracles** on the sides of the thorax and abdomen. A network of tubes carries the oxygen throughout the ant's body. Carbon dioxide, a waste product formed during energy production, leaves through the spiracles.

The blood system of the ant is responsible for bringing digested food to the organs, muscles, and nervous system. It also takes away waste material. The ant's heart is part of a long tube that runs along the top of the ant's body from the head to the gaster. Blood is sucked up into the heart through tiny openings along the tube. As the heart contracts, blood is forced toward the head of the ant. There, blood pours out through an opening, bathing the brain and then flowing backward through the rest of the body. The cycle repeats continuously, nourishing and cleansing the body.

An ant's digestive system is a long tube that extends from the mouth to the end of the gaster. Within the abdomen, the tube widens to form pouchlike organs. An important organ of the digestive system is the **crop**, or "social" stomach. Liquid food, gathered during feeding expeditions, is stored in the crop. Ants returning to their nest regurgitate (bring up) the food to share with colony members. Food that is not stored in the crop passes to the stomach, where it is digested, then to the hind gut, where most of the food is absorbed into the blood. Material that is not absorbed travels through the hind gut to the rectum. Waste absorbed from the blood also is deposited in the rectum. After most of the water is reabsorbed from the waste material, it passes out of the body through an opening called the **cloaca**.

▶THE LIFE OF ANTS

Although there is great variety in how ants live, there is one trait they all share—all ants live in colonies. Within the different colonies, ants perform similar tasks: making nests, producing young, and feeding.

Members of the Colony

Ant colonies contain male and female members. However, most of the time the colony is populated only by females. Each ant colony has at least one queen, who is more of an egg-producing factory than a ruler. Some ant species have several queens in a colony, while a few kinds have hundreds. Male ants have short life spans, appearing in great numbers during the mating season. Once their job—flying out and mating with the winged queens from another colony—is accomplished, they die. Most of the colony is composed of workers, small wingless females that do not breed. Some colonies also have larger, big-headed workers called major workers.

Members of an Ant Colony

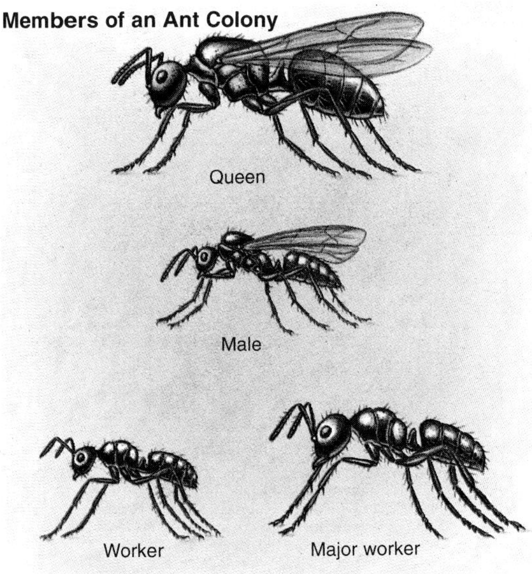

The Life Cycle of an Ant

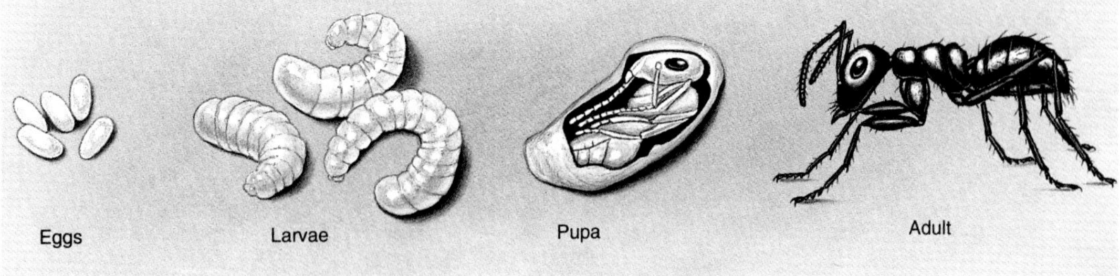

From the eggs the queen ant lays, wormlike larvae hatch. The larvae spend their time eating and growing. They enter the pupal stage when their growth as larvae is complete. During the pupal stage, an ant slowly takes on the adult form.

There may be more than one species of ant in a colony. For example, slave-making ants kidnap other ants and bring them back to work in the colony. Young queens of other kinds of ants leave their own colony to take over another species' colony. After killing the colony's queen, the invader queen forces the workers to raise its young. Eventually all the host ants are replaced by the invading ants.

Other kinds of animals, usually other invertebrates, may be "guests" of the colony. The guests are usually scavengers, eating leftover food or waste in the nest. Sometimes these invertebrates feed on the young or adult ants. The invaders may also use special chemicals to repel attacking ants or to fool ants into accepting them into the colony. In tropical rain forests, social wasps, bees, or even birds may live in part of an ant nest, or they may build separate nests nearby.

The Ant's Life Cycle

There are four stages in the development of an ant: egg, larva, pupa, and adult. The mating flights of males and young queens mark the beginning of the cycle. During the flight, a male deposits sperm (male sex cells) inside a queen's body. The queen stores the sperm until she is ready to lay eggs.

With mating accomplished, the male has fulfilled his only function for the colony, and he dies. The queen busily searches for a favorable location to start a new nest. When she finds a suitable place, she settles in, breaking off the wings she will never need again. After the queen prepares a nest, she lays a few eggs each day. As the eggs pass out of her body, they are fertilized by the stored sperm.

Within a few days of being laid, the eggs hatch. From the eggs, the wormlike forms called larvae (plural of larva) emerge. The larvae are fed by the queen. Depending on what they are fed, the larvae will develop into either queens or workers. The larvae, which spend most of their time eating, grow in size over the next few weeks. When their growth is complete, they enter the pupa stage. Some pupae (plural of pupa) spin a protective cocoon of silk; others are covered only by their skin. During the pupal stage, the ant slowly takes on the form of an adult. After about two or three weeks, its development is complete and the adult ant emerges.

The Ant's Home

Most ants make their homes in soil or rotting wood. Nests in soil or wood consist of chambers and narrow tunnels. Ants travel the tunnels to reach the chambers and the outside. In the tropics, many species nest in plants.

Some soil-nesting ants build a mound full of chambers and tunnels. The mounds are built of soil, small pebbles, twigs, grass blades, and leaf fragments. Some kinds of ants build nests without soil. They make nests with a paperlike

Did you know that . . .

ants were used as the first method of biological pest control? More than 2,000 years ago in southern China, farmers gathered the silk nests of the green tree ant. They took the nests from nearby forests and moved them to the orange groves on their farms. Because the ants are aggressive predators, eating any and all insects that cross their path, the ants helped keep the groves free of pests.

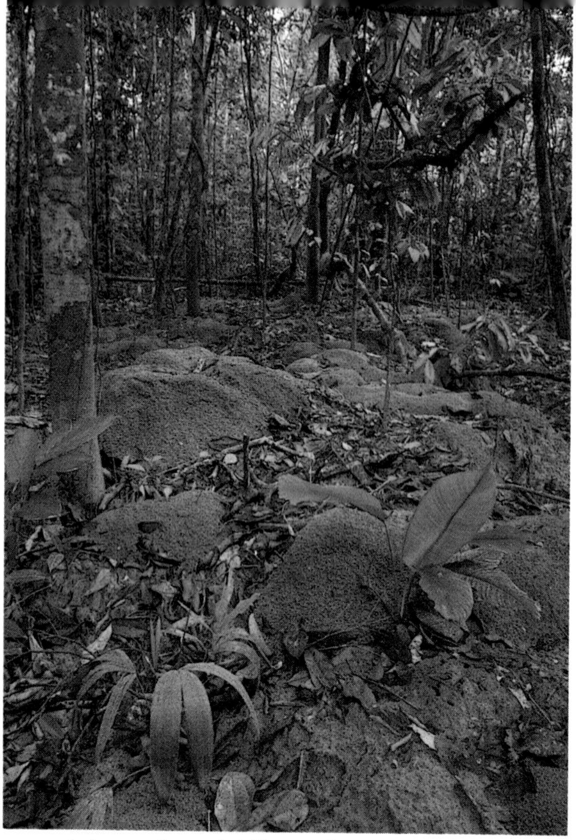

Ant mounds can hold interesting collections of objects. The chambers and tunnels of some have yielded fossils, minerals, even tiny nuggets of gold.

material, called **carton**, made of plant fibers stuck together with saliva. The carton nest may be simple sheets of material covering the spaces in bark or rocks in which the ants live. Or the nest may have a ball-like structure.

In addition to soil and carton, parts of plants also are used to make nests. Certain species of tropical tree ants weave a nest of leaves and silk. Groups of workers pull leaves together while others move silk-producing larvae (newly hatched ants) back and forth from the edge of one leaf to the other until the two leaves are firmly attached.

How Ants Obtain Food

Ants feed on a wide range of foods. Some ants eat only plant matter, such as seeds. Others feed on the fungus they carefully grow. But most kinds of ants are predators and scavengers—with a taste for sweets. They catch and eat small invertebrates, especially other insects, and they also eat already dead prey. They even steal prey from other small predators. Ants satisfy their taste for sweets by consuming plant sap, nectar, and fruit. The resourceful ants also get their sugary treats by raiding the hives of honeybees and the homes of human beings.

▶KINDS OF ANTS

Because ants have developed such elaborate and distinctive methods of feeding, they are often grouped together according to how they obtain food.

Harvester Ants

Seeds are part of the diet of many kinds of ants. However, they make up almost the entire diet of harvester ants, who gather seeds directly from plants or from the ground. These ambitious ants gather many more seeds than can be eaten at one time. The uneaten seeds are stored in special chambers in their nests, so there is always a ready supply of food.

Before the seeds can be eaten by the adults, they must be processed by the larvae. Workers break up the seeds into small pieces and feed them to the larvae. The larvae are able to digest the starchy seeds because they have a starch-digesting enzyme, which is missing in the adults. In the stomach of a larva, the seeds become a soft, pulpy mass. The larvae regurgitate some of this partially digested food for the adult ants. The different digestive abilities of the adults and larvae help ant colonies make use of food resources neither could use without the other.

Fungus-Grower Ants

Fungus-grower ants, found in the warmer portions of North and South America, have a very specialized diet. They have nests with large chambers deep in the soil. In these chambers, fungus growers cultivate special molds. The molds produce swellings that are eaten by the ants.

The fungus must be grown on beds of compost (decayed organic matter). Most fungus-grower ants farm their fungus crop on compost made from the droppings of plant-eating insects, such as caterpillars. Leaf-cutter ants are fungus-grower ants that make compost from pieces of fresh leaves, flowers, and fruits. The ants drink some of the plant juice from these materials but use most of it to raise the fungus that they and their larvae dine on.

Slave-Maker Ants

Slave-maker ants raid the nearby nest of a closely related species and steal its brood. The

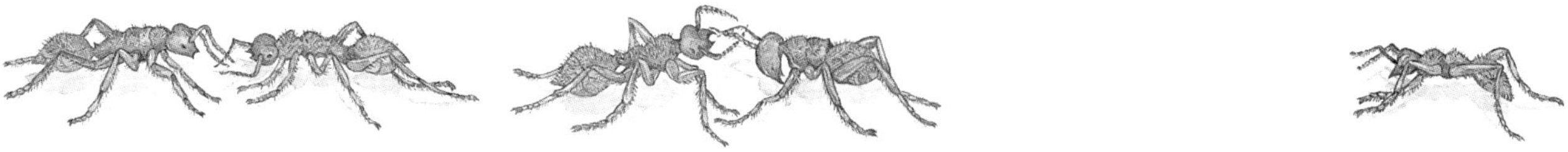

slavers carry the stolen brood to their home nest, where the slave ants already present eat most of the brood that is brought in. The brood that is not eaten matures and adds to the slave force of the colony.

To establish a new colony, mated slave-maker queens find a young or weak colony of a related species and invade it. The invaders kill the colony's queen and get the orphaned workers to raise their babies. The population of the colony increases as the slave-maker offspring mature and begin raiding other colonies. The colony remains a mixture of slave-maker ants and kidnapped ants.

Gatherer Ants

Several ant species have certain workers called **repletes** that, like other ants, store liquid food in their crops. Most replete-former ants are known as honey ants. They live in the deserts of North America and Australia. The liquid, usually honeydew or nectar, is gathered during the rainy season when plant growth is rapid and sap-feeding insects are abundant. Storing the liquid food allows these ants to have energy and water available during long dry spells.

Another replete-former lives in the oak woodlands of North America. This unusual ant is active in autumn, on warm winter days, and in early spring. Its main food is the rotting flesh of dead insects and earthworms. The ants collect the liquid from this softened meat during the time of year when many dead invertebrates are available. During summer, these "winter ants" stay underground and raise the year's brood with the liquefied invertebrate flesh stored in the crops of the repletes.

When its abdomen becomes so swollen with liquid food that it can barely walk (*left*), the gatherer ant called a replete must remain in the nest.

Slave-maker ants must depend on their slaves to perform such tasks as grooming the queen (*below left*), raising their brood, and building their nest.

Like miniature gardeners, leaf-cutter ants gather leaves (*below*) and other vegetation to prepare a bed on which to grow their fungus crop.

A herder ant "milks" aphids to get honeydew by stroking the insects with its antennae. It may also eat some of the aphids for meat.

Herder Ants

Herder ants live with sap-feeding insects in a special relationship that resembles the way human beings tend and herd cattle and other livestock. Some herder ants live underground with small insects called root aphids. The aphids feed on the sugary sap of the roots growing through the ant nests. To get rid of the excess sugar and water in their sap diet, the aphids discharge a sweet secretion called honeydew. Ants love to eat this sweet waste product. At times the ants also eat some of the aphids for meat. Ants that live this way often get all of their nutrition from aphids.

The herder ants of the Asian rain forest live with relatives of aphids called scale insects. These ants live in the warm, humid rain forest. The queen ant and her brood hide in the middle of swarms of workers on the soft new growth of forest shrubs. The scale insects suck sap from the plant twigs, and the ants harvest honeydew and scale insect meat for food. When the nest twig grows old and woody, the ants move, transporting their scale insects to a new "pasture"—that is, a new young twig.

Army Ants

When it comes to feeding, many ants are specialists, seeking out and preying on only one kind of food. Army ants are one such example. Many army ants only attack the nests of other ants, stealing and eating their broods. However, they have been accused of eating just about everything—from invertebrates to dogs, even humans!

Army ants have no permanent home. Each night the workers come together, creating a shelter out of their joined bodies. With the morning sun, bands of ants stream out from their temporary quarters, searching for food. When they find their prey, these ferocious ants swarm around it, attacking the victim with their long mandibles.

▶ANTS AND THEIR ENVIRONMENT

Ants serve several valuable functions. They help maintain the balance of nature by consuming large numbers of other insects and serving as a food source for other animals. They enrich the soil as they dig their burrows, loosening and mixing the dirt. Ants benefit human beings when they feed on insect pests, such as those that attack cotton plants and orange trees. But some of the same habits that make them helpful make them harmful. Ants can be household pests, infesting food and sometimes delivering painful stings. Some ants damage homes and other buildings by burrowing into the wood. They are agricultural pests when they feed on crops.

Over the years, myrmecologists have watched the same changes in the health of ant populations as in other species. Ants characteristic of endangered ecosystems—including the eastern tall grass prairie of North America, the rain forests of Asia, the savannas of northern Africa, and the hay meadows of Europe—are headed for extinction along with the other life-forms found in those habitats. In every way, the future of ants is linked to that of other life on our planet. Some species will increase; many others have already decreased and will continue to do so. Some may become victims of extinction.

James C. Trager
Editor, *Advances in Myrmecology*

See also Anteaters; Insects.

APACHE INDIANS. See Indians, American.

Size is the major characteristic that distinguishes the two groups of apes. The hulking gorilla (*above*) belongs to the group known as great apes, while the dainty gibbon (mother and daughter, *right*) belongs to the group known as lesser apes.

APES

Apes are hairy, long-armed animals without tails. They are intelligent creatures with large and complex brains, belonging to a group of mammals called **primates**. Human beings, monkeys (which are sometimes mistaken for apes), and a number of more primitive animals, such as lemurs, also are primates.

Of all existing animals, apes resemble human beings the most. The similarities between apes and human beings have led most scientists to believe that millions of years ago, apes and human beings shared a common ancestor. Some of the shared characteristics include highly developed nervous systems, excellent eyesight, broad flat chests, and flexible fingers and toes with nails instead of claws.

Although apes and human beings share many characteristics, there are significant differences. People, who are capable of more complicated tasks, have larger, more complex brains. Human beings also take longer to develop, have less body hair, and longer life spans. But probably the most important differences are that people have the ability to communicate with spoken language and to stand upright and walk on two legs.

▶CHARACTERISTICS OF APES

All apes are divided into two families, or groups, based chiefly on size. There are great apes and lesser apes. The great apes, which belong to the family Pongidae, include four species, or kinds, of apes: the gorilla, orangutan, chimpanzee, and bonobo, or pygmy chimpanzee. The largest of the great apes, and the largest primate, is the gorilla. A male can weigh about 600 pounds (272 kilograms) and stand more than 5 feet (1.5 meters) tall. The lesser apes, which belong to the family Hylobatidae, include nine species of gibbons. Gibbons are the smallest apes. They usually weigh 10 to 20 pounds (4.5 to 9 kilograms) and stand about 2 feet (0.6 meter) tall.

The various species of apes share many of the same characteristics. Their lively faces are more or less naked with flat noses and jaws that are thrust forward. Because they have mobile facial muscles, apes are able to display a wide range of facial expressions. Their eyes, which are directed forward, are capable of full-color vision. Hairless external ears are positioned on the sides of their heads. The trunk is well muscled with arms longer than legs. The siamang gibbon is the ape with the longest arms. Its arms, which may be more than twice as long as its body, span a distance of about 5 feet (1.5 meters). Apes have long-fingered hands with flat nails and opposable thumbs, that is, thumbs that can be placed against other fingers. Hair, varying in color from black to shades of reddish brown, covers their bodies.

Apes live in a variety of habitats. Gorillas are forest animals, found in tropical Africa. One population, the western lowland gorilla,

make sweet cider, hard cider, liqueurs, and apple cider vinegar. The processing remains can even be distilled to make perfumes used in shampoos and cosmetics.

ORIGIN OF THE APPLE

Although there are numerous kinds of wild, or crab, apples native to different parts of the world, the kind from which the familiar cultivated apple developed came from the mountains of southwestern and central Asia, between the regions of the Black and Caspian seas and eastward from there. This ancestor of the modern apple, which still grows wild, is smaller and more sour than our present varieties, but the tree on which it grows resembles our cultivated trees.

People selected the best fruit from the wild trees for eating and used seeds from the better fruit for planting. In this way the quality of apples was gradually improved.

VARIETIES

A number of distinct varieties of apples were raised in the lands north of the Mediterranean Sea several centuries before the time of Jesus. Since then thousands of varieties have been named and grown in different parts of the world. Most of these have now disappeared from commercial production, although many different varieties are still grown in various parts of the world.

In the United States and Canada, about 25 varieties are grown extensively, although there are small plantings of many other kinds. Apple varieties must meet certain requirements before growers are willing to invest time, money, and labor in them. First of all, the trees must be productive. Second, the fruit must be attractive-looking and of good size. Its flavor and texture must appeal to most people. Finally, the fruit must keep well in storage. This is why so few varieties are grown on a large scale.

Nearly all our present important varieties originated as chance seedlings. Since about 1900, scientific breeding work has resulted in the development of some fine new varieties. Most of these, however, are not yet widely grown.

The leading variety of apple in the United States is the Red Delicious, which originated from a seedling tree found on a farm in Peru, Iowa, about 1881. Most Red Delicious apples are now raised in the Northwest Pacific states and British Columbia, Canada, though some are grown in most apple-growing regions.

The McIntosh is the leading variety in Canada, New York, and the New England states. McIntosh trees are all descended from one chance seedling found on a pioneer farm in Ontario, Canada, in 1796. The original tree survived, bearing apples, until 1908, although it was badly damaged by a fire.

Other leading varieties include the Golden Delicious, Rome Beauty, Gala, Jonathan, and York Imperial.

Apples from Far Away

Among America's most popular apples are two that came from far away. The Granny Smith apple originated in Australia in the late 1860's. Mrs. Anne Smith found a young tree bearing large, hardy green apples that were good for cooking and eating. In the 1930's, the locally popular Granny Smith apples were exported from Australia. By the 1960's, successful strains were introduced to Wash-

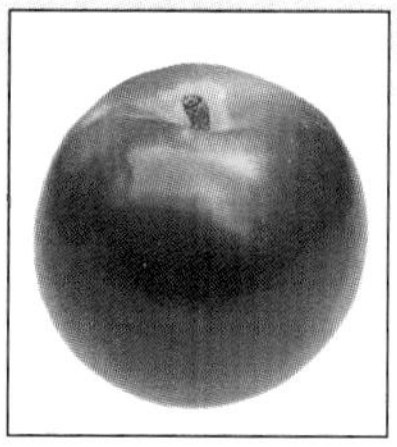

Of the many apple varieties commonly grown in the United States and Canada, these are some of the most popular for eating and cooking (*clockwise from far left*): Red Delicious, Rome Beauty, Granny Smith, Fuji, Yellow Delicious, and McIntosh.

Carefully maintained orchards—those that are properly fertilized, sprayed, and pruned—often produce a showy display of pink apple blossoms in the spring, followed by a bountiful crop of valuable fruit in the fall.

ington State. Now Granny Smith is one of Washington's leading apples. But the Granny Smith faces increased competition from another foreign apple, the Fuji, from Japan. This apple was first grown in 1939. It has gained popularity in the United States and, like the Granny Smith, is becoming one of Washington State's leading varieties.

Older Varieties

For more than 200 years, one of the most popular commercial apples was the Rhode Island Greening. Renowned even in the 1700's, this apple originated in Newport, Rhode Island. Up until the 1960's, the Rhode Island Greening was quite popular in the eastern United States. It is very difficult to find today. The Northern Spy was another American apple popular for more than a century. It arose from a seedling in a New York orchard around 1840. A major commercial apple until the 1960's, the Northern Spy is still grown on a small scale today. Its roots are resistant to some diseases, so the rootstock is commonly used for apple breeding. The Rome Beauty is an older variety that is still very common today. This apple, which dates to the 1840's, became famous for its bright red color and for its storage ability.

THE TREE

In good soils, unpruned apple trees will reach 30 to 40 feet (9 to 12 meters) in height. But when apples are grown for market, the trees are pruned to prevent them from becoming this tall. The trees in most commercial orchards are kept to a height of less than 20 feet (6 meters).

The apple tree is "rounded"—that is, it is about as broad as it is high. The branches are twisted and spreading. The fruit of most commercial varieties is red, but there are also varieties that bear yellow, green, russet (reddish brown), and striped fruit. Apple wood is dense, hard, and heavy. Because the tree has a short trunk and many branches, it is not used for lumber. Apple wood is sometimes used for carved ornaments and in furniture.

Apple trees generally do not begin to blossom and bear fruit until they are 5 to 8 years old. They reach maximum production at about 20 years, and commercial orchards are generally replaced when the trees are 35 to 40 years old. Although the trees would live much longer, the fruit produced on old trees is generally smaller and poorer in appearance.

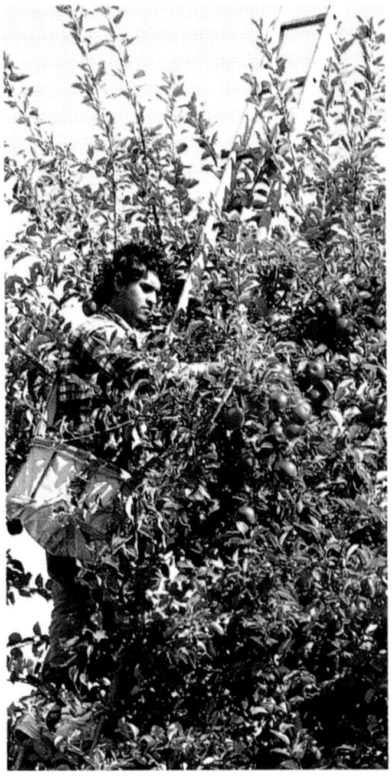

Apple pickers climb tall ladders to harvest ripe fruit from the treetops. Small batches of apples gathered from the trees are transferred to large containers on the ground.

MANAGING THE APPLE ORCHARD

A great deal of intensive work must be performed in the commercial orchard. Each year the trees should be pruned, usually in late winter. This prevents them from becoming too tall or too thick and bushy and results in larger, better-colored fruit. The trees must be fertilized to make them grow and bear properly. Nearly all apple orchards need nitrogen fertilizers. Other elements such as potassium and magnesium may also be needed.

Frost, insect pests, and fungus diseases are among the most serious problems the apple grower faces. Apple trees must be tended carefully throughout the growing season. Apple trees bloom in the early spring, bearing delicate, fragrant blossoms that range in color from white to dark pink. Because open apple blossoms die when the temperature drops a few degrees below freezing, crops are often lost when late frosts occur. Commercial orchards generally are planted on slopes or high ground to reduce this danger, since cold air tends to sink. Commercial growers may use heaters or spray the blossoms with water on cold nights. Water cools much more slowly than air, so a soaking with water can help keep blossoms from freezing even when the air temperature falls below 32°F (0°C). While the tree is in bloom, many growers bring in beehives so that there are plenty of bees to pollinate the flowers. The apple, which develops from the ovary of the flower, is the end product of the pollination.

Many insects attack the apple tree. One of the worst is the codling moth, which lays its eggs on or near the fruit. When the eggs hatch, the larvae bore into the fruit and a "wormy" apple results. Other insect pests include scales, aphids, and mites. Diseases caused by fungi and bacteria, such as apple scab and fire blight, can also infect the flowers, fruit, and leaves of the apple tree.

Repeated spraying is often necessary to keep the fruit free of insects and diseases. Be-

See For Yourself

How to Sprout Apple Seeds

1. The first step in sprouting apple seeds is to collect some seeds from an apple. Once you have gathered the seeds, soak them in warm water overnight.

2. There are a number of different kinds of containers you can plant your seeds in—flowerpots, milk cartons, or coffee cans. The container should have one or more drain holes in the bottom and be able to hold about 1 quart (0.9 liter) of moist soil. To prepare the container, place small stones or pebbles in the bottom and fill it to the top with soil. Water the soil and press it down farther into the pot. Make sure there is a dish underneath to catch the water that drains out of the soil. To plant the seeds, place a few seeds on top of the soil about 1 inch (2.5 centimeters) apart. Then push them about 1/2 inch (1 centimeter) under the surface with your finger. Gently pat the soil down and water it again.

3. The pot should be kept in a warm, sunny place. Be sure to check the soil every day and keep it moist. It may take several weeks for you to see tiny green stalks and leaves pop through the soil. Once the seedlings have grown about 2 inches (5 centimeters), each one can be put in its own container to grow. As they grow, the seedlings will continue to need sunshine and water. You also can fertilize them with houseplant fertilizer. Eventually the apple plants will need to be replanted in larger containers. Check with your local garden center to find out at what intervals they will need to be transplanted.

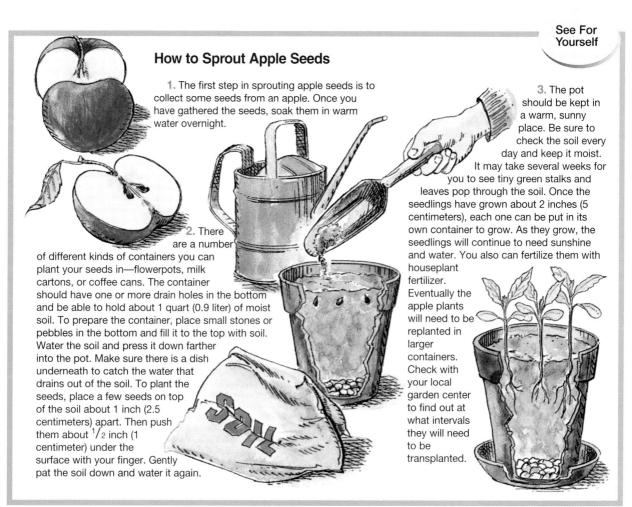

cause pests appear at different times of the growing season, some areas may need 12 to 14 sprays per year. New varieties of apples are now being bred that are resistant to certain kinds of insects and fungi. This reduces the need to spray so often.

PROPAGATION

Apple trees do not "breed true." That is, new trees grown from seeds do not produce fruit that is exactly like the parent tree's. Trees for orchards are therefore produced by budding or grafting. A bud or a short piece of a twig taken from a parent tree is inserted into a young seedling tree so that it grows and forms the top of the new tree. The new tree will then produce fruit exactly like that of the tree from which the bud was taken.

By budding or grafting onto certain kinds of roots, it is possible to produce trees that never become very large. Such trees are called dwarfs. Dwarf trees, besides being easier to spray, prune, and collect harvests from, usually bear fruit earlier. They are popular for home planting and are used commercially on a large scale. Since dwarf trees can be planted close together, the yield of fruit is generally increased.

HARVESTING AND STORAGE

Some varieties of apples mature in midsummer and others ripen in late fall. However, most kinds are ready for picking in September and October. The fruit must be picked by hand and carefully handled, for it will spoil if it is bruised.

The fruit is firm when picked but softens quite rapidly after picking unless it is put into cold storage. Apples will soften as much in one day at room temperature as they will in ten days in cold storage. Therefore, if the fruit is to be held for winter or early spring markets, it must be put into cold storage immediately and cooled rapidly to about 32°F (0°C). It is held there until time for marketing.

Apples will keep even better in controlled atmosphere storage: The fruit is put into airtight rooms, where the oxygen level is reduced from the 20 percent present in normal air to about 3 percent. At the same time the carbon dioxide content, normally present only in trace amounts, is increased to 2 to 5 percent. (The exact figures vary for different kinds of apples.) This slows down the life processes of the fruit cells and helps keep the fruit from softening. The controlled atmosphere, together with low temperatures, can keep some kinds of apples in good eating condition for up to a year. But very few apples are stored longer than nine months.

LEADING APPLE AREAS

Apples can be grown in nearly all the temperate areas of the world. Most kinds can endure winter temperatures down to –20°F (–29°C), and some kinds can withstand temperatures as low as –40°F (–40°C).

In the United States, the leading producers of apples are Washington, New York, Michigan, Pennsylvania, and California. In Canada, British Columbia, Ontario, and Nova Scotia lead. Other major apple-producing countries around the world include China, Italy, France, Poland, Turkey, Argentina, Chile, Spain, Russia, Germany, and Japan. Apples do not thrive in the tropics, for the trees require a period of cold and dormancy to grow and bear fruit properly.

Reviewed by ELIZABETH KAPLAN
Author, *Biology Bulletin Monthly*

See also FRUITGROWING.

APPLIQUÉ. See NEEDLECRAFT.

WONDER QUESTION

Who was Johnny Appleseed?

The legend of Johnny Appleseed is based on the life of a real person—John Chapman. Born in Massachusetts in 1774, Chapman became a wandering pioneer who made it his mission to spread the apple tree across the country. Throughout the early 1800's, he provided seeds and seedlings for settlers heading westward. He traveled thousands of miles, planting single trees and starting orchards in West Virginia, Ohio, and Indiana. Many apple orchards throughout the Midwest owe their start directly or indirectly to Chapman. Chapman's kindness to animals, love of nature, skill with herbal remedies, and love of the Bible inspired the stories behind the legend of the eccentric but much-loved character, Johnny Appleseed.

AQUINAS, SAINT THOMAS (1225?–1274)

Saint Thomas Aquinas was one of the great religious thinkers of the Middle Ages and had a powerful influence on his time. Yet as a student, his silence in the classroom and his heavy build earned him the nickname of "dumb ox." His fellow students and professors soon discovered, however, that he was not stupid, but rather a deeply intelligent, although humble, man.

Thomas was born in the castle of Rocca Secca near Aquino, Italy. His father was Landulf, Count of Aquino, and his mother was Theodora, Countess of Teano. When he was 5, he was taken to the abbey of Monte Cassino for his schooling. He stayed there until he was about 13 and later studied at the University of Naples for five years.

When Thomas was about 19, he joined the Dominican order, despite the objections of his family. He was eventually allowed to complete his studies in Paris and Cologne under Albertus Magnus, the most renowned professor in the Dominican order.

Thomas himself became famous as a teacher, winning admiration for the clarity and power of his thought. He developed a philosophy that combined Christian beliefs with the teachings of the Greek philosopher Aristotle.

About 1266, Thomas began writing his most famous work, the *Summa theologica*, a scientifically arranged study of theological teaching and Christian philosophy. He never finished it. On December 6, 1273, he experienced such a spiritual revelation at Mass that he could write no more. The revelation made all his writings appear as nothing to him.

Thomas died on March 7, 1274. He was made a saint in 1323 and a doctor of the Church in 1567. His writings fill 20 thick volumes and include much on Aristotle.

HARRY J. CARGAS
Editor, *The Queen's Work*

AQUINO, CORAZON C. (1933–)

Corazon Aquino served as president of the Philippines from 1986 to 1992. The widow of Benigno Aquino, Jr., a Filipino political leader assassinated by his opponents, she led a "People Power" revolution, in 1986, to overthrow President Ferdinand Marcos, who had held office since 1965. She campaigned to replace his government with one based on "justice, morality, decency, freedom, and democracy."

Corazon Cojuangco Aquino was born in Manila on January 25, 1933, the fourth of the six children of Jose Cojuangco and Demetria Sumulong. As a young woman she attended the College of Mount St. Vincent in the United States. In 1953 she married Aquino, a journalist and politician. They had five children.

Benigno Aquino rose quickly in politics. When in 1973 it appeared that he could win the Philippine presidential election, Marcos declared martial law and put his popular rival in jail. In 1980, Aquino was permitted to go to the United States for medical treatment, and Corazon accompanied him.

In 1983, Benigno Aquino was shot and killed when he returned to the Philippines. Many people held Marcos responsible for his death. Corazon, a housewife with no political experience, returned to the Philippines to lead the opposition movement against Marcos in her husband's place. In 1985, more than 1 million Filipinos petitioned her to run for president.

Marcos appeared to be the victor in the election of February 7, 1986, but many charged that he had tried to fix the election. With the support of the military, Aquino led the people in a campaign of nonviolent resistance and forced Marcos to resign.

When Aquino took office, she established a newly elected Congress, called for a new constitution, freed Marcos' political prisoners, and restored the people's civil liberties.

Aquino's new administration faced many serious challenges: Rivals tried to overthrow her government, and Communist rebels threatened the new democracy. Aquino was also faced with reviving the economy, which had suffered after years of corruption under Marcos. In 1992, Aquino was succeeded as president by her former defense minister, Fidel V. Ramos.

ISABELO T. CRISOSTOMO
Author, *Cory: Profile of a President*

ARABIA. See MIDDLE EAST; SAUDI ARABIA.

ARABIAN NIGHTS

Hundreds of years ago professional storytellers in India and the Middle East made up the stories now known as *The Arabian Nights*. Later on, groups of these stories were put together. One group was translated from Arabic to French by Antoine Galland in the early 1700's. His *Mille et une nuits*, or *A Thousand and One Nights*, introduced these Oriental tales to the Western world.

All the collections have one thing in common. A heroine, Scheherazade, tells the different stories. She recites the tales for a very good reason: She must save her life.

Scheherazade was married to Sultan Shahriyar, who had killed his first wife when she was unfaithful to him and then all his later wives in revenge against women. Scheherazade did not want to suffer the same fate. On her wedding night she began to tell her husband a story and stopped just before she reached the end. The Sultan allowed her to live another day in order to hear the end of her tale. The next night she finished the story and began another one even more fascinating than the first. Again she stopped before the ending, gaining another day of life.

And so it went, for a thousand and one nights. Finally the Sultan realized that Scheherazade was a good and faithful wife, and the couple lived happily ever after.

The stories supposedly told by Scheherazade are understandably popular. Nowhere does one find treasures more magnificent, beasts more fabulous, or magicians more cunning. Excerpts from two of the best-known stories follow.

In **Aladdin and the Wonderful Lamp** a magician poses as a long-lost uncle to the unsuspecting Aladdin. The two leave the city and arrive at a secret place, where the magician kindles a fire, throws powder on it, and says some magic words. The earth trembles and opens, revealing a flat stone with a brass ring to raise it by. With the help of more magic words, the stone is moved and steps appear.

"Go down," said the magician. "At the foot of those steps you will find an open door leading into three large halls. Tuck up your gown and go through them without touching anything, or you will die instantly. These halls lead into a garden of fine fruit trees. Walk on till you come to a niche in a terrace where stands a lighted lamp. Pour out the oil it contains and bring it to me." He drew a ring from his finger and gave it to Aladdin, bidding him prosper.

Aladdin found everything as the magician had said, gathered some fruit off the trees and, having got the lamp, arrived at the mouth of the cave.

The magician cried out in a great hurry, "Make haste and give me the lamp." This Aladdin refused to do until he was out of the cave. The magician flew into a terrible passion, and throwing some more powder on the fire, he said something, and the stone rolled back into its place.

The magician left Persia forever, which plainly showed that he was no uncle of Aladdin's, but a cunning sorcerer who had read in his magic books of a wonderful lamp which would make him the most powerful man in the world. Though he alone knew where to find it, he could only receive it from the hand of another. He had picked out the foolish Aladdin for this purpose, intending to get the lamp and kill him afterward.

For two days Aladdin remained in the dark, crying and lamenting. At last he clasped his hands in prayer, and in so doing rubbed the

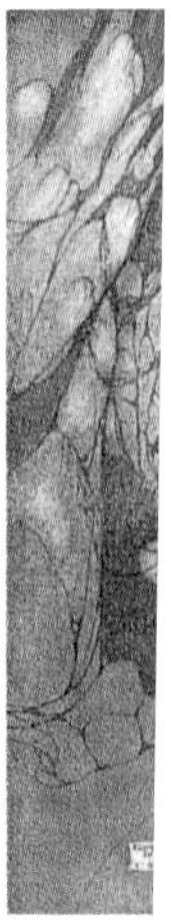

away from the site, leaving it unoccupied until other people settled there some time later. When people lived steadily on a site, one layer is much like the next. Only small changes occur in the shape of pots and tools and in ways of doing things. But in the second case, there may be very great changes from one layer to another. The great changes are caused in part by the longer amount of time between the building of layers, during which people may have discovered different ways of doing things. The changes are also caused by the fact that a different group of people may have moved in, with their own way of doing things. An early group of people may not have known how to bake pottery to make it hard. A later group may have made very good pottery. Thus, small and orderly changes tell an archaeologist that there probably was continual life on the site. But a sharp change in the way things were made or done indicates that there was a gap in living on the site or a strong influence from some outside group. Archaeologists may have to dig through several layers of artifacts before they find any from the period being studied.

Choosing the Most Promising Area To Dig

Once a site is found, archaeologists must decide where to dig. Excavating the whole site would be expensive and unnecessary—the archaeologist can get a good idea of what life at the site was like by carefully choosing places to dig. First, test pits are dug. The test pits may reveal the size of the settlement, interesting buildings, and areas that did not have many houses at all. One deep cut may also be dug into the side of the mound. The side cut shows approximately how many layers are in the site.

How the Digging Is Done

When the test diggings have shown the most promising areas, the archaeologists are finally ready to begin a full excavation. With surveying equipment, they divide the site into smaller units, marked on the ground with stakes and rope. The archaeological team then digs away the soil in the chosen areas. The excavators search the dirt carefully for clues. Sometimes the dirt is sifted through screens to recover small bits of bone and stone. Sometimes it is put in big tanks of water to recover plant material such as small seeds. After all the artifacts and other materials are carefully collected, the dirt goes to a dumping area near the site.

When the soil has been removed from the top of the digging area, the archaeologist begins to see the different layers. Sometimes they are natural layers of mud or clay left by heavy rainstorms. Sometimes they are cultural layers (layers deposited by people)—broken pots left on a floor inside a house, for example. The archaeologist tries to find and uncover each layer.

If archaeologists are excavating a site with many buildings, they may see the outlines of the lower parts of walls. Some walls made of packed mud or mud brick are very much like earth, but they are slightly harder. Careful excavators can feel this extra hardness. Using special small, light picks, they can usually tell by feel what they are hitting—a pot, a skeleton, or the wall of a house. Excavators also have trowels, brushes, and other special tools. They may use very delicate tools, like those of a dentist, to excavate a burial or uncover pieces of burned wood.

If the archaeologist is excavating a settlement with houses, the area inside each room is carefully cleared down to the floor. When this job is done, a whole house may appear or, if the area is large enough, several houses.

When the houses have been cleared, the archaeologist records the layout of the settlement. The staff photographer takes pictures of the houses, perhaps from a high photographic tower. Someone else draws an architect's plan of the houses, which includes careful measurements. Such records must be accurate and complete because once they are made, the walls and floors are cleared away, and this layer is gone forever.

The whole site may be excavated in this way. A representative sample of each layer is carefully dug out and recorded. If time and funds allow, the earliest layer may be reached.

Each of these great archaeological discoveries casts light on an ancient culture. The remains of the city of Machu Picchu, Peru (*opposite page*), hint at the extent of Inca civilization. The ruins of Pompeii (*above right*) reveal details of everyday life in the ancient world. Bakery millstones can be seen in this photograph. The discovery of King Minos' palace at Knossos, Crete (*below right*), provided evidence that Greek legends about Minos were based on fact.

A head of a man—called Tollund man after the site in Denmark where it was found—was preserved in a peat bog. Analysis of pollen grains dated it as 2,000 years old.

perature. The magnetic particles in the floor of an ancient clay oven, for example, are fixed in the pattern that they had when the oven was first fired. By comparing this pattern with the known shifts in the magnetic field, scientists can calculate the age of the oven.

Using these various methods of dating, an archaeologist can get a fairly good idea of when a certain people lived. And scientists are working on still other ways to help the archaeologist date materials.

Archaeology, as a scientific profession, is relatively new. There are many problems in human development and human history yet to be solved. But the methods by which they can be solved are becoming more scientific.

Even so, each problem that is solved often raises new problems, and new ways of solving these need to be found. The radioactive-dating methods were not even dreamed of until the late 1940's. And it is probably that future years will bring other new and important changes for archaeology.

▶THE TRAINING OF AN ARCHAEOLOGIST

As archaeology changed from a hobby and a picnic sport to a scientific profession, more and more importance was laid on the training of archaeologists. In particular, an archaeologist must know how to define an important problem. An archaeologist does not go out and dig just anywhere for the pleasure of discovering artifacts. There must be a purpose—an archaeological problem that needs solving.

It takes many years of hard work to become an archaeologist. The training may begin as early as high school. Young people who are interested in archaeology should realize that both a college and a graduate degree are needed. It may be necessary to read and speak several foreign languages, depending on where the students wish to work. Many important reports are published in French and German. Future archaeologists start one of these modern languages in high school. Latin and Greek are necessary if one is interested in classical archaeology. Students may also learn to type, and they may study mechanical drawing.

It is best to start with a well-planned liberal arts course. Students should learn to express ideas in writing easily and well, so that they can prepare clear and interesting reports. Particularly useful for students of prehistory are courses in geology, geography, botany, and zoology, to help them understand the natural environment. They need at least one year each of chemistry, physics, and biology so that they can understand methods for dating and the information the natural scientists will supply later on. In college, the students continue with foreign languages. They may try to learn the languages of the countries in which they are interested so that they can talk with workers there. They may also study ancient scripts such as Sumerian, Akkadian, or Egyptian, if they are interested in these periods. Finally, the archaeologist should have a good foundation in anthropology, history, and art history.

The Archaeologist Studies Anthropology

A study of anthropology helps the archaeologist to see how other peoples are different from ourselves. What is important to us may not matter at all to someone who lives in a different part of the world or has a different cultural background. Certainly the objects used in daily life in Arctic regions differ from those used near the equator. Archaeologists must realize that people today, like those in the past, do not necessarily all think and behave in exactly the same ways. Through anthropology, students of archaeology can learn how different peoples live and feel and think about things. This is very important because archaeologists depend heavily on their understanding of the present when they reconstruct how people lived in the past.

The Archaeologist Studies Recorded History

In the same way, an archaeology student needs to learn as much history as possible, especially the history of the chosen area. Usually we think of history as coming from the writings of an earlier people themselves. But these people probably did not describe everything they did, or how they lived, or what their countryside looked like. In ancient times—before the invention of paper, pens, and pencils—writing was difficult. Only a few scribes wrote what the priests and kings told them to write. These people may have left us only descriptions of battles, hymns to the gods, and a few business letters. Nevertheless, interesting ideas did slip in, and the archaeology student must learn as much as possible about these writings. From what the people wrote of themselves (and from the knowledge gained through anthropological training), the archaeologist forms a better picture of their lives. These writings may also show what the ancient people took to be good or bad, useful or worthless. All this helps archaeologists understand what they find.

A diver lifts an amphora (vase) from the wreck of a Roman ship that sank some 1,900 years ago off the coast of Turkey. Such discoveries add to recorded history.

For example, archaeologists study Greek writings about foreign trade carried on by ships. Now suppose that an archaeologist, working as a skin diver, discovers the underwater wreck of a Greek trading ship. The description of the ship can be recorded as well as the type of cargo. The direction in which the ship was headed may also be deduced. Such discoveries add much to Greek history as recorded by the Greeks themselves.

The Archaeologist Studies Art History

Most of the artifacts an archaeologist finds are everyday tools and objects. But occasionally, some art objects may be found—things that must have had special value to the people who owned them. This is why the study of art history is important. Greek vases and Egyptian tomb paintings, for example, often have wonderful pictures of Greeks or Egyptians doing all kinds of things. In the pictures, they are actually using many of the tools, weapons, and objects that the archaeologist finds.

Rounding Out the Training

On their own, archaeology students can learn much by trying to do things as ancient people did. For example, they can try to chip stone into a rough tool and use it to cut a small log. Or they can take wet clay, make a simple pottery bowl, dry it in the sun, and then bake it over an open fire.

During the summers, archaeology students will probably work on one of the digs that most large universities run. This gives them a chance to learn how digging should be done.

After college the archaeology student usually enters a graduate school to work toward a doctoral degree.

Archaeologists may find work with a university or museum after graduate school. After working with older and more experienced archaeologists on their digs, the young archaeologists may eventually have digs of their own and their own students working with them.

ROBERT J. BRAIDWOOD
GRETEL BRAIDWOOD MANASEK
University of Chicago

Reviewed by MAGGIE DITTEMORE
University of Chicago

See also ANTHROPOLOGY; PREHISTORIC PEOPLE; RADIOACTIVE DATING.

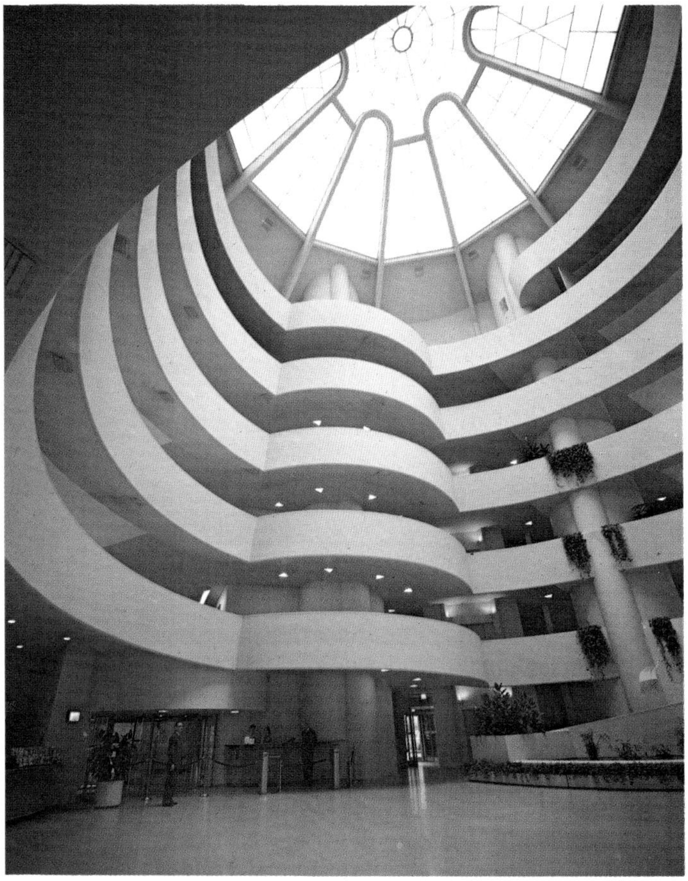

After 1950, concrete continued to be used to create bold, expressive forms. Above: Frank Lloyd Wright used a revolutionary spiral design for the Guggenheim Museum, in New York City. Below: Y-shaped buttresses support the thin concrete vault of the Little Sports Palace in Rome, designed by Pier Luigi Nervi.

Bear Run, Pennsylvania—designed by Frank Lloyd Wright—is one of the most impressive of the houses designed in this period. Called Fallingwater, the house extends out from a rocky slope and hovers over a waterfall. Its reinforced concrete platforms, or "trays," form a dramatic composition that blends architecture and landscape.

After World War II

After World War II almost the whole world came to embrace the international style. The masters of the style, each moving in a new direction, took the lead in the immediate postwar years. Gradually, architecture began to move away from the boxlike severity of the years between the wars.

Le Corbusier expanded the use of reinforced concrete. In the late 1940's, he designed the Unité d'Habitation, a big apartment building in the French city of Marseilles. He put the building on thick concrete legs instead of thin stilts. Le Corbusier made the entire structure of reinforced concrete, which was left rough to show the marks of the wooden boards that held the wet concrete in place while it dried. On top of the building he placed large concrete ventilators that look like big pieces of sculpture.

But the building that really pointed the way to new concrete forms was Le Corbusier's chapel Notre Dame du Haut at Ronchamp, France, designed in 1950. Its boldly curved

roof is made of a thin shell of reinforced concrete held together by concrete struts, like the metal struts inside the wing of an airplane.

In the early 1950's, Mies van der Rohe designed the Lake Shore Drive Apartments in Chicago. These were among the first big rectangular steel and glass towers. They set a standard for the steel and glass commercial buildings that came to dominate the skylines of cities all over the world during the great postwar building boom. A notable example is the 38-story Seagram Building (1956–58) in New York City, designed by Mies and Philip Johnson (1906–).The metal parts on the outside are bronze, and the glass is tinted gray. Because Mies was looking for general solutions that would fit almost any problem, he could design apartment and office buildings that are almost identical.

The Finnish architect Alvar Aalto (1898–1976) came to occupy a very important place in world architecture in the postwar years. Aalto moved away from the international style to develop buildings in which people would feel at ease. His buildings featured open, sky-lit spaces, curving lines, and natural materials such as pale birch wood. The best known of his designs were civic buildings constructed in Europe. Aalto's buildings often have unexpected shapes. These shapes reflect the purposes that the buildings serve. Baker Hall (1948), a dormitory at the Massachusetts Insti-

Above left: Alvar Aalto designed this stadium for the Polytechnial School in Otaniemi, Finland. Above right: Citicorp, in New York City, has energy-efficient double-glass and aluminum walls. Its slanted roof, which faces south, was designed to hold solar collectors.

ARCTIC

Surrounding the geographic North Pole is a deep, ice-covered ocean, the Arctic Ocean, which is bordered by the northern parts of the continents of North America, Europe, and Asia. This is the Arctic region. Here, periods of continuous daylight alternate with periods of continuous darkness for days to months at a time. Cold pervades the region. But unlike the southern polar region of Antarctica, which has no native human inhabitants, people have lived in the Arctic for thousands of years. Because of its location, its geography and climate, and its wealth of natural resources, the Arctic region is politically, scientifically, and economically important.

The boundaries of the Arctic region are measured in different ways. The Arctic is sometimes defined as the area north of the Arctic Circle, an imaginary line around the globe at 66° 30′ (66 degrees, 30 minutes) north latitude. Other ways of determining the region's limits include the tree line, the most northerly point at which trees will grow, and the extent of polar sea ice and of permafrost, or land that is permanently frozen.

GEOGRAPHY OF THE ARCTIC

The Arctic is dominated by the Arctic Ocean and a vast treeless plain called the tundra. Unlike Antarctica, which is an ice-covered continent, much of the Arctic consists of ice-covered seas.

The Arctic Ocean. The Arctic Ocean, which covers approximately 5 million square miles (13 million square kilometers), makes up about two thirds of the Arctic region. East of the island of Greenland, the Arctic Ocean connects with the Atlantic Ocean. West of Greenland the Arctic flows through Baffin Bay, Davis Strait, and shallow outlets between the northern islands of Canada. The Arctic Ocean joins the Pacific Ocean through the Bering Strait, which separates Alaska from what is now northeastern Russia (formerly part of the Soviet Union). Although its extent varies from summer to winter, ice covers the Arctic Ocean year-round, making navigation frequently difficult and dangerous. From October to June the ocean is completely ice-locked, and only submarines can cross it completely by passing under the ice. At times, icebergs, which break off the ends of glaciers, float south into the shipping lanes of the Atlantic Ocean and create hazards to navigation.

The Tundra. The tundra begins on the land area of the Arctic about where the tree line ends. When the summer sun melts the ice and snow cover, the Arctic tundra becomes a rich green living carpet of plants. But beneath a thin layer of soil lies ground that is always frozen. This permafrost forms whenever the temperature of the ground stays continuously

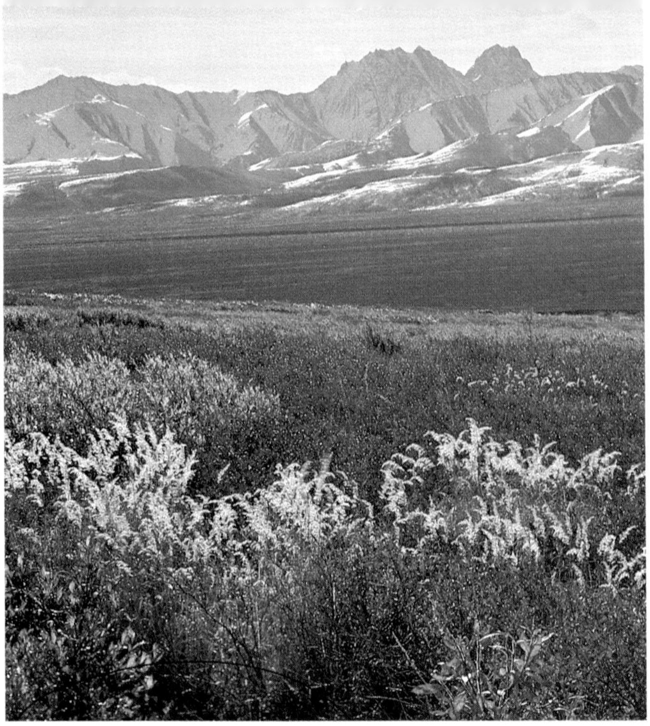

The frozen Arctic Ocean (*far left*) dominates the Arctic region. The people of the Arctic have survived in their harsh environment by developing simple but useful equipment, such as the dog sled (*center*). When the summer sun melts its covering of ice, the tundra (*left*) blooms with plants and flowers.

below the freezing point, 32°F (0°C), for two or more years. Most of Greenland, much of Alaska, half of Canada, and parts of Scandinavia, Russia, Mongolia, and Northeast China are affected by permafrost. Its greatest recorded thickness—4,900 feet (1,500 meters)—is in Siberia.

Not all of the land in the Arctic region is covered by the tundra. Rocky, mountainous islands quite different from the flat tundra are scattered around the Arctic Ocean. Greenland is almost completely covered by a large ice sheet, with mountains ringing its coast.

See the article TUNDRA in Volume T.

CLIMATE

Although low temperatures are the major characteristic of its climate, the Arctic is not always bitterly cold. During the summer, temperatures over the Arctic Ocean are near 32°F (0° C). Winter temperatures, however, average between –22° and –31° F (–30° to –35°C). It is colder over land areas, especially over the Greenland ice sheet, where a winter temperature of –87° F (–66° C) has been recorded. In the subarctic, a region just south of the Arctic, winters are colder but summers are warmer. The lowest temperature ever recorded here was –90° F (about –68° C) in Siberia.

Like Antarctica, the Arctic receives little precipitation (rain or snow). The generally low temperatures limit the amount of moisture that can be held in the air and consequently the amount of snow that will fall. In March and April, when the greatest amount of snow covers the ground, the average depth in the Arctic is 8 to 20 inches (20 to 50 centimeters). The snow remains for 10 months of the year.

The Arctic year is divided into a long, cold winter and a short, cool summer. Because of its geographical position, the Arctic is marked by long periods of darkness and daylight. At the North Pole the sun remains above the horizon for six months at a time and below the horizon for another six months, giving in effect six months of daylight, followed by six months of darkness.

PLANT AND ANIMAL LIFE

Plants and animals are plentiful in the Arctic. More than 90 types of plants grow not far from the North Pole. Closer to the Arctic Circle scientists have identified 450 varieties of plant life. In summer the tundra is covered with flowers and various plants, including lichens, mosses, grasses, and small shrubs. More than a hundred types of birds live in the Arctic. Musk oxen, caribou, reindeer, foxes, wolves, bears (including polar bears), valuable fur-bearing animals such as ermine and sable, snowshoe hares, and lemmings (small, mouse-like animals) thrive in the region. The Arctic waters are rich in fish, including salmon, cod, and rockfish, and many kinds of seals, whales, and porpoises.

ARCTIC PEOPLES

The Arctic has been populated by small groups of people for thousands of years. They probably followed herds of reindeer, caribou, and musk oxen from Central Asia northward and eventually adapted to the environment. One of the most widespread peoples in the region are the Inuit, formerly called Eskimos. They are found in Alaska and Canada, as well as Greenland and Siberia. Indians also live in some areas of the North American Arctic region, especially in Alaska and Canada. For more information on the Inuit, see the article INUIT in Volume I.

same time, its economic policies caused unemployment without curbing the inflation they were intended to remedy. The government collapsed after its ill-conceived 1982 invasion of the Falkland Islands and Argentina's defeat by Britain in the war that followed.

Raúl Alfonsín, the Radical Party candidate, won the 1983 presidential election. He restored political democracy but was unable to halt inflation. He was succeeded as president in 1989 by Carlos Saúl Menem. Although Menem was the candidate of the Peronistas, his political program ran strongly against the traditional positions of his party. He introduced severe austerity measures, which dramatically reduced inflation, and adopted free-market reforms. After the legislature passed a constitutional amendment making it possible for him to run for re-election, he won a second term as president in 1995. But in 1999, Menem was defeated by the Radical Party candidate, Fernando de la Ruá.

Carlos Saúl Menem was president of Argentina from 1989 to 1999.

To avoid the collapse of the nation's banking system, de la Ruá placed limits on banking withdrawals. But this extreme measure caused widespread riots, and de la Ruá was forced to resign. Congress appointed Eduardo Alberto Duhalde president until new elections could be scheduled. Meanwhile, Argentina's economic depression continued as the unemployment rate soared to more than 20 percent.

Robert L. Carmin
Ball State University

Reviewed by Robert J. Alexander
Author, *Juan Domingo Perón: A History*

ARIKARA. See Indians, American (On the Prairies and Plains).

ARISTOTLE (384–322 B.C.)

Aristotle was one of the most important citizens of ancient Greece. He never won a battle or held a political office, but he was a famous teacher and one of the greatest philosophers who ever lived.

Only a few facts are known about Aristotle's childhood. We know he was born in Stagira, a town in northeastern Greece, in 384 B.C. His father was court physician to Amyntas II, king of Macedonia, who was the grandfather of Alexander the Great. It seems likely that Aristotle learned something about science from his father.

ARISTOTLE THE STUDENT

When Aristotle was about 17 years old, he went to study in Athens, an important Greek city-state. He became a pupil of the finest teacher of his day, the philosopher Plato.

The young men at Plato's Academy spent several years studying mathematics, astronomy, and government. When they had mastered these studies, they were asked to think about some of the problems at the heart of Greek philosophy: What is happiness? What is the good life? Plato's method of teaching stressed learning how to think clearly.

Aristotle studied under Plato for about twenty years. He was an excellent student. Plato called him "the mind of the school." When Plato died in 347 B.C., Aristotle left the academy and began to develop his own method of teaching.

There was nothing, it seemed, that did not capture Aristotle's interest. How does the mind work? How can we learn what is true and what is false? What is the best form of government? These were only a few of the problems with which Aristotle wrestled.

Aristotle tried to find the answers by observing the world around him. He believed that every event had a logical explanation and that conclusions could be formed from investigation and observation.

ARISTOTLE THE TEACHER

Aristotle's fame was great by the time he left Plato's school. When King Philip II of

Macedonia was looking for a teacher for his son Alexander, he chose Aristotle. It is hard to know how much Aristotle influenced Alexander the Great, but we do know that teacher and pupil became lifelong friends.

After Alexander became king of Macedonia, Aristotle returned to Athens. In 335 B.C., with money contributed by Alexander, Aristotle opened a school called the Lyceum. It is from Aristotle's school that the high schools of France and Italy take their names: *lycée* and *liceo*.

Many subjects were taught at the Lyceum, and there were various aids for learning. Aristotle collected the first large library of ancient times. There was a museum of natural science, a garden, and a zoo.

After the morning classes Aristotle lectured to anyone who wanted to listen while he paced up and down the covered walk (called the *peripatos*) outside of his school. For this reason those who accepted his philosophy were called **Peripatetics**.

Aristotle lived and taught in a world that was very different from the one that Plato knew. In Plato's time every citizen understood the part he was to play in the life of Athens and his responsibility to the government of the city-state.

While Aristotle taught at the Lyceum, Athens lost its independence and became only a small part of Alexander's empire. As citizens of an empire, the Athenians had to adjust to a new form of government.

Aristotle urged each man to seek his own place in the world by learning how to live a good and useful life. A happy life could be found by living according to the "golden mean." By the "golden mean" Aristotle meant the middle way between two extremes. For example, he said the middle way "between cowardice and rashness is courage."

Twelve years after Aristotle opened his school, word reached Athens that Alexander the Great had died. At that time the people of Athens were divided into two groups—those who had learned to live under Alexander's rule and those who still hated it. When news of his death came, Alexander's enemies turned on his friends. Aristotle was prosecuted, like Socrates, for offending against religion. Rather than stand trial, he left Athens. He died soon afterward, in 322 B.C.

Copied from a Greek original, this Roman statue of Aristotle is in the Spada Gallery, Rome.

ARISTOTLE'S BOOKS

Of the 400 books that Aristotle is said to have written, only a small number have come down to us. But they are remarkable books. Aristotle's works seem to have been an encyclopedia of Greek learning of the 4th century B.C. There are books on astronomy, physics, poetry, zoology, oratory, biology, logic, politics, government, and ethics.

Aristotle's books were studied after his death. They were used as textbooks in the great centers of learning: Alexandria, Rome, and the universities of medieval Europe. No other man influenced the thinking of so many people for so long.

Even today Aristotle's books are an important influence because we still use his method of investigation and observation. He classified and related all the knowledge of his time about the world. Modern scientists have found that many of the observations he made more than 2,000 years ago are correct. He showed us that every statement should be supported by evidence. Aristotle's key to knowledge was logic and his basis for knowledge was fact.

Reviewed by GILBERT HIGHET
Author, *The Classical Tradition*

ARITHMETIC

When you keep score in a game, when you count your change, when you compare baseball batting averages or try to balance your checkbook, you are doing arithmetic. Arithmetic is a way of working with numbers. It is a branch of the science of mathematics.

▶NUMBERS AND NUMERALS

People begin using arithmetic when they are very young. Their earliest experiences, however, have to do with quantity, not with counting. Just by looking at them, a child too young to count knows that four toy blocks are more than two.

We think that early human beings had the same kind of **number sense**. They could not count, but they could tell by looking that they had as much of something as they needed or wanted.

As time passed, people needed more than just a sense of quantity. They needed to keep an actual count of things, such as how many sheep were in a herd or how many days it took to travel to a good hunting spot. People probably first used pebbles or their fingers to count. Then, at some unknown time thousands of years ago, numbers were discovered and number names were invented. These numbers are called **counting numbers**, which we also call **natural numbers**. Much later, zero was added to the counting numbers. Zero and the counting numbers together make up **whole numbers**.

People in ancient civilizations also developed different numeral systems, or ways of writing numbers. The Babylonians, Egyptians, Greeks, and Romans all had their own systems. These early systems were complicated and difficult to use. Then around 750 A.D., a new numeral system came into use. It was developed by the Hindus in India and was spread to other parts of the world by Arab traders. The Hindu-Arabic system includes only ten symbols. These symbols are 1, 2, 3, 4, 5, 6, 7, 8, 9, 0. The ten symbols of the Hindu-Arabic system can be used to write any number, no matter how great or how small, and they are still used today.

▶OPERATIONS WITH WHOLE NUMBERS

Once people had numbers and written numerals, they were able to work with them in different ways to solve everyday problems. They discovered that numbers can be used to perform four basic processes, or operations. These operations are addition, subtraction, multiplication, and division. Each operation is represented by a sign: + for addition, − for subtraction, × for multiplication, and ÷ for division. Another way to show division is with this sign: $\overline{)\quad}$

It is important to know when to use the different operations and how they relate to one another.

Addition

Addition is a way of operating with numbers. It is the process of putting groups of like things together to find their total number or quantity. Counting forward is another way of finding a total number or quantity. Addition is faster than counting forward except when you are counting forward only a few numbers.

In order to add, you must know the basic addition facts. An addition fact is made up of two parts: two numbers from 0 to 9 that are to be added, called the **addends**, and their **sum**, or the answer to the addition.

4 + 6 = 10　　**9 + 8 = 17**

In the first example, 4 and 6 are the addends and 10 is the sum. In the second example, 9 and 8 are the addends and 17 is the sum.

ADDITION TABLE

This table can be used to find the basic addition facts, the sums of any two numbers from 0 to 9. To find the sum of 3 + 4, for example, find the 3 in the far left-hand column. Go along that row until you get to the column with 4 at the top. You will be on the 7, and 3 + 4 = 7.

+	0	1	2	3	4	5	6	7	8	9
0	0	1	2	3	4	5	6	7	8	9
1	1	2	3	4	5	6	7	8	9	10
2	2	3	4	5	6	7	8	9	10	11
3	3	4	5	6	7	8	9	10	11	12
4	4	5	6	7	8	9	10	11	12	13
5	5	6	7	8	9	10	11	12	13	14
6	6	7	8	9	10	11	12	13	14	15
7	7	8	9	10	11	12	13	14	15	16
8	8	9	10	11	12	13	14	15	16	17
9	9	10	11	12	13	14	15	16	17	18

This next problem lets us compare addition and counting forward. Suppose you cycled 8 miles on Monday and 5 miles on Tuesday. You could find out how many miles you cycled in all by counting forward or by adding.

Counting forward	or	Addition	
8 9, 10, 11, 12, 13		8	addend
		+ 5	addend
		13	sum

When you are adding large numbers, it can be helpful to look at the numbers as if they were written in columns. Each column has a value and each one can be added in a sequence from right to left. The column names are **ones**, **tens**, **hundreds**, and **thousands**. If you were adding 1,268 and 2,159 this way, you would begin in the ones column to the far right and move left to the tens column, then to the hundreds column, and then to the thousands column.

Thousands	Hundreds	Tens	Ones
1	2	6	8
2	1	5	9
3	4	2	7

The greatest number you may write in any column is 9. What do you do when the sum in a column is more than 9?

In this example, the sum in the ones column is 17. You may think of 17 as 1 ten and 7 ones. Write 7 in the ones column and add the 1 ten to the other numbers in the tens column.

Add in the tens column: $1 + 6 + 5 = 12$. Think of the 12 tens as 1 one hundred and 2 tens. Write 2 in the tens column. Add 1 to the hundreds column.

Adding in the hundreds column, you get $1 + 2 + 1 = 4$. Write 4 in the hundreds column.

Adding in the thousands column, you get $1 + 2 = 3$. Write 3 in the thousands column. The sum is 3,427.

Subtraction

Subtraction is the opposite of addition. One kind of subtraction involves finding the number of objects remaining in a group after some of the objects have been removed. Counting back is another way of finding the number remaining. Subtraction is usually quicker than counting back. To use the subtraction method you must know the basic subtraction facts. For every addition fact there is a related subtraction fact. They can each be written down in two ways, which are shown below.

Addition Fact	Related Subtraction Fact
6 + 5 = 11	11 - 5 = 6
6	11
+ 5	- 5
11	6

When you use subtraction, you subtract from a number called the **minuend**. The number you subtract is the **subtrahend**, and the answer you get is the **difference**.

Suppose you had 15 postage stamps and you used 7 of them to mail letters. You could find out how many stamps you had left by counting back or by subtracting.

Counting back	or	Subtracting	
15 14, 13, 12, 11, 10, 9, 8		15	minuend
		- 7	subtrahend
		8	difference

When you are subtracting large numbers from one another, the idea of place value can be useful. For example, if you are subtracting 35 from 92, you could think of the numbers in this way:

92	=	9 tens and 2 ones
-35	=	3 tens and 5 ones

The 9 tens and 2 ones can also be written as 8 tens and 12 ones. All you do is change 1 ten into ten ones. This gives the following:

92	=	8 tens and 12 ones	minuend
-35	=	3 tens and 5 ones	subtrahend
57	or	5 tens and 7 ones	difference

You can check your results by adding the difference to the subtrahend. You should get the minuend.

Subtraction is also used to compare numbers. Suppose you compare the temperatures of a 19-degree day and a 35-degree day to find out how much warmer the 35-degree day is. You may think, What number added to 19 will make 35? You can do it this way:

19° to 20°	=	1 degree
20° to 30°	=	10 degrees
30° to 35°	=	5 degrees
		16 degrees

On paper, the operation of subtraction will provide a quick answer:

35 degrees
-19 degrees
16 degrees

x	1	2	3	4	5	6	7	8	9
1	1	2	3	4	5	6	7	8	9
2	2	4	6	8	10	12	14	16	18
3	3	6	9	12	15	18	21	24	27
4	4	8	12	16	20	24	28	32	36
5	5	10	15	20	25	30	35	40	45
6	6	12	18	24	30	36	42	48	54
7	7	14	21	28	35	42	49	56	63
8	8	16	24	32	40	48	56	64	72
9	9	18	27	36	45	54	63	72	81

MULTIPLICATION TABLE
This table can be used to find the basic multiplication facts, the products of any two numbers from 1 to 9. To find the product of 6 x 4, for example, find the 6 in the far left-hand column. Go along that row until you get to the column with 4 at the top. You will be on the 24, and 6 x 4 = 24.

Multiplication

Multiplication is a quick way of adding equal, or same-size, groups.

To do multiplication, you must know the basic multiplication facts. For example, you know that $3 \times 8 = 24$ is a basic multiplication fact. Read it as "3 eights equal 24." In a multiplication fact, the number being multiplied by another number is the **multiplicand**; the number used to multiply by is the **multiplier**; and the answer is called the **product**.

Suppose a pack of bubble gum contains 5 pieces; how many pieces are there in 3 packs? You can get the answer by adding equal groups or by multiplying.

Adding equal groups or **Multiplying**

$$\begin{array}{r} 5 \\ 5 \\ +\ 5 \\ \hline 15 \end{array} \qquad \begin{array}{rl} 5 & \textbf{multiplicand} \\ \times\ 3 & \textbf{multiplier} \\ \hline 15 & \textbf{product} \end{array}$$

Division

Division is the process of splitting a group into equal parts or groups. It is the opposite of multiplication.

To divide you must know some basic division facts. For example, $6 \div 3 = 2$ is a division fact. In a division fact, the number to be divided by another number is called the **dividend**; the number it is to be divided by is called the **divisor**; and the answer is called the **quotient**.

Suppose you have 24 soccer cards. If you can put 8 cards on each page in a photo album, how many pages will you fill? To find the number of pages, you can subtract equal groups or you can divide.

Subtracting equal groups of 8 or **Dividing by 8**

$$\begin{array}{r} 24 \\ -\ 8 \\ \hline 16 \\ -\ 8 \\ \hline 8 \\ -\ 8 \\ \hline \end{array} \qquad \textbf{divisor } 8\overline{)24}\ \textbf{dividend} \quad (3\ \textbf{quotient})$$

You can check your division results easily by using multiplication. Multiplying the quotient and the divisor should give you the dividend: $3 \times 8 = 24$.

In division you cannot divide by zero. For example, you may know that 24 cannot be divided into groups of 0.

Operations with Fractions and Decimals

You have been reading about addition, subtraction, multiplication, and division. All of the numbers in the examples you have seen are whole numbers. There are other kinds of numbers as well.

Fractions are numbers that represent parts of a whole, for example, one-half ($\frac{1}{2}$) of an apple, two-thirds ($\frac{2}{3}$) of a mile, or one-fourth ($\frac{1}{4}$) of a dozen.

Another way to express fractions is with decimals. For example, the fraction $\frac{1}{4}$ is 0.25 when written as a decimal.

Working with fractions and decimals is more complicated than working with whole numbers. However, the basic operations of arithmetic—addition, subtraction, multiplication, and division—can be applied to fractions and decimals.

▶USING CALCULATORS AND COMPUTERS

The operations of arithmetic can be performed by different methods. Calculations that may not have to be exact can often be done in your head. Sometimes using a pencil and paper helps you get an accurate answer quickly. When you need to do many operations or work with large numbers, calculators and computers are the most efficient way to work.

USING ESTIMATION STRATEGIES

Estimation is an important step in the process of using arithmetic operations to solve number problems. Estimation involves using clues to make a sensible guess, or estimate. For example, an estimate tells *about* how many of something there may be, or *about* how large or small something may be. You have probably used estimation many times. For example, you may have estimated how long it might take you to get to school, or how much money you might need to buy an outfit for a special occasion, or how much wood you might need to make a bench. Until you actually made the trip or priced the purchases or made specific measurements, you really did not have an accurate amount. But an estimate gave you a good enough picture to begin with. All estimation strategies involve using numbers that are easy to work with mentally.

Here are several strategies:

1. One way to estimate is to **round** each number to the nearest ten, hundred, thousand, and so on, before you add, subtract, multiply, or divide. For example, to estimate the sum of 48 + 11 + 42 + 29, round each number to the nearest ten, then add.

   48 ⟶ 50
   11 ⟶ 10
   42 ⟶ 40
   + 29 ⟶ + 30

2. **Clustering** is used when several numbers cluster near a single number. In the example 43 + 59 + 61 + 38, two of the numbers cluster near, or are close to, 40 and two are close to 60. The sum can thus be estimated as 2 × 40 plus 2 × 60, or 200.
3. **Comparison** also involves rounding numbers. In the example 47 + 39, comparison tells you that both numbers are less than 50. Therefore, their sum is less than 100.
4. Estimation can also be done by using front digits. This is called **front-end** estimation. To estimate 7,556 − 1,321, subtract the thousands: 7,000 − 1,000 = 6,000. Then adjust the answer: 556 is more than 321, so the answer must be *more than* 6,000.
5. A way to estimate quotients is to use **compatible numbers**, or numbers that are close to each other. For example, to divide 355 by 12, think of a number close to 355 that can be divided by 12 evenly: 360 ÷ 12 = 30.
6. In situations that require an exact answer, estimation is also helpful. Whether you compute with pencil and paper or with a calculator, it is a good idea to use estimation to check yourself and determine whether a particular answer to a problem is reasonable. If it is not, you should do the computation again.

Using estimation when you work with numbers will help you avoid careless errors.

Imagine, for example, that a recycling center collected 5,937 glass bottles, 7,365 plastic bottles, 3,779 metal cans, and 6,985 paper bags. What method would you use to calculate the total number of containers collected? It might be difficult to get an exact answer by performing this addition mentally. An accurate answer could be found in a reasonable amount of time using a pencil and paper. But a calculator would probably be the best choice to provide the correct answer quickly. Although computers can be used to perform lightning-fast calculations, they are best used for complex tasks, including organizing and displaying mathematical data, setting up graphs, and exploring mathematical patterns.

LYNN FLETCHER
Educational Writer

Reviewed by WILLIAM M. FITZGERALD
Professor of Mathematics
Michigan State University

See also DECIMAL SYSTEM; FRACTIONS AND DECIMALS; MATHEMATICS; NUMBERS AND NUMBER SYSTEMS; NUMERALS AND NUMERATION SYSTEMS.

ARIZONA

In 1736, a Yaqui Indian prospector discovered chunks of silver lying on the ground near a Spanish mining camp known as Arizonac. Pima Indians, who call themselves the O'odham ("the People"), lived in the region where the silver was found. Some scholars believe that the name Arizonac came from two Pima Indian words, ali *and* shonak, *which mean "small springs." Because many of the first European miners and settlers were Basques from northern Spain, other scholars think that the word derived from the Basque term* arritza onac *("valuable rocky places"). Whatever its origin, the name Arizonac eventually became Arizona.*

State flag

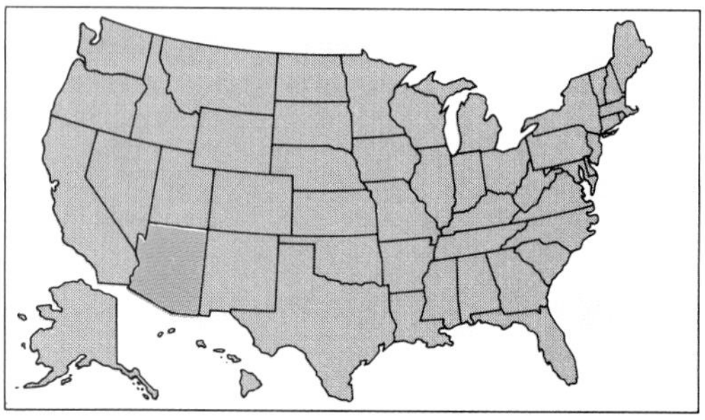

Because of its dry climate and sparse vegetation, Arizona is a state where the geological bones of the earth—its mountains, canyons, mesas, and valleys—dominate the landscape. In the north, the Grand Canyon of the Colorado River cuts a mile deep through rock formations that are nearly 2 billion years old. In the south, the Sonoran Desert stretches in a series of broad valleys and rugged mountain ranges deep into Mexico.

Arizona has one of the most varied natural environments in North America. North of Tucson, the Mount Lemmon Highway climbs 6,000 feet (1,830 meters) up the Santa Catalina Mountains, passing in the course of a one-hour drive through desert, oak woodland, pinyon pine and juniper woodland, pine forest, and spruce-fir forest.

Arizona's cultural environment is just as varied. Arizona is part of the American Southwest, a region where many different groups encountered one another and fought for control of water and land. The descendants of those peoples continue to live there today. Arizona is a state in which many different ways of life coexist.

It is also a place where the past exists side by side with the present. People have inhabited Arizona for at least 11,000 years; today it is one of the fastest growing states in the nation. Despite its well-deserved reputation for wide-open spaces, Arizona is one of the most urban states as well, with most of its population residing in metropolitan areas.

Most Arizonans work in those cities at manufacturing jobs or in service industries. Tourism is particularly important to the economy. Arizona's spectacular national forests, parks, and monuments draw millions of visitors to the state each year.

These national treasures underscore the importance of the federal government in Arizona. The U.S. government controls some 70 percent of Arizona's land. It also funded the giant water projects that provide much of the state with water for drinking, irrigation, and hydroelectric power.

LAND

Arizona is the sixth largest state in area. The Colorado River forms the western boundary with California. The northeastern corner touches the borders of Utah, New Mexico, and Colorado to form the Four Corners—the only point in the United States where four states meet. Although Arizona is landlocked, its southwestern border with the Mexican state of Sonora is less than 50 miles (80 kilometers) from the Pacific Ocean's Gulf of California.

Land Regions

Three major land regions—the Colorado Plateau, the Central Mountain Zone, and the Basin and Range—cross the state, giving Arizona great biological diversity as well as stunning natural beauty.

Clockwise from left: **A desert vista includes ancient rock inscriptions left by Arizona's first inhabitants. Sightseers descend into the Grand Canyon—the state's best-known landmark—on mules. Native American culture is a vital part of modern Arizona life.**

State flower:
Saguaro cactus blossom

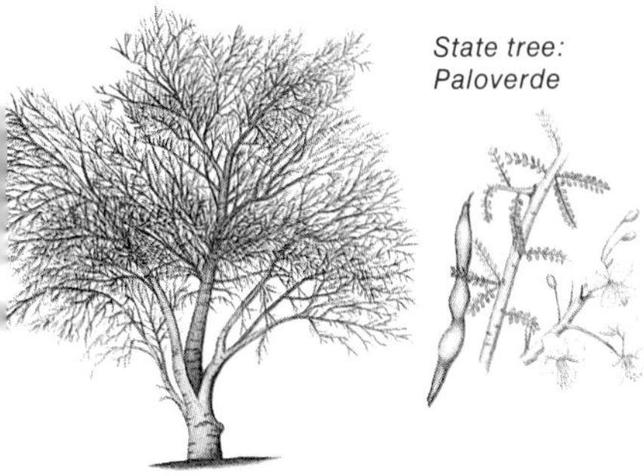

State tree:
Paloverde

FACTS AND FIGURES

Location: Southwestern United States; bordered on the north by Utah, on the east by New Mexico, on the south by Mexico, and on the west by Nevada and California.

Area: 114,006 sq mi (295,276 km^2); rank, 6th.

Population: 5,130,632 (2000 census); rank, 20th.

Elevation: *Highest*—12,633 ft (3,853 m) at Humphreys Peak; *lowest*—70 ft (21 m) along the Colorado River in Yuma County.

Capital: Phoenix.

Statehood: February 14, 1912; 48th state.

State Motto: *Ditat Deus* ("God enriches").

State Song: "Arizona."

Nickname: Grand Canyon State.

Abbreviations: AZ; Ariz.

State bird:
Cactus wren

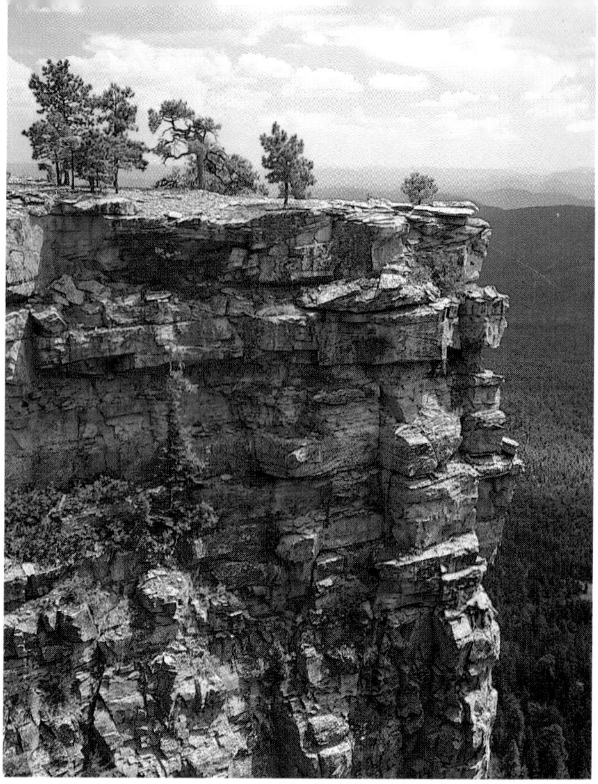

The Colorado Plateau is Arizona's largest land region. Stretching into Utah, Colorado, and New Mexico, it extends across Arizona from the northwest to the southeast. The Colorado River and its tributaries have carved steep gorges into the layers of sedimentary rock that form the region. The deepest and best known of these gorges is the Grand Canyon. In between are high **mesas** (flat-topped hills), broken by volcanic craters and peaks.

The southern edge of the Colorado Plateau is the Mogollon Rim, which rises north of Prescott and runs south and east into New Mexico. With elevations of more than 7,000 feet (2,130 meters), it supports the largest stand of ponderosa pines in the world. The rest of the Colorado Plateau is lower and drier, with sparser vegetation. It includes the Painted Desert, famous for its barren rock landscapes, and Monument Valley, where spires of eroded rock tower over the high desert floor.

The Central Mountain Zone, below the Mogollon Rim, is an arc of mountain ranges that separates the Colorado Plateau from the Basin and Range. It is one of the wildest, most rugged regions of Arizona. Ranges such as the Bradshaws, Mazatzals, and Sierra Anchas cross northwestern and central Arizona. To the east are the White Mountains and the Blue Range. Much of Arizona's mineral wealth is concentrated in this region.

The Basin and Range, Arizona's third land region, extends across the western United States and Mexico. Most of Arizona's Basin and Range belongs to the Sonoran Desert, two-thirds of which lies in Mexico.

The Basin and Range is composed of isolated mountain ranges separated by broad, fertile valleys. As the region approaches Tucson, the valleys narrow and the mountains loom higher, reaching elevations of 8,000 to 12,000 feet (2,440 to 3,660 meters). Biologists call these high ranges **mountain islands**. By that they mean that the mountains contain plants and animals not found on the valley floors—the desert "oceans"—that surround them. Mountain islands occur throughout the state, but they are most distinctive in southeastern Arizona.

Above: **The Mogollon Rim forms the southern edge of the Colorado Plateau.** ***Below:*** **The San Francisco Peaks, north of Flagstaff, are the state's highest mountains.**

Rivers and Lakes

Although much of Arizona is desert country, rivers have shaped its landscape and its history. The Colorado River, the greatest river in the West, flows through or along Arizona's borders for nearly half its length. All other major rivers and streams in Arizona empty their waters into the Colorado.

The major tributary of the Colorado in northern Arizona is the Little Colorado River, which arises in the White Mountains. The Gila River and its major tributary, the Salt River, drain central and southern Arizona. They also provide most of the water that irrigates Arizona farms. The Verde River in central Arizona and the Santa Cruz and San Pedro rivers in southern Arizona also flow into the Gila system.

All of Arizona's major rivers have been dammed to provide water for irrigation and hydroelectric power. Those dams have created artificial lakes where Arizonans fish, boat, and water-ski. Major dams along the Colorado River include Hoover Dam, which formed Lake Mead, and Glen Canyon Dam, which flooded magnificent Glen Canyon to create Lake Powell. Roosevelt Lake, Apache Lake, Canyon Lake, and Saguaro Lake are strung like beads along the Salt River.

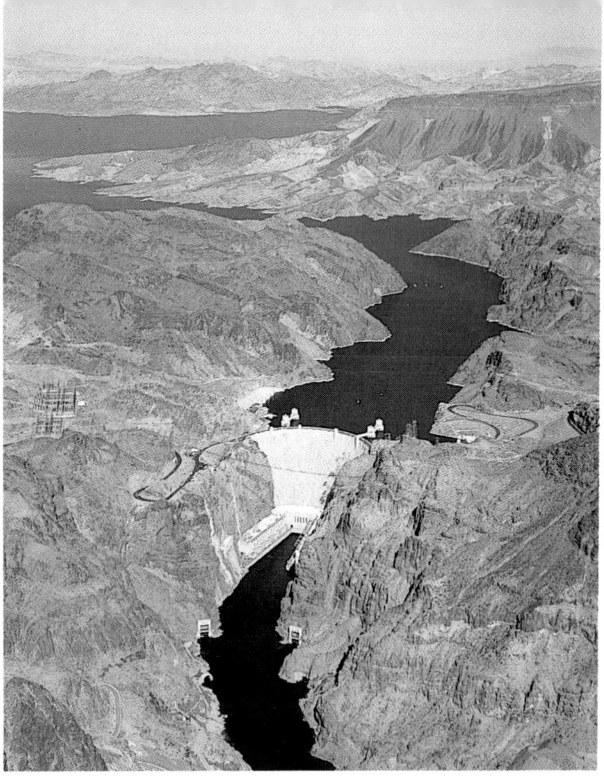

Hoover Dam, on the Colorado River between Arizona and Nevada, generates hydroelectric power and supplies water for agricultural and human use.

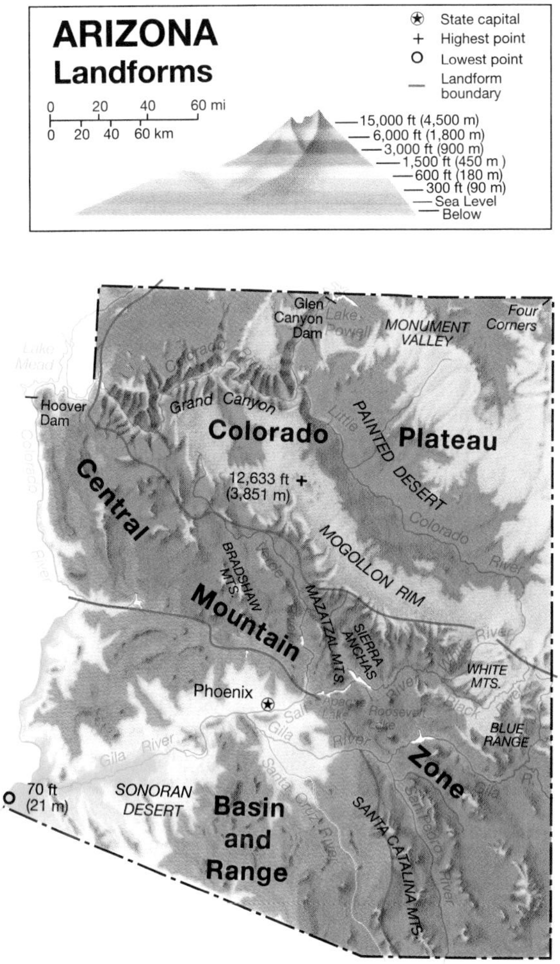

Climate

Most of Arizona has a very dry climate. Precipitation (rain and snow) varies throughout the state according to the elevation of the land. Lowland areas like Yuma in the southwest average less than 5 inches (127 millimeters) of rain a year. Rain or snow on the tallest mountain peaks may exceed 30 inches (762 millimeters).

Arizona's moisture arrives during two distinct rainy seasons. During July and August, summer thundershowers provide about two-thirds of the annual rain. Winter storms bring about one-third.

Much of Arizona is as hot as it is dry. Average temperatures for January range from 50°F (10°C) in the lowlands to 30°F (– 1°C) in the highlands. July temperatures average 90°F (32°C) in the lowlands and 65–75°F (18–24°C) in the mountains. Temperatures in the

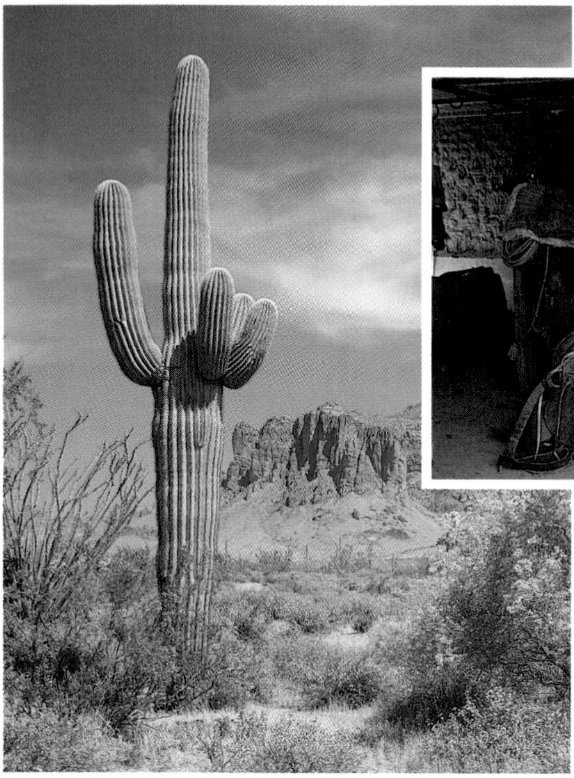

Far left: Plants, such as the saguaro cactus, that have adapted to the desert climate are a distinctive part of the Arizona landscape. *Near left:* The heritage of the Old West lives on in Arizonans such as this foreman of a ranch near Wilcox.

deserts occasionally reach 120°F (49°C) in summer. Many portions of the desert endure more than 100 days of 100°F (38°C) heat a year.

Because Arizona is so hot and dry, farming is impossible without irrigation. The average number of days without a killing frost ranges from 240 around Yuma to 100 days at higher elevations in northern Arizona.

Plant and Animal Life

Arizona's varied environments support many different species of plants and animals. Black bears and elk inhabit the Mogollon Rim and the high mountain country. Herds of pronghorn antelope dart across the grasslands while bighorn sheep clamber over the summits of desert mountain ranges. Coyotes, mountain lions, bobcats, and mule deer range from the deserts to the mountains.

Perhaps the most distinctive plants and animals are those that have adapted to the hot, dry climate of the desert. Cacti such as the giant saguaro and the thorny cholla have broad, shallow root systems that quickly suck up scarce moisture, which is stored in their spongy stems. The tiny kangaroo rat has specialized kidneys that enable it to extract moisture from seeds, so it does not need to drink.

Natural Resources

Arizona is rich in minerals, particularly silver, gold, and copper. Black Mesa in northern Arizona contains enormous deposits of coal. Forests of ponderosa pine and Douglas fir stretch across the Mogollon Rim, while broad valleys in central and southern Arizona have soils suitable for farming. The only limitation on agriculture is water.

Because there are no major rivers south of the Gila, southern Arizona obtains most of its water from aquifers (underground deposits of water). Until 1993, Tucson was the largest city in the United States that pumped all its water from below ground. Now the canals and pipelines of the Central Arizona Project bring water from the Colorado River 335 miles (540 kilometers) across the desert to Phoenix, Tucson, and the farmers of south central Arizona.

▶ PEOPLE

After 1940, Arizona transformed itself from a rural to an overwhelmingly urban state. On the eve of World War II, 499,261 people lived in Arizona. By the year 2000, Arizona's population had soared to more than 5 million. More than 85 percent of those people live in cities and towns.

Most Arizonans come from other places, particularly California and the Midwest. Arizona society is mobile: For every ten people who settle in Arizona, seven move away.

Native Americans, in contrast, have inhabited Arizona for thousands of years and today make up about 5 percent of Arizona's population. Most belong to the 14 major Native American groups that occupy Arizona—

the Navajos or Diné (the largest group), Hopis, Western Apaches, Yavapais, Hualapais, Havasupais, Quechans, Mojaves, Maricopas, Cocopahs, Akimel O'odham, Tohono O'odham (formerly called Papago), Yaquis, and Southern Paiutes. Some 70 percent of Native Americans live on the state's 22 reservations.

Hispanic Americans make up about 25 percent of the state's population. Most are recent immigrants from Mexico, particularly Sonora. Others come from families that have lived in Arizona for nine or ten generations.

Americans of European descent make up about 64 percent of Arizona's population. African Americans compose 3 percent, and about 2 percent of the state's residents are Asian Americans. All these relatively new arrivals join with American Indians and Mexican Americans to make Arizona one of the most multicultural states in the nation.

Authentic dances of old Mexico are performed at a festival in Sedona. Arizona shares many cultural traditions with Mexico, its neighbor to the south.

Education

The Arizona territorial legislature established the first public school system in 1871. There are three state universities. The University of Arizona in Tucson and the Arizona Territorial Normal School (now Arizona State University) in Tempe were founded in 1885. Northern Arizona University in Flagstaff was created in 1899.

Arizona also has numerous public community colleges, including Navajo Community College, which is run by the Navajo Nation. Private institutions include the University of Phoenix, in Phoenix; Prescott College, in Prescott; and the American Graduate School of International Management, in Glendale.

Libraries, Museums, and the Arts

Arizona has an active public library system, with bookmobiles and computers connecting rural communities with libraries in larger towns. The Arizona Historical Society, founded in 1884, operates its main museum in Tucson. Museums that focus on Arizona's Native American heritage include the Arizona State Museum of the University of Arizona in Tucson; the Museum of Northern Arizona in Flagstaff; and the Heard Museum in Phoenix.

Museums and botanical gardens devoted to the biological diversity of Arizona and the Sonoran Desert include the Arizona-Sonora Desert Museum west of Tucson, the Boyce Thompson Southwestern Arboretum near Superior, and the Desert Botanical Garden in Phoenix. The Phoenix and Tucson art museums contain important collections of Western, Mexican, and Native American art.

The Arizona Theater Company and other professional theater companies present plays in Tucson and Phoenix. Both Phoenix and Tucson have professional symphonies.

Arizona is internationally renowned for research in astronomy, anthropology, biology, and geology. One of the most important research institutions is the Desert Laboratory on

PEOPLE

Population: 5,130,632 (2000 census).

Density: 45 persons per sq mi (17 per km^2).

Distribution: 87% urban; 13% rural.

Largest Cities (2000 census):

Phoenix 1,321,045	Scottsdale 202,705
Tucson 486,699	Chandler 176,581
Mesa 396,375	Tempe 158,625
Glendale 218,812	Gilbert 109,697

Source: U.S. Bureau of the Census

Persons per sq mi	Persons per km^2
over 250	over 100
50-250	20-100
5-50	2-20
0-5	0-2

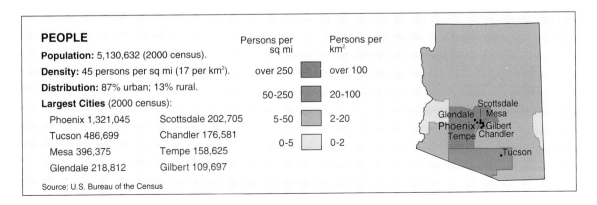

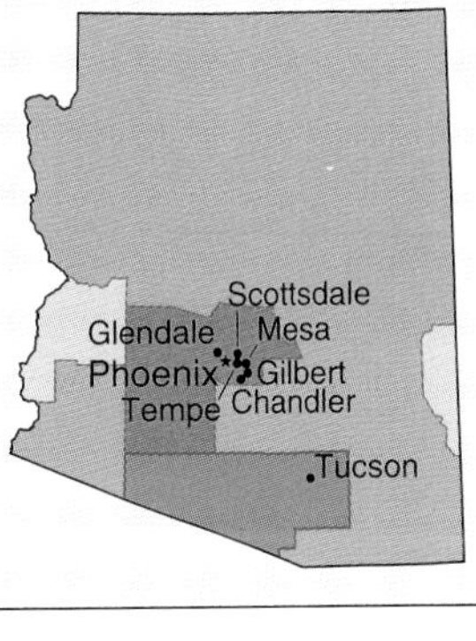

Above: Kitt Peak National Observatory, west of Tucson, is a world-renowned center of astronomical research. *Right:* Technicians inspect computer chips. Many Arizonans are employed in the electronics industry.

Tumamoc Hill in Tucson, where scientists have been studying the ecology of the Sonoran Desert for nearly a century. Another is the Kitt Peak National Observatory, west of Tucson.

ECONOMY

Before World War II, Arizona's economy was dominated by the so-called Three C's: copper, cattle, and cotton. Those industries remain important, but today most Arizonans work in the manufacturing or service sectors of the economy. More job growth was anticipated with the passage in 1994 of the North American Free Trade Agreement (NAFTA), which established a free-trade zone among Mexico, Canada, and the United States.

Services

More than 75 percent of Arizona's workers are engaged in service occupations. Many of these industries arose to serve the large numbers of tourists who visit the state each year. Businesses located along the Arizona-Sonora border rely heavily on customers from Mexico. Among the most important service industries are business, social, and personal services, such as banking, health care, and hotels and restaurants. Wholesale and retail trade are also important service activities.

Many Arizonans work for the local, state, or federal government, running public schools, administering federal and state lands, and managing Indian reservations and military installations. Other service industries are finance, insurance, and real estate and transportation, communicaton, and utilities.

Manufacturing

Manufacturing employs about 15 percent of Arizona's workforce. Leading products are machinery, transportation equipment, and electrical and electronic equipment.

Many manufacturing jobs are in the electronics and aerospace industries and rank high in terms of average annual salary. However,

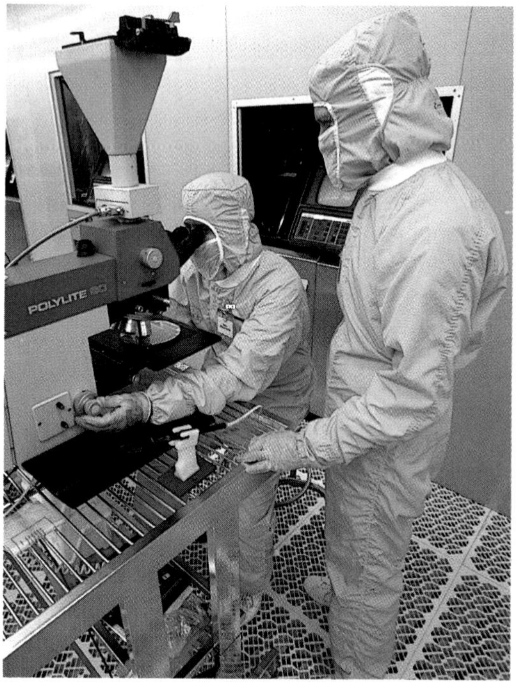

because many of these companies depend on government defense contracts, employment in manufacturing can be uneven. For example, the collapse of the Soviet Union and the end of the U.S.-Soviet arms race in the early 1990's led to layoffs in some Arizona electronics and aerospace companies. Nonetheless, the general trend in manufacturing seems to be expansion.

Mining and Construction

Mining, especially copper mining, was formerly the most important industry in Arizona. Today mining employs less than 1 percent of Arizona's workforce. The copper industry slumped in the 1980's, and although production rose again in the early 1990's, fewer miners were needed because of changes in technology.

A cattle drive on the Fort Apache Indian Reservation. Ranching, once a mainstay of the Arizona economy, remains an important industry in rural areas of the state.

Coal mining is restricted to Black Mesa in northern Arizona. On thousands of acres leased from the Navajo Nation and the Hopi tribe, coal is stripped from the ground with enormous draglines. Some of the coal fuels the Navajo Generating Station at Page. Mixed with water, the rest slides down a 274-mile (441-kilometer)-long pipeline to a power plant on the Colorado River in southern Utah.

Arizona's rapid growth has created employment opportunities in the construction industry. Federal projects such as the digging of irrigation canals also employ construction workers.

Agriculture and Forestry

Agriculture, ranching, and forestry remain important industries in rural Arizona. Arizona is a leading producer of cotton. Thousands of acres of alfalfa, wheat, vegetables, and citrus fruit are also cultivated. Although agriculture uses 80 to 85 percent of Arizona's water, it employs less than 3 percent of the state's workforce.

Ranching is a statewide industry, with most ranchers grazing their cattle and sheep on Arizona's public lands. About 40 percent of Arizona's total dollar value for agricultural production comes from livestock sales. The logging industry employs almost as many Arizonans as copper mining. Nearly all the timber is cut in northern Arizona, where most of the sawmills are located as well.

Transportation and Communication

Arizona is linked to the rest of North America by five interstate highways and two transcontinental railroads, the Santa Fe and Southern Pacific.

Two major international airports in Phoenix and Tucson connect Arizona to the nation and the world. More than 20 million people pass through Sky Harbor Airport in Phoenix each year. Because of its sunny skies, Arizona also has several major air bases, including Luke Air Force Base outside Phoenix and Davis-Monthan in Tucson.

All major Arizona cities have daily newspapers, and many rural communities have weekly newspapers. Radio and television stations, most originating from Phoenix and Tucson, broadcast throughout the state.

PRODUCTS AND INDUSTRIES

Manufacturing: Electrical and electronic equipment, transportation equipment, aerospace equipment, machinery.

Agriculture: Cattle, cotton, dairy products, lettuce, wheat, citrus fruit, sheep.

Minerals: Copper, silver, gold.

Services: Wholesale and retail trade; finance, insurance, and real estate; business, social, and personal services; transportation, communication, and utilities; government.

Percentage of Gross State Product* by Industry

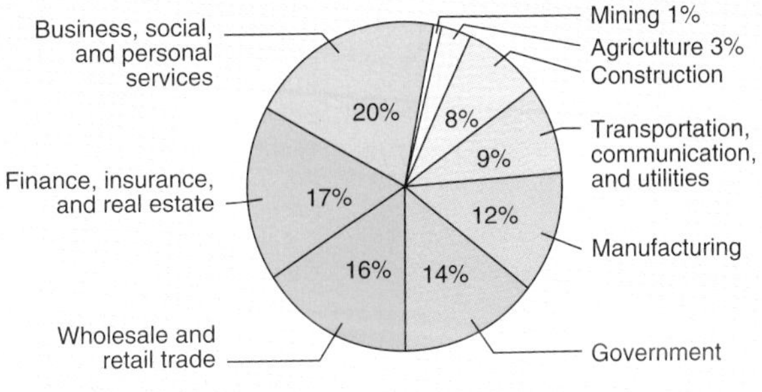

*Gross state product is the total value of goods and services produced in a year.

Source: U.S. Bureau of Economic Analysis

Places of Interest

Grand Canyon National Park

Mission San Xavier del Bac

Petrified Forest National Park

Betatakin Cliff Dwelling, Navajo National Monument

Many of Arizona's spectacular natural attractions are preserved as national forests, parks, and monuments. Some of the most outstanding are included in the descriptions below.

Canyon de Chelly National Monument, on the Navajo Nation in northeastern Arizona, is a sandstone canyon shaped like the talon of a hawk. At Spider Rock, a great sandstone spire, the cliffs rise nearly 1,000 feet (305 meters) above the canyon floor. Canyon de Chelly contains Anasazi Indian ruins built at the base of cliffs and in caves. The two most spectacular ruins are White House and Antelope House. Navajo (Diné) Indians farm small plots and graze their herds of sheep and cattle within the canyon.

Grand Canyon National Park is perhaps the most famous national park in the world. Set aside as a forest reserve in 1893 and a national park in 1919, the Grand Canyon attracts millions of tourists each year. An article on the Grand Canyon can be found in Volume G.

Kitt Peak National Observatory, on the Tohono O'odham Reservation, is a world-renowned center of astronomical observation and research.

London Bridge, in Lake Havasu City, is a historic stone bridge originally built in London, England, that was taken down and reassembled in Arizona. It spans an inlet of the Colorado River.

Mission San Xavier del Bac, south of Tucson, was founded as a Jesuit mission among the Pima O'odham Indians by Padre Eusebio Francisco Kino in 1700. The church itself, built by Franciscans in the late 1700's, is a magnificent example of baroque architecture and art. San Xavier continues to be used as a place of worship by the O'odham of the San Xavier Reservation.

Navajo National Monument, in northern Arizona, contains some of the most spectacular Anasazi cliff dwellings in the Southwest. Cliff dwellings such as Keet Seel and Betatakin appear to be timeless extensions of the sandstone cliffs to which they cling; in fact, anthropologists believe they were built, occupied, and abandoned between A.D.1267 and 1300.

Petrified Forest National Park, east of Holbrook, preserves prehistoric trees that turned to rock millions of years ago. The fallen trees and logs are scattered over thousands of acres. The park includes a portion of the **Painted Desert**, a barren area whose rock formations are tinted in shades of red, blue, and purple.

Roosevelt Dam, on the Salt River east of Phoenix, is the foundation of modern Arizona. Completed in 1911 by the National Reclamation Service, the dam controlled flooding along the Salt. It also provided the irrigation water and hydroelectric power to turn the Salt River Valley into one of the largest agricultural oases in the Southwest and Phoenix into the largest metropolitan center between California and Texas.

Saguaro National Park consists of two units east and west of Tucson. Both protect dense stands of giant saguaro cactus in the Tucson Mountains and the foothills of the Rincon Mountains. Tohono O'odham (Papago Indians) are still allowed to harvest saguaro fruit in the park in the early summer.

San Pedro Riparian Conservation District, along the San Pedro River in southeastern Arizona, was set aside by the federal Bureau of Land Management to preserve one of the last stretches of natural river habitat in Arizona. It protects great forests of cottonwoods and many species of birds and animals.

Tombstone, in Cochise County, became a mining boomtown after silver was found in the area in the 1870's. It is the site of the O.K. Corral, where Wyatt Earp, Doc Holliday, and other gunfighters took part in a famous shootout.

State Areas. Arizona maintains numerous state parks that preserve its natural beauty and its historical heritage. For more information, contact the Arizona State Parks Office, 800 W. Washington, Suite 415, Phoenix, Arizona 85007.

Above: The state capitol in Phoenix. *Below left:* The capital since 1912, Phoenix is also Arizona's largest city and a center of commerce and industry.

CITIES

Arizona has two major metropolitan areas. The largest is Phoenix and its satellites of Mesa, Glendale, Tempe, and Scottsdale. The other is the Tucson metropolitan area.

Phoenix is Arizona's capital and largest city. It became the territorial capital in 1889 and the state capital in 1912. Today it is a center of commerce and industry. Sun City, one of the first planned retirement communities in the United States, is part of the Phoenix metropolitan area. An article on Phoenix appears in Volume P.

Tucson, Arizona's second largest city, is located on the Santa Cruz River in the south central part of the state. Its name comes from a Pima Indian phrase meaning "the spring at the foot of the black mountain." Tucson was founded by the Spanish in 1775. It was the territorial capital from 1867 to 1877. An article on Tucson appears in Volume T.

Mesa, Arizona's third largest city, was founded by Mormon settlers in 1878. Originally an agricultural center, Mesa now anchors the rapidly urbanizing eastern portion of the Salt River Valley known as the East Valley.

Glendale began as an agricultural community promoted by canal-company developers in the late 1800's. Today it is the key city in the northwestern portion of the Phoenix metropolitan area. The American Graduate School of International Management is located there.

Tempe was known as Hayden's Ferry when it was founded in 1872 at a crossing on the Salt River. Like other cities in the Salt River Valley, its agricultural origins have largely given way to urban and industrial growth. Arizona State University is located there.

Scottsdale, located east of Phoenix, was founded in 1896 by Winfield Scott, a former army chaplain. Today the city, which calls itself "The West's Most Western Town," has many popular resorts and is a center of Western and Native American art markets.

Yuma, on the Colorado River in the southwestern portion of the state, is the center of a thriving agricultural area that includes the Wellton-Mohawk Valley along the lower Gila River. Thousands of tourists winter in the Yuma area each year.

GOVERNMENT

The state constitution was drafted in 1910 and approved by the people in 1911.

The governor heads the executive branch of the state government. The legislative branch is composed of a senate and a house of representatives. The judicial branch includes a supreme court of five justices.

Elected boards of supervisors administer Arizona's 15 counties. Most cities have city managers and city councils as well as mayors.

GOVERNMENT

State Government
Governor: 4-year term
State senators: 30; 2-year terms
State representatives: 60; 2-year terms
Number of counties: 15

Federal Government
U.S. senators: 2
U.S. representatives: 8
Number of electoral votes: 10

For the name of the current governor, see STATE GOVERNMENTS in Volume S. For the names of current U.S. senators and representatives, see UNITED STATES, CONGRESS OF THE in Volume U-V.

▶ HISTORY

People have occupied Arizona for at least 11,000 years. Early peoples survived by gathering wild plant foods and hunting game. Farming began about 1000 B.C. in well-watered areas such as the Tucson Basin.

Beginning about A.D. 200, Arizona's three major pre-European cultures developed. The Anasazi inhabited the Colorado Plateau, where they built cliff dwellings and large pueblos. The Mogollon occupied the highlands of eastern Arizona and western New Mexico. The Hohokam lived in central and southern Arizona. Along the Salt and Gila rivers, the Hohokam created the largest pre-European system of irrigation canals in North America.

Spanish Exploration and Settlement

The first European to enter Arizona was Fray Marcos de Niza, a Franciscan missionary. In 1539, the Spanish government sent him to search for the legendary Seven Cities of Cíbola, which were supposedly made of gold. A year later, a much larger expedition led by Francisco Vásquez de Coronado investigated de Niza's claims that he found the Seven Cities among the Zuni Indians of northwestern New Mexico. Those claims proved false, and Spain lost interest in Arizona until the late 1600's. Between 1687 and his death in 1711, Jesuit missionary Eusebio Francisco Kino established missions in northern Sonora and southern Arizona.

The arrival of the Europeans changed Indian life in Arizona in both good ways and bad. Old World diseases, such as smallpox and measles, killed thousands of Native Americans. But the Europeans also introduced horses, cattle, and sheep as well as crops, such as wheat, that could be grown in the winter.

Some Indians, such as the Pimas, became reluctant allies of the Spaniards. But others, particularly the Apaches, resisted the Spaniards and raided their settlements for horses and cattle. Because of Indian resistance, Spanish Arizona was confined to the valley of the Santa Cruz river. The first major Spanish settlement was Tubac, founded as a **presidio** (military garrison) in 1752. In 1775, the Spaniards transferred the presidio to Tucson.

Mexican Arizona

When Mexico won its independence from Spain in 1821, Arizona became part of the new republic of Mexico. The Mexican government awarded nine large land grants to Mexican ranchers in southern Arizona. However, by the 1840's the ranchers had been driven from the land by the Apaches.

In 1846, war broke out between Mexico and the United States. The Treaty of Guadalupe Hidalgo in 1848 ended the war and gave to the United States the territory of New Mexico, which included present-day Arizona north of the Gila River. Six years later, in 1854, Mexico sold southern Arizona to the United States under the Gadsden Purchase.

INDEX TO ARIZONA MAP

Akchin Indian Reservation		C4
Apache Junction	(Pinal)	D4
Apache Nat'l. Forest		F4
Avondale	(Maricopa)	C4
Benson	(Cochise)	E6
Bisbee	(Cochise)	F6
Buckeye	(Maricopa)	C4
Bullhead City	(Mohave)	A2
Cabeza Prieta Nat'l. Wildlife Refuge		F1
Camp Verde	(Yavapai)	D3
Canyon De Chelly Nat'l. Monument		F1
Carefree	(Maricopa)	D4
Casa Grande	(Pinal)	D5
Cave Creek	(Maricopa)	C4
Chandler	(Maricopa)	D4
Chino Valley	(Yavapai)	C3
Cibola Nat'l. Wildlife Refuge		A4
Clarkdale	(Yavapai)	C3
Clifton •	(Greenlee)	F4
Coconino Nat'l. Forest		D3
Colorado	(Mohave)	B1
Colorado River Indian Reservation		A3
Coolidge	(Pinal)	D5
Coronado Nat'l. Forest		E5,E6,F6
Cottonwood	(Yavapai)	D5
Douglas	(Cochise)	F6
Eagar	(Apache)	F3
El Mirage	(Maricopa)	C4
Eloy	(Pinal)	D5
Flagstaff •	(Coconino)	D2
Florence •	(Pinal)	D4
Fort Apache Indian Reservation		E4
Fort Mojave Indian Reservation		A3
Fredonia	(Coconino)	C1
Gila Bend	(Maricopa)	C5
Gila Bend Indian Reservation		B4
Gila River Indian Reservation		D4
Gilbert	(Maricopa)	D4
Glendale	(Maricopa)	C4
Globe •	(Gila)	E4
Grand Canyon Nat'l. Park		B1
Guadalupe	(Maricopa)	C4
Havasu Nat'l. Wildlife Refuge		A3
Havasupai Indian Reservation		C1
Holbrook	(Navajo)	E3
Hopi Indian Reservation		E2
Holbrook •	(Cleburne)	E3
Huachuca	(Cochise)	E6
Hualapai Indian Reservation		B2
Imperial Nat'l. Wildlife Refuge		A5
Kaibab Indian Reservation		C1
Kaibab Nat'l. Forest		C1
Kearny	(Pinal)	D4
Kingman •	(Mohave)	B2
Kofa Nat'l. Wildlife Refuge		B4
Lake Havasu City •	(Mohave)	A3
Lake Mead Nat'l. Rec. Area		A1
Mammoth	(Pinal)	E5
Marana	(Pima)	D5
Mesa	(Maricopa)	D4
Miami	(Gila)	E4
Navajo (Dine') Indian Reservation		D1
Navajo Nat'l. Mon.		E1
Nogales •	(Santa Cruz)	E6
Organ Pipe Cactus Nat'l. Mon.		C5
Oro Valley	(Pima)	E5
Page	(Coconino)	D1
Papago (Tohono O 'odham) Indian Reservation		C5
Paradise Valley	(Maricopa)	D4
Parker •	(La Paz)	A3
Payson	(Gila)	D3
Peoria	(Maricopa)	C4
Petrified Forest Nat'l. Park		F3
Phoenix ★	(Maricopa)	C4
Pima	(Graham)	F5
Pinetop- Lakeside	(Navajo)	E3
Prescott	(Yavapai)	C3
Prescott Nat'l. Forest		C3
Prescott Valley	(Yavapai)	C3
Safford •	(Graham)	F5
Saguaro Nat'l. Park		D5
St. Johns •	(Apache)	F3
Salt River Indian Reservation		D4
San Carlos Indian Reservation		E4
San Luis	(Yuma)	A5
San Xavier Indian Reservation		D6
Scottsdale	(Maricopa)	D4
Sedona	(Coconino)	D3
Show Low	(Navajo)	F3
Sierra Vista	(Cochise)	E6
Sitgreaves Nat'l. Forest		E3
Snowflake	(Navajo)	E3
Somerton	(Yuma)	A5
South Tucson	(Pima)	D5
Springerville	(Apache)	F3
Superior	(Pinal)	D4
Surprise	(Maricopa)	C4
Taylor	(Navajo)	E3
Tempe	(Maricopa)	C4
Thatcher	(Graham)	F5
Tombstone	(Cochise)	F6
Tonto Nat'l. Forest		D3
Tucson •	(Pima)	E5
Wellton	(Yma)	A5
Wickenburg	(Maricopa)	C4
Willcox	(Cochise)	F5
Williams	(Coconino)	C2
Winslow	(Navajo)	E2
Wupatki Nat'l. Monument		D2
Yuma	(Yuma)	A5

• County Seat   Counties in parentheses   ★ State Capital

ARIZONA
State capital
City or town
County seat
Urban area
National area
Highway
Interstate
U.S.
State boundary
Indian reservation
County names are shown in RED
0 20 40 60 mi
0 20 40 60 km
Albers Equal-Area Projection
North
A B C D E F
1 2 3 4 5 6 7
UTAH
NEVADA
CALIFORNIA
COLO
NEW MEXICO
SONORA
MEXICO
GLEN CANYON NAT'L. REC. AREA
Lake Powell
San Juan River
Colorado City
Fredonia
KAIBAB IND. RES.
Page
NAVAJO
(DINÉ)
INDIAN
RESERVATION
NAVAJO NAT'L. MON.
KAIBAB NAT'L. FOREST
GRAND CANYON NATIONAL PARK
Colorado River
Chinle Creek
Las Vegas
Lake Mead
Virgin River
HAVASUPAI IND. RES.
LAKE MEAD NAT'L. REC. AREA
HUALAPAI IND. RES.
KAIBAB NAT'L. FOREST
Little Colorado River
HOPI INDIAN RESERVATION
CANYON DE CHELLY NATIONAL MONUMENT
COCONINO
WUPATKI NAT'L. MON.
APACHE
NAVAJO
Lake Mohave
MOHAVE
Kingman
Williams
KAIBAB NAT'L. FOR.
Flagstaff
Winslow
Holbrook
Puerco River
Bullhead City
FORT MOJAVE IND. RES.
COCONINO
Sedona
NATIONAL
FOREST
PETRIFIED FOREST NATIONAL PARK
HAVASU NWR
PRESCOTT
YAVAPAI
Clarkdale
Cottonwood
Chino Valley
NAT'L.
Prescott Valley
Camp Verde
Prescott
FOREST
Lake Havasu City
Snowflake
Taylor
St. Johns
SITGREAVES NATIONAL FOREST
Bill Williams River
Santa Maria River
Verde River
Show Low
Payson
TONTO NATIONAL FOREST
Parker
Pinetop-Lakeside
Springerville
Eagar
COLORADO RIVER IND. RES.
LA PAZ
Wickenburg
Hassayampa River
Cave Creek
Carefree
Theodore Roosevelt Lake
FORT APACHE INDIAN RESERVATION
APACHE NATIONAL FOREST
Surprise
El Mirage
Peoria
SALT RIVER IND. RES.
Salt River
Black River
CIBOLA NAT'L. WILDLIFE REF.
Glendale
Paradise Valley
PHOENIX
Scottsdale
GILA
SAN CARLOS
INDIAN RESERVATION
Avondale
Buckeye
Tempe
MESA
Apache Junction
Miami
Globe
Guadalupe
Gilbert
Chandler
Superior
San Carlos Lake
GREENLEE
KOFA NATIONAL WILDLIFE REFUGE
MARICOPA
GILA RIVER IND. RES.
GRAHAM
IMPERIAL NAT'L. WILDLIFE REF.
GILA BEND IND. RES.
AK-CHIN IND. RES.
Kearny
Florence
Clifton
Gila River
Gila Bend
Casa Grande
Coolidge
PINAL
CORONADO
Thatcher
Pima
Safford
Wellton
Yuma
Somerton
Eloy
Mammoth
San Pedro River
YUMA
San Luis
San Luis Río Colorado
NATIONAL FOREST
Marana
Oro Valley
PAPAGO
(TOHONO O'ODHAM)
INDIAN RESERVATION
CABEZA PRIETA NAT'L. WILDLIFE REFUGE
SAGUARO NAT'L. PARK
TUCSON
CORONADO NATIONAL FOR.
Willcox
ORGAN PIPE CACTUS NAT'L. MON.
South Tucson
SAGUARO NAT'L. PARK
Santa Cruz River
COCHISE
SAN XAVIER IND. RES.
Benson
CORONADO NAT'L. FOR.
PIMA
Tombstone
CORONADO
Huachuca City
SANTA CRUZ
Sierra Vista
NAT'L. FOR.
Bisbee
Nogales
Douglas
Agua Prieta
Cananea
Magdalena
Caborca
114° 113° 112° 111° 110° 109°
37° 36° 35° 34° 33° 32° 31°

Famous People

Bruce Babbitt (1938–), who grew up in Flagstaff, was elected attorney general of Arizona in 1974. From this position he unexpectedly succeeded to the governorship of the state on the death of the incumbent governor in 1978. Elected to two terms in his own right, Babbitt crusaded against land fraud and forged the Groundwater Management Act, which strictly regulated the pumping of Arizona's groundwater. President Bill Clinton appointed Babbitt U.S. secretary of the interior in 1993.

Cochise (1810?–74) was chief of the Chokonen band of the Chiricahua Apaches. He was one of the greatest Apache war leaders and diplomats of the 1800's. From his homeland in southeastern Arizona, Cochise and his fellow Chiricahuas fought both the U.S. and Mexican governments. He finally made peace with the United States in 1871. Cochise spent the last years of his life trying to negotiate a lasting peace between the Chiricahuas and the United States government.

Barry Goldwater (1909–98), born in Phoenix, was one of the architects of the modern conservative movement in the United States. He served as U.S. senator from Arizona from 1953 to 1987. In 1964, he won the Republican nomination for president but lost the national election to Lyndon Johnson. Goldwater served as chairman of the Senate's Armed Services Committee and its Intelligence Committee.

Barry Goldwater

Carl T. Hayden (1877–1972) was born in Tempe. He grew up watching the farmers of the Salt River Valley battle floods and droughts, especially during the disastrous years of the 1890's, and developed a lifelong interest in water control. He pursued this interest when, upon Arizona's admission to the Union in 1912, he became the state's first representative in Congress. Hayden remained in Congress until 1927 and then entered the U.S. Senate, serving from 1927 to 1969. In 1968 he secured approval for the Central Arizona Project, fulfilling his lifelong dream.

George W. P. Hunt (1859–1934), a rancher in the Salt River Valley, was president of Arizona's constitutional convention (1910) and was elected the state's first governor (1912). He went on to win re-election six more times. Hunt was a champion of the Arizona labor movement and an enemy at times of the big copper companies. He also was the president of a bank in Globe.

Helen Hull Jacobs (1908–97), born in Globe, was a tennis champion in the 1930's. She was the first person to win the U.S. Open women's singles title four years in a row. She also took the singles title at Wimbledon, England,

Territorial Arizona

During the Civil War (1861–65), most Arizonans favored the South. Confederate troops occupied Tucson in 1862 but were soon driven out by Union forces. Arizona was separated from the territory of New Mexico in 1863. Prescott, the center of a mining district, became the first capital of the Arizona Territory.

After the Civil War, more prospectors, ranchers, and farmers moved to Arizona. The newcomers invaded the traditional lands of several Indian groups, who defended their homelands and tried to drive the miners and ranchers out. By the 1870's, most of these groups had been defeated and settled on reservations. But the Chiricahua Apaches, under such leaders as Cochise and Geronimo, waged brilliant campaigns of guerrilla warfare against both the U.S. and Mexican governments. With the surrender of Geronimo in 1886, Apache armed resistance ended.

Development and Statehood

The arrival of railroads in the early 1880's transformed Arizona's economy, enabling Arizona's major products—cattle, copper, and cotton—to be transported throughout the country.

The number of cattle in the territory increased from about 5,000 in 1870 to 1.5 million in the early 1890's. Arizona ranchers shipped most of their cattle by railroad to California or the Midwest to be slaughtered.

Copper mining did not become feasible until technological changes in the late 1800's enabled mining companies to extract low-grade ores. Huge underground and open-pit copper mines in Bisbee, Superior, Ajo, and other boomtowns made Arizona the largest producer of copper in the United States.

Large-scale agriculture could not take place in Arizona until rivers had been dammed to control floods and provide irrigation water. The Salt River Project, a federally funded irrigation project, constructed the Theodore Roosevelt Dam on the Salt River near Phoenix. The dam, which was completed in 1911, allowed farmers in the Salt River Valley to cultivate several hundred thousand acres of land.

A movement to make Arizona a state arose in the 1890's, but not until 1910 did Congress allow Arizona to draft a constitution and apply for statehood. Arizona became the 48th state on February 14, 1912. Phoenix, which had been made the territorial capital in 1889, became the state capital.

where she was a six-time finalist. Jacobs was elected to the Tennis Hall of Fame in 1962.

Estevan Ochoa (1831–88), with his partner Pinckney Randolph Tully, operated one of the largest long-distance freighting companies in the Arizona Territory. Ochoa also was a territorial legislator and a founder of the Arizona public school system. During the 1870's, he was a leading citizen of Tucson, serving as the first Mexican mayor of the city in 1875.

Estevan Ochoa

Helen Hull Jacobs

Sandra Day O'Connor (1930–) grew up on her family's ranch in Duncan. She served in the Arizona state senate and as a judge in the Arizona court system before becoming, in 1981, the first woman appointed to the U.S. Supreme Court. O'Connor is profiled in SUPREME COURT OF THE UNITED STATES in Volume S.

Linda Ronstadt (1946–), born in Tucson, is a well-known pop singer. Having first gained fame in the world of rock and country-rock, she later returned to her Southwest roots, recording albums of Mexican folk songs. Ronstadt springs from a musically prominent Tucson family. Her paternal grandfather, a native of Mexico who moved to Tucson as a young man, founded one of the city's first orchestras. Her aunt, **Luisa (Ronstadt) Espinel** (1892–1963), was a well-known performer of Spanish and Latin-American folk music during the 1920's and 1930's.

Stewart Udall (1920–), born in St. Johns, won fame as both a politician and an environmentalist. He practiced law in Tucson and served in the U.S. House of Representatives from 1955 until 1961, when President John F. Kennedy appointed him U.S. secretary of the interior. He held that post until 1969. His brother, **Morris Udall** (1922–98), succeeded him in Congress, serving from 1961 until 1991.

Later Developments

Beginning with World War II (1939–45), Arizona transformed itself from a rural to an urban state. Because of Arizona's good flying weather, the War Department built air bases throughout the state, training thousands of pilots there. The government also opened defense plants in Arizona. In addition, the war increased the demand for Arizona copper and other products.

Growth continued after the war ended. Wartime military and defense activities triggered a boom in electronics and aerospace manufacturing. The state's population grew as soldiers who had been stationed in Arizona returned there to live. Arizona's sunny, dry climate, now tempered by the use of air conditioning, attracted many new residents.

Arizona's Native Americans, who had been denied the right to vote in state elections until 1948, also profited from the economic boom. In the 1960's several tribes opened businesses on their reservations. In 1974 a long-standing land dispute between Hopi and Navajo tribes was settled by Congress. Land in northeastern Arizona that had been used jointly by the two tribes was divided between them. But the new boundary lines forced the relocation of many Indian families, and the settlement became a source of bitter controversy between Hopis and Navajos.

As the shift from rural to urban land uses continued, Arizona cities competed with farmers for water. The Salt River Project, which had turned the Phoenix area into an agricultural oasis in the early 1900's, now provided the water and power for Phoenix's phenomenal urban growth.

Arizona also tapped the water of the Colorado River. Under the terms of the Colorado River Compact, which Arizona signed in 1945, the state was entitled to 2.8 million acre-feet (3.5 billion cubic feet) of water from the Colorado each year. (An acre-foot equals enough water to cover an acre with a foot of water.) Congress finally approved the Central Arizona Project (CAP) in 1968. The CAP water was originally destined for agricultural use. By the time it finally reached Tucson in 1993, however, people were consuming much of it. As Arizona continues to grow, the struggle for water among various groups will undoubtedly intensify.

THOMAS E. SHERIDAN
Curator of Ethnohistory
Arizona State Museum

ARKANSAS

Early French explorers are credited with naming Arkansas after the Arkansa (or Arkansea) Indians. These Indians called themselves the Quapaw, meaning "downstream people," because they had settled in Arkansas after migrating down the Mississippi River. It was the tribes native to the region who named the newcomers the Arkansa, which in their own language meant "south wind people."

When the United States acquired Arkansas as part of the Louisiana Purchase of 1803, the spelling was changed to Arkansaw *to match its pronunciation, but it was soon changed back again. Ongoing confusion over the spelling and pronunciation finally prompted the state legislature to pass a law in 1881: The name of the state would be spelled* Arkansas, *but it would be pronounced* Arkansaw.

State flag

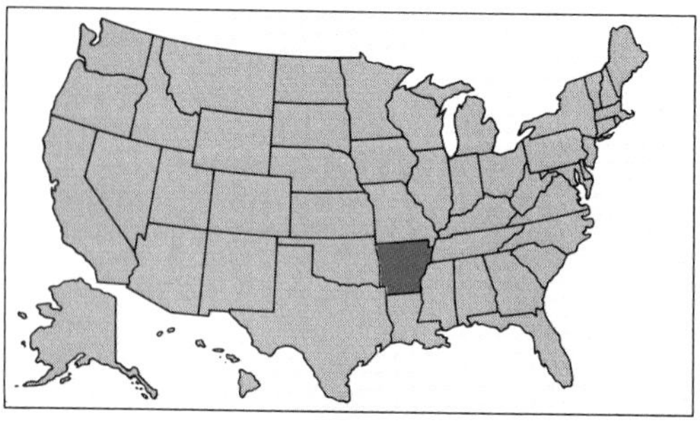

Arkansas is a southern state, located along the western bank of the Mississippi River. Its eastern and southern regions are covered by open plains that support large plantations on which cotton, soybeans, rice, and other cash crops are grown. To the north and west lie rugged highlands, featuring the beautiful Ozark Plateau and the Ouachita Mountains.

Much of Arkansas's history is linked to its agricultural past. Until 1865, state politics were dominated by slave-holding plantation owners, who supported withdrawal from the Union during the Civil War; in the 1880's dissatisfied small-scale farmers founded a new political party to protect their interests; and during the Great Depression of the 1930's, black and white tenant farmers and sharecroppers joined together to form the nation's first biracial farmers' union.

Despite the steady growth of manufacturing and the service industries in more recent years, the state continues to be associated with its agricultural production. Today Arkansas is the nation's leading producer of rice and poultry.

The largest segment of Arkansas's population lives in the farming regions in the south and east. However, the entire state is becoming increasingly urbanized and large numbers now live in central Arkansas, in or near Little Rock, the state's capital and largest city. The population in the northwest is also expanding due to the growth of tourism, the poultry industry, and retirement communities.

The state's official nickname, the Land of Opportunity, was adopted in 1953 to advertise the state's many assets and to attract new industries. The nickname the Natural State, which appears on Arkansas's state license plates, is the state slogan.

LAND

From east to west, Arkansas rises from the plains of the Mississippi Delta to the Ozarks and the Ouachita Mountains.

Land Regions

The land is divided into two main geographic regions—the lowlands in the southeast and the highlands in the northwest.

The Lowlands include the Mississippi Alluvial Plain, often called the Delta, and the West Gulf Coastal Plain. The Delta, which lies in the east along the Mississippi River, covers nearly one third of the state. The West Gulf Coastal Plain lies in the south-central part of the state and extends into neighboring Louisiana and Texas. The entire lowland area is relatively flat. It was once swampland, but most of it has been drained and put to agricultural use.

Natives of the Ozarks dedicate themselves to preserving regional customs and the unspoiled rural beauty of the Highlands. Ozark heritage celebrations, such as the annual Arkansas Folk Festival in Mountain View, feature traditional folk music, arts, and crafts.

State flower:
Apple blossom

State tree:
Shortleaf pine

FACTS AND FIGURES

Location: South central United States; bordered on the north by Missouri, on the east by Tennessee and Mississippi, on the south by Louisiana, and on the west by Oklahoma and Texas.

Area: 53,182 square miles (137,742 km^2); rank, 28th.

Population: 2,673,400 (2000 census); rank, 33rd.

Elevation: *Highest*—2,753 feet (839 m) at Magazine Mountain; *lowest*—55 feet (17 m) along the Ouachita River.

Capital: Little Rock.

Statehood: June 15, 1836; 25th state.

State Motto: *Regnat populus* ("The people rule").

State Song: "Arkansas."

Nickname: Land of Opportunity (official); Natural State; Diamond State.

Abbreviations: AR; Ark.

State bird:
Mockingbird

The Highlands are dominated by the Ozark Plateau and the Ouachita Mountains, with the Arkansas Valley between them. The Ozarks are sometimes referred to as mountains, but they are actually three eroded plateaus of increasing height: the Salem Upland, the Springfield Upland, and the Boston Mountains. The Ouachita Mountains, located in west-central Arkansas, rise more than 2,000 feet (610 meters). They are heavily wooded and known for their natural hot springs. The Arkansas Valley is lower-lying than the two regions it separates, and yet it has several high peaks of its own, including Magazine Mountain, the highest point in the state.

Rivers, Lakes, and Springs

Four great rivers flow through Arkansas: the Mississippi, the Arkansas, the Red, and the White. The Mississippi forms most of the state's eastern border. The Arkansas flows southeastward through the center of the state and empties into the Mississippi. Both rivers play important roles in transportation. Along with the White River and the Red River, they also serve as homes for wildlife and as places for recreation.

Dams have been constructed in a few of the smaller rivers, creating large artificial lakes. These lakes are chiefly in the Highlands and provide flood control, hydroelectric power, and recreation. Lake Chicot in the southeast is the state's largest natural lake.

Thermal springs attract tourists and other people who believe that bathing in them is good for their health. The water temperature at Hot Springs, a well-known resort, reaches about 140°F (60°C) at the surface. Mammoth Spring near the Missouri border is another well-known hot spring.

Climate

Arkansas enjoys a humid subtropical climate. Because of its inland location, Arkansas receives cold air masses from the heart of the North American continent in winter and hot air masses in summer. Far enough south, it also receives warm, moisture-laden winds from the Gulf of Mexico. The result is a relatively mild climate and an eight-month growing season that permits the cultivation of a wide range of crops.

July temperatures average about 80°F (27°C). The Highlands enjoy cooler summer nights than do the Lowlands. Similarly, the Highlands have somewhat colder winters. Average January temperatures in the state range between 36°F (2°C) and 48°F (9°C).

Most of the precipitation falls as rain, with the southern half of the state receiving more than the north. Snow sometimes falls in the northern mountains, but it is rare in the south. Arkansas ranks seventh among all 50 states in the amount of rainfall received. It averages about 49 inches (1,245 millimeters) per year.

Far left: **The sandstone cliffs of Petit Jean Mountain overlook the beautiful Arkansas Valley.** *Left:* **Agriculture thrives in Arkansas's fertile Mississippi Delta region.** *Right:* **The soothing effects of the natural hot mineral springs in the Ouachita Mountains attract tourists from all over the world.**

Plant and Animal Life

One hundred years ago, Arkansas was nearly covered by great forests of deciduous and evergreen trees, but today the majority of wooded land in the Mississippi and Arkansas river valleys has been cleared for farmland. Arkansas also has grasslands on its eastern prairies and in two counties in the northwest.

Many kinds of wildlife abound in Arkansas. Deer, fish, wild turkeys, and migrating ducks and geese, which feed in the rice fields, are abundant. Trout, largemouth bass, and smallmouth bass are among the many popular game fish. Squirrels, opossums, rabbits, weasels, and many other small mammals are found throughout the state. Black bears, which had nearly disappeared from the state, have been brought back and now thrive in the Boston Mountains.

Natural Resources

Arkansas's soils, forests, and minerals provide the raw materials that are so important to the economic life of the state.

The state's most fertile soils are its limestone and alluvial soils, which produce many different crops when properly fertilized and cultivated. The soils in the rice-growing areas have a subsoil that will not let water drain easily, which helps irrigate the rice.

Despite clearing by early settlers, forests still cover approximately one half of the state and are important economically. Softwood forests of shortleaf pine and loblolly pine are found in the south; hardwood forests of oak and hickory are found in the north, in the Mississippi Valley, and along southern streams.

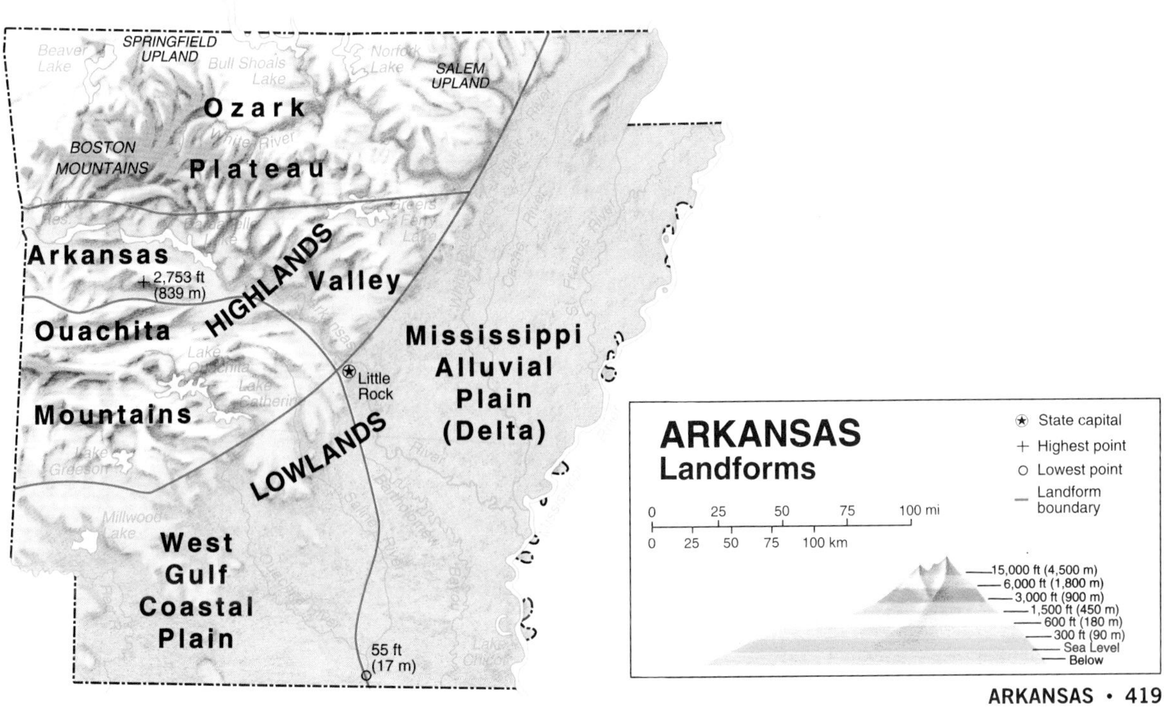

Left: **Arkansans who live in rural areas enjoy the benefits of country living. But increasing numbers are moving to urban areas in search of economic opportunities.** ***Above:*** **University of Arkansas football fans huddle for warmth at Razorback Stadium in Fayetteville.**

Most of the state's minerals are located in the West Gulf Coastal Plain and the Arkansas Valley. They include petroleum, natural gas, natural-gas liquids, clays, coal, and bauxite, from which aluminum is obtained. Stone is quarried in the highlands. Diamonds also are found in abundance, although they are no longer mined commercially.

▶ PEOPLE

The people of Arkansas are known as Arkansans or Arkansawyers. Approximately 54 percent live in urban areas; the other half live in rural areas—places with fewer than 2,500 residents. The Lowlands are more populous than the Highlands due to the Lowlands' productive agriculture, mineral wealth, and transportation facilities. The Highlands attract retired people because of the beautiful scenery, moderate cost of living, and pleasant climate.

The Caddo, Osage, and Quapaw Indians originally inhabited Arkansas, but few remain there today. In the 1800's, most were forced onto reservations in Oklahoma as a result of the westward expansion of Anglo-Americans.

Most of the Anglo settlers that first came to Arkansas were descendants of colonial southerners, most of whom had originally come from northwestern Europe. They brought with them to Arkansas the traditions and practices of the Old South, notably cotton production and slavery. Later settlers included Germans, Italians, Chinese, and Lebanese, who came to work on Arkansas's farms and railroads and in the lumber mills and mines.

Since the 1970's, Arkansas has shown a consistent gain in overall population. The African American population, however, has declined and today stands at about 16 percent.

PEOPLE

Population: 2,673,400 (2000 census).

Density: 50 persons per sq mi (19 per km²).

Distribution: 54% urban; 46% rural.

Largest Cities (2000 census):

Little Rock 183,133	Jonesboro 55,515
Fort Smith 80,268	Pine Bluff 55,085
North Little Rock 60,433	Springdale 45,798
Fayetteville 58,047	Conway 43,167

Source: U.S. Bureau of the Census

Persons per sq mi	Persons per km²
over 250	over 100
50-250	20-100
5-50	2-20
0-5	0-2

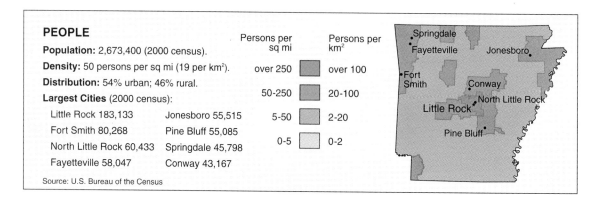

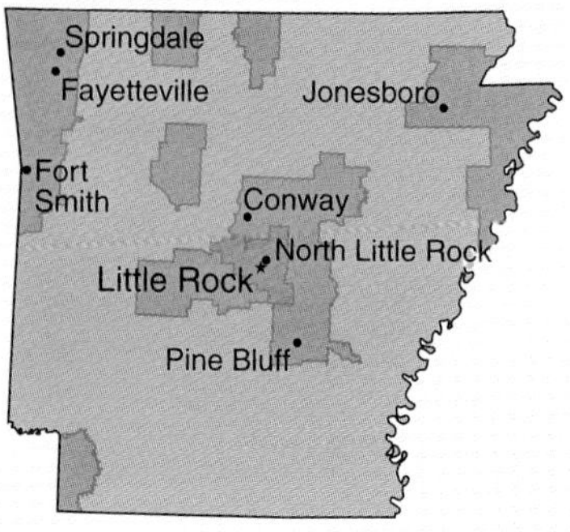

Education

When Congress created the Arkansas Territory in 1819, it set aside a section of land in each county for public schools. In 1843, the state legislature established a system for public education, but until the Civil War, most of the schools in operation were private. Today's public school system is largely based on a plan established by the state constitution in 1868.

Arkansas has 17 accredited four-year colleges and universites. The largest is the University of Arkansas, which has its main campus at Fayetteville; other campuses at Little Rock, Monticello, and Pine Bluff; and a medical sciences campus at Little Rock.

Other state-supported four-year institutions are at Jonesboro, Conway, Russellville, Magnolia, and Arkadelphia. Private four-year colleges include the University of the Ozarks in Clarksville, Hendrix College in Conway, and Harding University in Searcy.

Libraries, Museums, and the Arts

Arkansas's first library system was established in the mid-1800's. However, the growth of public libraries was slow, partly because the people lived in widely scattered rural areas. The Arkansas Library Commission was established in 1935 to address this problem. It maintains a book collection at Little Rock from which volumes are sent by mail to individuals, schools, and organizations. Bookmobiles operate throughout the state, and most of the cities support free public libraries.

The fine arts are represented in Arkansas by various activities. Little Rock has a choral society, an opera company, a repertory theater, and a symphony orchestra. Fort Smith and Pine Bluff also have symphony orchestras. Poets and writers have settled in Eureka Springs in northwest Arkansas where they have developed a lively and productive literary and artistic community.

The Arkansas Arts Center, in Little Rock, contains the state's most important collection of paintings and other fine arts. Also of note in Little Rock is the Museum of Science and History. The University of Arkansas Museum in Fayetteville contains Arkansas Indian artifacts and many science and natural history exhibits.

Arkansas is rich in folklore and legends. The Ozark Folk Center in Mountain View celebrates Arkansas folk culture. It provides live demonstrations of traditional arts and crafts during the summer. The library at the University in Fayetteville has a large and unusual Arkansas folklore collection that includes tape-recorded histories and stories told by Arkansas residents.

ECONOMY

In the past, Arkansas depended almost entirely on its farm products for its income. Products such as cotton, livestock, and poultry remain important income producers. However, in recent years services and manufacturing have become the state's primary economic activities.

Services

Arkansas's various service industries employ 70 percent of the state's entire work force. Wholesale and retail trade (the buying and selling of industrial and personal goods) are the most profitable within the services category. They are followed by financial services (banking, insurance, and real estate); professional and personal services (such as medical, tourist, and other social services); and government (which includes the maintenance of state-supported schools, hospitals, and the like). Remaining service industries are in transportation and communication.

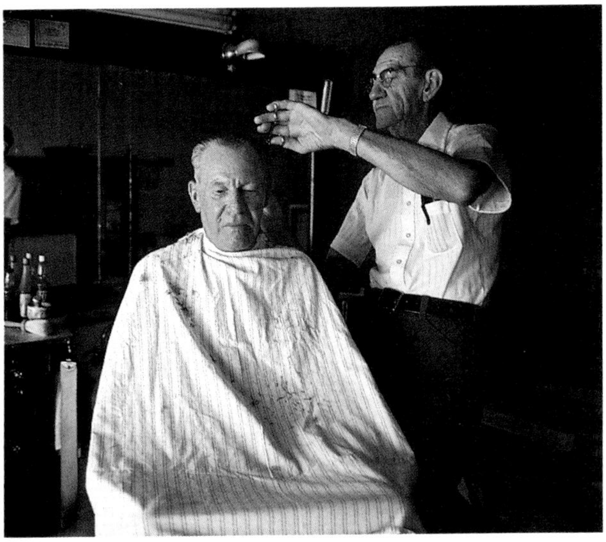

Most people in Arkansas make a living in the service industries. Personal services include such everyday activities as barbering and hairdressing.

Arkansas is the nation's leading producer of rice (*above*) and broiler chickens (*right*). The state's economy once depended on agriculture, but today it is based more on the service industries and on manufacturing, particularly food processing.

Manufacturing

Manufacturing employs about 25 percent of Arkansas's work force. The most important manufacturing industry is food processing, including the canning of fruits and vegetables and the processing of poultry and livestock.

Industries that make electrical equipment also are profitable. Among Arkansas's many products are electric motors, refrigerators and ranges, air conditioners, television sets, and lightbulbs. Arkansas factories also produce clothing, plastic and metal products, and chemicals.

Agriculture

Arkansas's Lowlands belong to a wider region of the South known as the Cotton Belt, and farmers there once grew only this crop. Cotton production has since declined in importance, but it still brings much income to the state. Today Arkansas ranks sixth in the nation in cotton production.

Today rice and soybeans are Arkansas's most profitable cash crops. In fact, Arkansas rice farmers supply an international market, including Japan. Arkansas is also the nation's leading producer of broiler chickens.

Arkansas's forests provide the raw material for many of its manufacturing industries. Pine is used for wood pulp, which is used to make paper; oak and hickory are used to make furniture, barrels, and railroad ties.

PRODUCTS AND INDUSTRIES

Manufacturing: Food processing, electrical machinery and equipment, lumber and wood products, paper products, fabricated metal products, chemicals, nonelectrical machinery, rubber and plastic products.

Agriculture: Broiler chickens, soybeans, rice, wheat, cotton, eggs, milk, beef cattle, turkeys, sorghum grain, cottonseed, hogs, oats, hay, corn, grasses, grapes, snap beans, tomatoes.

Minerals: Petroleum, natural gas and natural gas liquids, bauxite, barite, coal, granite, gypsum, sand and gravel, limestone, marble.

Services: Wholesale and retail trade; finance, insurance, and real estate; business, social, and personal services; transportation, communication, and utilities; government.

Percentage of Gross State Product* by Industry

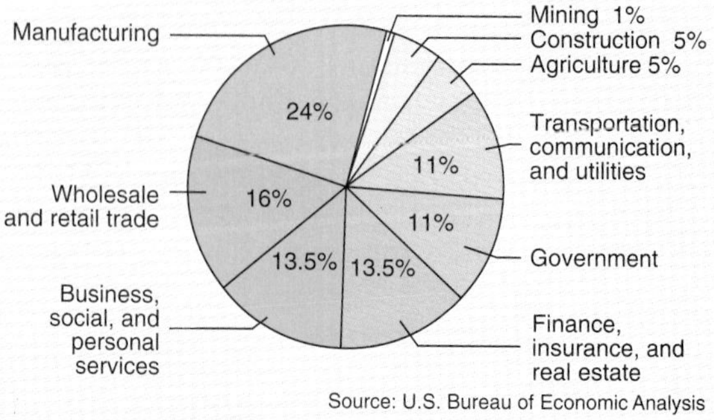

*Gross state product is the total value of goods and services produced in a year.

Source: U.S. Bureau of Economic Analysis

Mining and Construction

Petroleum and natural gas are important mineral products as are quartz crystals and crushed stone. Arkansas is the nation's leading producer of bauxite, the principal source of aluminum. It is also a leading producer of barite, a mineral used in the manufacture of paper, rubber, and other products. Mining and construction activities employ approximately 4 percent of the work force.

Transportation

The Mississippi River, the greatest river transportation system in the United States, has always been an important trade route to Arkansas. The Arkansas River also is used for limited amounts of freight traffic.

Four major and 24 short-line railways, covering 2,500 miles (4,000 kilometers) of tracks, operate within the state. Three of its rail systems are among the nation's largest: Burlington Northern, Inc.; the Union Pacific Railroad Company; and the Southern Pacific Transportation Company. Bus passenger service and bus and truck freight services also are important to the state's transportation systems. Arkansas has approximately 270 airports and airfields, and about one dozen commercial airlines serve the state. The principal airports are located in Little Rock and Hot Springs.

Communication

Until recently, Little Rock published two major daily newspapers, the *Arkansas Democrat* and the *Arkansas Gazette*. The *Gazette*, first published in 1819, had been the oldest newspaper in continuous publication west of the Mississippi River. The two newspapers combined to form the *Arkansas Democrat-Gazette*. More than 200 radio stations and 17 television stations broadcast throughout the state.

▶ CITIES

Six cities in Arkansas have populations exceeding 50,000. Only one, Little Rock, has more than 100,000 people.

Little Rock, the state capital and largest city, was founded in 1820. Its name comes from a rocky outcropping on the Arkansas River that marked the early settlement. Located near the center of the state, Little Rock is a major market for cotton, soybeans, and other agricultural products. It is also the leading transportation and trade center and the home of a large number of industries. Many historic buildings, such as the old Capitol, are located here.

Fort Smith, a historical border city between Arkansas and what was once called Indian Territory, grew up around a fort built in 1817. It is now an important market center on the Arkansas River, serving western Arkansas and eastern Oklahoma. It is also a leading industrial center, producing refrigerators, heating equipment, paper cups, light metal products, and furniture.

North Little Rock is an industrial city across the river from Little Rock. Among its products are clothing, cosmetics, wood products, ma-

Little Rock is Arkansas's capital and largest city. It was named after a small formation of rocks on the Arkansas River, where the city was founded in 1820.

Places of Interest

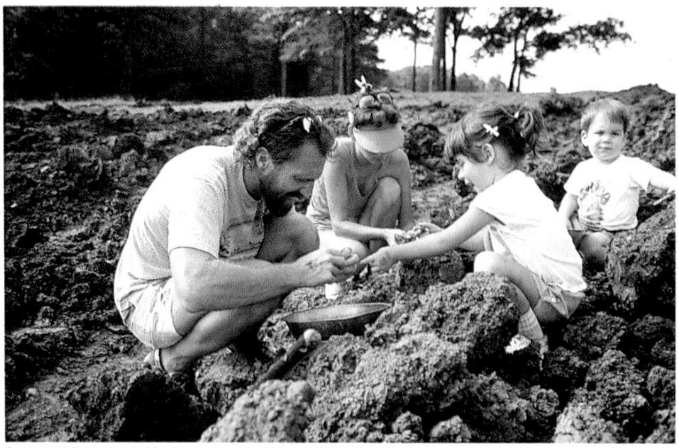

Crater of Diamonds State Park, near Murfreesboro

Ozark Folk Center, in Mountain View

Blanchard Spring Caverns, near Mountain View

Buffalo National River, in the Ozarks

Arkansas Post National Memorial, near Gillett at the mouth of the Arkansas River, marks the first permanent European settlement (1686) in the Lower Mississippi River Valley. Founded by Henri de Tonti, it served as Arkansas's first territorial capital (1819–21).

Buffalo National River was the first in the United States to be designated a national river (1972). Canoeists and rafters enjoy its exciting rapids and waterfalls and its scenic canyons, cliffs, and forests. It winds for 132 miles (212 kilometers) through the Ozarks.

Blanchard Spring Caverns, located near Mountain View in the Ozark National Forest, is one of the largest caverns in the United States. It contains many dramatic stalactite and stalagmite formations. The surrounding forest, one of three national forests in the state, is known for its rugged beauty.

Crater of Diamonds State Park, near Murfreesboro, is the only active diamond mine in North America. Discovered by farmer John M. Huddleston in 1906, it is no longer mined commercially. Visitors, however, may hunt for diamonds and keep whatever they find. More than 60,000 gems have been collected, some with a value of more than $100,000.

Eureka Springs, a resort town in the Ozarks, is known for its picturesque Victorian homes and tourist entertainments.

Hot Springs National Park, in Hot Springs, features a health spa and resort. Its naturally hot mineral waters reach a temperature of about 140°F (60°C). One million gallons flow from the spring each day. Visitors come to bathe in the mineral waters, which are said to be beneficial to one's health. The site was established as a national park in 1921. Thoroughbred racing is featured at nearby Oaklawn Park from February through April.

MacArthur Park, in downtown Little Rock, is home of the Arkansas Arts Center and the Museum of Science and History. The museum occupies the Old Arsenal Building, built in 1838, which was the birthplace of General Douglas MacArthur. The park is named for him.

Ozark Folk Center, in Mountain View, preserves Ozark folk arts. Craftspeople demonstrate traditional skills, such as blacksmithing, candle making, quilting, and weaving. Musicians also give live folk-music performances.

Pea Ridge National Military Park, located near Rogers, commemorates the largest Civil War battle fought west of the Mississippi River. More than 26,000 troops took part in the battle, which took place March 7–8, 1862. At the battle's end, Union forces had defeated the Confederate troops.

Toltec Mounds, in Scott, is an ancient ceremonial complex made of earthen mounds. The mounds once had buildings on them, probably used for religious purposes. They were built between A.D. 700 and 950 by people of the Plum Bayou Culture. Mistakenly named for Indians from Mexico, they are among the largest and most complex ancient sites in the Lower Mississippi River valley.

State Parks. Arkansas has 44 state parks and 3 state museums. For information, contact Arkansas State Parks, Department of Parks and Tourism, One Capitol Mall, Little Rock, Arkansas 72201.

chinery, and food products. Together with Little Rock it forms a large metropolitan area with a population of more than 580,000.

Pine Bluff, founded in 1819, is a commercial center in a rich agricultural region. It produces paper and other wood products, clothing, and light metal products. It is a major transportation hub for the southeastern part of the state.

GOVERNMENT

Arkansas's government is organized under the constitution adopted in 1874 (the state's fifth) and its various amendments. The first was adopted in 1836 when Arkansas became a state. The second was adopted when Arkansas withdrew from the Union in 1861. Others were adopted as a result of the Civil War and its aftermath.

All of the constitutions have provided for three branches of government, with largely separate powers. The legislative branch, called the General Assembly, consists of two bodies: the Senate and the House of Representatives. Senators are elected to 4-year terms, representatives to 2-year terms.

The executive branch consists of a governor and six other state officers—the lieutenant governor, secretary of state, attorney general, treasurer, auditor, and land commissioner. Each is elected by the people to a 4-year term. Other members of the executive branch are appointed by the governor, with approval by the state senate often required.

The judicial branch interprets and applies the law. Four kinds of state courts make up this branch. They are the minor courts, the circuit courts, the chancery courts, and the Supreme Court. The Supreme Court consists of a chief justice and six associate justices, all elected to 8-year terms.

County and city governments have authority in various local matters, including taxation. Important county officers are the county judge, county and circuit clerks, sheriff, assessor, collector, and treasurer.

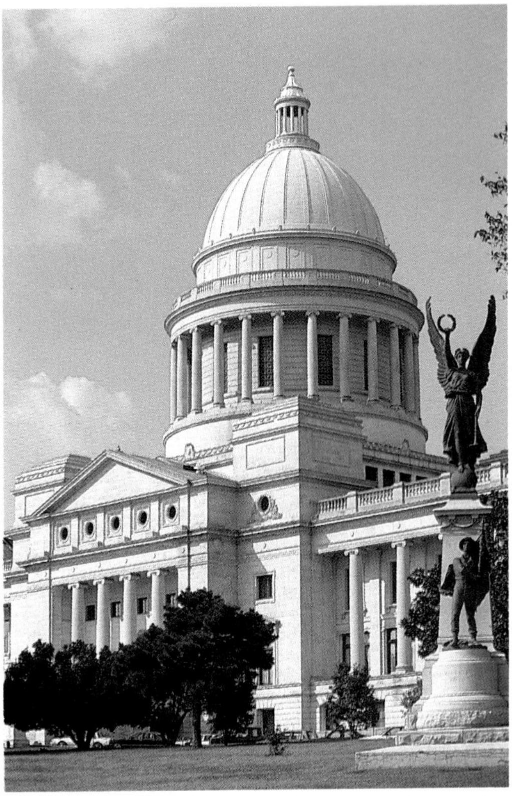

Arkansas's state capitol in Little Rock was modeled after the United States Capitol in Washington, D.C. The granite and marble structure was completed in 1915.

GOVERNMENT

State Government
Governor: 4-year term
State senators: 35; 4-year terms
State representatives: 100; 2-year terms
Number of counties: 75

Federal Government
U.S. senators: 2
U.S. representatives: 4
Number of electoral votes: 6

For the name of the current governor, see STATE GOVERNMENTS in Volume S. For the names of current U.S. senators and representatives, see UNITED STATES, CONGRESS OF THE in Volume U-V.

HISTORY

Three Indian groups lived in the Arkansas region at the time of first contact with European explorers: the Quapaw in the east, the Caddo in the Ouachita and Red river valleys of the southwest, and the Osage in the west.

European Exploration

The first Europeans to visit Arkansas were Spanish explorers, who arrived in 1541 looking for gold. They were led by Hernando de Soto, who died in Arkansas the following year.

The next wave of visitors came 130 years later, when French explorers Father Jacques Marquette and Louis Jolliet traveled by canoe down the Mississippi River and reached the Arkansas River in 1673.

In 1682, a French explorer and fur trader named Robert Cavelier, Sieur de La Salle, also traveled down the Mississippi to claim the river and its wide valley for the king

French explorers Father Jacques Marquette and Louis Jolliet first encountered the Quapaw Indians in 1673 when their expedition reached the Arkansas River.

of France. His faithful lieutenant, Henri de Tonti, returned to Arkansas in 1686, and at the mouth of the Arkansas River he founded a settlement the French called *Aux Arcs* (pronounced Ozarks), Arkansas's first permanent European settlement. Later it was renamed Arkansas Post.

The Louisiana Purchase and Statehood

Arkansas, which was claimed at various times by both France and Spain, was part of an enormous region that was called Louisiana. In 1803, the French emperor Napoleon I sold the territory to the United States. After the Louisiana Purchase, Arkansas was part of the Missouri Territory. Then in 1819 it became its own territory, with its own territorial governor. On June 15, 1836, Arkansas became the 25th state.

Withdrawal from the Union

In the early 1860's, with the threat of civil war surrounding the question of slavery, Arkansas voted against seceding (withdrawing) from the Union, unlike many other Southern states that seceded and formed the Confederate States of America. But after the Civil War began at Fort Sumter, South Carolina, on April 12, 1861, Arkansas joined the Southern states and seceded from the Union on May 6.

INDEX TO ARKANSAS MAP

Arkadelphia •	(Clark)	**B3**
Arkansas City •	(Desha)	**D4**
Ashdown •	(Little River)	**A4**
Ash Flat •	(Sharp)	**D1**
Augusta •	(Woodruff)	**D2**
Barling	(Sebastian)	**A2**
Batesville •	(Independence)	**D2**
Beebe	(White)	**D2**
Benton •	(Saline)	**C3**
Bentonville •	(Benton)	**A1**
Berryville •	(Carroll)	**B1**
Big Lake Nat'l Wildlife Refuge		**E2**
Blytheville •	(Mississippi)	**F2**
Booneville •	(Logan)	**B2**
Brinkley	(Monroe)	**D3**
Bryant	(Saline)	**C3**
Cabot	(Lonoke)	**C3**
Camden •	(Ouachita)	**C4**
Charleston •	(Franklin)	**A2**
Clarendon •	(Monroe)	**D3**
Clarksville •	(Johnson)	**B2**
Clinton •	(Van Buren)	**C2**
Conway •	(Faulkner)	**C2**
Corning •	(Clay)	**E1**
Crossett	(Ashley)	**D4**
Danville •	(Yell)	**B2**
Dardanelle •	(Yell)	**B2**
De Queen •	(Sevier)	**A3**
Dermott	(Chicot)	**D4**
Des Arc •	(Prairie)	**D3**
De Valls Bluff •	(Prairie)	**D3**
De Witt •	(Arkansas)	**D3**
Dumas	(Desha)	**D4**
Earle	(Crittenden)	**E2**
El Dorado •	(Union)	**C4**
England	(Lonoke)	**D3**
Eudora	(Chicot)	**D4**
Eureka Springs •	(Carroll)	**B1**
Fayetteville •	(Washington)	**A1**
Fordyce •	(Dallas)	**C4**
Forrest City •	(St. Francis)	**E2**
Fort Smith •	(Sebastian)	**A2**
Gosnell	(Mississippi)	**E2**
Greenwood •	(Sebastian)	**A2**
Hamburg •	(Ashley)	**D4**
Hampton •	(Calhoun)	**C4**
Harrisburg •	(Poinsett)	**E2**
Harrison •	(Boone)	**B1**
Heber Springs •	(Cleburne)	**C2**
Helena •	(Phillips)	**E3**
Hope •	(Hempstead)	**B4**
Hot Springs •	(Garland)	**B3**
Huntsville •	(Madison)	**B1**
Jacksonville	(Pulaski)	**C3**
Jasper •	(Newton)	**B2**
Jonesboro •	(Craighead)	**E2**
Lake City •	(Craighead)	**E2**
Lake Village •	(Chicot)	**D4**
Lewisville •	(Lafayette)	**B4**
Little Rock ★	(Pulaski)	**C3**
Lonoke •	(Lonoke)	**D3**
McGehee	(Desha)	**D4**
Magnolia •	(Columbia)	**B4**
Malvern •	(Hot Spring)	**C3**
Marianna •	(Lee)	**E3**
Marion •	(Crittenden)	**E2**
Marked Tree	(Poinsett)	**E2**
Marshall •	(Searcy)	**C2**
Maumelle	(Pulaski)	**C3**
Melbourne •	(Izard)	**D1**
Mena •	(Polk)	**A3**
Monticello •	(Drew)	**D4**
Morrilton •	(Conway)	**C2**
Mountain Home •	(Baxter)	**C1**
Mountain View •	(Stone)	**C2**
Mount Ida •	(Montgomery)	**B3**
Murfreesboro •	(Pike)	**B3**
Nashville •	(Howard)	**B4**
Newport •	(Jackson)	**D2**
North Little Rock	(Pulaski)	**C3**
Osceola •	(Mississippi)	**E2**
Ouachita Nat'l Forest		**A3,B3**
Ozark •	(Franklin)	**B2**
Ozark Nat'l Forest		**B2,C1**
Paragould •	(Greene)	**E1**
Paris •	(Logan)	**B2**
Perryville •	(Perry)	**C2**
Piggott •	(Clay)	**E1**
Pine Bluff •	(Jefferson)	**C3**
Pocahontas •	(Randolph)	**D1**
Prescott •	(Nevada)	**B4**
Rison •	(Cleveland)	**C4**
Rogers	(Benton)	**A1**
Russellville •	(Pope)	**B2**
St. Francis Nat'l Forest		**E3**
Salem •	(Fulton)	**D1**
Searcy •	(White)	**D2**
Sheridan •	(Grant)	**C3**
Sherwood	(Pulaski)	**C3**
Siloam Springs	(Benton)	**A1**
Springdale	(Washington)	**A1**
Star City •	(Lincoln)	**D4**
Stuttgart •	(Arkansas)	**D3**
Texarkana •	(Miller)	**B4**
Trumann	(Poinsett)	**E2**
Van Buren •	(Crawford)	**A2**
Waldron •	(Scott)	**A3**
Walnut Ridge •	(Lawrence)	**D1**
Warren •	(Bradley)	**C4**
West Helena	(Phillips)	**E3**
West Memphis	(Crittenden)	**E2**
White Hall	(Jefferson)	**C3**
White River Nat'l Wildlife Refuge		**D3**
Wynne •	(Cross)	**E2**
Yellville •	(Marion)	**C1**

• County Seat Counties in parentheses ★ State Capital

The Civil War and Reconstruction

The Civil War brought devastation and bitterness to Arkansas. About 60,000 Arkansans fought for the Confederacy; however, as many as 15,000 joined the Union forces. The largest battle that was fought west of the Mississippi River took place in Arkansas, at Pea Ridge on

ARKANSAS
State capital
City or town
County seat
Urban area
National forest
Highway
Interstate
U.S.
State boundary
County names are shown in RED
0 10 20 30 40 mi
0 10 20 30 40 km
Albers Equal-Area Projection
North
MISSOURI
KENTUCKY
TENNESSEE
MISSISSIPPI
LOUISIANA
TEXAS
OKLAHOMA
A
B
C
D
E
F
1
2
3
4
BENTON
CARROLL
BOONE
MARION
BAXTER
FULTON
RANDOLPH
CLAY
GREENE
LAWRENCE
SHARP
IZARD
WASHINGTON
MADISON
NEWTON
SEARCY
STONE
INDEPENDENCE
CRAIGHEAD
MISSISSIPPI
CRAWFORD
FRANKLIN
JOHNSON
POPE
VAN BUREN
CLEBURNE
JACKSON
POINSETT
CROSS
CRITTENDEN
SEBASTIAN
LOGAN
CONWAY
FAULKNER
WHITE
WOODRUFF
ST. FRANCIS
SCOTT
YELL
PERRY
PRAIRIE
LONOKE
LEE
MONROE
PHILLIPS
PULASKI
SALINE
GARLAND
MONTGOMERY
POLK
HOT SPRING
GRANT
JEFFERSON
ARKANSAS
HOWARD
PIKE
CLARK
DALLAS
CLEVELAND
LINCOLN
DESHA
SEVIER
LITTLE RIVER
HEMPSTEAD
NEVADA
OUACHITA
CALHOUN
DREW
BRADLEY
MILLER
LAYFAYETTE
COLUMBIA
UNION
ASHLEY
CHICOT
OZARK NATIONAL FOREST
OZARK NAT'L. FOREST
OUACHITA NATIONAL FOREST
ST. FRANCIS NAT'L FOREST
BIG LAKE NAT'L WILDLIFE REFUGE
WHITE RIVER NAT'L. WILDLIFE REFUGE
Bentonville
Rogers
Springdale
Fayetteville
Siloam Springs
Eureka Springs
Berryville
Harrison
Huntsville
Jasper
Yellville
Mountain Home
Salem
Ash Flat
Pocahontas
Corning
Biggott
Kennett
Paragould
Walnut Ridge
Jonesboro
Gosnell
Blytheville
Osceola
Melbourne
Marshall
Mountain View
Batesville
Newport
Trumann
Harrisburg
Marked Tree
Tahlequah
Sallisaw
Van Buren
Fort Smith
Barling
Greenwood
Ozark
Charleston
Paris
Booneville
Clarksville
Russellville
Dardanelle
Danville
Clinton
Heber Springs
Searcy
Augusta
Wynne
Earle
Marion
West Memphis
Memphis
Forrest City
Morrilton
Conway
Beebe
Cabot
Des Arc
Brinkley
Poteau
Waldron
Perryville
Jacksonville
Sherwood
Maumelle
North Little Rock
LITTLE ROCK
Lonoke
De Valls Bluff
Clarendon
Marianna
West Helena
Helena
Mena
Mount Ida
Hot Springs
Bryant
Benton
England
Stuttgart
Malvern
Sheridan
White Hall
Pine Bluff
De Witt
Clarksdale
Arkadelphia
Murfreesboro
De Queen
Nashville
Idabel
Ashdown
Hope
Prescott
Fordyce
Rison
Star City
Dumas
Camden
Hampton
Warren
Monticello
McGehee
Arkansas City
Dermott
Greenville
Cleveland
Greenwood
Texarkana
Lewisville
Magnolia
El Dorado
Hamburg
Crossett
Lake Village
Eudora
Mount Pleasant
Dyersburg
Jackson
Brownsville
Millington
Table Rock Lake
Beaver Lake
Bull Shoals Lake
Norfolk Lake
Greers Ferry Lake
Lake Dardanelle
Ouachita Lake
DeGray Lake
Millwood Lake
Lake Texarkana
White River
Buffalo River
Black River
Little Red River
Arkansas River
Caddo River
Saline River
Ouachita River
Little River
Red River
Sulphur River
Mississippi River
St. Francis River
40
55
62
63
67
65
30
79
95°
94°
93°
92°
91°
90°
89°
36°
35°
34°
33°

Famous People

Maya Angelou

Bill Clinton

Maya Angelou (1928–), born Marguerite Johnson in St. Louis, Missouri, was raised in Stamps. Her autobiography, about growing up during the civil rights movement, is entitled *I Know Why the Caged Bird Sings* (1970). Other works include *All God's Children Need Traveling Shoes* (1986) and *I Shall Not Be Moved* (1990). In 1993 she read a poem at the presidential inauguration of fellow Arkansan Bill Clinton that she wrote especially for the occasion.

Hattie Wyatt Caraway (1876–1950) was born near Bakersville, Tennessee, but later settled in Arkansas. A Democrat, she was the first woman elected to the U.S. Senate. In 1931 she completed her deceased husband's Senate term and was elected in her own right in 1932 and 1938. She sponsored an early version of the Equal Rights Amendment.

Johnny Cash (1932–), born in Kingsland, is a popular country music singer, guitarist, and composer. One of his first hit songs, "I Walk the Line," was recorded in 1956. He has won numerous Grammy Awards and has appeared in films and on television.

William Jefferson (Bill) Clinton (1946–), born and raised in Hope, was elected 42nd president of the United States in 1992. He had previously served twelve years as governor of Arkansas. A biography of Bill Clinton appears in Volume C.

Jay Hanna (Dizzy) Dean (1911–74), born in Lucas, was one of baseball's greatest pitchers. As a member of the St. Louis Cardinals, he led the National League in strikeouts for four years (1932–36) and in 1934 he won thirty games and the NL Most Valuable Player Award. In 1937 he injured his arm and was traded the following year to the Chicago Cubs. After his retirement in 1941 he became a sports announcer. He was elected to the National Baseball Hall of Fame in 1953.

March 7–8, 1862. Union forces won the battle and secured much of Arkansas and Missouri for the United States. After Union forces captured Little Rock in September 1863, the war was effectively over for Arkansas, although the civilians continued to suffer greatly. Arkansas was readmitted to the Union in 1868 but was occupied by federal troops until 1874.

Politics and Segregation

In the 1880's, many of Arkansas's tenant farmers and sharecroppers suffered due to low farm prices. In part, they blamed the Democrats who ruled the state legislature, and in 1886 they formed their own protest organization, the Agricultural Wheel, and ran "Wheeler" candidates for political office. The Democrats, in order to control dissent and drive a wedge between white "Wheelers" and black "Wheelers," passed laws that made it difficult for blacks to vote. Also, lynchings and other violence toward blacks increased.

Improvements and Reforms

In the early 1900's, during a period known as the Progressive Era, Arkansas's educational system was improved; a board of health was created; and a commission was formed to oversee the state's business interests. But in spite of this era of optimism, Arkansas soon faced many setbacks.

In the 1920's a major depression in agriculture ruined many farmers. Then a tragic flood in 1927 killed many people and destroyed much of that year's crops. Four years later, as the Great Depression of the 1930's was getting underway, a great drought again ruined crops. The government's New Deal programs brought relief to farm owners but to few farmworkers. As a result, black and white tenant farmers and sharecroppers banded together to form the Southern Tenant Farmer's Union, the first biracial union in the nation's history. The group succeeded in bringing attention to the plight of farm laborers.

In the early 1940's, World War II helped Arkansas's economy, but at the same time, thousands of people left the state, either to serve in the armed forces or to work in defense-related industries. With the work force depleted, farmers began to rely more on machinery to harvest the crops, and eventually agriculture became fully mechanized.

Integration

In 1954, the U.S. Supreme Court declared that segregating black and white students in separate schools was unconstitutional. Arkan-

James William Fulbright (1905–95) was born in Sumner, Missouri, but grew up in Fayetteville. A Rhodes scholar and lawyer, he served two terms as a U.S. representative (1942–45) and served five terms as a U.S. senator (1945–74) from Arkansas. In 1946 he sponsored the Fulbright Act, which provides scholarship funds to students studying abroad. As chairman of the Senate Foreign Relations Committee (1959–74), he was one of the chief congressional opponents of American involvement in the Vietnam War. The College of Arts and Sciences and the Institute of International Relations, both at the University of Arkansas, have been named for him.

John Harold Johnson (1918–), born in Arkansas City, founded (1942) the Johnson Publishing Company, which publishes *Ebony* and *Jet* magazines. Johnson has also been highly successful in the fields of book publishing, radio broadcasting, and cosmetics. He was awarded the Spingarn Medal in 1966.

Scott Joplin (1868–1917) was probably born in the border town of Texarkana. The son of former slaves, this musical genius became known as the King of Ragtime. Joplin's lively compositions include the still-popular "Maple Leaf Rag" and "The Entertainer." However, he was not recognized as a serious composer until long after his death; he was awarded a Pulitzer Prize in 1976.

Douglas MacArthur (1880–1964), born in Little Rock, was one of the United States' most brilliant generals. As commander of the U.S. Army in the Pacific during World War II (1941–45), his bold stategies helped defeat the Japanese. MacArthur also commanded (1950–51) the United Nations forces during the Korean War. A biography of Douglas MacArthur appears in Volume M.

Edward Durell Stone (1902–78), born in Fayetteville, was a noted architect. Often his buildings were designed around a courtyard, with bands of filtered light coming through the roofs and ceilings.

Douglas MacArthur

Among his best-known designs are the Museum of Modern Art (1937) in New York City; the U.S. Embassy (1954-58) in New Dehli, India; and the Kennedy Center for the Performing Arts (1964-69) in Washington, D.C.

In 1957 federal troops were sent to Arkansas to protect the first black students to enroll at the all-white Little Rock Central High School.

sas resisted the courts and continued to segregate the students until 1957, when nine black students attempted to attend the all-white Little Rock Central High School. Governor Orval E. Faubus called out the Arkansas National Guard to prevent them from entering the school.

In response to this, President Dwight D. Eisenhower ordered federal troops to Arkansas to enforce the integration. After a period of crisis and adjustment, the schools integrated without further incident.

Recent Trends

Today the farm economy of Arkansas is struggling, and some of its counties are among the poorest in the nation, especially those in the Delta region. However, the state's economy is growing overall, and population continues to rise. New businesses are coming to the state, and some industries are growing rapidly, especially tourism. Arkansas is working harder than ever to live up to its nickname as a land of opportunity for all.

JEANNIE M. WHAYNE
Arkansas Historical Association

ARLINGTON NATIONAL CEMETERY. See NATIONAL CEMETERIES.

ARMADA, SPANISH. See SPANISH ARMADA.

ARMENIA

The ancient homeland of the Armenians was a large, mountainous plateau in western Asia, which included part of what is now eastern Turkey. Armenians had inhabited the plateau continuously from the 500's B.C. Their kingdoms could be found in the region from earliest times to 1375. From this date until 1918, however, no Armenian state existed.

For most of this period its people were ruled as part of the Ottoman Turkish, Persian, and Russian empires. Between 1918 and 1920 a free Armenian republic struggled to survive, before becoming a part of the Soviet Union. Armenia remained a Soviet union republic until 1991, when it declared its independence. The present-day Republic of Armenia occupies a small area in the northeastern corner of its historic homeland.

THE PEOPLE

A Dispersed People. Armenians have been dispersed, or scattered, to many corners of the world. About half now live outside Armenia. Armenian communities have grown up in the Middle East, Russia, Western Europe, and the United States, among other places.

More than 90 percent of the Armenian republic's people are Armenian. Ethnic minorities include Azerbaijanis and Russians. The capital and largest city is Yerevan (sometimes spelled Erevan), with a population of more than 1 million.

Language and Religion. Armenian is a distinctive language with its own alphabet. Although it belongs to the large Indo-European language family, it is not related to any other living language.

Armenians have been Christians since the early A.D. 300's and claim to be the first to have adopted Christianity as their official state religion. Outside of Armenia, the church is often the center of Armenian social and community life. The head of the Armenian Apostolic Church is the Catholicos, who resides in the holy city of Echmiadzin, near Yerevan.

Custom and Tradition. Although Christmas and Easter are the most important holidays, two others are widely observed by Armenians. Vartanantz celebrates an event in A.D. 451, when Armenians under Vartan Mamikonian fought to the death against the Persians to preserve their religion. And on April 24th, Armenians commemorate the destruction, in 1915, of the Armenian community in Turkey. (See History section.)

Armenian foods are similar to that of other Middle Eastern peoples. A typical Armenian

FACTS and figures

REPUBLIC OF ARMENIA is the official name of the country.

LOCATION: Western Asia.

AREA: 11,500 sq mi (29,800 km²).

POPULATION: 3,300,000 (estimate).

CAPITAL AND LARGEST CITY: Yerevan (Erevan).

MAJOR LANGUAGE(S): Armenian.

MAJOR RELIGIOUS GROUP(S): Christian.

GOVERNMENT: Republic. **Head of state**—president. **Head of government**—prime minister. **Legislature**—parliament.

CHIEF PRODUCTS: Chemicals, electronic equipment, synthetic rubber, textiles, wheat, barley, cotton, fruits and nuts, copper.

meal might include lamb, rice pilaf, eggplant, yogurt, and a sweet dessert like baklava. Armenians pride themselves on their close family ties and the importance of hospitality. Children are taught respect for Armenian culture and traditions.

Notable Armenians. Armenians have gained renown in many fields. Among those prominent in Soviet life were the composer Aram Khachaturian, the astrophysicist Victor Ambartsumian, former world chess champion Tigran Petrosyan, and the onetime president of the Soviet Union, Anastas Mikoyan. Notable Americans of Armenian ancestry include the playwright William Saroyan, composer Alan Hovhaness, former California governor George Deukmejian, Jr., singer and actress Cher (who is also part Cherokee Indian), and businessmen Alex Manoogian and Kirk Kerkorian.

THE LAND

The Armenian plateau is a rugged highland averaging about 5,000 feet (1,500 meters) in elevation. It is crossed by numerous valleys and by swift-flowing rivers, broken by rapids and falls. Historic Armenia had its chief population centers in the valley of the Araks River (also called Aras or Araxes) and the region around Lake Van. Lake Van now lies within Turkey. Two other great lakes can be found on the plateau—Sevan in Armenia, and Urmia, now part of Iran.

The highest point on the plateau, Mount Ararat (Masis to Armenians), now lies in Turkey. Mount Aragats, the highest peak in the Armenian republic, rises 13,435 feet (4,095 meters) above sea level. The history of the land has been marked by destructive earthquakes. In 1988 two Armenian cities were devastated by a massive earthquake that killed more than 25,000 people.

Armenia has a generally dry climate, often with extremes of temperature. Winters are long and cold; summers are usually short and hot. Despite the harshness of the climate in winter, Armenia was one of the earliest agricultural areas cultivated by humans. The soil can be quite fertile, especially when irrigated. Copper is the chief mineral resource.

THE ECONOMY

Until the mid-1900's, most Armenians were peasant farmers. But with the great drive toward industrialization in the Soviet Union during the 1930's, Soviet Armenians began to

Most of Armenia consists of a high, rugged plateau ringed by mountains and crossed by numerous valleys and swift-flowing streams. The woman at right wears traditional Armenian dress.

move to the towns to work in factories. Today the majority of Armenians live in urban areas (cities and towns) and industry is the most important element of the economy. Major manufactured products include chemicals, electronic equipment, synthetic rubber, and various textiles, including fabrics.

The chief crops include wheat, barley, cotton, and fruits and nuts—particularly apricots, peaches, walnuts, and grapes for Armenian cognac, or fine brandy. Livestock include cattle, sheep, and goats.

HISTORY AND GOVERNMENT

Urartu to Tigranes I. The first important state in what became Armenia was the kingdom of Urartu, with its center around Lake Van. In the 600's B.C., new tribes migrated to the region, probably from the west. They mingled with the earlier inhabitants to form a distinct people, first mentioned as "Armenians" in the mid-500's B.C. Ruled for many centuries by the Persians, Armenia became a buffer state between contending Greeks and Romans to the west and Persians and Arabs to the south.

Armenia reached the height of its power under King Tigranes (or Tigran) I, the Great (reigned 95–55 B.C.). Tigranes founded an empire of many different peoples, but it was eventually conquered by the Romans.

Christianity and Conflict. In A.D. 314, the Armenian king Tiridates (or Trdat) III was converted to Christianity. In the early 400's, Saint Mesrop (known as Mashtots) created an alphabet for Armenian, and religious and historical works in that language began to appear. Yet the various noble houses of Armenia frequently fought with one another and with their kings. Although united by language and religion, Armenians were seldom unified under a single monarch.

The invasion of the Seljuk Turks in the 1000's led to the collapse of the independent Armenian kingdoms in Armenia. A new state, known as Lesser Armenia, was formed along the Mediterranean Sea. In 1375, however, this kingdom also fell, overrun by Mamelukes from Egypt. In the 1500's most of historic Armenia was conquered by the Ottoman Turks, who ruled it until the early 1900's. Eastern Armenia was under Persian rule until 1828, when it was absorbed into the Russian Empire.

Ottoman Rule. For centuries, Armenians in Turkey maintained relatively peaceful relations with their Ottoman masters. During the late 1800's, however, they began to suffer increasingly from discrimination, heavy taxation, and violence. In 1894–96, hundreds of thousands of Armenians were massacred with the approval of Sultan Abdul-Hamid II. Armenians were hopeful that when the Young Turk Revolution of 1908 overthrew Abdul-Hamid, a period of peace and cooperation would follow.

But when World War I broke out in 1914 and Turkey went to war with Russia, Armenians found themselves on both sides of the battlefield. In 1915 the Turkish government deported the Turkish Armenians, who were driven into the Syrian desert. In the process, between 600,000 and 1.5 million died of hunger and thirst or were killed outright, in what has been called "the first genocide of the 20th century."

Soviet Republic. Some survivors fled abroad. Others went to Russian Armenia, where in 1918, after the Russian Revolution, an independent Armenian republic was established. It survived only briefly. Threatened by a nationalist movement in Turkey, the government turned the new state over to the Soviet Communists in 1920. Armenia was the smallest of the 15 republics making up the Soviet Union. When the Soviet Union broke apart in 1991, the second independent Armenian republic came into being.

Armenia Today. The first president of the new republic, Levon Ter-Petrosyan, was elected in 1990 and again in 1996. A new constitution greatly strengthening the powers of the president was adopted in 1995. When Ter-Petrosyan stepped down in 1998, Premier Robert Kocharyan was elected to succeed him as president.

The new republic faces serious problems. Its economy is weak and many Armenians do not have enough to eat. Also, Armenians and Azerbaijanis have fought bitterly over the territory of Nagorno-Karabakh, which lies in neighboring Azerbaijan but whose people are mostly Armenian. In 1999, Prime Minister Vazgen Sarkisian was assassinated, plunging Armenia into further political crisis.

RONALD GRIGOR SUNY
University of Michigan
Author, *Armenia in the 20th Century*

The use of armor peaked between the 1300's and the mid-1500's. The soldier's suit was worn in France about 1550. The horse displays Venetian armor dating from 1575.

ARMOR

When primitive people began to use weapons, they were faced with new problems. Their bodies needed more protection. They learned to use shields of wood or tough animal hide to protect themselves from the enemy's clubs or stone axes. This was the earliest armor.

Later the ancient Egyptian and Assyrian soldiers wore heavy cloth jackets or shirts to add to their protection. These were made of many layers of quilted linen.

▶METAL ARMOR

The first metal armor was made of bronze. It was probably used by the Greeks about 2000–1800 B.C. They hammered bronze into helmets to protect their heads. They also covered their wooden shields with thin metal sheets.

The Romans were the first to make wide use of iron for armor. Roman soldiers protected their bodies with leather vests covered with thin strips of bronze or iron. Sometimes they covered their legs with metal shin guards. Helmets shielded the head. Roman helmets had broad, curving metal sidepieces to protect the cheeks. Brims came down to cover the forehead and the back of the neck.

Steel was not used in armor much before the Middle Ages. Armor made of steel was even stronger and more flexible than that made of iron. Whole suits of steel protected the medieval knight from head to toe. Sleeves, shin guards, and even gloves with jointed fingers were carefully shaped from thin metal plates. Hinges, joints, and rivets fastened the suits to make them flexible. Helmets had movable visors, or lids that dropped over the face when fighting began.

Some knights wore flexible armor of chain mail. Such armor was made of hundreds of tiny steel rings linked together to form a kind of steel cloth. Shirts of chain mail slipped over the head and reached to the knees.

Plate armor had to be carefully fitted to the body. The armorer heated the metal and

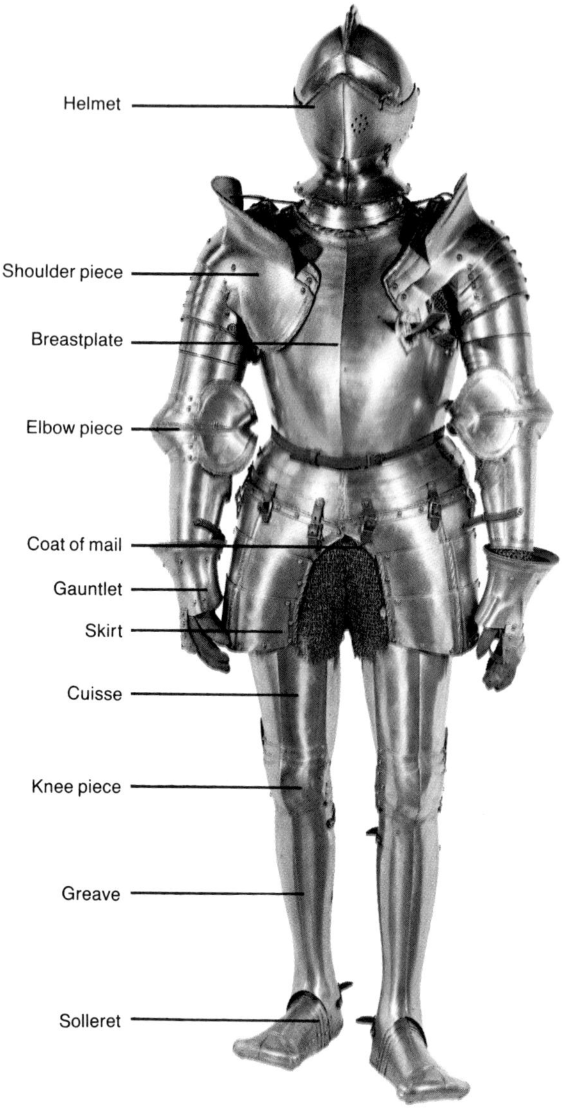

The fully covered "knight in shining armor" as shown at far left was a gradual development. Knights once wore shirts of chain mail, a fabric made from interlinked iron rings. Later, leather or metal plates were attached to the mail. In the 15th-century Italian suit at left, the steel plates have been made flexible by leather straps and rivets. Helmets, too, evolved. The bronze Corinthian battle helmet above dates from the 5th century B.C. The lion's head parade helmet at top is from Italy, 1460.

shaped it with tools. Working like a tailor, the armorer measured, tried on, and shaped again. Sometimes beautiful designs were etched into the steel. The shield was usually decorated with inlaid metal in several colors.

Full armor had many disadvantages. Because it was so expensive to make, only the well-to-do noble or knight could afford a suit of armor. Even worse was its great weight. A special servant or knight-in-training called a squire had to help the knight put on his armor and mount his horse. Drawings from the Middle Ages show knights being hoisted onto their horses by derricks or cranes. If the knight was thrown to the ground by his enemy, he was usually unable to struggle to his feet. His opponent could then easily kill him with his sword or spear.

THE DECLINE OF ARMOR

Gunpowder (invented centuries before by the Chinese) reached Europe about the end of the Middle Ages. A foot soldier with a gun could now pierce the heaviest armor that a man was able to carry on his body. Armor began to lose its usefulness. However, early explorers of the American continent continued to use armor against Indian arrows. But by the time of the American Revolution, armor appeared only in fancy-dress uniform.

Far left: A suit of Japanese armor dating from the 16th century is made of steel, silk braid, gilt bronze, deerskin, bear pelt, and gilt wood. Center: A suit of English armor dating from the 16th century is made of brass, leather, and velvet. It was fashioned at the Royal Workshop at Greenwich, the finest armor maker in England. Above: A parade helmet, made of silver and bronze, and shield, made of brass, silver, and gold, were crafted for King Louis XIV of France about 1700.

▶ARMOR IN MODERN FORM

In the two world wars, metal helmets were used to protect the head and neck from pieces of flying metal. Fliers in World War II and in Korea wore thick coveralls padded with fiberglass. These gave protection from cold as well as from shell fragments. Some police officers wear armor in the form of bulletproof vests. Still another type of modern armor is the protective helmet such as those worn by construction workers or motorcyclists.

Today a new type of armor has been designed to help astronauts explore outer space. Space suits are thickly padded and fit snugly from neck to toe. A helmet, covering the entire head, is fitted with earphones, microphones, and a supply of oxygen. With such protection astronauts can face the great strains of rocket launching and space travel. As long as people must protect their bodies against enemy weapons and the forces of nature, they will try to design better armor.

JAMES HOERGER
John F. Kennedy School
(Great Neck, New York)

ARMORED VEHICLES. See TANKS.

ARMS CONTROL. See DISARMAMENT.

ARMSTRONG, LOUIS. See LOUISIANA (Famous People).

ARMSTRONG, NEIL A. (1930–)

On July 20, 1969, American astronaut Neil Armstrong became the first man ever to walk on the moon.

Neil Alden Armstrong was born in Wapakoneta, Ohio, on August 5, 1930. After receiving his degree from Purdue University in 1955, Armstrong became a civilian research pilot for the National Advisory Committee for Aeronautics (NACA), later renamed the National Aeronautics and Space Administration (NASA). He worked seven years as a test pilot before being accepted in the astronaut program in 1962. Among his early major assignments was the command of the *Gemini 8* mission, which accomplished the first manual space-docking maneuver (March 16, 1966).

In January 1969, Armstrong was chosen to command the *Apollo 11* space mission. He was accompanied by fellow astronauts Edwin E. "Buzz" Aldrin and Michael Collins. On July 16, 1969, a *Saturn 5* booster rocket launched *Apollo 11* and its crew into space. Four days later, on July 20, the lunar module, the *Eagle*, landed on the moon, in a smooth region called the Sea of Tranquility. Armstrong thrilled the world when he radioed NASA with the declaration, "The *Eagle* has landed." Then, at 10:56 P.M. eastern standard time (EST), Armstrong became the first human being to set foot on the moon. The event was immortalized in his statement, "That's one small step for a man, one giant leap for mankind." For nearly 22 hours, Armstrong and Aldrin explored and collected samples of the moon's surface.

On July 24, the *Apollo 11* crew re-entered the Earth's atmosphere, splashing down in the Pacific Ocean at 12:50 P.M. EST. Hailed as heroes, the astronauts were each awarded the Presidential Medal of Freedom. Armstrong resigned from NASA in 1971.

Reviewed by AMOS J. LOVEDAY, JR.
Ohio Historical Society

ARMY. See CANADA, ARMED FORCES OF; UNITED STATES, ARMED FORCES OF THE.

ARNOLD, BENEDICT (1741–1801)

Benedict Arnold was a brave soldier, a patriot—and the most notorious traitor in American history.

Born in Norwich, Connecticut, on January 14, 1741, Arnold fought in the French and Indian War at the age of 14 and later became a captain in the Connecticut militia. When the Revolutionary War began in 1775, he helped Ethan Allen capture Fort Ticonderoga and then proposed a daring plan to capture Quebec, the key to British Canada. The attack failed, but Arnold proved himself a heroic soldier. In 1777 he played a key role in bringing about the British defeat at Saratoga, a major victory for the Americans.

In June 1778, Arnold was placed in command of Philadelphia, where he married Peggy Shippen, the daughter of a British sympathizer. In 1779 he was charged with using his position for personal profit and employing soldiers in his command as servants. A court martial cleared him of most of the charges, but General George Washington was required to reprimand him. Arnold, resentful of such treatment, plotted revenge.

In 1780, Arnold was given command of the strategic fort at West Point, New York, which he immediately plotted to surrender to the British. For this he was promised money and a promotion. But Arnold's British contact, Major John André, was intercepted by American soldiers and executed as a spy. Arnold fled to a British ship.

The British paid Arnold and gave him command of a small force, with which he fought against Americans in Virginia and Connecticut. After the war, he moved with his family to England. He died in London on June 14, 1801, scorned by Americans and British alike. Had he not betrayed his country, Arnold would be remembered today as one of the nation's greatest heroes.

Reviewed by RICHARD B. MORRIS
Editor, *Encyclopedia of American History*

ARNOLD, HENRY ("HAP"). See WORLD WAR II (Profiles: Allied Powers).

ART

Art is one of humanity's oldest inventions. It existed long before a single farm was planted, before the first villages were built. Art was already thousands of years old when writing appeared; in fact, the letters of the first alphabets were pictures. People were probably shaping objects and scratching out images even as they turned their grunts and cries into the first systematic spoken languages.

People are still making art; they have never stopped. Just about every society, from the oldest to the youngest and from the most primitive to the most advanced, has created works of art. No wonder that the sum of all this creation is called "the world of art." Art is a world in itself, a world as round and full and changeable as the world we live in and, like the earth, a whole of many distinct parts. Removing a wedge from the whole and studying it is like touring a country or visiting an era in the past. One wedge describes the ideals of the ancient Greeks. Another defines the interests of the French in the Middle Ages. Still another demonstrates the ideas that shaped the Renaissance in Italy. Another reflects the traditions that had meaning in Japan in the 1700's, or China in the 900's, or India in the 1600's. But seen as

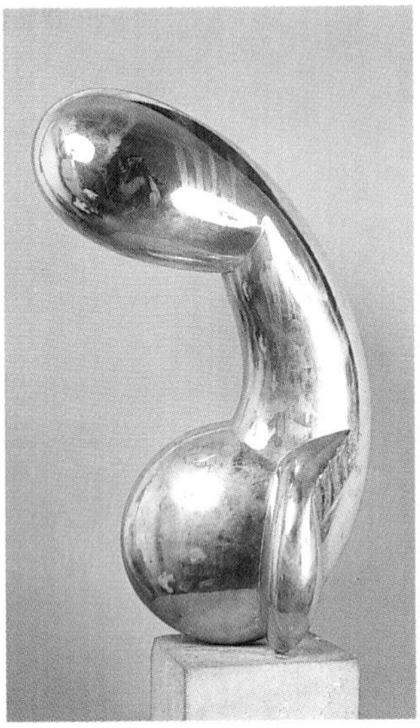

The Metropolitan Museum of Art, Gift of Renate Hofmann, 1975.

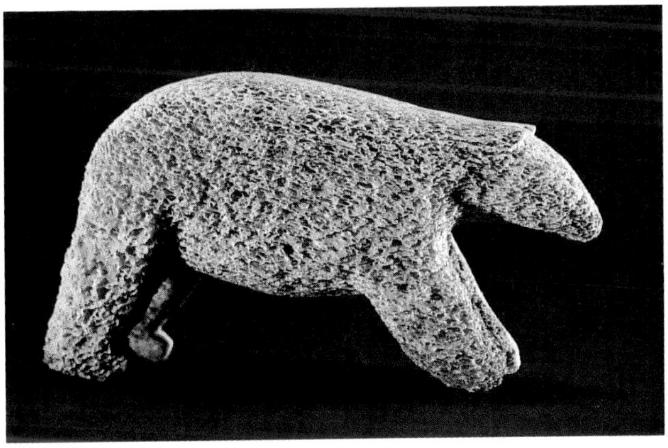

Every society, in every time and place, has created art. *Clockwise from top:* Artists use a variety of styles and techniques to depict the world around them, from the detailed realism of Albrecht Dürer's *Hare*, to the utter simplicity of *Princesse X*, by Constantin Brancusi. Hans Hofmann's *Rhapsody*, on the other hand, is completely abstract—it does not represent any recognizable object. The Inuit artist who carved a polar bear from whale bone chose a familiar subject and a readily available material.

This article discusses theories about the origins and meanings of art. It also suggests ways in which we can learn about a people or culture by studying the art they created. *The New Book of Knowledge* contains many articles that provide specific information on the arts of various cultures. For example, the arts of the peoples of Africa are discussed in AFRICA, ART AND ARCHITECTURE OF. The arts of individual countries are surveyed in numerous articles, including CHINESE ART; FRANCE, ART AND ARCHITECTURE OF; INDIA, ART AND ARCHITECTURE OF; JAPANESE ART AND ARCHITECTURE; LATIN AMERICA, ART AND ARCHITECTURE OF; and UNITED STATES, ART AND ARCHITECTURE OF THE.

Look up the names of periods and styles of art to find such articles as GOTHIC ART AND ARCHITECTURE, IMPRESSIONISM, ISLAMIC ART AND ARCHITECTURE, and MODERN ART.

The basic components of art are discussed in COLOR and DESIGN. There are also articles on art forms, such as COLLAGE, DRAWING, PAINTING, SCULPTURE, and WATERCOLOR. Other articles cover the history and collections of famous art galleries, including HERMITAGE MUSEUM, LOUVRE, METROPOLITAN MUSEUM OF ART, and NATIONAL GALLERY OF CANADA. Consult the Index to find the many biographies of artists contained in this encyclopedia.

Below: Prehistoric people may have created likenesses of animals, such as this bison carving, as a form of hunting magic. *Left:* Kachina figures made by Pueblo Indians are representations of ancestral spirits.

a whole, the world of art reveals a broad picture of all of humanity; it summarizes the ideals, interests, and ideas of all people in all eras. It tells us what has been on people's minds in generation after generation, from the dawn of humanity to the present day.

Art, then, is a product of the human mind and a mirror of that mind—a record of human progress. And like the mind, and like the societies that progress has created, art is rich, complicated, and sometimes quite mysterious.

THE MEANINGS OF ART

Actually, most people do know what art is. The trouble comes when they try to define it. No one definition satisfies everyone's idea. No one definition seems broad enough to cover every object in an art museum. And some definitions are too broad—they may apply to everything in the museum, but they also apply to many things that clearly are not art.

Despite the difficulty of defining art, we can make certain observations that help us to understand what art is. Art is a product made by people that expresses the uniqueness of the maker, of the society to which the maker belongs, of all humanity, or of all of these. The product appeals to the intellect and to the senses, especially to the sense of beauty. The product can assume a variety of forms—a musical composition, a ballet, a play, or a novel or poem. This article, however, deals only with the "fine" arts: drawing, painting, sculpture, and architecture.

It is our intellect that makes humans unique. People have created religion, science, and technology to make their struggle for survival easier. They have created art to measure the worth of these and all human enterprises against the quality of life. European medieval art dealt almost exclusively with religion. Italian Renaissance art reflected the growing interest in the sciences. Much Oriental art conveys the idea of a harmonious, well-ordered universe. Art of the modern era is very much a product of the age of technology.

Art—or at least great art—almost always gets at the truth. Great artists are expert observers and their work reflects life as they see it.

ART AS A RECORD

The earliest art that we know about was painted on the walls of caves during the Old Stone Age—roughly 20,000 years ago. Most of the pictures depict animals—bison, reindeer, ibex—the animals that early people hunted and depended on for survival. We cannot be completely sure why these images were painted, but we can guess that hunters created likenesses of their prey in order to capture its spirit. Having taken the spirit, the hunters found it easier to take the body. And since early people were very good hunters, whose mastery of weapons gave them an advantage over much stronger creatures, they must have believed that the magic worked.

About 5,000 years ago, the first great civilization began emerging from humanity's intelligent struggle for survival. And with them came monumental art—art created to proclaim the greatness of a civilization and to last forever. In Egypt and Mesopotamia gigantic pyramids were erected, the tombs within decorated with carvings and paintings showing the great deeds of the rulers buried there. Clearly, these ancient peoples had no intention of ever disappearing. Even their utensils and vessels were meant to last eternally.

Mesopotamian and especially Egyptian art dwelt on the achievements of rulers. This was so mainly because the rulers were thought to be gods, or at least to have intimate contact with gods. And it was fitting, too, because the ruler was regarded as the living embodiment of the nation: Pharaoh and Egypt were one and the same. The individuality of the human being was seldom even recognized, much less celebrated.

Then came the Minoans and Mycenaeans and the Greeks, and people had their day. The early statuary of the Aegean peoples was said to represent gods and goddesses, but the forms were becoming ever more recognizably human. This in itself seems to indicate that people were beginning to appreciate their own importance. Like the ancient Hebrews, they proclaimed themselves made in their gods' image—not perfect, perhaps, but nonetheless godlike. By the Classical Age (400's B.C.) in Greece, even that pretense was dropped. Greek sculptors began portraying spear bearers and charioteers with bodies as perfect as those of the gods Apollo and Dionysus.

Greek art idealized the human form. We do not believe that there were no Greeks with pot bellies or bowlegs; but we can conclude that the Greeks thought enough of themselves to find great satisfaction in showing themselves as ideal beings. And so we admire the Greeks not so much for what they were, but for the ideals they set up for themselves.

The Greeks' high regard for the individual is also reflected in their architecture. Greek architects took great pains to proportion their structures so that people could use them comfortably: The ceilings are never so high, the rooms never so massive that a person feels small or lost within. This is another example of how we use art, which expresses ideals, to learn about a people of the past.

Roman art, like Roman civilization, was based to a large extent on the Greek model. But the Romans carried their concern with the individual a step further. One Roman statue is a representation of an old, big-nosed citizen with a stern expression on his face. No one would call it an idealized portrait. Yet, as one studies it, the face gradually appears handsomer; it seems to reflect great character, wisdom, integrity. With such works the Romans are saying that the individual need not meet prescribed standards to be beautiful.

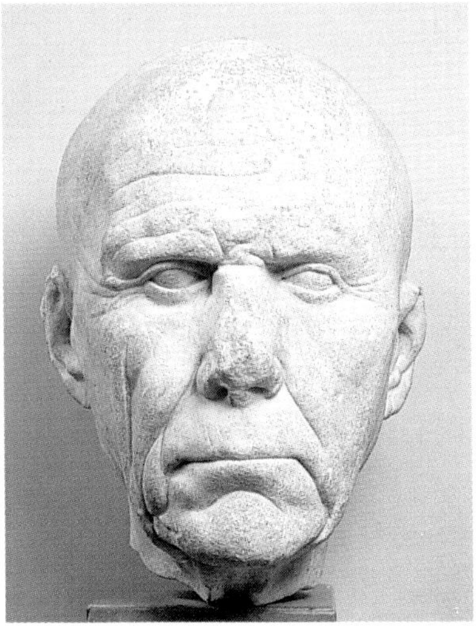

Portrait sculptures by Roman artists show their interest in portraying subjects realistically. The deeply lined face and stern expression of this sculpture of an old man reflect his individuality and character.

When invasions by Germanic tribes into western and southern Europe became too troublesome for the Romans to deal with, the emperor Constantine (280?–337) moved his capital eastward to the site of the old city of Byzantium. The new capital was called Constantinople, in his honor. Constantine also was the first Christian emperor, and thus his eastern empire, called the Byzantine Empire, became the first Christian civilization. There the traditions of ancient Greek and Roman art were remolded to fit the needs of Christianity. Under the emperor Justinian (483–565), Constantinople was built up as the first great Christian city.

The soaring heights and rich decoration of Gothic cathedrals, such as Reims Cathedral in France, were meant to inspire churchgoers with the glory of God.

The Roman Empire in western Europe came to an end in the A.D. 400's. The following period, from about 500 to 1500, is called the Middle Ages. The Germanic peoples who established kingdoms in the former empire were greatly influenced by Roman civilization. They learned the Roman tongue and adopted Christianity. They turned their artistic skills to making Christian art, using the intricately carved and decorated style that characterized their art.

The early Middle Ages were years of confusion and disorder in western Europe. Yet during this period the great Frankish king Charlemagne established a large empire that included much of western and central Europe. Elsewhere—in the Byzantine Empire, northern and western Africa, and the Far East—great civilizations flourished.

During the later Middle Ages, a new and monumental style of architecture called Gothic (the name was given to it much later) developed in the West. All over France, Germany, and England, grand cathedrals rose, one after another, each more lavish than the others. Nearly all the art of this period, which lasted into the 1500's in some parts of Europe, was devoted to decoration of the cathedrals. Columns were surrounded with statues; doorways were richly carved; beautiful stained-glass windows colored the sunlight pouring in; carefully cut and polished wood formed the altars; huge, heavy tapestries hung between chapels; mosaic tiles formed mazelike patterns on the floors. It was as if all artistic creativity was focused on the glorification of God and the church.

Gothic architecture tells us a great deal about how society regarded people. The Gothic cathedral is high, heaven-reaching, enormously empty. Inside, one cannot help feeling small and humble. And all the statues —the saints on the columns, the demons over the doors—are watching and warning.

Early in the 1400's, the God-centered outlook of the Middle Ages slowly began to change. First in Italy and then throughout Europe, the individual human being became a main concern of art. This attitude, known as humanism, is what distinguished the Renaissance from earlier periods. It is what made the Renaissance go down in history as a great age for humanity. And again, it was in art that the spirit of humanism was expressed most clearly.

Humanism affected not only the content of art but the very way in which art was created. For if art said that people were individuals, worthy of recognition for their beliefs, were not the people who made art very special individuals, deserving credit for their accomplishments? So, with the Renaissance, the artist took on a new importance. And the recognition that the artist received added a new facet to art.

In Eastern lands, as in the West, art from its earliest days was an ever-growing record of what was most important to people. Art in Japan often reflects an appreciation for the beauty of nature. Early Japanese painting tended to be delicate, airy, and romantic, reflecting the graceful life of the Japanese court. Later, when Japan was ruled by militaristic

The Metropolitan Museum of Art, Bequest of Mrs. H. O. Havemeyer, 1929.

Left: The Great Wave off Kanagawa, a woodcut by the Japanese artist Katsushika Hokusai. The development of woodcut techniques in Japan allowed prints to be reproduced inexpensively and helped bring Japanese art to a wider audience.

Below: Artists in the Eastern world developed original and expressive styles of manuscript illustration. This page is from a Persian manuscript of the 1400's.

emperors, art became harsher and more realistic. The 1700's and 1800's saw the development of the Japanese woodcut. Woodcuts, which are inexpensive to reproduce, were meant to reach a wider audience—to bring beauty within reach of the hardworking common people.

The arts in India have almost always had a religious content. However, this was often combined with an interest in earthly life. Sculpture, in particular, often portrayed gods and goddesses as vital and lifelike beings. Indian painters developed original and expressive styles of manuscript illustration.

China's artistic tradition is one of the oldest in the world, dating back to 5000 B.C. A respect for tradition and reverence for nature is reflected in Chinese art and architecture. Calligraphy, the art of beautiful writing, was considered one of the most important visual arts.

▶ART OF THE ARTIST

Art since the Renaissance has remained a record of humanity and a reflection of the ideas that concern people. But since the Renaissance this record has come down to us in a series of very personal statements.

The great Italian artist Michelangelo believed that the truth of any matter existed in nature. The artist's job was to seek that truth and capture it in his art. He once described sculpture as the act of "liberating the figure from the marble that imprisons it." In other words, the forms that he depicted so dramatically in his work already existed; his job was to find them and free them.

A later Italian painter, Caravaggio, sought the truth in everyday occurrences, such as the pleasures of making music. Even in his paintings of religious events, he clothed the participants in the apparel of his own time, and placed them in commonplace settings, such as taverns. Saints were often pictured as poor people with plain garments and bare feet. Caravaggio seemed to be saying that all people, even the most humble, have value.

The paintings of the Dutch artist Rembrandt may represent the peak of humanism. In a very special way, Rembrandt's subject matter was the soul of man. He painted religious subjects, portraits of prosperous Dutch citizens, and he painted simple portraits of poor people and of himself. But whatever he painted, his figures always appear lit from within, as if they were filled with all the suffering—and the beauty—of humanity. Rembrandt is telling us that with all the pain, corruption, and helplessness that characterize human life, the human spirit is still filled with all the glory and good of God's light.

The 1600's and 1700's were the "age of kings" in Europe. The courts of the European nations dominated much artistic activity. Many artists were dependent on the kings and aristocrats who

Above: **In his painting *The Jewish Bride*, Dutch artist Rembrandt van Rijn portrays the tender affection of a newly married couple. Rembrandt's work, in its expression of the dignity of the human spirit, may represent the peak of humanism in art.** ***Right:*** **In *The Third of May, 1808*, Spanish artist Francisco Goya protests the invasion of his country by Napoleon's armies—and attacks the nature of war itself.**

Collection, The Museum of Modern Art, New York. Gift of Mrs. Simon Guggenheim.

The Metropolitan Museum of Art, Purchase, 1983.

Near left: **A sculpture made by the Kota people of Gabon represents the spirit of the dead. It is constructed of wood covered with sheets of copper and other metals. The shapes and patterns of African art influenced many modern European and American artists, including Pablo Picasso. *Far left:* Picasso, like other modern artists, experimented with new ways of looking at things. *Girl Before a Mirror* uses bright colors and flattened shapes in its portrait of a young woman.**

ruled the continent. And yet great artists can never be slaves—except to the search for truth. As the abuses of the monarchs stirred the common people to greater and greater resentment, the artists often joined in the protests. For example, when Napoleon's armies invaded Spain in 1808, the Spanish artist Francisco Goya turned his talents to an assault on the French. His paintings and engravings include works that are savage attacks on the French invaders, and even more savage—and lasting—attacks on war itself.

Another Spaniard, Pablo Picasso, made a similar statement 130 years later. His well-known painting *Guernica* tells the story of the Spanish Civil War as directly as any text. And it is not only about a destroyed Spanish city; it is about war.

The 1800's and 1900's saw a remarkable increase in the speed at which civilization changes. We have come through an Industrial Revolution into an age of technology into a space age. Artists have kept pace with all these changes.

The ways in which artists approach art have been in a state of constant re-evaluation since the mid-1800's. The impressionists began a process that led to a breakdown in the importance of subject matter. With these French artists came an interest in the technique used to apply paint to canvas. Concern with forms for their own sake led to cubism and then to abstractionism, in sculpture as well as painting. By the mid-1900's painting and sculpture seemingly came together in a search for new forms.

The 1900's also saw a growing appreciation of the arts of non-Western cultures. Once dismissed as "primitive," the arts of African and Native American peoples were now admired for their vitality and directness of expression. African sculpture, in particular, influenced a number of modern artists, including Picasso. As modern communications have allowed ideas about art to become ever more widely spread, the influence of cultures on one another has continued.

What is the truth of our own age, as expressed in art? As we study the art of our age, each of us can draw our own conclusions.

David Jacobs
Author, *Master Painters of the Renaissance*

ART DECO. See Decorative Arts (The Industrial Age).

ARTEMIS. See Greek Mythology (Profiles).

ARTERIOSCLEROSIS. See Diseases (Descriptions of Some Diseases).

ARTHRITIS. See Diseases (Descriptions of Some Diseases).

CHESTER ALAN ARTHUR (1829-1886)

21st President of the United States

FACTS ABOUT ARTHUR

Birthplace: Fairfield, Vermont
Religion: Episcopalian
College Attended: Union College, Schenectady, New York
Occupation: Lawyer
Married: Ellen Lewis Herndon
Children: William, Chester, Ellen
Political Party: Republican
Age on Becoming President: 50
Office Held Before Becoming President: Vice President
President Who Preceded Him: James A. Garfield
Nickname: "The Gentleman Boss"
Years in the Presidency: 1881–1885
Vice President: None
President Who Succeeded Him: Grover Cleveland
Age at Death: 56
Burial Place: Albany, New York

DURING ARTHUR'S PRESIDENCY

Below, left: The U.S. Senate ratified (1882) the Geneva (or Red Cross) Convention of 1864. Congress passed the Pendleton Civil Service Act, which established the U.S. Civil Service Commission (1883). *Below:* The Brooklyn Bridge was completed (1883); at the time it was the world's longest bridge. Construction of the first building known as a skyscraper, the 10-story Home Insurance Building, was begun in Chicago (1883). The Linotype, the first practical typesetting machine, was patented (1884) by Ottmar Mergenthaler. *Above:* The Washington Monument in Washington, D.C., was dedicated (1885).

ARTHUR, CHESTER ALAN. On July 2, 1881, President James A. Garfield was shot in the back by an insane man. For two months the President lay between life and death. On September 19, Garfield died, and early the next morning Vice-President Chester Alan Arthur became the new president of the United States.

Arthur was a handsome man. Tall and broad-shouldered, he impressed people with his dignified bearing and elegant manners. He was courteous and friendly.

But many people considered the handsome vice-president unfit to be president. Arthur had long been associated with the spoils system. Under this system government jobs were awarded for service to a political party, whether the candidates were honest and able or not. In fact, the man who killed President Garfield explained that he did so because he had been refused a government job. People were alarmed that Arthur, a product of the spoils system, had become president.

Arthur's administration, however, proved to be quite different than his country expected. It was marked by honesty and by the replacement of the spoils system with the present Civil Service system based on merit.

▶ EARLY YEARS

Chester Alan Arthur was born October 5, 1829, in Fairfield, Vermont. He was the oldest son in a family of seven children. His father, William Arthur, was a Baptist minister.

The Arthur family moved about a great deal. The Reverend William Arthur was a man of strong beliefs and did not hesitate to speak his mind to his congregations. As a result, he did not stay in one place very long. At the age of 15, Chester entered Union College, in Schenectady, New York. He helped pay for his college expenses by teaching school during vacations. He studied hard and, in 1848, graduated with honors. Arthur then studied law. But he continued to teach to support himself until 1853, when he went to New York City to begin his career as a lawyer.

The future president first gained prominence when he became involved in the slavery question that was soon to lead to civil war. William Arthur had been opposed to slavery, and Chester shared his father's feelings. He sympathized with the plight of blacks and took part in two important cases in their defense. In one his law firm gained freedom for eight blacks accused of being runaway slaves.

The other case dealt with the problem of segregation. It arose when Lizzie Jennings was not allowed to ride on a streetcar in New York City because she was black. Arthur won $500 for her in damages. And the court decision stated that blacks had the same right to ride on New York streetcars as anyone else.

ARTHUR ENTERS POLITICS

Like most lawyers of the time, Arthur also took part in politics. In 1860 he helped organize the New York State Republican Party, and he supported its candidate for governor. As a reward the governor made Arthur engineer in chief and then quartermaster general of New York State. During the Civil War Arthur's position was very important, for all Union Army volunteers were equipped by the state before they were sent on to the Army. Arthur proved skillful and honest in providing thousands of New York soldiers with food, shelter, guns, tents, and other equipment.

COLLECTOR OF NEW YORK

Arthur's work for the Republican Party brought him to the attention of Senator Roscoe Conkling, the political boss of New York State. Arthur became Conkling's lieutenant and worked with him to win the election of Ulysses S. Grant in 1868. For his help President Grant in 1871 appointed Arthur collector of customs for the port of New York.

The collector was in charge of the New York Custom House, which received most of the customs duties of the United States. He also had the power to distribute more than 1,000 jobs. Under the spoils system these jobs went to faithful Republicans. They were expected to work for the party as well as for the Custom House. In the years that Arthur held the position, he simply followed the old system, although he himself remained an honest and able administrator.

In this newspaper cartoon of the 1880's (*above*), President Arthur turns his back on his old crony, Boss Roscoe Conkling. The woman represents the Republican Party. After President James A. Garfield was assassinated in 1881, Chester Arthur was inaugurated as 21st president at his home in New York City (*below*).

But many people were becoming angry about the inefficiency of the spoils system. They wanted a merit system, under which officeholders would be chosen on the basis of ability. In 1877 Rutherford B. Hayes, a believer in the merit system, became president. Hayes ordered an investigation of the New York Custom House, and in 1878 Arthur was dismissed from his post. The conflict caused a deep split in the Republican Party. The supporters of the old system became known as Stalwarts. The reformers were called Half-Breeds.

VICE-PRESIDENT

In 1880 the Republicans who met to pick a new candidate for president were still bitterly divided. The delegates voted 36 times before they agreed on a candidate whom no one had expected—James A. Garfield, a Half-Breed. However, Senator Conkling was Garfield's political enemy. And to gain the support of the Stalwarts, the Garfield men nominated Arthur for the vice-presidency. The Republicans won in a close election. Ten months later Garfield was dead, and Arthur became the 21st president of the United States.

Ellen Lewis Herndon (*below*) married Chester Alan Arthur in 1859. She died in 1880, before he became president. Their young daughter, Ellen, was raised in the White House by President Arthur's sister.

PRESIDENT ARTHUR SURPRISES MANY PEOPLE

As president, Arthur surprised both his friends and enemies. Arthur wished to make a good record for himself and was eager to be renominated and re-elected. He knew that he would never gain the support of reform and independent voters if he acted simply as a tool of Boss Conkling.

Arthur therefore determined not to let his administration be disgraced by the spoils system. He also tried earnestly to deal with some of the serious political problems the nation faced. But he was not so successful as he wished because he never had the full support of Congress.

For many years the Senate and the House of Representatives had gained power at the expense of weak presidents. Even such a strong personality as Abraham Lincoln had trouble with Congress. And his successors—Johnson, Grant, and Hayes—had let themselves be dominated by powerful Congressional leaders. Arthur was especially defenseless. He had become president by accident, and he did not command the support of any strong group in Congress.

Furthermore, Congress was itself divided. Both the Democratic and Republican parties were split into warring groups like the Stalwarts and the Half-Breeds. Some questions, such as the tariff (the tax on goods imported into the country), also divided the legislators. Other issues, such as the currency, set farmers, laborers, and manufacturers fighting one another.

Most important of all, the country was expanding and growing rich. Many people thought only of what they could get for themselves. Their representatives did not vote according to what was best for the nation as a whole. Instead they voted for laws that would gain the most for their supporters. Under such conditions it was difficult even for an able president to work out a good national policy. Arthur tried his best. But his achievements were limited.

The Pendleton Act and the Merit System

Before Arthur took office, it became known that some postal officials had collected money illegally in arranging mail routes. They were brought to trial in the famous Star Route cases. They were never convicted, but the

IMPORTANT DATES IN THE LIFE OF CHESTER ALAN ARTHUR

1829	Born at Fairfield, Vermont, October 5.
1848	Graduated from Union College.
1854	Became a lawyer in New York City.
1859	Married Ellen Lewis Herndon.
1860	Appointed engineer in chief of New York.
1862–1863	Quartermaster general of New York.
1871–1878	Collector of customs for the port of New York.
1880	Elected vice-president of the United States.
1881	Garfield assassinated; Arthur inaugurated president of the United States, September 20.
1881–1885	21st president of the United States.
1886	Died in New York City, November 18.

trial made many more Americans aware of the evils of the spoils system.

With President Arthur's support, Congress now tried to introduce the merit system. In 1883, Arthur signed a law that helped take thousands of government jobs out of politics. This was the Pendleton Civil Service Act. It required candidates for many government jobs to pass tests before they could be accepted. Men who qualified were protected against being dismissed for political reasons. The Pendleton Act was the beginning of the present United States Civil Service.

Too Much Money and Chinese Exclusion

During the 1880's the United States had an unusual problem: there was too much money in the treasury. In one year the government collected $80,000,000 more than it spent. This kept money out of circulation, hurt business, and caused prices to fall. Arthur wanted to solve the problem by lowering the tariff. Congress, however, refused to do so. It preferred to spend the money on a "pork-barrel" bill. This was a law that authorized federal funds to be spent on river and harbor improvements. Such a law won votes for the congressmen and senators of the favored states. Arthur rejected the bill even though he knew that this would make him unpopular. But Congress passed it over his veto, and the tariff problem was not solved during Arthur's term in office.

Congress also passed the Chinese Exclusion Act of 1882 against the president's wishes. Its aim was to prevent Chinese from immigrating to the United States. Arthur opposed the bill because it violated a treaty between China and the United States. His opposition forced Congress to rewrite the law so that it had fewer harsh restrictions against the Chinese.

NOT ALL WAS POLITICS

In 1859 Arthur had married Ellen Lewis Herndon, the daughter of a Virginia naval officer. Mrs. Arthur died in 1880, before her husband became president. Each day President Arthur honored her by placing fresh flowers in front of her picture.

The President's favorite sport was fishing. He was considered one of the best salmon fishermen in the country. Arthur was also fond of good food and companionship. He enjoyed the dinners to which he was invited and hated to leave. Since none of the guests could politely leave before the President, the dinners sometimes lasted until midnight.

Arthur liked elegant surroundings, and he had the White House completely redecorated. He installed new plumbing, a new bathroom, and the first elevator in the White House. His sister, who acted as hostess, helped him make it Washington's social center.

ARTHUR IS REJECTED BY THE REPUBLICANS

In 1884 the Republicans did not renominate Arthur for president. The Half-Breed reformers were still not satisfied with him, and his old Stalwart friends, of course, were now against him. James G. Blaine was nominated and later lost the election to Democrat Grover Cleveland.

Arthur returned to his old law practice. But his health was failing. On November 18, 1886, at the age of 56, he died at his home in New York.

Chester Arthur was an honest and courageous president. But the political situation of his times did not permit him to deal successfully with the country's great problems. The greatest achievement of his administration was the Pendleton Civil Service Act. However, he will be best remembered as the spoils system politician who became president by accident, and who proved himself a better man than anyone expected.

OSCAR HANDLIN
Harvard University

ARTHUR, KING

In romance and legend, in music and art, King Arthur and his Knights of the Round Table are among the world's best-known heroes. For centuries they have been favorites of storytellers in many different countries.

The tales, as they are most often told today, are set in Arthur's court at Camelot, in a castle with noble towers and a great hall. In the great hall stood the Round Table, where only the best and most valiant knights could sit. Because the table had no head and no foot, all the knights seated around it were of equal rank. Each knight has his own seat with his name carved on it. The knights were bound by oath to help one another in time of danger and never to fight among themselves.

The tales tell of the wise and courteous Sir Gawaine; the brave Sir Percival; Sir Lancelot, who loved King Arthur's wife, Guinevere; the traitor Sir Modred, who seized the throne and tried to wed Queen Guinevere; the noble Sir Bedivere, who received Arthur's last commands before he died; and Sir Tristram, the knight of many skills. One seat at the Round Table had no name on it. It was reserved for the knight who found the Holy Grail, the cup supposedly used by Christ at the Last Supper. The seat was finally won by Sir Galahad, the purest and noblest of all the knights.

Religion and magic run through all the stories about Arthur and his knights. On the side of good was the mighty magician Merlin, who was Arthur's adviser. On the side of evil was the wicked sorceress Morgan le Fay.

THE STORY OF ARTHUR

The story of King Arthur and his knights, as told in *Le Morte Darthur* ("The Death of Arthur") by Sir Thomas Malory, begins with the death of Arthur's father, King Uther Pendragon. Following the king's death, there was strife and civil war among England's nobles. The nobles finally gathered in a church to ask God to show them who their rightful king should be. As they came out of the church they saw a sword in an anvil mounted on a great stone. On the sword it was written that whoever could pull the sword out of the stone would be the next king of England. None of the nobles could withdraw the sword.

Although he was the king's son, Arthur was not with his father when he died. Arthur had been given to the magician Merlin for safekeeping shortly after his birth. Merlin had known that King Uther's death would cause a struggle for power among the nobles and that Arthur's life would be in danger, so Merlin gave the baby to Sir Ector and his wife to raise as their own, not telling them that the baby was King Uther's son.

Some months after the sword appeared in the stone, a great tournament was held and Sir Ector, his son Sir Kay, and the young Arthur all attended. When Sir Kay discovered that he had left his sword at the inn where they were staying, he sent Arthur after it. The inn, however, was closed because everyone had gone to the tournament. But Arthur remembered seeing a sword stuck in a stone in the churchyard nearby. Without knowing what it meant, he removed the sword easily, and, after further proofs, Arthur became king.

His reign was full of victories. Many of these he owed to another sword, an enchanted one called Excalibur. Here is Malory's tale, adapted by Mary MacLeod, of how he got it.

Leaving Sir Pellinore, King Arthur and Merlin went to a hermit, who was a good man, and skilled in the art of healing. He attended so carefully to the King's wounds, that in three days they were quite well, and Arthur was able to go on his way with Merlin. Then as they rode, Arthur said, "I have no sword."

"No matter," said Merlin, "near by is a sword that shall be yours if I can get it."

So they rode till they came to a lake, which was a fair water and broad; and in the midst of the lake, Arthur saw an arm, clothed in white samite, that held in its hand a beautiful sword.

"Lo," said Merlin, "yonder is the sword I spoke of."

With that they saw a damsel rowing across the lake.

"What damsel is that?" said Arthur.

"That is the Lady of the Lake," said Merlin, "and within that lake is a rock, and therein is as fair a place as any on earth, and richly adorned. This damsel will soon come to you; then speak you fair to her, so that she will give you that sword."

Presently the damsel came to Arthur, and saluted him, and he her again.

"Damsel," said Arthur, "what sword is that which yonder the arm holdeth above the water? I would it were mine, for I have no sword."

"Sir Arthur, King," said the damsel, "that sword is mine; the name of it is Excalibur, that is as much as to say *Cut-Steel*. If you will give me a gift when I ask you, ye shall have it."

"By my faith," said Arthur, "I will give you what gift ye shall ask."

"Well," said the damsel, "go you into yonder barge, and row yourself to the sword, and take it and the scabbard with you, and I will ask my gift when I see my time."

So King Arthur and Merlin alighted, and tied their horses to two trees, and went into the barge, and when they came to the sword that the hand held, Arthur lifted it by the handle, and took it with him. And the arm and the hand went under the water; and so they came to the land, and rode away.

Some years later, Arthur married Guinevere, the daughter of a king he had helped in battle. After their marriage, Arthur set up his court at Camelot. There he gathered the most chivalrous princes to be his Knights of the Round Table. The stories of their feats and adventures—tournaments, battles, and quests for the Holy Grail—are all part of the Arthurian legends.

At the end of Arthur's reign, while he was away from Camelot, Sir Modred tried to take over the kingdom and marry the queen. But Arthur returned and defeated Modred in battle, killing him with his own hands. As Modred fell, he lifted up his sword and mortally wounded Arthur. Arthur's body was mysteriously carried away to the island of Avalon. According to legend, King Arthur would return one day.

▶SOURCES OF THE ARTHURIAN LEGENDS

The book that is the chief source today for all the legends about Arthur and his knights was written by an Englishman, Sir Thomas Malory. It was printed in 1485 and was one of the first books to come from the press of the first English printer, William Caxton. Although the tales were written in English, the title of the book, *Le Morte Darthur* ("The Death of Arthur"), is French and most of the tales were adapted from various French versions of the legends.

Tales about Arthur were particularly popular in France during the 1100's and 1200's. Originally, however, the Arthurian tales came from Celtic sources—from myths belonging to the Irish and British races and from early accounts of the history of Britain.

The first of these histories to mention Arthur was written in Latin by Nennius, a Welsh priest who lived in the 800's. He tells of a Celtic military commander named Arthur who in the 500's won twelve battles against the Saxon invaders of Britain. This is the original Arthur and it is all we know of him. Legends grew up around him, however, and he became a popular Welsh hero. When some of the Celtic people migrated from Britain to France, they carried the tales about Arthur to their new neighbors, the French and the Normans. Wandering minstrels spread the tales even farther as they visited the courts of Europe and Followed European armies into lands of the eastern Mediterranean.

About this same time, in the 1100's, another Welsh priest, Geoffrey of Monmouth, wrote down some of these tales in a book called *Historia Regum Britanniae* (History of the Kings of Britain). Although he pretended that the book was a translation into Latin of "a very old book in the British language," it was his own creation. He made Arthur into a king and surrounded him with nobles and barons from western Europe. In 1155, a Norman monk named Wace translated Geoffrey's *Historia* into French, adding material from other sources and leaving out parts. His *Roman de Brut* contains the first mention of the Round Table. Wace's poem was used by a priest named Layamon, who was the first to write about Arthur in English.

Between 1170 and 1181, a Frenchman, Chrétien de Troyes, wrote poems based on the Arthurian legends that were highly regarded for their style. His material was probably taken from Celtic origins. He is an important source for the story of the Holy Grail.

The Arthurian legends have attracted many writers in English since Layamon. Stories about Arthur were written in the 1400's by Sir Thomas Malory; in the 1800's by Lord Tennyson, Algernon Swinburne, Matthew Arnold, and William Morris; and in the 1900's by T. H. White.

The Arthurian legends have also been expressed in music and art. In music, the most famous composer to make use of these legends was Richard Wagner. In art, several of John Singer Sargent's mural paintings depict the quest for the Holy Grail.

Reviewed by CAROLYN W. FIELD
The Free Library of Philadelphia

ARTICLES OF CONFEDERATION. See UNITED STATES, GOVERNMENT OF THE; UNITED STATES, HISTORY OF THE.

ARTIFICIAL INTELLIGENCE. See COMPUTERS.

ARTIFICIAL RESPIRATION. See FIRST AID (Rescue Breathing).

ARTILLERY. See GUNS AND AMMUNITION.

ART NOUVEAU. See DECORATIVE ARTS (The Industrial Age).

ASBESTOS

Asbestos is the common name for a group of fire-resistant minerals that are made up of soft and flexible fibers. The threadlike fibers can be woven into cloth or mixed with a binding material and molded into any shape.

Asbestos comes in two main forms. Ninety-five percent is chrysotile, from the mineral serpentine. The other form, amphibole, includes five minerals—crocidolite, amosite, anthophyllite, tremolite, and actinolite.

Both forms of asbestos developed when cracks in the earth's rocks filled with water containing many minerals. Over millions of years, heat and pressure evaporated the water but left the fibers of asbestos.

The biggest deposits of asbestos are found in Canada, the Russian Federation, and South Africa. Smaller deposits are located in the United States. Asbestos is mined like coal—from open pits or through tunnels.

Asbestos is a most valuable substance. It will not burn or melt. It resists acids as well as other strong chemicals, and it is a good insulator against heat or the flow of electricity.

The ancient Greeks and Romans were among the early users of asbestos. They wove the fibers into burial cloths, tablecloths, and long-lasting lamp wicks.

By the 1900's, asbestos was used in a wide variety of products, such as automobile brake linings, roofing shingles, furnace linings, floor tiles, and firefighter suits.

In the 1960's, scientists discovered that inhaling asbestos fibers can cause cancer or serious lung disease. In 1989, the U.S. government decided to phase out the manufacture, use, and export of most asbestos products while safer substitutes could be found. Asbestos was also removed from many schools and other buildings.

Some studies have shown that asbestos is not always harmful. Its danger depends on the type of asbestos and the amount and size of the fibers in the air. Still, experts urge people to avoid exposure to asbestos.

GILDA BERGER
Science Writer

ASCORBIC ACID. See VITAMINS AND MINERALS (Vitamin C).

ASHE, ARTHUR. See TENNIS (Great Players).

ASHLEY, WILLIAM HENRY. See FUR TRADE IN NORTH AMERICA (Profiles).

ASIA

Asia is the largest and most heavily populated of the world's continents. It occupies nearly one-third of the earth's total land surface and is home to about 60 percent of its people. Asia is bounded on three sides by oceans (and their various seas): the Arctic Ocean on the north, the Pacific Ocean on the east, and the Indian Ocean on the south. On the west its traditional boundaries are the mountains and bodies of water separating it from Europe. The Suez Canal divides Asia from Africa on the southwest; and the narrow Bering Strait, which links the Arctic and Pacific oceans, separates it from North America.

Asia is a continent of enormous extremes. It has the world's highest peak—Mount Everest, on the border between Tibet, a region of China, and Nepal. It also has the lowest point on the earth's surface—the shoreline of the Dead Sea, on the Israel-Jordan border. Asia has some of the most densely populated regions in the world, including the two most populous countries, China and India. At the same time, large areas of Asia are too dry, too cold, or too mountainous to support any but limited numbers of people.

Asia was the birthplace of the world's earliest civilizations and its major religions. It was the site of once-vast empires of great wealth and cultural and scientific achievement. These great empires declined with the rise to power

Some of the many aspects of Asia: *Opposite page:* the Royal Mosque in Isfahan, Iran, one of the glories of Islamic architecture; Bengal tigers, native to the Indian subcontinent; the skyline of Tokyo, capital of Japan; the Great Buddha at Kamakura, Japan. *Above:* fertile rice fields of Indonesia; the Great Wall of China; and a pensive boatman on the Jumna River at Agra, India, with the fabled Taj Mahal in the distance.

of European nations, several of which ruled large regions of Asia as colonies until the mid-1900's. The end of colonial rule marked the emergence of the nation-states of present-day Asia.

THE LAND

Physically, Asia forms the much larger, eastern portion of an enormous landmass known as Eurasia (Europe and Asia), which stretches from the Atlantic to the Pacific oceans. But although physically linked, Europe and Asia have had such distinct histories that they are usually considered separate continents. The generally accepted dividing line between them runs along the Ural Mountains, the Caspian Sea, the Caucasus Mountains, the Black Sea, and the Bosporus and Dardanelles straits that connect the Black Sea with the Mediterranean.

Numerous islands, including those making up the nations of Japan, Indonesia, and the Philippines, ring the continent and form part of it. The interior is marked by some of the world's most imposing physical features. In the heart of the continent, standing like an enormous wall, is the great chain of the Himalayas, of which Everest is a part. The Himalayas are themselves part of an even larger mountain system that runs from Turkey in the west to China in the east. Asia has some of the most forbidding deserts on earth, including the Gobi of Mongolia and China, the Syrian, and the Rub' al Khali (Empty Quarter) of

Saudi Arabia. Vast treeless plains, or steppes, cover much of Central Asia. Farther north is the broad belt of forest known as taiga.

Regions of Asia

Asia can be divided into a number of distinct regions, although geographers do not always agree on which countries belong in which regions.

East Asia is one of the centers of Asian civilization. It consists of China, Korea, Japan, and Taiwan. Historically and geographically, East Asia is dominated by China, which includes more than 75 percent of the region's territory.

Three important rivers flow through parts of China: the Huang He (Yellow River) of North China, the Chang Jiang (Yangtze) of Central China, and the Xijiang (Si Kiang) of South China.

Much of Southwest Asia consists of desert, such as the Rub' al-Khali of Saudi Arabia (*left*). Southeast Asia, by contrast, has large areas of tropical rain forest (*right*).

Korea is a long, mountainous peninsula, situated between China and Japan. Japan itself consists of four large islands and a number of smaller ones lying off the eastern coast of Asia. The island of Taiwan lies off the southeastern coast of the Chinese mainland. Historically a province of China, it is the seat of the Republic of China, which opposes the Communist government of the People's Republic of China on the mainland.

Central, or Inner, Asia is a rather imprecisely defined region. Included within it are Tibet and the Xinjiang-Uygur Autonomous Region of western China. Kazakhstan, Kyrgyzstan, Tajikistan, Turkmenistan, and Uzbekistan, which gained independence with the breakup of the Soviet Union in late 1991, are usually considered part of Central Asia, although they are sometimes included in North Asia. Mongolia is often considered a part of the region, too.

Covering a vast area, Central Asia consists mainly of high plateaus, mountains, deserts, and steppe land. Tibet, for example, forms one great plateau rising some 15,000 feet (4,500 meters). Because of its mountainous terrain, limited rainfall, and generally poor soil, however, the region has a relatively small population for its size.

South Asia includes India, Pakistan, Bangladesh, Afghanistan, Sri Lanka, Maldives, and the small Himalayan countries of Nepal and Bhutan. This region is mainly one of great population density, with a variety of climates. It extends from the high Himalayas in the north to the Indian Ocean in the south, forming a huge triangle, dominated by India. The Arabian Sea is situated on one side of this triangle and the Bay of Bengal is on the other.

Southeast Asia includes areas on both the Asian mainland and neighboring islands. Myanmar (Burma), Thailand, Laos, Cambodia, and Vietnam are situated on the mainland. East Timor, Indonesia, Singapore, and the Philippines are island countries. Malaysia lies on both the mainland and islands.

Mount Everest, the world's highest peak, rises in the great mountain chain of the Himalayas, which stands like an enormous wall in the heart of Asia.

Tiny, oil-rich Brunei, the smallest of the Southeast Asian nations, is located on the large island of Borneo, the rest of which belongs to Malaysia and Indonesia. Indonesia is the largest and most populous country.

The climate is tropical, with numerous areas of dense population. Four great rivers flow through mainland Southeast Asia—the Mekong, the Chao Phraya, the Salween, and the Irrawaddy.

FACTS and figures

LOCATION AND SIZE: Mainland Asia extends from: **Latitude**—1° 16′ N to 77° 41′ N. **Longitude**—26° 04′ E to 169° 40′ W. **Area**—approximately 17,297,000 sq mi (44,780,000 km²). **Highest Point**—Mt. Everest, 29,035 ft (8,850 m). **Lowest Point**—Dead Sea, about 1,300 ft (400 m) below sea level.

POPULATION: 3,737,000,000 (estimate).

PRINCIPAL LAKES: Aral, Baikal, Balkhash, Tungting, Urmia, Koko Nor.

PRINCIPAL RIVERS: Yangtze (Chang), Huang He (Yellow River), Amur, Lena, Mekong, Yenisei, Ob, Indus, Irtysh, Brahmaputra, Salween, Euphrates, Amu Darya, Ganges, Olenek, Kolyma, Syr Darya, Irrawaddy, Tarim, Xijiang (Si Kiang), Tigris, Chao Phraya (Menam).

PRINCIPAL MOUNTAIN RANGES: **Himalayas**—Mt. Everest, Kanchenjunga, Lhotse I, Makalu, Lhotse II, Cho Oyu, Dhaulagiri, Nanga Parbat, Annapurna; **Karakoram**—K2 (Mt. Godwin Austen), Gasherbrum I, Broad Peak; **Kunlun**—Ulugh Muztagh; **Hindu Kush**—Tirich Mir; **Tien Shan**—Pobeda Peak, Khan Tengri; **Elburz**—Mt. Demavend; **Altai**—Tabun Bogdo, Belukha; **Barisan**—Mt. Kerinchi; **Taurus**—Ala Dag; **Sulaiman**—Takht-i-Sulaiman, twin peaks; **Ural Mountains**—Naroda.

PRINCIPAL DESERTS: Gobi, Rub` al Khali, Syrian, Nafud, Taklamakan, Kara Kum, Thar, Kyzyl Kum.

Southwest Asia. Southwest Asia makes up most of the region called the Middle East. It includes the countries of Turkey, Iran, Syria, Lebanon, Israel, Jordan, Iraq, Kuwait, Saudi Arabia, Yemen, Oman, the United Arab Emirates, and the island nation of Cyprus. The Sinai Peninsula, a territory of Egypt lying east of the Suez Canal, is also considered a part of Asia geographically.

Southwest Asia has a generally hot and dry climate, with little rainfall. But an area of rich soil in the shape of a semicircle, called the Fertile Crescent, stretches between the Mediterranean Sea and the Persian Gulf. Here,

Bactrian camels graze on the high steppe that makes up much of Central Asia. Although one of Asia's largest regions, it has a relatively small population.

INDEX TO ASIA PHYSICAL MAP

Aden, Gulf of A5
Altai Mts. D3
Altyn Tagh E3
Amu Darya C3
Amur River F2
Anadyr Range F1
Andaman Islands D5
Andaman Sea E5
Arabian Sea B4
Arafura Sea H6
Aral Sea C3
Ararat, Mt. B2
Baikal, Lake E2
Balkhash, Lake D3
Baltic Sea B1
Banda Sea H6
Barents Sea C1
Bengal, Bay of D5
Bering Sea G1
Black Sea B2
Brahmaputra River D4
Borneo (Kalimantan) F6
Bosporus, Straits of A2
Caspian Depression B2
Caspian Sea B3
Caucasus Mts. B2
Celebes (Sulawesi) G6
Celebes Sea G6
Central Siberian Plain E2
Ceram H6
Chang River (Yangtze) F4
Chao Phraya (Menam) River E5
Cherski Range F1
Chukchi Sea F1
Dead Sea A3
Deccan Plateau C5
Demavend, Mt. B3
Don River B2
Dongting Lake F4
East China Sea G4
East Siberian Sea F1
Eastern Ghats D5
Elbrus, Mt. B2
Elburz Mts. B3
Euphrates River A3
Everest, Mt. D4
Flores G6
Formosa Strait F4
Ganges River D4
Gobi Desert E3
Godwin Austen, Mt. (K2) C4
Greater Khingant Mts. F2
Hainan F5
Halmahera G6
Helmand River C4
Himalayas D4
Hindu Kush C4
Hokkaido G2
Hong (Red) River E5
Honshu G3
Hwang Ho (Yellow) River F4
Indian Ocean C6
Indigirka River F1
Indus River C4
Iran, Plateau of B4
Irrawaddy River E5
Irtysh River D2
Japan, Sea of G3
Java F6
Java Sea F6
K2 (Mt. Godwin Austen) C4
Kamchatka Peninsula G1
Kara Sea D1
Kara Kum C3
Karakorum Range D4
Khyber Pass C4
Kolyma Range F1
Kolyma River F1
Koryak Range F1
Kunlun Mts. D4
Kuril Islands G2
Kuznetsk Basin D2
Kyrgyzstan Tien Shan D3
Kyushu G3
Kyzyl Kum C3
Laccadive Islands C5
Laptev Sea E1
Lena River E1
Luzon G5
Macassar Strait G6
Malacca, Strait of E6
Malay Peninsula E6
Maldives C6
Manchurian Plain F2
Mediterranean Sea A2
Mekong River E5
Mindanao G5
Mindoro G5
Minya Konka E4
Mongolia, Plateau of E3
Mount Sinai A3
Nafud (Red Desert) A4
Nan Shan E4
Negros G5
New Guinea H6
New Siberian Islands E1
Nicobar Islands D6
Ob River D2
Okhotsk, Sea of G1
Okinawa G4
Oman, Gulf of B4
Palawan G5
Panay G5
Persian Gulf B4
Philippine Sea G4
Qinghai Lake E4
Red Basin E4
Red Desert (Nafud) A4
Red (Hong) River E5
Red Sea A3
Rub' Al Khali B4
Ryukyu Islands G4
Sakhalin G2
Salween River E5
Samar G5
Sayan Mts. E2

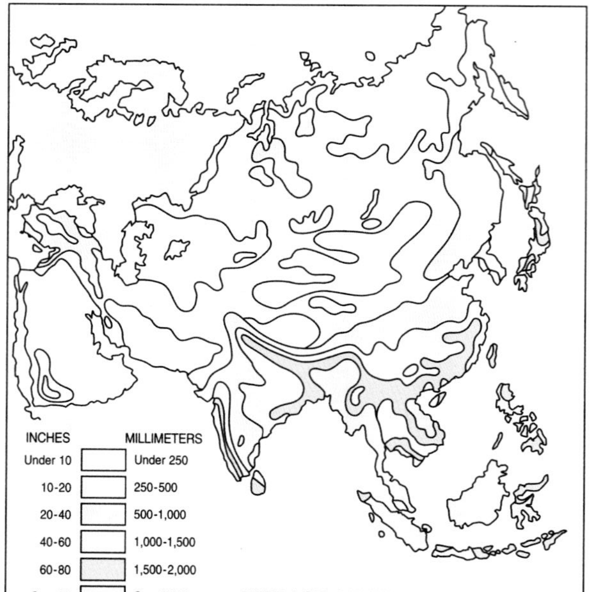

AVERAGE ANNUAL PRECIPITATION

Severnaya Zemlya E1
Shandong Peninsula F3
Shikoku G3
Si Kiang (West River) F4
Siberia E2
Sinai Peninsula A3
Socotra B5
South China Sea F5
Sri Lanka D6
Stanovoi Range F2
Suez Canal A3
Sulu Sea G5
Sumatra E6
Sumba G6
Sumbawa G6
Syr Darya C3
Syrian Desert A3
Taimyr Peninsula E1
Taiwan G4
Taklamakan Desert D4
Tarim River D3
Tarim Pendi Basin D3
Taurus Mts. A3
Thailand, Gulf of E6
Thar Desert C4
Tien Shan D3
Tigris River B3
Timor G6
Timor Sea H6
Tonkin, Gulf of F5
Tsinling Mts. E4
Turfan Depression D3
Ural Mts. C2
Ural River C2
Urmia, Lake B3
Ust-urt Plateau B3
Verkhoyansk Range E1
West River (Si Kiang) F4
Western Ghats C5
Western Siberian Plain D2
Wrangel Island F1
Xizang Plateau D4
Yaiu River F3
Yangtze (Chang) River F4
Yellow (Hwang Ho) River F4
Yellow Sea F3
Yenisei River D2
Zagros Mts. B3

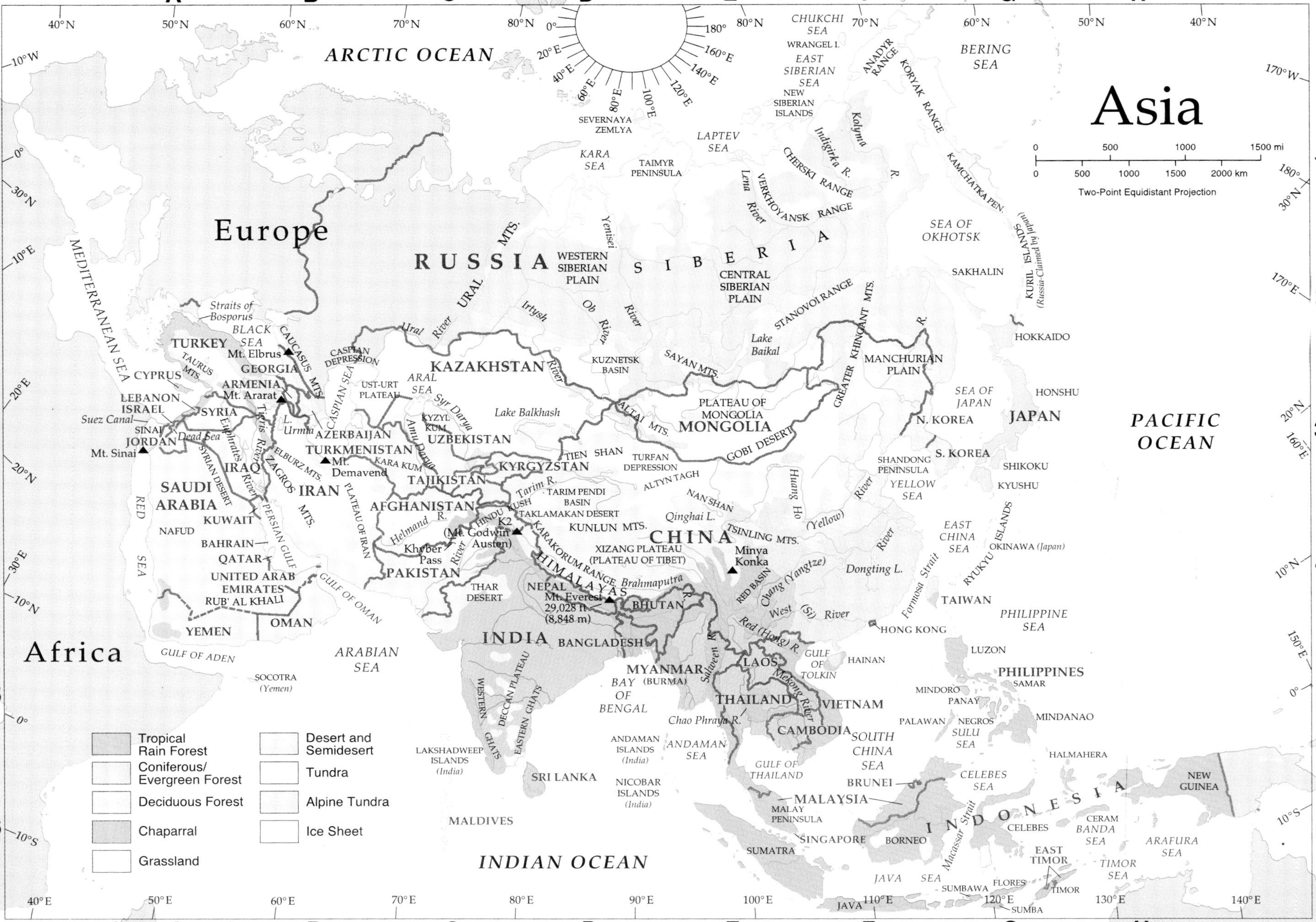
Asia
Two-Point Equidistant Projection
0 500 1000 1500 mi
0 500 1000 1500 2000 km
ARCTIC OCEAN
PACIFIC OCEAN
INDIAN OCEAN
Europe
Africa
RUSSIA
SIBERIA
WESTERN SIBERIAN PLAIN
CENTRAL SIBERIAN PLAIN
URAL MTS.
Ural River
Irtysh
Ob River
Yenisei River
Lena River
Indigirka R.
Kolyma R.
KARA SEA
LAPTEV SEA
EAST SIBERIAN SEA
CHUKCHI SEA
WRANGEL I.
NEW SIBERIAN ISLANDS
SEVERNAYA ZEMLYA
TAIMYR PENINSULA
VERKHOYANSK RANGE
CHERSKI RANGE
ANADYR RANGE
KORYAK RANGE
KAMCHATKA PEN.
BERING SEA
SEA OF OKHOTSK
SAKHALIN
KURIL ISLANDS (Russia-Claimed by Japan)
STANOVOI RANGE
Lake Baikal
SAYAN MTS.
KUZNETSK BASIN
GREATER KHINGAN MTS.
MANCHURIAN PLAIN
KAZAKHSTAN
CASPIAN DEPRESSION
CASPIAN SEA
ARAL SEA
UST-URT PLATEAU
Syr Darya
Amu Darya
KYZYL KUM
KARA KUM
Lake Balkhash
UZBEKISTAN
TURKMENISTAN
KYRGYZSTAN
TAJIKISTAN
AFGHANISTAN
PAKISTAN
IRAN
PLATEAU OF IRAN
Mt. Demavend
ELBURZ MTS.
ZAGROS MTS.
AZERBAIJAN
ARMENIA
GEORGIA
CAUCASUS MTS.
Mt. Elbrus
Mt. Ararat
L. Urmia
TURKEY
TAURUS MTS.
Straits of Bosporus
BLACK SEA
CYPRUS
MEDITERRANEAN SEA
LEBANON
ISRAEL
SYRIA
JORDAN
SINAI
Mt. Sinai
Suez Canal
Dead Sea
Euphrates
Tigris River
IRAQ
SYRIAN DESERT
SAUDI ARABIA
NAFUD
KUWAIT
BAHRAIN
QATAR
UNITED ARAB EMIRATES
RUB' AL KHALI
OMAN
YEMEN
PERSIAN GULF
GULF OF OMAN
GULF OF ADEN
RED SEA
ARABIAN SEA
SOCOTRA (Yemen)
Helmand R.
Khyber Pass
Indus River
HINDU KUSH
K2 (Mt. Godwin Austen)
KARAKORUM RANGE
HIMALAYAS
Mt. Everest 29,028 ft. (8,848 m)
NEPAL
BHUTAN
THAR DESERT
INDIA
BANGLADESH
WESTERN GHATS
DECCAN PLATEAU
EASTERN GHATS
SRI LANKA
LAKSHADWEEP ISLANDS (India)
MALDIVES
BAY OF BENGAL
ANDAMAN ISLANDS (India)
NICOBAR ISLANDS (India)
ANDAMAN SEA
Brahmaputra R.
TIEN SHAN
TURFAN DEPRESSION
Tarim R.
TARIM PENDI BASIN
TAKLAMAKAN DESERT
KUNLUN MTS.
ALTYN TAGH
NAN SHAN
Qinghai L.
XIZANG PLATEAU (PLATEAU OF TIBET)
ALTAI MTS.
PLATEAU OF MONGOLIA
MONGOLIA
GOBI DESERT
CHINA
TSINLING MTS.
Minya Konka
RED BASIN
Huang Ho (Yellow) River
Chang (Yangtze) River
Dongting L.
West (Si) River
Red (Hong) R.
HONG KONG
HAINAN
GULF OF TOLKIN
Formosa Strait
TAIWAN
N. KOREA
S. KOREA
SHANDONG PENINSULA
YELLOW SEA
EAST CHINA SEA
SEA OF JAPAN
JAPAN
HOKKAIDO
HONSHU
SHIKOKU
KYUSHU
RYUKYU ISLANDS
OKINAWA (Japan)
PHILIPPINE SEA
MYANMAR (BURMA)
Salween R.
LAOS
THAILAND
Chao Phraya R.
Mekong River
VIETNAM
CAMBODIA
GULF OF THAILAND
SOUTH CHINA SEA
MALAY PENINSULA
MALAYSIA
SINGAPORE
SUMATRA
BORNEO
BRUNEI
JAVA
JAVA SEA
PHILIPPINES
LUZON
MINDORO
PANAY
NEGROS
SAMAR
PALAWAN
MINDANAO
SULU SEA
CELEBES SEA
CELEBES
Macassar Strait
INDONESIA
HALMAHERA
CERAM
BANDA SEA
SUMBAWA
FLORES
SUMBA
TIMOR
EAST TIMOR
TIMOR SEA
ARAFURA SEA
NEW GUINEA
Tropical Rain Forest
Coniferous/ Evergreen Forest
Deciduous Forest
Chaparral
Grassland
Desert and Semidesert
Tundra
Alpine Tundra
Ice Sheet

North Asia is a vast but thinly populated region. It is often frozen in winter, when reindeer sleds (*right*) become a convenient form of transportation. The Chang Jiang (or Yangtze River) (*below*) is East Asia's major river and China's longest. Nearly half of China's people live in the river's great basin.

where the Tigris and Euphrates rivers provide sufficient water for irrigation, some of Asia's and the world's oldest civilizations arose thousands of years ago.

To the region's traditional nations three countries can be added—Armenia, Azerbaijan, and Georgia, which also gained independence from the former Soviet Union in 1991. They are sometimes called Transcaucasia or the Transcaucasian republics because of their location on or near the Caucasus mountain range between Europe and Asia.

COUNTRIES OF ASIA*

COUNTRY	CAPITAL
Afghanistan	Kabul
Armenia	Yerevan
Azerbaijan	Baku
Bahrain	Manama
Bangladesh	Dhaka
Bhutan	Thimphu
Brunei	Bandar Seri Begawan
Cambodia	Phnom Penh
China, People's Republic of	Beijing
Cyprus	Nicosia
Georgia	Tbilisi
India	New Delhi
Indonesia	Jakarta
Iran	Tehran
Iraq	Baghdad
Israel	Jerusalem
Japan	Tokyo
Jordan	Amman
Kazakhstan	Astana
Korea, North	P'yŏngyang
Korea, South	Seoul
Kuwait	Kuwait
Kyrgyzstan	Bishkek
Laos	Vientiane
Lebanon	Beirut
Malaysia	Kuala Lumpur
Maldives	Male
Mongolia	Ulaanbaatar
Myanmar (Burma)	Yangon
Nepal	Kathmandu
Oman	Muscat
Pakistan	Islamabad
Philippines	Manila
Qatar	Doha
Saudi Arabia	Riyadh
Singapore	Singapore
Sri Lanka	Colombo
Syria	Damascus
Tajikistan	Dushanbe
Thailand	Bangkok
Timor, East	Dili
Turkey	Ankara
Turkmenistan	Ashkhabad
United Arab Emirates	Abu Dhabi
Uzbekistan	Tashkent
Vietnam	Hanoi
Yemen	Sanaa

*Russia includes territory in both Asia and Europe, but the majority of its people live in Europe. Azerbaijan, Georgia, Kazakhstan, and Turkey also have areas of territory in Europe.

North Asia. This is another vast but thinly populated region, which extends across the northern part of the continent from the Ural Mountains to the Pacific Ocean. Most of North Asia consists of the region known as Siberia and lies within present-day Russia. Bordering the Arctic Ocean on the north, with the coldest winter temperatures on the continent, it is often inhospitable to human settlement, although it is rich in mineral resources.

See the separate articles on the Himalayas, the Middle East, Mount Everest, Palestine, Siberia, and Southeast Asia in the appropriate volumes.

Natural Resources

Minerals. Asia is rich in mineral resources, although a good part of its mineral wealth is still untapped. Deposits of coal, iron ore, and copper are found in East Asia, while South Asia is rich in manganese. Southeast Asia is

WONDER QUESTION

What and where is Asia Minor?

Asia Minor, also known as Anatolia, is a peninsula that forms the westernmost part of Asia and includes most of the land area of Turkey. It is bordered on the north by the Black Sea, on the south by the Mediterranean Sea, and on the west by the Aegean Sea, an arm of the Mediterranean. The land consists mainly of a high, rugged central plateau, ringed by mountains in the north and south.

Historically, Asia Minor was one of the earliest areas of human settlement. It was the site of numerous ancient kingdoms, most notably that of the Hittites, who flourished in the region from about 1900 to 1200 B.C. Some of the first Greek colonies were established on the peninsula's western coast. The legendary city of Troy (actually several cities), scene of Homer's *Iliad*, was located on the northwestern coast of Asia Minor.

The Greeks first used the name "Asia" to refer to the western part of the peninsula. Later, the name Asia Minor, meaning smaller or lesser Asia, was given to the entire region, to distinguish it from the rest of the vast Asian continent.

As a natural gateway between Europe and Asia, Asia Minor was a prize fought over by many conquerors through the centuries. Between 500 B.C. and A.D. 1500, it fell, in succession, to the Persians, the armies of Alexander the Great, the Roman and Byzantine empires, Arabs, Seljuk Turks, Mongols, and Ottoman Turks. With the collapse of the Ottoman Empire and the establishment of a republic in 1923, the region became the heartland of present-day Turkey.

Fishing begins at sunrise on the Mekong River, the chief waterway of Southeast Asia. The plains and delta of the river form a fertile rice-growing area, traditionally cultivated with the aid of water buffalo, probably the most useful domesticated animal of the region.

one of the world's chief sources of tin, with Malaysia being the world's largest producer. North Asia's extensive mineral resources include bauxite (aluminum ore), iron, gold, lead, zinc, and silver.

Southwest Asia, particularly the Persian Gulf area, is the world's single largest source of petroleum, with an estimated one-half of the total supply. Other important sources of petroleum are in Azerbaijan, China, and Indonesia. China also has the world's largest deposits of anthracite (hard coal) and tungsten. Turkey has large chromium deposits, and India has enormous deposits of mica.

Soils and Vegetation. Much of Asia has poor soils, particularly in the interior, which is too high, dry, or cold for good soil to have developed. Nor are the soils of the subtropical and tropical regions necessarily very productive. The most fertile places, where crops can most readily be grown, are located along the river valleys and some coastal areas, and it is here that the densest populations are found. In a few cases, such as the island of Java in Indonesia, the soils are fertile because of their volcanic origin.

Vegetation ranges from the mosses and other simple plant life of the frozen tundra along the North Asia coast to the lush tropical rain forests of Southeast Asia. Between the two lie the belt of northern forest (taiga), the grasslands of the semi-arid steppes, and deserts with little or no vegetation at all.

Its forests are among the continent's major natural resources. The taiga belt is the world's largest area of woodlands, and Southeast Asia's tropical rain forests include such valuable hardwoods as teak and mahogany. Logging, however, has suffered from a lack of transportation in some areas, and in others from overcutting.

Animal Life. Asia is home to a variety of wild and domestic animal life. Most wild animals inhabit the less-populated areas.

Polar and brown bears, Arctic foxes and hares, mouse-like lemmings, the rare Siberian tiger, reindeer, elk, and such valuable fur-bearing animals as ermine and sable are found in North Asia. The Bactrian (two-humped) camel is a vital beast of burden in the arid lands of Central Asia, while the Arabian (one-humped) camel performs the same function in the deserts of Southwest Asia. The hardy yak, a shaggy-haired ox, thrives in the high, wind-swept Tibetan plateau, where it is the most important form of livestock.

Animals unique to Asia include the Komodo dragon, largest of the lizards; the shy orangutan; and the Indian (or Asian) elephant, which has smaller ears than its African cousin.

Birds are found throughout the continent. The most gorgeously plumaged inhabit the tropical areas of South and Southeast Asia, which are also home to monkeys and apes. The orangutan lives only in the dense tropical forests on the islands of Sumatra and Borneo. India has a number of large mammals, including the Bengal tiger, the Indian rhinoceros, and the Indian (or Asian) elephant. The water buffalo is probably the most important domesticated animal of the region, invaluable in plowing its rice fields.

Large reptiles include crocodiles and a wide variety of snakes, among them the deadly Indian cobra and the enormous python. The Komodo dragon, the world's largest lizard, can be found on a few of the Indonesian islands. East Asia's most distinctive mammal is the giant panda, which is native only to the bamboo forests of interior China.

Climate

Asia has almost all the varieties of climates known. In general, it has what is called a continental climate—that is, one marked by wide seasonal and temperature ranges and limited rainfall. Much of the continent is cold and dry in the winter and warm and dry in the summer. Because of its great size, many areas are far from the sea. As a result, the interior of Asia is never touched by the winds that bring moisture from the oceans. Most of Central Asia is alternately cold and warm, but always dry.

Temperature. The high mountain ranges that cross Asia act as a huge wall. They keep the cold winds of the Arctic from blowing to the south and the hot winds of the south from blowing north. Therefore, average temperatures in the areas north of the mountains are lower than they would normally be at the same latitude elsewhere in the world. Siberian winters, for example, are among the coldest on earth. The average January temperature is about −60°F (−51°C). In the town of Verkhoyansk, in northeastern Siberia, the winter temperature has dropped to −90°F (−68°C).

The hottest parts of Asia are in the southwestern region. The area around the Persian Gulf is one of the hottest in the world, with land temperatures often reaching 120°F (49°C).

Rainfall. Rainfall in Asia is also affected by the size of the continent and its mountain ranges. Some regions receive a great deal of rain, while others receive little. Winds carrying moisture from the ocean bring rain to the near side of the mountains, leaving the far side of the high mountains generally dry.

Examples of this uneven rainfall can be seen throughout Asia. Parts of Southwest Asia receive as little as 4 inches (100 millimeters) of rain a year, while northeastern India is one of the wettest regions on earth. Southeast Asia is often hit by heavy rains, which may cause widespread flooding. Parts of southern China also receive much rainfall. Most of the rest of the continent tends to be dry.

Winds. Many parts of Asia are subjected to very strong winds. One such wind, called the Seistan, blows through Iran, in Southwest Asia, for about six months of the year at extremely high speeds. Many desert areas in Central Asia have similar winds. Winds from the plateau of Tibet have blown thousands of tons of soil (loess) hundreds of miles eastward to China. The heating and cooling of the land in interior Asia causes great masses of air to rush in and out of this area. Because of the height and location of the mountains, the winds usually move in an east–west direction.

The monsoons of the Indian Ocean are seasonal winds. For about six months each year they blow from northeastern India across the peninsula, carrying warm air out to the Indian Ocean. From June to September they reverse their direction and blow from the southwest. They then carry rain to the land, creating the wet monsoon season. If these returning winds do not carry enough rain, then crops fail and famine may result. The farmers of South and Southeast Asia are thus dependent upon the wet monsoon for their livelihood.

▸ THE PEOPLE

Asia's population, already very large, is growing rapidly. This is due partly to the high birthrate in some of the Asian nations and partly to the declining death rate. Modern medicines, better public health care, improved nutrition, and other advancements in living standards have helped increase the average life span of most Asian people.

Population Density

Asia's population is not spread out evenly over the continent. Most of the people live in three regions—South, Southeast, and East Asia. Therefore, even though more than one-half of Asia's land lies in North and Central Asia, less than one-tenth of Asians live there.

Population densities vary widely. Southwest Asia has fewer than 60 people per square mile (25 per square kilometer). But in South, Southeast, and East Asia, the highest population densities in the world are found. Often the population is even denser than the figures would indicate, since the bulk of the people are concentrated in the most fertile areas, usually along riverbanks or in coastal regions. In China, for example, the great majority of the people live in the eastern part of the country, along the coast and in the fertile basins drained by the great rivers. The average population density in these areas can be as high as four to six times the overall density of the country.

Racial and Ethnic Groups

Asians are as varied as their landscape. Attempts to classify them differ, but they can be divided into a number of broad categories.

Mongoloid peoples, including Chinese, most Japanese, Koreans, Mongols, and Tibetans, make up by far the largest group. The Han Chinese, who constitute most of China's population but are concentrated in the east, are the largest single ethnic group.

Turkic peoples occupy a vast area stretching from northwestern China across Central Asia to Turkey and Azerbaijan. North Asia is also home to some Turkic ethnic groups, as well as to considerable numbers of European Russians.

Malay peoples inhabit Indonesia and the Philippines, while most mainland Southeast

Asians are a Malay-Mongoloid mixture. South Asia includes two main ethnic groups: Indo-Aryans in northern India, Pakistan, Bangladesh, and most of Afghanistan and Sri Lanka; and Dravidians in southern India and part of Sri Lanka. Aside from Turkey, the Transcaucasian countries, and Iran (whose people are mainly Indo-Aryan), the great majority of Southwest Asians are Semites, chiefly Arabs but also including Jews, most of whom live in Israel. The people of Cyprus are of Greek (the majority) and Turkish ancestry.

Other distinctive Asian racial groups include the few remaining Ainu of northern Japan and the Negritos and hill people of South and Southeast Asia. These are believed to be the original inhabitants of the regions.

Languages

The peoples of Asia can also be defined by their languages. The language names are similar to, but not always the same as, the ethnic classifications.

South Asia has two major language divisions—the Indo-Iranian (or Indo-Aryan), part of the large Indo-European family; and the Dravidian. The Indo-Iranian branch is divided into dozens of languages, including Hindi, Urdu, Bengali, Punjabi, and Sinhala. The many languages of the Dravidian family of southern India include Tamil, Telugu, Kanarese, and Malayalam. Persian, spoken in Iran, and the Pashto and related languages of Afghanistan are also Indo-Iranian.

Chinese, Tibetan, and most of the languages of mainland Southeast Asia belong to the Sino-Tibetan family. Mandarin Chinese is the world's most widely spoken language. Japanese and Korean are separate languages, sometimes classified in the Altaic family. The Malayo-Polynesian family includes languages of Malaysia, Indonesia, the Philippines, and most of the Pacific islands.

The major language of Southwest Asia, Arabic, belongs to the Semitic family (as does Hebrew, spoken in Israel). The Osmanli Turkish of Turkey, the Azeri Turkish of Azerbaijan, and their related languages of Central and North Asia are Altaic. Armenian and the Greek spoken on Cyprus are Indo-European, while Georgian belongs to the small Caucasian language family.

Opposite page, clockwise from top left: **A wealthy Saudi Arabian with a gold-plated cellular telephone; elderly Tajiks from Central Asia; a Russian mother and daughter from Siberia, in North Asia; a Sri Lankan woman gathering tea leaves; and an Israeli woman.** ***This page, clockwise from right:*** **A girl from the Philippines; a boy from India; schoolchildren in Japan; a man from China.**

INDEX TO ASIA POLITICAL MAP

Abu Dhabi B4
Aden A5
Ahmadabad C5
Al Basrah B3
Almaty D3
Amman A3
Amritsar C4
Anadyr F1
Ankara A2
Ashkhabad B3
Astana C2
Baghdad B3
Baku B3
Bandar Seri Begawan F6
Bandung F6
Bangalore C5
Bangkok E5
Banjarmasin F6
Beijing F3
Beirut A3
Bishkek C3
Blagoveshchensk F2
Bombay (Mumbai) C5
Bratsk E2
Calcutta D5
Changchun F3
Chelyabinsk C2
Chengdu E4
Chita E2
Chongqing E4
Cochin C5
Colombo D6
Da Nang F5
Dalian F3
Damascus A3
Davao G5
Delhi D4
Dhaka D5
Dili G6
Doha B4
Dushanbe C3
Esfahan B3
Fuzhou F4
Gorkiy (Nizhnly Novgorod) B2
Guangzhou F4
Hanoi E5
Harbin F3
Hiroshima G3
Ho Chi Minh City F5
Hohhot F3
Hong Kong F4
Hyderabad (India) C5
Hyderabad (Pakistan) C4
Inchon F3
Irkutsk E3
Islamabad C4
Izmir A2
Jahrum B4
Jaipur C4
Jakarta F6
Jayapura H5
Jerusalem A3
Jiddah A4
Jinan F3
Kabul C4
Kandahar C4
Kanpur D4
Karachi C4
Karaganda D3
Kashi D3
Katmandu D4
Kerman B4
Khabarovsk F2
Kobe G3
Komsomolsk F2
Kota Kinabalu F6
Krasnoyarsk D2
Kuala Lumpur E6
Kunming E4
Kuwait B4
Kyoto G3
Lahore C4
Lanzhou E4
Lhasa D4
Lucknow D4
Macao F4
Madras (Chennai) D5
Madurai C5
Magadan F1
Magnitogorsk C2
Male C6
Manado G6
Manama B4
Mandalay E5
Manila G5
Mashhad C3
Mecca A4
Muscat B4
Nagasaki G3
Nagpur G3
Nanjing F4
Nanning F4
New Delhi C4
Nicosia A3
Norilsk D1
Novokuznetsk D2
Novosibirsk D2
Omsk D2
Osaka G3
Padang E6
Palembang F6
Pavlodar D3
Phnom Penh E5
Pyongyang F3
Qingdao F3
Quezon City G5
Riyadh A4
Sana A4
Sapporo G2
Semipalatinsk D3
Sendal G3
Seoul F3
Shanghai F4
Shenyang F3
Singapore E6
Srinagar C4
Sukkur C4
Surabaya F6
Tabriz B3
Taegu F3
Taipei F4
Taiyuan F3
Tashkent C3
Tbilisi B3
Tehran B3
Thimphu D4
Tianjin F3
Tokyo G3
Tomsk D2
Ujung Pandang G6
Ulaanbaatar E3
Ulan-Ude E3
Urumqi D3
Victoria F4
Vientiane E5
Vladivostok G3
Wenzhou F4
Wuhan F4
Xiamen F4
Xian E4
Yakutsk F2
Yangon (Rangoon) E5
Yekaterinburg C2
Yerevan B3
Yokohama G3
Zhengzhou F4

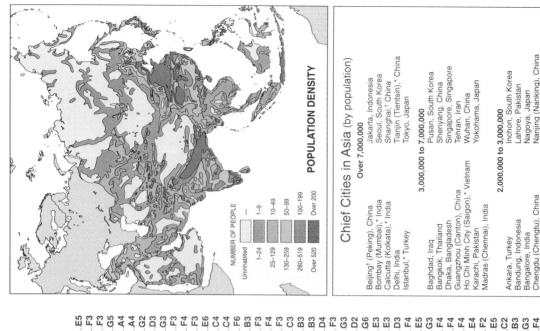

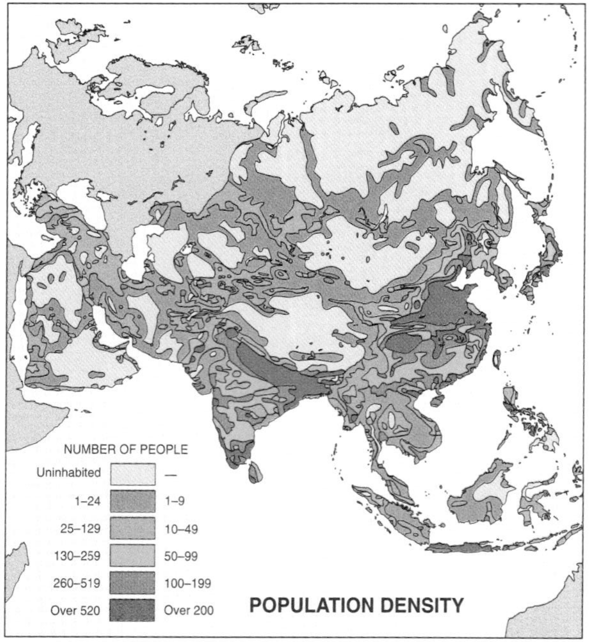

Chief Cities in Asia (by population)

Over 7,000,000

Beijing[†] (Peking), China
Bombay (Mumbai),* India
Calcutta (Kolkata),* India
Delhi, India
Istanbul,* Turkey
Jakarta, Indonesia
Seoul, South Korea
Shanghai,[†] China
Tianjin (Tientsin),* China
Tokyo, Japan

3,000,000 to 7,000,000

Baghdad, Iraq
Bangkok, Thailand
Dhaka, Bangladesh
Guangzhou (Canton), China
Ho Chi Minh City (Saigon),* Vietnam
Karachi, Pakistan
Madras (Chennai), India
Pusan, South Korea
Shenyang, China
Singapore, Singapore
Tehran, Iran
Wuhan, China
Yokohama, Japan

2,000,000 to 3,000,000

Ankara, Turkey
Bandung, Indonesia
Bangalore, India
Chengdu (Chengtu), China
Chittagong, Bangladesh
Chongqing (Chungking), China
Hanoi, Vietnam
Harbin, China
Hyderabad, India
Inchon, South Korea
Lahore, Pakistan
Nagoya, Japan
Nanjing (Nanking), China
Osaka, Japan
Pyongyang, North Korea
Surabaya, Indonesia
Taegu, South Korea
Taipei, Taiwan (Republic of China)
Yangon (Rangoon), Myanmar

*Metropolitan area
[†]Municipality, including surrounding counties

Asia
Two-Point Equidistant Projection
0 500 1000 1500 mi
0 500 1000 1500 2000 km
ARCTIC OCEAN
PACIFIC OCEAN
INDIAN OCEAN
Europe
Africa
RUSSIA
KAZAKHSTAN
MONGOLIA
CHINA
INDIA
TURKEY
GEORGIA
ARMENIA
AZERBAIJAN
CYPRUS
LEBANON
SYRIA
ISRAEL
JORDAN
IRAQ
SINAI
Suez Canal
SAUDI ARABIA
KUWAIT
BAHRAIN
QATAR
UNITED ARAB EMIRATES
OMAN
YEMEN
IRAN
TURKMENISTAN
UZBEKISTAN
KYRGYZSTAN
TAJIKISTAN
AFGHANISTAN
PAKISTAN
NEPAL
BHUTAN
BANGLADESH
XINJIANG-UYGUR AUTONOMOUS REGION
XIZANG AUTONOMOUS REGION (TIBET)
MYANMAR (BURMA)
LAOS
THAILAND
CAMBODIA
VIETNAM
N. KOREA
S. KOREA
JAPAN
TAIWAN
PHILIPPINES
MALAYSIA
BRUNEI
SINGAPORE
INDONESIA
EAST TIMOR
SRI LANKA
MALDIVES
KURIL ISLANDS (Russia)
OKINAWA (Japan)
SOCOTRA (Yemen)
LAKSHADWEEP (India)
ANDAMAN ISLANDS (India)
NICOBAR ISLANDS (India)
BARENTS SEA
KARA SEA
LAPTEV SEA
EAST SIBERIAN SEA
CHUKCHI SEA
BERING SEA
SEA OF OKHOTSK
SEA OF JAPAN
YELLOW SEA
EAST CHINA SEA
PHILIPPINE SEA
SOUTH CHINA SEA
SULU SEA
CELEBES SEA
BANDA SEA
ARAFURA SEA
TIMOR SEA
JAVA SEA
GULF OF TONKIN
GULF OF THAILAND
ANDAMAN SEA
BAY OF BENGAL
ARABIAN SEA
GULF OF OMAN
PERSIAN GULF
GULF OF ADEN
RED SEA
MEDITERRANEAN SEA
BLACK SEA
CASPIAN SEA
ARAL SEA
Izmir
Ankara
Nicosia
Beirut
Jerusalem
Amman
Damascus
Tbilisi
Yerevan
Baku
Tabriz
Baghdad
Al Basrah
Kuwait
Riyadh
Manama
Doha
Abu Dhabi
Muscat
Jiddah
Mecca
Sana
Aden
Tehran
Esfahan
Mashhad
Kerman
Jahrum
Ashkhabad
Tashkent
Dushanbe
Bishkek
Almaty
Kashi
Kabul
Kandahar
Islamabad
Srinagar
Amritsar
Lahore
Delhi
New Delhi
Jaipur
Sukkur
Karachi
Hyderabad
Ahmadabad
Kanpur
Lucknow
Katmandu
Thimphu
Dhaka
Calcutta (Kolkata)
Chittagong
Nagpur
Bombay (Mumbai)
Hyderabad
Bangalore
Madras (Chennai)
Cochin
Madurai
Colombo
Male
Yekaterinburg
Chelyabinsk
Magnitogorsk
Omsk
Astana
Novosibirsk
Pavlodar
Semipalatinsk
Karaganda
Tomsk
Krasnoyarsk
Novokuznetsk
Norilsk
Bratsk
Irkutsk
Ulan-Ude
Chita
Yakutsk
Magadan
Anadyr
Komsomolsk
Blagoveshchensk
Khabarovsk
Vladivostok
Ulaanbaatar
Urumqi
Lhasa
Lanzhou
Chengdu
Chongqing
Kunming
Xian
Zhengzhou
Taiyuan
Hohhot
Beijing
Tianjin
Jinan
Qingdao
Dalian
Shenyang
Changchun
Harbin
Nanjing
Shanghai
Wuhan
Wenzhou
Changsha
Fuzhou
Xiamen
Guangzhou
Hong Kong
Macao
Nanning
Taipei
Pyongyang
Seoul
Inchon
Taegu
Sapporo
Sendai
Tokyo
Yokohama
Kyoto
Kobe
Osaka
Hiroshima
Nagasaki
Mandalay
Yangon (Rangoon)
Hanoi
Vientiane
Da Nang
Bangkok
Phnom Penh
Ho Chi Minh City
Manila
Quezon City
Davao
Kota Kinabalu
Kuala Lumpur
Kuching
Medan
Padang
Palembang
Jakarta
Bandung
Banjarmasin
Surabaya
Ujung Pandang
Manado
Dili
Jayapura
A B C D E F G H
1 2 3 4 5 6
10°W 0° 10°E 20°E 30°E 40°E 50°E 60°E 70°E 80°E 90°E 100°E 110°E 120°E 130°E 140°E 160°E 170°E 180° 170°W
40°N 50°N 60°N 70°N 80°N 30°N 20°N 10°N 0° 10°S

Religions

Three of the world's great religions, Judaism, Christianity, and Islam, originated in Southwest Asia. Islam, the religion of the Muslims, eventually became the dominant faith of the region and spread to Central Asia and parts of South Asia (chiefly what are now Pakistan, Bangladesh, and Afghanistan) and Southeast Asia (mainly present-day Indonesia and Malaysia). Together with Hinduism and Buddhism, Islam remains one of the major religions of Asia.

Christianity was re-introduced to Asia by missionaries, and Judaism was re-established as the religion of Israel in recent times. Today, Christians predominate in Cyprus, Armenia, Georgia, and the Philippines, and make up about 40 percent of the population of Lebanon. Most of the Russians of North Asia are Christian, and there are significant communities in other parts of Asia.

Hinduism originated in India and is the chief religion of that populous country, which also has an important Muslim minority. India's religious heritage also includes Sikhs, Jains, and Parsees, or Zoroastrians. The origins of Zoroastrianism were in ancient Persia (Iran), where it was eventually supplanted by Islam. Buddhism also developed in India, based on the teachings of Siddhartha Gautama, called the Buddha. But it has relatively few followers in India today. Most Buddhists are now found in China, Japan, Korea, and mainland Southeast Asia.

Taoism is a native religion of China, which developed from the philosophy of Lao-tzu, while Shinto is the original faith of Japan. China has also been strongly influenced by Confucianism. Named for its founder, Confucianism is not a religion but a system of ethical teachings. Through China, it has influenced the thinking of other countries of East Asia as well as areas of Southeast Asia, partic-

Asia was the birthplace of the world's major religions: an orthodox Jew at the Western Wall in Jerusalem (*top*); Muslims kneeling in prayer (*right*); a Buddhist monk with statues of the Buddha (*below*); Christian dignitaries (*below right*); a Hindu holy man (*opposite page, top*).

ularly Vietnam. In addition, such early religious beliefs as animism and shamanism still survive in some parts of Asia.

Articles on the major religions of Asia can be found in the appropriate volumes. An article on Confucius appears in Volume C. Also consult RELIGIONS OF THE WORLD in Volume Q-R.

The Arts. Many Asian countries have a long tradition of cultural achievement in art, architecture, and literature. For detailed information on this aspect of Asia, see the following articles in the appropriate volumes of this encyclopedia:

ANCIENT WORLD, ART OF THE; CHINESE ART; CHINESE LITERATURE; INDIA, ART AND ARCHITECTURE OF; INDIA, LITERATURE OF; ISLAMIC ART AND ARCHITECTURE; JAPANESE ART AND ARCHITECTURE; JAPANESE LITERATURE; ORIENTAL ART AND ARCHITECTURE.

Education

The scholar has always been a respected member of the community in Asia. In China, the most revered figure, Confucius, was a scholar and teacher. Asia's tradition of learning is also very old, the first Chinese university having been founded in 124 B.C. But until modern times education was a privilege enjoyed only by the well-to-do, and the great mass of Asians could neither read nor write. Not until the latter half of the 1800's did most Asian countries begin to adopt the goal of universal education for all of their people.

The majority of Asian countries today have compulsory school attendance laws, and almost all of them have policies designed to keep children in school longer. Fees that prevented many children from attending school have been gradually abolished or lowered. The literacy rate (the percentage of people able to read or write) has risen dramatically, although it still varies widely from country to country. In higher education, there is at least one college in every major city, and many cities have several colleges and universities. The academic standards of many of them compare favorably with those of the best universities in the world.

CITIES

Although the majority of its people live in rural areas, Asia has some of the largest cities to be found anywhere in the world. Population trends are also marked by increasing urbanization, or the movement of people from rural areas to the cities.

The largest urban centers are located in East, South, and Southeast Asia. They include Tokyo, the capital of Japan; China's great municipalities of Shanghai; Beijing, the capital; and Tientsin (Tianjin); South Korea's rapidly growing capital of Seoul; the Indian cities of Bombay, Calcutta, and Delhi; and Jakarta, Indonesia's capital.

Many cities originated close to natural transportation routes. Istanbul, Turkey's largest city, one of the most favorably located, lies on the waters separating Europe and Asia. Formerly called Constantinople, it is a historic city and the only one situated on two conti-

Jakarta is the capital of Indonesia and the largest city of Southeast Asia. Like other rapidly growing Asian cities, it has new sections built in the most modern style.

Istanbul (*left*), Turkey's largest city, is strategically located on the waters separating Europe and Asia. Formerly called Constantinople, it was once the capital of the Roman Empire. Jerusalem (*above*) is an ancient city holy to three religions—Judaism, Christianity, and Islam.

nents. Other Southwest Asian cities, such as Iraq's capital of Baghdad, while smaller, are also of great historical and cultural interest. The importance of Jerusalem, a city holy to three religious faiths, far outweighs its relatively small size.

Articles on the cities mentioned can be found in the appropriate volumes.

THE ECONOMY

About two-thirds of Asia's people earn their livelihood from the land. The most fertile areas are in South and Southeast Asia and in the eastern part of East Asia. Here, where the continent's population is most densely concentrated, every bit of usable land is intensely cultivated. In recent decades, to keep up with population growth, Asian countries have used modern technology to increase farm output.

Industrialization has been the major goal of nearly every economic development program carried out in Asia since the end of World War II in 1945. Japan is the greatest example of an Asian nation that has succeeded dramatically in industrializing itself. Rich mineral deposits, particularly oil and natural gas, have also fueled regional growth. In addition, many international companies have moved their manufacturing activities to Asia to take advantage of its skilled workforce and relatively low wages. By the late 1990's, however, economic growth in much of East and Southeast Asia had slowed.

Agriculture

Rice, which needs a warm and wet climate to grow, is the major crop in the southern regions of Asia. Southeast Asia, eastern India, southern China, Korea, and Japan are the important rice-growing areas. Farther north, in the drier regions, cereal grains such as wheat, barley, and millet are grown. China, northern India and Pakistan, and Central Asia are major wheat- and corn-growing areas.

Rubber is an important commercial crop in Thailand, the world's leading producer of natural rubber, and other countries of Southeast Asia. Most of the world's tea comes from India, China, and Sri Lanka. Sugarcane is grown mainly in India, China, and Thailand. Cotton is a major product in China, India, and countries of Central Asia. Asia's soybeans and the world's silk come largely from China. Jute, used to make burlap and twine, is Bangladesh's chief export. Coconuts come from Indonesia and the Philippines, while peanuts are grown in China and India. Dates and oranges are specialties of Southwest Asia.

Nomadic herders in Southwest and Central Asia, where the land is often suitable only for grazing, depend largely on their livestock. Many small farmers throughout Asia raise poultry for food. India and North Asia produce much cheese and butter, and North Asia and China lead in beef, pork, mutton, and lamb. Wool is a major product in Central Asia.

Manufacturing

Japan is not only the most highly industrialized nation in Asia; it ranks among the top two or three world industrial powers. It is the world's chief shipbuilding country and, along with the United States, the largest producer of automobiles and other motor vehicles. It is either first or among world leaders in the manufacture of steel, aluminum, chemicals, television sets and videocassette recorders, and computers and other high-technology products. Japan has achieved this with few mineral resources of its own. It must import the raw materials with which to manufacture these goods for export.

India and China are a distant second to Japan in industrial output. India is an important producer of textiles, cotton clothing, steel, electrical machinery, and electronic equipment. China's industrial heartland has traditionally been in its northeastern region (sometimes called Manchuria), the site of large iron and coal deposits. A main goal of the country's leaders is to make China one of the world's major industrial powers by the early 2000's.

South Korea, Taiwan, Singapore, and Israel have developed modern industrial economies in recent decades, and Turkey has long had a significant industrial capacity. Until the late 1990's, when much of Southeast and East Asia experienced a serious economic downturn, countries such as Thailand, Indonesia, and Malaysia were also industrializing rapidly.

Mining and Fishing

Asia has virtually all the minerals needed for industrial growth, although some deposits remain to be developed, particularly in the lightly populated North Asia region. For detailed information on these minerals and where they are found, see the section Natural Resources (Minerals).

Fishing is an especially important industry in Asia. Japan's fishing industry is one of the most modern in the world, equipped with floating canneries that process the fish right after they are caught. China also has a major fishing industry, and Thailand has become the world's largest exporter of seafood (mostly farm-raised shrimp). The Persian Gulf waters

About two-thirds of Asians earn their livelihood from the land. Rice, here being planted in China's Sichuan province, is one of the continent's major crops. Automobiles are assembled at a plant in South Korea, which is rapidly becoming one of Asia's leading industrial areas.

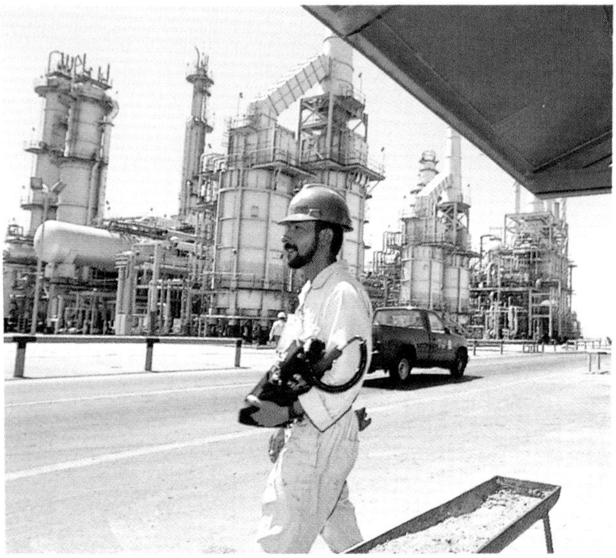

Oil refineries such as this one in Saudi Arabia process much of the world's fuel supply. Southwest Asia has about half of the world's known oil reserves.

are famed for their natural pearls, while Japan produces much of the world's supply of cultured pearls.

Lumbering

Russia is the world's leading producer of sawed wood, and a large part of its lumbering is done in Asia. Japan is also an important world producer of sawed wood. In spite of its rich forest resources, Asia as a whole has a shortage of lumber. Many Asian countries are now carrying out reforestation programs—that is, the planting of trees for future use. These projects, which replace lost timber areas, also help prevent floods and soil erosion.

Transportation

Geography has hindered the development of both transportation and trade in Asia. Transportation has been easiest on or near the coasts and along the great rivers, which have been the main avenues of transportation in much of the continent for centuries. In the North, however, the Arctic climate keeps the coastal areas icebound for the better part of the year. In parts of Asia transportation is still a matter of using old caravan trails. Merchants still cross the deserts of Southwest and Central Asia on camels, although the camels are gradually being replaced by vehicles designed for desert travel.

The first Asian railroads were built after the arrival of the Europeans, mainly during the late 1800's and early 1900's. Some new lines were built after World War II, and others are now under construction. The Trans-Siberian Railroad is the only rail line crossing the whole vast expanse of Asia. It is also the world's longest continuous railroad, linking the Russian capital of Moscow in Europe with the Pacific Ocean port of Vladivostok. The line was expanded in recent years, but the harsh climate and rugged terrain make further work difficult. Today, Japan, India, and China have the most extensive rail systems.

The roads and highways of Asia, with some exceptions, are generally poor. Increasingly, air transport is being used to reach formerly inaccessible areas.

Modern methods of transportation in Asia can be seen in Japan's system of turbo trains. Popularly known as "bullet trains" because of their shape and high speed, they can travel at 160 miles (260 kilometers) an hour. Here the bullet train passes Mount Fuji on the main Japanese island of Honshu.

The sculpture at left was discovered at Mohenjo-Daro, part of the Indus Valley civilization. One of three main sites of early Asian civilization, it flourished 5,000 years ago in what is now Pakistan. Later Greek and Roman influence is reflected in the ruins at Palmyra, in modern-day Syria, a city-state that briefly held power during the A.D. 200's.

▶ HISTORY

The history of Asia began in three great river valleys—the Tigris-Euphrates in Southwest Asia, the Indus in South Asia, and the Huang He (Yellow River) in East Asia. In these three areas, civilizations developed that give Asia its special place in the world today.

Early Civilizations

The Tigris-Euphrates Valley was the site of several early civilizations. From 3500 B.C. to 600 B.C., a succession of great states arose in the region. The Sumerians, Babylonians, and Assyrians developed writing, law, and commerce. The code of Hammurabi (about 1800 B.C.) was one of the first written law codes in the world. Around 600 B.C., the Persians, under Cyrus the Great, established an empire that stretched from the shores of the Mediterranean Sea to northern India. The empire was expanded by later Persian kings, among them Darius the Great.

The ruins of Harappa and Mohenjo-Daro are signs of early civilization in the Indus Valley of South Asia. In about 1500 B.C., Indo-Aryan invaders came through the mountains of northwestern India to establish the Hindu civilization. Traces of this early beginning remain to this day, and the tradition of Hinduism is still one of the most important influences in modern India.

For additional information on these periods of Asian history, see the articles ANCIENT CIVILIZATIONS (sections on Sumerian, Babylonian, and Indus Valley civilizations); and PERSIA, ANCIENT.

The earliest civilization in China developed along the northern reaches of the Huang He during the 1500's B.C. China's history was marked by successive dynasties, or ruling families. Some ruled for centuries; others for only a short period. The last dynasty, the Qing (or Manchu), was overthrown and a republic established in 1912.

Period of Development and Expansion

After 500 B.C., several great religions and empires grew up in Asia. In 334 B.C., Alexander the Great began his conquest of western Asia. His invasion brought Asia into direct contact with Greek civilization. Meanwhile the first great Indian empire, the Maurya, was established in the 320's B.C., creating unity in India. Under its greatest ruler, Asoka, Buddhism briefly flourished and the great monumental art of India began.

Farther east, in China, the Han dynasty (202 B.C.–A.D. 220) established an empire and extended its influence into Central and Southeast Asia. Under its great emperor Wu Ti, the Han adopted Confucianism. During this period other great religions took form. Chris-

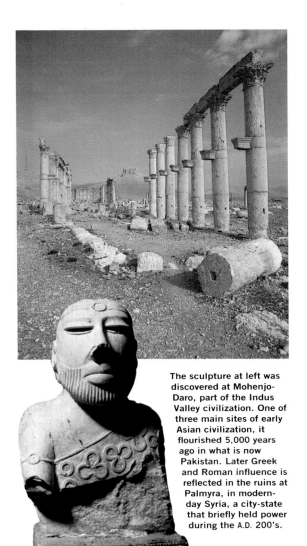

Confucius, China's great sage and teacher, lived from about 551 to 479 B.C. His system of ethics has influenced Chinese thinking from ancient times to the present.

IMPORTANT DATES

About 3200 B.C.	Beginnings of civilization: Sumerians develop cuneiform writing; early urban culture in the Indus Valley; China emerges from the Stone Age.
About 1750 B.C.	Hammurabi, king of Babylonia, introduces world's first uniform code of laws.
About 1500 B.C.	Shang dynasty flourishes.
About 1300's B.C.	Phoenicians develop the first alphabet.
1200's B.C.	Moses leads the Exodus, receives the Ten Commandments.
1028–25	Chou dynasty: beginning of China's Iron Age.
600–300 B.C.	Upanishads written; crystallization of the caste system in India.
500's B.C.	Cyrus the Great founds the Persian Empire.
274–232 B.C.	Asoka unites two-thirds of India; rules according to Buddhist laws; sends out missionaries.
202 B.C.–A.D. 220	Han dynasty: height of ancient Chinese civilization; paper and porcelain invented.
A.D. 330	Constantine I moves the capital of the Roman Empire to Byzantium, renamed Constantinople (now Istanbul).
618–906	Tang dynasty in China: printing invented.
622	Mohammed (570–632) flees from Mecca to Medina and organizes the Commonwealth of Islam.
632–1100	Growth of Arabic civilization under the influence of Islam.
960–1279	Sung dynasty in China: beginning of modernity; use of compass; gunpowder developed.
998–1030	Muslims invade Punjab: mixing of Hindu and Muslim cultures.
1096–1290	Era of Crusades: increased contact between East and West.
1206–27	Genghis Khan (1167?–1227) establishes the Mongol Empire, conquers large parts of Asia and Europe.
1260	Kublai Khan becomes emperor of China.
1271–95	Travels of Marco Polo bring first detailed knowledge of Asia to Europe.
1368–1644	Ming dynasty drives out Mongols, reunifies China.
1369–1405	Tamerlane conquers much of Southwest Asia, invades India.
1453	Constantinople captured by the Ottoman Turks: end of the Eastern Roman (Byzantine) Empire; beginning of the Ottoman Empire.
1498	Vasco da Gama sails to India, opens water route to the East.
1514	Portuguese make first landing in China.
1521	Ferdinand Magellan claims Philippines for Spain.
1526	Mogul Empire in India founded by Babur.
1549–51	St. Francis Xavier introduces Christianity in Japan.
1600–1868	Tokugawa period in Japan: ban on all foreigners begins a long era of isolation.
1644–1912	Qing (Manchu) dynasty rules China.
1756–63	Britain becomes dominant power in India after the Seven Years' War.
1839–42	Opium War between Britain and China.
1853–54	U.S. Commodore Matthew Perry lands in Japan: end of Japanese isolation.
1857–58	Sepoy Rebellion (Indian Mutiny) in India.
1868	Meiji Restoration begins in Japan.
1869	Suez Canal opens.
1894–95	Sino-Japanese War.
1898	Spanish-American War: United States acquires the Philippines.
1900	Boxer Rebellion in China.
1904–05	Russo-Japanese War: Japan emerges as world power.
1911–12	Revolution in China led by Sun Yat-sen: China becomes a republic.
1923	Turkey becomes a republic.
1931	Japan invades Manchuria.
1941	Japan attacks Pearl Harbor, bringing United States into World War II.
1945	Atomic bombs dropped on Hiroshima and Nagasaki; Japan surrenders; World War II ends.
1946	Jordan and the Philippines gain independence.
1947	India and Pakistan gain independence.
1948	Israel created; Burma (now Myanmar) and Ceylon (now Sri Lanka) become independent; North and South Korea established.
1949	Communists win control of mainland China: Nationalist government retreats to Taiwan; Indonesia gains independence.
1950–53	Korean War.
1950	Chinese troops enter Tibet.
1954	North and South Vietnam, Laos, and Cambodia established.
1957	Malaya gains independence.
1959	Tibetans revolt against China; Dalai Lama flees.
1960	Cyprus gains independence.
1961	Kuwait gains independence.
1963	Malaysia formed.
1965	Maldives and Singapore gain independence.
1967	Yemen (Aden) gains independence.
1971	Bangladesh gains independence.
1975	Vietnam War ends; civil war in Lebanon.
1976	North and South Vietnam united.
1979	Egypt and Israel sign peace treaty; Shah overthrown in Iran; Soviet forces invade Afghanistan.
1980–88	War between Iran and Iraq.
1984	Brunei gains independence.
1988–89	Soviet Union withdraws from Afghanistan.
1990	Yemen (Sana) and Yemen (Aden) are united; Iraq invades and occupies Kuwait.
1991	Gulf War ends with defeat of Iraq; breakup of the Soviet Union creates eight new Asian nations.
1993	First of a series of accords on Palestinian self-rule is signed by Israel and the Palestine Liberation Organization (PLO).
1997	Hong Kong is returned to China.
1998	India and then Pakistan conduct nuclear tests.
2000	North and South Korea hold their first summit meeting in 50 years.
2001	China is admitted to the World Trade Organization.
2002	East Timor gains independence from Indonesia.

tianity appeared in Southwest Asia, and Buddhism began to spread to East Asia.

The A.D. 600's saw the rapid rise of Islam. Its followers conquered most of North Africa, Southwest Asia, and northern India. In East Asia, China flourished under the Tang and Sung dynasties from about A.D. 600 to 1200. In the 1200's, Genghis Khan, the Mongol conqueror, gained control of much of Asia, from China to Russia.

Period of Colonialism

With the arrival in India of the Portuguese navigator Vasco da Gama in 1498, Europeans actively entered the life of Asia. Aware of Asia's many riches, the Europeans began to carve out colonial empires. In the 1500's, Portugal established colonies in India, and Spain acquired the Philippines. The English, French, and Dutch joined the rush for colonies in the 1600's. By the end of the 1800's, Britain governed most of what is now India, Pakistan, Bangladesh, Sri Lanka, Malaysia, Singapore, and Cyprus. France ruled modern Vietnam, Laos, and Cambodia; and the Netherlands controlled Indonesia. Among the few remaining independent Asian states were China, Japan, Korea, Siam (now Thailand), Persia (now Iran), and the Ottoman Turkish Empire. The United States won the Philippines from Spain, and Korea was later colonized by Japan, in 1910. Russia and the Soviet Union also ruled a great Asian empire.

Nationalism and Independence

The desire for self-rule and unity—called nationalism—was the most powerful force in Asia during the 1900's. Asian nationalism grew rapidly. It reached its height in the years after World War II, when the following nations were born: Mongolia in 1945; Jordan and the Philippines in 1946; India and Pakistan in 1947; Burma, Ceylon (now Sri Lanka), Israel, and North and South Korea in 1948; and Indonesia in 1949.

Amid great pomp, Suleiman I (*top*) ascends the Ottoman Turkish throne in 1520. The Ottoman Empire lasted nearly 400 years more, but gradually diminished in power. A British warship (*right*) fires on flimsy Chinese craft in the first Opium War (1839–42), which arose over Chinese efforts to bar imports of the drug. China's defeat forced it to cede Hong Kong to Britain and to open ports to foreign trade.

Mohandas K. Gandhi followed a policy of nonviolence, which eventually proved successful, in his struggle to win India's independence from Britain.

Cambodia, Laos, and North and South Vietnam became independent in 1954. The Federation of Malaya followed in 1957; Cyprus in 1960; and Kuwait in 1961. Malaysia established itself in 1963. Maldives won independence in 1965, as did Singapore, which seceded from Malaysia. Yemen (Aden) won its independence in 1967, and Bangladesh (formerly East Pakistan) did so in 1971.

In 1976, following the end of the long Vietnam War, North and South Vietnam were united. Brunei gained independence in 1984; and in 1990, Yemen (Aden) and the older nation of Yemen (Sana) were united into a single republic. Armenia, Azerbaijan, Georgia, Kazakhstan, Kyrgyzstan, Tajikistan, Turkmenistan, and Uzbekistan all won independence in 1991.

Perhaps the most far-reaching effect of Western tradition on Asia was in the introduction of its political ideas and institutions. Some of the newly independent Asian nations adopted Communist forms of government. Others developed parliamentary systems. Most Asian countries, however, assumed a nonaligned, or neutral, position in their dealings with the great powers. This policy had first been announced officially at the Bandung Conference in Indonesia in 1955.

Recent History

The nations of Asia are playing an increasing role in world affairs. Japan's economic strength makes it respected, and sometimes feared, by other nations. China, with more than one-fifth of the world's people, is a major power, especially since the breakup of the Soviet Union. India's size and great population make it dominant in South Asia, and the oil-producing countries of Southwest Asia are vital to the world economy.

The ideal of peace envisioned at the Bandung Conference, however, has been difficult to achieve. In the years since, wars and civil wars have broken out in many parts of Asia.

In South Asia, India and Pakistan have gone to war several times, chiefly over the state of Jammu and Kashmir. Afghanistan has experienced years of war and civil war. Sri Lanka has been torn by violent ethnic hatreds. Civil conflict also raged in Kampuchea, until a fragile peace was agreed to in 1991. Riots in Indonesia forced the resignation of its long-term president in 1998.

In Southwest Asia, Israel and the surrounding Arab nations have fought numerous wars. Lebanon was devastated by years of conflict. Iran and Iraq were at war from 1980 to 1988. And Iraq's invasion of Kuwait in 1990 led to war in the Persian Gulf. (For more information, see the article PERSIAN GULF WAR in Volume P.) Elsewhere in

A mushroom cloud marks the atomic bombing of Hiroshima, Japan, by the United States in 1945, which hastened the end of World War II.

Japanese commuters arrive for work. Japan recovered quickly from the destruction of World War II and became one of the world's top economic powers.

the Middle East, a series of accords signed by Israel and the Palestinian Arabs beginning in 1993 brought the Gaza Strip and nearly 43 percent of the West Bank under the control of an elected Palestinian government by March 2000. Israel and Jordan also signed a peace treaty in 1994. The United States and Vietnam restored diplomatic ties in 1995. In 2000, North and South Korea held their first summit meeting since the Korean War (1950–53).

However, conflict continued in parts of former Soviet Asia. After the September 11, 2001, attacks on the United States, a U.S.-led war on international terrorism ousted the Taliban regime in Afghanistan. By 2002, India and Pakistan were on the brink of nuclear war over Kashmir, and efforts to eliminate Iraq's ability to produce biological and chemical weapons had made little progress. The unstable situation in the Middle East was inflamed by a new wave of Israeli-Palestinian violence that halted the peace process and fueled Muslim discontent.

EDWARD W. JOHNSON
Montclair State College

HYMAN KUBLIN
Author, *The Rim of Asia*

See also articles on individual Asian countries.

ASIMOV, ISAAC. See SCIENCE FICTION (Profiles).

ASQUITH, HERBERT HENRY (1852–1928)

British statesman Herbert Henry Asquith, 1st Earl of Oxford and Asquith, served as prime minister from 1908 until 1916. He was the last leader of the Liberal Party to serve as prime minister.

Asquith was born on September 12, 1852, in Morely, Yorkshire. He was a brilliant student at Oxford University and later became a successful lawyer in London. In 1886, Asquith won his first election to Parliament. He quickly became a leader within the Liberal Party, serving as home secretary (1892–95) and as chancellor of the exchequer (1905–08) before succeeding to the premiership, following the death of Henry Campbell-Bannerman in April 1908.

Legislation passed during Asquith's first years in office included massive social reforms, including the provision of old-age pensions, unemployment insurance, national health insurance, minimum wage standards for miners, and protection of trade unions. However, Asquith was at his best when dealing with constitutional issues, such as limiting the power of the House of Lords, accomplished by the Parliament Act of 1911, and negotiating home rule for Ireland.

In 1914, Britain entered World War I. Unfortunately, Asquith did not prove himself an effective war leader, and in the third year of the war he was pushed out of office in favor of the more dynamic David Lloyd George. Although he continued to lead the Liberal Party until 1926, Asquith never again held office. In 1925 he was created Earl of Oxford and Asquith, and he entered the House of Lords. He died on February 15, 1928.

ROY JENKINS (LORD JENKINS OF HILLHEAD)
Author, *Asquith*

ASSINIBOIN. See INDIANS, AMERICAN (On the Prairies and Plains).

ASSYRIA. See ANCIENT CIVILIZATIONS.

ASTAIRE, FRED. See MOTION PICTURES (Profiles: Movie Stars).

ASTEROIDS. See COMETS, METEORITES, AND ASTEROIDS.

ASTHMA. See DISEASES (Descriptions of Some Diseases).

ASTOR, JOHN JACOB. See FUR TRADE IN NORTH AMERICA (Profiles).

Sally Ride, aboard the *Challenger*, learned how to eat in the weightlessness of space. Notice the special food tray designed for the astronauts.

ASTRONAUTS

Throughout history, a few people have dared to dream that one day human beings might leave the surface of the Earth and explore the heavens. During the last thirty years that dream has come true, and a select group of men and women from several nations have journeyed into space.

The men and women who travel in space for the United States are called **astronauts** (from a Greek word meaning "sailors of the stars"). Those sent into space by the former Soviet Union are called **cosmonauts** (from a Greek word meaning "sailors of the universe"). Astronauts and cosmonauts may be sent into space for different reasons. Their mission may be to gather information about the Earth, the moon, or the rest of our solar system; to perform experiments; to launch, repair, or retrieve space satellites or telescopes; to study how being in space affects people and other living organisms; and to learn what effect space has on nonliving substances.

Selecting Astronauts

The people who become American astronauts are selected by NASA, the National Aeronautics and Space Administration. Today, some astronauts are test pilots, others are scientists or engineers. All astronauts must have graduated from college and have at least a bachelor's degree. They must also have either extensive experience as jet pilots or an advanced degree or professional experience in engineering or in the biological or physical sciences. There is no age limit. The height limit ranges from 64 to 76 inches (163 to 193 centimeters) for pilots, and from 58½ to 76 inches (149 to 193 centimeters) for scientists and engineers. All astronauts must meet rigorous standards of physical health and mental fitness.

Training Astronauts

Today's American astronauts are trained to fly in the space shuttle. They must learn how to control the spacecraft, monitor its many systems, launch satellites, and conduct scientific experiments. Astronauts must also be prepared to handle any emergencies that might happen and to endure the physical and emotional stresses that occur during spaceflight.

Astronauts are trained at NASA's Johnson Space Center near Houston, Texas. They learn the space shuttle's propulsion, navigation, environmental, and computer systems. They learn how to use the shuttle's long robot arm to release satellites into orbit and how to use the tools and equipment carried on board the shuttle. Astronauts also learn how to put on, and work in, the space suits that must be worn if they venture outside the shuttle. In addition, they take classes in subjects such as astronomy, navigation, geology, oceanography, and meteorology.

Astronauts also fly a certain number of hours each month in training jets—the pilots practice flying, the scientists and engineers develop navigation and communication skills and practice working as part of a crew.

Once an astronaut is assigned to a spaceflight, she or he begins training with the other members of the crew. A typical crew is composed of two astronauts with test pilot backgrounds and three or more astronauts with either science or engineering backgrounds. The crew trains together to learn to work as a team and to learn about the experiments or space satellites on their particular flight. An important part of the training takes place in the spaceflight simulator—a device that reproduces many of the shuttle's maneuvers and responses during flight. In the flight simulators, astronauts practice all phases of spaceflight, including launch, orbit, re-entry, and landing. They also learn how to respond when a system malfunctions and how to communicate with mission control.

Living and Working in Space

Being in space is quite different from being on Earth. This is because astronauts and all the objects around them are weightless. Astronauts move around in the shuttle by pushing off from a wall and floating from one place to another. They can perform somersaults and can easily lift satellites that would weigh thousands of pounds on Earth.

Weightlessness also makes eating and sleeping different from what astronauts are used to on Earth. Most of the food is similar to what is eaten on Earth, but some of it is specially prepared. Foods that are sticky, like beef stew or pudding, are the easiest to eat because they stick to utensils instead of floating away before they can be eaten. A drink cannot be poured in space because the liquid would simply float out of the pitcher or glass. To solve this problem, liquids are served in closed containers, and astronauts drink through straws.

When they sleep, some astronauts strap themselves into sleeping bags, which can be attached to the walls with a fabric like Velcro so that they do not float around; others float freely in the middle of the room as they sleep. They can sleep right side up, upside down, or sideways—all positions feel exactly the same in weightlessness.

Compared with earlier spacecraft, today's shuttle is relatively roomy. The air inside is the same as in any living room and the temperature is controlled. Astronauts wear regular clothes during spaceflight. But if they have to go outside, either to conduct experiments or to repair something, they must put on pressurized space suits that provide breathable air and that protect them against the vacuum of space.

During spaceflight, astronauts are very busy conducting experiments, operating equipment, and monitoring different systems. There is some time, though, for just looking at the Earth through the small windows of the shuttle.

Milestones

Yuri Gagarin of the former Soviet Union became the first person in space on April 12, 1961. In February 1962, John Glenn became the first American to orbit the Earth. The first woman in space was Valentina Tereshkova of the former Soviet Union, who orbited the Earth in June 1963. In March 1965, Soviet cosmonaut Alexei Leonov became the first person to leave a spacecraft on a "spacewalk." On July 20, 1969, the American astronauts Neil Armstrong and Edwin Aldrin became the first human beings to set foot on the moon. John Young and Robert Crippen were the first astronauts to fly in the space shuttle, in April 1981. Sally Ride, who orbited the Earth in the shuttle in June 1983, was the first American woman in space.

The achievements of these and many other brave men and women have made the human dream of space travel come true. These individuals are truly sailors of the skies.

Sally K. Ride
Professor of Physics
University of California, San Diego

See also Armstrong, Neil A.; Glenn, John H., Jr.; Space Exploration and Travel; Space Shuttles.

WONDER QUESTION

Why are astronauts weightless?

During spaceflight, the space shuttle is held in orbit around the Earth by gravity. This means that astronauts are not "away from gravity," as many people think. Astronauts are weightless because they and the space shuttle are continually falling toward Earth under the force of gravity—just as you would be if you jumped out of an airplane. Imagine jumping out of an airplane carrying a scale to weigh yourself. If you could stand on the scale while you and it were falling, the scale would read zero—you would be weightless. This is exactly the same situation that astronauts find themselves in when they are in orbit. The shuttle and everything inside it, including astronauts, are weightless because they are not resisting gravity—they are all falling together under the force of gravity.

If the space shuttle is falling, why does it not crash into the Earth? The reason is that although the shuttle is falling toward Earth, it is also traveling very fast horizontally. The speed given to the space shuttle by its rockets when it is launched allows it to reach and travel at a certain altitude in space. It is the force of gravity at that altitude that forces the shuttle to fall just enough to stay in a circular orbit that is always at the same distance from the Earth.

ASTRONOMY

Astronomy is the study of everything in the universe. It is also one of the oldest sciences. For thousands of years, people have gazed at the sky to try to learn about the stars, the planets, and all of the other objects in the universe. Paintings of astronomical events thought to be about 10,000 years old have been found in caves in Europe; and marks that may represent the phases of the moon have been found on artifacts more than 30,000 years old. Aside from such examples, however, the earliest astronomers left no written records of their studies.

THE ORIGINS OF ASTRONOMY

Long before the invention of the telescope people noticed many things in the sky. They noticed, for example, that the stars move across the sky from east to west during the course of an evening. They noticed that certain other points of light, which we now know are planets, move through the sky at different speeds. They also observed that the moon goes through phases, or seems to change shape night after night.

Starting about 10,000 years ago, people used their knowledge of the changing positions of the sun and stars to determine when to plant and harvest crops. Between 4,000 and 5,000 years ago, people in England constructed a grouping of large stones to act as a kind of astronomical observatory. Known as Stonehenge, we believe this grouping of stones was used to measure the changing position of the sun as it rises. These positions could in turn be used to determine the changing of the seasons.

The movements of the sun, moon, and planets also became the basis for the study of **astrology**, which held that such movements had an effect on people's lives. Although astrology was unscientific, it led to careful studies of the heavens and to the development of the science of astronomy. The first records of astrologers date back to ancient Babylon about 3,000 years ago. But people also studied the skies in ancient Egypt, China, Mexico, and other parts of the world.

Stonehenge may have been an early observatory used to study the movement of the sun across the sky.

ASTRONOMERS OF ANCIENT GREECE

Since the earliest astronomers lived before recorded history, we can only guess at what they knew. Our first real knowledge of ancient astronomy dates from about 2,500 years ago, when ancient Greek astronomers carefully recorded what they had learned.

Among the earliest Greek astronomers was Thales (640–546 B.C.), who was supposed to have predicted an eclipse of the sun around the year 580 B.C. An eclipse of the sun occurs when the moon moves in front of the sun and blocks its light. Supposedly, the sudden darkness caused by this eclipse was so startling that soldiers laid down their arms in the middle of a battle and called a truce. Whether this story is true or not, it is probably true that Thales had the ability to predict eclipses. This tells us that Greek astronomy had reached a fairly advanced stage by Thales' time.

Our knowledge of other Greek scientists is more accurate. The mathematician Pythagoras (582?–500? B.C.) suggested that the Earth was round, which we now know is true. The astronomer Eratosthenes (275?–195? B.C.) calculated, quite accurately, the diameter of the Earth. He did this by comparing the length of shadows cast at noon in two different cities. He knew that the Earth must be round because the shadows were of two different lengths, which told him that the sun was shining at different angles on these two cities. By comparing the length of the shadows, he could calculate the Earth's diameter. In fact, he came very close to the correct diameter. The philosopher Aristarchus (310?–230? B.C.) suggested that the Earth and other planets revolved around the sun, but this idea did not catch on for more than 2,000 years.

Early astronomers, like those in this tapestry, helped change ideas about the order of the universe. By the 1500's, astronomy had become an important science, and careful measurements were being made of the changing positions of the sun, moon, stars, and planets.

The most famous and influential Greek astronomer was Aristotle (384–322 B.C.), a philosopher whose reputation extended into many areas of study. Aristotle's greatest contributions in astronomy dealt with **cosmology**, the study of the nature of the universe. Aristotle believed that the Earth was at the center of the universe and that the stars and other planets were inside crystal spheres surrounding it. According to Aristotle, these spheres rotated around the Earth at different speeds, which was why the stars and planets moved through the night sky at different speeds.

Like Aristotle, the Greek thinker Ptolemy (A.D. 90?–168?) also believed that the Earth was at the center of the universe. His book on astronomy, which became known as the *Almagest* (Arabic for "the greatest"), was one of the most influential books in the history of astronomy. The idea of an Earth-centered universe, known as the Ptolemaic System, was the accepted view for more than 1,000 years.

A number of articles cover topics relating to astronomy and space. For more information about them, see ASTRONAUTS; BLACK HOLES; COMETS, METEORITES, AND ASTEROIDS; CONSTELLATIONS; COSMIC RAYS; ECLIPSES; GRAVITY AND GRAVITATION; MILKY WAY; MOON; NEBULAS; OBSERVATORIES; PLANETARIUMS AND SPACE MUSEUMS; PLANETS; PULSARS; QUASARS; RADIATION BELTS; RADIO AND RADAR ASTRONOMY; ROCKETS; SATELLITES; SATELLITES, ARTIFICIAL; SOLAR SYSTEM; SPACE AGENCIES AND CENTERS; SPACE EXPLORATION AND TRAVEL; SPACE PROBES; SPACE RESEARCH AND TECHNOLOGY; SPACE SHUTTLES; SPACE STATIONS; SPACE TELESCOPES; STARS; SUN; TELESCOPES; UNIVERSE; and articles on the individual planets—MERCURY, VENUS, EARTH, MARS, JUPITER, SATURN, URANUS, NEPTUNE, and PLUTO.

A REBIRTH OF ASTRONOMY

During the Middle Ages in Europe, little scientific knowledge was accumulated, and the science of astronomy was nearly forgotten. However, the knowledge of the ancient Greeks was preserved by the Arabs, who translated Greek works into Arabic. If not for the Arabs, most Greek knowledge, including astronomy, would have been lost forever.

By the 1200's, Europeans had begun to reexamine Greek knowledge. But it was not until the 1500's that new ideas in astronomy had begun to form. One of the first people to suggest that Aristotle and Ptolemy were wrong was the Polish astronomer Nicolaus Copernicus (1473–1543). Copernicus believed that the sun, not the Earth, was at the center of the universe. He also revived Aristarchus' idea that the Earth revolved around the sun. In fact, Copernicus believed that all the planets revolved around the sun in circular orbits and that the moon revolved around the Earth. As it turned out, parts of his theory were wrong, but Copernicus was closer to the truth than Aristotle or Ptolemy.

One of the most significant points of Copernicus' theory was its explanation for the phenomenon of **retrograde motion**, in which some of the planets sometimes appear to slow down and even move backward in the sky. Copernicus explained that the planets all revolve in their own orbits around the sun. As

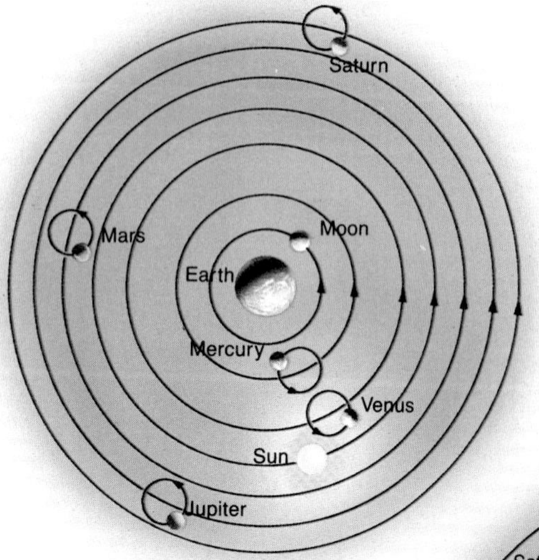

Ptolemy thought that the Earth was the center of the universe and that the sun and planets circled the Earth. Planets also moved in smaller circles, called epicycles.

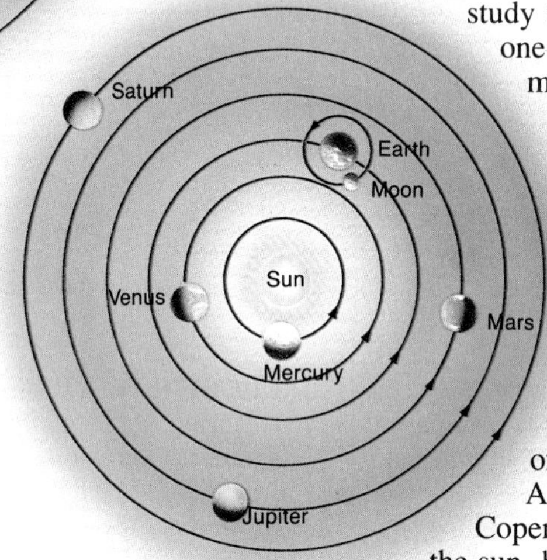

Copernicus was the first to realize that the Earth, moon, and planets orbit the sun. However, he was wrong in believing that the orbits were perfect circles.

the Earth overtakes another planet and passes it, it appears from Earth that the other planet is slowing down and then moving backward. In fact, the planet's direction is not changing at all. What the observer is experiencing is an effect that is similar to the feeling people have that objects in their field of vision are moving backward as they pass them. For example, a car moving next to your car will seem to go backward as you are going by it.

Copernicus' theories were published in 1543 in a book entitled *De revolutionibus orbium coelestium* ("On the Revolutions of the Heavenly Spheres"). This important book influenced the work of many generations of astronomers.

Later in the 1500's, Danish astronomer Tycho Brahe (1546–1601) built an observatory to study the heavens. Although telescopes had not yet been invented, Brahe designed sophisticated instruments to measure the movements of the stars and planets. Like Copernicus, Brahe believed that the sun was at the center of the universe. Brahe's young assistant, Johannes Kepler (1571–1630), also believed in the theories of Copernicus. When Brahe died, he left his records to Kepler, who used them to make a remarkable discovery about the planets. He discovered that the planets were moving around the sun in ellipses (ovals), rather than in circles as Copernicus had assumed.

At about this same time, the Italian scientist Galileo Galilei (1564–1642) was making even more remarkable discoveries. Galileo was the first astronomer to use a telescope to study the sky, and he saw things no one else had ever seen. He saw mountains and valleys on the moon, four moons around the planet Jupiter, and strange dark spots on the sun. He even saw something that he called "handles" sticking out of the side of the planet Saturn. They later turned out to be its famous rings. Galileo supported Copernicus' theories and attacked the ideas of the ancient Greeks.

Although Galileo believed, like Copernicus, that the planets orbited the sun, he could not explain why. The person who answered that question was the English scientist Isaac Newton (1642–1727). Newton discovered that all objects produce a force called gravity that attracts other objects. A large object like the sun produces enough gravity to hold the planets in orbit around it. Moons orbit planets for the same reason. Because of Newton's discoveries, scientists came to accept Copernicus' idea that the Earth and other planets revolve around the sun.

DISCOVERIES ABOUT THE UNIVERSE

The discoveries of Isaac Newton marked the beginning of modern astronomy. But there was still much to be learned about the solar system and the universe. Since Newton's time, astronomers have learned a great deal.

The Planets and Their Moons

Until the 1700's, astronomers believed that there were only six planets: Mercury, Venus, Earth, Mars, Jupiter, and Saturn. Then, in 1781, the astronomer William Herschel (1738–1822) and his sister Caroline Herschel (1750–1848) discovered a seventh planet. The discovery of this planet, called Uranus, caused

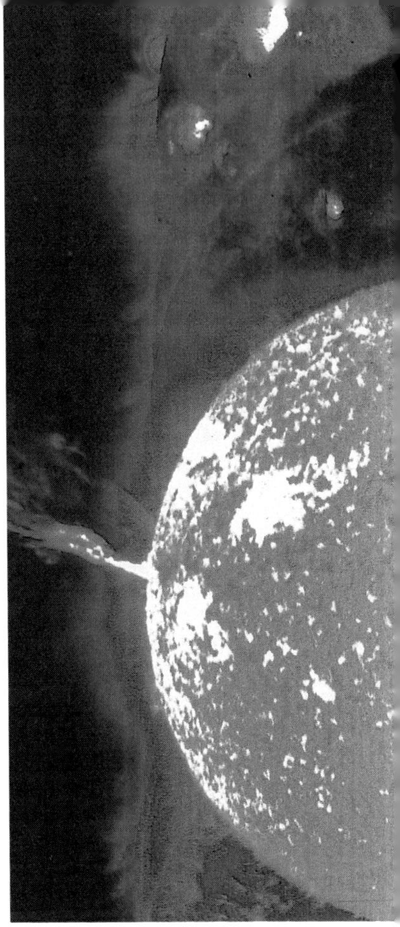

We have learned a great deal about objects in space. Comets like Halley's (*above*) are made of ice and dust. The sun (*right*) is a star made of hot gases that often shoot miles above its surface.

great excitement because it was the first new planet to be discovered since ancient times. Prompted by this discovery, astronomers began looking for other new planets. In 1846, the German astronomer Johann Galle (1812–1910) spotted the planet Neptune, although its presence had been predicted earlier by the English astronomer John Couch Adams (1819–92) and the French astronomer Jean Joseph Leverrier (1811–77). Finally, in 1930, the American astronomer Clyde Tombaugh (1906–97) located the planet Pluto, which had been predicted by the American astronomer Percival Lowell (1855–1916).

The existence of the Earth's moon has always been known. But the existence of other moons, or satellites, in the solar system was not known until Galileo discovered moons orbiting Jupiter in 1610. Gradually, other moons were discovered as well. The only planets that have no moons are Mercury and Venus.

Comets and Asteroids

For thousands of years, people had seen strange streaks of light pass through the night sky every few years. The English astronomer Edmund Halley (1656–1742) realized that these streaks of light were actually small objects orbiting the sun. These objects, known as comets, begin their long elliptical orbits far beyond the outermost planets. Attracted by the sun's gravity, they fall inward toward the sun and are then propelled back out to the outer reaches of the solar system.

Comets are made mostly of ice and dust. As a comet nears the sun, evaporation causes gases in its head, or **coma**, to glow. The solar wind (electrically charged particles from the sun) blows back some of these gases to form a brilliant, glowing tail that may be more than 60 million miles (100 million kilometers) long. Scientists think that comets come from a cloud of ice and dust orbiting the sun at a distance of more than 10 trillion miles (16 trillion kilometers). This cloud, called the Oort Cloud after Dutch astronomer Jan Oort (1900–92) who first predicted its existence, is left over from the earliest days of the solar system.

Another group of objects in the solar system are asteroids, a number of small bodies located between the orbits of Mars and Jupiter. Asteroids may be the remains of a planet that never quite formed. The first asteroid was discovered in 1801 and was named Ceres. Since then, thousands more have been discovered.

The Sun and the Stars

After Galileo observed dark spots on the sun, it was many years before other discoveries about it were made. Beginning in 1826, the German astronomer Heinrich Schwabe (1789–1875) began counting sunspots. Over time, he discovered that these sunspots appear in cycles during which their number varies. In 1851, the Scottish astronomer Johann von Lamont (1805–79) noted that disturbances in the Earth's magnetic field happened during the periods of greatest sunspot activity. These early discoveries opened the way for other discoveries about the sun's effects on the Earth, the sun's temperature, and the process that causes the sun's heat and light.

In time, astronomers realized that the universe is much larger than our solar system and that the sun is actually a star just like others in the night sky. These stars are globes of extremely hot gas heated by nuclear reactions in their interiors. One of the first to try to measure the distance to a star was the Dutch astronomer Christiaan Huygens (1629–95). Huygens was unsuccessful, but in 1838, the German astronomer Friedrich Wilhelm Bessel (1784–1846) measured the distance to a star named 61 Cygni (the star numbered 61 in the constellation Cygnus) and found that it was 66 trillion miles (106 trillion kilometers) away.

Stars beyond our solar system are so far away that astronomers invented a new unit to measure their distance. That unit, known as the **light-year**, represents the distance a beam of light travels in a year. Although light seems to travel instantly from place to place it does not. It actually moves at an extremely fast speed, about 186,000 miles (300,000 kilometers) per second. A light-year is about 6 trillion miles (9.6 trillion kilometers). The star 61 Cygni is therefore 11 light-years from Earth.

THE TWENTY NEAREST STARS

STAR	DISTANCE IN LIGHT-YEARS	STAR	DISTANCE IN LIGHT-YEARS
Sun	about 8.3 light-mins.	Yale 343.1*	9.0
		Ross 154	9.6
Proxima Centauri*	4.3	Yale 5736	10.3
Alpha Centauri A*	4.3	Epsilon Eridani	10.8
Alpha Centauri B*	4.3	Yale 5475	10.9
Barnard's Star*	6.0	Yale 2730	10.9
Wolf 359	7.7	61 Cygni A*	11.1
+36° 2147	8.3	61 Cygni B*	11.1
Sirius A*	8.7	Epsilon Indi	11.4
Sirius B*	8.7	Procyon A*	11.5

*member of binary or multiple star system

Omega Centauri, the brightest star cluster in the sky, is 22,000 light-years from Earth. Halley's comet, above it, is about 4 light-minutes from Earth in this picture.

Soon after Bessel measured the distance to 61 Cygni, the Scottish astronomer Thomas Henderson (1798–1844) measured the distance to Alpha Centauri at 4.33 light-years. A star's distance in light-years indicates how long ago the light we see now left that star. With Alpha Centauri, for example, the light we see today left the star 4.33 years ago. This means that we actually see Alpha Centauri as it was 4.33 years in the past. Most stars are millions of light-years away, and the light we see left them millions of years ago.

Binary and Variable Stars. Once astronomers began to study the stars beyond our solar system, they made a number of surprising discoveries. Most stars have other stars orbiting with them, making them part of multiple star systems. Some of these systems consist of only two stars, called **binary stars**. ("Binary" means "made up of two things.") Other systems consist of more than a dozen stars moving around one another in complex orbits.

Astronomers also discovered that stars do not always shine with a consistent brightness. Some grow brighter and dimmer over a period of time. These stars are called **variable stars**.

Classification of Stars. Some of the most important discoveries about stars have been based on their spectra, the plural form of **spectrum**. A spectrum is the range of colors observed in an object that produces light, such as a star. A rainbow is an example of a spectrum. Scientists can study the spectrum of a star by letting the light from the star pass through special instruments. Sometimes certain colors are found to be missing. Because these missing colors appear as dark or bright lines in the spectrum, they are called spectral lines. These lines tell astronomers about the chemical elements that the star is made of.

The first astronomer to photograph the spectrum of a star was Henry Draper (1837–82) in 1872. In the 1880's, American astronomers Edward Pickering (1846–1919) and Annie Jump Cannon (1863–1941) divided stars into classes based on the lines in their spectra and the bright background, or **continuum**, on which the lines are observed. The star classes they created, named O, B, A, F, G, K, and M, are arranged according to temperatures, with the hottest stars in class O and the coolest in class M.

Most stars fall in the area of the H-R diagram known as the main sequence because they obey the rule that hotter stars are brighter and cooler stars are dimmer. However, a few stars are cool and bright or hot and dim and they fall outside the main sequence.

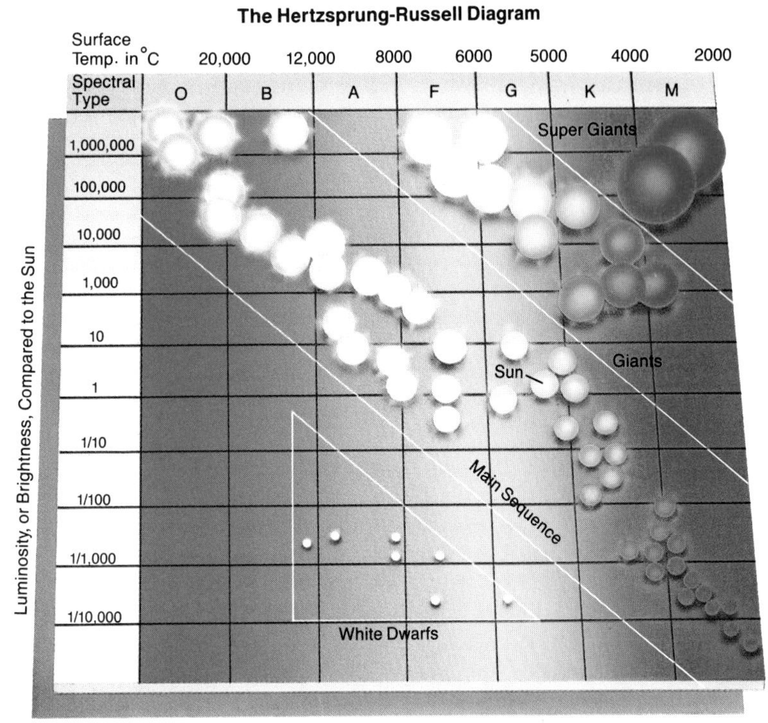

In the early 1900's, the Danish astronomer Ejnar Hertzsprung (1873–1967) and the American astronomer Henry Norris Russell (1877–1957) studied both the spectral classes of stars and their **luminosity**, or brightness. They discovered that temperature and brightness are closely related, with the hotter stars being brighter and the cooler stars being dimmer. These two scientists created a diagram, known as the Hertzsprung-Russell (or H-R) diagram, showing these relationships. This diagram has helped scientists learn how stars are born and how they die.

Detailed analysis of star spectra led British-American astronomer Cecilia Payne (1900–79) to conclude that most stars are made of the same chemical elements. This information also contributed to our understanding of the lifetimes of stars and why stars shine.

The Birth and Death of Stars. A star begins its life as a cloud of mostly hydrogen gas and dust floating in space. If something disturbs this cloud, such as a passing star, it can begin to collapse, and the gravity that is produced attracts other particles of gas and dust. As the cloud shrinks, the speed at which these particles fall toward the center of the cloud causes it to heat up and glow, forming what astronomers call a **protostar**. When the protostar reaches a certain temperature, a process known as hydrogen fusion begins, fueled by the hydrogen gas present. Hydrogen fusion creates such tremendous heat that the protostar tries to explode outward, but the powerful gravity of the gas and dust particles prevents this from happening. Instead, the protostar remains perfectly balanced between exploding and collapsing, and it becomes a star.

Stars have life expectancies ranging from a hundred or so million years to trillions of years, depending on their size. A very massive star uses up, or burns, its nuclear fuel very rapidly and has a relatively short life span. A star with a very low mass burns its fuel much more slowly and lasts much longer. Medium-sized stars, like our sun, use up their hydrogen in about 10 billion years.

Eventually, a star begins to run out of hydrogen gas and hydrogen fusion ceases. At that point, it begins to collapse again, generating even more heat. The star becomes so hot that other gases, such as helium, begin new processes of fusion. These new fusions generate such tremendous heat that the star expands greatly, becoming what is known as a **red giant**. While the outer layers of red giants are relatively cool, these stars are very bright because of their tremendous size.

As a red giant runs out of fuel, it collapses once more. If the original star was relatively small, the red giant will collapse into a small, dense form called a **white dwarf**. A white dwarf appears very dim because of its small size, but it is very hot. If the original star was massive, the collapsing red giant will generate so much heat that the star explodes. The resulting explosion is called a **supernova** and is millions of times brighter than an ordinary star. The part of the star left behind by the explosion becomes a **neutron star**, a rapidly spinning star that is even smaller and denser than a white dwarf. If the original star was extremely massive before it exploded, the neutron star would also collapse and would never stop collapsing. It would become a **black hole**, which is so dense and has such an enormous gravitational pull that even light cannot escape from it. A black hole has never been seen but would probably appear as a dark hole surrounded by a spiral-shaped halo of hot particles attracted by its gravity. Matter that falls into it can never escape.

Neutron stars often emit bursts of radio waves into space. Because the neutron stars spin rapidly, these radio waves are detected by radio telescopes as a pulsating signal, with a single pulse for every rotation. Because of these pulses, the first neutron stars discovered were known as pulsating stars, or **pulsars**.

Galaxies and Other Objects

For centuries, astronomers have been aware of small glowing clouds of matter in the universe. These clouds are called **nebulas**. Some are clouds of gas and dust left behind by supernova explosions like the Crab Nebula, which formed more than 900 years ago, or by other interstellar events. Others are protostars starting to form.

In the early 1900's, scientists discovered that some nebulas are actually very distant **galaxies**, or great clouds of stars. Our sun is part of the Milky Way galaxy. As astronomers studied these distant galaxies with telescopes that became more and more powerful over time, they saw that there are billions of galaxies in the universe. Most are clustered together in groups. The Milky Way galaxy is part of a small cluster known as the Local Group. When astronomers look at galaxies they see bright stars and glowing gases. But they have also learned that much of the matter in galaxies is invisible. This dark matter makes up about 90 percent of all the mass of the universe.

Certain galaxies, called Seyfert galaxies, appear to have violent explosions taking place in their centers, which may result from heat generated by giant black holes at their centers. There is some evidence that such a black hole may exist inside the Milky Way galaxy.

At the very edge of the visible universe, scientists have detected extremely bright objects known as **quasars** (short for "quasistellar objects"). Some of these quasars are billions of light-years away. Because the light from these distant objects takes billions of years to reach us, quasars may be galaxies at early stages of their existence.

The Development of the Universe

By the 1920's, astronomers had noticed that galaxies outside the Local Group were moving away from our galaxy. The American astronomer Edwin Hubble (1889–1953) also noticed that the farther away a galaxy was, the faster it was moving. In fact, clusters of galaxies were moving away from one another, suggesting that the universe was expanding.

Profiles

Friedrich Wilhelm Bessel (1784–1846) is considered to be one of the most skillful and diligent astronomical observers of his time. A self-educated astronomer, Bessel's calculations on the orbit of Halley's comet in 1804 brought him fame and a position at Lilienthal Observatory in Germany. His contributions included the determination of the positions of more than 75,000 stars and the first accurate calculation of the distance of a star from the earth, which was perhaps his greatest achievement.

Annie Jump Cannon (1863–1941) is recognized as one of the foremost woman astronomers. After studying astronomy at Radcliffe College, Cannon was appointed to the staff of Harvard College Observatory in 1896, where she worked for the rest of her life. She was one of the first women to receive a Harvard faculty appointment. One of her greatest achievements was her preparation of *The Henry Draper Catalogue*, a system still used to classify stars. Cannon proved that stars could be grouped into a few basic types arranged according to their color, which indicated a star's surface temperature. During her lifetime, Cannon classified well over 350,000 stars. She received numerous honors, including an honorary doctorate from Oxford University, the first awarded to a woman.

Annie Jump Cannon

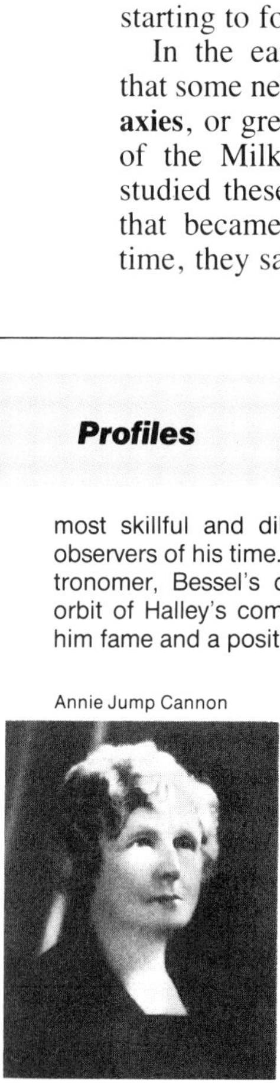

Sir Arthur Stanley Eddington

Sir Arthur Stanley Eddington (1882–1944) is noted for his work on the internal dynamics of stars. After graduating from Trinity College at Cambridge, England, Eddington served first as chief assistant at the Royal Observatory at Greenwich and then as director of the Cambridge Observatory. His pioneering work on stars proved that a star's energy is transported by radiation from its interior to its surface. He also determined the relationship between a star's mass and its brightness. Eddington became an important supporter of Einstein's theory of relativity. His observation that starlight is deflected (bent) around the sun during solar eclipses provided evidence to confirm Einstein's theory that gravitation causes light to bend. Eddington won many honors for his work.

Astronomers realized that if the universe is expanding, there must have been a time when all the galaxies were closer together. In fact, at some time in the distant past, all the galaxies may have been crushed into an area in space made up of a dense soup of particles smaller than atoms. By studying the speed at which galaxies are moving apart, astronomers theorized that about 10 to 15 billion years ago a tremendous explosion, which they call the Big Bang, may have started the expansion of the universe. At that time, these particles, which make up most of the matter in space, formed into hydrogen and helium atoms, and began to expand and move outward. Over millions of years, stars and galaxies began to form, but scientists are not sure how these particles formed galaxies in the shapes and patterns that exist in the universe today.

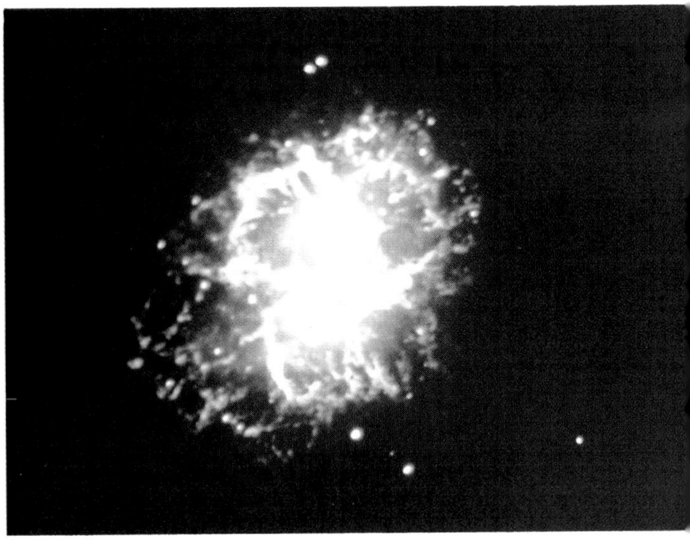

Telescopes help astronomers study the Crab Nebula, the remains of a supernova with a neutron star at its center, about 5,000 light-years from Earth.

THE TOOLS OF ASTRONOMY

Most objects studied in astronomy are so far away that astronomers must gather information about them from a distance by using special instruments. The first astronomical instrument, of course, was the human eye, and many early astronomers devised instruments to measure the motion of the stars and planets.

One of the most important instruments ever developed by astronomers is the optical telescope. ("Optical" means "making use of light.") The lenses and mirrors of optical telescopes focus the light entering them in such a way that distant objects appear larger and brighter. Optical telescopes also allow astronomers to see many more objects than are visible to the naked eye. The earliest type of optical telescope, developed in the 1600's, was the **refracting telescope**, which is basically a tube with a lens at each end. Another type of optical telescope is the **reflecting telescope**. In a reflecting telescope, one of the lenses is replaced with a mirror. Most of the larger telescopes are reflecting telescopes.

George Ellery Hale (1868–1938) was one of America's foremost astronomers. Hale studied physics at Massachusetts Institute of Technology but devoted much of his spare time to astronomy. One of his first achievements was the invention of the spectroheliograph, an instrument for photographing the sun. His greatest achievements, however, involved telescopes. His first triumph was in overseeing the construction of the 40-inch refracting telescope at Yerkes Observatory in Wisconsin—the largest of its kind in the world. Hale was also involved in the construction of a 100-inch reflecting telescope at the Mount Wilson Observatory in California and the 200-inch reflecting telescope at Mount Palomar Observatory in California.

The **Herschel Family** were distinguished English scientists of German origin who were noted for their work in astronomy. **William Herschel** (1738–1822) was a pioneer in almost every branch of modern astronomy. An avid builder of telescopes, he established his reputation in 1781 with the discovery of the planet Uranus. William is also noted for his classifications of star clusters and nebulas, his discovery of binary (double) star systems, and his theories on the structure of the universe. He was the first to establish the motion of the solar system and to try to determine the direction of its movement. He was also the first to suggest the existence of infrared radiation. **Caroline Lucretia Herschel** (1750–1848), William's sister, began her work in astronomy as her brother's assistant. However, she is also noted for her own research. In 1786 she observed her first comet, and by 1797 she had discovered seven more. She also discovered many new nebulas. **John Frederick William Herschel** (1792–1871), the son of William Herschel, began a career in mathematics and law but devoted himself to astronomy after his father's death in 1822. John Herschel discovered more than 1,000 binary stars and almost 2,000 nebulas and star clusters in the skies of the Southern Hemisphere. He also pioneered the use of photographic techniques in astronomy. A founding member of the Royal Astronomical Society, he received a knighthood for his achievements.

George Ellery Hale

William Herschel

ATLANTIC OCEAN

The Atlantic Ocean is the world's second largest body of water. Covering about one fifth of the earth's surface, it is exceeded in size only by the vast Pacific Ocean. As a link between four continents—Europe, Africa, North America, and South America—the Atlantic Ocean has played an important role in modern world history.

The word "Atlantic" is derived from Greek mythology, referring to the Titan Atlas, who gave his name to the Atlas mountain range of North Africa. To the later Romans, the Atlantic was the region beyond the Atlas Mountains. The Atlantic Ocean was also thought to be the site of the legendary land of Atlantis, which was said to have been swallowed up by the sea many centuries ago.

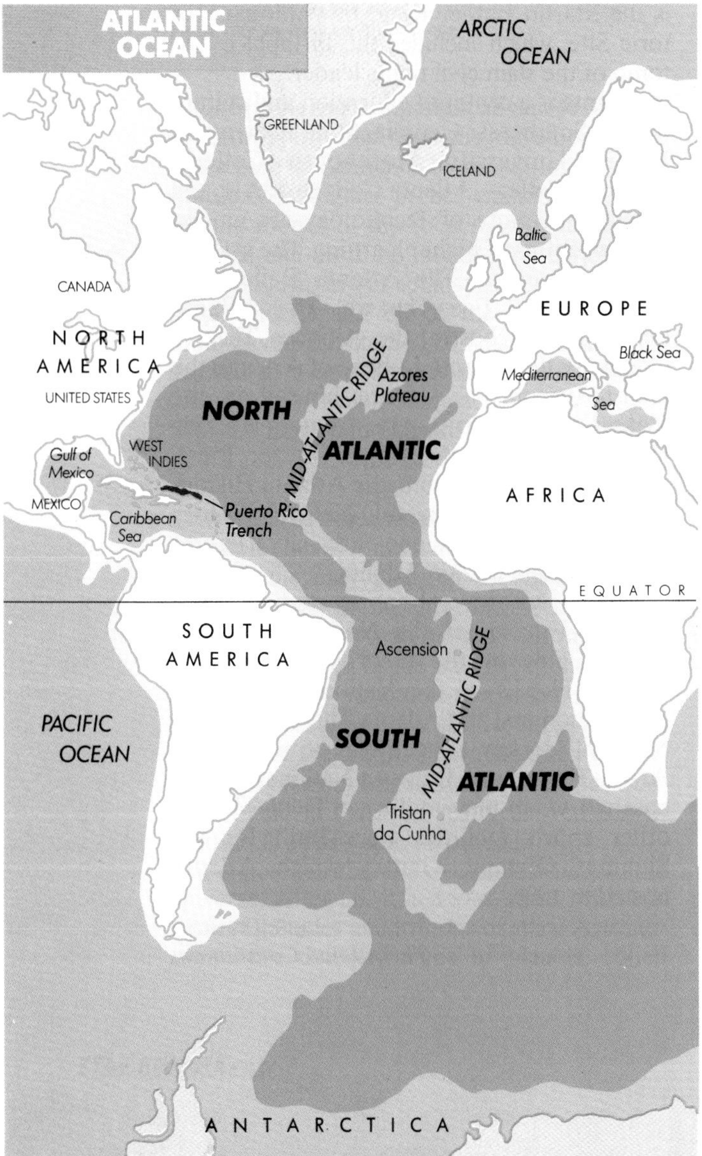

Area and Location. Counting all its adjacent seas, the Atlantic Ocean has an area of more than 41,000,000 square miles (106,000,000 square kilometers). Without them, the ocean still covers an area of some 31,830,000 square miles (82,440,000 square kilometers). The Atlantic Ocean extends from the Arctic region in the north to Antarctica in the south. Some geographers consider the Arctic Ocean to be a separate body of water, while others consider it a part of the Atlantic. The Atlantic is bounded on the east by Europe and Africa, and on the west by North and South America.

At its narrowest, between the bulge of Brazil (in South America) and the city of Dakar in Senegal (in Africa), the Atlantic is about 1,850 miles (2,980 kilometers) across. At its broadest, between Florida and the Strait of Gibraltar, it is more than 4,000 miles (6,400 kilometers) wide. The Atlantic Ocean is divided by the equator into two major parts, the North Atlantic and the South Atlantic.

The Ocean Floor. The Atlantic Ocean has an average depth of about 12,800 feet (3,900 meters). The deepest spot is in the Puerto Rico Trench, in the North Atlantic, which reaches a depth of 27,510 feet (8,385 meters).

The ocean floor is divided into two valleys by the Mid-Atlantic Ridge. This S-shaped ridge runs from north to south and rises about 6,000 feet (1,830 meters). Where it rises above the surface, the ridge forms a number of small islands, including the Azores, Ascension, St. Helena, and Tristan da Cunha.

Shorelines and Coastal Waters. Compared to the fairly straight coast of the South Atlantic, the North Atlantic has a very irregular shoreline. The greatest indentations are on the eastern side of the Atlantic. They are formed by the Baltic, North, Mediterranean, and Black seas. The coastal waters on the western side include Hudson Bay, the Gulf of Saint Lawrence, the Gulf of Mexico, and the Caribbean Sea. Water from most of the great river systems of the world flows into the Atlantic. These rivers give the Atlantic the largest drainage area of any ocean. Such drainage, from about half of the world's land area, includes many dissolved minerals and makes the Atlantic the saltiest of the oceans.

Currents: Warm and Cold. The North and South Atlantic have several strong currents that affect the climate of nearby land areas. The direction of these water currents is similar to that of the wind currents. In the North Atlantic they flow in a clockwise direction; in the South Atlantic, counterclockwise.

The Gulf Stream of the North Atlantic carries warm water northward from the tropics along the eastern coast of the United States and then turns northeast toward Europe. The Gulf Stream makes western Europe warmer than areas of the same latitude in eastern North America. The cold Labrador Current flows from the Arctic Ocean along the eastern coasts of Greenland and Canada until it meets the Gulf Stream. It is the Labrador Current that gives northern New England and eastern Canada their cold climates. It also carries icebergs and fog southward, where they often endanger shipping. In the South Atlantic the warm Brazil Current travels in a southerly direction from the equator along the eastern coast of Brazil.

The Sargasso Sea, a part of the Atlantic lying between the West Indies and the Azores, is a region of relatively still water and little wind. In the days of sailing ships, vessels were often becalmed there.

Historical Background. To the ancient Greeks and Romans, the Atlantic Ocean marked the boundary of the known world. Few early peoples, except for the seafaring and trading Phoenicians, ventured beyond the Mediterranean Sea. Vikings later colonized Iceland and Greenland, and in about A.D. 1000 founded a short-lived settlement in North America. It was not until Christopher Columbus' epic voyage of 1492, however, that large-scale exploration of the Atlantic began. Trade routes were established, followed by European settlement in the Americas. With improvements in technology, the Atlantic, which had once been a barrier to human expansion, became a vital highway between the Old World of Europe and the New World of America. In the centuries since, the importance of this link has continued.

DANIEL JACOBSON
Michigan State University

ATLANTIC PROVINCES. See NEW BRUNSWICK; NEWFOUNDLAND; NOVA SCOTIA; PRINCE EDWARD ISLAND.

ATLASES. See MAPS AND GLOBES.

ATMOSPHERE

The Earth is surrounded by layers of gases we call air, or our atmosphere. Our atmosphere serves us in many ways. It keeps a portion of the sun's radiation from reaching the Earth's surface, which prevents our planet from becoming boiling hot during the day. At night, it keeps the heat that is generated by the sun's rays during the day from escaping too quickly. This protects the Earth's surface from temperatures of extreme cold. Because the atmosphere moderates temperatures and screens out dangerous radiation from the sun, the Earth is able to support life.

The atmosphere also helps make the Earth a more pleasant place to live. Air carries sound waves, which let us hear voices and music. The molecules, particles, and water droplets in the air can scatter sunlight, giving rise to blue skies, red sunsets, and rainbows.

▶WHAT OUR ATMOSPHERE IS MADE OF

Air—our atmosphere—is a mixture of colorless gases, water vapor, and dust particles. Nitrogen is the most abundant gas in the atmosphere. Almost four fifths of air is made up of nitrogen. The next most abundant gas is oxygen. Nearly one fifth of air is oxygen, which is an essential element for almost all life. People need oxygen to breathe and to turn food into energy. Another gas in the atmosphere is carbon dioxide. Although it is present in very small amounts, it is vital to life on Earth. Green plants use carbon dioxide in the process of making their food.

Our air contains traces of still other gases. Helium and hydrogen are found in very small amounts, as are argon, krypton, neon, and xenon. Some gases, like methane, nitrous oxide, and dimethyl sulfide, are emitted into the atmosphere from the Earth's surface largely as a result of biological processes in plants and animals. Others, such as carbon monoxide and a class of molecules called *c*hloro*fl*uoro*c*arbons (CFC's), enter the atmosphere as a result of human activities, especially in industry. A third class of molecules, like ozone, is formed in the atmosphere usually as a result of chemical reactions caused by sunlight acting on the other molecules there.

Water vapor in the atmosphere is water in a gaseous form. It is found mostly in the lowest few miles of the atmosphere, but it can be found higher up as well. It enters the atmosphere from bodies of water such as oceans, lakes, and rivers, and by evaporation from the Earth's surface. When conditions are right, clouds and fog can form from this vapor. The water in clouds can evaporate back into the atmosphere or fall to Earth as precipitation, such as rain, sleet, or snow.

The lower atmosphere is filled with countless specks of dust—tiny particles of matter from soil, fires, plants, salt spray, volcanoes, or meteors, most too small to be seen.

AIR HAS MASS AND EXERTS PRESSURE

Although it may feel as though air does not have mass, it does. A cubic centimeter of dry air has a mass of about 0.00118 grams when it is at sea level and at a temperature of 77°F (25°C). If we could measure the mass of all of the molecules in the atmosphere, the total would be staggering, about 5,700,000,000,000,000 (quadrillion) tons.

The air presses down on us and against us from all sides. Something like a ton of air is pressing against you at this moment. You are not aware of this because pressure within your body balances the pressure of the air outside of it.

Air pressure is 14.7 pounds per square inch (1.036 kilograms per square centimeter) at sea level. It is greatest there because that is the bottom of the atmosphere. The higher you go, the thinner the air becomes. For example, at 10 miles (16 kilometers) above sea level, the density of the air is only about one tenth of the density at the Earth's surface.

OZONE DEPLETION

Scientists have been monitoring concentrations of ozone in the upper stratosphere since evidence for ozone depletion was found over Antarctica in the mid-1970's. Ozone acts as a shield that protects us from much harmful ultraviolet radiation from the sun. Ozone depletion occurs when chlorofluorocarbons exposed to the strong ultraviolet radiation in the stratosphere release chlorine atoms. The chlorine atoms help break down ozone into ordinary oxygen, reducing the amount and effectiveness of ozone in our atmosphere. Chlorofluorocarbons are industrially produced molecules used for air conditioning and refrigeration, as propellants for aerosol sprays, and as blowing agents for foams.

The total amount of ozone over a station in Antarctica where people were living and working was shown to have decreased by about one third between the mid-1970's and the mid-1980's. Measurements from a satellite showed this depletion occurred over all of the continent. By the early 1990's the amounts of ozone over Antarctica were about half those of the 1970's. The TOMS (Total Ozone Mapping Spectrometer) program continues to map daily levels of ozone over Antarctica from satellites in space. In this photograph, the wide bands of lavender and dark purple indicate areas of ozone depletion on this date.

LAYERS OF ATMOSPHERE

Our atmosphere is made up of the troposphere, the stratosphere, the mesosphere, the thermosphere, and the exosphere.

The Troposphere

This lowest layer of the atmosphere is where we live, and it is also the layer that we know the most about. Like the other atmospheric layers it varies in size. The troposphere extends from sea level to an altitude of almost 12 miles (19 kilometers) above the equator, but only about 5 miles (8 kilometers) above the North and South poles.

Most of the Earth's population lives within the area about 1 mile (1.6 kilometers) above sea level. But scientists have learned that peo-

A unique spectrometer maps levels of ozone in the Earth's atmosphere in Dobson units, a measure of the thickness of ozone over a broad area.

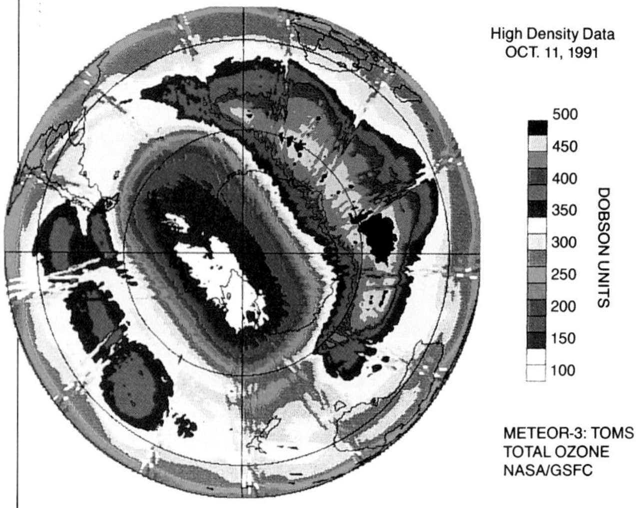

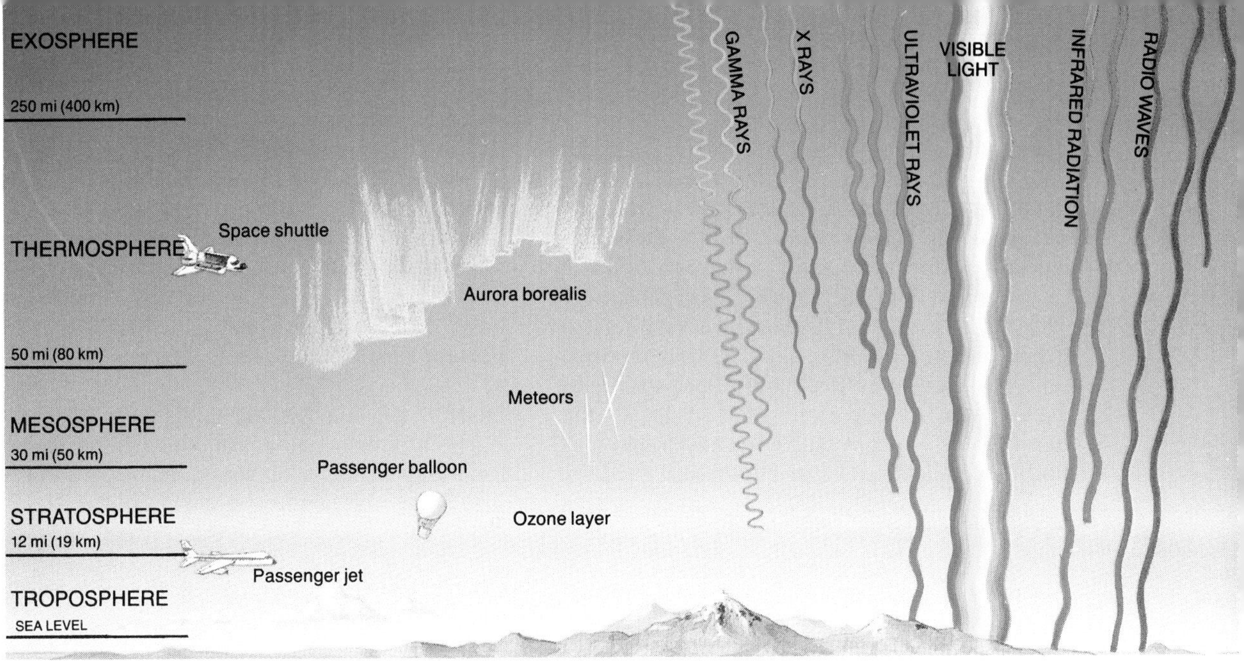

The many layers of the Earth's atmosphere—the troposphere, stratosphere, mesosphere, thermosphere, and exosphere—protect us from much harmful radiation from space.

ple can go about 3½ miles (5.6 kilometers) above the Earth's surface before they must use pressure suits and oxygen masks.

Most of our weather takes shape in the troposphere. Winds pick up water vapor from which clouds and rain form. Air currents move up and down, while winds blow north, south, east, and west, carrying warm or cold air.

Instruments carried aloft in balloons and on satellites have proven that the temperature in the troposphere drops steadily as one goes higher. There is a drop of about 3.5 to 5.5°F for each 1,000 feet (2 to 3°C for each 300 meters). At the top of the troposphere the temperature usually approaches −70°F (−56°C). Under certain conditions, temperatures as low as −117°F (−82°C) can be reached. This process slows near the top of the troposphere.

The area in which the temperature stops changing as you go higher in altitude is called the tropopause. This marks the boundary between the troposphere and the stratosphere. Winds reach their greatest force at the level of the tropopause. Most of the fast-moving winds called jet streams are found here. They move along at speeds of up to 200 miles (320 kilometers) an hour.

The Stratosphere

The second layer of air is the stratosphere. Temperatures in the stratosphere increase with altitude from the lower boundary (the tropopause) to the upper boundary (the stratopause). The stratopause is about 30 miles (50 kilometers) above sea level and the temperature there is typically about 32°F (0°C). The increase in temperature is caused by a layer of ozone. This gas absorbs most of the ultraviolet radiation that comes from the sun and changes it to heat energy, which is transmitted to other gas molecules in the stratosphere.

Ordinarily only between one and ten of every million molecules in the stratosphere are ozone molecules, but these molecules are very important to life on Earth. Ozone absorbs much of the sun's ultraviolet radiation, which can cause skin cancers and cataracts in people, so that only small amounts reach Earth.

The stratosphere is very stable, with little or no upward or downward movement of air. The air in the stratosphere is very dry, with only two to six molecules of water for every million molecules of air.

The Mesosphere

Above the stratosphere, the air becomes even thinner, and the temperature again falls. Beginning at a height of about 30 miles (50 kilometers) and extending up to about 50 miles (80 kilometers) is the mesosphere. At the top of the mesosphere, temperatures may be lower than −103°F (−75°C).

The Thermosphere and the Exosphere

The thermosphere reaches a height of perhaps 250 miles (400 kilometers) above sea level. It is remarkable for its electrical activity and range of temperatures. At the bottom of this layer, temperatures are below freezing. At the top, they exceed 2200°F (1200°C), caused by direct exposure to solar radiation.

Atoms and molecules of gas in the very thin air of the thermosphere are bombarded by radiation from the sun. They are broken into smaller, electrically charged particles called **ions** in a region referred to as the **ionosphere**. Here electric currents can flow, as they do in a neon tube or fluorescent light.

The ionosphere reflects some radio waves back to Earth. This allows radio communication between widely separated places on Earth. For example, radio waves beamed from North America bounce off the ionosphere and can be received in Africa. Without the bounce, the waves would simply continue out into space.

WONDER QUESTION

Is the Earth's atmosphere warming?

Many scientists think that small changes in its composition will cause the atmosphere at the Earth's surface to become warmer. They are alarmed because the amounts of gases such as carbon dioxide, methane, and nitrous oxide in our atmosphere are increasing. These gases tend to trap the radiation that reaches the Earth from the sun. Because the amount of radiation we receive tends to be constant, if less radiation escapes from our atmosphere, the atmosphere could become warmer.

The problem is complex because many factors need to be considered. For example, if the surface atmosphere of the Earth warms, glacial ice may melt, causing sea levels to rise. Also, more water may evaporate from the Earth's surface. This would affect the formation of clouds and the amounts and patterns of wind and rainfall. Both of these changes could affect temperatures around the world, but precisely how (and for how long) is not fully understood.

Records going back many years show a temperature increase, but the increase has been interrupted by cooling periods. The evidence continues to suggest, however, that "global warming" is occurring. Because the effects of global warming could be so serious, research is continuing on a global scale.

The exosphere, the outermost layer of the atmosphere, continues out into space until it eventually merges with the atmosphere of the sun. The atmosphere here is extremely thin. Atoms and molecules travel so rapidly, particularly at the upper levels, that they regularly escape the Earth's gravitation and become part of the gases in space.

CHANGES IN THE ATMOSPHERE

The atmosphere has remained fairly stable for many millions of years, but its temperature and composition change with time. Natural occurrences can cause changes in the composition of the atmosphere, for example, when ashes and hot gases are thrown into the atmosphere during volcanic eruptions.

People also cause changes in the atmospheric composition. The burning of fossil fuels such as coal and gasoline release carbon dioxide into the atmosphere. Agricultural activities such as cattle raising, rice production, and the burning of tropical rain forests and grasslands release methane, carbon monoxide, and nitrogen oxides. Many industrial processes release oxides of sulfur and nitrogen and traces of metals into the atmosphere. Some processes send chlorofluorocarbons into the stratosphere. Since the start of the Industrial Revolution during the late 1700's, the amount of carbon dioxide in the atmosphere has increased by 30 percent and the amount of methane has doubled.

Increased carbon dioxide in the atmosphere may cause temperatures on Earth to rise. Chlorofluorocarbons in the stratosphere cause the loss of ozone, which can allow unsafe levels of ultraviolet radiation to reach the Earth. Because of their impact, human activities that can cause changes in the Earth's atmosphere need to be better understood and controlled. Today there are many tools used to study atmospheric changes, including the research balloons, space shuttles, and space satellites that make observations and collect data and sophisticated computers that help scientists interpret it.

DR. JACK A. KAYE
Office of Space Science and Applications
Earth Science and Applications Division, NASA

See also AIR POLLUTION; CLIMATE; EARTH; WEATHER; WINDS.

ATOMIC BOMB. See NUCLEAR ENERGY.

ATOMIC ENERGY. See NUCLEAR ENERGY.

ATOMS

Atoms are the basic building blocks of our world. These tiny particles make up every type of matter in the universe—solid, liquid, or gas. Matter is anything that takes up space and has weight.

An atom is the smallest bit of uncombined matter that retains the properties or characteristics of larger portions of the same matter. A group of atoms bound together tightly is called a **molecule**. When atoms of the same type combine with one another, they form the molecules of a **chemical element**, usually referred to simply as an **element**. When different types of atoms combine, they form molecules of a **chemical compound**, often referred to as a **compound**—a substance made up of two or more elements in which the elements are always combined in exactly the same proportion. Water, for example, is a chemical compound made up of hydrogen and oxygen. A single molecule of water contains one atom of oxygen and two atoms of hydrogen. Most of the objects we encounter in everyday life are made up of such combinations of atoms.

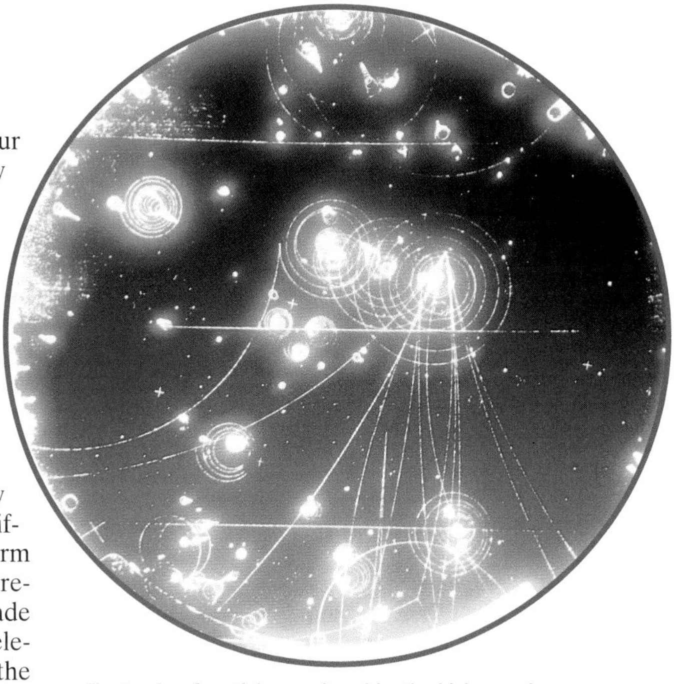

The tracks of particles produced by the high-speed collision between a photon and the nucleus of an atom of hydrogen can be seen in a bubble chamber, a particle detector used to expose such collisions for scientists to study.

PROVING THE EXISTENCE OF ATOMS

The idea of atoms is not new. More than 2,500 years ago, Greek scholars originated the idea of such tiny particles after reasoning that matter could be divided again and again but only so far before reaching a limit. They also imagined that the diverse and colorful world around them was built up from a relatively few different kinds of atoms. The word "atom" itself comes from the Greek word *átomos*, meaning something that cannot be cut or divided into smaller parts.

Even though the Greeks were able to imagine the idea of atoms, they could not prove that they existed. It was not until more modern times that scientists proved the existence of atoms. This scientific proof comes from both chemical and physical evidence.

Chemical Evidence

The laws of chemistry provide powerful indirect evidence for the existence of atoms. Every chemical compound has a precise recipe—it contains specific amounts of certain elements. This is known as the **law of definite proportions**. For example, when the elements hydrogen and oxygen combine to form water, the required amounts of each element, by weight, are eight parts of oxygen for every one part of hydrogen. It is not possible to combine hydrogen and oxygen in any other proportion and end up with water.

Furthermore, if a given set of elements can be used to create more than one compound, then the weights of the various compounds have simple relationships among them. This is known as the **law of multiple proportions**. For example, hydrogen and oxygen can also be combined to produce hydrogen peroxide instead of water. This compound contains 16 parts of oxygen for each part of hydrogen. Notice that this ratio—16:1—is twice the 8:1 ratio needed to produce water.

Scientists have concluded from these chemical laws that each molecule of water must contain two hydrogen atoms and one oxygen atom and that each molecule of hydrogen peroxide contains two hydrogen atoms and two oxygen atoms.

Physical Evidence

In 1827, the Scottish scientist Robert Brown observed a slight but continual and

Robert Brown

random motion of small visible particles in a liquid under a microscope. As a result of observations and analyses since that time, scientists know that this constant jostling of particles, called **Brownian motion**, is due to the randomly moving atoms or molecules of the liquid. It is possible to estimate the weight of atoms using measurements of Brownian motion because the abruptness of the jostling motion depends on the weight of the atom compared to the weight of the particle being jostled.

Two inventions of the late 1900's, the scanning tunneling microscope (STM) and the atomic force microscope (AFM), allow scientists to capture images of solid surfaces that clearly show arrangements of atoms on the surface. Although these images are not photographs in the ordinary sense, they provide additional physical evidence for the existence of atoms.

BASIC FACTS ABOUT ATOMS

Atoms are so small that they cannot be seen under the most powerful microscopes. But scientists have developed methods to determine the size of atoms and their **mass**, which is the quantity of matter in them regardless of their volume. Scientists also know how to identify and distinguish one type of atom from another.

The Size and Mass of Atoms

An atom is unimaginably tiny. The period at the end of this sentence has a diameter of about 0.02 inch (about 0.5 millimeter). If the period were made up of pure carbon, its diameter would contain about 2 million carbon atoms placed side by side. Another way to imagine the size of atoms is to think of magnifying the period so that each of the 2 million carbon atoms along its diameter is about as large as the period itself. The magnified period would be about 1.2 miles (2 kilometers) across. The diameters of the atoms that make up the other elements are not very different from those of carbon. The largest atoms have only about twice the diameter of the smallest atoms.

The mass of a single atom is also extremely small. Imagine fine grains of pollen, which have diameters of about 0.000004 inch (0.001

Figure 1. The Structure of an Atom

Scientists think that the inner structure of an atom looks like a tiny solar system. At its center is a nucleus made up of subatomic particles called protons and neutrons, which in turn are made up of particles known as quarks. Orbiting the nucleus are particles called electrons. Electrons are thought to be elementary particles, those that cannot be divided into smaller parts. The number of electrons in an atom is equal to the number of protons.

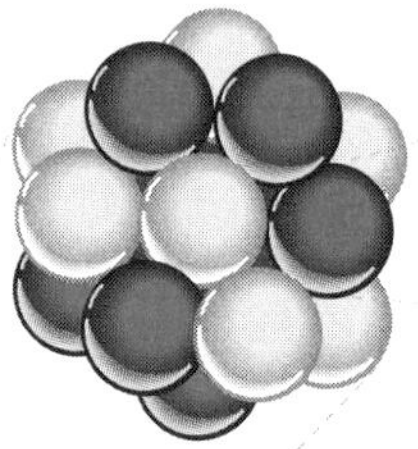

Protons and neutrons make up the nucleus of an atom.

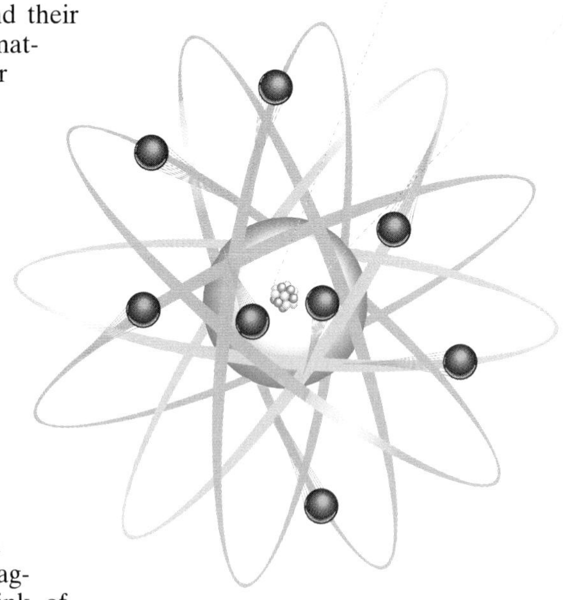

There are eight protons, eight neutrons, and eight electrons in the nucleus of an atom of oxygen.

millimeter). It would take about 2 trillion grains of pollen to make up 0.035 ounce (1 gram) of mass, which is about the mass of a paper clip. Yet each one of those tiny pollen particles would contain about 20 billion atoms.

The differences in the mass of atoms are more extreme than the differences in atomic size. Hydrogen, the lightest atom, has about one-twelfth the mass of a carbon atom. The heaviest known atom, unnilennium, has about 22 times the mass of carbon and more than 260 times the mass of hydrogen.

Types of Atoms

Although there are millions of different chemical compounds, their molecular structures are made from a limited collection of different types of atoms. A good way to understand this is to consider the following comparisons: The millions of different words in the English language have been constructed from an alphabet of only 26 different letters, and the thousands of musical tunes that exist have been created from twelve basic musical tones.

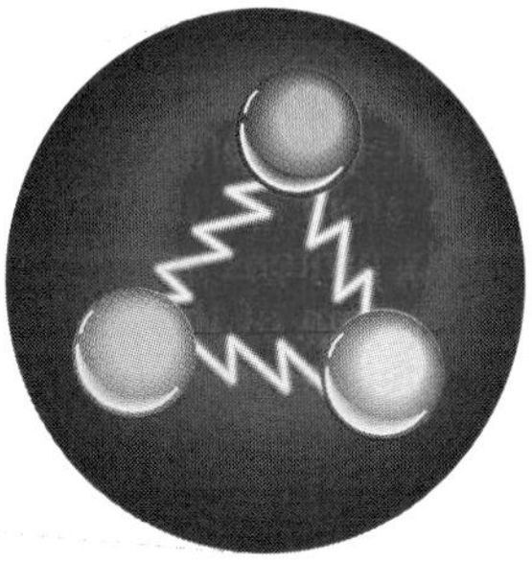

Each proton and neutron is composed of other particles called quarks.

Scientists have identified 92 elements that occur naturally on Earth, and each one represents a particular type of atom. Of these naturally occurring elements, the most common ones are oxygen, silicon, aluminum, iron, magnesium, calcium, potassium, and sodium. They make up more than 95 percent of all the atoms on Earth. Iridium, polonium, promethium, protactinium, and xenon, which make up fewer than one-billionth of the atoms on Earth, are the five rarest of the naturally occurring elements.

Another 20 elements, often called artificial elements, have been produced in limited quantities in nuclear reactors or scientific laboratories. All of the artificial elements are very unstable, which means they quickly decay or break down into other elements. This helps explain why they are not found in nature. Even if they had been present on Earth in the distant past, they would have decayed completely by now.

THE STRUCTURE OF ATOMS

Since the early 1900's, scientists have known that atoms contain even tinier particles of matter called **subatomic particles** and that these particles make an atom look like a miniature solar system (see Figure 1). At the center of the atom is a **nucleus** (the plural is **nuclei**). This nucleus contains two kinds of subatomic particles—protons and neutrons. A **proton** is a particle that carries a positive charge of electricity. A **neutron** is a particle that carries no electrical charge and has a mass about equal to that of a proton. Because protons and neutrons are found together in the nucleus, they are sometimes called **nucleons**.

Traveling around the nucleus are particles called **electrons**, which carry a negative electrical charge. In an atom of hydrogen, which is the simplest element, a single electron orbits a single proton. The force that binds these two particles together is an electrical attraction between the negatively charged electron and the positively charged proton. The two particles pull equally hard on one another. However, because the mass of a proton is more than 1,800 times greater than the mass of an electron, the proton barely moves in response to the electron's attraction. It is the electron that does most of the moving.

In its normal form, an atom has an equal number of electrons and protons, which means that it is electrically neutral. Some atoms, however, have fewer or more electrons than normal. An atom with fewer electrons than protons is called a **positive ion**. An atom with more electrons than protons is called a **negative ion**.

Atomic Number

Atoms differ from one another in the number of particles they contain. Oxygen, for example, has 8 electrons, 8 protons, and 8

ATTILA (406?–453)

Attila, the legendary king of the Huns, devastated the western half of the Roman Empire between A.D. 451 and 452. He was so feared by Christians, he became known as the Scourge of God, meaning the instrument of God's wrath.

The Huns were originally a nomadic tribe of Mongols, who came out of central Asia in the late 300's and invaded Europe. They were good horsemen, arming themselves with short, powerful bows, which they shot from horseback with devastating effect. About A.D. 400 they settled in the region later known as Hungary.

In 434, Attila succeeded his uncle as leader of the Huns. He won such respect as a warrior that Hunnish communities from the western borders of China to the Danube River accepted his kingship. In 445 Attila launched a campaign against the Roman Empire. In 447 his horsemen overran the Balkan lands, raiding the whole of Greece and threatening Constantinople, the seat of the Roman Empire in the East.

In 451 Attila turned westward and, in his most famous campaign, crossed the Rhine River, penetrating deeply into Gaul (France). Although he successfully besieged the city of Orléans, Attila was defeated later that year in the decisive battle of Châlons by the Roman general Flavius Aetius, who had formed an alliance with Theodoric I, King of the Visigoths.

The defeat did not prevent Attila from embarking on another campaign in 452. That summer his horsemen crossed the Alps to ravage Italy, and Pope Leo I allegedly paid Attila protection money to save Rome from attack.

Attila died suddenly in 453. Although he probably died from heart failure, legend says he was murdered by his bride, a Burgundian princess. His scattered empire disintegrated with his death, but so terrible was his impact on Christian Europe that Attila appears in the epic poems of several countries, most notably as Etzel in the German *Nibelungenlied.*

ALAN PALMER
Author, *Quotations in History*

ATTLEE, CLEMENT (1883–1967)

Clement Richard Attlee, leader of Great Britain's Labour Party from 1935 to 1955, served as prime minister (1945–51) following World War II. As the first prime minister to have a Labour majority in Parliament, Attlee introduced a series of social welfare programs, most notably the National Health Service.

Born in 1883 in a London suburb, Attlee studied at Oxford University, practiced law for four years, then became a social worker. His sympathy for the poor in London's East End slums led him to join the Labour Party.

Elected member of Parliament (MP) in 1922, he held junior cabinet posts in the short-lived Labour governments of 1924 and 1929–31 and became the Labour Party leader in 1935. During World War II, Attlee served as deputy prime minister (1942–45) in Winston Churchill's wartime coalition (multiparty) government. Then, with a landslide victory in 1945, he became prime minister.

At home, Attlee introduced national health care and brought the utilities and railroads into public ownership. In foreign affairs, he backed the creation of the North Atlantic Treaty Organization (NATO) and supported the United Nations' stand against Communist aggression in Korea. Attlee himself regarded the transition of the British Empire to a Commonwealth, marked especially by the government's granting of independence to India and Pakistan (1947), as his greatest achievement.

Although Attlee narrowly won the 1950 election, economic difficulties led to his defeat the following year. After his retirement in 1955 he was given a title of nobility as 1st Earl Attlee. He died on October 8, 1967.

ALAN PALMER
Author, *The Penguin Dictionary of Modern History*

ATTUCKS, CRISPUS. See REVOLUTIONARY WAR (Profiles).

AUDIO SYSTEMS. See HIGH-FIDELITY SYSTEMS; SOUND RECORDING.

AUDUBON, JOHN JAMES (1785–1851)

In the early 1800's John James Audubon was living on the American frontier. He dressed in buckskin and wore his hair long, but he was a different kind of pioneer. His work was the lifelike painting of birds in their natural surroundings.

Audubon was born on his father's plantation in Les Cayes, Santo Domingo (now Haiti), on April 26, 1785. The father, a trader and sea captain, returned to France in 1789, taking his son with him. In the town of Nantes, young Jean Jacques—the French for John James—went to school, but his real interests were the outdoors and painting.

In 1803 John was sent to live at Mill Grove, an estate his father owned near Valley Forge, Pennsylvania. After a short time he went back to France, returning to Pennsylvania in 1806. Audubon later moved to Louisville, Kentucky, where he set up a general store. In 1808 he married Lucy Bakewell, a neighbor from Mill Grove, and took her to Louisville. But the store soon failed, as did all the other business ventures that Audubon tried. Instead of attending to business, he was usually exploring the wilderness.

At first Audubon hunted for food and sport, but he became more and more interested in studying birds. He sketched them in the wild. Then, to get more detail, he began to bring specimens home. He made his paintings in watercolor and chalk. Audubon also made the first known banding experiments on American wild birds. He tied thread around the legs of baby birds and later observed that some had returned to their place of birth to nest.

By 1819, Audubon was bankrupt. He now had only one aim: to complete his collection of bird paintings for publication. In 1821 he traveled down the Ohio and Mississippi rivers, searching for birds and earning a little money by painting portraits. When he arrived in New Orleans, he sent for his wife and two sons. Lucy became a governess and was the main support of the family for the next twelve years.

Audubon began a search for someone to publish his work. Reproduction of his paintings required great skill and expense. In 1826, having failed to find a publisher in America, Audubon went to England and Scotland, where he was well received. He was elected to the Royal Society of Edinburgh in 1827.

A painting of meadowlarks nesting in a field by John James Audubon, who roamed the wilderness identifying, observing, and drawing the birds of North America.

In London that same year, Audubon finally found financial support, as well as an engraver who could reproduce his bird paintings. During the next eleven years, *Birds of America* appeared in four large volumes, one of the rarest and most ambitious works ever published. Between 1831 and 1839, with the help of the Scottish naturalist William Macgillivray, Audubon also wrote five volumes of text to accompany the engravings. This work contained life histories of nearly 500 bird species.

The books brought him money and fame. In 1841, Audubon was able to buy a Hudson River estate. He worked on a book and paintings of the animals of North America, which his sons completed after his death on January 27, 1851.

Audubon's interest in all wildlife is honored by today's National Audubon Society, which is dedicated to the protection of wild creatures and their habitats.

JOHN S. BOWMAN
Author and Science Writer

there in 1906. Beginning in the 1970's, the industry gained international attention though the work of filmmakers Bruce Beresford, Peter Weir, Gillian Armstrong, and Fred Schepisi. Many of these directors went on to further fame in Hollywood.

▸ THE LAND

Overview. Australia occupies an area roughly equal to that of the United States, excluding Alaska and Hawaii. It extends from Cape York in the north to South East Cape in the south—a distance of about 2,300 miles (3,700 kilometers)—and from Steep Point in the west to Cape Byron in the east—a distance of about 2,600 miles (4,000 kilometers). Off the northeastern coast lies the Great Barrier Reef, the world's longest coral formation.

Australia's major landforms are low mountains in the east and level plains and broad plateaus elsewhere. Three natural regions extend as broad bands from north to south across the continent. These are the Eastern Highlands, the Central Lowland, and the Western Plateau.

Eastern Highlands. The Eastern Highlands consist of a series of hills and plateau sections extending along the great curve of the Pacific coast. They form a series of watersheds dividing the flow of the rivers in the region. Elevation varies from between 1,000 and 2,000 feet (300 to 600 meters) over the northern half of the region to more than 3,000 feet (900 meters) in the more southerly part. Near the southeastern corner of the region are the Australian Alps, which are snow-covered in winter. Their highest peak, Mount Kosciusko, rises to 7,316 feet (2,230 meters).

The eastern slopes of the highlands are still largely forested and support logging in some areas. Rainfall is abundant, and rivers flowing to the coast are short and swift and subject to sudden flooding. Rivers on the western slopes flow into the Central Lowland. Here, however, rainfall is intermittent, and during the long dry spells, the same rivers become no more than a string of waterholes.

Central Lowland. This is an extensive, generally flat region with the lowest elevation in Australia. It has three shallow drainage basins. In the north are the rivers flowing into the Gulf of Carpentaria; in the center is the Lake Eyre Basin; and in the south is the Murray-Darling river system, which gathers together the main rivers flowing from the western slopes of the Eastern Highlands. The Murray River and its branches support a number of large irrigation areas, and the region ranks as Australia's most productive in

The Great Barrier Reef (*top*), the world's largest coral formation, extends for some 1,250 miles (over 2,000 kilometers) off Australia's northeastern coast. Farmland and vineyards are found in the relatively few fertile areas of South Australia (*right*). Queensland's varied landscape includes tropical rain forests (*opposite page*).

Ayers Rock rises 1,100 feet (335 meters) above the desert of northern Australia. It is called Uluru by the Aborigines, who consider it sacred.

terms of livestock raising and general output of farm products.

Lake Eyre, the lowest point on the continent, lies in the western part of the region. Its surface averages about 39 feet (12 meters) below sea level. For most of the time it consists of a vast expanse of dried, salty mud. Only two or three times in 100 years does it receive enough water to turn it into a true lake.

Underlying most of the Central Lowland is the Great Artesian Basin, a vast underground reservoir. When deep bores are drilled into the basin, warm water flows to the surface, making livestock raising possible when no other water is available.

Western Plateau. The largest of the three regions, the Western Plateau covers almost half of Australia. It has an average elevation of about 1,000 feet (305 meters), with a higher section in the northwest called the Kimberley Plateau. The arid interior includes three deserts—the Great Sandy Desert, the Gibson Desert, and the Great Victoria Desert. To the south is the Nullarbor (meaning "treeless") Plain. The most important agricultural area is in the southwest, where enough rain is received in winter for wheat and sheep farming. The Eyre Peninsula in the south is another significant farming area. Although often desolate, the region has much of Australia's mineral wealth.

Climate. Because Australia lies in the Southern Hemisphere, the seasons are reversed. Winter comes in June and summer in December. The northern third of the country has a tropical climate, marked in summer by warm, moist air and monsoon rains. Two or three times each year, the heavy rainfall along the coast results in serious flooding. The south has a temperate climate. Summers are generally hot and often rainless. But in

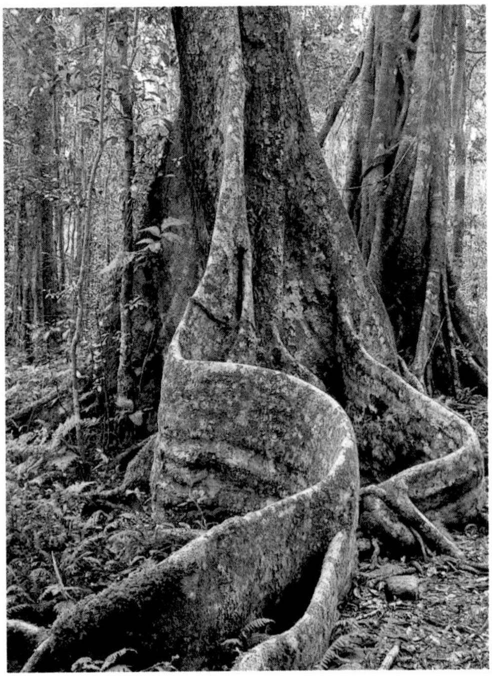

winter and spring the westerly winds bring rain to parts of Western and South Australia, most of Victoria and southern New South Wales, and Tasmania, thus sustaining the country's most fertile agricultural regions.

January and February are the hottest months and July is the coolest. Temperatures are highest in the tropical north and the arid interior. Darwin, on the northern coast, averages about 86°F (30°C) in January and about 77°F (25°C) in July, while Melbourne, on the southern coast, averages about 68°F (20°C) in January and 48°F (9°C) in July. In the desert interior and other arid regions, summer temperatures often exceed 100°F (38°C).

Rainfall can vary widely. The northern, eastern, and southwestern coasts receive more than 40 inches (1,000 millimeters) a year, while large areas of the interior receive less than 10 inches (250 millimeters). The areas of heaviest rainfall are along the Pacific coast, particularly in Queensland, which can receive as much as 160 inches (4,000 millimeters) annually.

Mineral Resources. Australia ranks among the wealthiest nations in terms of mineral resources. It is a leading producer of bauxite (aluminum ore), iron ore, copper, lead, uranium, industrial diamonds, gold, and silver. Huge coalfields have been opened up, while oil and natural gas fields (the largest are offshore) yield abundant energy. In addition, nearly 100 other minerals, including nickel and manganese, are mined in significant amounts.

A road sign alerts motorists to an approaching kangaroo crossing. Kangaroos are the country's best-known animals.

WILDLIFE

Australia's extraordinary varieties of animal wildlife are a result of its long isolation from other lands. When Australia split off from other continental landmasses, it included early forms of furred, warm-blooded animals as well as reptiles and birds. The earliest of the furred creatures had characteristics of both reptiles and warm-blooded animals. They were the ancestors of the present-day platypus and echidna (also known as the spiny anteater), which are unique in that they lay eggs and also produce a milk-like substance to feed their young. The platypus also has a duck-like bill and webbed feet.

Australia is home to most of the world's marsupials, or pouched mammals, of which kangaroos are perhaps the best known. There are a number of species, including the red kangaroo and the gray kangaroo, that grow to be as tall and heavy as human adults, and the wallaby, which is about the size of a small child. See the article on marsupials in Volume M. An article on kangaroos appears in Volume J-K.

Another distinctive animal is the tree-dwelling koala, which eats only the leaves of eucalyptus trees. The dingo, a wild dog, was brought to Australia by Aboriginal groups, who used it in hunting.

The emu is a large, flightless bird that, along with the kangaroo, appears on the Australian coat-of-arms. Its smaller relative is the cassowary. Another bird, the kookaburra, is known as the laughing jackass because its song sounds like rowdy laughter. Most numerous among the birds, however, are the parrots, which include many species in beautiful multicolored plumage.

Several animals introduced by Europeans have run wild in Australia. Among these are water buffalo, rabbits, goats, camels, and foxes. Rabbits, first brought in during the 1850's, multiplied so rapidly that they became major pests, and Australians have been trying to reduce their numbers ever since. Wild horses, known as brumbies, roam free in some mountain districts and in wilderness areas in the interior.

THE ECONOMY

A Diversified Economy. Australia has a diversified economy, combining agriculture, mining, and manufacturing. Although it has only limited fertile land, Australia is a major producer and exporter of agricultural products. Its wealth of mineral resources has made mining vital to the economy. Manufacturing is now central to the national prosperity, but the country's fastest-growing economic activity involves the provision of services. Australia's trade, which was once mainly with Britain and Europe, has increasingly been directed toward Asia and the Pacific.

Nearly as familiar as the kangaroo is the koala, which feeds only on leaves of the eucalyptus tree. Much of Australia's wildlife is found nowhere else on earth.

Manufacturing and Services. Australia's manufacturing industries grew in the 1950's and 1960's, eventually employing one-quarter of the workforce. But stagnation set in during the 1970's and a restructuring began, with the steel and metalworking industries leading the revival. New industries emerged in the 1990's, and manufacturing has rebounded to engage nearly one-fifth of the labor force.

The industries that have prospered the most are those associated with technological changes and rising standards of living. Factories are turning out, and often exporting, a wide range of goods. These include automobiles, construction materials, chemicals, and electronic equipment. In addition, Australian industry produces agricultural and earthmoving equipment, plastics, optical fibers, fertilizers, and pharmaceuticals.

Among service industries, finance, business and community services, and communications have risen the most in recent decades. Wholesale and retail trade have fallen slightly.

Agriculture and Livestock Raising. Australia has long been the leading sheep-raising coun-

Australia

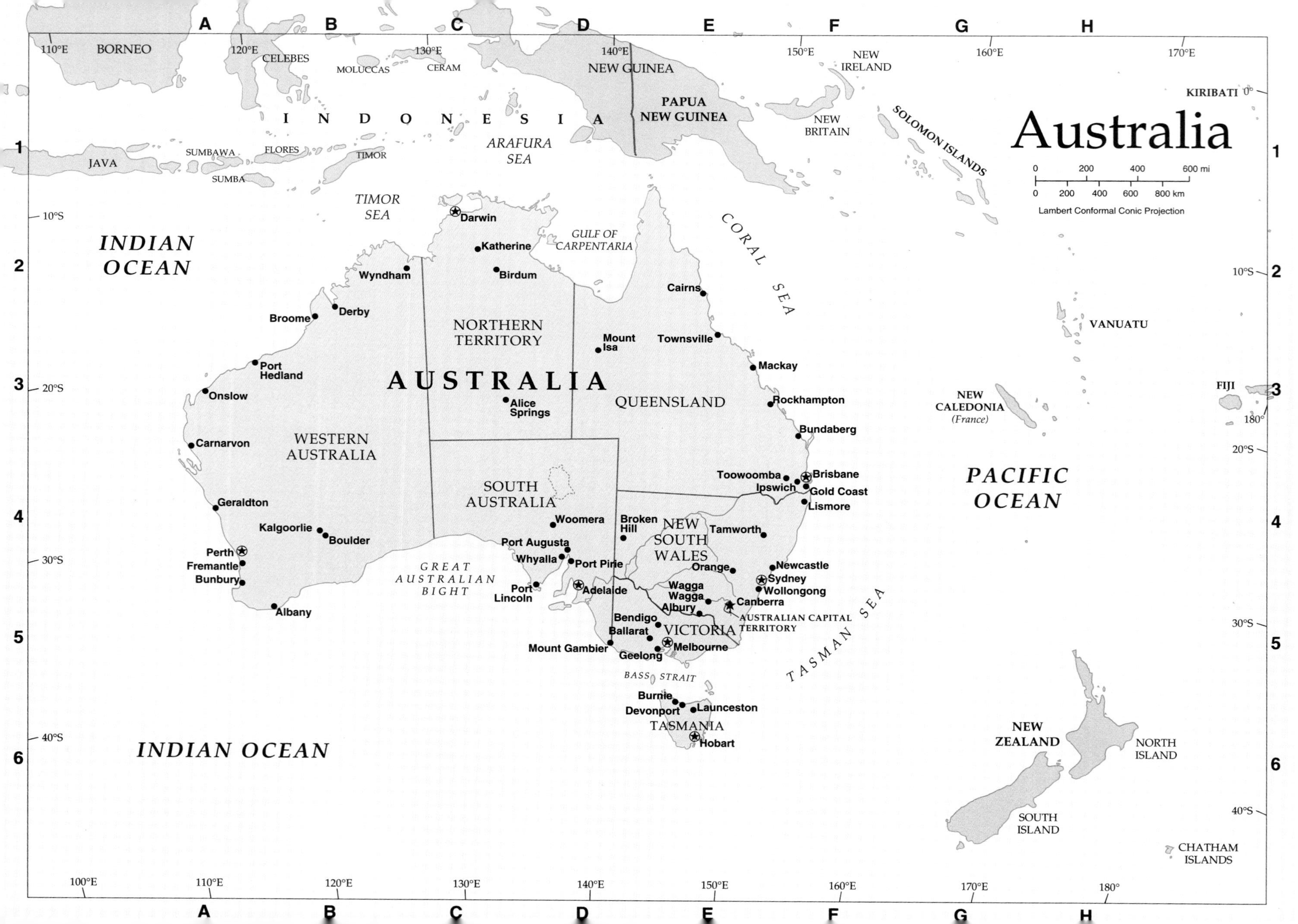

0 200 400 600 mi
0 200 400 600 800 km
Lambert Conformal Conic Projection
BORNEO
CELEBES
MOLUCCAS
CERAM
NEW GUINEA
PAPUA NEW GUINEA
NEW IRELAND
NEW BRITAIN
SOLOMON ISLANDS
KIRIBATI
I N D O N E S I A
JAVA
SUMBAWA
FLORES
SUMBA
TIMOR
ARAFURA SEA
TIMOR SEA
INDIAN OCEAN
GULF OF CARPENTARIA
CORAL SEA
VANUATU
FIJI
NEW CALEDONIA (France)
PACIFIC OCEAN
AUSTRALIA
NORTHERN TERRITORY
WESTERN AUSTRALIA
QUEENSLAND
SOUTH AUSTRALIA
NEW SOUTH WALES
VICTORIA
AUSTRALIAN CAPITAL TERRITORY
TASMANIA
Darwin
Katherine
Birdum
Wyndham
Derby
Broome
Port Hedland
Onslow
Carnarvon
Geraldton
Kalgoorlie
Boulder
Perth
Fremantle
Bunbury
Albany
Mount Isa
Alice Springs
Cairns
Townsville
Mackay
Rockhampton
Bundaberg
Toowoomba
Ipswich
Brisbane
Gold Coast
Lismore
Woomera
Port Augusta
Whyalla
Port Pirie
Port Lincoln
Adelaide
Broken Hill
Tamworth
Orange
Newcastle
Sydney
Wollongong
Wagga Wagga
Canberra
Albury
Bendigo
Ballarat
Melbourne
Geelong
Mount Gambier
GREAT AUSTRALIAN BIGHT
BASS STRAIT
TASMAN SEA
Burnie
Devonport
Launceston
Hobart
NEW ZEALAND
NORTH ISLAND
SOUTH ISLAND
CHATHAM ISLANDS
INDIAN OCEAN
100°E
110°E
120°E
130°E
140°E
150°E
160°E
170°E
180°
0°
10°S
20°S
30°S
40°S
A B C D E F G H
1 2 3 4 5 6

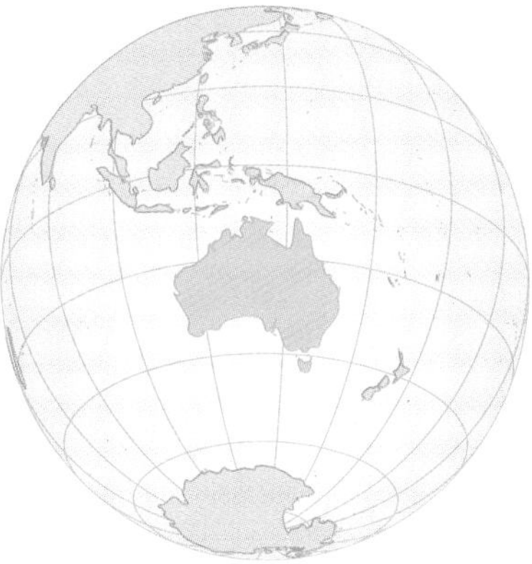

INDEX TO AUSTRALIA POLITICAL MAP

Adelaide	D5	Kalgoorlie	B4
Albany	B5	Katherine	C2
Albury	E5	Launceston	E6
Alice Springs	C3	Lismore	F4
Ballarat	E5	Mackay	E3
Bendigo	E5	Melbourne	E5
Birdum	C2	Mount Gambier	D5
Boulder	B4	Mount Isa	D3
Brisbane	F4	Newcastle	E4
Broken Hill	D4	Onslow	A3
Broome	B2	Orange	E4
Bunbury	A5	Perth	A4
Bundaberg	F3	Port Augusta	D4
Burnie	E6	Port Hedland	A3
Cairns	E2	Port Lincoln	D5
Canberra	E5	Port Pirie	D4
Carnarvon	A3	Rockhampton	E3
Darwin	C2	Sydney	E5
Derby	B2	Tamworth	E4
Devonport	E6	Toowoomba	F4
Fremantle	A4	Townsville	E3
Geelong	E5	Wagga Wagga	E5
Geraldton	A4	Whyalla	D4
Gold Coast	F4	Wollongong	E5
Hobart	E6	Woomera	D4
Ipswich	I4	Wyndham	C2

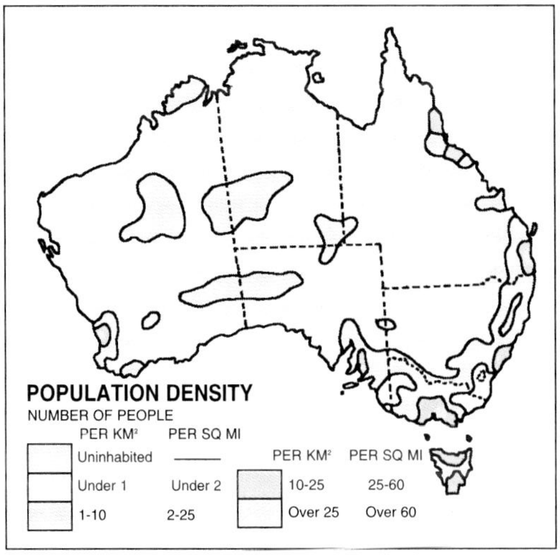

SOME AUSTRALIAN WORDS AND PHRASES

beano—a feast
billabong—a waterhole
billy—can for boiling water
bludger—idler
bonza—good, great
bush—forest country
dinkum—honest, true, genuine
ear basher—a talkative bore
galah—a silly, talkative person
give him the drum—tell the true facts
go crook—get angry
grizzle—to complain
larrikin—a hoodlum
never-never—back country
nong—useless person
no-hoper—a stupid person
ratbag—someone not to be taken seriously
ropeable—extremely angry
spine bashing—reclining
squatter—owner of a large sheep station
wake-up—someone sharp; no fool
whinge—complain
yacker—hard work

try, producing more than half of the world's fine-quality wool used in clothing. Its sheep population usually exceeds 150 million. Of these, two-thirds are merinos, which provide the finest wool. New South Wales has the largest number of sheep, with about 40 percent of the total.

Dairy farming is important near the main cities along the eastern and southern coasts and in irrigated areas in Victoria. Wheat and other grains are widely grown in eastern and southwestern Australia, usually on large, mechanized farms. Much of the wheat is exported. Most grain farmers also keep sheep as an additional source of income.

Australia produces a variety of fruits. Pineapples and other tropical fruits are grown on the north Queensland coast. Peaches, plums, and citrus fruits flourish in irrigated areas, and apples are produced in Tasmania. The Brossa Valley in South Australia is a wine-making center. Australia is one of the world's leading exporters of sugarcane, which is grown along the northeastern coast.

Mining and Energy. The discovery of large gold deposits in the 1850's made Australia

Agriculture and mining are an important part of the country's diversified economy. The vast flocks of sheep raised in New South Wales and other states (*below*) have made Australia the world's leading sheep-producing country, providing more than half of its supply of fine wool. Wheat farming (*left*) is highly mechanized. Gold is mined chiefly in Western Australia (*opposite page*).

the world's largest producer of the precious metal, and new goldfields continued to be found, although on a lesser scale, for decades. Kalgoorlie, in Western Australia, is the main gold-producing site. Iron ore, mined chiefly in the Pilbara region of Western Australia, is one of the country's most valuable exports. Australia leads the world in bauxite output, with 38 percent of the total production. The bauxite is mined in Queensland, in the Darling Range of Western Australia, and in the Northern Territory.

The discovery of oil and natural gas fields, beginning in the 1960's, transformed Australia's energy potential. Oil fields in Bass Strait, off the coast of Victoria; in southern Queensland; and in Western Australia supply most of the country's oil and natural gas needs. Increasing quantities of liquefied natural gas are now being exported from wells in the Timor Sea, particularly to Japan. Coal is mined in large quantities in central Queensland, both for export and for domestic use. Lignite (brown coal) is produced in Victoria.

Transportation and Communications. Transportation is generally well developed. Australia is one of the most highly motorized countries in the world, with an average of one motor vehicle for every two people, and there is an extensive network of roads along the coast. In the Outback, however, many of the roads are unpaved. Trains are fast and modern, and excellent internal air service is provided by Qantas Airways and Ansett Australia, along with regional airlines. Both airlines also operate international routes.

The basic telephone and fax services are government-owned. Radio and television programs, along with pay-TV, are offered by commercial stations, supplemented by the government-funded Australian Broadcasting Corporation. The use of satellites has opened up the remote areas that were previously served only by local stations. The larger cities each have several daily newspapers, including *The Australian*, which is published nationwide. A wide range of magazines and books are also published.

THE STATES AND TERRITORIES

New South Wales. Nearly one–third of Australia's people live in New South Wales, the most populous state. Most are concentrated along the eastern coast, and more than half live in Sydney, the capital and largest city. Sydney is also the heart of the state's manufacturing, commerce, finance, and transportation. Newcastle, the second largest city, is a center of steel production.

The narrow coastal lowlands of New South Wales have a succession of short river valleys well suited to farming. The country's highest point, Mount Kosciusko, is in the south, and the surrounding region is popular with skiers and other winter-sports enthusiasts. The western slopes of the Eastern Highlands include large areas of good crop and grazing land.

Nearly two-thirds of the state's area lies beyond the highlands. These western plains are crossed by the Darling and other rivers, which provide irrigation for growing citrus fruits, rice, and other crops. Wheat is also grown on the plains, and large numbers of sheep, particularly merinos, and some beef cattle are raised here as well.

Victoria. Victoria is the second smallest state in area and the second largest in population. Most of its inhabitants live in the south. Melbourne is the capital and largest city. Other important towns include Geelong and Ballarat.

Victoria occupies a wedge of territory in Australia's southeastern corner, in the heart

of what is known as the fertile crescent. With the state's mild, moist winter climate, Victoria's agriculture is highly productive, particularly its truck and dairy farms, which supply the main cities with fresh fruits, vegetables, and milk. The state's main energy source is its deposits of lignite, which have aided its industrial development. It also has offshore deposits of natural gas and oil. Victoria is the center of Australia's automobile production and manufactures a wide range of other goods as well.

Queensland. Queensland, Australia's second largest state in area, occupies the northeastern part of the country. Most of its people live along the narrow coastal strip, where

STATE	CAPITAL
New South Wales	Sydney
Queensland	Brisbane
South Australia	Adelaide
Tasmania	Hobart
Victoria	Melbourne
Western Australia	Perth
TERRITORY	**CAPITAL**
Australian Capital Territory	Canberra*
Northern Territory	Darwin

*National capital

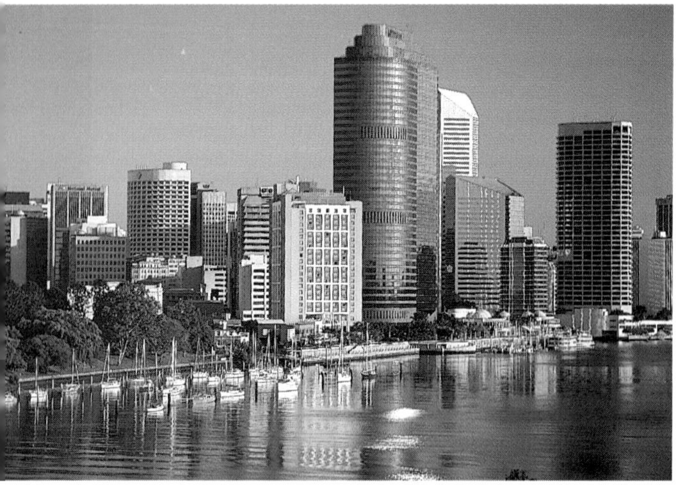

the north and west, making Queensland the chief beef-producing state.

South Australia. Most of South Australia's people, farms, and industries are situated in the southeastern part of the state. Adelaide, the capital, is home to about three-quarters of the state's population.

Only a very limited area of the state is suitable for farming. Wheat .and some barley is grown in the Eyre Peninsula and east of Spencer Gulf. Sheep also thrive in these regions. Along the lower reaches of the Murray River, irrigated land produces a variety of fruits, including grapes used in wine making. Dry, unproductive land makes up most of the remainder of the state, except for deposits of iron ore, uranium, and opals (a semi-precious stone). The Aboriginal groups have been granted title to vast areas of the virtually uninhabited interior.

Australia's major cities are located in the coastal areas. Brisbane (*top*), the capital of Queensland and the country's third largest city in population, is also an important port and manufacturing center. The newer Queensland city of Gold Coast (*left*) is a popular tourist resort.

Brisbane, the capital, and Gold Coast, the second largest city, are located. The interior is only sparsely populated.

Queensland's pleasant climate, beautiful beaches, offshore islands, and tropical rain forests have made tourism an important industry. Increasing numbers of retired people have also settled here. Mining is a major economic activity and includes the production of coal, copper, aluminum, and other minerals. The bulk of Australia's sugarcane is grown and processed in the tropical north, while the interior of the state is given over to sheep raising. Large numbers of cattle are grazed in

Western Australia. Nearly 400 years ago, Europeans first reached the coast of what is now Western Australia. They described it as a rugged, dry, and inhospitable land, and their description still fits all but its southwestern corner. The largest of Australia's states, it consists largely of barren desert, only occasionally broken by an isolated mining town or cattle station.

Nearly all of Western Australia's people and most of the wheat farms, sheep stations, and fruit orchards are in the southwestern part of the state. Perth, the capital, is the major urban center. Australia's only transcontinental rail line cuts across the empty Nullarbor Plain to the east.

Gold was first discovered in Western Australia in 1885, and mining towns sprang up overnight. The richest finds were at Coolgardie and nearby Kalgoorlie, towns lying on the fringe of the desert and dependent on a pipeline from Perth for their water. Kalgoorlie continues to be a world leader in gold production. The state is also rich in iron ore, mainly from the Pilbara region in the Hamersley Range. Oil is extracted at Barrow Island, and natural gas is piped in from the Timor Sea.

Tasmania. Tasmania, the island state, is the smallest in area of Australia's states. Sometimes called the Apple Isle because it produces most of Australia's apples, it is also famous for its rugged scenery. Hobart, the capital and largest city, lies at the foot of Mount Wellington. Other important towns are Launceston and Devonport. A ferryboat connects Devonport with Melbourne on the mainland across Bass Strait.

The western half of the island is mountainous, with heavy rainfall and dense forests. To the east, the climate is more suited to sheep raising and the cultivation of hops, various fruits, and potatoes. The abundance of water has encouraged hydroelectric development, and this has attracted industry to the island. Tin is also mined.

Northern Territory. The Northern Territory, which became self-governing in 1978, is the least populated and least developed part of Australia. Crocodiles and wild buffalo still live in some of the marshy coastal swamps. Darwin, the capital, is the only large settlement in the northern part of the territory. Almost entirely destroyed by a tropical cyclone in 1974, the city has since been rebuilt. Katherine (a former mining town) has grown with the establishment of an air force station and the development of tourism and cattle raising. Alice Springs, generally called Alice, is the largest town in the south and is linked by rail with Adelaide.

Australian Capital Territory. The Australian Capital Territory is an enclave within New South Wales surrounding the national capital, Canberra. The federal territory also includes the area of Jervis Bay, transferred from New South Wales in 1915 for use by the Royal Australian Navy.

Melbourne (*below*), the second largest city, is the capital of Victoria and a major port and financial center. Sydney (*right*), capital of New South Wales, is Australia's largest city and the country's chief port. The monorail is a distinctive feature of the city's transportation system.

MAJOR CITIES

Sydney, Australia's largest city, industrial center, and the capital of New South Wales, was founded in 1788. It was the first European settlement in the country. See the separate article on Sydney in Volume S.

Melbourne, the second largest city and the capital of Victoria, is a major port and a financial center of the nation. An article on Melbourne appears in Volume M.

The national coat of arms incorporates the kangaroo and the emu, a large, flightless bird that is also distinctive to Australia.

Brisbane, the capital of Queensland and third largest in population, is the only large Australian city with a subtropical climate. Numerous parks and gardens have made it one of Australia's most beautiful cities. It is Queensland's business and cultural center, and it handles much of the state's tourist trade. A monument in the city commemorates the cooperation between Australia and the United States during World War II.

Perth, the capital of Western Australia, has grown to become Australia's fourth largest city. Said to be Australia's most beautiful city, it reminds many Americans of cities in southern California. Its port is Fremantle, at the mouth of the Swan (Avon) River. The mining boom brought dramatic changes to Perth. At one time the highest building was 15 stories. Today several skyscrapers are many stories taller. Among the notable recent additions to the city are an entertainment center, a new art gallery, and extensive freeways. The Perth industrial complex extends to Fremantle, about 10 miles (16 kilometers) away, site of the world's largest wheat terminal.

Hobart, the capital of Tasmania, was founded in the early 1800's and is Australia's second oldest city. Mountains provide a beautiful background for the city, which is surrounded by a flourishing agricultural area. Ores, wood and metal products, and food and beverages are exported through the port of Hobart.

Canberra is an important seat of learning and scientific achievement as well as being Australia's national capital. See the article on Canberra in Volume C.

GOVERNMENT

Australia is an independent member of the Commonwealth of Nations. The federal government in Canberra conducts national affairs. Each state has its own parliament and

IMPORTANT DATES

1642	Abel Tasman sighted and named Van Diemen's Land (Tasmania).
1770	New South Wales was claimed for Britain.
1788	First British settlement was founded at Port Jackson (Sydney Harbour).
1803	Matthew Flinders circumnavigated (sailed around) the Australian coast.
1825	Van Diemen's Land separated from New South Wales.
1829	Swan River colony (Western Australia) was begun.
1836	Colony of South Australia was first settled.
1851	Victoria separated from New South Wales.
1853	Van Diemen's Land was renamed Tasmania.
1859	Queensland separated from New South Wales.
1862	John McDouall Stuart crossed Australia.
1892–93	Gold was discovered in Western Australia.
1901	Commonwealth of Australia was formed.
1914–18	Australia fought alongside Britain in World War I.
1927	Parliament moved from Melbourne to Canberra.
1939–45	Australia fought on the side of the Allies in World War II.
1945	Australia became one of the original members of the United Nations.
1950	Australia contributed forces to the United Nations in the Korean War.
1951	ANZUS Security Treaty between Australia, New Zealand, and the United States was signed.
1956	Melbourne hosted the Summer Olympic Games.
1978	The Northern Territory was granted internal self-government.
1988	Australia Day marked the bicentennial (200th anniversary) of British settlement in Australia.
1994	Legislation was enacted to give Aboriginal groups and Torres Strait Islanders authority to claim land under "native title."
2000	Sydney hosted the Summer Olympic Games.
2001	Centennial (100th) anniversary of Australia's federation.

governor. Australia was the first country to use the secret ballot, and every Australian citizen over 18 years of age is required to vote.

Legislative authority rests with the Federal Parliament, made up of the Senate and the House of Representatives. Each state has ten senators, and each territory has two. The House of Representatives is elected on the basis of population. Its membership is required to be, as nearly as possible, twice that of the Senate. A governor-general represents the British monarch, who is the ceremonial head of state. Political power rests with the prime minister, who heads the government. The prime minister is the leader of the governing party or parties in the parliament and is assisted by a cabinet of ministers.

The High Court of Australia is the supreme legal authority, with the power to override all other courts in the land. It interprets the constitution and settles disputes between the states.

▶ HISTORY

Discovery and Exploration. As early as the Middle Ages (and possibly earlier), stories were told about the existence of a large continent in the Southern Hemisphere. But Europeans had never seen it, and they referred to it as *terra australis incognita*, Latin for "the unknown southern land."

The Dutch were the first Europeans to see Australia, sighting it while making journeys between the Netherlands and their colonies in what is now Indonesia. But although they had seen the western coast of the continent, they did not know how far to the east it extended. In 1642 the Dutch navigator Abel Tasman was sent out to discover what lay in the east. Tasman sailed too far south to see the mainland, but he did visit the island that is now called Tasmania in his honor but which he named Van Diemen's Land. Tasman then continued eastward to New Zealand and later explored Australia's northern coast.

No careful explorations of the continent were made until 1770, when James Cook, a British naval officer and explorer, sailed along its eastern coast and named it New South Wales. He visited Botany Bay, near what is now modern Sydney, and reported that the bay and much of New South Wales looked suitable for settlement. See the article on James Cook in Volume C.

First Settlements. The first settlement came about after Britain had lost its colonies in what is now the United States. Looking for an alternate place that it could use to relieve its overcrowded prisons, the government decided to establish a penal colony at Botany Bay. The first shipload of convicts and a few British soldiers commanded by Captain Arthur Phillip landed on January 22, 1788. Four days later, Phillip moved the settlement a little farther north to a better location at Port Jackson, which he named Sydney. More convicts followed, and new colonies were established in Tasmania and other parts of the continent.

Further Exploration. Most of the coastline was only vaguely known at this time and further explorations were carried out. In 1798, George Bass, a naval surgeon and explorer, sailed along the southern coast and showed that Tasmania was an island. Bass Strait, which separates the island from the mainland, was named after him. In 1801, Matthew Flinders, a captain in the Royal Navy, discovered and charted Kangaroo Island and Spencer and St. Vincent gulfs along the south coast. (Flinders Ranges and Flinders Island were named for him.) The Blue Mountains, which lay behind Sydney, were first crossed in 1813.

The first British settlement in Australia was established at Port Jackson (Sydney Harbour) in 1788 by Captain Arthur Phillip, after their initial landing at Botany Bay.

The Early Colonies. Life was very difficult during the early years in Sydney. Attempts at farming failed in the poor soil, and it was not until better land was found along Nepean Bay, to the west, that successful farms were established and food supplies improved. The successful breeding of Merino sheep, which proved well suited to the climate, led to the development of a flourishing wool industry. At the same time, whaling in the South Pacific brought trading ships to Sydney.

Free English settlers began arriving in the 1820's, and the first free colony was established at Swan River, in what is now Western Australia, in 1829. South Australia was settled in 1836, and settlers from Tasmania crossed Bass Strait and occupied the Port Phillip district from 1835 to 1837. This later became the colony of Victoria.

Expansion Inland. In the 1820's, settlers had begun taking their flocks of sheep across the Blue Mountains. Hoping to find more good land, explorers went farther inland. Captain Charles Sturt first explored the Darling River; then in 1829–30, he followed the Murrumbidgee River to the Murray. Continuing on to sea, he reported on the excellence of the grassy plains. In 1836, Major Thomas Mitchell found fertile land south of the Murray River. Close behind the explorers came the sheep herders, settling where they found good pasture.

In spite of optimistic hopes, later explorers found dry and mainly unrewarding land. One was Edward John Eyre, who in 1841 discovered the great salt lake that bears his name. Another was Wilhelm Ludwig Leichhardt, who in 1844–45, traveled overland from Brisbane to the northern coast. In 1862, John McDouall Stuart crossed Australia from Adelaide in the south to the site of Darwin in the north.

The six colonies grew rapidly and all became self-governing during the latter half of the 1800's.

Nationhood. Realizing the merit of acting together on matters of common interest, the colonies decided to seek a basis for federation. A first constitution was drawn up in

Exploration of Australia's rugged interior (*above*) was essential to its development. Nationhood was finally achieved in 1901, after which the first federal parliament was convened (*below*) in Melbourne, the early national capital.

Australians celebrated the 200th anniversary of British settlement in 1988. The event was highlighted by a fireworks display in Sydney Harbour.

1891, and a second in 1898. After it won approval from Australian voters, the British Parliament passed a constitution act, and on January 1, 1901, the six colonies became states in the new Commonwealth of Australia.

With the outbreak of World War I in 1914, Australia joined forces with Britain and its allies. During World War II (1939–45), Australia again fought on the side of Britain, and after the entry of the United States into the war, it became a support base for U.S. forces. Its forces took part in campaigns first in the Middle East and then in the Pacific. In 1942 the city of Darwin was bombed by Japanese planes.

Australia became increasingly active in world affairs after World War II. It was an original member of the United Nations, and in 1950, when the Korean War erupted, Australian troops were sent to Korea as part of the United Nations command. In 1951, Australia signed the ANZUS defense pact with New Zealand and the United States. A significant proportion of Australia's national income each year is allocated to assisting the developing countries.

Economic Growth and Immigration. Growing demand and scarcity of imports during World War II provided a major stimulus to Australian industry. To strengthen development after the war, the government encouraged immigration from Britain and other parts of Europe, and over time, millions of new Australians were resettled successfully.

During the 1980's, however, the large-scale immigration from Britain and Europe fell off sharply. Many of the new arrivals were from countries in Asia—especially refugees from Vietnam, China, and Cambodia and business and professional people from Hong Kong.

Recent History. In 1988, Australians marked the 200th anniversary of British settlement. The occasion became one of review and redirection. This was especially so in relations with the Aboriginal people, who had suffered dispossession from their lands during the settlement of the country. Among the government's measures to bring about reconciliation for past injustices were increased welfare spending and other social programs. In 1994 legislation was enacted to give Aborigines and Torres Strait Islanders authority to claim land under "native title."

Economically, financial deregulation in the mid-1980's led to a speculative boom, which collapsed in 1990 and was followed by a sharp recession. Many industries declined, causing high levels of unemployment. The government, meanwhile, has been advocating the removal of barriers to international trade. It is also directing its efforts to gaining access to markets in the fast-growing Asia and Pacific area, where Australian trade is now increasingly based.

Proposals to replace the constitutional monarchy with a republican form of government gained ground in the mid-1990's. But in 1999, Australians voted to keep Great Britain's monarch as their head of state.

In 2000, Sydney hosted the Summer Olympic Games, just as Melbourne had 44 years earlier. And in January 2001, Australia celebrated the centennial, or 100th, anniversary of its federation.

CHARLES M. DAVIS
University of Michigan
R. M. YOUNGER
Author, *Australia and the Australians*

Austria's cultural heritage includes many great figures in music, literature, and art. Among the most important are (*top row, from left*) composers Joseph Haydn, Wolfgang Amadeus Mozart (as a boy), and Franz Schubert; (*bottom row, from left*) authors Arthur Schnitzler and Franz Kafka; and painter Oskar Kokoschka (in a self-portrait).

CULTURAL HERITAGE

Austria and lands that were once a part of the Austrian empire have produced many important figures in the world of music, literature, and art. Only a relatively few names can be cited here.

Music. Much of the world's great music was written by Austrians or by composers who made Austria their home.

The greatest period of Austrian music, from about 1730 to 1830, produced Joseph Haydn, Mozart, Ludwig van Beethoven (who lived in Vienna most of his life), and Franz Schubert. The two giants of music in the 1800's were Johannes Brahms (who spent the last twenty years of his life in Vienna), and Anton Bruckner. The Strauss family, especially Johann, Jr., and Johann, Sr., made the Viennese waltz world famous. Gustav Mahler continued the great Viennese tradition into the early 1900's. Arnold Schoenberg and Alban Berg were two of the leading modern composers.

Austria is also the birthplace of one of the most famous Christmas carols—"Silent Night" (*Stille Nacht*), written on Christmas Eve, 1818, by Franz Gruber and Joseph Mohr.

See the article on German (and Austrian) music in Volume G.

Literature and Art. In literature, Austrians have made important contributions to drama, poetry, the short story, and the novel. The dramatist Franz Grillparzer, in the 1800's, combined the German classical tradition with Austrian and modern elements. Hugo von Hofmannsthal wrote plays and poems, as well as librettos for operas by the German composer Richard Strauss, in the late 1800's and early 1900's. At about the same time, Arthur Schnitzler was writing plays and stories on psychological themes.

The poet Rainer Maria Rilke and the short-story writer and novelist Franz Kafka are two of the greatest literary figures from this same period. Kafka (whose short life was spent in Prague, the capital of today's Czech Republic) wrote symbolic stories about the anxiety of modern life. Other important authors from the first half of the 1900's include novelists Robert Musil, Stefan Zweig, and Franz Werfel.

The beginnings of the modern period of Austrian art are reflected in the paintings of Gustav Klimt. Klimt, who died in 1918, was a leader in the movement that led to expressionism. His work influenced two other important 20th-century Austrian artists, Oskar Kokoschka and Egon Schiele.

▶GOVERNMENT

Austria is a federal republic made up of nine provinces: Burgenland, Carintha, Lower Austria, Upper Austria, Salzburg, Styria, Tyrol, Vienna, and Vorarlberg.

The president of Austria, who is elected for six years, is the head of state. The national legislature is the Federal Assembly, composed of the National Council and the Federal Council. The National Council is elected by the people for 4-year terms. The Federal Council, which has only limited powers, is elected by the provincial legislatures. The president appoints the chancellor (prime minister) to head the government. The chancellor and ministers of the government are usually members of the political party with the largest number of seats in the National Council, and they are responsible to that body.

Each of the provinces has its own legislature and governor, with control over its local affairs.

▶HISTORY

Early History. The discovery of ancient burial grounds shows that Austria was inhabited in prehistoric times. About 15 B.C. the region was conquered by the Romans. One of their settlements, Vindobona, eventually became the city of Vienna. With the collapse of the Roman Empire in the West in the A.D. 400's, the region fell to eastern invaders. Not until the time of Charlemagne's empire in the 700's was a stable government re-established.

In 976 the Holy Roman emperor Otto II gave part of Austria to Leopold of Babenberg. The Babenbergs ruled for 300 years. When the line died out, Austria passed to the kingdom of Bohemia (now part of the Czech Republic).

Rise of the Habsburgs. In 1278, Rudolph of Habsburg, who was then Holy Roman emperor, defeated the Bohemian king Ottokar II at the Battle of Marchfeld. Rudolph acquired the Austrian lands, which he and his descendants were to govern continuously until 1918. During that time, Austria became the center of a vast Habsburg empire that often dominated the rest of Europe. The German princes elected a Habsburg to rule the Holy Roman Empire for all but five years between 1438 and 1806, when the empire came to an end.

Austria's real power came from those lands that it owned outright and ruled by heredity. The Habsburgs expanded these possessions, often by military alliances with other countries. They frequently sealed these alliances by offering their sons and daughters in marriage to the children of other rulers.

The greatest matchmaker of all was Emperor Maximilian I. His marriage to Mary of Burgundy in 1477 eventually gave him control of the prosperous Low Countries and parts of northern France. Maximilian then arranged for his son Philip to marry Juana, heiress to the throne of Spain.

Height of Power: Charles V. In 1516, Philip's son, Charles of Ghent, inherited the throne of Spain as King Charles I. When Charles's grandfather Maximilian died in 1519, he became emperor, as Charles V, as well. Charles ruled over more territory than any previous European monarch.

Charles's empire was so vast that he gave Austria to his younger brother Ferdinand in 1522. Through his marriage to Anne of Hungary and Bohemia, Ferdinand was chosen ruler of both these kingdoms in 1526. The House of Austria now governed two empires. Through Charles V, the Spanish branch ruled Spain, the Low Countries (the Netherlands, Belgium, and Luxembourg), much of Italy, and Spain's American colonies. At the same time, the Austrian branch headed by Ferdinand ruled in Austria, Hungary, what is now Germany, the Czech Republic, Croatia, Slovenia, half of Romania, and parts of northern Italy.

A painting from about 1515 depicts three generations of the Habsburg family, which ruled Austria for some 600 years. The emperor Maximilian I is at the left.

In some factories, such as this cannery, products move from start to finish along an assembly line, and no human assistance is necessary.

Coordination of Movements

Another important property of automated equipment is self-coordination. A machine that is self-coordinated can perform several different actions at the same time. Some delicatessen meat slicers are self-coordinated. The deli worker places a large piece of meat into the carriage of the slicer, selects the slice thickness by adjusting the distance from the carriage to the slicing blade, and turns the slicer on. The slicer then coordinates three motions. The blade that will cut the meat is spun, the meat is pushed into the blade by the carriage, and the carriage automatically moves back and forth across the blade. Each pass across the blade yields a uniform slice of meat without any effort from the worker.

Sequencing of Actions

Automated equipment that is self-sequencing can execute several different actions one after another in a correct order. Some of the electronic animated figures found at amusement park attractions are run by self-sequencing automation. An **audio-animatronic** figure of a man that moves its mouth, face, hands, and body in a synchronized way with a sound track appears to be singing and dancing along with the music each time the sound track is played. The animatronic man is able to act out a scene for an amusement attraction many times each day without becoming tired or hoarse, as a human might.

In some factories, self-sequencing automation is used to ensure the correct assembly of products. Automated conveyor belts or trolley cars transport products from one work site to the next. At each work site, another step toward finishing the product is carried out. For the product to be assembled correctly, the work sites must be visited in the proper order. Some semiconductor processing factories operate in this manner to produce integrated circuits for electronics products.

Decision-Based Automation

Automation that is decision-based can choose its next action based upon the outcome of a decision. The decision that the equipment makes may be conditional, requiring only if-then decisions. Or it may be more complex and involve artificial learning or artificial intelligence. (Artificial intelligence is software that tries to simulate certain aspects of human intelligence. For more information see the article COMPUTERS in Volume C.) Coin sorters found in banks use if-then decision making. The bank teller places unsorted coins into a bin and turns on the machine. The conditional logic the machine uses is simple: If the coin is the size of a dime, then it is dropped into the dime container; if it is the size of a penny, it is dropped into the penny container, and so forth.

▸ ROBOT SYSTEMS

Robots are a sophisticated and versatile type of automation. While most automated equipment is designed for one specific task, robots can be set up and programmed to perform several different jobs and to change

Audio-animatronic figures, such as this life-size Furby, sometimes attract large audiences who are fascinated by their lifelike movements.

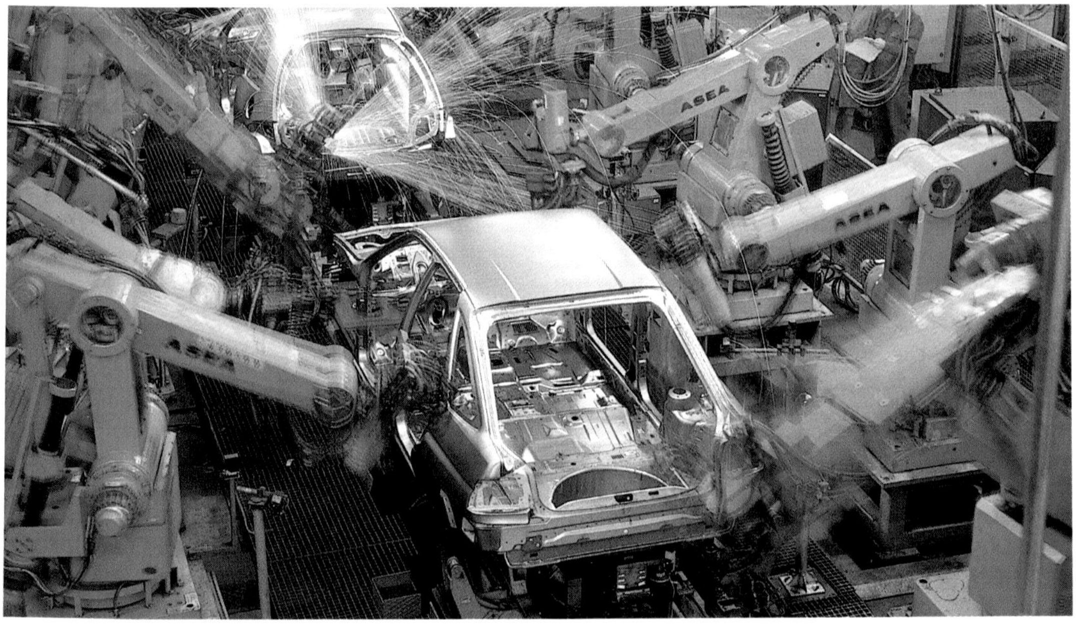

Robot arms, each programmed to perform a precise sequence of tasks, work tirelessly on an automobile assembly line.

their own operation in response to the working environment. Some of today's automated factories use robots that have all the characteristics of automation listed above.

Consider a robot that removes parts from a conveyor belt and assembles them into a product. The robot has mechanical devices, called **actuators**, that control its movements. Each actuator self-adjusts to reach a programmed position. The robot has a control computer that coordinates the movements of each actuator. The motions of the robot are also self-sequenced so that each part is picked up from the conveyor belt in the proper order and placed in the correct location to assemble the product.

Robots use decision-based action to handle unexpected conditions. For example, if the robot reaches for a part but does not obtain one, it automatically makes a decision about how to continue based upon its program. It may be programmed to try to grasp the part again, to reach in an alternative location for the part, or to stop and notify the operator that something has gone wrong.

Further, the robot may be programmed with the ability to assemble several different types of products. If so, it would have an internal computer listing the components needed for each different type. The robot would consult its computer before assembling each product to determine the proper parts to use and their locations. For more information about how robots work, see the article ROBOTS in Volume R.

AUTOMATION TODAY

Automation has been developed for almost every aspect of our daily lives. Factory automation frees laborers from dangerous or repetitive work. Automation within the home saves hours of undesirable chores. Automation within our communications systems allows fast and limitless connections to people around the world. Automation in the farming industry enables a few workers to grow enough food to feed thousands of people. And automation within our transportation system permits the organized and safe transport of millions of passengers each day.

Industrial Automation

There are many examples of automation used in industry. Some factories use automation for a single process. In others, production lines are fully automated from start to finish. The automobile industry was one of the first to use automation on a large scale. A robot with a welding tool can be set up to automatically weld a set of joints in an automobile assembly line. Another robot carrying a spray painting gun can be set up to smoothly pro-

HOW AN AUTOMOBILE WORKS

Modern automobiles are complex machines made up of thousands of metal, plastic, glass, and rubber parts. They are reliable, comfortable, and safe. Although the sleek, modern automobile has changed greatly from the noisy and smelly cars of the 1890's, it has the same basic systems.

Most cars are powered by an internal-combustion engine. An **electrical system** provides the power to start the engine and, in gasoline engines, provides the sparks that ignite the fuel. Electricity is also required for electric devices such as lights, horns, radios, and heater fans.

Engines have **lubrication systems** to reduce the friction of their moving parts. They have **cooling systems** to carry away the great heat created by combustion. They have a **fuel system** to store and carry fuel to the engine. An **exhaust system** carries away the waste products of combustion.

The engine and all the parts that carry power to the wheels make up the **drive train.** In addition to the engine, the parts of the drive train include the **transmission,** the **drive shaft,** the **differential,** the axles, and the wheels that move the car, called the **drive wheels.** Some cars have the drive wheels in the front, some have drive wheels in the rear, and in other cars, all four wheels are drive wheels.

All cars have a **steering system** to connect the steering wheel to the front wheels. A **brake system** slows and stops the car. A **suspension system** protects the car and passengers from the bumps and dips in the road.

The basic structure to which all these parts are attached is the **chassis.** The **body** of the car consists of the external parts such as the fenders, hood, roof, doors, and trunk lid and the internal fittings of the passenger compartment. These fittings include the seats and the dashboard, which displays instruments that monitor such things as engine temperature, oil pressure, speed, and distance driven.

The Engine

The engine is the first part of the drive train. Most cars today are powered by internal-combustion engines. These engines burn a gaseous mixture of air and either gasoline or diesel fuel inside hollow cylinders. Most modern automobile engines have four, six, or eight cylinders. The cylinders in four-cylinder engines are generally arranged in a line. The cylinders in six-cylinder engines are arranged either in a

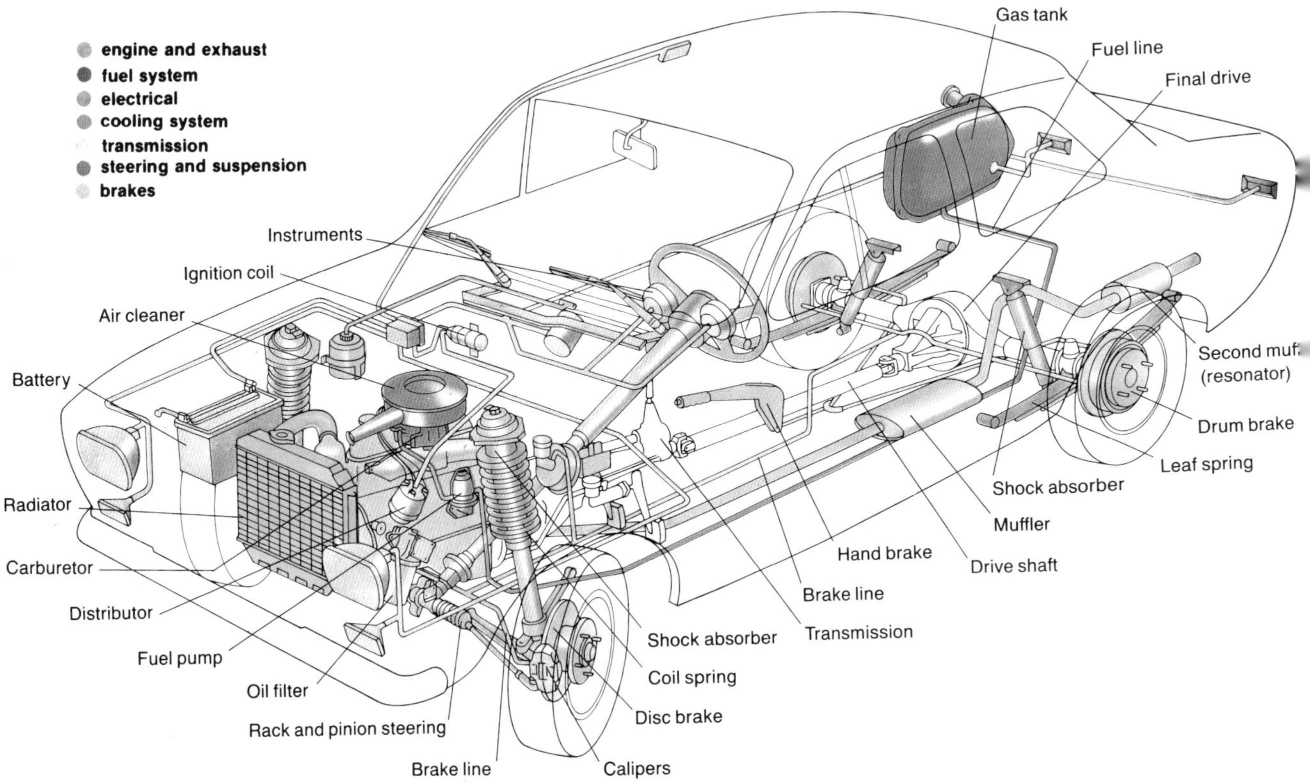

line or in a V-shape with three cylinders in each arm of the V. These engines are called V-6's. The cylinders in an eight-cylinder engine are nearly always arranged in a V, and such engines are called V-8's. Generally, the more cylinders that an engine has, the more powerful that it is.

When an internal-combustion engine is running, the burning gas expands, pushing a piston inside the cylinder. This happens very rapidly, one piston after the other, in each of the engine's cylinders. A connecting rod connects each piston to a shaft, called the **crankshaft**. As each piston is pushed by the gas, it forces the crankshaft to turn. This turning motion is passed through the drive train to the drive wheels. For more information on how these engines work, consult the articles INTERNAL-COMBUSTION ENGINES and DIESEL ENGINES in this encyclopedia.

The Fuel System

Fuel stored in the automobile's fuel tank is drawn to the engine by a **fuel pump.** A **carburetor** then mixes the fuel with air and sends the gaseous mixture to the **intake manifold** and on into the cylinders of the engine. Instead of a carburetor, some cars have a **fuel-injection system** that sprays controlled amounts of gasoline into intake ports close to the cylinders. The fuel-air mixture goes into the cylinder when an **intake valve** opens.

Filters in the fuel line clean the fuel, but they can block the flow of fuel when they get clogged with dirt. They need to be changed regularly or the engine will not run properly.

Some modern, high-performance cars have **turbochargers** that suck in extra air and force it into the cylinders of the engine. This creates more pressure as the fuel is burned and enables the engine to produce greater power.

The Exhaust System

When the fuel burns inside an engine, gases are formed. These gases must be removed from the engine so that new fuel may be burned. This is a fast-moving, continual process. The operation of the piston in each cylinder forces the gases out an **exhaust valve** and then into an **exhaust manifold** that collects exhaust gases from all the cylinders. The gases then pass through **mufflers**, into **tail pipes**, and out the rear of the automobile. They must be forced away from the car because they are poisonous and can cause death when breathed by the driver or passengers.

Most automobiles have one or more mufflers in the exhaust system to muffle the loud noise of the burning fuel. Modern cars also have **emission-control devices** to reduce the amount of carbon monoxide, hydrocarbons, and nitrogen oxide, the harmful chemicals in the exhaust gases. Some cars pump some of the exhaust back through the engine to use every last bit of the fuel. Others have devices such as a **catalytic converter** to convert (change) the harmful gases to a less harmful form. Most states have laws to regulate the maximum amounts of harmful chemicals that may be present in automobile exhaust gases.

The Electrical System

Electrical energy is stored in a rechargeable battery that, on most modern cars, provides 12 volts of electricity. Whenever the engine is running, the battery is kept charged by an electrical generator called an **alternator.** The alternator is driven by a **belt,** a flexible loop attached to an engine-driven wheel. You will find more information on generators and alternators in the article ELECTRIC GENERATORS in Volume E. An article explaining how BATTERIES work is in Volume B.

When a driver turns the ignition key to the "start" position, power from the battery operates the electric starter motor. This motor turns the crankshaft, which pushes the pistons up and down, thus causing the gasoline engine to start. One part of the electrical system, called the **ignition system,** provides power to

The Ignition System

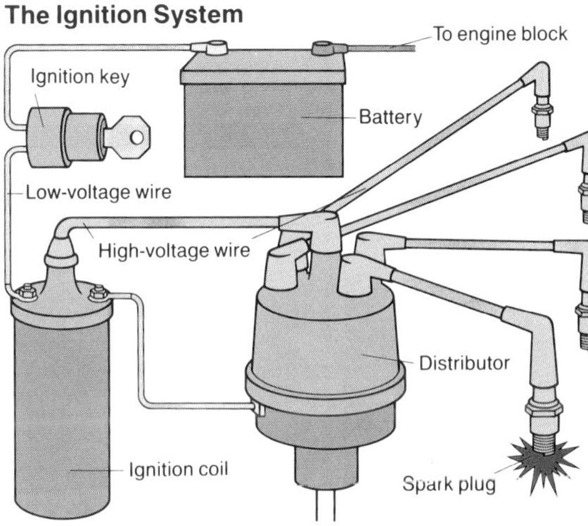

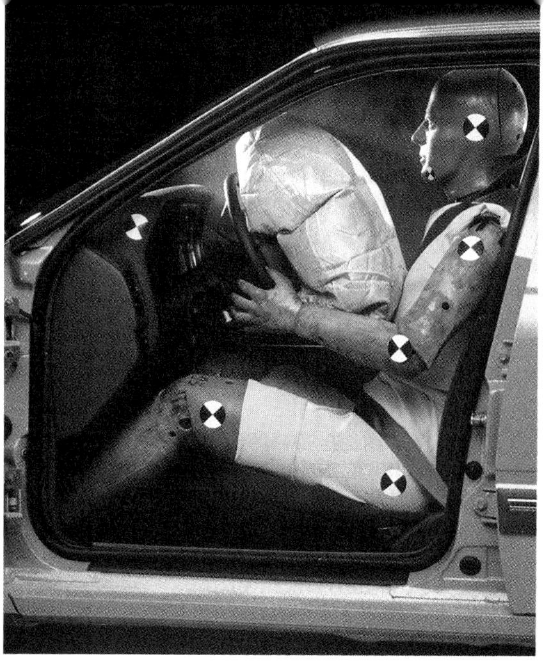

Left: In a test crash, an air bag inflates in a fraction of a second. The air bag prevents the dummy from smashing into the steering wheel or the windshield when the car stops abruptly. *Above:* Cars for sale in the United States are built so that the front end of the car will crumple and absorb some of the force that stops the car in a front-end accident.

remove a wheel, as in case of a flat tire. Modern tires are called **pneumatic tires** because they are filled with air that helps to cushion the ride. There are three kinds of tires used on automobiles: bias-ply, belted-bias, and radial. For more information about each type, see the article TIRES in Volume T.

Safety Features

All cars today have seat belts or some other restraint system to protect drivers and passengers in case of an accident. Many states now require people to fasten their belts every time they get into the car. In 1978 the state of Tennessee passed a law requiring that infants and children be placed in special restraints, and since then many states have passed similar laws. Seat belts have been proven to help prevent injury and save lives.

Since the mid-1990's, most new cars have also had "air bags" that rapidly inflate from the steering wheel hub, the dashboard, or the doors if the car suddenly stops, such as in a collision. The resulting "balloons" keep the driver and passengers from slamming into the front or the sides of the car, or from flying out the windshield or the windows. Air bags have been credited with saving thousands of lives. However, some early air bags inflated too forcefully, posing a threat to children and small adults. Engineers are refining air bag systems to make them safer for everyone.

Other safety laws exist. Automobile bodies must be strong and often reinforced with steel bars in critical areas such as doors to protect the driver and passengers in case of accidents. Doors must have special locks that are crash resistant. Bumpers are now built to absorb some of the force of an impact. Brakes must meet certain performance standards, and fuel systems must be able to withstand crashes without spilling their flammable contents. Interiors of cars must be well padded, and outside mirrors must be available. Even the steering column on a modern car must be built to collapse, or otherwise absorb the impact of a crash. Tires, transmissions, and windshields must all be built with safety rules in mind.

How a New Model Is Created

A new model is made as a blend of what the public wants and needs and what the manufacturer thinks the public will buy. When the manufacturer decides to build a new model, the ideas of many people are considered. Engineers, stylists, designers, and economists decide how the car should look and perform and how much it should cost. Detailed drawings are then sent to hundreds of skilled specialists who plan the actual production of the car. Step-by-step they build the car from the ground up. They design and make working models of the various parts that will go into the car. Engineers may design and build a new engine for the new model. Other engineers may experiment with various types of axles, gears, brakes, and other components to see which will perform best for the new model.

Styling engineers select paint finishes, interior fabrics, and trim and also design the instrument panel and other accessories.

Finally a prototype, or sample version, of the car is built. It has probably taken months, even years, of careful research, design, and engineering to produce the final model. But questions still remain. Will the car perform correctly? Is it really the car the public wants?

Testing A New Model. The sample car is put through test after test to see if anything is wrong with it. It is placed in special "torture chambers" where it is frozen and thawed, drenched with water, heated and allowed to cool, and shaken and twisted until any flaws have been spotted and corrected. When the laboratory tests have been completed, the sample car is driven over a test track at the company proving ground. There it is subjected to far more severe punishment than the average automobile will have to face. Sample cars are also road tested to see how they perform on steep twisting mountain roads, on long flat straight roads, and in crowded city traffic. All this testing often leads to changes in design and then to more testing.

Mass Production of Automobiles

While the prototype model is going through its tests, engineers are planning how to manufacture the car in quantity. They design machines that will turn out the various parts of the car. Some of these machines, such as those that stamp out the roofs or fenders or doors, are the size of a small building. Other machines are designed so that parts, such as engine blocks, automatically move from one machine to another as different drilling, grinding, and other operations are performed.

Today's mass production of automobiles takes precise timing of every operation. Before mass production starts, engineers must determine the most efficient way to assemble the cars. Their plan must make sure that each machine manufacturing a part works in coordination with all the other machines so that the right parts meet at the right time and place on the final assembly line.

When everything is organized, full-scale production begins. Modern automobile production is like a great river. The main river is fed by side rivers, which are fed by streams. The "main river" of an automobile factory is

Right: Computers play a major part in the development of a new model. The shape of the car and the way people will fit in the car can be tried on a computer before even a model is made. *Below:* For some models, a new engine may be designed and tested to achieve the desired performance. *Below right:* A model of the new car is scanned by a device that records the car's shape. The data will be used in determining the final design.

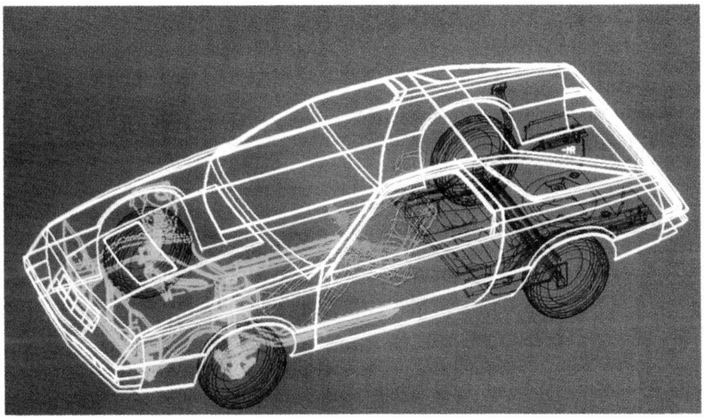

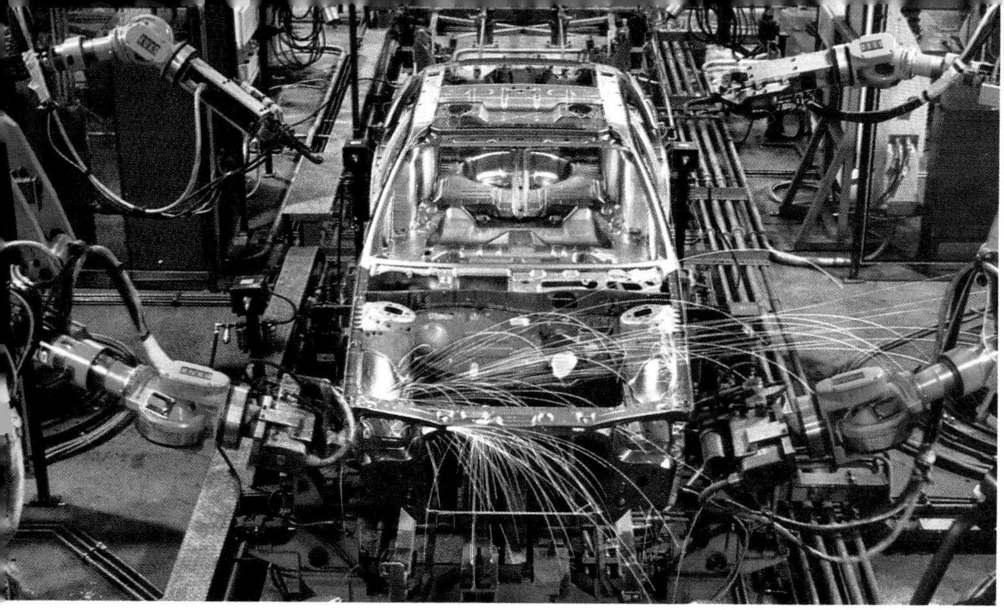

Left: Computer-controlled robots do much of the tedious and dangerous work in assembling cars. Robots weld the several pieces of stamped sheet steel together to create the automobile body. *Right:* Final assembly and checking of an engine still require a skilled human. *Far right:* As the car nears completion, body and engine come together.

the final assembly line, an endless moving belt or chain that carries main components such as engine blocks.

The many sub-assembly lines are like the side rivers and streams, bringing parts and assembled sub-units—such as carburetors, fuel pumps, or alternators—into the main assembly line where they are attached by automatically controlled machines or by workers. A modern automobile has almost 20,000 separate parts, ranging in size from the roof and engine hood to tiny screws used inside the speedometer. Almost every part has been transported on an assembly line before it becomes a part of a finished automobile.

Once the engine and other sub-assemblies have been completed on their assembly lines, they are ready to be attached to the three major parts of the car—the chassis, the engine, and the body. With some models, the first two sub-assembly lines—carrying the chassis and the engine—meet and are fitted together. Then the chassis-engine assembly is joined to the body to produce a nearly completed car.

Other car models use an integrated, or single-unit, type of construction. Here, the body and chassis are welded together to make one instead of two major sub-assemblies.

Many additional operations are performed as the car moves down the assembly line. Parts are added at each station. Seats and floor carpets are installed, and the electrical systems are hooked up. Water hoses are attached, and various pieces of trim are added. Finally, at the very end of the line, gasoline is pumped into the tank and coolant into the radiator. Oil has already been added to the engine on the engine's assembly line. A worker slides behind the wheel, starts the engine, and drives the car off the line.

But it is still not ready for its first owner. Quality-control inspectors examine the car for flaws. They adjust headlights and check details such as door, hood, and window fit.

Finally, the car is ready for the road.

The Automobile Industry

The automobile industry is one of the world's biggest producers and merchandisers of a product. It is also one of the biggest buyers. The industry consumes huge quantities of raw materials such as iron, copper, and rubber. In the United States it uses up one fourth of the country's steel production.

Excluding agricultural work, one out of every nine jobs in the United States is directly related to the manufacture, sale, and use of motor vehicles. These jobs support approximately 14 million Americans. The center of automobile manufacturing in the United States is the Detroit area in Michigan, although major manufacturing plants are located in several other states.

Beginning in the early years of the industry, manufacturers of automobiles have merged to form large corporations. In the United States, the three major manufacturers have traditionally been General Motors, Ford, and Chrysler, each of which has produced cars that still bear the names of the original independent companies. General Motors cars include Chevrolet, Pontiac, Oldsmo-

bile, and Cadillac. Cars manufactured by the Ford Motor Company include Ford, Mercury, and Lincoln. Chrysler Corporation cars include Chrysler, Plymouth, and Dodge. In Great Britain the major manufacturer of automobiles is the Rover Group, which produces the Land Rover and the Range Rover. Rolls-Royce Motor Cars in England produces the famous Rolls-Royce and Bentley cars. In Germany the leading manufacturing companies are Volkswagen, Daimler-Benz (Mercedes), and BMW (Bayernische Motoren Werke). In France the leading manufacturing companies are Peugeot-Citroen and Renault. In Italy, the largest manufacturer of passenger cars is Fiat. In Japan, the leading producers are Toyota, Nissan, and Honda.

In the 1990's, automobile companies continued to merge. BMW took over the Rover Group. The makers of Mercedes and Chrysler joined to form DaimlerChrysler. And Volkswagen bought Rolls-Royce.

In the mid-1990's more than 50 million motor vehicles were manufactured worldwide each year. Of these, more than 37 million were passenger cars and the remainder were trucks and buses. The five leading producers of passenger cars are Japan, United States, Germany, France, and South Korea, in that order. Other countries that have a sizable automobile industry include Spain, Canada, the United Kingdom, Brazil, and Italy. All of these countries export a large percentage of their output.

Throughout the world there are more than 646 million cars on the road. If every person around the world climbed into an automobile at the same moment, there would be an average of twelve people in each car. But the number of people per automobile varies widely throughout the world. In the United States there are about two people per car, in Europe there are about five people per car, in Russia there are about 24 people per car, but in China there are more than 1,300 people per car.

In the mid-1990's, there were more than 135 million passenger cars on the road in the United States. More than two thirds of all the households in the United States have more than one motor vehicle. American motorists traveled just about 2 trillion miles in one year.

People in the United States own more than 30 percent of the world's cars, trucks, and buses. Japan is in second place in the number owned. Other countries where ownership is high are Germany, France, Italy, the United Kingdom, and Canada.

When the automobile rolls off the assembly line, a number of businesses become involved. Trucking firms haul new cars from the factory to the dealers. The dealers employ staffs of salespeople and mechanics. Their advertisements bring business to newspapers and radio and television stations. Service stations supply gasoline and oil to keep the cars running. Service stations in turn purchase their supplies from oil companies. Cars need regular servicing, and this keeps many thousands of mechanics busy. In the United States, the automobile industry accounted for nearly $300 billion in sales of motor vehicles in 1997 alone.

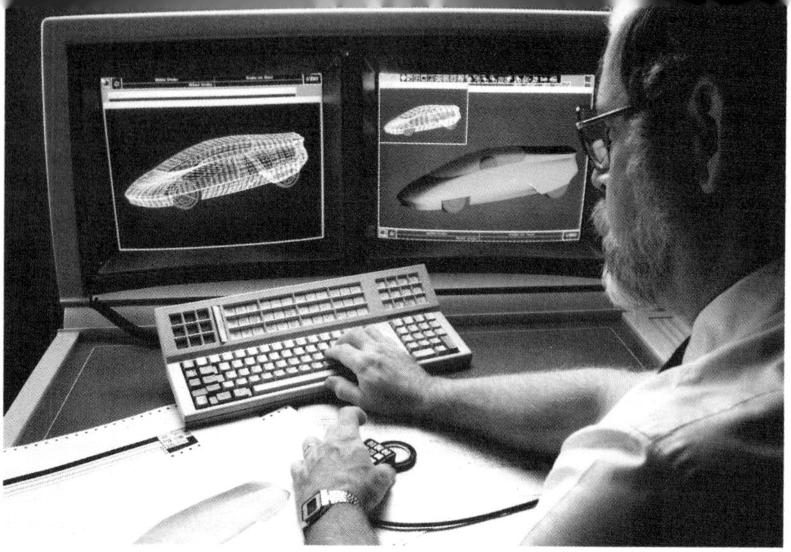

The car of the future may look like some cars of today, but it will be very different in the way that it operates. As new ideas and developments take place, they will be tried on a computer long before they are tested on the road.

Careers in the Automobile Industry

Manufacturing, selling, and servicing cars offer a wide range of career opportunities. Manufacturers employ many college graduates. Marketing experts determine what features the customers may want. Engineers, scientists, and artists design the cars. Production experts decide how to build them.

Manufacturing employees, such as machinists and tool and die workers, may have learned their skills in trade schools. They may serve several years as apprentices learning particular manufacturing skills. Others may be trained on the job to assemble cars.

Car dealers employ salespeople who are skillful in persuading customers to buy cars. Salespeople must be able to explain the cars' features and tell why these are desirable. This requires some mechanical knowledge.

Servicing cars offers a wide range of jobs—from pumping gas to making complicated repairs. Mechanics may be specialized in repairing certain areas such as transmissions, electrical systems, or car body repairs. Some of these skills may be learned in trade schools. Others may be taught by manufacturers' representatives or learned on the job. Large repair facilities have service managers and supervisors who make sure the work is done properly and efficiently.

The Car of the Future

The modern automobile is a marvelous machine. It is fast, sleek, comfortable, and beautiful to look at. But most automobile engineers know that the modern car will look like yesterday's noisy, smelly car when compared with the automobile of the future.

Experts predict that cars of the future will be made of plastics and carbon fibers that will be much stronger than steel and much lighter in weight. Even engines will be made of these materials.

Cars of the future will be smaller and lighter, but their design will probably be similar to the sleekest of the modern sports cars. There will probably not be any extreme design changes for a long time.

The real frontier for cars of the future lies not in body design but with computer activation. Cars may someday actually drive themselves. Highways would be wired so that cars could be programmed to travel a certain route and could make the trip with or without a driver. Everyone in the car would be able to relax, even take a nap, as the car speeds along at 200 miles (322 kilometers) per hour. The car would be radar- and computer-controlled to never touch other driverless cars or trucks and buses on the road. Changes of destination along the way could be made from the car, and a central computer could notify a computer at home.

Eventually the car would ease over to the right and pull off the high-speed roadway, navigate the city streets, and finally stop at the programmed destination.

Most automobile engineers believe that these cars are certain to be built, maybe even in the early 21st century—which would make it in your lifetime.

Ross R. Olney
Author, *Car of the Future*

See also Buses and Bus Travel; Diesel Engines; Internal-Combustion Engines; Transmissions; Trucks and Trucking.

AVALANCHES AND LANDSLIDES

On a sunny winter day, snow on a steep slope fractures and tumbles down a mountainside. The avalanche, a violent movement of snow that can also contain ice, soil, and rock, buries everything in its path.

On a rainy spring day, a huge water-soaked mass of land suddenly breaks away and falls down a steep hill, taking entire houses and roads along with it. Such a large movement of rock and soil is called a landslide.

Avalanches and landslides start for different reasons. However, they can both have a devastating impact on nearby settlements and recreation areas.

The violent movement of snow can be seen in this photo of an avalanche on Mt. McKinley, Alaska. Avalanches can occur wherever snow accumulates on steep slopes.

AVALANCHES AND THEIR CAUSES

In order for avalanches to occur, there must first be an accumulation, or buildup, of snow on a steep mountainside over time. During the winter, storms continually deposit fresh layers of snow on existing snow, creating a snowpack. Because each layer is built up under different weather conditions, the tiny ice crystals making up the snow may form strong bonds between some layers but weak bonds between others. If the bonds between layers are too weak, the top layers of snow can barely resist the downward pull of gravity.

At this stage, all that is needed for an avalanche to start is a so-called trigger event. This could be anything from the weight of new snow or a passing skier or animal to the impact of small chunks of snow and ice falling from above. Even a loud noise can set off an avalanche.

There are two main types of avalanches. A loose snow avalanche occurs when snow on or near the surface does not bond with the snow beneath it and begins to slide down a slope, gathering more and more snow as it continues down. The more common and deadly slab avalanche occurs when a weak layer of snow buried under a strong layer makes an entire snowpack unstable. A trigger event can then cause a single large plate, or slab, of snow to break off and fracture as it falls down the slope.

Snow builds up on a mountainside in layers. If a weak layer is buried under a strong one, the weight of a skier could trigger an avalanche.

Avalanches are a danger wherever snow accumulates on steep slopes. The deadliest avalanche ever occurred in 1970, when an earthquake off the coast of Peru triggered an ice avalanche near the summit of Mount Huascarán. The descending mass of ice and rocks accelerated to a speed of more than 170 miles (280 kilometers) an hour, destroying villages below. More than 18,000 people were killed.

▸ LANDSLIDES AND THEIR CAUSES

A landslide occurs when part of a hillside becomes too weak to support its own weight. This weakening can be caused by earthquakes or when the ground becomes soaked with rain or melting snow. Some types of landslides move seasonally, during rainy periods of the year. Others may lie dormant (inactive) for long periods of time, moving only once every number of years.

A landslide on this California hillside caused these houses to collapse. Soaking rains of the season had weakened the ground.

Landslides are more frequent in areas where there is a lot of erosion—the gradual wearing down and carrying away of land. Erosion is especially noticeable along some streams, rivers, and seacoasts. But landslides also occur far from areas of active erosion.

Human activities can also contribute to landslides. For example, the construction of buildings on hillsides may involve excavating material from the bottom of a slope and adding material higher up to create a more level lot. As a result, the slope can become overloaded, meaning that it cannot safely support the weight of the added material.

There are three main types of landslides: slides, falls, and flows. Slides are large bodies of land that move together along a sloping surface. Slides that rotate backward along a curved surface are called slumps. Translational slides are slides along a straight sloping surface. Slumps and translational slides can move up to 100 feet (30 meters) a day, although some move much more slowly. Debris slides and rockslides can move slowly or rapidly.

Falls of rock and soil occur on cliffs and steep slopes. Large rockfalls can be catastrophic events. Even small falls can be hazardous. Every year, small amounts of falling rock kill motorists, hikers, and campers in mountainous areas.

Flows are landslides in which materials move more like a fluid. Debris flows are rapid movements of wet mud and debris, while earthflows are movements of wet, clay-rich material. Debris flows triggered by storms have caused many deaths and much property damage in the United States. There are also dry flows, in which dry materials flow rapidly over long distances. In 1920, an earthquake in China's Gansu Province triggered a large, rapid flow of dry loess (silt deposited by wind) that killed some 100,000 people.

▸ PREVENTION AND DAMAGE CONTROL

In ski areas and along highways and railways, explosives are used to intentionally trigger small avalanches rather than allowing the slabs to build up to large and destructive avalanches. Heavy-duty fencing can hold snow in place, and specially designed deflecting walls can turn snow away from an area to be protected. Avoiding avalanche-prone slopes when skiing or hiking is the best way to prevent triggering an avalanche or being caught in one.

A number of methods are used to prevent landslides as well. One way is to capture and drain excess water before it reaches a potential landslide area. Walls and buttresses are used to prevent deep-seated landslide movements. Special fences and nets can keep falling rocks from reaching highways. And maps of landslide-prone areas help builders and planners avoid dangerous areas.

Reviewed by DALE ATKINS
Colorado Avalanche Information Center

REX L. BAUM
U.S. Geological Survey

See also EARTHQUAKES; FLOODS.

The ancient dream of flying has come true. These air show pilots are giving a thrilling demonstration of aerobatic flying, trailing white smoke to mark their paths in the sky.

AVIATION

People have always wanted to fly. The dream of flight appears in legends and myths of many cultures. It has been painted on cave walls, carved in stone, and inscribed on clay tablets. Through the centuries, stories have been told of magic flying carpets, winged horses, and chariots pulled by flying dragons.

The materials for simple aircraft have always been available. It would have been possible for ancient Chinese, Egyptians, or Incans to have made a hot-air balloon or a simple glider. Perhaps in a tiny village or on a remote mountainside someone did make a successful flight that was never recorded.

In the 20th century, the dream finally became a reality. Millions of people have flown in aircraft as varied as hot-air balloons, gliders, helicopters, 400-passenger airliners, and supersonic military fighters.

▸EARLY ATTEMPTS TO FLY

One of the earliest concepts of flight came from watching the effortless soaring of birds. Many individuals tried to fly by strapping wood and fabric wings to their arms and jumping from a tower or a cliff—only to plunge straight to the ground.

A successful introduction to flight appeared in China several centuries before the birth of Christ. In a war a soldier could be sent up on a large kite to spy on the enemy army. But it was not the answer to the dream of flying, because the kite had to be attached to the ground by a long rope.

In the 16th century the great Italian artist, scientist, and inventor Leonardo da Vinci had many ideas for ways in which humans could fly. He drew designs for parachutes, helicopters, and human-powered ornithopters (aircraft with flapping wings) and may have experimented with kites and balloons. Da Vinci's sketches did not get people off the ground, but his work did prepare the way for the scientists of the 18th and 19th centuries who in turn set the stage for the explosion of flight that would take place after 1903.

This article is an overview of the subject of aviation. It covers major events in the history of flight. The development of commercial, military, and private aviation is discussed. Other subjects covered here are government regulations and safety standards, aircraft manufacture, and careers in aviation.

Descriptions of specific kinds of aircraft appear in the articles AIRPLANES; BALLOONS AND BALLOONING; GLIDERS; and HELICOPTERS. The physical laws of flight are found in AERODYNAMICS; the subject of flying faster than the speed of sound is covered under SUPERSONIC FLIGHT. The kinds of engines used on aircraft are described in detail in JET PROPULSION; INTERNAL-COMBUSTION ENGINES; and ROCKETS.

Other articles containing information related to aviation are AIRPORTS; NAVIGATION; PARACHUTES; RADAR, SONAR, LORAN, AND SHORAN; and UNITED STATES, ARMED FORCES OF.

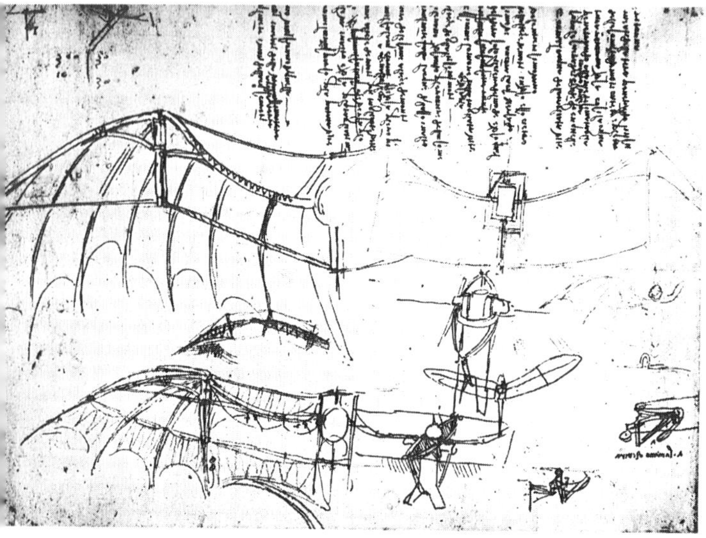

Balloons

Over the centuries, people have observed that the smoke and sparks from a fire are carried upward in the currents of hot air. But no one thought to catch the hot air in a bag until the 18th century when the French brothers Joseph Michel and Jacques Étienne Montgolfier began experiments with balloons. They made a huge balloon, 100 feet (30.5 meters) around, which was a linen bag lined with paper. Lifted by hot air from a straw-fed fire, the balloon rose into the air on June 5, 1783. It was the first successful step on the road to flight.

About the same time, another French scientist, J. A. C. Charles, found that the newly discovered element hydrogen, which is lighter than air, could also lift a balloon. On August 27, 1783, he demonstrated his hydrogen balloon in Paris to a group that included an American inventor, Benjamin Franklin.

These two methods of balloon flight—gas-filled and hot-air balloons—are still in use today. Because hydrogen is flammable, helium now fills weather balloons, blimps, and even toy balloons. Hot-air ballooning has become a popular sport. Several people ride in a "basket" carried aloft by a large, brightly colored balloon that travels with the wind.

But balloons were not the solution for practical air transportation. Although they could lift heavy loads into the air, there was no way of controlling the direction of their flight.

Airships

In the late 18th century, efforts were being made to develop a balloon with power and a means to steer it. But it was not until 1852 that the first powered airship was flown. A French engineer, Henri Giffard, flew over Paris in a hydrogen-filled **dirigible**. Dirigible is the French word for "steerable" and is sometimes used as a name for powered, steerable lighter-than-air craft. Giffard's dirigible had a steam-powered propeller. Later dirigibles were powered by electric batteries or internal-combustion engines. Giffard's dirigibles were **nonrigid airships**, which means their shape was maintained by the pressure of the gas with which they were filled. They were shaped like huge, fat cigars. The British called them **blimps**, a term that is still used today.

In 1900 the first **rigid airship** flew. It was built by a German company owned by Ferdinand von Zeppelin. The shape of these **zeppelins**, as rigid airships are often called, was maintained by an internal metal framework which contained hydrogen-filled bags. Zeppelins had internal-combustion engines to power their propellers. More than 100 of these rigid airships were built, but they were not the ideal aircraft. The future of aviation was with the more slowly developing heavier-than-air craft.

Gliders

In the early 1800's, Sir George Cayley, an English inventor, believed it would be possible to build a heavier-than-air craft. Based on his observation of the flight of birds such as seagulls, which soar for long distances without flapping their wings, he built model gliders with wings curved like a bird's wing. He added a combination rudder-elevator to make the glider turn and to climb or descend. These inventions are so important to all later

◀ Leonardo da Vinci drew plans for a glider (*far left*) in the 16th century. Otto Lilienthal (*left*) flew his first successful glider in 1891.

▶ The Wright brothers had studied Lilienthal's designs. In 1903 they made the first powered flight at Kitty Hawk, North Carolina.

aircraft designs that Cayley is often called the "father of aeronautics."

Power-driven model airplanes were being flown by the middle of the 19th century. The first was a steam-powered model designed and built by John Stringfellow, an English engineer. Steam remained the most popular source of power until the end of the 19th century. While tiny steam engines worked well enough in small model airplanes, steam engines large enough to power a full-size plane were too heavy to be practical. The development of the internal-combustion engine, light yet powerful, would one day be the solution. However, before powered flight was achieved, experiments with gliders large enough to carry a pilot solved the many problems of aircraft design and control.

Otto Lilienthal, a German, was one of the most successful designers of gliders. His first glider, built in 1891, was made of wood and cloth. The pilot hung from a frame in the center of the wing. Lilienthal took off in his glider by running down a hill with it until he was moving fast enough for the wind to lift the craft. He controlled the direction of flight by moving his body to one side or the other. Lilienthal made more than 2,000 flights. He was killed in 1896 while testing one of his new gliders.

▶POWERED FLIGHT

Lilienthal was the first engineer-pilot, designing, building, and flying his own aircraft. His work was an inspiration to two brothers from Ohio who made their living building bicycles. They were Wilbur and Orville Wright.

The Wright Brothers

In the amazingly short time of four years, the Wright brothers identified and solved the basic problems of flying a heavier-than-air craft. These were:

(1) Wings with enough surface area and the proper curve to provide lift.

(2) A means to control the direction of the aircraft's movement.

(3) Proper placement of weight to keep the aircraft balanced.

(4) A lightweight source of power.

(5) Efficient propellers.

(6) Piloting skills needed to fly the aircraft.

While the Wright brothers were solving these problems, others were also racing to be the first to fly in a powered aircraft. The Wrights' closest competitor may have been Samuel Pierpont Langley of the Smithsonian Institution.

After years of patient experiments and trials with models, Langley completed a full-size airplane called the *Aerodrome* in 1903. Langley's gasoline-powered machine was to be launched from the top of a houseboat in the Potomac River. On the first flight the *Aerodrome* crashed into the river. It was fished out and repaired and then launched again, only to crash a second time. Discouraged by the failures and by heavy criticism in the newspapers, Langley gave up his experiments.

The Wrights meanwhile had been creating a series of gliders. They had also built a wind tunnel, in which a fan forced air through a large tube. In this they could observe the effects of airflow on models of their aircraft designs. By 1903 they also had designed and built a lightweight internal-combustion engine and propellers to be connected to the engine by bicycle chains.

The First Flight

On December 17, 1903, a windy day at Kitty Hawk, North Carolina, Wilbur and Orville Wright made the first successful powered flight in a heavier-than-air craft. The first flight, made by Orville, was short—120 feet (36.6 meters) in 12 seconds—but it was followed by three more flights with the brothers taking turns. The last flight that day was made by Wilbur. It lasted for 59 seconds and covered 852 feet (260 meters). That distance would have been longer if there had not been a strong headwind.

Early Designers and Pilots

After the Wright brothers had solved the basic problems of powered flight, more people became excited about aviation and began to build and fly their own planes, often learning by trial and error. In Canada, Alexander Graham Bell, the inventor of the telephone, established the Aerial Experiment Association in 1907. One of the association's members was Glenn Hammond Curtiss, a designer of lightweight engines and a record-setting motorcycle racer. The association built several aircraft including the *June Bug,* in which Curtiss won a prize offered for flying more than 1 kilometer (.62 miles).

In France, interest in aviation was very high. Alberto Santos-Dumont, a Brazilian who lived there, made the first European flight in a powered biplane in 1906.

In 1909, Louis Bleriot, of France, became the first person to fly a plane across the English Channel. He made the flight in a monoplane that he had designed himself. Bleriot had added several new features to his airplane. The pilot sat in the cockpit of a covered fuselage (the body of the craft). He controlled the flight with a control stick and pedals, just as airplanes are flown today. The rudder and the elevators were at the rear of the plane. Bleriot's design became the standard for later airplane builders.

Soon the new designs created in Europe surpassed those in the United States. One reason for these rapid advances was that the military forces of the various European governments supported aviation development.

▶WORLD WAR I, 1914–1918

Although aircraft were only a small part of the total military effort in World War I, aviation was important right from the beginning of the conflict.

Airships were used by both sides for gathering information behind enemy lines. The British used blimps for spotting enemy submarines that could then be attacked by airplanes or ships. The Germans continued their pre-war development of zeppelins and used them in 53 bombing raids against England. Such raids were more notable for the fright they caused than for actual damage. By the end of the war, the disadvantage of airships was apparent. Zeppelins moved very slowly, making them easy targets. Gunfire from hostile airplanes or ground artillery could cause the hydrogen gas to burst into flames.

During the early years of the war, airplanes were also used for flying over enemy lines to gather information. But soon there were also squadrons of fighters and bombers with specialized airframes, engines, and weapons.

In 1914 a typical British aircraft was the B.E. 2a, a fragile biplane with a 35-foot (10.6-meter) wingspan and weighing only 1,274 pounds (573 kilograms). With its 70-horsepower Renault engine, it had a top speed of 70 miles (113 kilometers) per hour. It carried a pilot and an observer. Its weapons were pistols and hand-held bombs.

At the war's end, in November, 1918, the British Royal Air Force was flying the Handley-Page V/1500. The V/1500 had a wingspan of 126 feet (38.4 meters), weighed 24,000 pounds (10,800 kilograms), and was powered by four 375-horsepower Rolls-Royce engines. Its top speed was 97 miles (156 kilometers) per hour. The fighters were capable of speeds in excess of 140 miles (225 kilometers) per hour and strong enough to make the high speed turns, dives, and other maneuvers of air combat. There were aircraft carrying five machine guns and bombs weighing hundreds of pounds.

▶PEACETIME AVIATION, 1919–1938

After the war, former military pilots and many others used aircraft for peaceful purposes. They crossed the oceans, flew to unexplored areas of the world, and always tried to fly higher and faster.

Record Flights

In the ten years after World War I, the speed record went from 171 miles (275.2 kilometers) per hour to 370 miles (595 kilometers) per hour. The altitude record increased from 33,113 feet (10,093 meters) in 1920 to 43,166 feet (13,157 meters) in 1930.

The first aircraft to cross the Atlantic Ocean was the U.S. Navy's Curtiss NC-4. This four-engine **flying boat** (an aircraft that takes off and lands on the water) completed the trip in 19 days in May, 1919. The first nonstop flight across the Atlantic was made in the next month. British Lieutenants John Alcock and Arthur Whitten Brown flew a two-engine Vickers Vimy from Newfoundland to Ireland, a distance of 1,890 miles (3,043 kilometers), in 16 hours and 28 minutes.

In May, 1923, the first nonstop flight across the United States was made in a U.S. Army Air Service Fokker T-2, that was flown coast to coast in 26 hours and 50 minutes. In September, 1924, two U.S. Army Douglas World Cruisers completed a round-the-world flight that had taken 175 days.

The record-making flight that most excited the public was Charles A. Lindbergh's solo flight from New York to Paris. On the morning of May 20, 1927, he took off from Roosevelt Field on Long Island in a silver Ryan monoplane named the *Spirit of St. Louis.* Thirty-three hours and 30 minutes later, he landed in Paris where he was given a hero's welcome. His later flights and many public appearances created enthusiasm for aviation that speeded its progress for the next decade.

Early Commercial Aviation

For several years after World War I, the practical use of airplanes was limited because they were not large enough, reliable enough, or able to fly in bad weather. This meant that businesses could not make a profit by carrying passengers, nor could they compete economically with the railroads as freight carriers.

One thing airplanes could carry was the mail. In 1918 the United States Government established its own airmail service, with airfields and beacon lights across the country. In 1925, private companies were given the job of carrying the mail. They also began to carry other cargo and some passengers.

Aircraft design and construction improved, and the number of passengers began to grow. In 1926, Congress passed the Air Commerce Act, which set a system of licensing for airlines and pilots and established a federal airways system with light and radio beacons to mark the routes. Safety was improved with the addition of de-icers—devices on the wings that reduce the accumulation of ice in bad weather. Ice is dangerous because it destroys smooth airflow thus reducing lift. It also adds weight. Fire-extinguishing systems were installed, and new instruments and radio aids were developed to improve navigation and to allow safer flying. In 1927 more than 18,000 passengers traveled on commercial airlines.

Charles A. Lindbergh (*left*) stands beside the plane in which he made the first solo flight across the Atlantic Ocean (1927). Amelia Earhart (*right*) was the first woman to fly alone across the Atlantic (1932) and from Hawaii to California (1935).

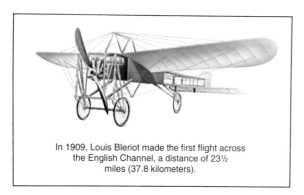

In 1909, Louis Bleriot made the first flight across the English Channel, a distance of $23\frac{1}{2}$ miles (37.8 kilometers).

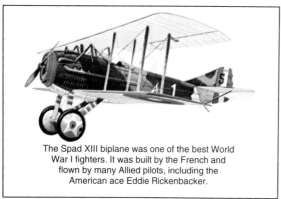

The Spad XIII biplane was one of the best World War I fighters. It was built by the French and flown by many Allied pilots, including the American ace Eddie Rickenbacker.

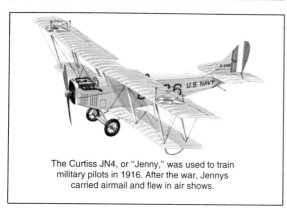

The Curtiss JN4, or "Jenny," was used to train military pilots in 1916. After the war, Jennys carried airmail and flew in air shows.

The all-metal Ford Trimotor, a ten-passenger plane, was one of the first successful airliners.

Zeppelins. As airplanes began their first commercial flights, they had growing competition from rigid airships. The Germans built giant zeppelins. The first, in 1900, had been 419 feet (128 meters) long. By 1938 they had built a zeppelin that was 803 feet (245 meters) long, had four diesel engines, and could carry 30 tons of cargo across the ocean.

But the possibility of damage by storms or from the use of highly flammable hydrogen gas made airship travel hazardous. When the zeppelin *Hindenburg* burst into flames while docking in Lakehurst, New Jersey, in May, 1937, the public rejected them as a passenger aircraft. By that time, airplanes had become safer and more convenient. In 2001 a German company began offering commercial airship flights again. The new zeppelins are filled with nonflammable helium.

Successful Airliners. One of the first successful passenger planes was also used for explorations such as the pioneering flights made by American Rear Admiral Richard E. Byrd in Antarctica. The plane was the Ford Trimotor, one of the first all-metal aircraft. This ten-passenger plane was introduced in 1926, and many were still flying in the late 1930's.

In 1933, Boeing Aircraft Company introduced the 247, an all-metal plane with many new design features. Its cantilever wings were routed through the fuselage. The two engines had streamlined **cowling** (covers) into which the landing gear retracted. The new features were successful, but this plane also carried only ten passengers—too few for the growing airline businesses. However it paved the way for the first passenger plane capable of earning a profit. This was the legendary Douglas DC-3, introduced in 1936.

Douglas Aircraft Company engineers incorporated into the DC-3 all of the current technical developments of the time—all-metal structure, engine cowling, and retractable landing gear. It had **radial engines** (cylinders in a circle around the crankshaft) that were cooled by the air flowing over them, so they did not need heavy, complicated liquid cooling systems. The controllable pitch propellers could be changed to the most efficient angle for taking off or cruising. The landing flaps allowed the plane to land at lower speeds. In addition, the DC-3 carried 21 passengers. This plane made the United States a world leader in airline travel.

In the 1930's, intercontinental air travel increased. Giant zeppelins (*left*) carried passengers between Europe and North and South America. Flying boats, such as the Boeing 314 (*above*), were able to land on harbors and rivers next to many of the world's major cities.

The DC-3 was copied by many manufacturers in other countries and was the basis for airline growth all over the world. In World War II it was called the C-47 for use as a military transport. More than 13,000 civilian and military versions were built, many of which were still flying in the late 1980's.

Flying Boats. Another important passenger aircraft used in the 1930's was the flying boat. It was particularly useful for traveling long distances over oceans. It could land at many of the world's major cities that had no airports but were located on oceans, lakes, or rivers. Small flying boats were used for short trips in Europe, but only those built in the United States were capable of traveling long distances such as the 2,400 miles (3,900 kilometers) across the Pacific Ocean from California to Hawaii. Special piers were built for the flying boats to unload passengers and cargo. Sikorsky Aircraft Company's S.40 and S.42, the Martin M-130, and the Boeing 314 flew to the Far East, South America, and Europe. Flying boats were popular from the late 1930's until the end of World War II. By then, large airfields had been built all over the world, and there were land aircraft capable of carrying more passengers than the flying boats.

WORLD WAR II, 1939–1945

The technical advances used in the design of the DC-3 were also applied to the fighters and bombers of all the air forces that fought in World War II. The German Luftwaffe (air force) had already tested modern military aircraft such as the Messerschmitt Bf 109 fighter and Heinkel He 111 bomber in the Spanish Civil War. Civilians had learned the terrors of air warfare when German planes bombed and destroyed the Spanish city of Guernica. In 1939 and 1940 the Luftwaffe used tactics it had developed in Spain to support the German army in the conquest of Europe.

The English had matched the German aircraft development with its own fighters, the Spitfire and Hurricane. These were used to fight the Battle of Britain in August and September of 1940. By maintaining control of its own skies, the British Royal Air Force was able to prevent the Germans from invading or forcing a British surrender by heavy bombing. Although London and many British industrial cities were bombed, production of aircraft continued and the people's morale remained high.

The British had developed four-engine heavy bombers—the Short Stirling, Handley-

Page Halifax, and Avro Lancaster. These, with the American Boeing B-17s and Consolidated B-24s, eventually carried large bomb loads deep into German territory, sometimes maintaining round-the-clock bombing of military, industrial, and railroad targets, as well as of major cities.

The Japanese and Allied forces used aircraft in combination with ships throughout the war in the Pacific. On December 7, 1941, the Japanese used carrier-based aircraft to attack Pearl Harbor, the U.S. Naval base in Hawaii. The first important aerial blow struck by the United States was a bombing raid in April, 1942. B-25s, normally land-based, were launched from aircraft carriers to attack Tokyo and other Japanese cities. Allied strength in the air grew, with carrier-based and land-based planes playing important parts in the war in the Pacific. The last blow of the war was struck in August, 1945, by two B-29s, each carrying a single atomic bomb.

The B-29 was one of two aircraft that demonstrate the effect the war had on aircraft design and technology. It could fly at 400 miles (644 kilometers) per hour, had a range of 5,333 miles (8,583 kilometers), and could carry up to 10,000 pounds (4,545 kilograms) of bombs. This was later increased to 20,000 pounds (9,000 kilograms).

The second plane was Germany's 550-mile (885-kilometer)-per-hour Messerschmitt Me 262 fighter, whose jet engines and swept wings clearly showed the way for future aircraft design.

Other important aviation developments came out of the war. One was the use of radar for aircraft identification, control, navigation, and bombardment. Another was the helicopter, which was used as a rescue aircraft.

Military Airplanes

The British Spitfire was a World War II fighter. It could fly at more than 350 miles (560 kilometers) per hour.

The B-17 Flying Fortress, a World War II bomber, could carry 3 tons of bombs to targets 600 miles (966 kilometers) away.

The MiG 15, shown here with North Korean markings, was a Russian-built fighter used in the Korean War. Its top speed was 668 miles (1,075 kilometers) per hour.

The B-52 Strato Fortress was in service from the late 1950's through the 1980's. It can carry bombs to targets 12,500 miles (20,000 kilometers) away.

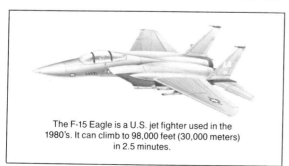

The F-15 Eagle is a U.S. jet fighter used in the 1980's. It can climb to 98,000 feet (30,000 meters) in 2.5 minutes.

Other developments included a worldwide network of landing fields, navigational aides, meteorological (weather forecasting) facilities, and repair sites. These helped the huge expansion of air travel in the next decade.

1945 TO THE PRESENT

Before World War II, new designs of aircraft had been limited by the power available from current engines. The jet engine changed this situation. It was so powerful that stronger, more streamlined airframes were required.

New Designs. One of the most visible design changes was the swept wing that had been used on the Me 262. These wings were used on the new fighters and bombers and, in 1954, on the prototype (original model) of the Boeing 707, which became the world's first successful jet airliner. New metals and new manufacturing techniques were also developed to meet the special needs of high speed and high altitude flight.

The jet engine was not the only new form of propulsion. In October, 1947, the Bell XS-1 research rocket plane flew faster than the speed of sound (about 760 miles, or 1,225 kilometers, per hour). Rockets were usually used in research aircraft and as auxiliary power to help heavily loaded military planes take off.

The North American F-100, the first supersonic fighter, was put into service in 1953. Three years later the first supersonic bomber, the delta-winged Convair B-58, followed. In 1969, co-operative effort by Britain and France made possible the flight of the Concorde, the first successful supersonic airliner.

New Records. The new technology meant that speed and altitude records would continue to be challenged and broken. An intense international rivalry developed. The first official postwar speed record of 603 miles (971 kilometers) per hour was set in 1945 by a British Gloster Meteor F4.

In 1956 a British Fairey Delta 2 exceeded the 1,000-miles-per-hour mark at a speed of 1,132 miles (1,823 kilometers) per hour. A Russian Mikoyan Type E166 raised this to 1,666 miles (2,682 kilometers) per hour in 1962. By 1976 a U.S. Lockheed SR-71A—nicknamed the "Blackbird"—flew at 2,193 miles (3,531 kilometers) per hour. After the war, speeds were referred to in **"Mach" numbers**—multiples of the speed of sound, which is called Mach 1.

Although the records are not official, the highest and fastest aircraft ever flown is the North American X-15 research plane. In 1963 the X-15 reached an altitude of 354,200 feet—over 67 miles (108 kilometers). Because this is considered to be a space flight, the pilots were awarded astronaut wings. In 1967 the X-15A-2 achieved a speed of Mach 6.72, or 4,534 miles (7,300 kilometers) per hour.

While speed and altitude records were made and broken, one major goal of flight in the atmosphere had not been achieved. This was a nonstop, nonrefueled flight around the world. In December, 1986, this goal was reached in *Voyager,* a fragile-appearing airplane built by Burt Rutan, an American aircraft designer. It had a wingspan of 111 feet (33.8 meters)—longer than a Boeing 727—weighed 2,680 pounds (1,206 kilograms), and carried almost 1,200 gallons (4,560 liters) of fuel, which weighed four times as much as the plane itself.

The flight of 26,718 miles (43,016 kilometers) was made in 9 days by pilots Dick Rutan and Jeana Yeager. It was a triumph of high-technology materials, computer-aided design, and the personal skill and bravery of its pilots.

Left: The DC-3, introduced in 1936, is one of the oldest airplanes in use today. This one is dropping fire fighters near a forest fire.

Right: *Voyager* is one of the latest airplane designs. In 1986 it made the first nonstop, nonrefueled flight around the world.

The 400-seat Boeing 747 (*above*) has its cockpit above the passenger area. The supersonic Concorde (*right*) has an adjustable nose section, shown here in the lowered position, allowing the pilot to see the runway better.

COMMERCIAL AVIATION TODAY

Air travel has changed our lives in many ways. Where once only the wealthy traveled from country to country, now the average citizen can do it, too. Two things that make this possible are larger airplanes and more fuel efficient engines. An airplane like the Boeing 747 can carry 400 people at a cost 25 percent lower per person than the 100-passenger 707.

Another factor in lowering the cost of flying is deregulation of the airlines. In 1984 the United States government dissolved the Civil Aeronautics Board (CAB), the agency that had controlled the routes, fares, and some other airline activities. Now airlines compete for passengers by offering lower fares, better schedules, or different routes—things that once were set for them by the CAB.

Growth and Problems. After deregulation there was tremendous growth in the U.S. airline industry. But this growth has created problems, one of which is crowded airports. One of the busiest, O'Hare Field in Chicago, serves about 70 million passengers a year. In such busy conditions, baggage sometimes gets lost, or more tickets are sold for a flight than there are seats on the airplane. Delays caused by weather or maintenance problems may result in lines of airplanes waiting for takeoff or circling overhead waiting for their turn to land. Air traffic controllers must direct growing numbers of flights of arriving and departing aircraft as well as those en route. Airport administrations, airline companies, and the federal government are all trying to solve these problems.

The growth in passenger flying has created a need for new large and small airliners. The United States is the world leader in the manufacture of large planes such as the Boeing 767 and McDonnell Douglas MD11. But U.S. airlines also buy from foreign manufacturers. Regional airlines use smaller planes such as the German Fokker 100 and the British de Havilland DHC-7.

Although many technical improvements have been made in passenger airplane construction, speeds have increased very little. The original Boeing 707s had a maximum cruising speed of about 600 miles (966 kilometers) per hour. A modern 747 can attain about 625 miles (1,006 kilometers) per hour. Except for the supersonic Concorde, most airliners fly at about 550 miles (885 kilometers) per hour. As a result, flight times have remained constant for the last 30 years.

FLIGHT SAFETY

The airlines have had a very good safety record, and statistics show it is safer to travel by airplane than by car. But many people remain concerned about the dangers of flying. The government agency setting and maintaining aviation safety standards is the Federal Aviation Administration (FAA). The FAA regulates air traffic, investigates accidents, and makes rules for aircraft construction and maintenance and pilot licensing and training.

Because accident investigations often focus on pilot error, the FAA pays close attention to the training requirements of pilots. It gives pilot candidates written and flying tests for different levels of skill. A pilot is not allowed to fly for purposes beyond the level of the license earned. Airlines also test their pilots periodically.

Following the September 11, 2001, terrorist attacks, new security measures were established to ensure flight safety. The responsibility for airport security was assumed by the federal government. Also, all cockpit doors were strengthened and locked, and flight crews received additional training for handling emergency situations. (Also see HIJACKING in Volume H.)

GENERAL AVIATION

Aviation other than military or airline is called general aviation. The United States has long led the world in the number of private planes registered and in the total number of pilots licensed. In the mid-1990's, there were over 180,000 active general aviation aircraft, flown by some 640,000 active pilots.

Flying corporate executives in swift jets and fighting forest fires in water bombers are general aviation activities. Others include delivering organs for transplants, controlling traffic and other police work, and sport flying.

The number and variety of airplanes using large airports have created problems: Each type of plane flies at a different airspeed when approaching to land, yet it is necessary to maintain a safe distance between them. The pilots may be students in training or experienced flyers.

In the late 1980's, pilots, owners and manufacturers of small planes, and the FAA were seeking ways to protect flyers without overly restricting the use of the public airports. Controlled airspace around large airports is restricted to planes with two-way radios. In many such areas an aircraft must also have a **transponder**—a device that sends a signal identifying its position on the controller's radar screen.

AIRCRAFT MANUFACTURING

The cost of the new electronic equipment is high, as are the costs of buying, insuring, and maintaining aircraft. Flying lessons and renting airplanes are also expensive. This reduced by about 85 percent the number of new general aviation aircraft sold between the late 1970's and the late 1980's.

Total shipments of U.S. aircraft were about 2,400 in 1995 (not including off-the-shelf military aircraft). During World War II, U.S. manufacturers produced 100,000 aircraft per year. But modern planes are far more com-

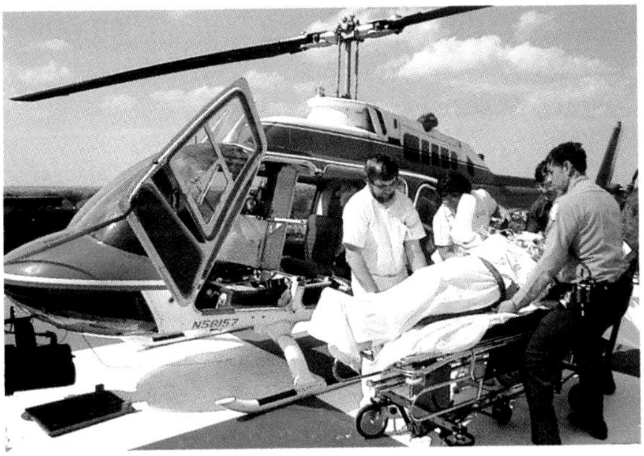

Aircraft serve many important purposes. Helicopters can be used to carry the ill or injured to hospitals (*top left*). Seaplanes carry people and supplies into remote areas where there are no airports (*bottom left*). Airplanes drop chemicals or water on forest fires (*below*).

plex. It may take seven years from the initial design to production of a warplane, and four years for a commercial airliner.

Every aspect of the design must be considered in order to achieve the combination of large size, high speed, and requirements for safety, reliability, and fuel economy. Engineers use many computer-aided design techniques. Before the first parts are built, there are computer tests of the design for strengths and weaknesses. New metals and composite materials such as plastic resins and graphite fibers are used because they combine strength and light weight. Sophisticated electronic equipment is also designed with the aid of computers.

The new materials and equipment and the time spent designing and building new planes are very costly. But planes are far more durable today than in the past. Whereas the early jet engines had to be overhauled every 25 hours of flying time, modern jet engines serve for tens of thousands of hours with much less maintenance. They last so long that weather-induced corrosion is more of a problem than are parts worn out by use. With careful maintenance and replacement of some parts with ones of newer design, an airliner can last 20 or 30 years, flying thousands of hours. This repays the owner's investment many times over.

▶CAREERS IN AVIATION

As airline services grow, so does the need for highly trained pilots and other aviation professionals. Because there are often a large number of qualified pilots seeking positions with the airlines, the standards for hiring can be very high. However, many new pilots are required every year as older pilots retire. For this reason, airlines are looking for ways to have enough pilots with the necessary training and experience. Some are providing their own training programs in which the entire training of a pilot is done by the airline's methods, right from the start. These may be combined with college degree programs.

Another source of qualified pilots is former military flyers. Military flying training standards are very high, and the equipment used is up to date. However, pilots earning their wings in the military service have to serve a number of years before returning to civilian life. In addition, the military pay is now more competitive with that of civilian pilots.

There are also a number of independent civilian flight training schools. It may cost a student as much as $25,000 to earn ratings to qualify as a professional pilot. Such a course would include 260 hours of flying time. Graduates of these schools might work for small commuter airlines, air taxi services, businesses owning airplanes, or in other jobs in which they are paid to fly with passengers. For all of these positions, candidates must be 18 years old and have a commercial license, which requires at least 250 hours of flying time. They must also take a written test and pass a physical examination.

Airline pilots must meet stricter requirements. To obtain an Airline Transport Pilot license, extensive training and experience with airline equipment is required. As well, written, physical, and flight examinations must be passed. Many airline pilots start out as flight engineers, for which they usually

In 1988, world records were set for distance and time aloft in a human-powered plane. Greek cycling champion Kanellos Kanellopoulos pedaled the American-built *Daedalus* for 3 hours and 54 minutes to complete the 74-mile (119-kilometer) flight between the Greek islands of Crete and Santorini.

The Beech Starship, a business plane, is built of light, strong composite materials. It has small forward wings, called canards, and winglets—sharply angled wingtips.

need both a commercial pilot's license and a flight engineer's license earned by passing written and practical tests.

Two licenses can be earned to become an airplane mechanic—either an airframe or engine mechanic's license; some positions require both. Aircraft mechanics maintain the complicated modern airliner. They often receive further training by the airline and by the manufacturer of the planes they maintain.

Each airline sets its own requirements and training for flight attendants. Their most important job is to see that the passengers are safe in normal operations and in emergencies. They also try to make the flight comfortable and enjoyable for the passengers.

Manufacturers employ engineers in many fields to design aircraft. Mechanics, electricians, and other expert workers are involved in the construction of the aircraft, and pilots are employed to test-fly them.

The FAA employs and trains air traffic controllers to work in airport control towers and other control centers. FAA pilots check the performance of commercial pilots, give flight exams to people seeking a pilot's license, and perform many safety-related tasks. Agency investigators try to discover the causes of all aviation accidents in order to prevent future ones.

THE FUTURE IN AVIATION

Since the first brief powered flight in 1903, aviation has undergone huge changes and has brought equally great changes to the world. Millions of people fly for business and pleasure. Two world wars and many other conflicts have shown the devastation of aerial conflict. And world leaders fly from one capital to another to attempt settlements of small wars before they become large ones.

The field of aviation will continue to change. New ideas in aircraft design will result in higher speeds and greater fuel economy. In the early 21st century, it may be possible to fly from New York City to Tokyo in less than two hours in a plane that flies at the edge of space.

Short flights from city center to city center will become more frequent with the further development of vertical-takeoff aircraft. The helicopter is a familiar version. Others will be similar to the tilt-rotor Bell XV-22, on which the angle of the engines can be changed for vertical or horizontal flight.

Cargo planes will be larger and able to carry heavier loads. The total weight of an aircraft, its fuel, and cargo might be as much as 1,000,000 pounds (450,000 kilograms). Cargo aircraft may be built in different shapes to carry certain large items. There are already specially modified planes that carry a single huge rocket engine. A modified 747 is used to carry the space shuttle on its back. More such uses will be devised.

Military aircraft will also have new shapes and be built of new materials. Some already have wings swept forward, and others have wings that can be moved from straight to swept positions. On-board computers assist in

MILESTONES OF AVIATION

1783 Jacques Étienne and Joseph Montgolfier of France launched first balloon (June).

1785 Jean Pierre Blanchard, French balloonist, made first successful voyage across English Channel.

1804 First winged glider made by Sir George Cayley, English aviation pioneer.

1848 John Stringfellow (English) constructed first successful power-driven model airplane.

1852 Henri Giffard flew steam-driven airship over Paris.

1891 Otto Lilienthal of Germany began his glider experiments.

1903 Wright brothers made first sustained, controlled flights in powered heavier-than-air craft at Kitty Hawk, North Carolina.

1909 Louis Blériot (French) made first crossing of English Channel in an airplane.

1911 Galbraith P. Rogers flew across United States, New York to California; flying time, 49 days.

Eugene Ely accomplished first landing on deck of a ship.

1912 Harriet Quimby flew across English Channel, first woman to perform this feat.

1918 First airmail route established in United States.

1919 First crossing of Atlantic by air, accomplished by U.S. Navy seaplane; flying time, 54 hours.

First nonstop air crossing of Atlantic made by two English airmen, Captain John Alcock and Lieutenant Arthur Whitten Brown.

1923 Two U.S. Army pilots made first nonstop transcontinental flight, New York to San Diego, California, in 26 hours, 50 minutes.

1924 U.S. Army pilots made first round-the-world flight, which was also first transpacific flight; flying time, 175 days.

1926 Lieutenant Commander Richard E. Byrd and Floyd Bennett flew across the North Pole, May 9.

1927 Charles A. Lindbergh made first solo nonstop transatlantic flight, New York to Paris; flying time, 33 hours, 30 minutes.

1929 Lieutenant James H. Doolittle, U.S. Army, made first flight using instruments only.

Commander Richard E. Byrd and crew made first flight across South Pole, November 29.

Fritz Opel of Germany flew first rocket plane.

1932 Amelia Earhart became first woman to fly Atlantic solo.

1939 First flight by jet aircraft made, in Germany.

1947 Captain Charles Yeager, USAF, made first supersonic flight.

1949 A USAF B-50, *Lucky Lady II*, completed first nonstop round-the-world flight.

1963 The X-15 flew to an altitude of 67 mi (108 km).

1965 Commander J. R. Williford, U.S. Navy, made longest direct helicopter flight—2,105 mi (3,388 km).

1967 First nonstop crossing of North Atlantic made by two USAF helicopters.

The X-15A-2 achieved the speed of Mach 6.72 (4,534 mi, or 7,300 km, per hour).

1969 First flights of Supersonic Transports (SST's) —Soviet TU-144 and Anglo-French Concorde.

1970 Boeing 747's made first commercial flights.

1976 Concorde began first passenger-carrying supersonic service.

1979 A human-powered aircraft, the *Gossamer Albatross*, was flown across the English Channel.

1981 Space shuttle orbiter *Columbia*, the first reusable spacecraft, made an airplane-like landing after completing its first space mission.

Stephen Ptacek flew *Solar Challenger*, powered by electricity from solar cells, across the English Channel.

1986 Richard Rutan and Jeana Yeager flew *Voyager* on the first nonstop, nonrefueled flight around the world.

1988 Record for distance (74 mi, or 119 km) and time aloft (3 hours, 54 minutes) set in a human-powered plane, the *Daedalus*.

1997 Linda Finch successfully flew the round-the-world route attempted by Amelia Earhart in 1937.

Steve Fossett flew a record distance (9,672 mi, or 15,572 km) in his balloon, *Solo Spirit*, from the United States to India.

the controlling of the aircraft and its weapons. New materials for the surface of the aircraft will make it less visible on radar.

New fuels such as hydrogen, methane, or nuclear fuels will be used. Solar energy has already been used to power a very lightweight experimental aircraft. Other experiments are being conducted in which ground antennas beam microwaves to an aircraft where they are converted to electric power.

New materials and designs will also be used in general aviation aircraft. Some of these ideas will come from those modern aviation pioneers, the designer-pilots. These pilots follow the path of the Wright brothers, sometimes setting world records and leading the way for aircraft manufacturers. Many of the pilots and companies exchange information and encouragement through such organizations as the Experimental Aircraft Association of Oshkosh, Wisconsin.

Sport planes may soar with the birds at 20 miles per hour, fighters may roar 10 feet above the terrain in darkest weather, and airliners may whisk 1,000 passengers from New York City to Honolulu. All of these aircraft will be products of the human spirit that produced the original dream of flight. They are a tribute to the men and women who devote their lives to aviation.

WALTER J. BOYNE
Former Director
National Air and Space Museum
Smithsonian Institution

See also AERODYNAMICS; AIRPLANES; AIRPORTS; BALLOONS AND BALLOONING; GLIDERS; HELICOPTERS; INTERNAL-COMBUSTION ENGINES; JET PROPULSION; NAVIGATION; RADAR, SONAR, LORAN, AND SHORAN; ROCKETS; SUPERSONIC FLIGHT; TRANSPORTATION; UNITED STATES, ARMED FORCES OF THE.

AZERBAIJAN

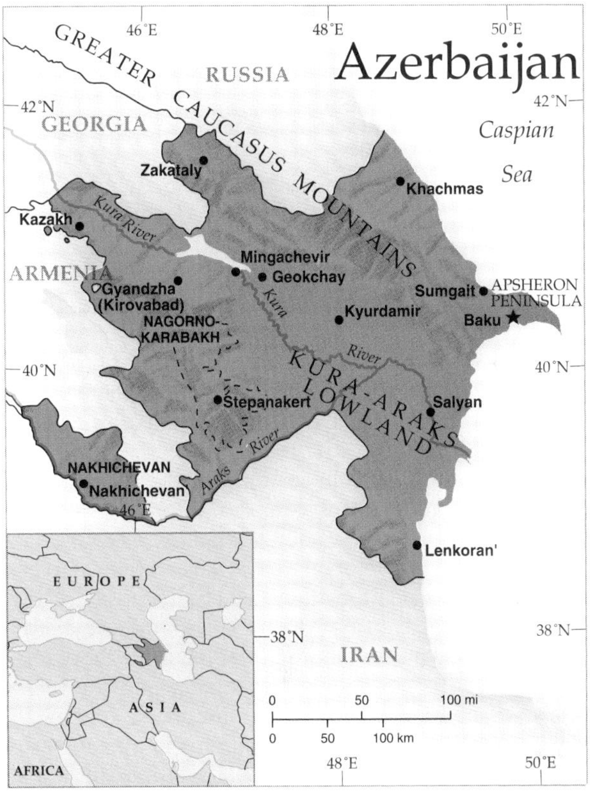

Azerbaijan is a country situated in the eastern part of Transcaucasia—the region lying along the great Caucasus Mountain range, which traditionally forms part of the dividing line between Europe and Asia. The present-day borders of Azerbaijan date from the early 1800's, when it was divided between Russia and Persia (now Iran). Russian, or northern, Azerbaijan was briefly independent, from 1918 to 1920, before it was absorbed by the Soviet Union, which succeeded the Russian Empire. When the Soviet Union itself fell apart in late 1991, northern Azerbaijan declared its independence.

The People. The Azeri, or Azerbaijanis, are descended from Turkic-speaking peoples who migrated to the region from Central Asia in ancient times. Today, Azeri Turks make up about 85 percent of the country's population. The two largest ethnic minorities are Russians and Armenians. Azeri Turkish is the official language, although Russian continues in common usage. (In Iranian Azerbaijan, Persian is widely used.) The Azerbaijanis are Muslims, the Russians and Armenians Christians. There are also a small number of Jews, some of whom have preserved their faith since the days of the Khazar Kaganate, a once-powerful Turkic state in the region.

About half the people live in urban areas. The capital and largest city, Baku, is Azerbaijan's chief port on the Caspian Sea. With some 2 million people in its metropolitan area, Baku has more than one-quarter of the country's total population.

Azerbaijan's territory includes the Nagorno-Karabakh and Nakhichevan regions. Nagorno-Karabakh has been the scene of much bloody fighting between ethnic Armenians and Azeris. The Armenians, who make up a majority of its population, seek unification with Armenia.

The Land. Azerbaijan has a ruggedly beautiful landscape. Nearly half the land is covered by mountains. The Greater Caucasus forms Azerbaijan's natural boundary on the north; the Lesser Caucasus separates it from Armenia on the west; and the Talysh Mountains border Iran to the south. Eastern Azerbaijan lies open to the Caspian Sea, which, despite its name, is the world's largest lake. Beyond the Caspian Sea are the deserts of Central Asia.

Looking as rugged as the mountains of her homeland, a woman of Azerbaijan contemplates her country's future. Azerbaijan was a constituent republic of the Soviet Union, before winning its independence as a result of the Soviet Union's collapse in 1991.

The Kura-Araks Lowland, which makes up the remaining land, takes its name from the country's two major rivers, the Kura and the Araks. The Araks marks the boundary with Iran. Fertile lowland plains, watered by the rivers and streams, stretch from the mountains to the Caspian Sea. The Apsheron Peninsula juts into the Caspian Sea.

Climate and Natural Resources. The climate varies widely, depending on elevation. The lowlands generally have mild winters and long, hot, and dry summers. Lowland temperatures in summer average 80°F (26°C). In the upper valleys and highlands, snow covers the ground in winter, while summers are comfortably cool.

Azerbaijan is rich in mineral resources. In the early 1900's it produced half of the world's petroleum. Most of the crude oil now comes from offshore oil fields in the Caspian Sea. Pipelines have been built to transport oil to ports on the Black Sea.

The Economy. Economically, Azerbaijan has well-developed industry as well as a diversified agriculture that meets almost all of the food needs of its people. Heavy industry is by far the most important segment of the economy. It includes oil processing and the manufacture of petroleum products, chemical fertilizers, electrical equipment, machinery, metals, and related goods. Light industry, also important to the economy, includes processed agricultural products, textiles, footwear, and electrical household appliances and other consumer goods.

The varied climatic zones enable Azerbaijani farmers to grow a variety of crops. These include wheat and other grains, cotton, tea, tobacco, and almost all kinds of vegetables and fruits. Sheep are grazed on mountain pastures in summer and in the lowlands in winter. The Caspian Sea teems with fish, including sturgeon, whose roe (eggs) are the source of the finest caviar.

History. As the only convenient land route through the Caucasus between Europe and Asia, Azerbaijan has been crossed by invading armies and migrating peoples since earliest times. The formation of Azerbaijan nationality dates from the A.D. 1000's, with the arrival of the last Turkic tribes, whose common language became Azeri Turkish. At only one period in its history, however, was all of Azerbaijan united under a single national ruler. In the 1500's, a native Azeri dynasty of the Safavids (or Safawids) created a great empire that eventually reached from Central Asia to the Persian Gulf. But in the 1600's the Safavid state fell under Persian rule.

The 1700's were marked by the struggle between Persia, Ottoman Turkey, and Russia for control of Azerbaijan and the rest of Transcaucasia. Under treaties signed in 1813 and 1828, Russia acquired the half of Azerbaijan north of the Araks River.

After the Russian Revolution of 1917, Azeri leaders, on May 28, 1918, proclaimed an independent Azerbaijani republic. It lasted only until 1920, when Azerbaijan was invaded by forces of the Soviet Union. It became a constituent republic of the Soviet Union in 1922.

With the collapse of the Soviet Union in December 1991, Azerbaijan regained its independence. A 1995 cease-fire halted the fighting in Nagorno-Karabakh, but tensions between Azerbaijan and Armenia over control of the region continued.

Government. The country's legislative body is the National Assembly (Milli Mejlis). Executive authority is held by the president, who appoints a council of ministers, headed by a prime minister, to handle the day-to-day operations of the government. Geidar A. Aliyev was elected president in 1993. That same year the National Assembly approved Azerbaijan's entry into the Commonwealth of Independent States (CIS). Aliyev was re-elected in 1998, although the opposition claimed he did not win the two-thirds majority of votes required.

ALEC RASIZADE
The W. Averell Harriman Institute
Columbia University

FACTS and figures

AZERBAIJANI REPUBLIC is the official name of the country.

LOCATION: Eastern Transcaucasia.

AREA: 33,436 sq mi (86,600 km²).

POPULATION: 8,000,000 (estimate).

CAPITAL AND LARGEST CITY: Baku.

MAJOR LANGUAGES: Azeri Turkish (official), Russian.

MAJOR RELIGIOUS GROUP: Muslim.

GOVERNMENT: Republic. **Head of state**—president. **Head of government**—prime minister. **Legislature**—National Assembly (Milli Mejlis).

CHIEF PRODUCTS: Agricultural—wheat and other grains, cotton, tea, tobacco, vegetables and fruits, livestock. **Manufactured**—petroleum products, chemical fertilizers, electrical machinery, metals, processed agricultural products, textiles, consumer goods. **Mineral**—petroleum and natural gas, aluminum, iron, copper, and zinc ores.

AZTECS

The Aztecs were an American Indian people of central Mexico, best known as the builders of an empire that swiftly fell under Spanish control during the years 1519 to 1521.

The defeat of the Aztecs was no ordinary conquest. The capital of their empire was a city larger than Rome. In its beauty it resembled Venice, set in the middle of a lake with canals for streets.

Although the city was demolished in the final battle of 1521, its fame has endured. Aztec civilization is remembered today for its elaborate religious life, complex social organization, elegant literature, and monumental works of sculpture.

▶ SOCIAL ORDER

What made Aztec society run smoothly? How was it organized?

Such questions cannot be answered fully. Yet there is a wealth of information in the writings of conquerors and missionaries. Aztecs themselves learned to use alphabetic script, and some of them wrote descriptions of life as it had been before the Spanish Conquest. These early accounts are our sources.

Family and Community

When a man tied the end of his cloak to the corner of a woman's blouse, she became his wife and he could marry no other. Though he might take one or more secondary "wives," only the children of his actual wife could inherit his property.

A man's duties included farming, soldiering, and the various trades, such as carpentry and metalwork. A woman took care of the home, wove cloth, or practiced medicine.

Children had responsibilities of their own. Girls helped with the weaving. Boys fetched firewood or went to the marketplace to pick up scraps of maize (corn) and beans left by the merchants.

Settlements. Families lived in villages, towns, or cities. Every town had neighborhoods, each with its chief. A city with many neighborhoods might be divided into four quarters, each quarter with its chief. These divisions made it easy to recruit people for military service or large work projects.

In the Valley of Mexico, the center of the Aztec world, there were dozens of cities. The largest was the capital, called Tenochtitlán, which may have had a population of 200,000. Tenochtitlán and its twin city, Tlatelolco, were located on islands in the middle of a shallow lake. The islands were connected to the mainland by earthen causeways.

Today the capital of the republic of Mexico is Mexico City. It is on the same site, but the lake, over the years, has been mostly drained.

Social Classes. Like cities today, the Aztec capital was a place of bustling activity, filled with people of all kinds. Everybody, however, fit into one of three categories: nobles, commoners, and *tlatlacotin*. The *tlatlacotin* were poor people who had sold themselves as permanent workers. Their children, however, were born free.

This drawing by Ignacio Marquina shows the Aztec capital Tenochtitlán as it appeared in 1519. It is based on the descriptions of Spanish conquerors and the remains of Aztec monuments.

High officials were usually chosen from the noble class. Commoners were also selected, if of proven ability.

Government

Each city was ruled by a king, who gave orders to neighborhood chiefs and to kings of cities under his control. There was no single chain of command but several, each ending with one of the important kings. These kings made alliances among themselves. Since Tenochtitlán was the strongest of the cities, its ruler can be called emperor or king of the empire.

Tribute. The reason for controlling other cities was to make them pay taxes, or tribute. Tribute goods included cloaks, hides, timber, stone, precious feathers, jewels, gold, and various foods.

Warfare. People did not like giving tribute to a king in a distant city. They were loyal to their own town. But if they refused to pay, they were threatened with armed attack.

Aztec armies were well equipped with bows and arrows, spears, and a kind of wooden sword, called *macana*, which was edged with sharp bits of stone.

If the governors or emperor heard of a faraway city rich in goods, they sent warriors to conquer it. Afterward they divided up the tribute and made sure that it kept coming regularly. This is how the empire grew.

▶WAY OF LIFE

Traditional Aztec wisdom preached caution. The saying "The world is slick and slippery" meant it is easy to make mistakes in life. Aztecs also said, "Not twice on earth," meaning you only live once, so enjoy life while you can.

From Birth to Death

When a girl was born, she was presented with a tiny sewing basket. A boy was given a miniature shield and four little arrows. Before the age of 4, children had their ears pierced. At 5 or 6, children could go out to play, if they had finished their chores.

Education. At 10, children were legally responsible for their actions and could be sentenced to punishment. At this age all boys and girls were sent to neighborhood boarding schools. Some students learned trades. Others studied history, music, the art of speaking, and the interpretation of dreams.

At 15 a young woman was ready for marriage. The typical young man became a warrior and would marry later.

Dress. Men wore loincloths and simple cloaks knotted over one shoulder. Women wore sleeveless blouses and wrap-around skirts of cotton cloth.

Shelter and Food. Houses were of one story and might have several rooms, each facing a central courtyard. The kitchen with its fireplace was in the rear. A young family often lived in a single room in the house of the husband's father.

Maize, beans, squash, and turkey were important foods. Crops were grown on island gardens called *chinampas*, made of fertile soil scooped from the lake bottom.

Commerce. More unusual foods, such as cacao, pineapples, and vanilla, were brought by merchants from the lowlands. Cacao beans, the source of chocolate, were often used as money in the great marketplaces, where goods from all over the Aztec world were traded.

Goods came to market on the backs of porters. There were no beasts of burden and no wheeled vehicles. Water transport was by dugout canoe.

Old Age. Alcohol was restricted by law. But the elderly could drink as much as they wanted. This, along with retirement from work, was a privilege of old age.

Fragment of an Aztec Song

We merely come to stand sleeping,
we merely come to dream. It
is not true, not true that
we come to live on earth.
We come to do as herbs in spring:
and though our hearts come
sprouting, come green, those
few flowers of our flesh
that open wither away.

— translated by John Bierhorst from *Cantares Mexicanos*, a manuscript written in the 1500's.

Aztec statues are noted for their massive size and mysterious details. *Left:* The great statue of the earth goddess Snake Skirt wearing a carved necklace of human hands and hearts. *Above:* The famous "calendar stone." In the center is the face of an Aztec earth god.

Funerals. Long prayers were said for a dead person. The corpse was either buried or cremated, together with a sewing basket and weaver's tools (for a woman) or weapons (for a man).

It was believed that most people went to the dead land beneath the earth. Those who had drowned went to the paradise of the rain god. The most honored dead were men killed in battle and women who had died in childbirth. They went to the sky to live with the sun.

Religion

Aztecs worshipped many gods in addition to the rain god and the sun. There was the fire god, called Old God. There was an earth goddess, called Snake Skirt, and a goddess of love, named Flower Plume.

Merchants and hunters had special gods who received their prayers. The city of Tenochtitlán had a tribal god, Huitzilopochtli (wee-tseel-oh-POACH-tlee), who protected the city's warriors.

Feasts and the Calendar. The year was divided into 18 "months," each with 20 days. In each of these months there was a feast in honor of one or more gods. The rain god and the maize god were remembered in the spring. One of the fall months was devoted to Cloud Snake, god of hunting. Religious feasts were marked by parades and music. At the end of the year were five unlucky days, when people stayed indoors.

At the close of every 52 years a special ceremony was held. All fires were put out. Then a priest kindled a new fire using a drilling stick. Runners with torches carried the new fire to each of the settlements in the Valley of Mexico.

The Payment. Aztecs believed that the gods demanded payment, perhaps an offering of food or a sacrifice of quail. For the new fire ceremony and other important feasts it was necessary to make the "human payment"—the sacrifice of a human being.

Arts

Architects, painters, and musicians were skilled professionals who enjoyed prestige in Aztec society.

The most impressive works of architecture were the pyramids, built in tiers like a wedding cake. At the top of a pyramid were one or more temples, housing statues of gods.

Gods were also depicted in books, made from long sheets of bark paper, rolled or folded. There were no words, only numbers and pictures that were outlined with black and filled in with brilliant colors. The books were used to record history, to explain the functions of gods, and to list the tribute each city had to pay.

Aztec literature as we know it today was not preserved in these old-style books. It was written after the Spanish Conquest, using the alphabetic script learned from missionaries.

It includes poetic speeches, myths, histories, and the texts of songs.

Songs, both before and after the Conquest, were accompanied by two kinds of drums: a skin drum, played with the hands, and a two-toned log drum, played with mallets. Songs, as well as speeches, often touch upon historical incidents that are explained more fully in other longer works of literature.

▶ HISTORY

Traditional Aztec histories begin with myths of world creation. They continue with legends about the Aztecs' predecessors, the Toltecs, who archaeologists have determined flourished between A.D. 900 and 1200. Their capital, Tula, now in ruins, is located 45 miles (72 kilometers) north of Mexico City. These legends are followed by historical accounts of the kings who built the Aztec empire.

Origin of the Aztecs

Aztecs claimed to have come from a region far to the north, migrating south toward Tula and into the Valley of Mexico. At about this time—according to legend—Tula's last ruler, the priest-king Quetzalcóatl (keh-tsahl-KOH-ahtl) broke his priestly vows and fled in disgrace to the eastern seashore. He disappeared over the water, promising one day to return. After he had gone, an Aztec tribe called Mexica founded Tenochtitlán, in 1325.

The Rise and Fall of the Aztec Empire

After years of warring with its neighbors, Tenochtitlán formed an alliance with two other cities, Texcoco and Tlacopán. This occurred about 1430. The new alliance, or empire, grew rapidly. By the time of the emperor Montezuma II, Aztecs controlled a territory stretching from the Pacific Ocean to the Gulf of Mexico and south to the present border of Guatemala.

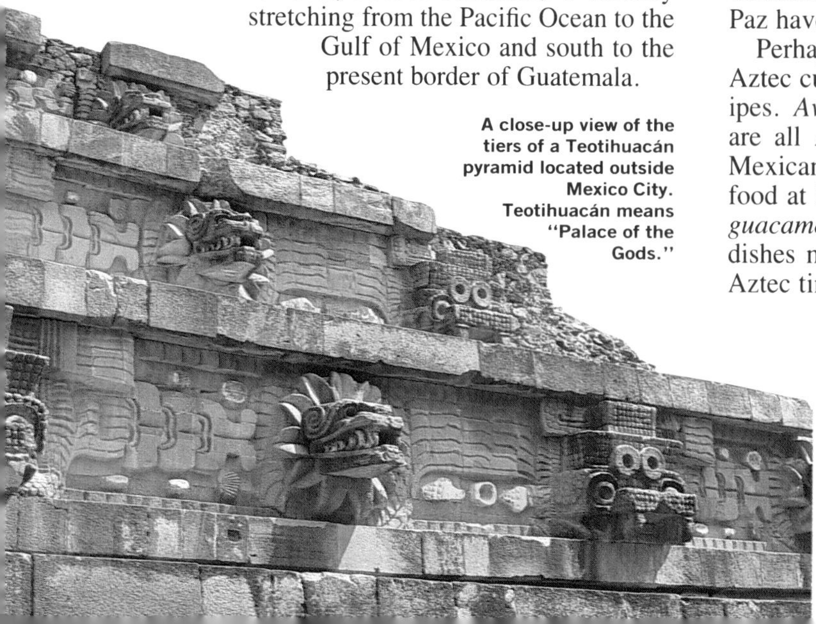

A close-up view of the tiers of a Teotihuacán pyramid located outside Mexico City. Teotihuacán means "Palace of the Gods."

Spanish Conquest. It was Montezuma II who greeted the conqueror Hernando Cortés in 1519 (or the year 1 Reed by the Aztec calendar). According to legend, Montezuma believed Cortés was the legendary Quetzalcóatl, who was to return in the year 1 Reed, and was hesitant to give offense.

Montezuma was taken prisoner by the Spanish and mysteriously killed. Unable to restrain the populace by peaceful means, Cortés resorted to force. Firearms, horses, and steel armor gave the Spanish an edge. But they could not have won without the help of other Aztec cities, eager to see Tenochtitlán humbled. The capital was reduced to rubble during the fierce battle of the summer of 1521. A new Spanish city began to rise in its place.

Aftermath. Smallpox and other diseases brought from Europe greatly diminished the Aztec population. The succession of kings continued through the 1500's. Now known as *gobernadores* (governors), they served under Spanish authority. Although the *gobernadores* eventually lost what remained of their powers, people continued to read and write the Aztec language through the 1700's and to keep up many of the ancient customs.

Legacy of the Aztecs

The modern Aztec language, known as Nahuatl or *mexicano*, is still spoken by more than a million Nahua, who continue to plant maize, weave cotton cloth, and play instruments like the log drum. The Nahua live mostly in small towns and villages in central Mexico.

Nationally, Aztec art is recognized as an essential feature of Mexico's heritage. Aztec painting and sculpture have influenced Mexican artists such as Diego Rivera and Miguel Covarrubias. Modern poets such as Octavio Paz have been inspired by Aztec literature.

Perhaps the most widely known legacy of Aztec culture is in the realm of foods and recipes. *Avocado, chili, chocolate,* and *tomato* are all Aztec words. If you have been to a Mexican restaurant or have prepared Mexican food at home, you may have had *enchiladas, guacamole, tacos,* and *tamales.* These are dishes made with ingredients that go back to Aztec times.

JOHN BIERHORST
Author, *The Mythology of Mexico and Central America*

See also CORTÉS, HERNANDO; INDIANS, AMERICAN; MONTEZUMA II.

HOW TO USE THE INDEX

When travelers visit a large city, they use maps or guides to find their way about. When you want to find information in an encyclopedia, you need a guide, too. The Index is your guide to all the information in THE NEW BOOK OF KNOWLEDGE.

Each volume of THE NEW BOOK OF KNOWLEDGE contains the corresponding alphabetical division of the Index.

USING THE INDEX

When you look something up in this encyclopedia, you should always refer to the Index first. It will tell you where you can find what you want to know. Sometimes, if you need just one key fact, it will tell you all you want to know.

The Index brings together all the references to information about a particular subject. It tells you where that subject—and every subject related to it—is discussed. In most cases when you use the Index to look up a topic, you will find along with it a short definition or identifying phrase. This brief definition explains a term that may be unfamiliar to you and helps you make sure you have found the topic you are looking for.

HOW THE INDEX IS ARRANGED

The model entry and text in the next column and the diagram below explain what you will see if you look up a subject in the Index.

Anthropology (study of human beings and human culture) **A:300–305** *see also* Human beings; Sociology
archaeology related to **A:**349, 362
Boas, Franz **B:**261
Leakey family **L:**96–97
Mead, Margaret **M:**195
prehistoric people **P:**438–42
races, human **R:**28–31

The subject you are looking up, **Anthropology**, is called the **heading** and is in boldface type. Next to the heading are a few words that identify the topic —"study of human beings and human culture." These words are called the **identification**. A volume letter and page numbers follow the identification—**A:300–305**. The volume letter is always in boldface type and tells you in which volume to look for the information about the subject. The page numbers tell you on which pages of the volume to look. If they are also in boldface type, they are directing you to an entire article about the subject; if they are in lightface type, the information is in another article. The heading, its identification, and its volume and page numbers together make up the **entry**.

Following the page number of the entry, you will find the words "*see also*," followed by two index headings. The "*see also*" listings are called **cross-**

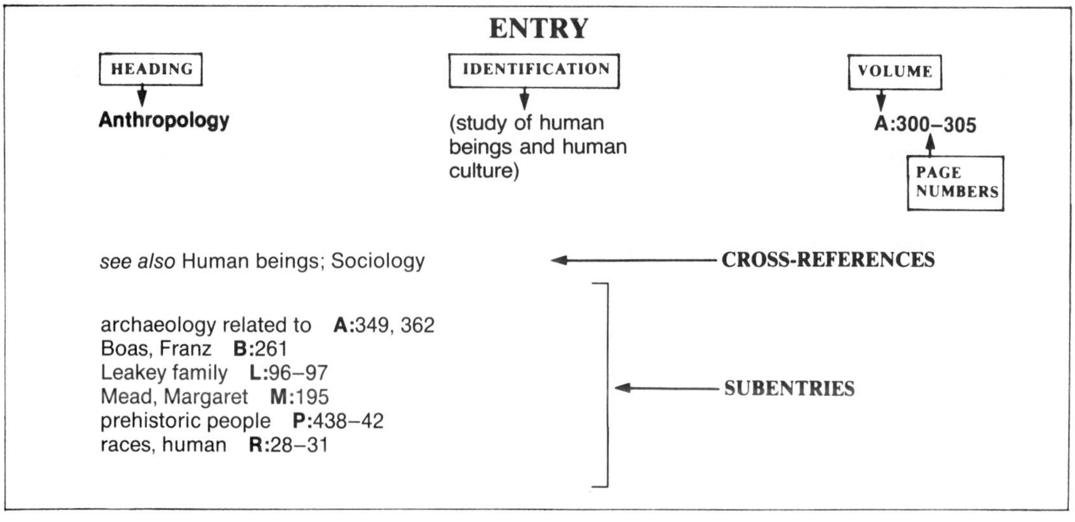

references. They tell you where to look to find more information related to your subject. Cross-references are guides to Index entries, not to article titles.

Beneath the entry there is a list of additional references to your subject. These references are called **subentries**. They are indented and arranged in alphabetical order. The subentries refer to all the important information about your subject throughout the set. Unless you look in the Index, you may not think of all the points about your subject that have been covered in the encyclopedia. (Subentries, in turn, may appear as main entries in other parts of the Index under their own initial letters.)

In the case of **Anthropology** there are only a few subentries. But if you look up a broad topic, such as **Vocations**, you may find dozens of subentries. Subentries are helpful if you want to review the whole of a particular field.

Illustrations are indicated by the words *"diagram(s)"* or *"picture(s)"* following the subject entry and its subentries.

Circles (in geometry) *diagram(s)* **G**:122
Bridges **B:395–401**
  picture(s)
    swinging bridge **J**:157

Country, state, and province articles each include at least one map, often with its own index. These maps are not listed in the Index, but other types of maps are indicated by the word *map(s)*, following the subject entry and its subentries.

Pigs
  map(s)
    world distribution **W**:265

Parentheses are used to enclose identifications. They are also used to enclose initials, alternative forms of names, and dates.

Initials: **Civilian Conservation Corps (CCC)**
Alternative forms of names:
Madison, Dolley (Dorothea Payne Todd Madison)

Dates: Dates are given for historical events that are summarized briefly in the Index.
Mayflower Compact (1620)

What should I look for?
Think of the specific word about which you need information and look for that. Go directly to the name you usually use for the thing you want. If you want to find out about baseball, turn directly to **Baseball** in the Index. You do not have to hunt first under **Sports**, although you would find baseball listed there, too.

How do I look up a person's name?
Look for the last name, just as you do when you use the telephone book.

Blake, William (English poet and artist) **B:250b**

How do I look up names that begin with "Mac" or "Mc"?
Names beginning with "Mac" and "Mc" are placed in alphabetical order, just as they are spelled.

MacArthur, Douglas
Macbeth
Mac Cool
Machine language
Maze
M' Bochi
McAuliffe, Christa
McKinley, William

What if the person is known by more than one name?
Some persons are known by more than one name. Such entries are listed by their best-known names—**Buffalo Bill**; **Twain, Mark**; **Napoleon**. However, if you should look under the person's official name, a cross-reference will tell you the right place to look.

Bonaparte, Napoleon *see* Napoleon I
Clemens, Samuel Langhorne *see* Twain, Mark
Cody, William Frederick *see* Buffalo Bill

How do I look up names beginning with "Saint" or "St."?
Saint is always spelled out. Place names beginning with Saint are listed under **Saint**.

Saint Louis (Missouri)

But the names of saints are listed according to the name. "Saint" is placed after the name.

Paul, Saint

What if there is more than one spelling for my topic?
If you use a different (but correct) spelling from the Index, you will also find a *"see"* reference.

Aleichem, Sholem *see* Aleykhem, Sholem

How are the headings in the Index arranged?
Because this is a Dictionary Index, it is arranged like a dictionary, letter by letter.

Mink
Minneapolis
Minnesingers
Minnesota

What if a heading is made up of more than one word?
Even when headings are made up of more than one word, they are still arranged alphabetically, letter by letter.

New Amsterdam
Newark
Newbery, John
New Castle

When there is a comma in the heading, the letter-by-letter arrangement goes through to the comma only—so that all the same names will be brought together.

Black (color)
Black, Hugo La Fayette
Black, Joseph
Blackball
Black Hills
Black market

What about words in parentheses, titles, and Roman numerals?
The alphabetical arrangement of headings is not affected by words in parentheses, titles, or Roman numerals. Just look up the heading as if it did not contain these added words or symbols.

John I, II, and III (books of the New Testament)
John (king of England)
John II (king of France)
John XXIII (pope)
John, Saint (apostle of Jesus Christ)

How do I look up a heading that begins with a number?
If a number is the first word in a heading, the number is spelled out and put in its alphabetical place.

Seven Cities of Cíbola
Seven Sisters
Seventeenth Amendment (to the United States Constitution)
Seven wonders of the ancient world

When numbers appear in any other place in a heading, they come before letters.

Carbon
Carbon-14
Carbon black

Do I look up "A," "An," and "The"?
"A," "an," and "the" are not used in alphabetizing. If any one of these words is part of the title of the book or play, the word is put at the end of the title.

Cat in the Hat, The
Midsummer Night's Dream, A

How are initials indexed?
You will find initials in their proper alphabetical order. A *"see"* reference along with them will lead you to the heading for which the initials stand.

CIA *see* Central Intelligence Agency

How do I look up the abbreviation "Mt."?
Mount is always spelled out and is placed after the name.

Everest, Mount

The word "lake," too, as a geographical term, is placed after the name.

Michigan, Lake

But you can look up the names of forts, towns, and rivers just as you would say them.

Fort Dearborn
Lake Placid
Mississippi River
Mount Vernon

How do I look up a poem?
Poems are listed individually by name and also by their authors.

"Jabberwocky" (poem by Carroll) **N:**273

Carroll, Lewis
"Jabberwocky" **N:** 273

How do I look up a story?
If the story you are looking for has been included in its complete form, you will find it listed under the heading **Stories** (told in full). If the story you want is part of a longer work, you will find it listed individually by its name.

Oliver Twist (book by Charles Dickens)
excerpt from **D:**151–52

Other listings similar to **Stories** are **Experiments and other science activities; Hobbies; How to.**

Index

Angelico, Fra (Italian painter) **A:259; I:**396; **P:**20
Renaissance art **R:**166
picture(s)
Angel (painting) **R:**166
Angeli Laudantes (Praising Angels) (tapestry designed by Burne-Jones)
picture(s) **T:**21
Angelou, Maya (American writer, stage performer, and composer) **A:**428 *profile*
picture(s) **A:**428
Anger, feeling of (in psychology)
divorce, attitudes toward **D:**231
grief **G:**380
Angerstein, John Julius (English merchant and art patron) **N:**35
Angina pectoris (chest pains) **D:**193; **H:**82
Angiogenesis (formation of blood vessels) **C:**95
Angiosperms (division of the plant kingdom) **F:**280, 374; **P:**301, 302
Angkor (ancient city in Cambodia) **C:**35, 37
Angkor Thom (temple in Cambodia)
picture(s) **S:**335
Angkor Wat (temple in Cambodia)
picture(s) **C:**35
Angle, Edward (American orthodontist) **O:**237
Angle bars (steel pieces joining sections of railroad track) **R:**77
Angle of incidence (in physics of light)
diagram(s) **L:**212
Angle of reflection (in physics of light)
diagram(s) **L:**212
Angler fish **A:**281; **F:**182
picture(s) **F:**183
Anglers (persons who fish for sport) **F:**209
Angles (Germanic people, invaders of Britain) **E:**236
Angles (in geometry) **G:**121
bevel gauges **T:**230
optical instruments that measure angles **O:**182–83
trigonometry **T:**312–13
diagram(s) **G:**121
Angleworms *see* Earthworms
Anglican Church (Protestant Episcopal Church) **P:**491, 492, 493, 494 *see also* England, Church of
Christianity, history of **C:**293
Cranmer's prayer books **E:**243
Reformation **R:**132
saints **S:**18c
United States **C:**294
Angling *see* Fishing
Anglo-Burmese wars **B:**459
Anglo-Egyptian Sudan *see* Sudan
Anglo-Norman French language **F:**434
Anglo-Saxon Chronicle **E:**268–69
Anglo-Saxon (Old English) language **E:**265
compared with Anglo-Norman French **F:**434
names **N:**4
Anglo-Saxon literature **E:**268–69
Beowulf **B:**144a–144b
Anglo-Saxons (Teutonic peoples who settled in England) **E:**237
Celtic and Anglo-Saxon art **E:**256–57
rulers of England, list of **E:**236
Angola **A:260–61; C:**610; **P:**402
map(s) **A:**261
picture(s)
flag **F:**226
Luanda **A:**260
Angora (now **Ankara**) (capital of Turkey) **T:**347
Angry young men (in English literature) **D:**303; **E:**290
Anguilla (one of the Leeward Islands in the Caribbean Sea) **C:**114; **S:**13
Angus (breed of beef cattle) **C:**151
picture(s) **C:**152
Anhinga (bird)
picture(s) **A:**277
Anicetus, Saint (pope) **R:**292
Animal behavior *see* Animal intelligence and behavior
Animal bites **F:**161; **S:**3–4
Animal breeding *see* Breeding, animal
Animal communication **A:**284; **C:**462–63
ants **A:**318–19
bee "dances" **B:**120
birds **B:**227
cats, wild **C:**143–44
coyotes **C:**580
dogs **D:**247
elephants **E:**180
foxes **F:**396a
llamas **L:**278
Animal defenses *see* Protective coloration; Protective devices
Animal diseases *see also* Distemper
anthrax **D:**188; **K:**291
Can people get parrot fever? **B:**249
cattle **C:**154
chickens can catch many diseases **P:**414
endangered species **E:**209
fish as pets **F:**205
lung disease in penguins **P:**124
rabies **D:**199–200
treating sick animals in zoos **Z:**392–93
vectors of disease **V:**282–85
veterinarians and what they do **V:**323
Animal experimentation
cloning **L:**210
dogs **D:**243–44
Pavlov, Ivan **P:**103
primates **P:**457
What kinds of animals have traveled in space? **S:**350
Animal Farm (novel by Orwell) **E:**289; **O:**238
Animal feed *see* Feeding and feeds, animal
Animal husbandry (art and science of livestock raising)
aquaculture **A:**336
fish farming **F:**205–8
livestock **L:**271, 273
Animal intelligence and behavior
beetles **B:**124–25
birds **B:**224–27
conditioning experiments in learning **L:**98–99
dinosaurs tended their young **D:**171
dolphins **D:**277–78
Lorenz, Konrad **L:**302
play **P:**333, 334
Animal kingdom **A:**265–67; **K:**253, 254–55; **L:**208, 209
classes of animals **A:**264
eggs and embryos **E:**95–98
Animal locomotion **K:**255
beetles **B:**124
birds **B:**218–19
dinosaurs **D:**168, 170–71, 172, 173
dolphins **D:**275
feet **F:**81–82
fish **F:**198–99
hands **F:**83–84
how animals move from place to place **A:**278–79
mammals **M:**71–72
marsupials **M:**115
protozoans **P:**496–97
snakes **S:**213–15
spiders, ballooning of **S:**406
starfish **S:**426
turtles **T:**356–57
diagram(s)
clams **O:**291
Animal rights **F:**504, 505
vegetarian diet for ethical reasons **V:**293

PHOTO CREDITS

The following list credits the sources of photos used in THE NEW BOOK OF KNOWLEDGE. Credits are listed, by page, photo by photo—left to right, top to bottom. Wherever appropriate, the name of the photographer has been listed with the source, the two being separated by a dash. When two or more photos by different photographers appear on one page, their credits are separated by semicolons.

A

2 © Terry Madison—The Image Bank
6 The Granger Collection (all photos on page).
6a The Bettmann Archive; The Granger Collection; The Granger Collection; The Granger Collection.
6b The Bettmann Archive
7 © Jack S. Grove—Liaison Agency
8 Giraudon/Art Resource
10 © John Elk III—Bruce Coleman Inc.; © Fletcher & Baylis—Photo Researchers.
11 The Granger Collection
12 The White House Collection, © copyright White House Historical Association; The Granger Collection.
13 National Gallery of Art, Washington; Gift of Mrs. Robert Homans.
14 Courtesy of Maryland Historical Society
15 Yale University Art Gallery
16 Corcoran Gallery of Art; The Granger Collection; The Bettmann Archive.
18 The Bettmann Archive; The Granger Collection.
19 The Bettmann Archive
20 The Granger Collection
21 Historical Pictures Service
24 © Jeff Isaac Greenberg—Photo Researchers
29 Courtesy of Binney & Smith Inc.
30 Courtesy of Young & Rubicam, New York
31 © Danilo Boschung—Leo de Wys; Courtesy of the American Cancer Society.
32 Courtesy of Grolier Enterprises Corp.
35 Warshaw Collection of Business Americana
37 British Aerospace
41 © Steve Swope—Indy 500 Photos; © Yogi, Inc.
42 © Jackie Foryst—Bruce Coleman Inc.; © Reuters/Oleg Popov—TimePix.
43 © Emil Muench—Photo Researchers
44 © Arthur C. Twomey—Photo Researchers; © Peter Knapp—The Image Bank.
45 © Laura Rauch—AP/Wide World Photos
46 © Sally Mayman—Stone; © R.I.M. Campbell—Bruce Coleman Limited; © Gerald Cubitt; © Fridmar Damm—Leo de Wys; © Gerald Cubitt.
47 © Hiroyuki Matsumoto—Black Star; © Pedro Coll—The Stock Market; © Michael J. Howell—Leo de Wys.
48 © Robert Everts—Stone; © Hiroyuki Matsumoto—Black Star.
49 © Carl Frank—Photo Researchers
50 © Robert Frerck—Stone
52 © James P. Rowan—Stone
53 © M. Philip Kahl—Black Star; © Alan Binks—Anthony Bannister Picture Library; © Mitch Kezar—Stone.
54 © Gerald Cubitt; © Betty Press—Woodfin Camp & Associates; © Nicholas DeVore—Stone; © Pedro Coll—The Stock Market.
55 © Kerstin Beier—Anthony Bannister Picture Library; © Stone; © Martin Rogers—Stone.
56 © Marc & Evelyn Bernheim—Woodfin Camp & Associates; © Paul Stepan—Photo Researchers.
57 © Michael Coyne—Black Star; © Gerald Cubitt; © Marc & Evelyn Bernheim—Woodfin Camp & Associates.
58 © J. Bertrand—Leo de Wys
60 © Betty Press—Woodfin Camp & Associates; © Kerstin Beier—Anthony Bannister Picture Library.
61 © Betty Press—Woodfin Camp & Associates
62 © Hubertus Kanus—Photo Researchers (all photos on page).
63 © Victor Englebert—Photo Researchers
64 © Pierre Boulat Cosmos—Woodfin Camp & Associates; © Jason Laure—Woodfin Camp & Associates.
65 The Granger Collection
66 The Granger Collection (all photos on page).
69 © Brooks Kraft—Corbis-Sygma
70 © Richard Saunders—Leo de Wys
71 © George Holton—Photo Researchers; Photographed by Kathy Corday. National Museum of African Art, Eliot Elisofon Photographic Archives, Smithsonian Institution.
72 Photographed by Franko Khoury. National Museum of African Art, Eliot Elisofon Photographic Archives, Smithsonian Institution (all photos on page).
73 Photographed by Dick Beaulieux. Ethnographic Museum, Antwerp; © Lee Boltin; © Lee Boltin.
74 Photographed by Franko Khoury. National Museum of African Art, Eliot Elisofon Photographic Archives, Smithsonian Institution. Gift of Dr. Ernst Anspach and museum purchase; © Lee Boltin; © Lee Boltin.
75 Photographed by Franko Khoury. National Museum of African Art and National Museum of Natural History, Eliot Elisofon Photographic Archives, Smithsonian Institution; Photographed by Jim Young. National Museum of African Art, Eliot Elisofon Photographic Archives, Smithsonian Institution.
76 © Strauss—Curtis—The Stock Market
76a © Marc & Evelyn Bernheim—Woodfin Camp & Associates
77 © Paul Funston—Anthony Bannister Picture Library; © Bill Kaufman—Leo de Wys; © Marc & Evelyn Bernheim—Woodfin Camp & Associates.
79a © Jeffrey Henson Scales; © George Olson—Woodfin Camp & Associates.
79b © Nick Kelsh—Kelsh Wilson Design Inc.; © Yva Momatiuk/John Eastcott—Woodfin Camp & Associates.
79c © Tom Raymond—Stone/Getty Images
79d The Granger Collection
79e Peter Newark's American Pictures; Schomburg Center for Research in Black Culture—The New York Public Library—Astor, Lenox and Tilden Foundations.
79f The Granger Collection
79g The Granger Collection; Peter Newark's American Pictures.
79h Schomburg Center for Research in Black Culture—The New York Public Library—Astor, Lenox and Tilden Foundations
79i Peter Newark's American Pictures; The Bettmann Archive.
79j The Granger Collection; Peter Newark's American Pictures.
79k UPI/Bettmann Newsphotos; The Bettmann Archive.
79l © Driggs Collection—Magnum Photos; © David Diaz, courtesy of HarperCollins Publisher; The Bettmann Archive; National

Museum of American Art, Smithsonian Institution, Washington, DC. Gift of the Harmon Foundation—Art Resource; Schomburg Center for Research in Black Culture—The New York Public Library—Astor, Lenox and Tilden Foundations.

79m Philadelphia Museum of Art: Gift of Dr. and Mrs. Mathew T. Moore; Peter Newark's American Pictures.

79n UPI/Bettmann Newsphotos; © Topham—The Image Works.

79o © Ted Russell—Corbis-Sygma; © Charles Moore—Black Star.

79p © Kenneth Jarecke—Contact Press Images; Peter Newark's American Pictures.

80 © Jonathan Barth—Getty Images; © Ulf Andersen/Newsmakers/Getty Images; © Jamal A. Wilson/Newsmakers/Getty Images; © Chris Kasson—AP/Wide World Photos; Albert Trotman—Allford Trotman Associates.

81 Hulton/Archive by Getty Images

82 © Dugald Stermer

84 © William Hubbell—Woodfin Camp & Associates

85 © Phil Huber—Black Star; © Ira Wyman—Corbis-Sygma.

86 Gerald Davis—Contact

87 The Bettmann Archive

88 © Earl Roberge—Photo Researchers

89 © Jules Bucher—Photo Researchers

90 © Andrew Holbrooke—Wheeler Pictures; © Ronny Jacques—Photo Researchers.

91 © Andrew Holbrooke—Wheeler Pictures

92 © Bill Backman—Photo Researchers; © George Holton—Photo Researchers.

93 © Louis Goldman—Photo Researchers; © Ulrike Welsch—Stock, Boston.

94 © Joe Munroe—Photo Researchers

95 © Photo Action Press—Photo Researchers

96 © Grant Heilman Photography

98 The Pierpont Morgan Library

99 National Gallery of Art, Washington, DC, Garbisch Collection

100 © Liane Enkelis—Stock, Boston

100a U.S. Department of Agriculture

104 Model Airplane News

106 Robert Schleicher

107 Courtesy of Byron Originals

108 © James A. Anderson—Unicorn Stock Photos; PhotoEdit; Courtesy, Cessna; Brent Jones.

110 © R. Caton—H. Armstrong Roberts, Inc.

111 © Ingrid Johnsson—Journalism Services

112 Courtesy, British Aerospace

113 © Dennis Barnes; © David Brownell.

114 © Heinz Steenmans—Wheeler Pictures; Leonard Lee Rue III—Bruce Coleman Inc.

115 © Joseph Jacobson—Journalism Services

116 © Lepper & Miller—H. Armstrong Roberts; NASA.

117 © Randa Bishop

119 Courtesy, Boeing Aircraft Co.

120 Courtesy, McDonnell Douglas Corporation; © PhotoEdit.

121 NASA; Courtesy, Bell Helicopter Textron.

122 © John V. A. F. Neal—Photo Researchers

124 © Peggy Kahana—Peter Arnold, Inc.; © Dave Davidson—Tom Stack & Associates.

125 © DeSazo—Rapho Guillumette; © George Hall—Woodfin Camp & Associates.

126 © Ruud Taal—Capital Press

128 Courtesy, Airports Commission, City & County of San Francisco; © Martin Rogers—Stock, Boston.

129 © Ruud Taal—Capital Press

131 © F. Sieb—H. Armstong Roberts; © Marc Bondarenko; © Wally Argus.

133 © Rob Outlaw—Root Resources; © David Haynes—Photo Options.

134 © University of Alabama; © Ed Malles—Pic's.

135 © Sonja Reiger—Photo Options

136 © Marc Bondarenko

137 © William H. Allen, Jr.

138 © R. Krubner—H. Armstrong Roberts; © Richard T. Nowitz; © David Haynes—Photo Options.

139 © Leo de Wys

140 The Granger Collection

142 The Bettmann Archive; © Charles Phelps Cushing—H. Armstong Roberts; The Bettmann Archive.

143 UPI/Bettmann Newsphotos

145 © James Balog—Photo Researchers; © Bob & Ira Spring; © Sullivan & Rogers—Bruce Coleman Inc.

146 © Ken Graham—Bruce Coleman Inc.

147 © James Balog—Bruce Coleman Inc.

148 © Thomas Kitchin—Tom Stack & Associates; © John Shaw—Bruce Coleman Inc.; © Mark Kelley.

149 © Rod Planck—Photo Researchers; © Ken Graham—Bruce Coleman Inc.

150 © Bob & Ira Spring (all photos on page).

151 © Jim Nilsen—Tom Stack & Associates; © Lael Morgan—Stone.

152 © Thomas Kitchin—Tom Stack & Associates

153 © Ken Graham—Bruce Coleman Inc. (all photos on page).

154 © Thomas Kitchin—Tom Stack & Associates

156 Alaska State Library—Early Prints Collection; The Granger Collection; Alaska State Library—Centennial Commission.

157 © Michael Penn—Liaison Agency; Alaska State Library—Eric A. Hegg Collection.

159 © Soren Rasmussen—Sipa Press; © Filip Horvat—SABA.

160 © Facelly—Sipa Press

161 © Chris Niedenthal—Black Star

162 © Tom Stoddart/Katz—SABA; © Paolo Koch—Photo Researchers.

163 The Granger Collection; The Bettmann Archive.

165 © Von Rhijn—Miller Comstock, Inc.

166 © E. Otto—Miller Comstock, Inc.; © Malak—Miller Comstock, Inc.

167 © Thomas Kitchin—Tom Stack & Associates

169 © George Hunter—Miller Comstock, Inc.

170 © Paolo Koch—Photo Researchers; © E. Otto—Miller Comstock, Inc.

174 Orchard House

175 Concord Free Public Library

176 Giraudon/Art Resource; The Granger Collection.

177 The Granger Collection; Pella Museum—Courtesy, The Art Institute of Chicago.

179 The Granger Collection

180 © Bob Evans—Peter Arnold Inc.; © Walter H. Hodge—Peter Arnold, Inc.; © Michael P. Gadomski—Photo Researchers; © James Bell—Photo Researchers.

181 © Biophoto Associates/Science Source—Photo Researchers; © Manfred Kage—Peter Arnold, Inc.; © Manfred Kage—Peter Arnold, Inc.; © Walter H. Hodge—Peter Arnold, Inc.

182 © Scott Barrow

185 © Jacques Pavlovsky—Corbis-Sygma

186 © Victor Englebert—Photo Researchers

187 © SuperStock

188 © Helen Marcus—Photo Researchers

191 © Manfred Kage—Peter Arnold, Inc.

192–193 Art Resource

194b © Ray Manley—SuperStock

194d University of California, Lawrence Livermore Berkeley Laboratory

194e © Chislaine Morel—Liaison Agency

194f © Malcolm S. Kirk—Peter Arnold, Inc; © Chislaine Morel—Liaison Agency.

196 The Granger Collection; The Granger Collection; The Bettmann Archive.

197 The Granger Collection

198 The Granger Collection; Culver Pictures; The Granger Collection; North Wind Picture Archives; Culver Pictures.

199 The Free Library of Philadelphia; The Granger Collection; The Granger Collection; The Bettmann Archive; The Granger Collection.

200 Culver Pictures; The Granger Collection; Culver Pictures; North Wind Picture Archives; The Granger Collection.

201 The Granger Collection; The Granger Collection; Culver Pictures; The Granger Collection; Culver Pictures.

206 Culver Pictures

209 The Bettmann Archive; The Bettmann Archive.

210 The Granger Collection

214 The Everett Collection

214b © E. S. Ross—California Academy of Sciences

216 © Joe McDonald—Animals Animals

217 © Bill Bachmann—Photo Network

219 © Georg Gerster—Photo Researchers

220 Giraudon/Art Resource

222 © Lee Boltin

223 Egyptian Collection, Staatlichen Museum, Berlin—Art Reference Bureau; Ancient Egyptian Paintings, Oriental Institute, University of Chicago.

224 © Georg Gerster—Photo Researchers

225 © S. Fiore—SuperStock

226 Art Resource; © E. Boubat—Agence Top.

227 © SuperStock

228 © Margot Wolf—Scala, New York; Roland-Ziolo—National Archeological Museum, Athens.

229 © Roland-Ziolo—Acropolis Museum, Athens; Scala, New York.

230 Art Resource; By permission of the Trustees of the British Museum.

231 Art Resource

232 © Richard Nowitz—Photo Researchers; The Granger Collection; The Granger Collection.

233 By permission of the Trustees of the British Museum—Art Reference Bureau

234 The Granger Collection; Oriental Institute; University Museum, University of Pennsylvania.

235 © Lee Boltin

236 The Granger Collection

237 © John Baker—SuperStock; © Raymond V. Schoder.

239 Hirmer Verlag; © Josephine Powell.

240 The Granger Collection

241 Art Resource; The Granger Collection.

242 © Ray Manley—SuperStock

243 Staatlichen Museum, Berlin

244 Art Reference Bureau; Courtesy of the Trustees of the British Museum; Tomb of the Leopards, Tarquinia—Art Reference Bureau.

246 The Metropolitan Museum of Art, Fletcher Fund, 1956

249 © Jack Delano

251 Courtesy of Marian Anderson, RCA Records

252 © Maurice and Sally Landre—FPG

253 Lisl Steiner—Grolier Inc.; © Jerry Frank.

255 © Tom Hollyman—Photo Researchers; © Peter Wichman—Birnback.

256 Boston Medical Library, Massachusetts Medical Society

259 Art Resource

260 © Joao Silva—Black Star

264 © Michel Viard—Peter Arnold, Inc.; © Matt Meadows—Peter Arnold, Inc.; © Science Photo Library—Photo Researchers.

265 © Tom McHugh—Photo Researchers; © Bob Winsett—ProFiles West/Index Stock; © Nicole Duplaix—Peter Arnold, Inc.; © Manfred Kage—Peter Arnold, Inc.

266 © M. P. Kahl—Photo Researchers; © R. Andrew Odum—Peter Arnold, Inc.; © E. R. Degginger—Animals Animals; © Joe McDonald—Tom Stack & Associates.

267 © Gregory G. Dimijian—Photo Researchers; © Carl Roessler—Animals Animals; © Jeff Foott.

268 © Richard R. Hansen—Photo Researchers; © M. P. Kahl—Photo Researchers; © Nigel Dennis—Photo Researchers.

270 © Joseph T. Collins—Photo Researchers; © Kathie Atkinson—Animals Animals; © Toni Angermayer—Photo Researchers; © Robert A. Tyrrell—Animals Animals.

271 © Tom McHugh—Photo Researchers; © Kevin Schafer—Tom Stack & Associates.

272 © Stephen J. Krasemann—Photo Researchers

273 © Zig Leszczynski—Animals Animals

274 © Thomas Kitchin—Tom Stack & Associates

275 © Breck P. Kent—Animals Animals

276 © Tom Stack—Tom Stack & Associates; © Chlaus Lotscher—Peter Arnold, Inc.

277 © Jeff Foott; © Richard Kolar—Animals Animals; © Dave Watts—Tom Stack & Associates.

278 © Fred Bavendam—Peter Arnold, Inc.

279 © Anup & Manoj Shah—Animals Animals; © Mark Chappell—Animals Animals.

280 © Bruce Davidson—Animals Animals; © Jany Sauvanet—Photo Researchers.

281 © J. H. Robinson—Animals Animals; © Allen Russell—ProFiles West/Index Stock.

282 © Jeff Lepore—Photo Researchers; © Jeff Foott.

283 © Stan Wayman—Photo Researchers

284 © Jeff Foott

285 © Nancy Sefton—Photo Researchers; © William J. Jahoda—Photo Researchers; © Brian Parker—Tom Stack & Associates.

286 © S. R. Maglione—Photo Researchers

287 © Bradley Smith—Animals Animals

288 Photofest

289 © 1951 Warner Bros. Inc.; © Will Vinton Productions, The California Raisins, © CALRAB; © Touchstone Pictures—Amblin Entertainment, Inc.

290 © 1988 Pixar

291 © 1937 The Walt Disney Company; © The Walt Disney Company.

292 © Douglas T. Cheeseman, Jr.—Peter Arnold, Inc.; © Russ Kinne—Photo Researchers.

293 © Schoeck—Leo de Wys

296 © François Gohier—Photo Researchers

297 © Bruce Davidson—Animals Animals; © Stephen J. Krasemann—Photo Researchers.

298 © Arthur Gloor—Animals Animals

299 The Bettmann Archive

300 © DeZolduondo—Anthro-Photo

301 © Robert Frerck—Odyssey Production
302 © Anthony Bannister and Peter Johnson; © George Holton—Photo Researchers; © Robin Smith—SuperStock; © V. Phillips—Leo de Wys; © Alvis Upitis—SuperStock.
304 © Michal Heron
306 The Granger Collection; Courtesy, Stuart B. Levy, M.D. from *The Antibiotic Paradox: How Antibiotic Drugs Are Destroying the Miracle*, © Plenum Press, 1992.
307 The Bettmann Archive (all photos on page).
308 Courtesy, Professor Greenwood—University Hospital Queen's Medical Centre—Nottingham (all photos on page).
309 Raymond T. Testa—Lederle Laboratories
311 © Dennis Kunkel, University of Hawaii
312 © James Holmes—Celltech Ltd/Science Photo Library—Photo Researchers
315 Yale University Art Gallery, Mabel Brady Garvan and C. Sanford Bull, B.A. 1893, Collections (by exchange); © SuperStock; © SuperStock.
316 Cooper-Hewitt Museum; Sandwich Glass Museum; National Museum of American History, John Paul Remansnyder Collection.
316a Buten Museum of Wedgwood; Abby Aldrich Rockefeller Folk Art Center; Yale University Art Gallery, William Inglis Morse Collection, Gift of his daughter, Mrs. Frederick W. Hilles.
316b © Stan Aggie—Picture Group; Cooper-Hewitt Museum.
317 Art Resource
318 © Satoshi Kuribayashi—Nature Production; © Satoshi Kuribayashi—Nature Production.
322 © Michael Fogden—DRK Photo
323 © Varin—Jacana—Photo Researchers; © Mark Moffett—Minden Pictures; © Mark Moffett—Minden Pictures.
324 © Dwight Kuhn—DRK Photo
325 © Gerry Ellis Nature Photography; © Gerry Ellis—Bruce Coleman Inc.
326 © BIOS—Peter Arnold, Inc.; © Gerry Ellis Nature Photography.
327 © Peter Davey—Bruce Coleman Inc.; © Gerry Ellis Nature Photography
328 © Roberto Hoesch
330 Photo courtesy of NY Apple Association; © Alan L. Detrick—Photo Researchers; © Alan L. Detrick—Photo Researchers; © Alan L. Detrick—Photo Researchers; © Alan L. Detrick—Photo Researchers; Photo courtesy of NY Apple Association.
331 © Eric Crichton—Bruce Coleman Inc.; © Martha McBride—Unicorn Stock Photos.
333 The Granger Collection
336 © Michael Yamashita
337 © Phyllis Picardi—Photo Network; © Gerd Ludwig—Woodfin Camp & Associates.
340 *Stories From Arabian Nights* retold by Lawrence Housman. Illustrated by Edmund Dulac. Charles Scribner's Sons, 1907.
341 The Granger Collection (all photos on page).
342 The Granger Collection
343 © K. Scholz—H. Armstrong Roberts, Inc.; © Bernard Gerard—Viesti Associates, Inc.
344 © Wendy Chan—The Image Bank; The Granger Collection.
345 © Marge George—Spectrum Stock; Brannan Linsley—AP/Wide World Photos; Jeremy Ferguson—Spectrum Stock; © Jeremy Ferguson—Spectrum Stock.
347 © Peter Paz—The Image Bank
348 © Anthony Mercieca—Root Resources; © Patti Murray—Animals Animals; © J. H. Robinson—Photo Researchers.
350 The Granger Collection
351 © Lee Boltin
352– © Bruno J. Zehnder—Peter Arnold, Inc.; ©
353 Dan Porges—Peter Arnold, Inc.
354 © Charles Perry Weimer
355 © Stockpile; © Fritz Henle—Photo Researchers.
356 © Lee Boltin
357 © Cameramann International Ltd. (all photos on page).
358 © Jacques Jangoux—Peter Arnold, Inc.
359 © Yoram Kahana—Peter Arnold, Inc.
360 © Lee Boltin; © Lee Boltin.
361 Courtesy of the Oriental Institute, University of Chicago, Prehistoric Project
362 Danish National Travel Office
363 © John Cochran
364 © Douglas Mazonowicz—Bruce Coleman Inc.; © Jock Montgomery—Bruce Coleman Inc.
366 © Focus on Sports
368 © Jiri—Leo de Wys; © Don Sparks—The Image Bank; © Cameramann International Ltd.
369 © Peter Pearson—Leo de Wys; © Steve Vidler—Leo de Wys; © Steve Vidler—Leo de Wys; © Cameramann International Ltd.
370 © Filmbureau Niestadt
372 © Norman Owen Tomalin—Bruce Coleman Inc.
373 © Pellegrini—Madeline Grimoldi
375 © Gerald Clyde—FPG
377 © Dennis Hallinan—Alpha
379 Giraudon/Art Resource
380 © Inge Morath—Magnum Photos
381 © Karen McKinnon—Art Resource; Art Resource.
382 © Elliott Erwitt—Magnum Photos; Ezra Stoller.
383 Photographie Giraudon
384 © Michael Vaccaro; Solomon R. Guggenheim Museum, New York.
385 Finnish Tourist Bureau; © A. J. Levin—Black Star.
386 © Ann Chwatsky—Art Resource
386a © Peter Aaron—Esto
386b © SuperStock; © Ted Spiegel—Black Star.
386c © Stephen J. Krasemann—Peter Arnold, Inc.
388 © Loren McIntyre
390 © Allen Green—Photo Researchers
391 © Victor Englebert—Photo Researchers; © David Barnes—Stone.
392 © J. Zeister—Z.E.F.A./Leo de Wys
393 © Loren McIntyre
394 The Bettmann Archive
395 UPI Bettmann Newsphotos
396 © Diego Goldberg—Corbis-Sygma
397 Alinari—Art Reference Bureau
403 © Larry Ulrich; © Tom Bean—The Stock Market; © Jerry Jacka.
404 © Willard Clay; © Bob Clemenz.
405 © Bob Clemenz
406 © Bob Clemenz; © Jerry Jacka.
407 © Bob Clemenz
408 © Joe Bator—The Stock Market; © Cameramann International Ltd.
409 © Jane R. Kriete—Root Resources
410 © Larry Ulrich; © M. Schneiders—H. Armstrong Roberts; © Willard Clay; © Larry Ulrich.
411 © Jerry Jacka; © George Hunter—H. Armstrong Roberts.
414 © Steve Leonard—Black Star
415 Arizona Historical Foundation; © Everett Collection.
417 © Matt Bradley; © Matt Bradley; © Bob Firth.
418 © Terry Donnelley—Stone; © Bill Barksdale—Root Resources.
419 © Matt Bradley
420 © Matt Bradley (all photos on page).
421 © Matt Bradley
422 © Garry D. McMichael—Root Resources; © Don Smetzer—Stone.
423 © H. Abernathy—H. Armstrong Roberts
424 © Garry D. McMichael—Root Resources; © John Elk III; © Terry Donnelley—Stone; © Matt Bradley.
425 © John Elk III
426 1993 National Gallery of Art, Washington, Paul Mellon Collection
428 © Wide World; © Karl Gehring—Liaison Agency.
429 UPI/Bettmann Newsphotos; Historical Pictures—Stock Montage, Inc.
431 © Alex Borodulin—Leo de Wys; © Eugene G. Schulz.
433 The Metropolitan Museum of Art
434 Photographie Giraudon—Musee de l'Armee; The Bettmann Archive; The Metropolitan Museum of Art; The Metropolitan Museum of Art; The Granger Collection.
435 The Metropolitan Museum of Art (all photos on page).
436 Archive Photos
437 Bridgeman/Art Resource; Giraudon/Art Resource; The Metropolitan Museum of Art, Gift of Renate Hofmann, 1975; © Lee Boltin.
438 Scala/Art Resource; Musee des Antiquities Nationales, St. Germaine-en-Laye, France.
438a Scala/Art Resource
438b Giraudon/Art Resource
438c The Metropolitan Museum of Art, Bequest of Mrs. H. O. Havemeyer, 1929. The H. O. Havemeyer Collection; General Egyptian Book Organization, Cairo.
438d Art Resource; Scala/Art Resource.
438e Collection, The Museum of Modern Art, New York. Gift of Mrs. Simon Guggenheim; The Metropolitan Museum of Art, Purchase, 1983.
438f The White House Collection, © copyright White House Historical Association; The Bettmann Archive; The Granger Collection.
438g The Bettmann Archive; The Granger Collection.
438h © The White House Collection, © copyright White House Historical Association
444 © Bill Holden—Leo de Wys; © Roland Seitre—Peter Arnold, Inc.; © Charles Gupton—Stone; © Charles Gupton—Stone.
445 © Dian Duchin—Bruce Coleman Inc.; © Steve Vidler—Leo de Wys; © David Ball—The Stock Market.
446 © Robert Azzi—Woodfin Camp & Associates; © Nigel Dickinson—Stone.
447 © Colin Prior—Stone; © George Holton—Photo Researchers.
450 © Bryan Alexander—Black Star; © Jeffrey Aaronson—Network Aspen.
451 © Jeffrey Aaronson—Network Aspen; © Norman Meyers—Bruce Coleman Inc.
452 © Norman Owen Tomalin—Bruce Coleman Inc.
453 © Wardene Weisser—Bruce Coleman Inc.; © Manoj Shah—Stone.
454 © Alain Nogues—Corbis-Sygma; © Ned Gillette—The Stock Market; © Clark James Mishler—The Stock Market; © Anthony Cassidy—Stone; © Zviki-Eshet—The Stock Market.
455 © Catalyst—The Stock Market; © Ian Lloyd—The Stock Market; © Anthony Cassidy—Stone; © Paul Steel—The Stock Market.
458 © Benjamin Rondell—The Stock Market; © Gerd Ludwig—Woodfin Camp & Associates; © Steve Vidler—Leo de Wys; © Luis Villota—The Stock Market.
459 © Paolo Koch—Photo Researchers; © D & J Heaton—First Light.
460 © Lawrence Manning—First Light; © Steve Vidler—Leo de Wys.
461 © Bruno Barbey—Magnum Photos; © P. J. Griffiths—Magnum Photos.
462 © Jacques Langevin—Corbis-Sygma; © Stone.
463 © Jon Hicks—Leo de Wys; National Museum of Pakistan, Karachi; The Granger Collection.
465 The Granger Collection (all photos on page).
466 Margaret Bourke-White—*Life* magazine—© Time Inc.; © Keystone—Corbis-Sygma.
467 © Ken Straiton—First Light
468 Lyndon B. Johnson Space Center/NASA
470 © Brian Seed—Stone
471 The Rohss Museum of Arts and Crafts, Gothenburg
473 © 1986 Australian National University/California Institute of Technology; NASA.
474 © Fred Espenak—Science Photo Library—Photo Researchers
476 The Granger Collection; UPI/Bettmann Newsphotos.
476a NOAO; The Granger Collection; North Wind Picture Archives.
476b The Granger Collection; UPI/Bettmann Newsphotos.
476c UPI/Bettmann Newsphotos; North Wind Picture Archives.
476d © Roger Ressmeyer—Starlight
477 © Greg Probst—Stone
480 NASA
483 © Omikron—Photo Researchers
484 The Granger Collection
486 Brown Brothers
489 © Phototake
490 North Wind Picture Archives
491 National Audubon Society
494 The Bettmann Archive
496 © Harvey Lloyd—The Stock Market; © John Carnemolla—Australian Picture Library; © Michael Coyne—Black Star.
497 © Luis Villota—The Stock Market; © Bill Bachman—Photo Researchers; © Michael Coyne—Black Star; © David Austin—Stone.
498 © David Austen—Stone; © Nick Rains—Australian Picture Library.
499 © Ulrike Welsch; © Denis O'Byrne—Stock Photos Pty Ltd.
500 © Robert Garvey—Black Star; © David Davies—Stone
501 The Art Gallery of New South Wales; © Jack Vartoogian; The Bettmann Archive; © AP/Wide World Photos; © Rick Maiman—Corbis-Sygma.
504 © Paul Chesley—Stone
505 © SuperStock; © Robin Smith—Stone; © Kevin Schafer—Stone
506 © Paul McKelvey—Stone
507 © Ben Simmons—The Stock Market
510 © Robert Frerck—Woodfin Camp & Associates; © J. Burry—Australian Picture Library.
511 © J. Burry—Australian Picture Library; © Patrick Ward—Stone

512 © John Carnemolla—Australian Picture Library; © Hideo Kurihara—Stone
513 © Raga—The Stock Market; © Noeline Kelly—Australian Picture Library.
514 © John Carnemolla—Australian Picture Library
515 The Tate Gallery, London—Art Resource
516 The Granger Collection; Image Library.
517 © Robert Garvey—Black Star
518 © Joachim Messerschmidt—Leo de Wys
519 © Stone; © Herlinde Koelbl—Leo de Wys; Austrian Information Service.
522 The Granger Collection; Scala/Art Resource; The Granger Collection; The Granger Collection; The Granger Collection; The Bettmann Archive.
523 Giraudon/Art Resource
530 © SuperStock; © Tim Boyle—Getty Images.
531 © Adam Lubroth—Stone
532 © Paul Shambroom—Photo Researchers
533 © David Young-Wolff—Stone
534 © Robert Schleicher
535 © Robert Schleicher; Aurora Plastics Corp.
536 UPI; © Diana Burnett—Focus on Sports.
537 © J. DiMaggio—Focus on Sports; © Jeffry W. Meyers—Alpha.
538 © SuperStock
539 Ford Motor Company
541 The Bettmann Archive; © Cindy Lewis—All Rights Reserved; © 1981 Henry Austin Clark, Jr.—Mr. Donald M. Scott, Penfield, New York; © 1970 Henry Austin Clark, Jr.—Mr. Frank H. Gardner, West Newton, Massachusetts; © 1972 Henry Austin Clark, Jr.—Mr. Willard W. Newman, Tampa, Florida; © 1980 Henry Austin Clark, Jr.—Mrs. William C. Donze, Strongsville, Ohio.
542 © Cindy Lewis—All Rights Reserved; © 1981 Henry Austin Clark, Jr.—Mr. Morris Stone; © Henry Austin Clark, Jr.; © Cindy Lewis—All Rights Reserved; From the collections of Henry Ford Museum & Greenfield Village.
543 From the collections of Henry Ford Museum & Greenfield Village
544 © Henry Austin Clark, Jr.; © Chet Bahn—Volkswagen Corp.; From the collections of Henry Ford Museum & Greenfield Village; © Ron Kimball; From the collections of Henry Ford Museum & Greenfield Village.
545 © Cindy Lewis—All Rights Reserved; Acura; Toyota Motor Sales; 1998 GM Corp.—Used with Permission of GM Media Archives. All Rights Reserved; Mercedes Benz; Ford Corporation; Honda Automobile News Bureau; Reprinted with permission of Chrysler Historical Foundation; Volvo Corporation; 1996, 1997 GM Corp.—Used with Permission of GM Media Archives.
552 Ford Motor Company; General Motors.
553 © John Zoiner—Nawrocki Stock Photos; Chrysler Corporation; Chrysler Corporation.
554 Ford Motor Company.
555 © Ovak Arslanian; © Cameramann International Ltd.
556 Ford Motor Company.
557 © William Bacon—Photo Researchers
558 © Spencer Grant—Photo Researchers
559 © Jim Sugar—Black Star
560 The Bettmann Archive; Science Museum, London.
561 National Air & Space Museum—Smithsonian Institution
563 The Granger Collection; Culver Pictures, Inc.
565 Photo by Ed Castle from the *Smithsonian Book of Flight* by Walter J. Boyne © 1987, Smithsonian Institution; The Bettmann Archive.
566 © David Falconer—Bruce Coleman Inc.
567 © James Sugar—Black Star
568 © David O. Hill—Photo Researchers; © Mel M. Boughman—Bruce Coleman Inc.
569 © Journalism Services; © Matt Bradley—Bruce Coleman Inc.; © Jean-Claude Carton—Bruce Coleman Inc.
570 © Mike Smith—MIT
571 © Michael Melford—Wheeler Pictures
573 © Serguei Fedorov—Woodfin Camp & Associates
575 Courtesy Department of Library Services—American Museum of Natural History
577 © Buddy Mays; © Comstock.
578 © George H. Harrison—Grant Heilman Photography